The Theoretical Fo of Criminology

To confront the challenges criminologists face today and to satisfactorily critique the theories on which criminology is founded, we need to learn from the past. To do this we must give context to both theorist and theory. Written from a critical perspective, this book brings criminological theory to life. It presents the core theories of criminology as historical and cultural products and theorists as producers of culture located in particular places, writing in specific historical periods and situated in precise intellectual networks and philosophical controversies.

This book illustrates that theory does not arise 'out of the blue' and highlights the importance of understanding how and why ideas emerge at certain points in time, why they gained currency and the influence that they have had. It follows the trajectory of criminology from pre-Enlightenment society through to the present day and the proliferation of criminological thinking. It explores:

- Setting the Stage for the Emergence of Criminology
- Classicist Criminology: The Search for Justice, Equality and the Rational 'Man'
- The Positivist Revolution, Physiognomy, Phrenology and the Science of 'Othering'
- Chicago School of Sociology: An Explosion of Ideas
- Developing a Sociological Criminology: Durkheim, Du Bois, Merton and Tannenbaum
- Feminism: Redressing the Gender Imbalance
- Confronting the Establishment: The Emergence of Critical Criminology
- From Theoretical Innovations to Political Engagement

The Theoretical Foundations of Criminology provides an invaluable contribution to the growing conversation about criminology's 'origin story' and the level that this is grounded in the idiosyncrasies of the North Atlantic world and its historical development. This book will be invaluable reading to students and academics engaged in studies of criminology and criminal justice.

Jayne Mooney is an associate professor of sociology at John Jay College of Criminal Justice and a member of the doctoral faculties in sociology and women studies at the Graduate Center, City University of New York. Her focus of scholarship is on the history of crime and punishment, gender and crime, the sociology of violence, social deviance and critical criminology. She was previously on the criminology faculties of Middlesex University and the University of Kent at Canterbury in the UK.

'Mooney is like the best of urban tour guides leading us through a complicated metropolitan landscape where the evolution of space is a multivalent story of corporate interests, state power, local zoning, and diverse working populations struggling to get to work, raise kids, and seek respite in a night on the town. This book is exciting because it offers us a sophisticated guide for criminological theory charted by an author with a historian's depth, and ethnographer's instincts, and a poet's heart. The writing is elegant yet accessible; the purpose clear and serious. Students of criminology will not only learn about theories and their contexts, but about the importance of theory itself for understanding the world as it is and for changing it.'
    Corey Dolgan, *Professor of Sociology and Criminology, Stonehill College, USA and President-Elect for the Society for the Study of Social Problems*

The Theoretical Foundations of Criminology

Place, Time and Context

Jayne Mooney

Routledge
Taylor & Francis Group
LONDON AND NEW YORK

First published 2020
by Routledge
2 Park Square, Milton Park, Abingdon, Oxon OX14 4RN

and by Routledge
52 Vanderbilt Avenue, New York, NY 10017

Routledge is an imprint of the Taylor & Francis Group, an informa business

© 2020 Jayne Mooney

The right of Jayne Mooney to be identified as author of this work has been asserted by her in accordance with sections 77 and 78 of the Copyright, Designs and Patents Act 1988.

All rights reserved. No part of this book may be reprinted or reproduced or utilised in any form or by any electronic, mechanical, or other means, now known or hereafter invented, including photocopying and recording, or in any information storage or retrieval system, without permission in writing from the publishers.

Trademark notice: Product or corporate names may be trademarks or registered trademarks, and are used only for identification and explanation without intent to infringe.

British Library Cataloguing-in-Publication Data
A catalogue record for this book is available from the British Library

Library of Congress Cataloging-in-Publication Data
A catalog record for this book has been requested

ISBN: 978-0-415-73395-3 (hbk)
ISBN: 978-0-131-96010-7 (pbk)
ISBN: 978-0-429-32272-3 (ebk)

Typeset in Garamond
by Apex CoVantage, LLC

For Joseph and Fin

Contents

List of figures xii
List of boxes xiii
Acknowledgements xiv

**The theoretical foundations
of criminology: place, time and context** 1
Introduction 1

1 **Setting the stage for the emergence of criminology** 5
  'Justice' and the ancien régime *5*
     Torture 11
     Regicide: the ultimate crime of the ancien regime 11
        Robert-François Damiens: a quest for justice 16
        The significance of Damiens for criminology 21
  *'The tide is turning; the tone of life is about
  to change' 21*
     The intellectuals 21
        Montesquieu 22
        The philosophes *24*

2 **Classicist criminology: the search for justice, equality
  and the rational 'man'** 29
  The Enlightenment and the origins of classicist criminology 29
     Human nature and the basis of society 31
     Crime, justice and the influence of classicism 34
     Cesare Beccaria 35
        On Crimes and Punishments *36*
        On Crimes and Punishments: *a manifesto for
        its time 43*

The historical influence of On Crimes and
   Punishments 45
Jeremy Bentham 48
   Bentham on torture 52
   *The panopticon: 'The more strictly we are watched,
      the better we behave'* 55
*The critique of Enlightenment ideas and classicist
   criminology 60*
   The problem of the social contract 60
   Who is equal before the law? 60
      Colonialism 60
      Gender and class bias in classicist thought 62
   The distinction between the public and private spheres 64
   *The 'Classicist Contradiction': between formal and
      substantive equality 65*
      The problem of legal categorisation 65
      The focus on the criminal act 66
   *Responses to undermining or violating the social contract:
      banishment and the birth of the penitentiary 66*
      Banishment 66
      The Birth of the Penitentiary 68
Modifying classicist ideas 70
Defending Beccaria: the issue of social class 71
*Contemporary application of classicist
   thought in criminology 75*
   'Just Desserts' 75
   Rational-choice theory: 'opportunity makes the thief' 76

3 **The positivist revolution, physiognomy, phrenology and
    the science of 'Othering'**   83
   Positivism 83
   *André-Michel Guerry and Adolphe Quetelet: 'moral
      statistics' 86*
   The Italian school of criminology 88
      Cesare Lombroso 88
         Lombroso's Criminal Man: *atavism and phrenology 90*
         A note on Lombroso's museum 97
         Criminal characteristics and tattooing 99
         Lombroso on women and crime 101
         Towards a more multi-factorial explanation 103

Raffaele Garofalo and Enrico Ferri 104
The application of Lombroso's theories 105
*Early critiques of Lombroso and the ideas of individual
  positivism 108*
Creating the 'other': the presentation of the Irish 114
*'The persistence of the positivist paradigm': the twentieth century
  and beyond 117*

4 Chicago School of Sociology: an explosion of ideas 132
Chicago School of Sociology 133
  The University of Chicago 135
  Women of the university 136
    *Annie Marion MacLean: the 'mother of contemporary
    ethnography' 137*
    *University women, criminology and criminal justice
    policy: a mixed legacy 140*
  Men of the university 149
    The Park and Burgess years 150
  The Hull House settlement 158
    Theory and practice 160
    A women-centred approach 161
    Hull House Maps and Papers *by the Residents of Hull
    House 162*
    Improving social conditions 163
    Crime policy 164
    Painting a rosy picture? 165
    Contributing to an intellectual climate 166
  Achieving a better tomorrow? 167

5 Developing a sociological criminology: Durkheim, Du Bois, Merton and Tannenbaum 172
Émile Durkheim 172
  Society, social facts and social integration 178
  Society and punishment 180
  The perils of modern society 181
  The 'normal' and the 'pathological' 183
  L'affaire Dreyfus 185
  Durkheim's legacy 189
Across the Atlantic 190
  W.E.B. Du Bois 190

Slavery and the convict lease system 193
The Philadelphia Negro 195
Post-Philadelphia: the Atlanta School 198
A snapshot of 1930s America 203
Robert Merton and the American Dream 205
Frank Tannenbaum and 'the dramatization of evil' 209

6 **Feminism: redressing the gender imbalance** 219
French women revile Lombroso 219
'Feminist' and 'feminism' 220
The nineteenth century 223
The suffragette movement 225
The use of surveillance tactics against the suffragettes 226
Feminist activism in Europe 227
Early feminism, crime and criminal justice 228
The Contagious Diseases Acts and the work of Josephine Butler 228
Violence against women 232
A critique of the treatment of women in prison 235
Feminism in the contemporary period 240
The late 1960s onwards 241
Liberal feminism 242
Socialist feminism 243
Radical feminism 245
Radical feminism and violence against women 247
Feminism and criminology 250
Rethinking 'feminism' 257
Achieving the feminist 'political project' 261
The new radical feminist politics: 'The suffragettes wouldn't stand for this' 262

7 **Confronting the establishment: the emergence of critical criminology** 267
The historical context: poverty, resistance and the transformation of society 268
Karl Marx and Friedrich Engels 268
Marx and Engels on crime 269
W.A. Bonger 275
Georg Rusche and Otto Kirchheimer 279
The rise of critical criminology 282

The National Deviancy Conferences 283
The New Criminology 284
The Centre for Contemporary Cultural Studies 289
Anarchism and criminology 295
Problematising critical criminology 299
Critical criminology: developments in Europe and the United States 300
Addressing the politics of the time: critical criminology: from the 1980s to the early 2000s 303
Left realism 303
The 'exceptional' state 309

8 **From theoretical innovations to political engagement** 316
Never boring: cultural criminology 317
'Beyond the horizon, across the divide': Southern criminology and green criminology 321
Southern criminology 321
Thinking about the planet: 'greening' criminology 327
Concluding thoughts 334
Political engagement 335

References 339
Index 374

Figures

1.1	'The Execution of Damiens'	14
2.1	Lapi's engraving in *On Crimes and Punishments*	44
2.2	*Panopticon, or The Inspection House*	56
3.1	Phrenology	91
3.2	'Types of Criminals', from C. Lombroso's *Criminal Man*	95
3.3	'The Irish Frankenstein', from *The Tomahawk*, 18 December 1869	115
3.4	'The Irish Frankenstein' from *Punch* magazine, 20 May 1882	116
4.1	'A Young Toiler'	139
4.2	'Map of the radial expansion and the five urban zones'	153
5.1	Alfred Dreyfus	189
5.2	The 'American Dream'	204
6.1	A postcard sent to Christabel Pankhurst	225
6.2	A secretly taken photograph of suffragettes Evelyn Manesta and Lillian Forrester	226
6.3	ID sheets that were used to help police officers identify suffragettes	227
6.4	'The Modern Inquisition – Treatment of Political Prisoners Under a Liberal Government'	238
6.5	Newspaper billboard from the *Evening Standard*, 1914	239
6.6	Reclaiming the direct action campaigns of the suffragettes	264
6.7	Sisters Uncut's die-in on the red carpet of *Suffragette*	264
7.1	News coverage of the Handsworth 'mugging'	293
8.1	Samuel Augustus Mitchell map of the world on the Mercator projection	321

Boxes

1.1	Voltaire and *la lettre de cachet*	7
1.2	The persecution of 'witches' in the time of the *ancien régime*	8
2.1	Voltaire's advocacy for human rights: thought into action	31
2.2	Alessandro Manzoni, Beccaria's grandson and Italian debates on torture	47
2.3	Tormenting Beccaria	73
3.1	The work of Johann Caspar Lavater: physiognomy and the identification of a 'criminal type'	85
3.2	Phrenology	91
3.3	Extract from *The New York Times*, 4 Aug. 1907: 'Lombroso Tricked Again?'	109
3.4	An extraordinary meeting: Lombroso and Leo Tolstoy	110
4.1	Silencing the academy: the case of Edward Bemis	144
5.1	A note on Durkheim and the Chicago School of Sociology: the establishment of a discipline	177
5.2	The necessity of activism, the transformation of society and the 'Red Scare'	199
5.3	Frank Tannenbaum: convict criminologist	209
6.1	Excerpt from the 'Declaration of Sentiments'	223
7.1	Death of a criminologist: W.A. Bonger	278
7.2	*The New Criminology*: A new approach to theory	287
7.3	The Berkeley School: a critical teaching agenda 1972–1973	302

Acknowledgements

There are many people who have helped me along the way with writing this book. Firstly, I must thank Thomas Sutton, Hannah Catterall and Jake Rainbow from Taylor & Francis for their endless support and patience. Keith Hayward and Shadd Maruna – the ideas we discussed in planning *Fifty Key Thinkers in Criminology* inspired me to explore further the historical and theoretical foundations of criminology. I am extremely grateful for early conversations with Deborah Talbot on the need to go back to primary sources and especially for comments on some of my original work on Beccaria and Lombroso. To Phil Carney, who supplied me with material on the *ancien régime*. To Susan Opotow and Wendy Smith for reigniting my interest in the Chicago School and the activities of Hull House. To Danny Kessler and Louis Kontos, who kindly read every chapter and provided the most insightful advice – I really owe you both a few drinks at Reynolds! To the students at the University of Kent, John Jay College of Criminal Justice and the Graduate Center, City University New York, who made use of draft chapters in their criminology and sociology courses. To Larry Sullivan, Jeff Ferrell, Walter DeKeseredy, Eugene McLaughlin and Sandra Walkate, who either gave feedback or just encouraged me to write. I owe a special debt to Claire Martin, Ruth Jamieson and Anne Mackinnon for getting me back on my feet again after a rough few years. To Dave Brotherton, Lisa Koffler, Juliet, Anny and Jesse Ash, Sara Salman, Yolanda Ortiz-Rodriguez, Theresa Rockett, Jacqui Young, Terri Brajewski, Susan Cohen Lasky, Diane D'Alessandro, Joe Whittaker, Kate Rigden, Jenny Cobine, Peter Marina, Albert de la Tierra, Emily Troshynski, Lynn Chancer, Marcia Esparza, Carla Barrett, Martha Rose, Marty Schwartz, Andy Karmen, Robert Weide, Lucia Trimbur, Gill Gower, Nancy Kaminash, Melissa Myers, Cyann Cox Zoller, Candace McCoy, Valerie West, Barry Spunt, Gregg Barak, Jan Jordan, Alex Steers McCrum, Andrew Taylor, Alisa Thomas, Kerry Carrington and Rafa Gude and the incredible activism of Sisters Uncut. I am also appreciative to have received the support of Dan Stageman and the Office for the Advancement of Research, John Jay College of Criminal Justice; the CUNY Office of Research and to the chairs of my department, Henry Pontell and Bob Garot. Special thanks must go to

Polly, Faith and Erin, who got me into the 'writing groove' – Polly's beautifully drawn daily work timetable stuck to my computer screen was a valuable reminder of what I had to do. I must not forget Piper Doodle, our dog, who kept me company and was often found buried under paper. Finally, while working on this book I lost the love of my life, my soul mate, my partner in crime. Jock – I know that wherever you are you will be breathing a sigh of relief that I have managed to finish and refrained from going down yet another rabbit hole. I hope the stars and the whales are keeping you company. This book is dedicated to my other two loves, our sons Joseph and Fin.

This book has had a long journey, and I am grateful to the *European Journal of Criminology* and to Routledge for allowing me to use parts of earlier writing on Damiens and British critical criminology, respectively. And to Sisters Uncut, the Museum of London, the University of Chicago Library, the National Archives and Getty Images for permission to use illustrations and photographs from their collections.

Jayne Mooney, May 2019, Red Hook, Brooklyn

The theoretical foundations of criminology
Place, time and context

Introduction

Traditionally, sociology (and thus sociological criminology) has been seen as a nomothetic discipline that seeks generalisation irrespective of place and time, whereas history is one that is idiographic, which depicts the unique. This is an implausible division, as all sociological research is idiographically situated, and as Edward Carr pointed out in his classic book *What Is History?* (1961), all history involves at least implicit generalisation. This has not, of course, stopped sociologists in search of social 'laws' from eschewing the culturally specific nor historians from believing that history is the mere documentation of the 'facts' as they happened. C. Wright Mills's famous critique of abstracted empiricism in *The Sociological Imagination* (1959) was a forthright denunciation of such a nomothetic tendency in positivist sociology. In this he insisted on a triangular analysis based on the individual in concrete situations set in a historical context. For him, the rise of abstracted empiricism involved precisely such an elimination of the idiographic, in that not only was the social actor detached from history but the individual was removed from his or her particular cultural and structural setting.

It is this critique that I have used as the basis for an exploration of the foundations of criminology. Hence, the aim of this book is to present the core theories of criminology as historical and cultural products and theorists as producers of culture located in particular places, writing in specific historical periods and situated in precise intellectual networks and philosophical controversies. For far too often we find that theorists and theories of crime have been presented as if they were isolated from the social, historical and philosophical debates of their times. Sometimes a couple of lines of context are offered, but often little else. My intention, therefore, has been to reverse this. For Mills the 'sociological imagination' involved viewing the sentiments, troubles and opinions of the individual in the context of the social structure and the history of their time. We should do this for the theorists and theories we wish to study. For example, to really attempt to understand Beccaria, it is necessary to look beyond that one small volume, *An Essay on Crimes and*

Punishments (*Dei deliti e delle pene*), to consider his ideas in the context of the Enlightenment in terms of his relationship with Voltaire and the Verri brothers and their 'academy of fists' and the dangerous times in which he lived. It is only in this fashion that we can begin to understand the text, to truly make sense of Beccaria's insights and his hesitancies. Likewise, with Lombroso – the so-called father of biological positivism – we have to see him as the controversial character he was: the target of ardent feminist criticisms of the time, the person who bemused newspaper journalists. We must place his insidious racism in relation to his animosity towards Southern Italians. And the arguments of nineteenth-century feminists on crime and criminalisation must be considered alongside the activism of the suffragette movement and the often vitriolic and violent response that this engendered. In taking this approach I attempt to draw on the strengths of sociological criminology and the work of criminal justice historians – the former, as Paul Lawrence has put it, is identified by a 'strong sense of contemporary purpose, and a shallow time/depth perception', the latter 'a weak, or at least diffuse, sense of contemporary purpose, and a strong sense of time perception' (2012, p. 5).

Students often ask, 'why study theory?' The response to this is that crime is a subject of continuous fascination and, as such, it is the case that popular theories of crime causation abound. When I asked women for a previous study what they thought caused men to use violence against their wives or girlfriends, very few said they 'didn't know'. Their responses ranged from a commentary on a poor criminal justice system that failed to convey the message that such behaviour was not to be permitted, to a focus on individual factors (alcohol, mental instability, emotional insecurity), to the wider culture (representations of women in the mass media, pornography) and social structure of society (unequal power relations between men and women, social pressures such as poverty and unemployment). The arguments presented were thoughtful and well considered and, without realising, drew on some of the core tenets of criminological theory. Certainly, they show, as Jock Young (1981) commented, that it is not only criminologists who are capable of 'thinking seriously about crime'. But, popular explanations can be contradictory, for example, with respect to the factors involved in causation and the policy implications that are drawn. It is theory that helps us to organise our thoughts about crime and what to do about it. Theory provides 'us with an image of what something is and how we might best act toward it', it names 'something this kind of thing and not that' and it helps 'to transform a mass of raw sensory data into understanding, explanations, and recipes for appropriate action' (Pfohl, 1985, pp. 9–10).

Theory, however, does not arise 'out of the blue': we need to understand how and why ideas emerge at specific points in time, why they gained currency, whether they are indicative of the interests of a particular social group and the influence that they have had. The dominant theories of crime largely emerged from Northern European societies (the 'Global North'), and consequently the links to an exclusionary world order and colonial past are inescapable. Yet criminology has been affected by what Paul Rock (2005) described as 'chronocentrism' and a myopic take on the past in which we ignore continuities and forget the history of the discipline and the stain of 'dangerous knowledge' on people and communities. As Stephen Pfohl writes, it is those ideas that have 'captured the theoretical imagination of western society at various points in history. . . [that] have often been used as justifications by the west for defending against and/or subordinating its non-western "others"' (1998, p. 1). In being a largely policy-oriented discipline the theoretical origins of criminology have and continue to have a tremendous influence on the treatment of those labelled as 'criminals'. For example, a century after the emergence of classicism, the majority of legal and penal systems of administration in Europe were reformulated to reflect its core principles. Indeed in having related to an extant hierarchal social order, criminological theory has frequently been entangled with – and sometimes placed in opposition to – the power of the state.

Further, in documenting the past, it is necessary to make the leap from one historical situation to another, to relate the assumptions over individual predisposition to criminality that were perpetuated by Lombroso and his colleagues to the eugenicist movement and the horrors of the Holocaust; the debate about torture that preoccupied Voltaire, Beccaria and their compatriots to contemporary political rhetoric on the function of torture and the accounts of what has occurred in the detention centres of Guantanamo Bay, Iraq and Afghanistan. The development of critical criminology must be examined in relation to the writings of Marx and Engels and be seen against the backcloth of the civil rights movement and the counterculture that occurred in the 1960s and the subsequent proliferation of critical thinking. In the current period what has come to constitute both past and present 'criminological knowledge' is not dismissed for its influence is unavoidable, but is critiqued for being grounded in the idiosyncrasies of the North Atlantic world and its historical development: this has had an imperialistic hold on the production of knowledge, with that generated accepted as being of universal relevance (Willis et al, 1999; Carrington and Hogg, 2017; Carrington et al, 2018). The development of southern criminology serves to challenge that produced by the Global North and in so doing highlights the importance of specificity and context.

Finally, in the introduction to our book, *Fifty Key Thinkers in Criminology* (2010), Shadd Maruna wrote that criminology is a 'messy, dynamic intellectual process characterized by collaboration and cross-fertilization' (*ibid*, p. xxv), and this is what I have tried to uncover and reflect in this current project. I start with exploring pre-Enlightenment society – which in being placed in opposition to a developing 'enlightened world' set the scene for the emergence of criminology – and proceed to present a historical survey of the major tenets of criminological theory from classicism to positivism to early sociological theories, feminism and developments in critical criminology. Although I have taken a roughly chronological approach (that some might describe as somewhat conventional or whiggish) to maintain a degree of coherence and clarity, the ideas that underpin criminology have not necessarily developed sequentially – some emerged in the same historical time frame, and there is a constant to-ing and fro-ing as ideas are picked up and discarded and then picked up again. Moreover, the coverage is by no means exhaustive. Writing from a critical perspective, I focus on when ideas occurred, the influence that they were to have and what this means for the discipline of criminology and its future. The main themes that I discuss will be familiar to most criminologists, but some of the stories and key protagonists may be less so. In order to make sense of how criminology has developed as a major social science in the contemporary period and the impact that it has had, it is necessary to reflect on the trajectory of the discipline over time. If we are to move forward into the present and the challenges that face us today and to satisfactorily ground and critique the theories on which we have based criminology, we should understand and learn from the past, and to do this we must, as best we can, give context to both theorist and the theory.

Chapter 1

Setting the stage for the emergence of criminology

'Justice' and the *ancien régime*

In order to place the development of modern criminology historically, it is useful to begin with the state of 'justice' in much of continental Europe from the fourteenth to mid-eighteenth centuries, the period dubbed the *ancien régime* by the French revolutionaries.[1] Whilst historical research is fraught with difficulties when it comes to making sense of what actually happened and there is debate on the way that 'justice' was delivered during this time, there is nonetheless a great deal of evidence to be found in first-person accounts, letters, newspapers and public records to show that by and large 'justice' was arbitrary, dominated by religious bigotry, frequently decided in secret and featured interrogation and punishment techniques that could be excessive and brutal. Indeed, I have chosen to place inverted commas around the word 'justice' to problematise its usage when employed in contexts that clearly resulted in the unjust treatment of alleged offenders.

What is significant about this early history is that the resentment that was felt against the way in which 'justice' was administered was one of the forces that spurred on the Enlightenment movement; this, in turn, gave rise to the French and American revolutions, the values of which have come to symbolise the modern age. It is in the opposition of Enlightenment thinkers to the *ancien régime* that we can identify the origins of criminology.[2] Moreover, this period witnessed the beginning of discourses on 'human rights' that remain important to debates on the treatment of those accused and convicted of crimes. Yet the history of criminology is not an easy one, for it is a history of silencing and exclusion. Criminology and criminologists have traditionally glossed over the terrible crimes committed by the state and in the name of colonialism. Slavery is rarely discussed.[3] The nomothetic tendencies of the discipline and its resulting quest for generalisations that are independent of nation, space or time have contributed to the erasing of voices at the periphery and especially those from non-Western social contexts (Young, 2011; Walklate, 2016). Moreover, the 'science' of criminology has proved a powerful tool in the hands of the state, contributing to the 'othering' and repression of historically marginalised people and those who have dared to resist its workings. As Biko Agozino (2014) and others have pointed out, it is highly significant that the discipline of criminology originated in Northern Europe, the centre of colonial power.

But to try to 'set the stage', let us consider what was meant by the *ancien régime*. '*Ancien*' refers simply to the 'former' regime that preceded the French Revolution of 1789. The term was used in a derogatory way to signify what the revolutionaries thought they were bringing to an end (Doyle, 1986). The *ancien régime* was both a system of government and a form of society permeated by religion (*ibid*). It was characterised by a monarchy in which the king had absolute power and was seen as appointed by and answerable only to God. As such, the king maintained the God-given right to intervene in all aspects of life – that is, in all political, financial and personal affairs. He was God's representative on earth and therefore to question him was to question God. Commentators on this period have often held up Louis XIV of France (1638–1715) as the closest example of an absolute monarch. With the monarch at the top, society was then divided along hierarchical lines into three estates: the first estate being the clergy, the second estate the nobility and the third the rest of the population. Privilege was concentrated in the clergy and nobility, who had special status, enjoyed certain legal rights and were exempt from most of the taxes. The third estate were the majority, yet they had comparatively few rights and paid most of the taxes. Where you were placed in the hierarchy was for many people determined by virtue of birth.

The administration of 'justice' under the *ancien régime* was criticised for its inconsistencies. The king, as God's representative on earth, was above the law. Indeed, his word was regarded as law: as the last king of France, Louis XVI reportedly said when challenged by one of his subjects, 'It is legal because I wish it'. There was seemingly little rational basis to the notion of 'justice': it was an unequal system with an offence against a nobleman being punished more severely than that against a commoner, there was no obvious scale of punishment and the laws governing crime and punishment varied from region to region. As Voltaire, whose work we will turn to in more depth in the next chapter, sardonically reflected on France, 'a man who travels in this country changes his law almost as often as he changes horses' (1764, 1901 ed, p. 49). There are, he said, 'as many laws as there are towns; and even in the same parliament, the maxims of one chamber are not the maxims of another' (1801, p. lxxvi). Many of the problems were due to the various jurisdictions modifying and enforcing different aspects of the old Roman law (which had been resurrected in the twelfth century), together with the constant additions of new laws in a manner seemingly devoid of system or forethought (Maestro, 1942). As Cesare Beccaria was to despairingly comment,

> [S]ome remnants of the laws of an ancient conquering people, which a prince who reigned in Constantinople some 1200 years ago caused to

be compiled, mixed up afterwards with Lombard rites and packed in the miscellaneous volumes of private and obscure commentators – these are what form that set of traditional opinions which from a great part of Europe receive nevertheless the name of laws.

(1880 ed, p. 111)

Judicial appointments were for sale, and yet judges had ultimate power because the king had delegated to them the authority that had been bestowed on him by God. Trials were typically secret affairs with the judge, attended only by his clerk, questioning each witness separately. Abuses of the system were, not surprisingly, commonplace. Vulnerable witnesses could easily be pressurised by the judge to give false testimony. Sometimes a trial was not even necessary. In France people could be imprisoned or exiled on the basis of a *lettre de cachet*: an order – that did not always have to specify a charge – signed by the king, which could be obtained, and not infrequently bought, by a 'person of influence'. This was typically without the possibility of legal redress. It is estimated that during the reign of Louis XV, between 1715 and 1774, 60,000 *lettres de cachet* were issued (MacFarlane, 1844).

Box 1.1 Voltaire and *la lettre de cachet*

In 1726 a *lettre de cachet* was issued against Voltaire – who was by birth from the bourgeoisie, that is, a wealthier member of the third estate – following a quarrel with a nobleman, Chevalier de Rohan-Chabot. As a result, Voltaire was imprisoned in the Bastille for six months before going into exile in England. This had occurred in response to some uppity banter following which Rohan-Chabot asked of Voltaire, 'Who is the young man who talks so loud?' Voltaire cuttingly retorted, 'He is one who does not carry about a great name, but wins respect for the name he has' (Morley, 1913, p. 53). Following a beating by Rohan-Chabot's servants, Voltaire challenged him to a 'gentlemanly' duel in a bid to resolve the matter but received instead the *lettre de cachet*. Such an unpleasant experience underscored for Voltaire that despite being increasingly recognised for his literary talents, social status was what mattered in pre-revolutionary France. To have been born outside of the nobility, to lack a 'great name', meant he counted for little in the eyes of the law and was left powerless in the face of accusations from an aristocrat.

Religion ensured that crime was equated with sin. Carl Ludwig von Bar (1916) pointed out in his examination of continental criminal law in this period that the Mosaic Law and the principle of the '*talio*' (as in 'an eye for an eye, a tooth for a tooth') became influential in many jurisdictions. Whilst originally intended to limit excessive punishment, it was interpreted as a law of retribution, 'the product of a vengeful deity' (Granucci, 1969, p. 839) and, thus, a divine command. It was applied particularly stringently to offences that were perceived as a direct affront to religion and helped to ensure the criminal law was often harshly and cruelly applied; hence, it was written in the Swedish-Finnish penal codes of the 1500s to 1700s, 'the legislator shall seek to soften the wrath of the Deity and save the realm from his vengeance by the most severe punishments' (von Bar, 1916, pp. 295–296). The divine origins of the criminal law ensured there was little in the way of compromise or mitigation (Ganucci, 1969).

The influence of the Church was particularly evident in the persecution of witchcraft and heresy that saw hundreds of thousands of 'witches' – three-quarters of whom were women – tortured and executed between the fourteenth and mid-seventeenth centuries. Widely embraced were the Dominican Order's[4] theories of witchcraft that were founded on a dualistic conception of the world which, as Nachman Ben-Yehuda describes, involved, 'a battlefield in which a struggle between the godly sons of light and the satanic sons of darkness was being played out' (1980, p. 5). Thus, witches were regarded 'as the exact qualitative opposite of the conception of Christ, and witchcraft as the exact opposite of what was supposed to be the true faith, Christianity' (*ibid*). Pope John XXII was the instigator of much of the early hysteria that occurred in the fourteenth century by suggesting the practice of witchcraft was gaining in influence and encouraged inquisitors to seek out and put on trial all sorcerers, enchanters and other heretics (Lea, 1901). There is an extensive literature on this period, much of which has drawn attention to the sheer number of women executed.[5]

Box 1.2 The persecution of 'witches' in the time of the *ancien régime*

Women identified as witches were, certainly at the start of the hysteria, often older women who were seen as non-conformist in the sense of living outside of the traditional family structure. 'Witches' may therefore have represented a misplaced fear over the changing position of women in Northern European society. For this was a period that saw growth in the number of unmarried women, the move from a subsistence-level to a cash-based economy that resulted in women entering the labour market, more women involved in prostitution and the use of contraception and infanticide, which brought into question women's role as mothers

(Ben-Yehuda, 1980). At the same time women's inferior status in comparison to men and lack of political power and organisation made them easy targets for such large-scale persecution (*ibid*).

Women were often presented as at one with the devil. The infamous *Malleus Maleficarum* (*The Witches' Hammer*), written around 1486 by Heinrich Kramer and James[6] Sprenger, two members of the Dominican Order, portrays women as naturally more wicked than men and susceptible to the influence of the devil. Women are 'credulous', have 'slippery tongues', find it easy to deceive and are more carnal, 'all witchcraft comes from carnal lust, which in women is insatiable' (1486, 1971 ed, p. 47). Women are either good or bad, there is no in between, and 'when they are governed by a good spirit, they are most excellent in virtue; but when they are governed by an evil spirit, they indulge [in] the worst possible vices' (*ibid*, p. 42). Thus, we speak of witches rather than wizards, 'and blessed be the Highest who has so far preserved the male sex from so great a crime' as that of witchcraft (*ibid*, p. 47). 'All wickedness' they argue, 'is but little to the wickedness of a woman' (*ibid*, p. 43). The *Malleus Maleficarum* aimed to prove not only the existence and menace of witchcraft and Satanism – indeed not to believe in this was a manifestation of heresy – but to function as an authoritative guide for the civil and ecclesiastical courts as to the identification and prosecution of witches. Once apprehended, the 'witch' was to be put on trial, stripped of her clothes in case there is some 'instrument of witchcraft sewn into her clothes; for they often make such instruments, at the instruction of devils' (*ibid*, p. 225), horrifically tortured to secure a confession and then it was recommended that she be burnt in order to banish the devil from her body. Ben-Yehuda (1980) credits part of the success of the *Malleus Maleficarum* with its wide circulation: for the printing press had recently been invented, and it was one of the first books to be printed using this means. There were at least twenty editions published. It was a 'best seller', outselling even the Bible.

The German theologian Friedrich von Spee fervently spoke out against both torture and the callous prosecutions of women suspected of being witches, attracting condemnation from political and ecclesiastical authorities. In 1631 his book *Cautio Criminalis* (Precautions for Prosecutors), published anonymously due to fear of prosecution, exposed the illogicality of using torture to secure confessions, for many 'are so weak they will state any lie rather than suffer torture' (p. 74) and that in order to escape the torture, those who are innocent will not only confess but are liable to implicate others who are just as guiltless. He pleaded with the princes to 'observe with their own eyes the savagery of tortures that now flourish everywhere' (*ibid*, p. 29). Von Spee had spent much of his early priesthood in some of the worst areas affected by the witch hunts and, as part of his duties, ministered to women suspected of witchcraft. Indeed, when asked by Johann Philipp von Schönborn, who was to become archbishop of Mainz, why his hair had turned grey so early, von Spee retorted,

> [G]rief has turned my hair white, grief on account of the witches whom I have accompanied to the stake . . . Not only grief at such inhuman punishments, but grief at the malice and stupidity of the whole procedure of the witch hunts raging throughout Franconia and Westphalia.
>
> (Knowles, 2007)

Let us pause for a moment to reflect on the utter humiliation, despair, terror and extreme physical pain that these women endured. And although there is debate over the level of which it was endorsed by the Catholic Church, there is no doubt that the *Malleus Maleficarum* was influential and provided the rationale for the torture and murder of hundreds of thousands of women in Europe.[7] This has been described as nothing less than 'gendercide', for neither before this time nor since have women been so extensively and selectively the focus for killing (see Jones, 2006; gendercidewatch.com). Yet as Randeep Singh Chauhan reminds us, while the witch hunts gradually ceased during the 1700s, with 'the patriarchs of history claim(ing) that women would no longer face such gross structural persecution', on an ideological level, the legacy of sexism and the 'othering' of women who were seen as nonconformist continued (2005, p. 5).[8] In criminology this was to be reflected, for example, in the works of Cesare Lombroso, Otto Pollak and Hans Eysenck.

Further Reading:

Ben-Yehuda, N. (1980) 'The European witch craze of the 14th to 17th centuries: A sociologist's perspective', *American Journal of Sociology*, Vol. 86, No. 1, pp. 1–31.

Admittedly, the persecution of witches began to wane as opposition to the social order represented by the *ancien régime* grew, there were still troubling instances. Voltaire (1801) writes of an old woman of Wurtsburg who was convicted of witchcraft and burnt as late as 1748. Moreover, the Bavarian Penal Code of 1751 covered the crime of witchcraft and stated that 'those who zealously spread heretical doctrines, or mislead others, or incited them against the authorities, such seducers of the faithful were to be executed with the sword and their bodies burned upon a funeral pyre' (Maestro, 1942, p. 4). The horror of the numbers killed during this period was powerfully underscored by Voltaire, who said that if we were to add to this figure those heretics who were executed, 'our part of the globe will appear one vast scaffold covered with executioners and victims, and surrounded by judges, guards and spectators' (1801, p. xxv).

Torture

The judicial system in continental Europe was laid down in a number of legal codes, the most frequently referenced being the Constitutio Criminalis Carolina of 1532. As noted earlier, one of the predominant characteristics of the judicial system, or 'anti-system' as Dale Van Kley (1984, p. 262) chose to describe it, was the secret investigation of the crime by the judge who heard each witness on oath and questioned the alleged offender. In cases where there was neither eyewitness evidence nor a voluntary confession, torture could be used to achieve a confession.[9] According to the Constitutio Criminalis Carolina, torture was to be administered in such a way that the alleged offender would also reveal facts about the crime which 'no innocent person can know' (1532, p. 5). Thus, it was not just reserved for 'witches,' but rather was part of the ordinary judicial process – that is, for those of the third estate. The clergy and nobility were generally exempt or treated with leniency. In France, torture, *'la question'*, could be administered at two points in a trial: *question préparatoire* to secure a confession and *question définitive* or *préalable* to reveal accomplices.

Regicide: the ultimate crime of the ancien regime

> *"My God, give me strength, give me strength. Lord, my God, have pity on me. Lord, my God, I am suffering so much. Lord, my God, give me patience."*
>
> (*The words of Robert François Damiens during his punishment for the crime of regicide at the Place de Grève, Paris, 26 March 1757*)[10]

The persecution of women as witches and the utilisation of torture in the time of the *ancien régime* illustrates the harshness of the judicial system; it also serves to remind us of the cruelty that people can inflict on one another. The notorious case of Robert-François Damiens, a lowly domestic servant who was convicted of the attempted murder of Louis XV of France, has come to be seen as symbolic of the barbarity of the *ancien régime* (Mooney, 2014). The level of inhumanity expressed in the incident is quite simply appalling. There is no mercy, no pity in the administration of his punishment. For criminology students, the treatment of Damiens particularly resonates through its utilisation by Michel Foucault in the dramatic opening to his seminal work, *Discipline and Punish: The Birth of the Prison* (1975).

On 5 January 1757, Damiens approached the king as he went to board his carriage and stabbed him with a pen knife. This was reported as resulting in a 'small wound' below his fifth rib. Damiens made no attempt to escape. The king, on seeing that he had been hurt, said, 'There is the man who struck me. Let him be seized, and no harm done to him' (*The Monthly Review*, 1757, pp. 64–65). However, as the king was God's representative on Earth, a crime against the king was a crime against God and, as such, warranted the greatest of punishments. *L'affaire Damiens* caused immense excitement; the Archbishop of Paris ordered the reciting of prayers for forty hours without rest (MacKinnon, 1902). Condemned as a regicide, Damiens's fate was therefore to mirror that of François Ravaillac, a known religious fanatic, who had assassinated Henry IV of France in 1610. Like Ravaillac, Damiens was first to be taken 'in a tipcart naked' to make the *amende honorable* before the main door of the Church of Paris, where he was to hold 'a burning wax torch weighing two pounds' and 'there on his knees he will say and declare that he had committed a very mean, very terrible and very dreadful parricide, and that he had hurt the King'; he was to then 'repent and ask God, the King and Justice to forgive him' (Anon, 1757, *Pièces originales et procédures du procès, fait à Robert-François Damiens*). From the Church of Paris, Damiens was taken to the Place de Grève, and the hand that had held the knife was burnt with sulphur; 'red-hot' pincers were used to tear at the flesh on his arms, thighs and chest. Molten lead, wax and boiling oil were poured into every wound. He was asked if he wanted to say anything and replied, 'No'. Priests approached and held the crucifix for him to kiss. He was then 'quartered', that is, his arms and legs were harnessed to four wild horses to be pulled apart and, if this was not horror enough, 'though they (the horses) were driven to four contrary points, none of the members gave way, though all drawn to an amazing degree of extension'. His screams reverberated around the Place de Grève. After an hour of being pulled in this way, they cut the sinews and even 'after both thighs and one arm were off' Damiens still breathed. When all four limbs were eventually severed from his torso, he was thrown on a 'burning pyre' (As recounted in the *Gazette d'Amsterdam*, 1 April 1757).

Numerous commentators – both then and now – have expressed disgust at the enormous crowd that gathered to watch Damiens's demise. Rooms overlooking the execution site were rented out to nobles for great sums of money. Accounts of the time reveal a gory fascination and even a delight in the witnessing of such a spectacle; Giacomo Casanova's memoirs (1791) describe how an acquaintance, a guest at his social gathering, becomes sexually aroused as the events unfold in the square below and Damiens 'piercing shrieks' fill the air.

The *l'affaire Damiens* was the main topic of public discussion for the next twelve months or so; it was the theme of songs, poems, engravings and religious sermons (Graham, 2000). Both the trial and execution were widely reported – nationally and internationally – in the newspapers of the day. The international press at first condemned Damiens for his 'horrid attempt' (*London Gazette*, 5–9 April 1757, p. 2) on the king's life but then expressed revulsion at the manner of his death, which was written about in excruciating detail. In a review of the case in *Lloyd's Evening Post* on 5 August of that year, it was stated that it 'was the result of nothing but the madness of a poor wretch', that Damiens should have been the 'object of the deepest compassion, than of those infernal tortures at which humanity shudders and can hardly admit of a case where they should be allowable to use them, or to forget, in any criminal, his being a fellow creature' (p. 60). It was, as a popular nineteenth-century publication, *The Penny Cyclopaedia*, put it, 'altogether one of the most disgraceful exhibitions that ever took place in a civilized country' (Long, 1837, p. 298).

There is an enormous amount written about the execution of Damiens. Charles Dickens, who as a boy had read about the fate of Damiens in *The Terrific Register* ('Dreadful Execution of Damiens', 1825, Vol. 1, p. 1), included it in *A Tale of Two Cities* (1859), where he writes both of the horror of Damiens's death and the disturbing nature of the spectacle:

> 'Listen once again then, Jacques!' said the man with the restless hand and the craving air. 'The name of that prisoner was Damiens, and it was all done in open day, in the open streets of this city of Paris; and nothing was more noticed in the vast concourse that saw it done, than the crowd of ladies of quality and fashion, who were full of eager attention to the last – to the last, Jacques, prolonged until nightfall, when he had lost two legs and an arm, and still breathed!
>
> (p. 112)

Further, in *Rights of Man*, authored during the early stages of the French Revolution, Thomas Paine comments on the case of Damiens in a section that ominously warns of the impact of such barbarous punishments on the populace, particularly the lower orders, against whom it was disproportionately employed. Such punishments 'either tortures their feelings or hardens their hearts, and in either case, it instructs them how to punish when power falls into their hands' (1791, p. 36). Thus,

> Lay then the axe to the root, and teach governments humanity. It is their sanguinary punishments which corrupt mankind. In England, the punishment in certain cases is by *hanging*, *drawing* and *quartering*; the heart of the sufferer is cut out and held up to the view of the populace. In France, under the former Government, the punishments were not less barbarous. Who does not remember the execution of Damien, torn to pieces by horses? The effect of those cruel spectacles exhibited to the populace, is

Figure 1.1 'The Execution of Damiens'. *Bibliothèque nationale de France.*

to destroy tenderness or excite revenge; and by the base and false idea of governing men by terror, instead of reason, they become precedents. It is over the lowest class of mankind that government by terror is intended to operate, and it is on them that it operates to the worst effect. They have sense enough to feel they are the objects aimed at; and they inflict in their turn the examples of terror they have been instructed to practise.

(*ibid*)

For Michel Foucault, this 'gloomy festival of punishment' was representative of a by-gone era: one that was to be replaced by a criminal justice system that was based on imprisonment. In *Discipline and Punish* Foucault recounts at length the treatment of Damiens before turning to compare it to the daily 'rules' of Leon Faucher's House of Young Prisoners in Paris in 1838 (for example, 'Art. 17. The prisoners' day will begin at six in the morning in winter and at five in summer ... Art. 18. *Rising*. At the first drum-roll, the prisoner must rise and dress in silence, as the supervisor opens the cell doors' (*ibid*, pp. 6–7)). For Foucault, the execution and prison rules, which were separated by less than a century, defined two distinct penal styles and the move from one to the other symbolic of a wider political change in the way that power is exercised (*ibid*, p. 23). The public spectacle of torture and the body as 'the major target of penal repression' (*ibid*, p. 8) were gradually replaced by the more private, regulated practices centring on discipline and surveillance: in just a few decades 'the tortured, dismembered, amputated body, symbolically branded on face or shoulder, exposed alive or dead to public view' disappeared (*ibid*, p. 8). Punishment occurred in private and in silence. No longer was it the obvious horror of punishment that functioned as a deterrent, but its inevitability.

The new system is seen by Foucault to be just as insidious, for it symbolises a shift in focus from the body to the soul of the prisoner. As Daniel Maier-Katkin notes, the argument presented in *Discipline and Punish* is that

> the subtlety of contemporary technologies of punishment has allowed them to become more widespread and more effective in imposing docility on the human spirit. The symbolism of the medieval system of criminal punishments was focused on the power and glory of majesty and authority: the symbolism of the modern era is focused on internalized discipline and conformity. For Foucault, the history of punishment is not an account of humanity's advance from barbarism and brutality, it is an epic tale of the substitution of one form of social control for another; and in his view the subjugation of the individual has grown deeper and more widespread.
>
> (2003, p. 165)[11]

The emphasis moves from the need to avenge crime to the 'correction' of the offender. The resulting subjugation of the individual is, in fact, much more 'widespread' than that which occurs in the prison, for the same mechanisms for achieving discipline and conformity are evident in factories, military barracks, schools, hospitals and so on.

Yet the transition from public spectacle and the torture of the body to penal discipline and a focus on the soul of the offender was not quite as straightforward as Foucault presents. While Foucault saw the soul as a modern invention (and we can debate what it was that he actually meant by the 'soul'),[12] it is perhaps worth mentioning at this juncture that the *ancien régime*, with all of its religious undertones, was certainly concerned with the transformation of the soul when inflicting punishment. Witness the instructions given to Damiens – to repent and ask for God's forgiveness – and the handing to him of the crucifix to kiss during his execution (Anon., 1757). Punishment is not just concerned with the avenging of crime but with the salvation of the soul and, as such, with the 'correction' of the offender before he or she meets their maker.

Whether there was such a qualitative leap or sea-change in attitude towards punishment is questionable. The centrality of torture in the judicial process was not to disappear with all of its horrors of bodily suffering. Indeed, despite extensive opposition from Enlightenment figures, the practice continued long after this period in history. Although it is true to say that it is mostly hidden, it is there nonetheless in the actual practice of prison and police interrogations, and is more overtly apparent in the actions towards those considered separate from and/or 'unworthy' of citizenship by state elites. This was obvious from the treatment of slaves, and to this day in the treatment of combatants in war and suspected terrorists.

What is of interest at this point in the story is that Foucault saw Damiens as the object of punishment, yet there is much more to the case. He can, for example, be seen as a symbol of resistance. Indeed, the events that ultimately led to Damiens's crime represented a general social movement that was sweeping through France, which was questioning the way that society was structured and the role of 'justice' within this structure. It is in this period that some of the core theoretical principles of what was to become the discipline of 'criminology' emerged. Further, this case provides an early illustration of how those who speak out against political injustice find themselves targeted by the 'justice' system in a bid to silence dissent.

Robert-François Damiens: a quest for justice

Robert-François Damiens was a fairly unremarkable man; he is reported to have been a 'good servant', although there are accusations of him 'chasing women' and having an overfondness for wine. He was dismissed from several positions for drunkenness and in one case for poor service and a 'sinister physiognomy' (Van Kley, 1984, p. 21). As an aside, the use of this phrase is of interest, as 'physiognomy', the means of determining character and behaviour from a person's external, especially facial, features, appeared in debates on criminality from the late eighteenth century. Damiens was also portrayed as somewhat unstable: 'he would often talk to himself and mutter inwardly' (Anon, 1757, *Lloyd's Evening Post and British Chronicle*, 3 Aug.). Voltaire described him in rather derogatory terms as a 'mad dog' and 'a crazy monster' (*Lettres*, cited in Davidson, 2004, p. 48), this being some years before his own campaigns on miscarriages of 'justice'. Damiens's alleged state of mind at the time of the offence was to fuel comparisons with the English 'regicide' Margaret Nicholson, who attempted to stab George III in 1786. Nicholson was certified 'insane' and confined to Bethlam Royal Hospital, where, as a commentary in *The Gazetteer and New Daily Advertiser* noted, she would be 'treated with every degree of humanity' and would receive 'every attention and comfort' (13 Dec. 1786, see Mooney, 2014). Although the reality was that Nicholson was to be confined for life, spent part of the time shackled to her bed and was subjected to the most derogatory and painful treatments.

At time of Damiens's attack on the king, there was considerable political unrest in Paris. The ordinary working people – those at the bottom of the third estate – felt unsupported by the government; they felt that their 'expectations', namely the right to food and protection, were not being met. The king was seen as failing in his duty to look after his people. Disquiet over the level of social iniquity that affected the lower orders was openly and stridently voiced, and correspondingly the authorities became increasingly concerned about the possibility of social upheaval. Police agents and informers regularly reported on the public mood (Graham, 2000; Jassie, 1996; Farge, 1994). Let us look at some of the events that incited popular discontent, which in turn were to influence Damiens in the commission of his crime. These help us to understand more clearly the symbolic nature of his actions and the extent to which they can be considered to have a harbinger quality, in the sense of contributing directly (through actions and statements) and indirectly (in their representation by commentators) to the significance of this particular moment in history. For they were interpreted by those in power and by radical commentators as evoking criticism of the present and as a portent for the future.

Problems with the harvest, transportation difficulties, bureaucratic hold-ups and corruption resulted in a shortage of bread and grossly inflated prices (Jassie, 1996). Many Parisians faced starvation and often their response was to take to the streets in protest. Local bakeries came under attack by groups of people, who would use or threaten violence in order to force the bakers to reduce their prices. But it was not the bakers who were held responsible for the hunger of the people – it was the authorities, and by the early 1750s the blame fell at the feet of the king of France (Jassie, 1996; Kaplan, 1982). Indeed, although at the start of the crisis many still believed in a paternalistic and benevolent monarch who had the welfare of his subjects at heart, as time went on criticism of the king grew to the extent that he was even accused of directly profiting from the sale of grain so badly needed by his subjects (Jassie, 1996). The working people expressed their dissatisfaction in 'loose talk', letters and placards. The need for popular justice was underscored by one such placard that complained, though 'the people' are 'dying of hunger' there was 'neither [official] aid nor justice, except what comes from our hands and arms' (cited in Jassie, 1996, p. 108).

Rioting was also to occur in response to the rounding up and incarceration of children found on the streets. Royal orders had been issued in November 1749 to 'arrest all the mendicants (beggars) in the Kingdom' (d'Argenson, 1857–8 ed, p. 80) in a bid to clean up the streets; in Paris the police targeted 'young mendicants' who were, according to one police agent, Sebastien LeBlanc, largely the 'children . . . of working people' (cited in Jassie, 1996, p. 85) and who were often simply hanging about the streets. Between May 1749 and May 1750 200 children were arrested. It was rumoured that they were to be shipped to the colonies (Farge and Revel, 1991; Van Kley, 1984). Again, people took to the streets and directly confronted those who were seen 'kidnapping' children. Many were arrested for their actions, and there were widespread allegations of police brutality.

The people openly complained about the unfair manner in which 'justice' was meted out both in response to the riots and in relation to more everyday events. The authorities executed a number of those involved, but as the rioters believed their actions were legitimate, this was seen to be shockingly unjust, as having resulted in the deaths of those who had committed no crime. As Kenneth Jassie (1996) points out in his insightful thesis on this period, this not only exacerbated the level of discontent but also served to emphasise the differences between official and popular conceptions of the meaning of justice. In more everyday cases the degree to which the law favoured the powerful was increasingly resented. Those who committed crimes against those of higher social status were often treated with extreme severity, such as the case in 1726 when a cook was hanged for allegedly writing a threatening letter to his employer. The people were outraged that such a punishment could be meted out to someone who had 'neither killed, stolen, or ever committed any serious misdeed' (Barbier, 1847–56, Vol. 1, p. 232).

Perhaps what is even more important in terms of our understanding of *l'affaire Damiens* was the highly contentious dispute over the Jansenists (see Van Kley, 1984). Regarded as one of the most momentous episodes in the political history of this period in France, this dispute brought the monarchy into direct confrontation with the magistrates of the *parlement* of Paris and, of course, many of the king's subjects. The Jansenists, a religious minority within the Catholic Church, were popular with the working people. Jansenist priests were known for their acts of humanity and charity. They supported many of those living in poverty and hardship. As Jassie comments, 'the poor and disenfranchised considered Jansenists "true Christians"' (1996, p. 151). The Jansenists, however, had long been denounced for their beliefs: in 1713 the papal bull *Unigenitus* was issued at the request of the previous king, condemning 101 Jansenist propositions contained in Pasquier Quesnel's *Nouveau Testament*. Jansenists were not afforded the status and privileges typically granted to the clergy in this period. The French monarchy came to regard the Jansenists as politically dangerous; the memoires of the Duc de Saint-Simon records that for Louis XIV they were to be seen as 'enemies of the Church and State, as republicans, as enemies of his authority and person' (cited in Campbell, 1996, p. 44). This view continued into the reign of Louis XV, fuelled no doubt by the extremely popular underground Jansenist journal, *Nouvelles ecclésiastiques*, which came into being in 1728 and continued to be published until 1803. On the pages of this journal were to be found vehement opposition to the *Unigenitus* and stories detailing resistance to religious persecution (Jassie, 1996). According to James Breck Perkins's (1899) account of France under Louis XV, the Archbishop of Paris threatened members of his congregation with excommunication if they dared to read *Nouvelles ecclésiastiques* – but they read it all the same! Jansenist priests and their supporters were routinely harassed and, not infrequently, arrested and imprisoned, often by *lettre de cachet*.

The working people of Paris were known to have been particularly angered when the government attempted to prevent the worship of the deceased Jansenist deacon, François de Paris (Jassie, 1996; Farge, 1994). François de Paris was in life an extremely charismatic person, a man of wealth who had given away all he had to the poor; in death, miracles were ascribed to him. In January 1732 the cemetery of the Church of St Médard, where he was entombed, was closed to prevent pilgrimages to his graveside; in response a placard was attached to the doors of the church on which it was written in a parody of the royal ordinance, 'By the King's order: God is forbidden to perform miracles in this place' (Barbier, 1847–56, 2, p. 246).[13] The king's role as God's representative on Earth was clearly being doubted by the working people. They were openly saying 'that the king will not live very long. It will be as punishment for his treatment of the Abbe Paris' (Barbier, cited in Jassie, 1996, p. 140). The dispute was to reach a climax when Louis XV supported an order by the Archbishop of Paris, Christophe de Beaumont, to refuse to give the sacraments to Jansenists; this was opposed by the magistrates of the *parlement* of Paris, many of whom, for various reasons, were sympathetic to the Jansenists (see Van Kley, 1984). The people were more direct in their opposition. The memoires of the Marquis d'Argenson (1859) recall how in 1753 market women from Les Halles approached 'the bugger' de Beaumont and tried to drown him in the Seine. A full-scale political crisis ensued, leading to the resignation of *parlement* in mid-December 1756, just prior to Damiens's assault on the king.

There are, therefore, three possible positions on Robert-François Damiens: the first regards him as a poor, misguided eccentric, or 'mad man'; the second perceives him to be part of an organised conspiracy; and the third sees him as signifying a society in transition. These explanations reappear in contemporary discussion of criminality, especially those that try to make sense of terrorist attacks (Mooney and Young, 2005) or violence arising from political protest. Even though Damiens's prosecutors certainly appear to have been under the assumption that Damiens was part of an organised plot and in the pay of wealthy dissidents (why else would someone of such 'humble social status' commit such an act?) (Van Kley, 1984, p. 36), he revealed no names under interrogation, and he was interrogated over fifty times. It seems likely, as Jassie puts it, that Damiens was 'one member of the common people' who 'gave "resistance" new meaning' (1996, p. 143). There are a number of published testimonies from Damiens in which he explains the reasons for his assault on the king. These, together with records of his conversations with people prior to the incident, reveal he shared the concerns of the working people. Hence, his actions symbolise the level of discontent expressed by the people of Paris. In one testimony he says he had not wanted to kill Louis XV, but 'to touch the King' and thus 'prompt him to restore all things to order and tranquility in his states' (Anon, 1757, *Pièces originales et procédures du procès, fait à Robert-François Damiens*). In another Damiens is reported as saying that the 'poverty of the French people' (*ibid*) was a factor; at this time bread in Paris was 50 per cent above its usual price. It was widely rumoured that Damiens had declared that his attention was 'to deliver the country from a tyrant who made the people die of hunger'; the king, he argued, 'governed badly and that it would be doing the kingdom a great service to kill him' (d'Argenson, 1857, p. 327).

According to contemporary sources, throughout the torturous interrogation process, Damiens consistently maintained that the cause of his action lay in the religious controversy over the Jansenists, and it was alleged that he had on him a copy of the New Testament at the time of his assault on the king, which was used by the authorities as indicative of a religious motivation. At one point during the interrogation process, Damiens was reported to have said that he 'planned on doing it three years ago because of the Archbishop's bad behavior'; by this he meant the aforementioned refusal of sacraments to Jansensists (Anon, 1757, *Pièces originales et procédures du procès, fait à Robert-François Damiens.*). For 'No one should refuse Sacraments to good people who pray in Churches every day, from morning to evening' (*ibid*) and, as such, his wish was to get the king to listen to the concerns being voiced in his kingdom, 'to render [Louis XV] more disposed to hear [his *parlement's*] remonstrances, to dispense justice, and cease heeding the pernicious advice of his ministers' (cited in Van Kley, 1984. p. 39).

In this context, Robert-François Damiens can be seen as on a quest for justice on behalf of the ordinary people of France. The radical philosopher William Godwin described Damiens as being 'deeply penetrated with anxiety for the eternal welfare of mankind' and for this was willing to sacrifice his life and expose himself to torture and death (1793, p. 99).

Thus, whilst I have commented on the disquieting way in which people were attracted to the spectacle of Damiens's gruesome death, there were many who openly supported his actions and would have been outraged at the manner of his execution. There is ample evidence of this in the official records of the procurator general of the Paris *parlement*. Documented by Dale Van Kley (1984), these records, which include police reports made at the time, reveal one peasant to have said that if he were Damiens, 'he would not have missed the king and would have pierced his guts with an awl' and a Rémond Dupont, who proclaimed, 'it would have been better for the king and queen to have been reduced to ashes rather than Damiens'. A cloth shearer who had been unable to find work described Louis XV as 'the cause of his misery' and apparently called the king a 'bugger' who 'would not be alive in eight days'. A day labourer, Marie-Marguerite Gadibois, complaining over the price of grain, grumbled that Damiens 'had done badly to have missed his coup, since the said Damiens would have been just as dead in the one event as in the other'. She reported that all the working people were saying this. Another day-labourer described Damiens as a 'saint' and a 'martyr' and claimed he 'appeared daily at the [place de] Grève demanding vengeance for his execution' (Van Kley, 1984, p. 247).

Damiens's attack brought into question the sacredness of the king, for in highlighting the 'vulnerability of the king's mortal body', it served to raise the possibility of a world that was no longer centred on the monarch (Graham, 2000, p. 139) or indeed might exist without the hierarchal structure that typified the *ancien régime*. Not surprisingly, the period following *l'affaire Damiens* witnessed an increased clampdown by the authorities on the ordinary people – as is typical of regimes that are under threat. As Lisa Jane Graham (2000) notes, in the two-year period after the execution of Damiens more people were arrested for crimes of *mauvais discours*, which covered a range of offences from seditious speech and literature to anti-monarchist plots, than at any other time during the rule of Louis XV. So although Damiens's execution was intended to remind the people of the almighty power of the monarchy, it did not succeed in quieting the voices of popular opposition. Calls for the king's death or dethroning were being heard throughout the streets of Paris and beyond. The rumblings of change could not be stopped. As Van Kley puts it,

> For all Damiens' eccentricities and in part because of them, he aspired to be mainly that [a good citizen]; his real 'folly' consisted in thinking that someone like him could directly participate in the political conflicts of the day and in actually doing so in the only way available to him. Before long there would be many more like him.
>
> (1984, p. 96)

The significance of Damiens for criminology

Damiens's act of violence against the king represents a popular sense of injustice which was eventually to transform society, demolish the *ancien régime* and attempt to bring about a society characterised by liberty, equality and fraternity. Such a social order involved not only a freeing up of the social and economic system from the ties of feudalism but correspondingly led to a criminal justice system which professed to embody the principles of freewill, equality of all before the law and punishment proportional to the harm committed. Further, the outrageous atrocity which Damiens suffered was born out of the extreme anxieties of the authorities with regard to social change; this act of savagery embodied precisely the principles of the *ancien régime* that Voltaire and Beccaria and the founders of the classicist school of criminology were to rally against. That is, it involved punishment totally disproportional to the act, inequality before the law – the assailant being from the lower orders and the victim the king himself – and a gory spectacle created to instil terror in the general population rather than punish the individual offender himself.

'The tide is turning; the tone of life is about to change'

(Van Kley, 1984, p. 270)

The intellectuals

The working people were by no means alone in their opposition to the monarchy and the administration of 'justice' under the *ancien régime*. From the sixteenth century there was a steady flow in published work that critiqued the structure of society and the dominance of religion, pointed out both the futility and brutality of judicial torture, opposed the persecution of alleged witches and, importantly, started to lay the theoretical framework for a concept of humanity which advanced the rights of the individual. Of particular importance in terms of the development of criminology are the writings Montesquieu and the *philosophes*.

Montesquieu

Towards the end of the 1740s in France, Charles Louis de Secondat, Baron de Montesquieu, published the enormously successful *The Spirit of Laws* (*L'espirit des lois*). It was described by David Hume in his *An Enquiry Concerning the Principles of Morals* as the 'best system of political knowledge that, perhaps, has ever been communicated to the world' (1751, p. 27). In France the Chevalier d'Aydie praised Montesquieu for 'discovering for mankind the ways to become more just and consequently happier' (Carrithers et al, 2001, p. 2). In 1892 Emile Durkheim wrote his Latin dissertation (one of two theses that were required for a doctorate degree) on Montesquieu's methodology. Today *The Spirit of Laws* is regarded as a classic within Western political philosophy. Acknowledged for its profound impact on the United States Constitution, *The Spirit of Laws* outlines different modes of government and argues for the need for a separation of powers within government in order to prevent the concentration of power in the hands of one person or group.

Furthermore, and of importance to this present exploration of the origins of criminology, Montesquieu made the case for the need for 'justice' to be administered fairly with an emphasis on protecting the rights of the accused. He opposed the use of severe and disproportionate punishments not just in terms of their obvious cruelty but also because they are ineffective:

> If an inconveniency or abuse arises in the state, a violent government endeavours suddenly to redress it; and, instead of putting the old laws in execution, it establishes some cruel punishment, which instantly puts a stop to the evil. But the spring of government hereby loses its elasticity; the imagination grows accustomed to the severe as well as the milder punishment; and, as the fear of the latter diminishes, they are soon obliged, in every case, to have recourse to the former. Robberies on the high-way were grown common in some countries. In order to remedy this evil, they invented the punishment of breaking upon the wheel; the terror of which put a stop, for a while, to this mischievous practice: but, soon after, robberies on the highways became as common as ever.
> (1748, 1766 ed, p. 121)

There was, as Montesquieu discovered, no historical evidence that severe punishments were more effective in terms of deterrence than lenient ones.

Indeed, extreme punishment risked inciting hostility amongst the population which, in turn, could threaten the stability of the existing social order. And, as we have seen, this was beginning to be the situation in France. There was, he believed, a direct link between moderate punishment and liberty: 'it would be easy to prove that in all or nearly all the states of Europe, penalties have decreased or strengthened to the extent they have drawn closer to or farther from liberty' (1748, 1766 ed, p. 61). 'The spirit of moderation' is key to the overall argument of the text, for 'political evil, like moral evil', is to be found 'lying between two extremes' (*ibid*, p. 286; see Carrithers, 2001, p. 318).

For Montesquieu it is the certainty of punishment that deters would-be offenders. Moreover, there should be no arbitrariness in the administration of punishment; it should arise from the nature of the crime rather than 'the capriciousness of the legislator' (1766 ed, p. 271). Although Montesquieu wrote little on torture, believing the main arguments to have already been made, 'so many men of learning and genius have wrote against the custom of torturing criminals' (1766 ed, p. 114),[14] he saw the practice as a feature of 'despotic states, where what inspires fear is the fittest spring of government' (*ibid*). He believed religious offenses should be decriminalised and wrote against the equation of crime with sin: sin is to 'offend the Deity' and, 'where there is no public act, there can be no criminal matter, the whole passes between man and God' (*ibid*, p. 227). Crime, on the other hand, is that which presents an actual threat to the tranquillity and security of the individual and the state. However, it should be noted that some of Montesquieu's ideas bear a similarity to early positivist thought in criminology: in *An Essay on Causes Affecting Minds and Characters* (1736–1743) he argued that climate, temperature, the nature of soil and agricultural conditions have a determining influence on human behaviour. Further, he proposed an experiment where the bones of a Dutchman were compared to those of a man from the Pyrenees in order to establish whether there were differences in the condition of their bones' fibres which had in turn created 'the differences between their characters' (1736, p. 422).

Montesquieu was undoubtedly a progressive voice in the time of the *ancien régime*, an advocate for equality between 'men'. Numerous early biographies make much of the story of his birth, when a beggar presented himself at the family chateau and was welcomed into the home as his godfather to 'remind him all his life that the poor were his brothers' (Holmes, 1900, p. v). Yet there is much in Montesquieu's writing that causes disquiet, to say the least. Rather confusingly, given his stance on moderation, he advocated for the retention of the death penalty – although in a restricted form – for he saw it as functioning as a form of deterrence. In *The Spirit of Laws* he argues 'the penalty of death is actually very favourable to the liberty of the citizen since the deterrence provided by this ultimate punishment is that it protects the liberty of all citizens' (Carrithers, 2001, p. 315). This can be seen as a precursor to the pro-death penalty arguments often voiced today, particularly in the United States. He does, however, argue that it serves no purpose to punish a soldier's desertion with death, for 'a soldier accustomed to venture his life, despises or affects to despise, the danger of losing it' (Montesquieu, 1766 ed, p. 104). It would be better to 'shame' him, but the shame involves this: 'the nose broken and the ears cut off' in order to 'brand him with infamy for life' (*ibid*). Furthermore, in *An Essay on Causes Affecting Minds and Characters*, Montesquieu writes,

> It has been discovered that the savages of America are immune to discipline, incorrigible, and incapable of any enlightenment or instruction. Instead, trying to teach them something, trying to bend their brain fibres, is like trying to make totally crippled people walk.
> (1736, 1977 ed, p. 435)

The dreadfulness of this is underscored when one considers the atrocities perpetrated against the Indigenous North American people in the early days of colonialism and continued by the founders of the new 'democracy' (Mann, 2005). Colonialism resulted in the most appalling violence on every level – from physical to psychological to structural – resulting in the decimation of Indigenous populations, but it required as Raewyn Connell points out, 'an intellectual workforce' (2014, p. 213). The writings of Montesquieu and other Enlightened thinkers were to contribute to the establishing of this 'intellectual workforce': instrumental to the enforcing of what Mudimbe (1988) calls the ' "colonizing structure" – controlling space, integrating the economy and changing the native's minds" ' (*ibid*). Additionally, David W. Carrithers urges the reader, in relation to Montesquieu's solution to the soldier's desertion, 'not to exaggerate the humanitarianism of such Enlightenment era reformers of the criminal law as Montesquieu' (2001, p. 318).

The philosophes

In France the major impetus for change is usually attributed to the work of the *philosophes*, a group of forward-thinking intellectuals with whom Montesquieu was associated. The *philosophes* included Denis Diderot, Jean Le Rond d'Alembert, Claude Helvetius, Baron d'Holbach, Nicolas de Condorcet, Chevalier Louis de Jaucourt and Voltaire. The *philosophes* embraced science and rationality, voiced (often loudly) a distrust of organised religion and were openly critical of the absolute power of the French monarchy and the injustices of the system. For Diderot,

> [A] society should first of all be happy; and it will be so if liberty and property are assured . . . if all the orders of citizens are equally subjected to laws; if taxes are paid according to resources, or are well distributed [and] if they do not exceed the needs of the state.
> (From *Observations sur le Nakaz*, 1992 ed, p. 124)

As Friedrich Engels wrote, the *philosophes* subjected everything 'to the most unsparing criticism; everything must justify its existence before the judgment seat of reason, or give up existence. Reason became the sole measure of everything' (1877 ed, p. 31). The influence of the ideas of the *philosophes*, together with the actions of Damiens, are underscored by William Harrison Ainsworth, who wrote of them '[t]hey . . . who mend their pens with the penknife of Damiens will someday overthrow the monarchy' (1844, p. 269).

Diderot and d'Alembert were responsible for compiling what has been described as the 'great manifesto' of the Enlightenment era: the *Encyclopédie*. The aim of the *Encyclopédie* was 'to collect knowledge disseminated around the globe; to set forth its general system to the men with whom we live, and transmit it to those who will come after us' (from the entry 'encyclopédie' [*The Encylopedia of Diderot and d'Alembert*]).[15] Published between 1751 and 1772, this was a hugely ambitious project involving contributions from over one hundred French writers. Given the numbers involved it is not surprising that even a cursory glance at *Encyclopédie*[16] reveals it to be extremely variable in both quality and political astuteness. Hence, we have Louis Chevalier de Jaucourts's progressive (for the time) commentary on the African slave trade in which he emphatically denounces slavery as a violation of human rights:

> [T]his purchase of Negroes to reduce them into slavery is a negotiation that violates all religion, morals, natural law and human rights . . . men and their freedom are not objects of commerce; they can be neither sold, nor purchased, nor bought at any price . . . Who is permitted to become wealthy by robbing his fellow man of their happiness? Is it legitimate to strip the human species of its most sacred rights, only to satisfy one's own greed, vanity, or particular passions? No . . . European colonies should be destroyed rather than create so many unfortunates!
> (From the entry 'Traite des nègres)

Alongside this is the entry simply entitled 'negroes' in which the author declares that 'the least valued of all the *negroes* are the Bambaras . . . they are lazy, drunken, gluttonous and great thieves'. Enlightened times, indeed!

In the *Encyclopédie* 'crime' is discussed from a secular perspective. No longer is it equated with sin. As Clive Emsley notes, 'crime' is described in a literal, commonsensical way, 'a criminal was quite simply someone who had been convicted of a crime' (2007, p. 42). In the entry on 'tolerance', 'the essence of crime' is described as

> the intention to act directly against our judgment, to do what we know is wrong, to cede to unjust passions, and to trouble on purpose the laws of order that we know; in a word, the entire morality of our actions is in our consciences, in the motives that make us act.

The seriousness of crime was to be judged firstly, in terms of its impact on 'human society in general', then came those 'that trouble the order of civil society' and finally 'those that affect individuals' (the *Encyclopédie*, cited in Elmsely, 2007, p. 41). With respect to the latter, these are to be 'rated according to the evil that they cause' (for example, 'a thief who attacks people is more criminal than one who simply fleeces them') and 'the rank and relationship of the victim to the offender' (*ibid*). When determining guilt, the person's past should not be taken into consideration (from the entry on 'probability'), and once guilt is established, punishment should be applied with moderation. For many of the *philosophes* torture had no place in a civilised society. For it contravenes the laws of humanity and fails to fulfil its intention of ascertaining guilt. As Chevalier de Jaucourt argued in his section on *la question*, building on the work of early oppositionists, such as that of the famous French essayist Michel de Montaigne (1580):

> It is a sure way to condemn an innocent person with a weak and delicate constitution and to save a guilty individual who was born robust. An individual who can bear torture and one who lacks the strength to stand it, both lie. The torments that people suffer under torture are certain and the crime of people undergoing are not.
> (The *Encylopedia of Diderot and d'Alembert*)

Significantly, the *philosophes* did not openly support Robert-François Damiens's actions. In fact, his crime was met with general condemnation. In the entry on 'regicide', it is written that 'France will always shudder at the crime . . . the tears that the French people shed following a . . . recent assassination attempt will take a long time to dry'. It is probable that the *philosophes* simply saw Damiens as a religious fanatic and, in so being, as representative of what they hoped would someday be a by-gone age. However, the *philosophes* were not particularly concerned with the 'common man': they represented bourgeois interests – hence their rallying against the privileges bestowed on the nobility by virtue of birth. Indeed, Diderot expressed contempt for the 'multitude', describing them as 'ignorant and stupefied'. For Voltaire, the masses would always be fanatical, and as Robert Darnton notes, he opposed education for them 'because, he said, someone had to tend the fields' (2018, p. A19).

Yet the *Encyclopédie* was to be directly implicated in the spread of subversive ideas against the church and state, which formed the backcloth to the *l'affaire Damiens*. The Archbishop of Paris, Christophe de Beaumont, described the *Encyclopédie* as anti-religious propaganda, and the Bishop of Montauban wrote of it, that 'up to now Hell has vomited its venom, so to speak, drop by drop. Today there are torrents' (cited in Herrick, 1985, p. 79). In the aftermath of Damiens's attack on the king in 1759, the manuscript was seized by police, and the Jesuits twice halted its publication. Before issuing the first decree against its publication, the attorney general of Paris stated that 'there is a project formed, a Society organized, to propagate materialism, to destroy Religion, to inspire a spirit of independence, and to nourish the corruption of morals' (*ibid*, p. 80). Nevertheless, the spirit of progress was not to be stopped. Society was changing and with this came new debates on the nature of crime, justice and the treatment of offenders.

Notes

1. As William Doyle points out, *ancien régime* was a term that was retrospectively employed to cover the period before the French Revolution: nobody at the time 'thought of themselves as living under something called the *ancien régime*' (1986, p. 1). The first usage of the term appears to have been made by a pamphleteer in 1788, with it becoming by early 1790 'the standard term' for what had occurred before the revolution (*ibid*).
2. According to Nicole Rafter (2009), the term 'criminology' did not enter into popular usage until the late nineteenth century.
3. With notable exceptions, as in the work of W.E.B. Du Bois (see Chapter 5) and Frank Tannenbaum (1947).
4. Catholic and Protestant theologians were united in their endorsement of the persecution and punishment of witches; thus, as Carl Ludwig von Bar noted in his 1916 *A History of Continental Criminal Law*, 'there may often be found in libraries bound together in the same volume the products of this insane superstition of both Catholic and Protestant theologians, who in other matters were contending furiously' (p. 228).
5. In America fears over witchcraft were to reach new heights in Salem in 1692. The hysteria over witches in New England has been subject to much scholarly attention. See for example, Carol F. Karlson's *The Devil in the Shape of a Woman: Witchcraft in Colonial New England* (1987).
6. In some accounts Sprenger's name is listed as 'Jakob' rather than 'James'.
7. The rise of colonialism and the imposition of Christianity and Northern traditions on colonised lands meant that the *Malleus Maleficarum* and its ideas spread to the Americas. However, although I found copies of the *Malleus Maleficarum* in historical collections in Mexico City, and allegations of 'witchcraft' were undoubtedly used to persecute women, the situation in Latin America is more complicated (Behar, 1987). The conquistadors were known to dismiss women who were so accused as simply deluded (thus, they may not have been perceived as a destabilising force), whereas within their own communities witchcraft was often seen as a means of gaining power in a world in which women were structurally disadvantaged. Whilst 'witches' were typically those who were living unconventional lives – sex workers, widows, those co-habiting with men outside of marriage – they appeared to be not only feared but admired. They therefore may well have represented the rebel/deviant woman – albeit one who has garnered societal respect, acceptance and status. A woman who has chosen to break away from accepted gender role expectations: an important theme within contemporary feminist debates.
8. Randeep Singh Chauhan's fascinating dissertation *". . . And he Shall Rule Over Thee" The Malleus Maleficurum and the Politics of Misogyny, Medicine and Midwifery (1484 to Present)* (2005) advances a Foucauldian 'history of the present' in placing the struggles over the contemporary regulation of midwifery in Canada in terms of their historical and cultural context.
9. As Julius Ruff (2001) notes in *Violence in Early Modern Europe 1500–1800*, the major law codes of this period in continental Europe – the Constitutio Criminalis Carolina (1532) of Germany, the Ordinance of Villers-Cotterets (1539) of France, the Nueva recopilacion (1567) of Spain and the Criminal Ordinance (1572) of the Spanish Netherlands – all provided for the practice of torture as part of the judicial proceedings.

10 Source: Anon, 1757, *Pièces originales et procédures du procès, fait à Robert-François Damiens* (Paris: Pierre Guillaume Simon).
11 See also David Garland (1990) *Punishment and Modern Society*, Oxford: Clarendon (Chapter 6 'Punishment and the Technologies of Power: The work of Michel Foucault')
12 Garland in *Punishment and Modern Society* comments that 'Foucault uses the notion of "the soul" to refer to what psychologists variously term the psyche, the self, subjectivity, consciousness, or the personality. He appears to use it for its metaphoric resonance – "the soul is the prison of the body" – but also to avoid using a more theoretical term of art that might seem to commit him to a particular psychology of one kind or another. For Foucault it is the soul that is "the seat of habits" and thus the target of disciplinary techniques.' (1990, p. 137).
13 There are many contemporary pamphlets documenting the response of the people to these events. Breck Perkins (1897) and Jassie (1996) particularly draw on the journals of Barbier.
14 Those 'men of learning and genius' who wrote against torture include those of Juan Luis Vives (1493–1540), Michel de Montaigne (1533–1592), Friedrich von Spee (1591–1635) and Christian Thomasius (1655–1728). In his *Essay on Cruelty* (1580) Michel de Montaigne criticises both the level of cruelty and the pleasure exhibited in the punishment and execution of offenders. He ends with the words of the Roman philosopher Seneca, who objected to the impassioned way in which it was carried out:

> For my part, even in justice itself, all that exceeds a simple death appears to me pure cruelty; especially in us who ought, having regard to their souls, to dismiss them in a good and calm condition; which cannot be, when we have agitated them by insufferable torments. . . . I could hardly persuade myself, before I saw it with my eyes, that there could be found souls so cruel and fell, who, for the sole pleasure of murder, would commit it; would hack and lop off the limbs of others; sharpen their wits to invent unusual torments and new kinds of death, without hatred, without profit, and for no other end but only to enjoy the pleasant spectacle of the gestures and motions, the lamentable groans and cries of a man dying in anguish. For this is the utmost point to which cruelty can arrive:

> ["That a man should kill a man, not being angry, not in fear, only for the sake of the spectacle."–Seneca, Ep., 90.]

15 The entries from the *Encyclopédie* in this section are largely taken from the *Encylopedia of Diderot and d'Alembert*, Collaborative Translation Project, Michigan Publishing (accessed at: https://quod.lib.umich.edu/d/did/).
16 From the *Encylopedia of Diderot and d'Alembert*, Collaborative Translation Project.

Chapter 2

Classicist criminology
The search for justice, equality and the rational 'man'

The Enlightenment and the origins of classicist criminology

The historical era known as the Enlightenment, of which Montesquieu, Voltaire and the *philosophes* were part, was to form the basis of modern liberal democracy.[1] The philosophy of the Enlightenment reflected the political and social overthrow of the *ancien régime*. Much of the impetus for change stemmed from the reaction of the emerging bourgeoisie to the constraints of feudalism, for example, with respect to property, finance, manufacture and travel, which limited the development of trade and industry. The *ancien régime* was to be superseded by a political framework based on a radical re-conceptualisation of the nature of the individual and the formation of society. This found its most concrete expression in the American Declaration of Independence and the French Declaration of the Rights of Man and of the Citizen, which were put in place following the American War of Independence (1775–1783) and French Revolution (1789–1799). Central to this were the notions of freedom, equality and fraternity. The Enlightenment also challenged the way in which punishment was enforced under the *ancien régime*. In France, as the Robert-François Damiens case exemplifies, punishments were often unfair, cruel and affected by religious superstition and prejudice (see Text Box 2.1). Enlightenment thinkers sought to introduce a new and more equitable approach to dealing with crime and punishment; these ideas are commonly described in criminology as 'classicist' and represent the first systematic discussion of crime and the response to it.

Attitudes towards the Enlightenment are complex and contradictory. Yet as Nikita Dhawan points out, we cannot escape its intellectual and political legacies for they 'endure in our times' and 'whether we aspire to orient ourselves by them or contest their claims' and 'whenever norms of secularism, human rights, or justice are debated', what we are doing is 'positioning ourselves vis-à-vis the Enlightenment' (2014, p. 9). On the one hand, the Enlightenment is considered representative of the start of the long march of progress: freeing individuals from the shackles of absolutism,[2] religion and tradition. It is the inspiration for social, political and revolutionary movements, with emancipatory arguments for suffrage, the abolition of slavery and rejection of torture and the death penalty being traced back to the Enlightenment. For some, the Enlightenment project is far from complete but it is still one that is worth pursuing (Bahr, 1988; Carey and Festa, 2009).

On the other hand, the Enlightenment's claims of freedom, equality and fraternity have been dismissed as a 'hollow myth' (Dhawan, 2014, p. 10). The Enlightenment represents the philosophy of the bourgeoisie, who were intent on solidifying a position of power and privilege for themselves. It marked the beginnings of agrarian capitalism and the birth of the free market: an economic policy based on free trade is inevitably one that will favour the rich, for they have the most to trade (Young, 1981; Ashcroft et al, 2013). The new system for dealing with offenders that Enlightenment thinkers sought to put in place was largely to be about protecting their rights and interests. Although the intention may have been to create a collective vision with collective values – a theory based on 'We, the people' and the principles of 'the Rights of Man' – this was ultimately to translate into a revolutionary and transnational proclivity to advance across borders, creating a stranglehold on ideas and how ideas translated into practice in the Global North and parts of the Global South. Moreover, the 'civilizing mission' of the Enlightenment and its notion of progress meant the 'development of the idea of modernity' as 'a distinctive period in the history of humanity' and with this a 'sense of superiority over those pre-modern societies and cultures that were "locked" in the past – primitive and uncivilized peoples whose subjugation and "introduction" into modernity became the right and obligation of European powers' (Ashcroft et al, 2013, p. 130). Hence, the Enlightenment's promise of 'attaining freedom through the exercise of reason' was 'ironically [to] result in [the] domination by reason itself' and 'along with progress and emancipation, it brought colonialism, genocide and crimes against humanity' (Dhawan, 2014, p. 9), with the democracies it spawned being better described as 'ethnocracies', that is, as representing democracies for one ethnic group (Mann, 2005) to the exclusion and disempowerment of 'others'. The Enlightenment was therefore to mean imperial conquest, subjugation and a Eurocentric creation of universal truths. Classicism as a theory of crime signified the start of an imperialistic train of thought that was to ensure the dominance of European and North American ideas on the discipline of criminology. Of any theory of crime, classicism's history is the longest, and it continues to exert a profound influence not only on criminological debate but also on institutions of social control.

This chapter attempts to make sense of the complicated legacy of Enlightenment thought in relation to crime and justice and seeks to situate the position of key thinkers within the nuances of their time. In order to do this, it is first necessary to explore the fundamental tenets on which classicist theories of crime are based.

Human nature and the basis of society

In Enlightenment thought the individual was presented as rational and governed by free will. All 'men'[3] were considered to be formally equal, in that all were endowed with these attributes. Human behaviour was seen as purposive and founded on hedonism, with the individual rationally calculating the drawbacks and rewards of 'his' actions, thus avoiding that which gave pain and seeking that which resulted in pleasure. Individuals were described as originally living in the 'natural state', where they were governed by what the English philosopher John Locke called 'the law of nature' in which 'no one ought to harm another in his life, health, liberty or possessions' (1690, p. II.6). However, as transgressions of this law occurred, 'men' were described as giving up some portion of their natural freedom to 'contract' together to protect their rights. Thomas Hobbes theorised that without such a contract, individuals pursuing their own self-interest would lead to a 'war of all against all'; only the social contract prevented the 'natural state' from degenerating into chaos. The basis of society is therefore the 'contracting' together of free and equal individuals to form a fraternity; a state for their individual and mutual benefit.[4] As the creation of the state involved placing restrictions on individual freedom, and given the absolute authority of the monarchy that was a feature of the *ancien régime*, it was deemed its power should be contained by carefully delineating the boundaries in which it could operate; in particular, distinctions were made between the public and private spheres of life. Regulation was to be permitted in the public sphere but not the private. The private sphere was seen as including the family; it represented the personal side of life. Other areas immune from state control included freedom of speech, of worship and of the right to own private property. Enlightenment thought, as we have seen, represented an attack on the authority of the monarchy and the church. Voltaire and Diderot are both reported to have said that freedom from oppression would only occur when 'the last King is strangled with the bowels of the last priest' (abbé Barruel, 1799, pp. 98–99). The Enlightenment was to substitute the dogma of religion with that of reason, implying as Anthony Thomson has noted, 'that everyone who was willing to reason about things would, by the quality of argument and evidence, eventually arrive at a shared agreement' (2010, p. 37).

Box 2.1 Voltaire's advocacy for human rights: thought into action

Voltaire became a celebrity on the French literary scene with the critical success of his first tragedy, *Oedipe*. He went on to be a prolific writer of verse dramas, poetry, histories and political and social commentaries.

Today he is perhaps best remembered for his satirical novel, *Candide* (1759). He can also be seen as one of the first campaigners for human rights through his work to right the miscarriages of justice that had befallen Jean Calas, whose case is discussed in detail below; Pierre Paul Sirven, wrongly convicted of murdering his daughter; and nineteen-year-old Jean-François de La Barre, who was gruesomely tortured and executed for failing to take off his hat to a religious procession, singing blasphemous songs and allegedly vandalising an old wooden cross.

Jean Calas

Jean Calas was born in 1698 in Castres, France, and had worked in Toulouse for over forty years at the time of his death. He was a respectable, hardworking man, a good husband and father. His temperament was 'gentle as well as serious' (Sanderson, 1902, p. 166). Calas was, and this is of significance, a Protestant. For at that time Catholicism was the only religious faith recognised in France. Protestants were routinely discriminated against and persecuted for their beliefs. As we have seen from the discussion of Damiens and the Jansenist dispute, during the reign of Louis XV religious policy was controlled by the powerful Jesuits. Hostility towards Protestants, however, had long been commonplace in French society. In the sixteenth century thousands and thousands of Protestants were killed in a series of massacres, culminating in the deaths of 70,000 in Paris on the Feast of St Bartholomew on 24 August 1572.

One of Calas's sons, Louis Calas, had previously converted to Catholicism, apparently with his father's approval. Indeed, Jean Calas appears to have been tolerant of religious difference, having employed for over thirty years an extremely devout Catholic woman, Jeanne Viguier, who had helped raise his four sons and two daughters. The trigger for the extraordinary events that were to occur to Calas and his family was the discovery on 13 October 1761 of the death of another of his sons, Marc-Antoine, at the family home. Marc-Antoine was allegedly found hanging from a rope attached to a doorway. Marc-Antoine, known as a 'man of letters', was a troubled man: he failed to gain a position in his chosen field of law and had lost considerable sums of money from gambling, and had been reading about suicide. Pierre Calais, a younger son, and Lavaisse, a family friend, on finding Marc-Antoine's body, ran for the doctor and authorities. Whilst Calas and his wife were grieving over their dead son's body, a crowd gathered outside the house and, at some point, someone shouted out that Marc-Antoine had been murdered by his father, as he, too, was about to convert to Catholicism. Jean Calas was put on trial and, despite the only evidence being that of hearsay and superstition, was found guilty and put to death. Like Damiens, the manner of Calas's execution was brutal: the wheel was used, which was a cartwheel on which the condemned would be stretched out along the spokes.

In early 1763 Voltaire published *A Treatise on Toleration: In Connection with the Death of Jean Calas* in which he rallied against the prejudice of the local people who had condemned Calas: 'they are superstitious and impulsive people; they regard as monsters their brothers who do not share their religion'. He emphasised the way in which 'a deluded religion took the place of proof' (1763, 1994 ed, pp. 147–149). Jean Calas, he noted, was an 'old man of sixty-eight years, whose limbs had long been swollen and weak'; it would have been impossible for him to have murdered a twenty-eight-year-old who was 'above average in strength'. Moreover, if he had been helped by other members of the household – his wife, Pierre and Lavaisse were originally implicated – why wasn't there 'a long and violent struggle' which 'would have aroused the neighbours' with 'repeated blows and torn garments'? When Marc-Antoine was found, 'his shirt was unruffled, his hair neatly combed, and he had no wound or mark on his body'. With respect to the trial, Voltaire expressed outrage that the verdict condemning Calas 'to the most frightful death' was passed by a mere eight votes to five. He argued that given there were so few instances of fathers killing their children on account of religion, such an event deserved a unanimous verdict: 'the slightest doubt in such a case should intimidate a judge who is to sign the death sentence' (*ibid*, pp. 147–151). Largely due to the efforts of Voltaire, on March 9, 1765, Calas was posthumously exonerated of any wrongdoing and his family was compensated financially by the king.

Voltaire's activism on behalf of Calas led him to be described as

> the prototype committed artist . . . the creative writer and man of letters who used his literary standing as a platform from which to launch a prolonged campaign against the oppressive intolerance, injustice and inhumanity which he found in the society into which he was born.
>
> (Barber, 1993, p. xxxvi)[5]

Voltaire was a man who was not afraid, despite the dangerous times he lived in, to express his dislike of the way in which 'justice' was delivered and to put his words into action. His *Lettres philosophiques* were seen as 'one of the first public calls for political, religious and philosophic freedom in France' (Staff, 2007, p. 29) and, as such, it was seized by the authorities and condemned by the *parlement* of Paris to be burnt, having been deemed 'likely to inspire a license of thought most dangerous to religion and civil action' (*ibid*). Forced into exile on several occasions due to the seditious nature of his writing, Voltaire has been seen as a forerunner to generations of committed artists not content with merely criticising the world around them but intent on changing it. It is notable that although the discipline of criminology has historically advanced the rights of white men with property to the detriment of other groups within society, many criminologists have chosen to apply their ideas to issues of injustice and have worked to promote social change. Criminology in the contemporary period developed alongside critiques of inequity, of capital punishment and of imprisonment.

Voltaire was writing and campaigning as the values of the Enlightenment were gaining greater and greater support. The Calas case was important for igniting discussion amongst the intellectuals of the time both within and outside of France: for if Robert-François Damiens was symbolic of the unrest being felt by the 'common' people, the reaction to Calas was symptomatic of the rumblings of disquiet within the bourgeoisie as to the level of inequity and injustice represented by the *ancien régime*. Certainly, the impassioned response to the cruelty inflicted on Jean Calas and the level of bodily violation that occurred in the name of 'justice' helped to clarify the importance of those key Enlightenment concepts of humanitarianism and individual rights. Yet this emphasis on a few cases – whilst acknowledging the horror of the acts – is rightly controversial. For as Biko Agozino asks, why does 'the execution of a single innocent Frenchman count for more in the conventional history of criminology than the genocidal trans-Atlantic slavery in which millions of Africans were destroyed or the genocide of Native Americans and Aboriginal Australians by the European *conquistados*' (2003, p. 346)?

Further Reading:

Agozino, B. (2003) *Counter-Colonial Criminology: A Critique of Imperialist Reason*, London: Pluto Press

Davidson, I. (2004) *Voltaire in Exile*, London: Atlantic Books

Crime, justice and the influence of classicism

Classicist theory began to emerge in the latter half of the eighteenth century. The impact of this work was such that within a century the majority of the legal and penal administration systems in Europe were reformulated to reflect classicist principles. Montesquieu had written about different systems of government, the futility of harsh punishments and the need for justice to be administered fairly, with importance placed on protecting the accused; Voltaire dealt with miscarriages of justice and argued for penal reform, and the philosophes' *Encyclopédie* went some way towards initiating a dialogue on the meaning of crime per se. However, it is Cesare Marchese di Beccaria, an Italian mathematician and economist, who is credited with systematically applying Enlightenment ideas to the subject of crime and criminal justice. His short book, *An Essay on Crimes and Punishments* (*Dei delitti e delle pene*), published in 1764, was a runaway success. In the preface to the 1801 English edition it is noted that it was repeatedly published in Italy, translated into every European language with four editions in England and it 'has received the approbation of every friend of liberty' (Anon., p. i). This edition also includes a commentary by Voltaire, who describes having read it with 'infinite satisfaction' and suggests that the book in terms of morality, 'as in medicine, may be compared to one of those few remedies, capable of alleviating our sufferings' (*Commentaire*, p. i). Moreover, there is evidence from a letter dated 1772, included in a later translation of *Dictionnaire philosophique* under the section on 'Justice', that Voltaire had corresponded with Beccaria on the Calas, Sirven and Jean-François de La Barre cases. On the de la Barre case Beccaria is alleged to have replied that the judges were 'assassins'.[6] The publication of Voltaire's *Commentaire* alongside *On Crimes and Punishments* helped, given the writer's considerable celebrity, to attract further interest in Beccaria's text and widened the book's circulation, especially in America, where early translations list Voltaire's name ahead of Beccaria's on the title page. Given the length of *Commentaire* – it is nearly as long as *On Crimes and Punishments* – one might entertain the idea that Voltaire had been thinking about writing a book along the same lines.

Cesare Beccaria

Beccaria was born on 15 March 1738 to a Milanese noble family. As a young man he met two brothers, Pietro and Alessandro Verri, who were very much at the centre of the Milan intellectual scene. The Verris were the originators of a society that became known as the 'academy of fists' (*'accademia dei pugni'*), which was, according to Henry Paolucci's introduction to a later edition of *On Crimes and Punishments*, 'dedicated to waging relentless war against economic disorder, bureaucratic petty tyranny, religious narrow mindedness, and intellectual pedantry' (1963 ed, p. xii). Whilst focused largely on the problems of Lombardy and the need for political and social change, the intellectual inspiration for the 'academy of fists' largely came from Paris. For Pietro Verri, d'Alembert, Voltaire, Helvétius, Rousseau and the Scottish philosopher David Hume were 'men of a superior order destined to live for centuries to come' (Cassatti, 1879–81, p. 116; cited in Limoli, 1958, p. 259). The confrontational name given to the group was meant to underscore its intention to combat with vigour the stuffy traditions of both the academy and Milanese society. In 1764 the group began to publish *Il Caffè*, which has been described by Rebecca Messbarger as 'the most eminent and influential periodical of the Italian Enlightenment' (1999, p. 355). Modelled on the English journal, *The Spectator*, *Il Caffè* stirred controversy in Milan for 'the broadside attacks delivered against all prevailing abusive conditions – the idleness of the nobility, the corruption of the tax farmers, backward agricultural practices, and prejudice against going beyond the inadequate model of language provided by Dante' (Limoli, 1958, p. 259). The influence of the Verri brothers on Beccaria was immense: they encouraged him to read the work of the *philosophes*, Hume and other European Enlightenment figures. It was they who suggested he write, with their help, *On Crimes and Punishments*. Both brothers had some experience of penal matters; Alessandro had undertaken the official post of 'protector of prisoners', and Pietro had started work on a history of torture (between 1770 and 1777 Verri wrote *Osservazioni sulla tortura* [*Observations on Torture*], which was to be published posthumously in 1804).[7] It has at various times been suggested that the brothers, especially Pietro Verri, contributed directly to *On Crimes and Punishments* (Paolucci, 1963; Bellamy, 1995; Draper, 2000). Beccaria certainly acknowledged his debt to Pietro in a letter to Andre Morellet. He wrote that Pietro 'encouraged me to write and it is to him that I owe my not having thrown into the fire the manuscript of *On Crimes* which he kindly copied out himself in his own hand' (Beccaria, 1995 ed, p. 123).

On Crimes and Punishments

Let us now focus on the main arguments of *On Crimes and Punishments*. The extracts used in this section are taken from the 1801 English translation, which included Voltaire's *Commentaire*. This is regarded as the closest of the early translations to the original text, as it restored several passages omitted from previous editions. As I have noted, at the centre of Enlightenment thought was a philosophy on the nature of 'man'. It is therefore important to begin with Beccaria's perspective on human nature and the social order, as this provides the framework for his ideas on crime and criminal justice.

- *Human nature and the establishment of social order*

Reasserting the fundamental principles of Enlightenment thought, Beccaria saw individuals as following their own self-interest; the individual 'would always endeavour not only to take away from the mass his own portion but to encroach on that of others' (1801 ed, p. 6). He acknowledges that 'no man ever gave up his liberty, merely for the good of the public. Such a chimera exists only in romances. Every individual wishes, if possible, to be exempt from the compacts that bind the rest of mankind' (*ibid*, p. 8). Thus, in order to 'avoid living in a continual state of war' a state or society is formed whereby individuals give up part of their natural freedom, agree to follow certain rules – 'the social contract' – in order to live in 'peace and security'. And if every individual is bound to society, then society also has a responsibility to the individual; the 'social contract' by 'its nature binds both parties' (*ibid*, p. 10). According to Beccaria, justice is seen as essential to the orderly functioning of society; it is at the centre of the social contract. Justice is what binds individuals together; without it we would return to the original barbarous state of nature.[8]

- *The importance of good laws, fairly and equally administered*

Beccaria writes in the introduction to *On Crimes and Punishments* on the need for 'good laws' so justice can be dispensed equally and to all:

> In every human society, there is an effort continually tending to confer on one part the height of power and happiness, and to reduce the other to the extreme of weakness and misery. The intent of good laws is to oppose this effort, and to diffuse their influence universally and equally.
>
> (*ibid*, p. 1)

There should be no arbitrariness in the system; it is essential that society is governed by an agreed legal code that is fixed in advance. The law should be rational and just. This legal code must be clear and accessible to all; 'obscurity' prevents the people from understanding and adhering to the laws. Further, Beccaria argued that too much power had been given to the judges; this is particularly undesirable, for

> Every man hath his own particular point of view, and at different times sees the same objects in very different lights. The spirit of the laws will then be the result of the good or bad logic of the judge; and this will depend on his good or bad digestion; on the violence of his passions; on the rank and condition of the accused, or on his connections with the judge; and on all those little circumstances which change the appearance of objects in the fluctuating mind of man. Hence we see the fate of a delinquent charged many times in passing through different courts of judicature, and his life and liberty victims to the false ideas or ill humour of the judge; who mistakes the vague result of his own confused reasoning for the just interpretation of the laws. We see the same crimes punished in a different manner at different times in the same tribunals; the consequence of not having consulted the constant and invariable voice of the laws, but the erring instability of arbitrary interpretation.
>
> (*ibid*, pp. 14–15)

This underscores both the fallibility of individuals and the iniquities in the system of legal administration whereby judges were allowed unlimited discretion in deciding the punishment of those convicted of crime. Thus, the power of the judges was to be restricted. Their role was not to interpret the penal code and prescribe punishment but simply to determine whether an act is in accordance with the written law or not. Furthermore, it should be the work of legislators, as representatives of the whole of society, to establish and administer the laws. Punishment is fixed and therefore not open to interpretation in the penal code.

At the core of Beccaria's system is a written penal code, where the laws of the land and the system of punishments should be written down and known and understood by all. It was the 'obscurity' of the law that prevented people from understanding and adhering to it – and the arbitrariness of punishment fermented a sense of iniquity and unfairness.

- *Definition of crime and levels of seriousness*

Crime is behaviour which violates the social contract; it is that which is against the common interests of individuals residing in society. Levels of seriousness must be established in terms of the harm that has been done to society; hence,

> [A] scale of crimes may be formed, of which the first degree should consist of those which immediately tend to the dissolution of the society, and the last, of the smallest possible injustice done to a private member of society. Between these extremes will be comprehended, all the actions contrary to the public good, which are called criminal, and which descend by . . . degrees, decreasing from the highest to the least.
>
> (*ibid*, p. 22)

Any action that is not on this scale will not be called a crime. For Beccaria, the 'highest degree' crimes are those that threaten the very fabric of society and therefore all members of society with destruction. These are called crimes of '*lèse-majesté*', or high treason; then comes those that 'attack the private security of the life, property, or honour of individuals', and a third level 'consists of such actions, as are contrary to the laws which relate to the general good of the community' (*ibid*, p. 29). The latter refers to crimes that disturb the peace and quiet of public streets. In order for the system to remain impartial, all other factors in determining seriousness should not be taken into consideration, including the motivation of the offender. This is because determining motivation is complex and 'depend[s] on the actual impression of objects on the senses, and on the previous disposition of the mind; both which will vary in different persons, and even in the same person at different times, according to the succession of ideas, passions and circumstances' (*ibid*, p. 25); taking account of this would make it very difficult to administer the law for every crime, and criminals would have to be assessed on an individual basis.

> Upon that system, it would be necessary to form not only a particular code for every individual, but a new penal code for every crime. Men often with the best intention, do the greatest injury to society, and with the worse do it the most essential services.
>
> (*ibid*, p. 25)

This being said, Beccaria undoubtedly saw the extent of crime as limited. The implication of the social contract is that whilst crime is undoubtedly a problem, it is unlikely, in a society governed by the rule of law, to be an endemic problem extensively affecting and involving the majority of the population. The social contract, after all, is formed precisely because of this: to minimise the 'war of all against all'; because of this, most rational people will agree to act within the rule of law.

- *On punishment*

As with the administration of the law, Beccaria held that punishment should be applied on the basis of equality and in accordance with the crime, not the person: 'I assert that the punishment of a nobleman should in no wise differ from that of the lowest member of society' (*ibid*, p. 78). Punishment should be proportional to the crime and act as a deterrent. Parallel to the scale of crimes, Beccaria argued for a fixed scale of punishments proportional to the harm done to society. For 'if an equal punishment be ordained for two crimes that injure society in different degrees, there is nothing to deter men from committing the greater, as often as attended with greater advantage' (*ibid*, p. 24). Thus, if the theft of a horse and a loaf of bread merited the same punishment, then the offender might as well steal the horse. Beccaria acknowledged that the setting of punishments involves a careful balancing act: the punishment should be enough to achieve deterrence but not so great that it becomes in itself an act of injustice:

> (T)he intent of punishments, is not to torment a sensible being, nor to undo a crime already committed. . . . The end of punishment, therefore, is no other, than to prevent the criminal from doing further injury to society, and to prevent others from committing the like offence. Such punishments, therefore, and such a mode of inflicting them, ought to be chosen, as will make the strongest and most lasting impressions on the minds of others, with the least torment to the body of the criminal.
>
> (*ibid*, pp. 41–42)

For punishment to be both 'just' and 'useful' it must be swift and inevitable. By being swift, it will be just 'because it spares the criminal the cruel and superfluous torment of uncertainty, which increases in proportion to the strength of his imagination and the sense of his weakness' (*ibid*, p. 72) and useful 'because the smaller the interval of time between the punishment and the crime, the stronger and more lasting will be the association of two ideas of *crime* and *punishment*; so that they may be considered one as the cause, and the other as the unavoidable and necessary effect' (*ibid*, pp. 73–74). On the inevitability of punishment, crimes are most effectively prevented by the certainty of punishment, rather than the severity; the certainty of milder punishment will make more of an impression on individuals than one that is more severe, especially if there is the possibility of escape. Beccaria believed that what 'unites the fabric of the human intellect' is the association between ideas, an awareness that an action leads to a consequence. Thus, the most effective deterrent is achieved by making an association between *crime* and *punishment*, which is strengthened in the minds of individuals by the immediacy and inevitability of punishment.

- *On the mildness of punishment*

Given the horrors of punishment witnessed under the *ancien régime*, it is not surprising that Beccaria supported milder forms of punishment. If punishment is too severe, 'men are naturally led to the perpetuation of other crimes, to avoid the punishment due to the first' (*ibid*, p. 85). For example, a person intent on theft may be more likely to murder their victim to ensure there is no witness to the crime. Moreover,

> the countries and times most notorious for severity of punishments, were always those in which the most bloody and inhuman actions and the most atrocious crimes were committed; for the hand of the legislator and the assassin were directed by the same spirit of ferocity.
>
> (*ibid*, p. 95)

For punishment to be just, it should only have the level of severity necessary to deter others in the future. Severe punishments can only be justified when the harm that has been done to society is commensurably immense; these should therefore be administered relatively rarely.

- *On torture*

Beccaria argued forcefully against the use of torture. Because he believed individuals should be regarded as innocent until proven guilty, he saw torture used before or during the course of a trial as inflicted on the innocent.

Central to this argument is that if someone is found guilty, they should receive the punishment proscribed by the law and if innocent, there are simply no grounds for torture. Echoing the words of early oppositionists to torture, Beccaria writes that when torture is used, pain becomes 'the test of truth, as if truth resided in the muscles and fibres of a wretch in torture' (*ibid*, p. 56) and, moreover, 'by this method the robust will escape, and the feeble [be] condemned' (*ibid*, p. 56); the ridiculousness of this is underscored by the mocking tone of this passage written from a judge's perspective:

> *I, the judge, must find someone guilty. Thou, who art a strong fellow, hast been able to resist the force of torment; therefore I acquit thee – Thou, being weaker, hast yielded to it; I therefore condemn thee. I am sensible that the confession which was exhorted from thee, has no weight; but if thou dost not confirm by oath what thou hast already confessed, I will have thee tormented again.*
>
> (*ibid*, p. 64)

- *On the death penalty*

Beccaria's arguments against the death penalty are the most passionate and eloquently expressed in the book. On the most fundamental level the death penalty is against the social contract; individuals gave up part of their liberty so that they would be protected. He questions,

> What right . . . have men to cut the throats of their fellow creatures? Certainly not that on which the sovereignty and laws are founded. The laws, as I have said before, are only the sum of the smallest portions of the private liberty of each individual, and represent the general will, which is the aggregate of that of each individual. Did anyone ever give to others, the right of taking away his life? Is it possible, that in the smallest portions of the liberty of each, sacrificed to the good of the public, can be contained the greatest good of all, life?
>
> (*ibid*, p. 99)

The death penalty damages society, for 'the laws, which are intended to moderate the ferocity of mankind, should not increase it by examples of barbarity' (*ibid*, p. 108). Further, 'is it not absurd, that the laws which detest and punish homicide, should in order to prevent murder, publicly commit murder themselves' (*ibid*, p. 108)? The death penalty creates contradictions in the minds of individuals, for how do we reconcile the horror of death with the cold and clinical way in which this most ultimate of sentences is carried out?

Here Beccaria highlights the potential damage that the death penalty can inflict on society:

> What must men think, when they see wise magistrates and grave ministers of justice, with indifference and tranquillity, dragging a criminal to death, and whilst a wretch trembles with agony, expecting the fatal stroke, the judge who has condemned him, with the coldest insensibility, and perhaps with no small gratification from the exertion of his authority, quits his tribunal to enjoy the comforts and pleasures of life? They will say, 'Ah! those cruel formalities of justice are a cloak to tyranny, they are a secret language, a solemn veil, intended to conceal the sword by which we are sacrificed to the insatiable idol of despotism. Murder, which they would represent to us as a horrible crime, we see practised by them without repugnance or remorse. Let us follow their example'.
>
> <div align="right">(<i>ibid</i>, p. 109)</div>

Beccaria contends that there is no evidence that the death penalty, or any severe punishment, has ever acted as a deterrent to crime. It is too obscure, sensational and of the moment to affect that association of ideas between an act (crime) and a consequence (punishment) which, as we have seen from the general discussion of punishment, is suggested as necessary for deterrence.

> It is not the intenseness of the pain that has the greatest effect on the mind, but its continuance; for our sensibility is more easily and powerfully [e]ffected by weak but repeated impressions, than be a violent, but momentary impulse. . . . The death of a criminal is a terrible but momentary spectacle.
>
> <div align="right">(<i>ibid</i>, p. 101)</div>

- *On the trial process and protecting the rights of the accused*

For Beccaria to ensure fairness, equality and that trials are conducted in accordance with the fixed penal code, it is essential that they are public events. This ensures the judge's powers are not exceeded and allows the people to say 'we are protected by the laws; we are not slaves' (*ibid*, p. 50). There should be no secret accusations or trials; these, 'are a manifest abuse', and as we have seen in the use of the *lettre de cachet*, this was commonplace in eighteenth-century French society. Likewise, there must be no suggestive interrogation, that is the utilisation of 'questions which having an immediate reference to the crime, suggest to the criminal an immediate answer' (*ibid*, pp. 148–149) and in so doing leads the accused to acquit or implicate 'himself'. This is akin to the provision against the use of leading questions by opposing counsel in trial settings today. For Beccaria, what is important is evidence, the 'facts' of the case at hand, that the accused is innocent until proven guilty and that everyone is equal before the law. Anyone of 'common sense' can be a witness; their suitability should only be questioned in terms of hatred of, or previous friendship, or other involvement with the accused. However, one witness is not enough, and the best administrations are those where a person is tried by their peers. And to ensure absolute fairness, Beccaria proposed that when a crime has been committed against someone of a different status, half the judges should be peers of the accused, the other half peers of the accuser so the interests of both parties are represented. Advancing the rights of the accused further, he also advocated that the accused should be allowed to exclude a certain number of judges before the trial commenced.

- *On prevention of crimes*

Despite the overall concern with just punishment, the aim of good legislation is to prevent crime from happening in the first place. To assist with prevention, Beccaria reiterates some of the points made throughout *On Crimes and Punishments*:

> [L]et the laws be clear and simple; let the entire force of the nation be united in their defence; let them be intended rather to favour every individual, than any particular classes of men; let the laws be feared, and the laws only.
>
> (*ibid*, p. 157)

It should be clear that it is in the interests of everyone not to commit crime. There are a number of ways to assist in the prevention of crime, for example, through the rewarding of virtue and by perfecting a system of education, although Beccaria acknowledges that such methods are outside the scope of the book.

Finally, Beccaria sums up *On Crimes and Punishments* with this general statement on punishment:

> That a punishment may not be an act of violence, of one, or of many against a private member of society, it should be public, immediate and necessary; the least possible in the case given; proportional to the crime and determined by the laws.
>
> (*ibid*, pp. 169–170)

On Crimes and Punishments: *a manifesto for its time*

Like Voltaire's written work and activism, which can be seen as paving the way for *On Crimes and Punishments*, Beccaria's short text is notable for its humanitarianism and opposition to the often barbaric and arbitrary way in which justice was administered. His most polemical writing is in the chapters on torture and the death penalty, and the impact of his words was considerable. As Coleman Phillipson notes, 'Montesquieu is against torture, but expresses himself rather guardedly; Voltaire vigorously denounces it; Beccaria gave it its death blow' (1923, pp. 33–34). The themes of *On Crimes and Punishments* are further underscored by Giovanni Lapi's engraving, commissioned and designed by Beccaria, that forms the frontispiece to the 1765 edition; here we see Justice turning from the horror of capital punishment, as represented by the severed head, to look at what would have been considered as more benign instruments of correction, for example, tools for hard labour, shackles and a precariously balanced scale of justice.

Many commentators have provided detailed critiques of *On Crimes and Punishments*, identifying its influences and philosophical contributions. Often criticism is voiced with respect to detail and inflection, but the intention of Beccaria's short volume was to be a manifesto advancing Enlightenment ideas,

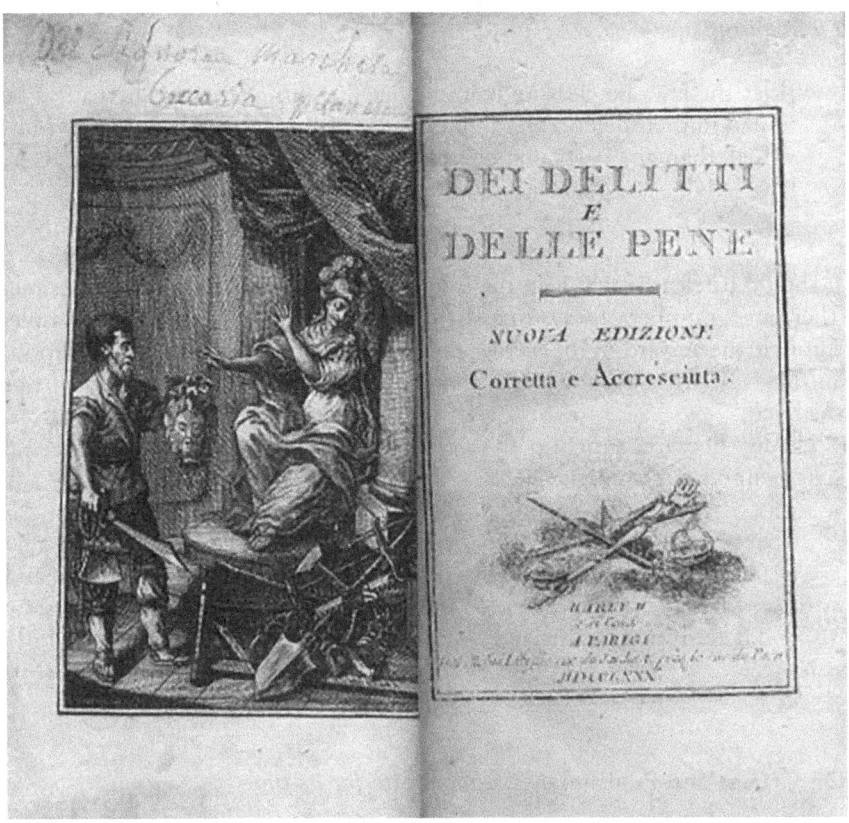

Figure 2.1 Lapi's engraving in *On Crimes and Punishments*.

and it is on this level that it should be judged. Thus, it provides a list of key principles to be included in a more rational and equitable system of justice but makes little reference to intellectual context. *On Crimes and Punishments* is uncluttered by references: Montesquieu is briefly mentioned, and the Hobbesian conception of the state of war that proceeded the establishment of society is referred to in a later introduction added by the author, but that is all (see Beccaria, 1995 ed). In recognising the work as a manifesto, it is therefore not surprising that changes were made to the original manuscript by several of the translators and by Beccaria himself as it went through new editions. André Morellet, one of the French *philosophes*, who was the first to translate *On Crimes and Punishments* into French, made the most substantial alterations to the text by reordering the chapters and most of the paragraphs to give greater clarity to 'the truths he [Beccaria] wished to teach'.[9] In a letter to Morellet, Beccaria praises these changes and the 'excellent' preface in which Morellet had written: 'once a book which pleads the cause of humanity is published, it belongs to the world and every nation' (1995 ed, p. 120). *On Crimes and Punishments* is clearly a tract for change, and its proposals were intended to be built upon as the progressive ideals of the Enlightenment took hold; hence, the quotation by Francis Bacon, the sixteenth-century statesman, essayist, philosopher and early advocate for progress, that is used on the title page:

> In all negotiations of difficulty, a man may not look to sow and reap at once; but must prepare business and so ripen it by degrees.

Francis Bacon, *Essays* XLVII ('Of Negotiating')[10]

The historical influence of On Crimes and Punishments

As previously noted, *On Crimes and Punishments* was a huge success. Elio Monachesi commented that Beccaria's book 'appeared at a moment marked by a growing revolt against despotism and absolutism – it was the product of an era given to the serious questioning of the sanctity and utility of prevailing social institutions' (1955, p. 446). The changes proposed to the legal administration were generally regarded, at least by the intelligentsia, as desirable and were publicly supported. The French *philosophes*, whom Beccaria so greatly admired, were enthusiastic[11] and invited him to Paris to discuss his work. Catherine the Great of Russia and Empress Maria Theresa of Austria both declared their intentions to utilise his proposals to reform their countries' penal codes. Catherine, who claimed to be a 'humble pupil' of the French *philosophes*, corresponding frequently with many of them, was so impressed with *On Crimes and Punishments* that on receiving Morellet's translation, she is said to have written the entire book out in hand and incorporated the full manuscript into her legislative guide, *Nakaz* (Cizova, 1962). Moreover, following the French Revolution, Beccaria's ideas were incorporated into the

French Declaration of the Rights of Man and of the Citizen (Article VIII) and provided the foundation for the French Penal Code of 1791.

In colonial America, John Adams, the young lawyer who went on to become president, invoked the name of Beccaria in his 1770 defence of the English soldiers involved in the Boston massacre. Adams, in a later diary entry, quotes Beccaria on tyranny, which is indicative of the level of importance that was to be placed on Beccaria's words by the founding fathers of America.

> 'Every Act of Authority, of one Man over another for which there is not an absolute Necessity, is tyrannical.'
>
> *'Le Pene the oltre passano la necessita di conservare il deposito della Salute pubblica, sono ingiuste di for natura.'* Beccaria.
>
> The Sovereign Power is constituted, to defend Individuals against the Tyranny of others.
>
> Crimes are acts of Tyranny of one or more on another or more. A Murderer, a Thief, a Robber, a Burglar, is a Tyrant.
>
> Perjury, Slander, are tyranny too, when they hurt any one.
>
> (Adams, 20 July 1786)

Thomas Jefferson, principal author of the Declaration of Independence, was to use *On Crimes and Punishments* to revise the laws of Virginia, and in his *Commonplace Books* (1762–1767) there are twenty-six extracts from *On Crimes and Punishments* copied out in his own handwriting (Maestro, 1942). Numerous commentators have pointed out the obvious contradiction between Jefferson's support for justice and equality for all and the fact that he enslaved more than 600 people during his lifetime (Wiencek, 2012). Moreover, as Michael Mann writes, 'Jefferson [and Washington] forgot about the Enlightenment when Indians sided with the British' (2005, p. 92). Jefferson 'repeatedly recommended the root-and-branch destruction of hostile tribes or driving them beyond the Mississippi: "nothing [he said] is more desirable than total suppression of their savage insolence and cruelties"' (*ibid*).

Meanwhile, in England, William Blackstone, the eminent legal theorist, was likewise influenced by Beccaria's ideas. The final volume of his *Commentaries on the Laws of England*, published in 1769, makes explicit reference to Beccaria's words on punishment:

> It is the sentiment of an ingenious writer, who seems to have well studied the springs of human action, that crimes are more effectively prevented by the *certainty*, than by the *severity*, of punishment.
>
> (1860 ed, p. 16)

Blackstone was, however, to remain in favour of the death penalty in limited circumstances and supported corporal punishment. More dramatically, the philosopher and penal reformer Jeremy Bentham supposedly exclaimed on reading *On Crimes and Punishments*,

> Oh! my master, first evangelist of Reason, you have raised your Italy so far above England, and I would add above France . . . you have made so many useful excursions into the path of utility, what is there left for us to?
> (Paolucci, 1963, p. x)

Yet Bentham did feel there was more to do and is regarded as one of the early founders of the classicist school in criminology.

Box 2.2 Alessandro Manzoni, Beccaria's grandson and Italian debates on torture

Beccaria's grandson was the celebrated poet and novelist Alessandro Manzoni (1785–1873); he was the son of Beccaria's daughter Giula, and his father was thought to be Giovanni Verri, the younger brother of Pietro and Alessandro. Manzoni also was to write against torture in *The Column of Infamy* (1845), which dealt with the torture and 'fearful death' that was inflicted on those falsely accused of causing the terrible plague of Milan in 1630 by smearing the walls of houses with substances intended to spread disease. As Martin (2014) notes, this alleged event and the miscarriage of justice that was to follow dwelled heavily on future generations of Milanese. As part of the punishment one of the houses of the accused, a barber named Giangiacoma Mora, was demolished and 'upon its site a column . . . raised . . . called the Column of Infamy, bearing an inscription which should transmit to prosperity a knowledge of the crime and of its punishment' (Manzoni, 1845, p. 213).

Whilst Manzoni does refer briefly to Beccaria's book, 'the little work, *Crimes and Punishments* which promoted, not only the abolition of torture but the reform of the entire system of legislation' (p. 257), it is with Pietro Verri's *Observations on Torture* (1804) that he particularly engages with and critiques. For Verri – in keeping with the arguments of the Enlightenment – the Mora case was symbolic of the 'ignorance of these times' (Manzoni, 1845, p. 214) and a barbarous judicial system that permitted and endorsed the use of torture. Certainly, erecting the Column of Infamy was in keeping with the needs of what Montesquieu called 'despotic states' (1751 ed, p. 114): old regimes that find themselves under threat typically create a spectacle to instil fear and compliance in the populace.

However, in *The Column of Infamy* Manzoni aims to tell the 'truth' of these events, which is not to see them as the fault of the legal system but as arising from the judges who interpreted – wrongly – that system for their own ends. He thus moves the debate from the level of the social structure (the state) to that of the individual (the judges). For Manzoni, the legal system alone cannot explain what happened to those accused. The judges were fuelled by the people's terror over the spread of the plague and had become 'passionate' in their desire to convict and condemn the accused by any means necessary. Here it is possible that Manzoni was influenced by Beccaria's arguments on the power of the judges, but unlike Beccaria he de-emphasises unlimited judicial discretion as symptomatic of the problems facing the judicial system as whole and the resulting need for systemic reform. Furthermore, Manzoni finds the laws governing the utilisation of torture to be ambiguous and argues at length that the judges had chosen to ignore those statutes that restricted its use, particularly in cases such as this one, where it had led the men to incriminate themselves. Manzoni points out that it is futile to place the blame on a political or judicial system 'for ignorance in natural philosophy may produce inconvenience, but not iniquity and a bad institution does not enforce itself' (1845, p. 214). The responsibility lies with the individuals concerned and the way they chose to interpret the law and to use the word of law to justify their actions against the accused. It seems that for Manzoni (significantly, a Catholic convert) that our concern should be with the morality of individuals (Martin, 2014) rather than the workings of the state.

The reality is that torture occurs as a result of both the actions of the state and the lack of morality or cruelty of individuals, as was evident from the atrocities that were perpetrated at Abu Ghraib prison (see Box 2.3 Tormenting Beccaria). If the 'truth' of this case – which is what Manzoni wanted to reveal – is that it was a terrible event but an aberrant one caused by a few judges intent on abusing their powers, torture would not have persisted into the present day.

Jeremy Bentham

Bentham, who was born in 1748, was a particularly gifted young man who graduated from Oxford University at the tender age of twelve. He was a stern critic of the English constitution and travelled widely, meeting and corresponding with many of the leading intellectuals and politicians of his day in Europe, America and Spanish/Latin America (Williford, 1980; Rosen, 1982; Rancine, 2010; Gómez, 2014). Indeed, during his lifetime he seems to have been somewhat better known outside of his home country. William Hazlitt in 1825 described Bentham as one 'of those persons who verify the old adage, that "A prophet has most honour out of his country": that he was known 'better in Europe, best of all in the plains of Chili and the mines of Mexico' (p. 2). In terms of Spanish America – which had a special hold on him to the extent that he thought of emigrating to Mexico and, when that idea was thwarted, to Venezuela – it is estimated that 40,000 copies of Bentham's translated works were sold there before 1830.[12] He would later boast that young men in Spanish America were not thought of as having received a full education if they had not read his writing (Rancine, 2010, p. 446). As a man of some financial means and with the patronage of the influential politician Lord Shelburne, Bentham was able to dedicate himself to his writing. His best-known book, *An Introduction to the Principles of Morals and Legislation*, was printed in 1780 and published in 1789. The intellectual father of what has become known as the 'Benthamite' movement in liberalism – which included leading liberals such as James Mill (father of John Stuart Mill) and David Ricardo – Bentham was to have an major impact on nineteenth-century liberal thought (O'Malley, 2010).

Bentham is credited with developing the utilitarian[13] approach to individuals and society whereby actions are evaluated in terms of their consequences, that is, the benefits and/or costs that result. For Bentham, the aim of an action, and likewise that of good government, should be to promote the greatest happiness of the greatest number, sometimes referred to as 'the greatest happiness principle'. In *An Introduction to the Principles of Morals and Legislation* Bentham writes that 'an action then may be said to be conformable to the principle of utility . . . when the tendency *of it* . . . to augment the happiness of the community is *greater* than any it has to *diminish* it' (1879 ed, p. 5, author emphasis). Happiness is associated with pleasure and the avoidance of pain: individuals – in line with the largely hedonistic conception of human behaviour that was favoured by Enlightenment thinkers – are thus considered to seek that which gives them pleasure and avoid that which results in pain. As Bentham put it,

> Nature has placed mankind under the governance of two sovereign masters, pain and pleasure. It is for them alone to point out what we ought to do, as well as to determine what we shall do. On the one hand the standard of right and wrong, on the other the chain of causes and effects, are fastened to their throne. They govern us in all we do, in all we say, in all we think.
>
> (1879 ed, p. 1)

Bentham's 'happiness principle' is suggested by some commentators to have come directly from Beccaria. In the early English translations of *On Crimes and Punishments*, which are likely to have been used by Bentham, it is written that the aim of the laws should be to promote 'the greatest happiness of the greatest number' (1801 ed, p. 2). Yet this is a mistranslation; in the original, it is stated that the laws should aim to bring about 'the greatest happiness *shared* by the greatest number' (author emphasis). According to the political theorist Richard Bellamy, the correct translation underscores Beccaria's desire for 'social welfare to be best maximized by showing equal consideration in the securing of basic human interests' (1995, p. 25). The word 'sharing' serves to emphasise the need for the benefits of the law to be equally distributed so that they would promote the happiness of all, rather than some select members of society.[14] It is important to be aware of the problems of translation. In this case, Beccaria's ideas may have been interpreted as lending weight to a more individualistic interpretation of the happiness principle.

Further, Bentham does not share Beccaria's humanism (see the section, 'Defending Beccaria: The Issue of Social Class'); his philosophy is founded on a notion of scientific calculus – human beings are presented as rational-choice actors who are making calculated decisions. In *Hard Times* Charles Dickens represents Bentham in the character of Mr Gradgrind who says to the young Louisa, 'Louisa, never wonder!', and with this,

> Herein lay the spring of the mechanical art and mystery of educating the reason without stooping to the cultivating of the sentiments and affections. Never wonder. By means of addition, subtraction, multiplication, and division, settle everything somehow, and never wonder.
>
> (1854, p. 58)

There is no need to cultivate 'sentiments and affections', for they are of little relevance. The idea of human beings as rational-choice actors re-appears in neo-classicist approaches to crime and crime prevention that developed in the late 1970s and early 1980s.

It is probably fair to say that Bentham, despite his influence, is only 'tangentially a criminologist' (O'Malley, 2010, p. 9). His concern was really with penal theory and reform. Bentham regarded penal law as a core component of government, with its primary role being that of defending the security of society and individual welfare and property. As Pat O'Malley notes, it is when security exists that people can plan for the future, and 'Bentham regarded the generalisation of this capacity as what differentiated an Enlightened society from one populated by barbarous hordes' (2010, p. 11). The ability to have 'foresight' is what brings together the rational-choice actor with the principle of happiness (*ibid*). Bentham believed that punishment in itself is an 'evil' but 'upon the principle of utility' it should be used 'in as far as it promises to exclude some greater evil' (1879 ed, p. 170). Offences, or what he called 'mischief', fell into two parts: 'the first he called "primary" mischief which related to the pain sustained by an assignable individual or individuals'; the second 'he labelled "secondary" mischief, for, whilst clearly originating from the former, this secondary mischief extended throughout the whole, wider society, affecting innumerable unknown, unassignable, individuals' (Draper,

2002, p. 10). Punishment was to be rationally administered in proportion to the 'harm' that had occurred: it was to result in only enough pain to ensure compliance and the prevention of crime. Indeed, it was because of the failure to establish 'harm' that Bentham opposed the criminalisation of consensual sexual acts, resulting in the first systematic legal defence of homosexuality in England (Compton, 1978; Crimmins, 2015) and pre-empting work on victimless crimes (Schur, 1965; Meier and Geis, 1997). He argued in his essay on paederasty (written around 1785 but remaining unpublished in his lifetime) that homosexuality, in contravention to prevailing attitudes, does not weaken men, does not threaten society or marriage and was commonplace in Ancient Greece and Rome. Significantly, as Louis Compton (1978) documents, Bentham's notes on the manuscript reveal his worries over expressing such opinions given the moral and legal reaction towards homosexuality at the time.

For Bentham, punishment had three aims: the prevention of crime, correction of offenders and compensation of victims (Bedau, 2004). It had to be proportional so that potential offenders would always have an incentive to commit a less serious rather than a more serious offence. In terms of crime prevention, it should operate not just on the person being subjected to it but also on those who may be tempted to offend. Punishment changes the balance between the avoidance of pain and the seeking of pleasure as seen by would-be offenders. Hence,

> The immediate principal end of punishment is to *control action*. This action is either that of the offender, or of others: that of the offender it controls by its influence, either on his will, in which case it is said to operate in the way of reformation; or on his physical power, in which case it is said to operate by disablement: that of others it can influence otherwise than by its influence over their wills; in which case it is said to operate in the way of example.
> (Bentham, 1879 ed, pp. 170–171; author emphasis)

The prevention of offending by 'example' is, Bentham argued, 'beyond comparison the most important' part of penal law: 'for in the case of *reformation*, and *incapacitation* for further mischief, the parties in question are no more than the *comparatively small number of individuals*, who having actually offended, have moreover actually suffered for the offence', whereas, 'in the case of example, the parties are *many individuals as are exposed to the temptation of offending*; that is, taking the character of delinquency in the aggregate, the whole number of individuals of which the several political communities are composed – in other words, *all mankind*' (1843 ed, p. 174; author emphasis). To help lawmakers with the difficult task of proportionating punishment to harm, Bentham laid out detailed instructions in the form of thirteen rules, or 'canons'. While, as Tony Draper points out, there were several precursors to Bentham's line of reasoning – most notably Montesquieu and Beccaria, but also lesser-known thinkers such as Sollum Emlyn (1730) – the rules provided 'the formation of a mechanism for a calibrated assessment and application of pain that was simply unknown to earlier analyses' (2009, p. 10) and was 'an obvious contribution to the Enlightenment project of rational explanation, and better regulation, of existing practice' (2002, p. 10).

Bentham on torture

In the writings of Beccaria, Pietro Verri and other key Enlightenment figures, torture is dismissed as an abhorrent practice that is symbolic of the abuse of tyrannical power. Writing some years later, Beccaria's grandson, Alessandro Manzoni, presents torture as morally repugnant, condemning in his celebrated work, *The Column of Infamy* (1845), the treatment of those who were falsely accused of the 1630 plague of Milan. Given their opposition, it is perhaps surprising to discover that Jeremy Bentham put forward a justification for the benefits of torture from a utilitarian standpoint.[15] Bentham explored his thoughts on the subject in unpublished manuscripts dating between 1777 and 1779 held by the Bentham project at University College London,[16] which were brought to light in the early 1970s by W.L. Twining and P.E. Twining. In them, Bentham acknowledges that he is at odds with the progressive voices of the day. He writes that his words are likely to 'seem singularly strange and unexpected', given 'all Europe knows with what strength of reason this practice has been combatted by M. Beccaria', which is 'to say nothing of writers of less merit or less fame' (Bentham Manuscripts, Twining and Twining, 1973, p. 308).

However, for Bentham, discussions of torture are affected by sentiment, and one should not be swayed by 'the delusive power of words' (Bentham Manuscripts, Twining and Twining, 1973, p. 308). It is, he wrote, only through 'scrupulous examination' that 'a man learns ... to correct the first impressions of sentiment by the more extensive considerations of utility' (*ibid*, p. 308). He therefore has 'given the subject a very attentive consideration, and the result is that I am inclined to think there are a very few cases in which for a very particular purpose. Torture might be made use of with advantage' (*ibid*).[17] Bentham's torture is that of bodily torture: it is 'where a person is made to suffer any violent pain of body in order to compel him to do something or to desist from doing something which done or desisted from the penal application is immediately made to cease' (*ibid*, p. 309). It is justified against a person if the 'community has an interest in his doing' what has been asked of him and if 'he is obstinate and in despite of Justice' refuses. In such cases, he writes, 'where is the harm done' in inflicting torture to achieve compliance (*ibid*, p. 312). For Bentham, if through the use of torture we can be sure that the person will do what has been asked of them, this may well be better than judicial punishment. As Rod Morgan notes, this is based on the utilitarian justification for punishment which lies in 'deterrence' or 'reformation' with the assumption that there 'is always a risk, the future being uncertain, that more punishment will be used than is necessary. . . [w]ith torture, [Bentham] suggests there is no such risk' for the torture stops as soon as the person complies (2000, p. 187). To provide clarification, Bentham puts forward this example: 'two men are caught setting a house on fire; one of them escapes: set the prisoner on the rack, ask him who his Accomplice is, the instant he has answered you may untie him' (Bentham Manuscripts, Twining and Twining, 1973, p. 311). In contrast to a situation where

> a man may have been lingering in prison for a month or two before he would make an answer to a question . . . just as a Man will linger on a month with the Toothache which he might have saved himself from at the expense of a momentary pang.
>
> (ibid)

Bentham further clarified how torture is justified through the application of a 'calculus of harms' (Davies, 2012, p. 3; Bufacchi and Arrigo, 2006) – the benefits (i.e. for the 'greater good') being found to outweigh its harms (the pain caused to an individual). For Bentham, torture becomes necessary when information needs to be extracted quickly, as the 'slow formalities of justice' in such cases move either too slowly or inefficiently. Hence,

> Suppose an occasion, to arise, in which a suspicion is entertained, as strong as that which would be received as a sufficient ground for arrest and commitment as for felony- a suspicion that at this very time a considerable number of individuals are actually suffering, by illegal violence inflictions equal in intensity to those which if inflicted by the hand of justice, would universally be spoken of under the name of torture. For the purpose of rescuing from torture these hundred innocents, should any scruple be made of applying equal or superior torture, to extract the requisite information from the mouth of one criminal, who having it in his power to make known the place where at this time the enormity was practising or about to be practised, should refuse to do so? To say nothing of wisdom, could any pretence be made so much as to the praise of blind and vulgar humanity, by the man who to save one criminal, should determine to abandon a 100 Innocent persons to the same fate?
>
> (Bentham, 27th May, 1804, Twining and Twining, 1973, p. 346)

Torture, for Bentham, is justified if many lives can be spared through 'extract[ing] requisite information' from one person. Unlike that which typified the *ancien régime*, Bentham's torture is here concerned with future actions rather than the past (Davies, 2012). However, this is based on flawed logic: for Bentham, as Morgan points out, 'simply asserts that the suspect knows that which his interrogators wish to know and we know what the suspect and his accomplices intend. But how do we know that he knows? And how do we know what they intend' (2000, p. 188). Further, it contradicts the classicist emphasis on the criminal act, for the offence has yet to occur.

In the contemporary period, the torturing of one person to save the lives of '100 Innocent persons' has reappeared as part of the 'War on Terrorism'. This has become known as the 'ticking bomb' argument. Put simply, this defends the inflicting of torture on a terrorist who is believed to be withholding information on the location of a bomb that is soon to be detonated in a populated area, e.g. a shopping centre, putting many lives at risk. Indeed, in a section following that of the '100 Innocent persons' Bentham wrote that we need only to 'look to Ireland' in terms of the use of torture. As Jeremy Davies notes, it is 'in the aftermath of the 1798 Irish Rebellion' that 'Bentham envisaged the use of torture specifically as a way of dealing with terrorism' and, in all likelihood, he 'outlined his fully fledged version of the ticking bomb as a direct response to a cycle of insurgency and counter-insurgency that had shaken the British imperium and that was still ongoing in 1804' (*ibid*, p. 5). Torture, as is well documented, has been used throughout Ireland's history by the English in a bid to suppress rebellion.

The popularity of the 'ticking bomb' argument today is such that Justin Clemens (2017) found that nearly every published justification for torture in the twenty-first century is based upon it. It has routinely been deployed to support a state-sanctioned programme of torture, especially since 9/11. Alan Dershowitz, the prominent legal scholar, who cites the 'liberal Jeremy Bentham' who 'made the most powerful utilitarian case for limited torture' (2003, p. 275), suggested that a 'ticking bomb' scenario would inevitably lead to the torture of potential informants, and, as such, it should be regulated by the state in the form of 'torture warrants'. This would, he said, reduce its illicit use and 'we would not be winking an eye of quiet approval at torture while publicly condemning it' (in *L.A Times*, 8 Nov. 2001). But when an activity is state sanctioned or carried out by representatives of the state – e.g. the police, prison guards or the military – this must force us to consider or reconsider the fundamental principles on which the state is founded.

Thus far in this book I have drawn attention to the cruelty of torture (see also Box 2.3). Bentham's definition of torture – with its hedonistic conception of human behaviour – 'ignores the extreme defenselessness of the torture victim and destruction of hope and trust, which aggravate the stress and cruelty of torture beyond that of ordinary punishment' (Card, 2008, p. 10). Torture is an immoral act: our morality is dependent on treating 'each and every human being with due concern and respect' (Bufacchi and Arrigo, 2006, p. 357). The words of Michael de Montaigne, Chavalier de Jaucourt and Beccaria served to illustrate not only the grim horror of torture but also its futility as a means of gaining information.[18] Bufacchi and Arrigo reference the French general, Paul Aussaresses, the chief intelligence officer in the Battle for Algiers (1955–1957), who described in his memoir terrorists 'dying under torture with their secrets or exasperating him to the point of murdering them himself' and the Israeli General Security Service, who 'officially interrogated 23,000 Palestinians, torturing the great majority, yet terrorism flourished' (2006, p. 361). Moreover, the introduction of state-sanctioned torture in the form of torture warrants would violate the 1975 United Nations Declaration Against Torture and the Convention Against Torture and Other Cruel, Inhuman or Degrading Treatment or Punishment, which was passed by the UN General Assembly in 1984. The United Kingdom, the United States and all other liberal democracies are signed up to this convention (*ibid*; ACLU, 2019). By 2006 141 countries had ratified the convention (ACLU, 2019). State-sanctioned torture potentially leads, as Bufacchi and Arrigo argue, to 'the degeneration of the core values on which the liberal democratic state rests' (2006, p. 365). For any state that establishes torture interrogation units stands to 'lose its moral legitimacy, and therefore [will] undermine the political obligation of its citizens' (*ibid*, p. 366). For the French in Algeria there was an obvious and stark contradiction with the foundational proclamations of the Declaration of the Rights of Man and of the Citizen. As Claudia Card asks, can 'a nation defended by torture – especially so-called "one-off" torture – be worthy of the trust of its citizens' (2008, p. 13)?

The panopticon: 'The more strictly we are watched, the better we behave'

Bentham is largely remembered today for his efforts to reform systems of punishment by the invention of a new prison design: the 'panopticon' ('all-seeing', in Ancient Greek). It is important to be aware that until the eighteenth century prisons were crude constructions and not intended for long-term stay: as Beirne and Messerschmidt point out, 'their uses were limited to act as holding institutions for torture before trial, for debtors, for confinement prior to execution, and (especially in England and France) for the period between conviction and transportation to a penal colony' (2014, p. 63). Bentham's panopticon was designed with the idea that prisoners would be under constant surveillance and that this would have an impact on their conduct. The idea was originally suggested by his brother, Samuel. According to Philip Schofield, director of the Bentham Project at University College London, Samuel Bentham was working on an estate in Russia, and as his employees were largely unskilled, he had arranged them in a circle around his desk so he could easily see what everyone was doing (cited in McMullan, 2015, p. 2). When Bentham visited his brother, he realised that this structure could be applied to other situations, including the prison, factory, school and hospital (*ibid*). At the centre of Bentham's prison was to be a tower in which a guard or guards were housed: they would see into every cell and be seen by every prisoner. The prisoners could never be sure whether they were being observed or not. It was hypothesised that this constant surveillance, whether actual

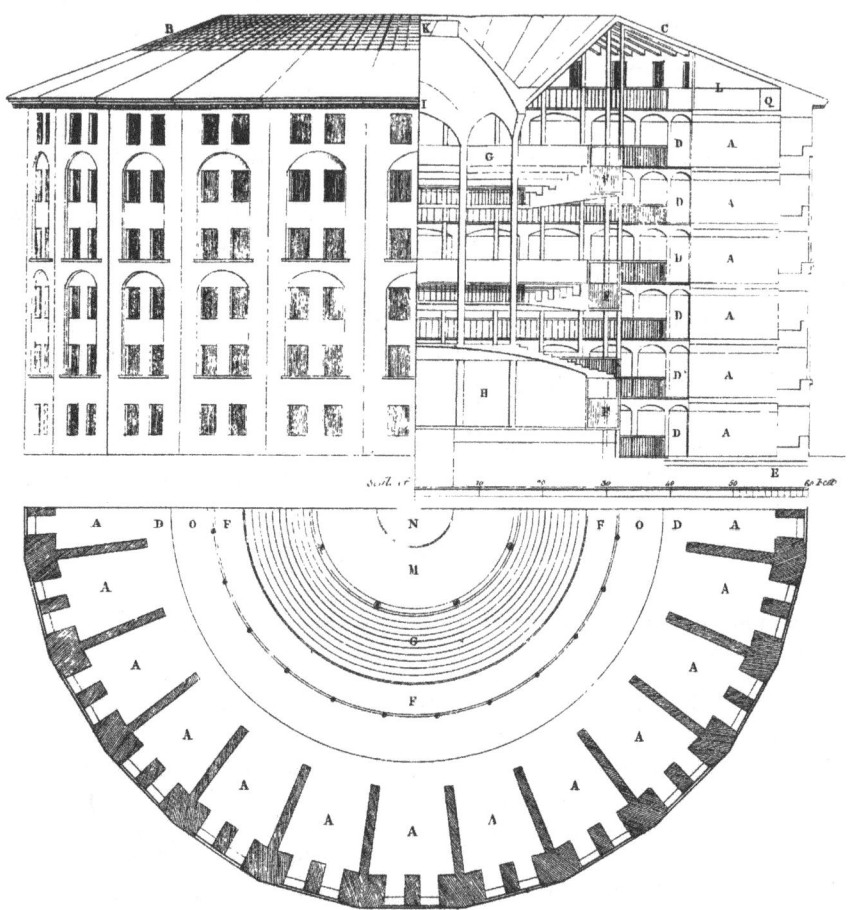

Figure 2.2 Panoptican, or The Inspection House, J. Bentham, 1791, 2008 edition.

or suggested, would stop the prisoners from acting in a wrongful manner. Bentham believed it to be 'one of the corner stones of political science' and an 'indisputable truth' that 'the more strictly we are watched, the better we behave' (The Bentham Project, 2010).

Bentham believed that the panopticon was more economical and efficient than the current scheme of transportation: his main rival for achieving government support for his proposals was the penal colony that was being established in New South Wales in Australia. There was, he said, 'on earth no more accessible spot more distant than New South Wales' (1802b, p. 186). Bentham saw transportation as akin to the punishment that typified the *ancien régime* – although it is, in fact, the logical outcome of having undermined the social contract. The New South Wales colony, Bentham argued, undermined the principal aim of punishment: that of deterring potential offenders, which 'was more likely to be achieved by making an example of convicts in a strictly run penitentiary than by shipping them off to the other side of the world' (Jackson, 1998, p. 370). Bentham's panopticon prison was to be situated within the city to ensure that it would be *visible to all*. Thus, visibility was to function not just within the institution but was to work on the outside as a reminder – as an 'example' – of the consequences of crime. Indeed, the site that was chosen is where the art gallery Tate Britain now stands on the banks of the River Thames in London.

Bentham's prisoners would also work at profitable trades. They could, however, choose whether to work or not, although Bentham believed that the majority would, for it was in their interests to do so:

> If a man won't work, nothing has he to do, from morning to night, but to eat his bad bread and drink his water, without a soul to speak to. If he will work, his time is occupied, and he has his meat and his beer, or whatever else his earnings may afford him, and not a strike does he strike but he gets something, which he would not have got otherwise.
>
> (Bentham, 1791, p. 54)

The panopticon was to be privately managed. As Bentham put it, monetary reward was 'the best way to unite the duty of the contractor with his interest', with 'the welfare of prisoners . . . to be assured by financial penalties on the contractor: £100 for every death in custody, fines for escapees and those convicted of a new offence after discharge'(*ibid*). This differed from current thinking, which had advocated that the fee system should be abolished and for prisons/jails to come under the control of the authorities (Cooper, 1981). While critics have suggested he believed it would also make him a fortune (Himmelfarb, 1968; Jackson, 1998), Pat O'Malley (2010) explains that his position is entirely in line with his philosophy of utilitarian liberalism: Bentham 'believed that the principle of economy as a public good would be most efficiently and effectively served by the private sector' and that 'competition would ensure low costs to the state' (p. 8). In the contemporary period, the proliferation of privately run prisons appear to benefit only the corporations that run them, and it is doubtful whether they actually save money for the state (Joy, 2018).

Despite initial enthusiasm for the panopticon project, to Bentham's great disappointment, it was eventually rejected. Bentham's displeasure was such that in 1823 Francis Place refused to pen an article on the panopticon for the *Westminster Review* 'out of fear that a single misplaced word might bring down Bentham's wrath, not to mention the surety that Bentham would be continually hovering about until the article was complete' (Cooper, 1981,

p. 679).[19] The closest to Bentham's panopticon prison model was eventually constructed in the 1920s: the Presidio Modelo complex in Cuba. The Presido Modelo subsequently became infamous for corruption and the cruel treatment of prisoners and was eventually abandoned (McMullan, 2015).

THE 'PANOPTICON' AS A METAPHOR

Largely through Foucault's discussion of the panopticon in *Discipline and Punish* (1975), the word 'panopticon' has since become 'a metaphor for a continuous, anonymous and all-pervading power and surveillance operating at all levels of social organization' (Barker and Jane, 2016, p. 103). Representing a change in the operation of state power from pre-Enlightenment times, the panopticon, for Foucault,

> Reverses the principle of the dungeon; or rather of its three functions – to enclose, to deprive of light and to hide – it preserves the first and eliminates the other two. Full lighting and the eye of the supervisor capture better than darkness, which ultimately protected. *Visibility is a trap.* The major effect of the Panopticon [is] to induce in the inmate a state of conscious and permanent visibility that assures the automatic functioning of power.
>
> (1975, 1977 ed, p. 200, 201; author emphasis)

Domination in modern society is therefore no longer dependent on 'bars, chains, and heavy locks' (p. 202). The observer is in a position of power, for the observed visibility equates to powerlessness. The achievement of 'permanent visibility' – of constant surveillance – becomes emblematic of the modern state that 'watches its citizens, collects information about them and thereby maintains power over them' (Bentham Project, 2010). 'Is it surprising', Foucault asks, 'that prisons resemble factories, schools, barracks, hospitals, which all resemble prisons' (1977 ed, p. 228)? Bentham's panopticon becomes symbolic of the rise of modern disciplinary society; 'on the whole' writes Foucault, 'one can speak of the formation of a disciplinary society in this movement that stretches from the enclosed disciplines, a sort of social 'quarantine', to an indefinitely generalizable mechanism of "panopticism"' (*ibid*, p. 217). While the Bentham Project (2010) argues that Foucault's reading of Bentham is misleading – as 'Bentham wanted open and accountable government, in which the people watched, and commented upon the actions of officials' – what is relevant in a similar way to the 'ticking bomb' scenario is how these ideas can be taken up by the state and its agents to shore up the power of the state to the disadvantage of its citizens.

As Foucault stresses, the panopticon has to be seen as 'a generalizable model of functioning': it is 'a way of establishing power relations in terms of the everyday life of men . . . it programmes, at the level of an elementary and easily transferrable mechanism, the basic functioning of a society penetrated through and through with disciplinary mechanisms' (1977 ed, p. 205). As a metaphor the panopticon is employed in myriad ways and not just for 'total institutions'. For example, as Ashcroft, Griffiths and Tiffin point out, in postcolonial studies it is used to understand how the surveillance of colonial space has been a dominant element of exploration and travel writing: the desire to achieve a 'commanding view' became a means

> by which European explorers and travelers could obtain a position of panoramic observation, itself a representation of knowledge and power over colonial space. The desire for a literal position of visual command is metaphoric of the 'panoptic' operation of the imperial gaze in which the observed find themselves constituted. When a writer takes this position, as occurs time and again in Orientalist discourse, the invulnerable position of the observer affirms the political order and the binary structure of power that made that position possible. As in the panopticon, the writer 'is placed either above or at the centre of things yet apart from them so that the organization and classification of things takes place according to the writer's own system of value' (Spurr, 1993, p.16).
>
> (2003, p. 187)

This contributes to the 'othering' of people, a reinforcing of the powerlessness of the observed. 'Othering' invites oppression and facilitates acts of violence against individuals and communities. This is an important theme in recent criminological discourse (see Mooney and Young, 2005) and is discussed further in the next chapter.

The danger of increased surveillance was illustrated by George Orwell in his novel *1984* where the characters live under constant surveillance; hence, the notion of 'Big Brother is watching you'. In the last few decades surveillance has increased dramatically: closed circuit television (CCTV) is everywhere – infiltrating both the public and private spheres, the latter in contradiction to the liberal/classicist emphasis on individual privacy. The use of this form of surveillance as a crime prevention initiative, especially in the public sphere, has remained a feature of contemporary classicist approaches such as that of rational-choice theory. In today's Internet age, our security and privacy and the ease with which we can be surveilled are constantly questioned, especially in the wake of the Edward Snowden case and the Cambridge Analytica scandal in which the company gained access to 50 million Facebook accounts – again encroaching into private lives. Like the imperial gaze, this panoptic model is largely invisible: 'there is no looming tower, no dead-eye lens staring at you every time you enter a URL' (McMullan, 2015). But it is there nonetheless.[20]

The critique of Enlightenment ideas and classicist criminology

Criticism has been directed both at the fundamental principles on which classicism is based and its application in terms of the judicial process.

The problem of the social contract

For Enlightenment thinkers society is based on the social contract. The social contract is what binds individuals together. But who were these individuals? In the time of the *ancien régime* rights, liberties and freedom had belonged to a minority largely by virtue of birth – now these were claimed by the bourgeoisie. But they assumed these 'rights' not in the name of their class but by using the language of universality – 'We, The People'. What is significant is that for much of the early history Enlightenment thinkers did not even think that these rights had a wider application: Indigenous people, Black people, women, slaves and the labouring poor were excluded from the social contract. Moreover, the notion of the contract – that between free and equal individuals – allowed men to hire the labour of others, to sell goods and acquire private property or, in the time of slavery, to sell and hire the human property of others. The international division of labour, dependent as it was on slavery and colonialism, could not allow for 'all men' to be created equal in any serious sense. It was therefore necessary to theoretically justify their exploitation by making them endure lives of bondage and servitude, denied even the pretence of formal equality. Seen as something other than 'men', they were to be classed as unfit for citizenship and party to the social contract. The rights of citizens to employ the labour of others, acquire property and accumulate wealth supported the growth of a society based on a competitive individualism that resulted in a massively unequal distribution of advantages and disadvantages.

Who is equal before the law?

Colonialism

'Rationality', and thus equality, was ascribed to Northern Europeans. 'Inferior' cultures being outside of the social contract were liable to a more tyrannical rule. Indeed, in *On Crimes and Punishments* Beccaria writes that punishment should be proportional to the state of the nation. Hence, in those nations that are less advanced, punishment 'should be most severe, as strong impressions are required' (1801 ed, 169). Indigenous populations were necessarily inferior. Voltaire, for example, in a 1763 letter to Madame Calas, uses 'Iroquois', the name of the Indigenous people who lived (and continue to live) in what is now New York State and eastern Canada, to describe the people of Toulouse – the implication being that they are nothing more than savages (Sanderson, 1902, p. 153). The Indigenous populations of America were seen, as Dario Melossi points out, by the English colonialists 'as foreign nationals' and were 'continuously pushed West, until their land was almost completely taken over by white colonists' (2001, p. 410). They were to be consigned to reservations. Michael Mann, in *The Darkside of Democracy*, comments on the contradiction between California's constitution of 1850 that enshrined full white male suffrage, which was 'the most advanced form of democracy of the age', with its authorisation of 'the forcible detention and placing of indentured labour in perpetuity for any Indians who fled the reservations or were found wandering' and as the reservations were on land that was either too small or impoverished, or both, to sustain those sent there, many ended up being killed by settler militias (2005, p. 90).[21] Large numbers also died from disease, malnutrition and starvation. The result was that 'between 1848 and 1860 the Indian population of California fell from 150,000 to 31,000 whilst the white population rose from 25,000 to 350,000' (*ibid*, p. 89). The colonialists made no apology for the destruction that they caused. Andrew Jackson, under whose presidency the franchise became extended to all white men, described the Indigenous people as 'deceitful' and 'unrelenting barbarians' and bragged that 'I have on occasions preserved the scalps of my killed' (*ibid*, p. 93). Theodore Roosevelt declared that the elimination of the Indigenous 'was as ultimately beneficial as it was inevitable' and infamously was to say, 'I don't go as far as to think that the only good Indians are dead Indians, but I believe that nine out of ten are, and I shouldn't like to inquire too closely into the case of the tenth' (*ibid*, p. 94). As Mann wonders: how many of these early presidents of the new republic would today be prosecuted by an international war crimes tribunal (*ibid*, pp. 94–95)?[22] Additionally, the lauded Scottish Enlightenment philosopher, David Hume, was to write of Black people, 'I am apt to suspect the Negroes, and in general all other species of men to be naturally inferior to the whites' (cited in Smith, 2013, p. 1). And as we saw in the last chapter, such racist sentiments were likewise expressed in the writings of Montesquieu and the French *philosophes*.

In his ground-breaking assessment of the history of criminology, *Counter-Colonial Criminology: A Critique of Imperialist Reason* (2003), Biko Agozino points out that the time of the Enlightenment was to coincide with the height of the slave trade. The 'human rights' perspective that has been discussed in this chapter – with the exception of Louis Chevalier de Jaucourts's commentary on slavery in the *Encylopédie* – was not extended to slaves. Until the mid-nineteenth century there was little formal challenge to the treatment of slaves, their lack of 'rights' or the way in which punishment was arbitrarily meted out to those who had done no wrong. Agozino (2003) observes that slavery and colonialism had the effect of punishing the innocent as if they were offenders and asks, what sort of punishment would be proportional to the crimes of slavery and colonialism as experienced by those of African descent? As with the situation of the Indigenous population, 'the European slave trade provides the testing ground for the Enlightenment's credentials as liberatory thought' (p. 346). Further, as Temitope Babatunde Oriola argues, in a commentary on Agozino's book, the experience of colonized peoples must be seen as 'a study in plunder, wanton destruction and total disruption of a pattern of existence' and, as a result, those countries that participated in slavery and colonialism should be held to account as 'criminal states' and pressurised by today's criminologists 'to pay for their sins' (2006, p. 12). Indeed, as Stephen Pfohl writes, 'there is something hauntingly unreal about a scholarly discipline dedicated to the study of crime, the criminal and the criminal law that focuses almost exclusively upon the actions of lawbreaking individuals while turning a blind eye to the mass terrorism imposed upon innocent people by slavery, colonialism and their continuing legacies' (2003, p. 1).

The bitter irony of how the United States – a country founded on liberal democratic principles – was to treat its Indigenous and African American people was not lost on early social reformers. In her 1837 *Society in America*, which was based on two years of travel in the United States, Harriet Martineau outlined the way that African Americans suffered:

> Their homes and schools . . . pulled down, and they can obtain no remedy in law. They are thrust out of offices, and excluded from the most honourable employments, and stripped of all the best benefits of society by fellow citizens who, once a year, solemnly lay their hands on their hearts, and declare that all men are born free and equal, and that rulers derive their just powers from the consent of the governed.
>
> (1837, 1, p. 96)[23]

Gender and class bias in classicist thought

The gender and class bias of classicist thought is well documented.[24] By being denied the vote, women and men without property were excluded from full participation in the new democracies. The word 'man' was not employed in a generic way: 'man' *was* a property-owning male. It was this bourgeois male who was endowed with the attributes of free will and rationality; it was he who had formal equality, that is, of course, with other bourgeois men. Indeed, with respect to women there was general agreement amongst the principal Enlightenment thinkers that women's biological make-up was such that they could not be considered rational individuals (Bryson, 1992). In the writings of Diderot, Montesquieu and Rousseau, for example, we find women described as governed by their emotions and passion. Women are seen as having an important function as wives and mothers, but their biology is presented as rendering them unfit for life in the public sphere. Women, therefore, did not have the 'capacities' for citizenship in the liberal state and, as such, were excluded from full participation in society and deemed subject to man's authority. Rousseau wrote in *Emile* that

> [A woman] cannot fulfil her purpose in life without [a man's] aid, without his goodwill, without his respect; she is dependent on our feelings, on the price we put upon her virtue, and the opinion we have of her charms and her deserts. Nature herself has decreed that woman, both for herself and her children, should be at the mercy of man's judgement.
> (1974 ed, p. 328)

And John Locke, having overthrown the old patriarchs as represented by the absolute monarchs of the *ancien régime*, still accepted the patriarchy of the household; arguing that since the husband is 'the abler and the stronger' (*Second Treatise*, 1690, p. 22), he has natural authority over his wife and children. As Carole Pateman has pointed out, these theorists constructed 'sexual difference as a *political* difference, the difference between man's natural freedom and women's natural subjection' (1988, p. 5, original emphasis). It is not surprising that Mary Astell, writing in 1700 on marriage, questioned the assumptions of early classicist thought:

> If Absolute Sovereignty be not necessary in a State, how comes it to be so in a Family? or if in a Family why not in a State? since no Reason can be alleg'd for the one that will not hold more strongly for the other?
>
> For if Arbitrary Power is an evil in itself, and an improper Method of Governing Rational and Free Agents, it ought not to be Practis'd any where.
> (1986 ed, p. 76)

Even though in Italy *Il Caffè*'s 'Defense of Women' (1764–66) by Carlo Sebastiano Franci was intended, as Rebecca Messbarger's (1999) informative article shows, to be a progressive discussion of the 'woman question', defending women from 'infinite complaints' with respect to their 'idle, indolent lifestyle of utter uselessness to human society' (Franci, cited by Messbarger, 1999, p. 359), it likewise presents women's place as the domestic or private sphere.[25] Indeed, Franci is concerned that women have been moving into the public sphere for this is seen as threatening the stability of society. As Messbarger puts it, 'Franci's modern women endanger private and by extension, public tranquillity when "they go with an incessant movement scurrying through every quarter of the city" out of fear that they may not be seen "at every ball, at every visit, at every assembly"' (1999, p. 360). Social stability is presented as dependent on women returning to and maintaining their traditional role of wife and mother and men assuming their role as the authority figure in both the private and public spheres. Although in the 'midst of his laud to female domesticity' (*ibid*, p. 362) Franci does proscribe a role for woman as workers in the commercial marketplace, it is clearly not meant to be on par with that of the male worker, as is evident by his reference to traditional representations of femininity. He writes, 'it is not beyond the scope of the well-regulated mind of a female citizen to manage a workshop . . . there are many arts compatible with female delicacy and modesty that are commonly practiced by plebeian women without risk to their beauty' (cited by Messbarger, 1999, p. 363). The mention of 'plebeian women' in this context also underscores the level of class-based prejudice that was exhibited by many Enlightenment thinkers. At the end of 'Defense of Women' Franci praises the monarch, Maria Theresa of Austria, who is, of course, representative of a woman in public life, a woman in command of a state, a woman with power. Yet as Messbarger observes, 'he venerates, above all, Maria Theresa's womanly virtues: her piety, sweetness, devotion to her husband and tender love for her children' and, in doing so, 'a potent figure of female authority backslides from public prominence to an "innocent and regular lifestyle" immured in the domestic sphere' (1999, p. 366).

Moreover, in France, Olympe De Gouges argued for the new democracy to give women the same rights as men. She put forward her own Declaration of the Rights of Women and the French Citizen (1791), which employed the same language and format as the French Declaration of the Rights of Man. Article 1 states that 'woman is born free and lives equal to man in her rights'. Article 2 continues, 'the purpose of any political association is the conservation of the natural and imprescriptible rights of woman and man; these rights are liberty, property, security, and especially resistance to oppression'. De Gouges continued to protest the position of women in France, and her activism against the injustices of Robespierre's government eventually resulted in her being tried for treason and executed by the guillotine in 1793. Women were to be held politically responsible whilst, at the same time, denied full political rights.[26]

Similarly, in terms of class, it was accepted that those without property – the poor – would not only be disenfranchised but would be subject to authority and subordination. In today's society, repeated studies of the service delivery of the criminal justice system show that the less powerful, whether they be women, Black or minorities or the working class, have unequal access to law and to legal protection. It is not just that substantive inequalities are ignored by laws which seek to guarantee formal equality, but that formal equality is denied because of substantive inequalities in power.

The distinction between the public and private spheres

The division of society into public and private spheres is likewise problematic for women and children. Women's 'natural' role is seen as that of wife and mother; they are defined in terms of their family relationships, and the private sphere is their domain. For classicists, crime and violence exist outside of the family, in the public sphere. Yet it is in the sanctuary of the family that domestic violence and child abuse largely occur. As the private sphere is designated by the liberal state as the sphere of the least state interference, this has serious implications. Firstly, power relations in the family have remained until relatively recently unchallenged, for the state left power with the husband and father. Second, women historically have had little formal legal protection against domestic violence.

The 'Classicist Contradiction': between formal and substantive equality

> *The law, in its majesty equality, forbids the rich as well as the poor to sleep under bridges, to beg in the streets and to steal bread.*
> Anatole France, *The Red Lily*, 1894, Ch. 7

It can be argued that the logical extension of the classicist project is the extension of equal rights to all. But this will still leave untouched the 'classicist contradiction' (Young, 1981, p. 264) between formal and substantive equality. Classicism neglects the material conditions that govern people's lives, the inequalities caused by differences in gender, race and class. For example, for women, substantive inequalities make them financially dependent on men and/or the welfare state, and this compounds the problems of women in domestically violent relationships. Even if violence against women and men were treated equally by the law, the impact of such violence on women would be greater because of their economically more disadvantaged situation (see Mooney, 2000).

The problem of legal categorisation

The reliance on objective definitions by classicists – such as legal categories – cannot convey the subjective impact of the act and the context of the crime. What is classed as a 'common assault' will mean different things in different situations – it can be the result of a fight between two teenage boys in a school playground or the result of a psychiatric patient hitting a nurse or part of a long-standing history of violence against a woman by her husband or boyfriend. The underlying problem of legal categorisation stems directly from the classicist contradiction: that is, an attempt to measure social harm in terms of formal categories. For we must be aware that social harm will be proportional to the substantive degree of vulnerability of the person so afflicted. The legal notion of judging objectively similar offences as if they were equal in harm and inflicted on equal victims ignores the substantive differences of an economic, emotional and psychological nature between victims. The problem of definition was to become one of the key themes in left realism, which developed in the 1980s.

The focus on the criminal act

The focus of classicism is on the criminal act; what led up to the act is not to be considered in a rational and uniform justice system. The causes of crime, whether these originate within the individual or are socially induced, are neglected. Although Beccaria, whose position on social class is discussed later, was aware of poverty and lowly class position as *causes* of crime, these factors are largely ignored in terms of the practical application of classicist principles to criminal cases. The deterrence equation is that crime is willed where opportunities occur and deterrence is low: an argument that has been used in the contemporary period to endorse crime prevention measures, such as target hardening and increased surveillance, and also to justify harsh sentencing, the latter being in direct contravention to the ideas of Beccaria and other Enlightenment thinkers.

Responses to undermining or violating the social contract: banishment and the birth of the penitentiary

For classicists the crime rate should generally be low: after all, the social contract was formed to minimise the 'war of all against all'. Peace and security should prevail. But what should happen if the legal system determines that a harm has been committed against society? Beccaria actually said very little about how his ideas translated into practice. However, he did suggest that in the case of those 'accused of an atrocious crime' that are to the detriment of the social contract, in the sense of 'he . . . who violates the conditions on which men mutually support and defend each other', should 'be excluded from society, that is banished' (1801 ed, p. 80). Beccaria wrote briefly of imprisonment but only entertained its use in a rational system of justice once it becomes 'less horrible' and 'compassion and humanity shall penetrate the iron gates of dungeons' (*ibid*, p. 113). As Enlightenment ideas started to take hold, both banishment, mostly in the form of transportation to the colonies, and imprisonment emerged as ways to deal with problem populations i.e. those that were perceived as threats to the development and smooth working of the nation-state.[27] Although both systems have their advocates and apologists, there can be little doubt that they resulted in the replacing of the barbarity of the *ancien régime* with other forms of cruelty, contravening the Enlightenment's protestations of the need to treat people with 'compassion and humanity'.

Banishment

Beccaria recommended banishment for citizens rather than strangers. For the crimes of those who had signed up to be part of their communities were worse than those of strangers, for they were without fraternal obligations.

Yet banishment was to be used for those with citizen and non-citizen status and often for those who had committed petty crimes or no crimes at all. In the United States and Australia, Indigenous people were to be banished from their lands by the white colonialists to shore up their claims on these countries. In the 1800s Britain was to become particularly associated with the use of banishment, in the form of transportation, to remove those who were found to have offended against its laws or engaged in political agitation.[28] Prisoners[29] were first sent to the colonies in America, mostly those of Virginia and Maryland, where they were sold into servitude (Maxwell-Stewart, 2010). However, following the American War of Independence it became apparent that the new republic would no longer tolerate the practice. Famously Benjamin Franklin, using reprehensible language – 'human serpents' – to describe those transported to the American colonies, suggested rattlesnakes should be sent in exchange to populate the parks of England and the gardens of politicians:

> In the Spring of the Year, when [Rattlesnakes] first creep out of their Holes, they are feeble, heavy, slow, and easily taken; and if a small Bounty were allow'd *per* Head, some Thousands might be collected annually, and *transported* to Britain.
>
> The Newgates and Dungeons in Britain are emptied into the Colonies. It has been said, that these Thieves and Villains introduc'd among us, spoil the Morals of Youth in the Neighbourhoods that entertain them, and perpetrate many horrid Crimes: But let not *private Interests* obstruct *publick Utility*. Our *Mother* knows what is best for us.
>
> I would only add, That this Exporting of Felons to the Colonies, may be consider'd as a Trade, as well as in the Light of a Favour. Now all Commerce implies Returns: Justice requires them: There can be no Trade without them. And Rattle-Snakes seem the most suitable Returns for the Human Serpents sent us by our Mother Country.
> (Franklin (1751) 'Felons and Rattlesnakes', *The Pennsylvania Gazette*, May 9th; original emphasis)

West Africa was also for a time a destination for transportation, with prisoners being put to work in slave forts. Many died from disease. Finally, in January 1788 a penal colony was established in New South Wales, Australia. Until 1868 over 168,000 prisoners were to be transported from Britain to Australia. Banishment to Australia – given how far it was and the difficulties of getting back – meant that it was a life sentence. People were uprooted from their families and friends. Deborah Swiss (2010) writes of Ludlow Tedder, who was transported to Tasmania. Tedder was a widow with four children. She had stolen eleven spoons and a bread basket that she had pawned to send Arabella, her youngest child, to school. She was sentenced to ten years. Arabella was transported with her and placed in an orphanage on arrival. She had to leave her other children behind and never saw them again.

A sizable minority of those banished to Australia were political prisoners. Of these, many were Irish rebels. As Glynis Ridley notes, the Irish were effectively 'stripped of their history and denied recognition of the political struggle that transported them from home' (2002, p. 215). The dreadfulness of their conditions of enforced labour were recognisable even to the Aboriginal population, 'for whom the word "croppy" (a term for Irish convict [also in Ireland for a rebel from the 1798 uprising]) was shorthand for getting the worst in any situation' (*ibid*, pp. 215–216). In 1834 the Tolpuddle Martyrs were transported to Australia for starting trade union activism among farm workers. One of the martyrs, James Hammett, did eventually return to his native village. He spoke little of what happened to him in Australia; only when he was pressed on the subject did he say, 'If you'd been sent into the interior of New South Wales and there been sold like a sheep for a pound, would you want to talk about it?' (Waterson, 1994, p. 1).

The Birth of the Penitentiary

Though Beccaria made only passing reference to imprisonment in *On Crimes and Punishments*, the prison or penitentiary as a method for dealing with crime and disorder within society developed as Enlightenment ideas on criminal justice began to take hold in the Global North. For Jeremy Bentham incarceration was 'one of the most signal improvements that have ever yet been made in our criminal legislation' (1843, p. 5). In the United States early prison reformers and advocates made extensive use of the ideas of key Enlightenment figures in shoring up their proposals for the development of new criminal codes and penitentiaries. Thomas Eddy the founder of the penitentiary system for New York City and the first warden of the New York State Penitentiary – known as Newgate possibly after the prison in London – refers extensively to Montesquieu and Beccaria and the English prison reformer John Howard in his 1801 book, *An Account of the State Prison or Penitentiary House, in the City of New York*. This book, which was known to have been read by Jeremy Bentham with whom he corresponded, outlined his concept of the penitentiary – it was to emphasise solitude, preferably solitary confinement, and work. Such a regime was to reform an offender's character so that they would not break the law again. It would enable them to 'be introduced into a conversation with their fellow men – the very prerequisite for democracy' (Melossi, 2001, p. 409). For Eddy believed that in solitude the prisoner would be left 'to ruminate' on 'his present condition and past conduct' and 'may sooner or later perceive the wickedness and folly of his former course of life', and by inspiring 'penitence' he or she would come to 'feel the bitter pangs of remorse, and be disposed to future amendment' (1801, p. 32). He was to boastfully suggest that the penitentiary system would 'reflect lasting honour on the State; become a durable monument of the wisdom, justice, and humanity of its legislators, more glorious than the most splendid achievements of conquerors or kings' (1801, p. 70). Yet New York City's early penitentiaries were to be denounced as failures, affected by outbreaks of rioting amongst the prisoners, leading on one occasion to the military being called in to restore order (McLennan, 2008; Mooney and Shanahan, 2020).

Dario Melossi (2001) comments on the role that the penitentiary played in the development of the new republic. It was, he says, 'quite a coincidence' that Alexis de Tocqueville, who arrived in 1831 to write about the penitentiaries, would find himself penning *Democracy in America*. 'Could it', Melossi continues, 'be that the two topics had so much in common' (2001, p. 408)? By the estimation of Declaration of Independence signatory Benjamin Rush, such measures would represent the 'monumental Gateway to the Republic' (*ibid*, p. 409). They would help to produce

> 'Republican machines', human beings, that is, that were supposed to turn from men who were uncivilized, or who had lost their civilization, into good workers and citizens, able to be introduced into a conversation with their fellow men – the very prerequisite for democracy.
>
> (*ibid*)

In other words, those who were to be party to the social contract were those who were deemed 'civilized': the function of the penitentiary was to integrate or reintegrate those who were similar enough to those whose membership of the new society was already assured. Those who were 'perceived as unable, or unwilling, to enter into enlightened, republican, democratic, dialogue' were not permitted to cross the 'Gateway' (*ibid*, p. 410). There was, therefore, in this period 'no place' for Indigenous people and slaves 'in the white men's penitentiaries,' excluded as they were from the social contract. For the Indigenous people, this is underscored by banishment from their lands and the atrocities of genocide that was perpetrated against them. Whilst slaves could be subjected to punitive incarceration in the South, this was not a routine practice. For they were, after all, already without their freedom. Free Black people, on the other hand, were more readily seen as the subjects of penal control being at the bottom end of the labour market. This provides an explanation for why in 1850 Black incarceration rates in the Southern states were less than half those of whites, with the opposite being the case in the North (Melossi, 2001; Mooney and Shanahan, 2020). As Melossi suggests the 'special status' of slaves meant 'they could not be admitted to the honors of the penitentiary', whereas in the North, 'despite the small number of black men and women, their "free" condition opened to them the gates of the penitentiary' (2001, pp. 410–411).

The penitentiary was to serve as a way of maintaining control over rapidly expanding urban populations, over the so-called 'vagabonds and idle beggars' or the newly emerging 'dangerous classes', who could destabilise the workings of the new republic. Thus, it is not so incongruent that 'the American Republic, praised then and later as the most direct vessel to ferry peoples and intellects from the Land of the Social Contract to that of Democracy, would at the same time be the harboring place of an institution, the prison, that however enlightenedly conceived, would become identified with pain, suffering and oppression'(Mclossi, 2001, p. 408; 2008), with its disproportionate impact on Black and minority communities and for having paved the way for mass incarceration. Moreover, for many commentators, the Thirteenth Amendment of the United States Constitution, ratified in 1865, which forbade slavery and involuntary servitude, 'except as a punishment for crime where of the party shall have been duly convicted', was simply to lead to another form of slavery, but this time within the confines of the penitentiary (Hirsch, 1991; Berger and Losier, 2018).

The prison is central to the way in which the modern criminal justice system deals with law breaking. Yet as Mary Bosworth reflects, it is clearly much more than 'bricks and mortar', for it represents 'a set of ideas that are continuously being debated', and 'it is these on-going discussions that the form and nature of our society are articulated; it is here we distinguish between the good from the bad, the deserving from the undeserving' and, in so doing, 'we map out no less than our sense of national identity' (2010, p. 10). When we think about the role of banishment and the violence inflicted on those who were not seen as 'rightful' citizens, it is obvious that 'the question we must ask ourselves, then, is what kind of nation has been formed through the exclusion of so many' (*ibid*)?

Modifying classicist ideas

In classicism it is the *act* that is the concern of criminal justice; all criminals should be treated the same: however, this led to difficulties when the French Penal Code of 1791 was put into practice. For example, first-time offenders were treated the same as more seasoned criminals; children were treated the same as adults, and no allowance was made for a person's mental state. Opposition to this led to the reintroduction of discretion into the judicial process so age, psychological problems and other factors that might have had a bearing on the act could be considered. Classicism was henceforth adapted using some of the ideas drawn from positivism. This gave rise to what was subsequently termed neo-classicism, where individual circumstances of mental state and age and delineated mitigating circumstances are considered, providing a more individualised system of justice. Needless to say, more substantial and *substantive* factors of, for example, class, gender and racial discrimination are not permissible.

For modern classicists the prison is largely discounted as a means of dealing with law breakers for it does not embody the classicist principles of 'justice', and its current manifestation aims to 'treat the individual rather than to punish him' (Young, 1981, p. 14). Hence, David Fogel writes, 'justice-as-fairness represents the superordinate goal of all agencies of the criminal law' and 'when correction becomes mired in the dismal swamp of preaching, exhorting, and treating ('resocialization') it becomes dysfunctional as an agency of justice' (1975, p. 184). The aim of correctional agencies should be to 'engage prisoners as the law otherwise dictates – as responsible, volitional and aspiring human beings' (*ibid*).

Defending Beccaria: the issue of social class

Philip Jenkins (1984) presents Beccaria as a fundamentally conservative figure who promoted a system of justice which avoided the revolutionary and materialist implications of Enlightenment thought, with the result that his work can be reduced to nothing more than a bureaucratic tool. In other words, Jenkins sees him as not going far enough in terms of confronting the deep social divide within society caused by unequal access to wealth and property. As we have seen, *On Crimes and Punishments*, like other classicist works, has generally been criticised for ignoring the causes of crime, especially those that relate to poverty, and for being overly concerned with bourgeois interests. *How far are these criticisms justified?*

First it must be noted that Beccaria lived in dangerous times, and, as I stress throughout this book, it is important for theorists and theoretical developments to be situated in terms of their historical and political context. The nobility and the church were powerful forces in much of continental Europe. The harassment of the French *philosophes* by the authorities is well known. Fearing persecution, they published much of their work anonymously, and it was not uncommon for them to deny authorship. Voltaire was thrown into prison for writing satirical verses that angered the Prince Regent and was forced into exile on several occasions. A copy of his *Dictionnaire philosophique*, identified as a particularly seditious work, was thrown on the fire alongside the body of the ill-fated Jean-François de La Barre. In Italy the Verri brothers were under suspicion and feared prosecution. *On Crimes and Punishments* was first published anonymously, and in the letter to Morellet, Beccaria made clear his concerns, acknowledging that some passages in the book are deliberately obscure, for 'I could hear the rattling chains of superstition and howls of fanaticism stifling the faint moans of truth . . . I wish to defend truth without being a martyr to it' (1995 ed, p. 121). Beccaria had a wife and family; he had no wish to risk his life for a book. He wrote that in Milan his views were very much those of a minority, 'in a capital of 120,000 inhabitants there are hardly twenty individuals who desire to instruct themselves and who devote themselves to truth and virtue'; the people were riddled with prejudice and superstition and 'unforgiving' to those who wished them to change (*ibid*, p. 123). Moreover, whilst *On Crimes and Punishments* was acclaimed in progressive circles, it was attacked by legal scholars concerned with upholding the old systems of government and by religious groups. The Church of Rome put it on its index of banned books in 1766 where it stayed for over 200 years. As Mike Ahearne puts it in his thoughtful essay on Beccaria, taking a swipe at the critics who reside safely in today's universities, 'The sylvan comforts of [the] University and the freedom to write with impunity were privileges Beccaria and his companions did not enjoy let alone take for granted' (1994, p. 11). In the light of this, it would not be surprising if *On Crimes and Punishments* was cautious and covert in its approach.

However, there is plenty of evidence in the text to indicate that Beccaria was very aware of class-based inequality and that this had been reflected in the law. He notes how the laws have 'favoured the few and outraged the many' (1801 ed, p. 98), that they should 'favour every individual, than any particular classes of men' (*ibid*, p. 157) and 'diffuse their influence universally, and equally' (*ibid*, p. 1). On the causes of crime, Beccaria clearly relates the crime of robbery to poverty: 'this crime, alas! is commonly the effect of misery and despair; the crime of that unhappy part of mankind, to whom the right of exclusive property (a terrible, and perhaps unnecessary right) has left but a bare existence' (*ibid*, p. 80). Pecuniary punishments will therefore only compound the problem and impact unjustly on the family. Questioning the right to private property is, of course, a revolutionary idea and one which Jeremy Bentham was to strongly oppose:

> It is astonishing that a writer so judicious as Beccaria has interposed in a work dictated by the soundest philosophy, a doubt subversive of the social order. *The right of property*, he says, *is a terrible right which perhaps is not necessary.*
>
> (1864, p. 114; original emphasis)

Perhaps not surprisingly, Karl Marx referred to Bentham as 'a genius . . . of bourgeois stupidity' (1864, 1921 ed, p. 668). Moreover, it is in Beccaria's use of the words of the thief that we find him at his most socially aware:

> What are the laws, that I am bound to respect, which makes so great a difference between me and the rich man? He refuses me the farthing I ask of him, and excuses himself, by bidding me have recourse to labour with which he is unacquainted. Who made these laws? The rich and the great, who never deigned to visit the miserable hut of the poor; who has never seen him dividing a piece of mouldy bread, amidst the cries of his famished children and the tears of his wife. Let us break those ties, fatal to the greatest part of mankind, and only useful to a few indolent tyrants. Let us attack injustice at it source.
>
> (1801 ed, pp. 105–106)

As Ahearne (1994) notes, the radical connotations of this passage are apparent and yet Beccaria was writing almost a century before Marx. The charge levelled against Beccaria in 1765 by the Dominican monk Ferdinando Facchinei of a new heresy that he called 'socialism' was perhaps an apt one. Maestro (1942) has suggested that this was the first time the word socialist ('socialista') was used in Italian, and it is likely that Beccaria was the first person to be publicly called a socialist.

Box 2.3 Tormenting Beccaria

Classicist ideas are considered central to the criminal justice systems of liberal democracies throughout the world. At the core of the legal systems of the United Kingdom and the United States are the notions that everyone has the right to a fair and equal trial by a jury of one's peers, that the accused is considered innocent until proven guilty and the importance of evidence and witnessing of the act. In the historical period discussed in this chapter, we see the emergence of discourses on human rights and campaigns to right miscarriages of justice. In 1948 the United Nations drafted and adopted the Universal Declaration of Human Rights. This document is written in the language of the Enlightenment; thus, Article 1 declares: 'All human beings are born free and equal in dignity and rights. They are endowed with reason and conscience and should act towards one another in a spirit of brotherhood'. Article 5 of the declaration declares, 'No one shall be subjected to torture or to cruel, inhuman or degrading treatment or punishment'.[1] The use of torture, as documented in the main text, is prohibited.

It is well over 200 years since Beccaria wrote his little book as a manifesto for change and to overhaul the 'justice' system as represented by the *ancien régime*. He argued that punishment should be proportional to the crime committed and that the use of secret trials, torture and the death penalty had no place in a rational system of justice. It is over 200 years since Voltaire launched his campaigns to help the cases of Jean Calas, Pierre Paul Sirven and Jean-François de La Barre, who were brutally tortured and executed. Beccaria would be tormented to discover that there are in today's world numerous examples of harsh and unjust sentencing and that many countries still use secret trials, torture and the death penalty.

For example, at the peak of 'The Troubles' in Northern Ireland in the 1970s, the British government established secret trials at Long Kesh internment camp near Belfast for those accused of politically motivated offences; the right to trial by jury was suspended and, in many cases, special branch officers gave evidence without the defendant being present

(Campbell et al, 1994; Jamieson, 2015). In the United States after 9/11 President George W. Bush signed an order authorising special military tribunals to try suspected terrorists from abroad; they would, therefore, be denied the right to be tried in public in front of a jury. As Barbara Olshansky (2002) of the Center for Constitutional Rights has pointed out, under Bush's military order a person could be tried on evidence that may not have been examined or adequately tested, convicted by two-thirds of a vote, sentenced to death and executed, without Congress, the judiciary or members of the public knowing about the proceedings. As she notes, 'under President Bush's new Military Order, the checks and balances that define democracy are eliminated, public knowledge is censored, and the President, free from accountability, is invested with totalitarian power' (*ibid*, p. 33).

It is remarkable that the United States, whose Declaration of Independence is a document of the Enlightenment and whose founders were influenced by Voltaire and Beccaria, has come under constant criticism for its harsh sentencing, especially for drug offences under the Rockefeller laws, where the selling of drugs could lead to a sentence as long as that for second-degree murder, for the retention and use of the death penalty in many states and the use of torture against alleged terrorists. Organisations such as Amnesty International and Human Rights Watch have documented the many instances in which torture is still employed as a means of interrogation and punishment by the United States and by other countries; the rhetoric of the 'War on Terrorism' has been used to justify or intensify old patterns of repression, including the use of torture (Amnesty International, 2015). This is how Abu Omar describes his experiences of torture, during a fourteen-month period of secret detention, having been first abducted in Italy and flown by U.S. agents to Egypt, 'I was hung like slaughtered cattle, head down, feet up, hands tied behind my back . . . and exposed to electric shocks all over my body and especially the head area' (*ibid*). The United States has authorised the use of stress positions (for example, standing for forty hours), sensory deprivation and waterboarding in its detention centres in Iraq, Guantanamo Bay and Afghanistan. Indeed, the very fact that acts of rendition frequently occur where suspects are transported beyond the borders of the United States or the European democracies so they can be tortured, outside of the rule of law, indicates a remarkable acknowledgement and cynicism about the illegality of such procedures. The abuse of prisoners at Abu Ghraib, in Iraq, and Guantanamo Bay is now well documented.

The practice of waterboarding, which is intended to simulate drowning, dates from the time of the *ancien régime*.[30] Its use was especially evident during the time of the Spanish Inquisition (Lea, 1901). The case of Jean Calas, as we have seen, involved water torture; he was forced to drink ten gallons of water, which would have caused extreme discomfort and the feeling of being suffocated. Waterboarding or water torture was commonly employed against those accused of religious crimes during this period. The U.S. government has admitted to using this on Khalid Sheikh Mohammed, Abu Zubaydah and Abd al-Rahim al-Nashiri, suspected Al-Qaeda terrorists. Given that the 'War on Terror' is sometimes characterised as a clash between the Christian (West) and Islamic (East) worlds, the utilisation of this form of torture against those of a different faith also causes us to question how much has changed since the days of the *ancien régime*.

Contemporary application of classicist thought in criminology

Despite the considerable and wide-ranging influence of classicism on the criminal justice system and jurisprudence, classicism as a criminological theory was given little thought for much of the twentieth century as the emphasis switched to trying to understand, as Sutherland and Cressey put it, 'the criminality of behavior, not behaviour, as such' (1970 ed, p. 73). From the late 1970s there was a revival of some of the ideas of classicism in response to the perceived failures of the rehabilitative model of criminal justice and the apparent lack of relevance of criminological theory to those dealing with crime in the real world. Rather patronisingly, Marcus Felson and Ron Clarke suggested that theories of criminality were 'mostly beyond the reach of everyday practice' and 'extremely complicated for those who want to understand crime, much less do something about it' (1998, p. 1). With the rise in crime that occurred in the 1970s and 1980s in the Global North, it was suggested that 'nothing works' and, accordingly, new perspectives on crime policy were encouraged – including a move away from welfarism – and mainstream theory started to lean 'toward explanations couched in terms of social control and its deficits' (Garland, 1999, p. 353). After all, critics of sociological explanations argued that social conditions had improved in the post-Second World War years and yet the crime rate rose. In this climate two applications of classicist thought were to emerge – 'just desserts', which focuses on punishment and sentencing, and rational choice theory, which emphasises the classicist notion of human behaviour as rational and purposive.

'Just Desserts'

In the 1970s the perceived failure of the 'welfare' or rehabilitative model of criminal justice reignited debate on what should form a just policy on sentencing. The welfare model, which had been particularly prevalent in the United States since the late nineteenth century, was influenced by positivist ideas and, as such, focused on the offender and the need for individualised treatment (see the following chapter). In line with this, 'indeterminate sentencing' was introduced in which the length of sentence was decided – regardless of the crime – in relation to whether the offender was deemed to have improved or not. It could therefore result in some offenders receiving long sentences for low-level crimes if they were seen to be insufficiently rehabilitated to warrant release. 'Just desserts' proposed the emphasis of sentencing should be put back on the *criminal act* rather than the *actor*. The leading proponent of 'just desserts' is Andrew von Hirsch, who restated the basic classicist principles of proportionality, fixed sentencing, a more milder approach to punishment and the importance of non-discretional decision-making in the judicial process. This is evident in the following extract from 'Giving Criminals Their Just Desserts,' which discusses the importance of proportionality and the dangers of punishments that are too severe:

> The severity of punishment should comport with the seriousness of the crime. Stringent punishments should be limited to crimes that are serious; as the gravity of the crime diminishes, so should the severity of the punishment. When the principle is not observed, the degree of blame becomes inappropriate. If an offender convicted of a lesser crime is punished severely, the moral obloquy which so drastic a penalty carries will attach to him – and unjustly so, given the not-so-very wrongful character of his offense.
>
> (1996, p. 320)

With the focus placed on the criminal act, a sentencing system is proposed which would include the following features: the irrelevance of the offender returning to crime in deciding sentencing; that sentences should be fixed ('since the seriousness of crime is known at the time of verdict, there would be no need to delay the decision on sentence length to see how well the offender is adjusting'); and imprisonment for only serious offences. Prison 'should be the sanction only for crimes, which cause or risk grievous harm – such as assault, armed robbery, and rape' (*ibid*, pp. 320–321). 'Just desserts', however, suffers from the same problems of traditional classicism: namely, that it does not pay attention to what led up to the act (i.e. the causes of law breaking) and that substantive inequalities in power not only affect the administration of justice but result in its differential impact on individuals and communities.

Rational-choice theory: 'opportunity makes the thief'

Rational choice theory is particularly associated with the work of Derek Cornish and Ron Clarke (1986) and Clarke and Cornish (2001 ed). Its classicist roots are clearly evident in its presentation of crime as the product of wilful, rational action. As the name implies, the criminal is portrayed as having rationally weighed up the costs and benefits of the criminal act. People are seen as liable to commit crime when there is little to prevent them from doing so. Crime is viewed as opportunistic, in that it mainly occurs when situations arise which prevent possibilities for criminal advantage. However, the traditional classicist emphasis on the use of the criminal justice system as deterrence is considered palpably ineffective. Clarke (1980) argued, prisons merely encourage recidivism and policing has little proven record of effectively apprehending offenders. The policy proposals arising out of rational-choice theory emphasised restricting the opportunities for crime, rather than looking at the motivations of the criminal, and by building up new social control mechanisms. This led to support for situational crime prevention measures such as target hardening and increasing the level of surveillance. Clarke is particularly known for the development of such initiatives during his time at the UK's Home Office Research and Planning Unit in the 1980s – a body of work that was termed 'new administrative criminology'. The proposals included: better locks and bolts on houses, improving architectural design and the use of CCTV cameras for surveillance purposes. Such policy proposals, as Downes and Rock have put it, are in accord with their perception 'of criminals as reasoning people implicated in chains of decision making' for 'rational criminals confronting critical choices are fairly susceptible to intelligent control strategies' (1988, p. 229). Their ideas combine the utilitarianism of traditional classicism with theories of deterrence (see Zimring and Hawkins, 1973) and economic approaches to crime, for example, that of Travis Hirschi, 1969).

Related to this strand of thinking is Marcus Felson's (1998) routine activities approach, which focuses on the conditions in which crime occurs. For 'the chemistry of crime to occur' – crime being reduced by Felson to a chemical reaction – there has to be a likely offender, a suitable victim (who he refers to as a 'target') and the absence of 'capable guardians' against crime (1998, p. 354).[31] We need, he suggests, to understand how our daily lives result in criminal opportunities and invent 'routine precautions' to prevent such opportunities occurring (*ibid*, p. 115). For rational-choice theory and the routine activities approach, the 'root cause' of crime is 'opportunity'. Hence (and this is also relevant to crime pattern analysis), Clarke and Felson write that they are building 'on the old saying that "opportunity makes the thief"'. They offer this example in their report for the British Home Office:

> Any store that makes shoplifting easy causes more crime to occur in two ways: by encouraging more people to participate in the crime and by helping each shoplifter to be more efficient as a thief. On the other side of the coin, stores that have thwarted shoplifting with careful design and

management reduce the problem by producing fewer thieves and cutting the efficiency of each offender.

(1998, p. 1)

In this they paint a very different picture of the thief to that presented by Beccaria. For Clarke and Felson, the thief will be stopped and thievery reduced through 'careful design and management'. For Beccaria, we need to understand the inequities within the judicial system, laws that have been made by the 'rich and the great' of use to only them and the impoverished circumstances that lead to theft. These circumstances are largely invisible to those in power, for it is they 'who never deigned to visit the miserable hut of the poor' (1801 ed, pp. 105–106).

It is somewhat telling that the position of Clarke and Felson, unlike that of traditional classicism or von Hirsch's 'just desserts', does not have an emphasis on social justice. Indeed, the policy proposals of rational-choice theory are attractive to centre-right administrations, such as the Conservative governments of Margaret Thatcher (1975–1990) and John Major (1990–1997) that are concerned with reducing public spending and pulling back on welfare provision; to put it simply, it is much cheaper to target-harden, i.e. put in metal bars at windows to prevent break-ins, than to tackle the social problems on poor, run-down estates. Those who argue that we must consider the causes of crime – whether these reside in individual or social factors – are seen by rational-choice theorists to exaggerate the situation. For, as Clarke argued, eradicating poverty offers no solutions:

> [E]ven if it were possible to provide people with the kinds of jobs and leisure facilities they might want, there is still no guarantee that crime would drop; few crimes require much time or effort, and work and leisure in themselves provide a whole range of criminal opportunities.
>
> (1980, p. 137)

As with traditional classicism and 'just desserts', the most frequently heard criticism of rational-choice theory is that it does not address the causes of crime. If the motivation for crime and its causes are disregarded, the way in which people strive to overcome and get around target hardening and surveillance measures will also be ignored. Further, the problem with the varied and intrusive measures of social control – everything from CCTV to phone tapping – is that they encroach on individual human rights.

In recent years rational-choice theory has been subject to scathing commentaries from cultural criminologists (Hayward and Young, 2004; Ferrell et al, 2008; Hayward, 2007), with the picture of 'the rational calculator and the mechanistic actor' being derided for its narrow essentialist view of human behaviour and for presenting crime as a mundane activity. The victim 'is a likely target to be understood through their attempts to calculate their optimum security strategies' (Hayward and Young, 2004, p. 263), which has to be admitted is a slippery slope towards 'victim blaming'. With rational choice and similar 'cost–benefit' analyses of criminality, as with the control theory of Gottfredson and Hirschi (1990), 'there is no special deviant or pathological criminality . . . criminal behaviour is simply understood as the result of calculative strategies aimed at utility maximization' (Ferrell et al, 2008, p. 66). The rise of rational choice served to 'open the door' to what David Garland (1997) described as a 'culture of control', 'a strategy of crime control closely attuned to the fields of risk and resource management, and calculative governmental approaches regarding the containment and management of social problems' (Ferrell et al, 2008, p. 67).

Keith Hayward, one of the leaders of cultural criminology, highlights the impoverishment of rational choice as a model of criminal behaviour. As he points out, developments in the field of rational-choice theory 'now test the efficiency of crime prevention initiatives by reducing the mind of the potential offender to a statistical formula: $Yi = A + \beta(Xbi) + \beta(Xci) + \varepsilon i$ (e.g. Exum, 2002)'. With such a rubric 'the human purposes and existential meanings of crime are thus literally banned from the equation' with 'the intractable question of criminality reduced to a two-inch formula' (2007, p. 234). Cultural criminologists point out that the actual experience of committing crime and its outcome bear little relationship to such a narrow essentialist framework (Hayward and Young, 2004, p. 264). Crime is 'seldom mundane' – and, as such, 'the adrenalin rush of crime, that takes place (as Jeff Ferrell puts it) between "pleasure and panic", the various feelings of anger, humiliation, exuberance, and fear' (*ibid*, p. 264) just does not fit a Clarke and Felson analysis. Further, crime does not necessarily have rational-choice theory's 'instrumental payoffs', for example,

> The armed robber, as ex-con John McVicar (1979) once remarked, could make more money as a day labourer; the juvenile delinquent, as Albert Cohen pointed out a long time ago, spends much of his time making mischief and mayhem while in school: 'the teacher and her rules are not merely something onerous to be evaded. They are to be flouted' (1955, p. 28). And, following Jack Katz's seminal *Seductions of Crime* (1988), the sensual, visceral, bodily nature of crime is ignored in the orthodox academic depictions of criminality – in remarkable contrast, of course, with the accounts of offenders or indeed of much crime fiction.
>
> (*ibid*, p. 264)

The existential motivational structure that cultural criminologists explore counters that of rational choice, routine activities and control theory. For the motivation to commit crime 'is not mundane but the revolt against the mundane, rules are transgressed because they are there, risk is a challenge not a deterrent' (Young, 2003, p. 391). Rational choice with its images of opportunism and control is the criminology of neo-liberalism.

In the next chapter the focus switches from the criminal act to that of the actor by considering the development of positivist theory within criminology. Identified by its 'scientific' search for the determinants of criminality, positivism also has a long history within criminology with wide-ranging implications for individuals, their families and communities.

Notes

1 As Eric Hobsbawn points out in *The Age of Revolution, 1789–1848*, 'If the economy of the nineteenth-century world was formed mainly under the influence of the British Industrial Revolution, its politics and ideology was formed mainly by the French. Britain provided the model for its railways and factories..but France made its revolutions and gave them their ideas, to the point that the tricolor of some kind became the emblem of virtually every emerging nation . . . France provided the vocabulary and the issues of liberal and radical-democratic politics for most of the world' (1962, p. 73). France, aside from Russia, was the most 'powerful and populous state in Europe in 1789 something like one European out of every five was a Frenchman' (*ibid*, p. 74).
2 'With the exception of Britain, which had made its revolution in the seventeenth century, and a few lesser states, absolute monarchies ruled in all functioning states of the European continent; those in which they did not rule fell apart into anarchy and were swallowed by their neighbours, like Poland' (Hobsbawn, 1962, p. 36).
3 As is usual in early texts, 'man' is here being used to mean all of humankind. However, that being said, in Enlightenment thought, 'man' meant a white man with property; 'rights' were not extended to women or to Black or Indigenous people. They were excluded from the social contract. (See the section in the text, 'Who Is Equal Before the Law?').
4 The key social contract theorists are Thomas Hobbes (1588–1678), John Locke (1633–1704) and Jean-Jacques Rousseau. (1712–1778).
5 Voltaire has additionally been described as the 'father of the innocence campaign' (Staff, 2007, p. 29). For the strategy that he employed for Calas parallels that of a modern-day campaign against a miscarriage of justice, that is, an investigation in order to secure evidence of innocence; publicity to stir up public feeling and thus pressurising officials to re-investigate the case; the acquiring of financial aid to support the case and, following the declaration of innocence, monetary compensation (*ibid*).
6 1901 translation by William F. Fleming of Voltaire's *Dictionniare philosophique*.
7 Pietro Verri had previously written a pamphlet against torture in 1763, the *Orazione panegirica sulla giurisprudenza milanese* ('Panegyric speech on the Milanese judiciary') (see Baldoli, 2009).
8 This is indicative of Hobbes's influence on Beccaria.
9 Cited in Bellamy (1995, p. xlii) 'Note on the texts of *On Crimes and Punishments*'.
10 Translated in Bellamy (1995), title page.
11 In a letter to André Morellet, Beccaria excitedly acknowledges the influence and respect he has for Morellet, d'Alembert, Diderot, Helvétius, Buffon and Hume, all key Enlightenment thinkers, who had praised *On Crimes and Punishments*:

> Your immortal works are my constant reading, the object of my studies during the day and of my meditations at night . . . I find myself repaid beyond my hopes in receiving signs of respect from all these famous men whom I consider my teachers
>
> (Beccaria, 1995 ed, p. 121).

12 Bentham never ended up going to Spanish/Latin America. Yet he enjoyed lengthy correspondence with well-known Spanish/Latin American political figures, including Francisco de Miranda, Simón Bolívar, Francisco de Paula Santander and José del Valle, some of whom he met during their sojourns to England. According to Karen Rancine, Bentham 'enthusiastically responded to their requests to draft constitutions and other laws for Colombia, Buenos Aires, Guatemala, and Venezuela' (2010, p. 424). In his fascinating essay 'José del Valle: A Benthamite in Central America' (2014), Alejandro Gómez describes his influence on José del Valle's writing and government proposals between 1810 and 1834 in Guatemala. Valle wrote to Bentham, 'your works give you the glorious title of legislator of the world', and when Bentham died on June 6th 1832 requested that the Federal Government wear mourning to honour 'my dear and respected Maestro' (*ibid*, p. 14, 31). The influence of Bentham's ideas on Spanish/Latin America supports the critique of southern theorists who draw attention to the dominance of European and North American thought on the Global South to the exclusion of Indigenous and other voices (Connell, 2007a).

13 Apparently Bentham came up with the term 'utilitarian' following a dream in which he imagined himself 'a founder of a sect; of course a personage of great sanctity and importance. It was called the sect of the *utilitarians*' (Crimmins, 2015; text of the dream in Crimmins, 1990, p. 314). However, an early influence on Bentham's thought was Claude Adrien Helvétius, whose writing he had read at university.

14 Pietro Verri also wrote on 'happiness'. Being mindful of translation difficulties, Verri's take on happiness seems similar to that outlined by Beccaria, which is not surprising, given the level of collaboration that occurred between Beccaria and the Verri brothers. For Verri, the societal aim was to have 'the greatest possible happiness distributed with the greatest possible equality' (1763, cited in Porta and Scazzieri, 2002, p. 87); the equitable and shared nature of the happiness principle is underscored by Verri's use of the term 'public happiness'.

15 This is not to suggest that all Enlightenment thinkers were against torture. Voltaire 'vigorously denounces' torture but does not completely dismiss its use, and Denis Diderot presented an argument for its retention that is in line with Bentham and that of the 'ticking bomb' scenario: 'think how a few minutes of torturing a villain may save the lives of a hundred innocents whose throats his accomplices are going to cut, and you will consider that the *question* is an act of clemency' (cited in Clemens, 2017, p. 10)

16 The Bentham Project is at: www.ucl.ac.uk/bentham-project

17 To remove the prejudice 'that are apt to be entertained against' torture, Bentham provides examples of its common usage in the 'domestic jurisdiction' in '*which nobody suspects it to be wrong*' (author emphasis). Hence,

> If a Mother or Nurse seeing a child playing with a thing which he ought not to meddle with, and having forbidden him in vain pinches him till he lays it down, this is neither more nor less than Torture: If a parent having put a question to his child and upon the child's obstinately refusing to answer whips him till he complies, this too is neither more nor less than Torture.
>
> (*ibid*, p. 310)

While it is important to show how the meaning that is ascribed to an action changes according to context, Bentham's words are clearly illustrative of an outmoded past. For what counts as permissible or impermissible violence changes over time: most people today would see the pinching and whipping of children as not only bad child rearing practice but as simply wrong! The negative consequences – the physical and psychological harm – far surpass any potential benefits, i.e. the preventing of 'bad' behaviour. His arguments for the justification of torture in other situations should similarly be dismissed as archaic.

18 Admittedly, at one point, Bentham does appear to acknowledge that torture might be counterproductive: imprisonment, he suggests, 'breaks the spirits' but 'torture raises a

passion, which in persons of firm temperaments may support them' (Bentham Manuscripts, Twining and Twining, 1973, p. 323).
19 Panopticon features were, however, incorporated into a number of prison designs. In the United States, Pittsburgh's Western State Penitentiary in 1826 used some of Bentham's ideas, but the construction was eventually denounced as being 'wholly unsuited for anything but a fortress' and from 1926 to 1935 Illinois planned the Statesville Prison along panopticon lines, but 'after four of the circular cell houses were built and occupied their impracticability was so obvious that it was decided to change to a more conventional plan in completing the institution', with a prison architect commenting 'that it was "the most awful receptacle of gloom ever devised and put together with good stone and brick and mortar"'(Geis, 1955, p. 170).
20 As some commentators suggest, we are today living in a 'surveillance society' (see, for example, Clive Norris and Gary Armstrong (1999) and David Lyon (2001)).
21 Dario Melossi cites Ronald Takaki's (1979) account of Alexis de Tocqueville's visit to America in the early 1830s in which the French nobleman was 'amazed' at 'the ability of white society to deprive Indians of their rights and exterminate them "with singular felicity, tranquility, legally, philanthropically . . . It is impossible to destroy men with more respect for the laws of humanity"' (2001, p. 410; Tocqueville, 1961 ed, pp. 352–353, 364).
22 'Colonial terrorism' in the form of taking land and genocide occurred to Indigenous populations throughout the colonised world. See Asafa Jalata's (2013) article on how the Indigenous people of Australia were almost destroyed by English colonial settlers and the recent special report in *The Guardian* newspaper, 'The Killing Times: The Massacres of Aboriginal People Australia Must Confront' (3 March 2019).
23 Cited in Thomson, 2010, p. 125. As Thomson has pointed out, 'Martineau's writing and activism against slavery helped arouse public opinion in Britain in favour of abolition' (*ibid*, pp. 125–126).
24 See, for example, Pateman (1988), Naffine (1990), Bryson (1992), Donovan (1997), Phillips (1998), Okin (1998).
25 It should be noted that the articles in *Il Caffè* represent a collective endeavour on behalf of the Verri brothers and members of their intellectual circle.
26 Appendix to Helen Maria Williams, the eighteenth-century writer and supporter of women's rights and the French Revolution, *Letters Written in France: in the Summer 1790*, edited by Fraistat and Lanser (2001), London: Broadview Press.
27 See the excellent Digital Panopticon project, which has pieced together the experiences of London convicts in Britain and Australia, 1780–1925, from Old Bailey Records (P.I. Barry Godfrey, www.digitalpanopticon.org/). Hamish Maxwell Stewart's section on Australian transportation on the same site is a useful source on Australian transportation (www.digitalpanopticon.org/Transportation).
28 Penal transportation, however, was not the prerogative of the British. As Hamish Maxwell-Stewart points out, 'the use of convicted labour to aid the process of European colonization of overseas territories dates back at least to the Portuguese invasion of Ceuta in North Africa in 1415' (2010, p. 1222).
29 There is much discussion over the use of words such as 'convict', 'prisoner', 'inmate' and so on (see the Marshall Project, 2015). From a political perspective, the term 'prisoner' is preferred because it underscores an individual's lack of power over their situation.
30 It was also common to the U.S. penitentiary system in the nineteenth century.
31 Clarke has described rational choice as a micro theory 'dealing with the ways that offenders make decisions to take advantage of criminal opportunities', whereas routine activities is a macro theory, 'dealing primarily with the ways that opportunities for crime rise or decline with broad changes in society' (2010, p. 273).

Chapter 3

The positivist revolution, physiognomy, phrenology and the science of 'Othering'

Positivism

> *Those who follow criminal trials and study the results by visiting prisons or examining statistics are disheartened by the endless debate over punishment. . . . Those who have had direct contact with offenders, such as members of their families or prison wardens, know that they are different from other people, with weak or diseased minds that can rarely be healed. Psychiatrists in many cases find it impossible to neatly distinguish between madness and crime. And yet legislators, believing exceptions to free will are rare, ignore the advice of psychiatrists and prison officials. They do not understand that most criminals really do lack free will. In past years, having decided that reform is the greatest goal of their terrestrial mission, legislators established legal criteria that failed to recognise any gradations whatsoever among healthy, diseased and guilty minds.*
> (Cesare Lombroso in the preface to his classic text, L'uomo delinquente [Criminal Man], first published in 1876)

As we saw in the last chapter, Enlightenment thought and traditional classicist approaches to crime and criminal justice typically placed an emphasis on the criminal act and largely saw individuals as governed by free will. Central to this was the debate over what a just system of punishment should look like. In the opening quotation, Cesare Lombroso challenged this particular way of thinking, most radically with respect to conceptions of the criminal.

Positivism as a theory of crime developed during the latter half of the nineteenth century, influenced and supported by the general enthusiasm for science that dominated the time. This was the era in which Charles Darwin introduced the idea of evolution by natural selection in *On the Origin of the Species* (1859) and *The Descent of Man* (1871), that saw the birth of psychoanalysis through the work of Freud and his followers and witnessed numerous advances in the fields of medicine, physics and technology. In 1822 Auguste Comte, the French philosopher credited with naming 'sociology', published 'Plan of the Scientific Operations Necessary for the Reorganizing of Society', in which he argued for the need to develop a 'positive science' which would be founded on empirical investigations designed to make and scrutinise abstract laws of social organisation.[1] The belief that human beings and their social environment could be subjected to scientific analysis became widely accepted.

As a criminological theory, unlike classicism, positivism's focus is on the criminal and the causes of crime rather than the criminal act. It presents crime as something that individuals are driven to by forces that are largely beyond their control and, in keeping with the importance afforded to science, exhorts the use of the 'scientific method' to identify and investigate those factors that differentiate between criminals and non-criminals. Theorists have variously classified these 'forces' or determining factors as biological, psychological or social – or simply multi-factorial, combining elements of each. One of the central tenets of the 'scientific method' is to apply those instruments and methods that are used in the study of our physical surroundings and in animal biology to human beings. The shift in focus from classicism to positivism was seen by both advocates of positivism and social commentators at the time as an intellectual revolution. For the principles on which positivism are based result in 'almost a mirror image of classicism' for 'free-will disappears under determinacy, equality bows before natural difference and expert knowledge, and human laws that are created become scientific laws that are discovered' (Young, 1981, p. 267). Moreover, in moving the focus from the act (crime) to the actor (criminal) and the forces that propel him or her, positivists have recommended the replacement of the jury system with 'a team of experts . . . to investigate the causes propelling the individual into crime, diagnosing him and prescribing an appropriate therapeutic regime' (Taylor et al, 1973, p. 22). Taking this to its extreme, if criminals are determined, then they cannot be held responsible for their actions and, as a result, a punitive response is deemed inappropriate.

To an extent such a characterisation is an exaggeration, for although classicism did hold that in *most* circumstances a person can morally assess a situation and make free and rational choices, the notion of determinacy was acknowledged. Jeremy Bentham, despite being a leading proponent of the classicist view of human nature, includes in his *Introduction to the Principles of Morals and Legislation* (1823 ed) a chapter called 'Circumstances Influencing Sensibility' that discusses, albeit briefly, thirty-two biological, psychological and social factors that have a determining impact on human behaviour, for example, strength, bodily imperfection, firmness of mind, insanity, occupation, education and climate. Anthony Walsh observes that 'the fact that he recognized internal and external constraints on rationality and free will places Bentham both among the last of the old classical criminologists and among the first of the positivist criminologists' (2003, p. 2). Further, there were thinkers in the eighteenth and early nineteenth century, at the height of the classicist ascendancy, who were focusing primarily on the physiological causes of human behaviour and crime; as can be seen in the development of ideas about Lavater's physiognomical approach (see Box 3.1 'The Work of Johann Caspar Lavater'). One of the founding fathers of the United States, Benjamin Rush, wrote several essays, most notably that of 'The Influence of Physical Causes Upon Moral Faculty' delivered to the American Philosophical Society in 1786, which also places him among the first to examine the relationship between biology and crime (see Rafter, 2009). In the contemporary period, debates over free will versus determining factors have continued: positivism did not supersede classicist approaches, as is evident with the development of both 'just desserts' and rational choice theory.

More seriously what both approaches have in common as theories of crime is their neglect of crimes committed in the name of colonialism and at the hands of the state and the level that they have contributed to the upholding and reinforcement of an exclusionary world order. Classicism was founded on the notion of formal equality, which was a myth, for most 'men' were not born free and equal. 'Rationality' was ascribed to white men, originally those with property, and those who were outside of this group, especially if they were from so-called 'inferior' cultures, were not worthy of inclusion within the social contract and, thus, for them democracy and a fair and equitable system of justice were to be denied. Positivist ideology was to provide the justification for keeping them outside of the social contract and subordinate to a rule that was no less tyrannical than that of the *ancien régime*. As Biko Agozino points out, the criminal anthropology that won Lombroso the French Legion Medal of Honor was utilised 'to prove that African Americans and white women, like Africans and Asians, were unfit for self-determination through universal suffrage' (2003, pp. 4–5) and contributed to the 'othering' of historically marginalised people that continues to this day.

Box 3.1 The work of Johann Caspar Lavater: physiognomy and the identification of a 'criminal type'

Johann Caspar Lavater (1741–1801) was a deeply religious man with a passion for drawing and painting portraits. It was through his artistic endeavours that he came to observe a relation between a person's external, especially facial, features and their qualities and conduct; this was termed 'physiognomy'. In *Essays on Physiognomy*, which was first published in 1772, he wrote, 'the experienced eye of the painter perceives a thousand small shades and colours which are unremarked by common spectators, so the physiognomist views a multitude of actual or possible perfections which escape the general eye of the despiser, the slanderer, or even the more benevolent judge of mankind' (1804 ed, p. 3). With the man to be avoided is:

> He who carries high, and bends backwards, a large or remarkably small head ; displaying feet so short as to attract notice; who making his large eyes larger, continually turns them sideways, as if he must see everything over his shoulder; who listens long in proud silence, and then answers dryly, short, and disapprovingly, concluding with a cold laugh, and superciliously imposing silence as soon as a reply is attempted – has at least three unamiable qualities – conceit, pride, ill- nature – and most probably adds to these a disposition to lying, maliciousness, and avarice.
>
> (1804 ed, p. 490)

Some of these ideas can be traced back to the works of the Ancient Greeks. Aristotle, for example, highlighted the importance of analysing facial features; this is acknowledged by Lavater in *Essays on Physiognomy*, although he disagreed with Aristotle's contention that those who have the smallest heads are the wisest! As is discussed in the main text, physiognomy influenced the development of phrenology, and the idea of the criminal as being a distinct physical type was central to Lombroso's theoretical position.

Further Reading:

Lavater J. (1878 ed) *Essays on Physiognomy*, London: W. Tegg.

André-Michel Guerry and Adolphe Quetelet: 'moral statistics'

There are two positivist traditions within criminology: a sociological perspective intent on examining society as a whole in the search for the causes of crime that dates from the work of André-Michel Guerry and Adolphe Quetelet in the mid-nineteenth century and one which searches for causes within the individual – although social factors are inevitably also considered. The work of Guerry, a French lawyer, and Quetelet, a Belgian scientist, involved the analysis of the first annual crime statistics collected in France from 1827. The use of crime statistics was very much in keeping with the need to develop a scientific approach to the study of crime and criminal behaviour. Their work was to establish the study of 'moral statistics', which has remained a feature of sociological and criminological research. Additionally, it was to inaugurate a cartographical tradition within criminology. The early nineteenth century was, in fact, a 'golden age' for cartography. Piers Beirne has pointed out that 'like movements in public health, in prison reform and statistics the development of cartography was closely linked with the vastly expanded sphere of state activities' (1993, p. 111) that also characterised this time and with the need to record newly discovered and colonised lands.

Whereas the earliest maps of moral statistics are believed to have been produced by Charles Dupin in France, possibly as early as 1819 (*ibid*; Friendly, 2007), André-Michel Guerry and his colleague Adriano Balbi, a Venetian geographer, were the first to use shaded maps to show crime rates. Guerry and Balbi's *Statistique comparée de l'état de l'instruction et du nombre des crimes* (1829 ed) included three shaped crime maps illustrating the rate of crime against the person, property crime and education (Friendly, 2007). The maps produced by Guerry (which included England) and the slightly later ones of Quetelet allowed for the exploration of the spatial patterning of crime.

This chapter, as the title implies, is mainly concerned with individual positivism within criminology, but let us briefly consider the ideas of Quetelet,[2] as some of these reappear in later sociological discussions on the causes of crime. One of Quetelet's initial observations was that the crime rate was relatively constant from year to year and that this was true for all crimes, even that of murder, which often appears unplanned and of the moment and would therefore be expected to show greater yearly variation. Quetelet took this to indicate that the causes of crime are to be found in the structures of society. He therefore writes in *A Treatise on Man and the Development of His Faculties*,

> In everything which relates to crimes, the same numbers are reproduced so constantly, that it becomes impossible to misapprehend it – even in respect to those crimes which seem perfectly beyond human foresight, such as murders committed in general at the close of quarrels, arising without a motive, and under other circumstances to all appearance the most fortuitous or accidental: nevertheless, experience proves that murders are committed annually, not only pretty nearly to the same extent, but even that the instruments employed are in the same proportions.

And, therefore,

> Society includes within itself the germs of all the crimes that will be committed, and at the same time the necessary facilities for their development. It is the social state in some measure, which prepares these crimes, and the criminal is merely the instrument to execute them.
>
> (1835, 1842 ed, p. 6)

Quetelet found that those with the greatest propensity to commit crime were young men, the peak age being 25 years, who were living in poverty. However, he argued that poverty alone was not a sufficient explanation, and this shows him to move beyond positivism. What was relevant for Quetelet is how poverty is experienced, as 'poverty is felt the most in areas where great riches have been amassed' (*ibid*, p. 88) and where economic changes have resulted in individuals passing 'from a state of comfort to one of misery' (*ibid*). It is this that gives rise to crime, 'particularly if those who suffer are surrounded by materials of temptation, and are irritated by the continual aspect of luxury and of the inequality of fortune, which renders them desperate' (*ibid*). Crime is a response to the feeling of deprivation, 'the inequality between riches and wants' (*ibid*, p. 89), and the impact of this was seen as greater in urban areas: 'the giant cities . . . present an unfavourable subject, because they possess more lurement to possessions of every kind' (*ibid*). As we shall see, in presenting such a perspective on crime, Quetelet's work is a precursor to those sociological theories that have focused on the gap between the 'haves' and the 'have-nots' and how individuals are affected and respond to their socio-economic circumstances. The experience of relative deprivation is key to much sociological criminology in the contemporary period.

Furthermore, in identifying men as being the usual offenders, Quetelet made explicit the male/female differential in the crime rate: 'the propensity to crime in men is about four times as great as in women' (*ibid*, p. 90) and women, with the exception of infanticide, were more likely to commit non-violent property crime – themes that were to be developed in subsequent discussions on gender and crime. As Piers Beirne (1987)[3] points out, the importance of Quetelet's ideas was acknowledged: Karl Marx described *A Treatise on Man* as 'an excellent and learned work' (1853, p. 229), and Emile Durkheim refers to Quetelet in his seminal works, *Rules of Sociological Method* (1895) and *Suicide* (1897).

The Italian school of criminology

With respect to early positivist thought that places an emphasis largely on individual factors – as opposed to the broader sociological analysis of Quetelet – the most frequently referenced examples are those from the 'Italian school of criminology', as represented by the writings of Cesare Lombroso and his followers, Enrico Ferri and Raffaele Garofalo, which emerged in the late nineteenth century. Lombroso's most important works on crime are *Criminal Man* (1876) and *Criminal Woman, the Prostitute, and the Normal Woman* (*La donna delinquent*, 1893) written with Guglielmo Ferrero, who was to become his son-in-law.

Cesare Lombroso

> *In the history of criminology probably no name has been eulogised or attacked so much as that of Cesare Lombroso.*
>
> (Marvin Wolfgang, 1960, p. 232)

Marco Ezechia (Cesare) Lombroso, a doctor from Verona, was acclaimed by some as a genius, as a dangerous maverick by others. He is variously described as either the founding father of biological positivism or, more grandly, 'the father of modern criminology' (Wolfgang, 1960, p. 168), as 'a crank who wrote "silly stuff" about criminals with malformed heads' (Pick, 1986, p. 61) and high armpit temperatures or, more sinisterly, as one of the 'men of science' who made racist ideology theoretically acceptable and leant weight to eugenicist ideas through his popularising of the belief that we are determined by our biology and in applying this to the criminal. Like Cesare Beccaria, Lombroso was a graduate of the University of Pavia. Given their later theoretical positions, Beccaria's and Lombroso's studies at the University of Pavia are of significance, symbolising a shift in focus from the criminal act and penal responses to the act to seeing criminality as a medical problem to be scientifically examined by experts. Beccaria had graduated in law in 1758; Lombroso studied medicine, graduating in 1858 after writing a thesis on endemic cretinism.

During his lifetime, Lombroso and his work became well-known in Europe, North America and Latin America, no doubt helped by his inflammatory and excitable style of writing. In Latin America Dain Borges and Pablo Piccato suggest that 'his concoction of anthropology, biology, medicine and law' became 'a compelling rationale for monitoring, categorizing, disciplining and centralizing control over . . . fragmented and regionalized populations' (see Salvatore et al, 2001, p. xv). In the Global North, by the time of Lombroso's death in 1909, his name was a 'household word' (*The Times*, 15 June 1911, p. 11).[4]

According to Marvin Wolfgang (1960), it was during Lombroso's university days that he found himself in opposition to the idea of free will that had characterised Enlightenment thought. Among his key influences were Charles Darwin, German phrenologist Franz Joseph Gall and German biologist Ernst Haeckel, along with Bénédict-August Morel, a Franco-Austrian psychiatrist who argued that criminality, insanity and other forms of social deviancy were symptoms of an underlying medical condition – *degeneracy* – that was passed from generation to generation (1857, cited in Wetzell, 2000, p. 46), and Auguste Comte, who had put forward the notion that human behaviour was subject to natural, scientific laws and it was 'our business' to uncover these laws to devise solutions to social and moral problems (1822, p. 5). Daniel Pick comments that whilst Lombroso was not directly a Comtist, nor is there a direct lineage from Comte's positivism to that within criminology, he did share Comte's 'confidence in natural science as the great key to social advance and social explanation and viewed knowledge itself as an evolution from religion to metaphysics to "positive" science' (1993, p. 131).[5]

Soon after completing his thesis, Lombroso volunteered as a soldier-physician for the Sanitary Corps of Piedmont in 1859. This was the time of the wars of the *Risorgimento*, or the Second War of Italian Unification, which were to consolidate the different states of the Italian peninsula into a single Kingdom of Italy. During his four years in the army, Lombroso served in several regions, most notably in the southern province of Calabria, where he was sent as part of the war against peasant 'brigandage'. What was meant by 'brigandage' is contested: it was loosely applied by the new government to cover outbreaks of violent opposition to its laws in the South.[6] Hence, 'peasant unrest' or 'rebellion' might more accurately describe what happened. Those labelled 'brigands' were seen as at odds with the development and cohesiveness of the new nation-state. Yet the factors behind the unrest were, as Dickie (1992, 1999) points out, the extreme levels of economic hardship experienced in the South, conscription and the eroding of collective land-use rights. It was the bourgeois landowners who were the main benefactors of the *Risorgimento*. Prejudice by the North towards those from the South was long-standing; Southerners were thought of as 'a form of other world, racially different, a space to be explored, penetrated, contained, colonised' (Pick, 1986, p. 62). Conservative newspapers spoke of the South as 'barbaric Italy' and as the 'Italian Africa' (Cimino, 2014). But for the ordinary people of the South, 'brigands' – such as Giuseppe Musolino, who was to feature in Lombroso's article *The Last Brigand* (1902) – were romantic Robin Hood figures; outlaws that hid in the mountains, fighting on their behalf the conquerors of the North. The war between the North and South was to see thousands of soldiers deployed to the South and the massacre, execution and arrest of hundreds of thousands of 'brigands' and working people accused of directly supporting or hiding the 'brigands'. Villages were either razed to the ground or depopulated in an attempt to sever the ties between the 'brigands' and their peasant supporters (Matthews, 2010).

As a physician, Lombroso was not involved in direct combat, and when serving in Calabria, he 'beguiled' his 'ample leisure' by conducting anthropometrical research on 3,000 soldiers with the intention of exploring the physical and ethnic diversity of the various regions of Italy and the differences between the 'honest soldier' and his more 'vicious comrade' (Lombroso, 1911, p. xii). Lombroso's Calabrian research was to provide the foundation for much of his later studies. He was to associate the South with criminality and savagery: their people were presented as 'other', as 'inferior', serving to uphold the superiority of the North.

Lombroso's Criminal Man: atavism and phrenology

It was Lombroso's student, Garofalo Ferri, who was to credit him with 'demonstrating . . . that we must first understand the criminal who offends, before we can study and understand his crime' (1905, p. 15). Lombroso was to propose that there was a criminal anthropological type, and his school of thought became known as criminal anthropology, which he defined as 'the Natural History of the Criminal' (1911 ed, p. 5). In *Criminal Man* (1876)[7] he argued that male offenders were biological throwbacks to an earlier evolutionary stage of development; they were more primitive and less highly evolved than non-criminals. Lombroso, as numerous commentators have been at pains to stress, was, however, not the first to utilise biological explanations of criminal behaviour (Savitz and Johnston, 1982; Lilly et al, 2011) Johann Caspar Lavater and Franz Joseph Gall and the phrenological school predates the work of Lombroso.[8]

Box 3.2 Phrenology

Lombroso was influenced by phrenology, a development of physiognomy. Based on the belief that the brain is the instrument of the mind and each of its parts, known as 'organs', has a specific function, the

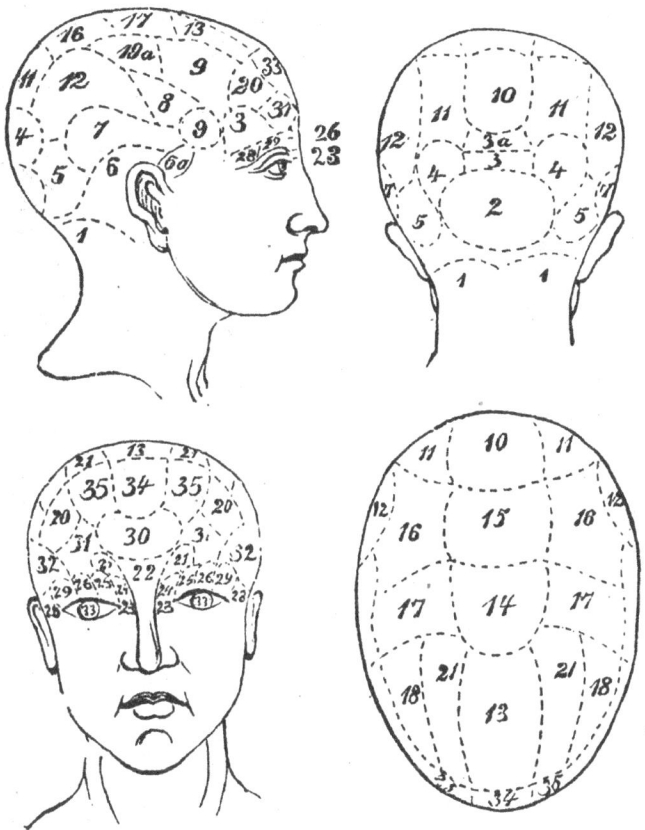

A Chart of Phrenology.

1 Amativeness · 2 Philoprogenitiveness ; 3 Concentrativeness ; 3 *a* Inhabitiveness ; 4 Adhesiveness ; 5 Combativeness ; 6 Destructiveness ; 6 *a* Alimentiveness ; 7 Secretiveness ; 8 Acquisitiveness ; 9 Constructiveness ; 10 Self-esteem ; 11 Love of Approbation ; 12 Cautiousness ; 13 Benevolence ; 14 Veneration ; 15 Firmness ; 16 Conscientiousness ; 17 Hope ; 18 Wonder ; 19 Ideality ; 19 *a* (Not determined) ; 20 Wit ; 21 Imitation ; 22 Individuality ; 23 Form ; 24 Size ; 25 Weight ; 26 Coloring ; 27 Locality ; 28 Number ; 29 Order ; 30 Eventuality ; 31 Time ; 32 Tune ; 33 Language ; 34 Comparison ; 35 Causality. [Some raise the number of organs to forty-three.]

Figure 3.1 Phrenology, Webster's Dictionary, circa 1895.

primary focus of phrenology was on the shape of the skull, which was seen as corresponding to its interior in such a way that character and mental capabilities could be revealed through its examination. This is illustrated by the entry on 'Phrenology' in an early edition of Webster's Dictionary.

Franz Joseph Gall is hailed as the founder of phrenology. As the president of the Congress of the International Centenary of Phrenology stated, 'it is to Dr Gall that the glory of the discovery of the true physiology of the brain belongs, which he called the science of Human Nature' (Fowler, 1896, p. 5). Gall, a physician from Vienna, was known early on for his acute scrutiny of the physical appearance of those he came in contact with. In *On the Function of the Brain and of Each of its Parts*, he wrote that one of his first observations related to his fellow students; those with good verbal memories were distinguished by 'large prominent eyes projecting from the head' (1835 ed, p. 58). Gall travelled widely, gathering 'innumerable facts' from 'schools, the great establishments of education, in the asylums for orphans and foundlings, in the insane hospitals, in houses of correction and prisons, in judicial interrogatories, and even in places of execution', all of which 'contributed greatly to correct and confirm my opinions' (*ibid*, p. 21). Skulls were frequently sent to him for analysis, and from this he concluded that features of murderers were similar to those of carnivorous animals. Gall's work was popularised in Europe by his former assistant, Johann Spurzheim; in the United States by Charles Caldwell, who had been his student in Paris; and by George Combe in Britain. Much of its appeal resulted from the visuals developed by Spurzheim and Combe – the familiar phrenological heads, charts and so on – that illustrated the different mental faculties by region of the brain and mapped to locations on the surface of the skull. Despite the controversial nature of phrenology and the derision that it generated – especially through its association with fortune telling and showmanship – we should, not as Nikolas Rose reflects, 'underestimate the risky radicalism' of the early researchers, for 'most held explicitly materialist philosophical positions, asserting that human mental capacities could be explained without reference to any metaphysics or religion, and without invoking an immaterial soul' (Rose and Abi-Rached, 2013, pp. 62–63). Thus, again we see a 'scientific' move away from a religious world order and an acceptance of religious 'truths' in Europe: there is no soul, only brain (*ibid*). Work in this area was to provide the foundation for future work in neuroscience and anatomy, with ideas on how outward cranial appearance could help with the identification of the 'criminal type' enduring.

In the introduction to Gina Lombroso Ferrero's summary of *Criminal Man*, Lombroso discusses making the acquaintance of the 'famous brigand' Giuseppe Villella while studying criminals in prison, 'a man who possessed such extraordinary agility, that he had been known to scale steep mountain heights bearing a sheep on his shoulders' and who 'openly boasted of his crimes' (Lombroso, 1911 ed, p. xiv). When he died on a gloomy, cold November morning, Lombroso was tasked with Villella's post-mortem. In an oft-quoted passage, Lombroso describes his excitement at discovering in the man's skull a clearly defined depression, which he named *median occipital fossa* because of its resemblance to the 'middle of the occiput as in inferior animals, especially rodents'.

> At the sight of that skull, I seemed to see all of a sudden, lighted up as a vast plain under a flaming sky, the problem of the nature of the criminal – an atavistic being who reproduces in his person the ferocious instincts of primitive humanity and the inferior animals. Thus were explained anatomically the enormous jaws, high cheek bones, prominent superciliary arches . . . found in criminals, savages and apes. . . [their] love of orgies, and the irresistible craving for evil for its own sake, the desire not only to extinguish life in the victim, but to mutilate the corpse, tear its flesh, and drink its blood.
>
> (1911 ed, p. xv)

On his desk Lombroso was to keep a phrenological bust and Villella's skull to remind him, as Nicole Rafter notes, of 'criminological anthropology's predecessor in the science of deciphering the human brain while the skull incorporated almost all the wisdom of criminal anthropology' (Rafter, 2008, p. 68). As she wryly observes, 'this was a lot to infer from the skull of one old man' (*ibid*, p. 67).

Lombroso's description of Villella's skull displays a similarity to the words of Charles Darwin, who argued in the *Descent of Man* that:

> [I]njurious characters . . . tend to reappear through reversion, such as blackness in sheep; and with mankind some of the worst dispositions, which occasionally without any assignable cause make their appearance in families, may perhaps be reversions to a savage state, from which we are not removed by very many generations. This view seems indeed recognized in the common expression that such men are the black sheep of the family.
>
> (1874, p. 134)

For Lombroso, 'criminals' were to be characterised as 'born criminals', and 'atavistic' was the label he gave to their features. By comparing criminals to non-criminals, he claimed to have identified a number of physical anomalies that indicated a propensity to criminality. In the third edition of *Criminal Man* he wrote:

> Atavism remains one of the constant characteristics of the born criminal ... many of the characteristics of primitive man are also commonly found in the born criminal, including low sloping foreheads, overdeveloped sinuses, frequent occurrence of the medium occipital fossetta, overdevelopment of the jaw and cheekbones, prognathism, oblique and large eye sockets, dark skin, thick and curly head hair, large or protuberant ears, long arms.
>
> (1876, 2006 ed, p. 222)

Although Lombroso described himself as being encouraged by this 'bold hypothesis', which was supported by his studies on Verzeni, a man convicted of sadism and rape, 'who showed the cannibalistic instincts of primitive anthropophagists and the ferocity of beasts of prey' (1911, p. xvi), this was for him still an incomplete story of the causes of criminality. The 'final key' was the case of Misdea:

> [A] young soldier of about twenty-one, unintelligent but not vicious. Although subject to epileptic fits, he had served for some years in the army when suddenly, for some trivial cause, he attacked and killed eight of his superior officers and comrades. His horrible work accomplished, he fell into a deep slumber, which lasted twelve hours and on awaking appeared to have no recollection of what had happened. Misdea, while representing the most ferocious type of animal, manifested, in addition, all the phenomena of epilepsy, which appeared to be hereditary in all the members of his family. It flashed across my mind that many criminal characteristics not attributable to atavism, such as facial asymmetry, cerebral sclerosis, impulsiveness, instantaneousness, the periodicity of criminal acts, the desire of evil for evil's sake, were morbid characteristics common to epilepsy, mingled with others due to atavism.
>
> (1911, p. xvi)

Criminals were henceforth disturbingly to be presented as atavistic and/or epileptic, 'epilepsy frequently reproduced atavistic characteristics, including even those common to lower animals' (*ibid*). Musolino, the 'last brigand', according to Lombroso (1902), also had a strong family history of epilepsy. The history of epilepsy is a frightening one, marked by the persecution of those who suffer from seizures. The *Malleus Maleficarum* or *The Witches' Hammer* (1486), referred to in Chapter 1, considered epilepsy a characteristic of witches. In 1895, concerns over the transmission of epilepsy from one generation to another resulted in Connecticut becoming the first U.S. state to prohibit marriage for people with the condition, and from 1907

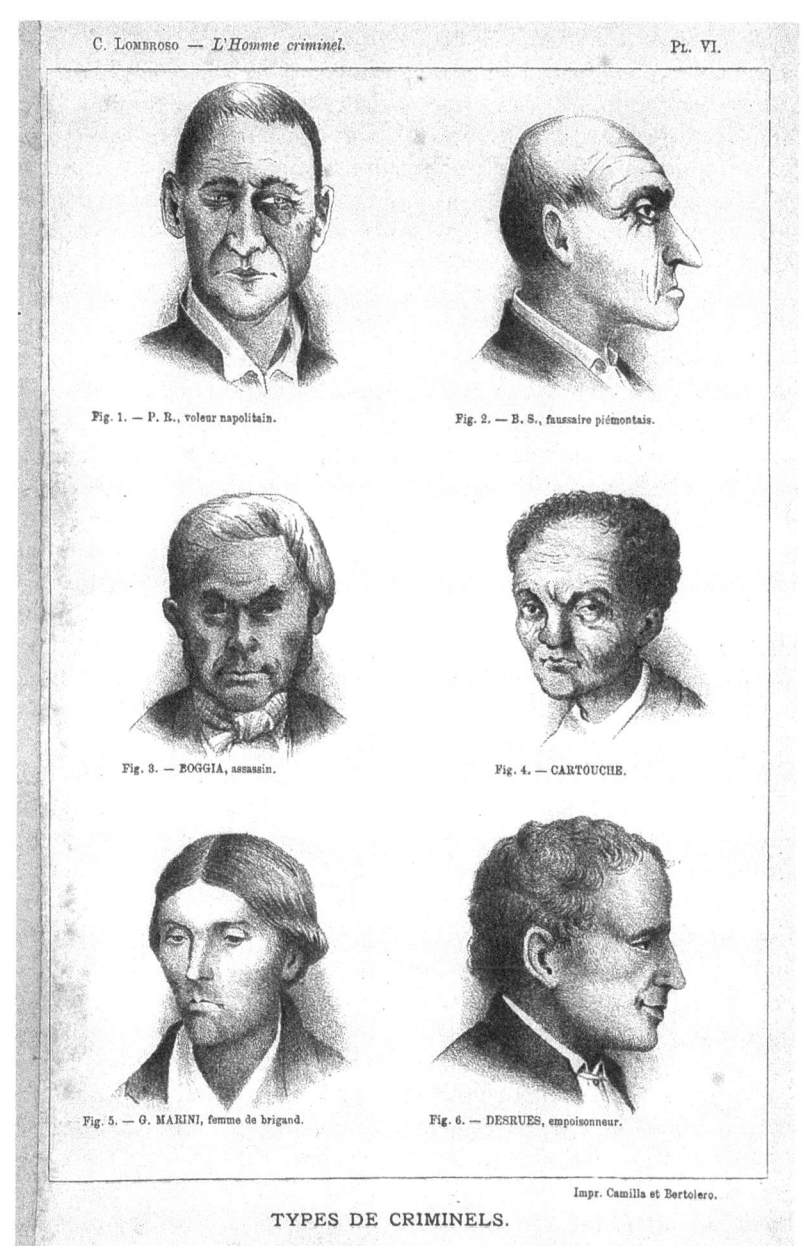

Figure 3.2 'Types of Criminals', from C. Lombroso's *Criminal Man*, Wellcome Collection, CC BY.

epileptics were subject to America's eugenicist laws in relation to the forced sterilisation of individuals.

In *The White Man and the Man of Colour*, which was published in 1871, five years before *Criminal Man*, Lombroso put forward his belief in race as a determinant of behaviour and that certain racial characteristics were indicative of atavism. This book, based on lectures on 'popular science for the ladies' (1871, p. 5), is important in terms of understanding the trajectory of Lombroso's thought: the centrality afforded to scientific racism. The lectures and their subsequent publication are further illustrative, as Mary Gibson suggests, of 'the positivists' urge to spread their ideas beyond an academic audience, or even the male political class, to the general public' (2002, p. 99). In *The White Man and the Man of Colour*, Lombroso describes Black people as 'the most imperfect' and whites the 'most perfect'. The African still exhibited 'that infantile and monkey-like manner of smiling and gesturing ... the brain is undeveloped in the back and weighs less than ours. As for the skull which holds it ... the face predominates over the forehead as [their] passions drown [their] intelligence' (pp. 84, 27–28; cited in Gibson, 2002, p. 107). He constantly reinforces – as he did throughout his work – his belief in the superiority of whites: 'only we whites have touched the most perfect symmetry of the form of the body' and, in a passage serving to support one of the contentions of this book that liberalism is at the behest of white men, 'only we have bestowed the human right to life, respect for old age, women and the weak. ... And only we have with Washington and Franklin and Mirabeau, proclaimed the concept of the true nation' (pp. 219–223). In *Criminal Man*, criminals 'resemble savages and the coloured races' (Lombroso, 1876, 2006 ed, p. 91).

Lombroso deduced from his Calabrian research that the Southern Italian was lazy, generally inferior, uncivilised and evidencing a 'criminality of blood' (Lombroso, 1898, in D'Agostino, 2002, p. 323) and that this could, in part, be attributed to North African influences on the population. The South was classified as racially mixed, with those from Sardinia, Calabria and Sicily sharing a proclivity for murder with their African and 'Oriental' ancestors (Lombroso, 1911, p. 140). Brigandage in Sicily could be traced back to the 'blood' of the Berber and Semitic tribes (Lombroso, 1897 ed, p. 26). Giuseppe Musolino, in 'The Last Brigand', was described as anatomically degenerate with 'a receding forehead, protruding eyebrows, and an asymmetrical face' (Pick, 2004, p. 641) and 'an instinct for killing and revenge' (Lombroso, 1902). His physique was representative of 'his regional type'. The way that Lombroso and his followers, most prominently, Alfredo Nicefero were to portray the people from the South gave, as Daniel Pick (1986) argues, a scientific credibility to the notion that they were biologically different, innately criminogenic and, hence, were not part of the new Italy. Lombroso is one of Antonio Gramsci's 'propagandists of the bourgeoisie', in which

> the South is the ball and chain which prevents the social development of Italy from progressing more rapidly; the Southerners are biologically

inferior beings, semibarbarians or total barbarians, by natural destiny; if the South is backward, the fault does not lie with the capitalist system or with any other historical cause, but with Nature, which has made the Southerners lazy, incapable, criminal and barbaric.

(2000 ed, p. 173)

This depiction justified and facilitated the continued subjugation of the South and the islands, reducing them to exploitable colonies (*ibid*).

The inescapable fact of Lombroso's virulent racism makes it difficult to comprehend why he is still often treated respectfully by commentators on criminality, with references made to the progressive nature of his thought, his 'brilliant intuition' (Gatti and Verde, 2012) and a need for a 'revisionist' assessment of his work (e.g. Raine, 2013). Lombroso's association of criminality with savagery and his 'othering' of those of 'inferior' cultures infused racism into the emerging field of criminology (Gabbidon, 2010).

A note on Lombroso's museum

In 1892 Lombroso opened a museum in Turin to house what had become a huge collection of relics relating to his research, including over 200 skulls that, as he wrote for *The New York Times* in 1907, ranged from the 'barbarous to the most intellectual' (17 Feb., p. 9). The collection dated from his early studies of soldiers when serving in the army, which was added to over the years by donations of 'criminal' artefacts from students and friends. Exhibits include, for example, photographs depicting the born criminal, epileptics, psychiatric patients and prostitutes, objects made by prisoners and preserved sections of tattooed skin. The opening of the museum, as Gibson and Rafter comment, 'marked a triumph of positivism, with its emphasis on empirical research and scientific induction' (2006, p. 27). Some of Lombroso's acquisitions had previously been publicly exhibited, for example, at the Torino Exposition in 1884, the International Penitentiary Congress in Rome in 1885 and the Second International Criminal Anthropology Congress in Paris in 1889. It is a collection that Lombroso himself admitted in *The New York Times* article that came about in a 'more or less legitimate manner from the spoils of old abandoned tombs in Sardinia, Valtellina, Lucca, and Piedmont' (17 Feb., p. 9). Indeed, he writes of committing 'one of these scientific crimes' in the Piedmontese valleys, 'with the complicity, no less exalted, than that of the Royal Procurator' and with the 'good fortune that the villagers who bore on their bent backs sacks filled with skulls did not guess their content' (*ibid*).

Amongst the skulls on display in the museum were those of Giuseppe Villella, previously been kept by Lombroso on his desk, and the anarchist, Giovanni Passannante. Passannante was an impoverished cook from the Basilicata region who tried unsuccessfully to assassinate King Umberto I of Savoy in 1878. The king had been riding in a carriage through the streets of Naples, a visit paid for by the imposition of a special tax (Vitelli, 2009), when Passannante struck with a small knife, which caused little more than a scratch. The failed regicide, much like Robert-François Damiens's attack on the king of France in 1757 and Margaret Nicolson's on George III in 1786 (Mooney, 2014), was symptomatic of the level of disgruntlement being felt by the ordinary people.[9] Passannante, who claimed to have been acting alone, said he was fighting against the level of indifference being shown to the poor, especially in relation to increases in the flour tax. At first he was sentenced to death, but this was commuted to life imprisonment and he was to endure the most horrendous torture and captivity on the island of Elba before being transferred to an asylum, where he died. His family members were either jailed or committed to asylums. After Passannante's death, his skull and brain were sent to the Lombroso museum to be examined by Lombroso's followers for criminal features. Both Villella and Passannante are seen as symbols of Southern oppression, with calls for their remains and those of others stored in the museum (who were mostly 'soldiers who lost a war, and whose remains were desecrated and put on display' (J. Matthews, 2010, p. 1) to be returned to their homes and families for proper and respectful burial.

It is not surprising that the Lombroso Museum's 2009 re-opening to mark the centenary of his death was met with fierce opposition. The *NoLombroso* committee was formed, condemning the museum as 'obscene, inhuman and racist', a symbol of the North's suppression of the South and its failure to acknowledge the atrocities committed against the Southern people – the 'erasing of a historical memory' – and the level that it had criminalised and demonised a population who were 'simply defending their land and right to life' (Iannantuoni, *NoLombroso* 2009). The *NoLombroso* committee has even gone so far as to argue that Lombroso's name should be removed from textbooks. Even though several commentators have emphasised that since its re-opening care has been taken to place the collection more sensitively within its historical context, which enables the viewer to 'ponder on the complex relationship to the here and now . . . to consider how a science on "monsters" has now metamorphosed into what some saw, and still see, as a monstrous science' (Knepper and Ystehede, 2013, p. 4), the director of the museum, Silvano Montaldo, is somewhat dismissive of the controversy. He suggests that the protestors are 'proponents of a prejudiciary hostile interpretation of the national unification process', which has resulted in a 'somewhat contrived interpretation of the past and against objective reality' (2013, p. 108). Yet, in actuality, how we interpret the past and what is meant by 'objective reality' depends on the evidence that is found to be most compelling: the history of Italy in this period is certainly complicated, there is nonetheless a significant amount of verifiable scholarship and archival material that supports the complaints voiced by those opposed to the museum. Moreover, there are obvious ethical implications that need to be considered with respect to the displaying of the body parts of Southern Italians, those labelled as criminal or insane and so on, many of which were acquired by less-than-legal means. For, whether commentators like it or not, as Wayne Morrison argues, 'museums are not passive places, a reflection of facts, but the result of a desire to master, control and order objects and to celebrate that power on display' (2013, p. 70).

Criminal characteristics and tattooing

In addition to the physical characteristics discussed so far, Lombroso noted in the born criminal other factors such as a lack of moral sense (for example, vanity, cruelty, idleness), various sensory and functional features (for example, greater tolerance to pain and touch, ambidexterity, greater strength in the left limbs), the use of criminal slang and a penchant for tattooing. In *Criminal Man* Lombroso devotes a chapter to tattooing; he also wrote an article, 'The Savage Origin of Tattooing', for *Popular Science Monthly* in 1896. As is indicated by the title of the article, he also equates tattooing with atavism; it is a characteristic of 'primitive man': 'there is not a single primitive tribe that does not use tattooing' (1876, 2006 ed, p. 62) and thus, the practice is linked with a propensity to criminality. His studies revealed that between 8 and 10 per cent of the criminal population were tattooed, and the tendency of some to decorate their genitals with tattoos was not only 'shameless' but supported his belief that criminality was marked by insensitivity to pain (*ibid*, p. 59). Lombroso's writings established him as a leading expert on the relationship between tattooing and criminality. His views on tattooing, as well as the work of Alexander Lacassagne (1880), who observed and recorded the tattoos of criminals serving out their sentences in the French army, were extensively discussed in the leading newspapers of the day.

The Pall Mall Gazette described Lacassagne's work, noting that many criminal men 'were tattooed on every part of the body, except the inner side of the thighs' and that 'it would be interesting to know whether English criminals . . . tattoo themselves as assiduously as do the French and the Italians' (25 October 1881). The work of Lombroso and Lacassagne was further popularised in the United States through an address by Robert Fletcher entitled 'Tattooing Among Civilised People' made to the Anthropological Society of Washington in 1882. Much of the commentary on the practice likewise considered it to be representative of barbarism and savagery. An article in *The Pall Mall Gazette* concluded in a racist tone, illustrative of the superiority expressed by colonialists, that 'the only moral that can be drawn from this practice is that savagery is always very close to our civilisation and that the criminal and indolent easily glide back into the manners of Australians and Red Indians'.

Perhaps not surprisingly, having identified its links with criminality and 'savagery', the popularity of tattooing amongst women and the aristocracy in the eighteenth century was condemned by Lombroso and Lacassagne and other commentators. Lombroso expressed concern on being told that 'the fashion of tattooing the arm exists among women of prominence in London society' (1896, p. 793). This cannot, he argued, be 'a good indication of the refinement and delicacy of the English ladies' (*ibid*). For Lombroso this would 'indicate inferior sensitiveness, for one has to be obtuse to pain to submit to this wholly savage operation without any other object than the gratification of vanity; and it is contrary to progress, for all exaggerations of dress are atavistic' (*ibid*). In *Criminal Woman*, Lombroso expressed his disgust at the elderly lesbians of Paris who 'often tattoo the name of their mistresses between their genitals and the navel, thus confirming their obscene habits' (1896, p. 152).

The Newcastle Weekly Courant reported that tattooing introduced 'a relic of barbarism into the end of a century of enlightenment and progress' (5 November, 1898). In linking the practice to criminality, barbarism and savagery, the tattooed also risked being stigmatised or 'othered': on the outside of what is considered to be 'civilised' society. Indeed, Fisher (2002) suggests that the Greek word 'stigma(ta)' was first used to describe tattooing and shows how the practice was used punitively from the time of Ancient Greece and Rome.

In Ancient Greece and Rome, 'stigmata' was employed to mark those designated as criminals or slaves: to distinguish the 'other' from the rest of the population. As Fisher notes, 'by indelibly marking the nonconsenting bodies of criminals and slaves, the Roman state could more easily control their movements by means of the external mark upon these individuals', with their bodies therefore acting 'as agents of the state emitting a visible sign of their social role' (*ibid*, p. 92). African and African American slaves in colonial times would also routinely have the initials or other identifying marks of their slave owners tattooed on to their skins as a form of identification and punishment (Johnson, 2016). And, as is well documented, the tattooing or branding of Holocaust victims by the Nazis came 'to symbolize the utter brutality ... of the concentration camps and the attempt of the Nazis to dehumanize their victims' (Rosenthal, ND).

The historical and contemporary practice of tattooing is one that is imbued with 'multiple levels of constructed meaning' (Fisher, 2002, p. 91):[10] spanning the physical, social and cultural. Now considered the 'fashion accessory of the 21st century', it is suggested that one out of every five adults in the United States has one or more tattoos (Harris Poll, 2012). The tattoos of celebrities are frequently discussed on Internet sites and photographed by the popular press. In contravention to the positivist model, people are not driven to tattoo their bodies, but – providing it is not forced upon them – choose to tattoo. The practice is thus at odds with deterministic arguments, fitting with sociological perspectives that focus on how we choose to create and express identity. In the case of gangs or other subcultural groups, tattoos become symbolic of group identity or belonging. It is additionally of interest that women's tattoos of the late nineteenth and early twentieth centuries often depicted the new inventions of the time, such as the motor car, and hence can be interpreted as a sign of modernity rather than degeneracy (Bailkin, 2005). For many women tattooing was likely to have represented a rebellion against the stuffier aspects of Victorian society.

Lombroso on women and crime

In Lombroso and Ferrero's *Criminal Woman* (1893), women criminals were investigated in a similar way to men – that is the emphasis was placed on uncovering the various physiological and pathological anomalies associated with criminality. However, although they noted certain physical characteristics (for example, 'certain wrinkles, such as the fronto-vertical, the wrinkles on the cheek bones, crow's feet and labial wrinkles on the cheek bones are more frequent and deeply marked in criminal women of mature age' (1893, 2004 ed. p. 72.), they found much less variability amongst women. In *Criminal Woman*, women (criminal and non-criminal) were described in derogatory terms, which reflect the attitudes of the time towards respectable and 'other' women – as was obvious from Lombroso's attitudes towards women and tattooing. Women were generally presented as less developed than men, for instance, as similar to children and with less sensitivity to pain and, in so being, all had the potential to commit crime (*ibid*, p. 151). In the 'normal' woman these deficiencies were usually kept in check by piety and maternity. Women therefore had low offending rates, and Lombroso and Ferrero found them more likely to be occasional rather than born criminals: 'the natural form of retrogression in women being prostitution and not crime. The primitive woman was impure rather than criminal' (1893 p. 52). But when a woman was a born criminal – born criminals were found to be more frequent amongst prostitutes – she was presented as much worse than a man: 'they are often much more ferocious . . . a monster' (1893 pp. 150–152). The following quotation summarizes Lombroso and Ferrero's position on women and the woman offender:

> We have seen that the normal woman is naturally less sensitive to pain than a man, and compassion is the offspring of sensitiveness. If one be wanting, so will the other be.
>
> We also saw that women have many traits in common with children; that their moral sense is deficient; that they are revengeful, jealous, inclined to vengeances of a refined cruelty.
>
> In ordinary cases these defects are neutralised by piety, maternity, want of passion, sexual coldness by weakness and an undeveloped intelligence. But when a morbid activity of the psychical centres intensifies the bad qualities of women, and induces them to seek relief in evil deeds; when

> piety and maternal sentiments are wanting, and in their place are strong passions and intensely erotic tendencies, much muscular strength and a superior intelligence for the conception and execution of evil, it is clear that the innocuous semi-criminal present in the normal woman must be transformed into a born criminal more terrible than any man.
>
> (*ibid*, pp. 150–151)

Frances Heidensohn has drawn attention to the duality of such an analysis: 'women are both wicked and saintly, whores and mothers' (1985, p. 112). And as Carol Smart argued in her cutting-edge critique of mainstream criminology, *Women, Crime and Criminology* (1976), for positivists such as Lombroso, ' "true" female criminals are biologically abnormal, because first they are rare and second they are not fully female'. This 'produces a situation in which female offenders are doubly damned for not only are they legally sanctioned for their offences, they are socially condemned for being biologically or sexually abnormal' (1976, p. 34). As with male 'criminals', race is a determining factor: 'prostitution, like crime' he argued, was 'a normal fact of life from the dawn of evolution. It is still normal in the life of savages' (1893, 2004 ed, p. 100). Black women were depicted as both 'savage' and masculine (*ibid*).

Feminist commentators such as Smart (1976), Heidensohn (1985, 1994), Carlen (1985) and Morris (1987) point out that biological positivist theories have dominated the study and treatment of women offenders. As Smart commented:

> [V]ariations on the belief in biological determinism, both of crime and the nature of women, on sexist beliefs in the inferiority of women and an implicit support of double-standards of morality, along with the failure to take account of the socio-economic, political and legal context in which 'crime' occurs, all appear in later works on female criminality.
>
> (1976, p. 36)

Indeed, Pat Carlen has demonstrated that they had a detrimental effect on the treatment of female offenders by the criminal justice system: 'in the nutshell of Lombroso and Ferrero's theory of 1895. . . are all the elements of a penology for women which persists in misogynous themes' (Carlen, 1985, p. 3).

Nicole Rafter and Mary Gibson observe that it is no accident that *Criminal Woman* was published in a period when members of the early feminist movement in Italy were becoming more organised and 'vociferously demanding access to education, entrance to the professions, equality within the family, and the right to vote' (2004, p. 16). *Criminal Woman* can be interpreted as indicative of Lombroso's fears over the growth of the movement and what it might mean in terms of the restructuring of gender roles: hence, the allocating of the first major section of *Criminal Woman* to providing evidence of the inferiority of women in general and 'the female's place in the hierarchy of animal life' (Lombroso and Ferrero, 1893, 2004 ed, p. 42). Like many of the Enlightenment thinkers (see Chapter 2), Lombroso saw women's natural habitat as the private sphere: pointing 'to the movement of the sperm and the immobility of the egg' to provide the justification for 'male public activity and female domestic passivity' (Rafter and Gibson, 2004, p. 21). As Rafter and Gibson further remark, 'his ridicule of intellectual women and his insistence on maternity as the proper aspiration for all women scientifically affirmed traditional stereotypes and directly challenged the vision of female emancipationists' (*ibid*). Written by a well-established and influential intellectual, *Criminal Woman* was to have serious implications for the movement: for in purporting to present 'modern empirical proof of women's inferiority', it served to 'weaken the Italian women's movement in its quest for expanded legal and political rights for women' (*ibid*, p. 18).

Towards a more multi-factorial explanation

Following criticism and more extensive investigation, Lombroso did modify his theory. By the second edition of *Criminal Man*, he had begun to concede that not *all* criminals were born criminals and went on to develop a typology. There were, he argued, born criminals, insane criminals, 'criminaloids' (occasional criminals) and criminals of passion or of impulse which 'involve people of full-blooded or nervous temperament' who are often young and previously 'known for honourable conduct' (2006 ed, p. 105). Furthermore, Lombroso gave more attention to factors in the physical and social environment of the male offender, for example, the effects of population density and increased industrialisation. He made use of Henry Mayhew's (1861) work on the London poor and Charles Loring Brace's *Dangerous Classes of New York* (1874) and emphasised several environmental conditions that cause or have an effect on criminality, including poverty; the relationship between prices of various staple foods and categories of crime; the influence of alcohol; the effects of criminal association in prisons not built on the cellular system and so forth (see Gina Lombroso Ferrero's summary [1911]). Moreover, *Crime: Its Causes and Remedies* (1899) opens with 'Every crime has its origin in a multiplicity of causes'.

After Lombroso's death on 19 October 1909 many of the obituaries were to pay tribute to his research on the Italian poor; he had found that certain deficiencies in the diet of those in agricultural areas resulted in various physical, behavioural and psychological problems. The consumption of maize that had been badly grown and cured resulted in pellagra, a disease causing malnutrition, dermatitis, aggression and irritability and that can be characterised by features of dementia. Accordingly, he was critical of the levels of taxation that were crippling the tenant farmers and labourers, which contributed to the wide-scale production and distribution of poor-quality maize. There is admittedly somewhat of a contradiction between his biologically determined racist analyses and sympathy for the poor. Nonetheless, despite this and a widening out of his initial theory, Lombroso held on to his conviction that the major determining factors were biological and continued to see the criminal as a degenerate, inferior being, with his work firmly positioned within the tradition of scientific racism.

Raffaele Garofalo and Enrico Ferri

Lombroso's followers, Garofalo and Ferri, whilst never renouncing Lombroso's biological positivism, put more emphasis on other determining factors. Garofalo's focus was on the importance of psychological factors. In the introduction to *Criminology* he commented that his work should only be included in Lombroso's school of criminal anthropology on the proviso that 'it be granted that of this science criminal psychology is the most important chapter' (1885, 1914 ed., p. xxx). His position was that criminals had psychological or moral anomalies which could be transmitted through heredity: 'crime cannot escape the inflexible laws of psychologic heredity' (*ibid*, p. 251).

Ferri, on the other hand, gave more attention to social, economic and political factors. In his major text, *Criminal Sociology*, he contended that 'the causes of crime have their seat not in the criminal alone, but to a large extent also in the physical and social medium which surrounds him' (1905, 1917 ed, p. 3). He refers to the importance of Quetelet's work on the social causes of crime and engages with the ideas of Durkheim, describing him as 'the most original and the most genuine positivist of contemporary French sociologists' (*ibid*, p. 82). In *The Positive School of Criminology*, the impact of poverty is highlighted, which, in turn, 'leads to intellectual and moral poverty' and is represented by criminality (1906 ed, p. 121). Referring to the city of Naples he writes, 'we have a city in which some hundred thousand people rise every morning and do not know how to get a living, who have no fixed occupation, because there is not enough industrial development' (*ibid*, p. 122). Ferri believed that social reform was necessary to create a more equitable society. He also argued for improvements in housing (he was particularly critical of living conditions in the tenement buildings and 'slum hotels'), better nourishment, education which focused on learning by experience and example and was adapted to the individual, divorce (this would 'prevent many bigamies, adulteries and homicides' [1917 ed, p. 272]) and a social focus on neglected children. Ferri regarded a neglected childhood to be 'the source and the seed of habitual criminality and recidivity' (*ibid*, p. 274), and this was the result of poverty and inequality within the class structure. For in order to survive parents have to 'labour day and night' and this 'has destroyed all family life, forcing the children of the proletariat to grow up in the mud of the streets, and hence, to become accustomed to begging, petty thievery and offenses of immorality' (*ibid*, p. 274). Lilly et al have commented that these observations and recommendations were 'reflective of his socialistic belief that the state is responsible for creating better living and working conditions' (1989, p. 30).

Ferri, known for his charisma and good looks, was a socialist for nearly fifty years. Lombroso was also a member of the Socialist Party, but as Marvin Wolfgang (1960) points out, he was never a regular party worker and was opposed to revolution and class war and to the 'common man' being vested with too much power. Ferri's earlier political views are outlined in *Socialism and Modern Science* (1900 ed). In this text, whilst proclaiming his support for the evolutionists Charles Darwin and Herbert Spencer, he aimed to

> demonstrate that Marxian Socialism – the only socialism which has a truly scientific method and value, and therefore the only socialism which from this time forth has power to inspire and unite the Social Democrats throughout the civilized world – is the only practical and fruitful fulfilment, in the social life, of the modern scientific revolution.
>
> (p. 9)

Yet Ferri shared Lombroso's scientific racism and systems of classification. In his book on homicide – in line with the cartographical approach that was gaining in popularity – he made use of shaded maps to depict a more criminogenic Southern Italy (Rafter, 2008). Not surprisingly, Gramsci was to express his disgust of the Socialist Party for giving its blessing to Enrico Ferri and the 'clique of writers of the so-called positivist school' (2005 ed, p. 10).

Ferri went on to achieve notoriety for endorsing Mussolini and fascism. As many have pointed out, (Quinney and Wildeman, 1977; Vold and Bernard, 1986; Lilly et al, 1989), positivist approaches, with their emphasis on the scientific expert, are easily adapted to totalitarian styles of government. For Vold and Bernard,

> [Positivism] is centred on the core idea of the superior knowledge and wisdom of the scientific expert who, on the basis of scientific knowledge, decides what kind of human beings commit crimes, and prescribes treatment without concern for public opinion and without consent from the person so diagnosed (i.e., the criminal). [As such]there is an obvious similarity between the control of power in society advocated in positivism and the political reality of centralized control of the life of the citizen by a government bureaucracy indifferent to public opinion.
>
> (1986, p. 42)

Ferri's support, and that of other Lombrosians, for Mussolini's party resulted in the intertwining of criminal anthropology with Fascism.

The application of Lombroso's theories

Lombroso intended his theoretical ideas to have practical implications in terms of policy: they were to make, as he put it, 'useful suggestions in the struggle against crime [and] in the practice of psychiatry and forensic medicine'

(2006 ed, p. 350). Although classicism had been introduced to counteract the often arbitrary and unjust administration of the law, its emphasis on the criminal act had led to injustices, for by treating everyone the same, there was little discretion in terms of sentencing. The jury system was problematic due to the susceptibility of jury members to corruption. For Lombroso, the current system was seriously lacking in its delivery of justice and equality, with legislators having 'failed to recognise any gradations whatsoever among healthy, diseased and guilty minds' in terms of deciding on punishment. In contrast, Lombroso argued for individualised treatment, for 'crime is like an illness that requires a specific remedy for each patient' (*ibid*, p. 242) and that punishment should be proportional not to the gravity of the crime, but to the dangerousness of the criminal. Instead of a jury, each type of criminal should be assessed by experts, and punishment should vary 'according to whether the criminal is young or old; male or female; a country or a city dweller; and a criminal of passion, occasional criminal, born criminal or insane criminal' (*ibid*, pp. 343–344). Lombroso was frequently called upon to give expert testimony in criminal cases. In the case of 'criminals of passion', he thought punishment unnecessary, as the remorse they themselves feel is punishment enough – they are not dangerous. Similarly, he saw little to be gained from sending an elderly person to prison 'when they are already crippled and unable to commit harm' (2006 ed, p. 346). For other criminals Lombroso was generally wary of imprisonment for he felt prisons incited recidivism by bringing occasional criminals into contact with more habitual criminals.

In the fifth edition of *Criminal Man* Lombroso expressed enthusiasm for the Elmira reformatory model, designed for young offenders aged sixteen to thirty years who had committed non-serious crimes, which he believed was inspired by an early edition of *Criminal Man*. Zebulon Reed Brockway, the founder of the New York State–based Elmira reformatory, studied the psychological condition, family background and other factors he believed of relevance to crime causation of those sentenced to Elmira. He used this information to design an individualised programme of reform that typically included exercise, showers, massage, gymnastics, a good diet and education.[11] There were no fixed sentences; instead the sentence was adjusted according to the offender and whether reform, defined by Brockway (1870) as 'correction or amendment to life or manners', was judged to have been successful. On release, parole was introduced to ensure continuing good behaviour. The Elmira reformatory was symbolic of a change in policy in the United States from a focus on the criminal act and punishment to fit the crime to a system of rehabilitation. In line with the positivist model, importance was placed on the expert knowledge of doctors, social workers and administrators in deciding the best course of action for dealing with individual offenders. This change in focus incited considerable debate in the press. *The New York Times* discussed a paper given at the New York State Medical Association conference in which it was argued that the current jury and legal system were faulty, that retaliative punishment should be condemned and that criminals 'should be sent to reformatories as patients to remain, until cured and not for a fixed time'. The work of the Elmira reformatory under Superintendent Brockway was hailed as exemplary in its application of reformist procedures (18 Oct. 1895, p. 1). By 1900 it was announced that indeterminate sentencing had made its way into the legislation of many states and that it was generally recognised that 'crime is a diseased condition which demands cure rather than punishment' (*Chicago Daily Tribune*, 13 Aug. 1900, p. 6). Katharine Bement Davis, a graduate of the Chicago School, associate of W.E.B Du Bois and Jane Addams and the first woman commissioner of corrections for New York City, was to become a firm advocate of indeterminate sentencing.

Brockway and the Elmira reformatory were hugely controversial: indeterminate sentences meant prisoners often had no idea of the length of their stay (*The New York Times*, 20 Mar. 1894, p. 9). When indeterminate sentences have been introduced, there is debate over the way that the key factor of 'dangerousness' is defined, and critics have drawn attention to the fact that some people have found themselves locked up for years despite not committing a serious crime. The use of indeterminate sentences was partly what provided the impetus for the revival of classicist ideas in the form of 'just desserts'. Moreover, in Elmira, control over the inmate population was to be achieved through religious education and military training and drills, and when these methods failed to work, Brockway and his staff would resort to corporal punishment. It is documented that approximately 30 per cent of those detained at Elmira were beaten twice a week with a waterlogged 22-inch whip (Rothman, 1980). Solitary confinement and shackling were also commonplace. This is, as Michael Welch writes, 'in sharp contrast to the genuine ideals of rehabilitation': reform at Elmira was 'reinforced by instilling a sense of fear in the prisoners' (2013, p. 66).

With regard to the treatment of 'insane' criminals, Lombroso stressed the need to reconcile treatment with the protection of society. As a result, he argued for their permanent confinement in criminal asylums; this would also 'prevent insane criminals from transmitting their disease through heredity, from associating with ordinary criminals, and from forming criminal gangs' (2006 ed, pp. 347–348). The born criminal, however, was more problematic; treatment models such as Elmira's would be 'largely ineffective' for criminals with no 'moral sense'. The born criminal must 'be interned in special institutions for the incorrigible', although it might be possible to 'put them to work in occupations that are repugnant to normal men but suited to their atavistic instincts: war for murderers, police spying for blackmailers' (*ibid*, p. 355). Failing this, the solution to the born criminal was to impose the death penalty. For although in the first edition of *Criminal Man* Lombroso does not support the death penalty, acknowledging that in Italy public opinion wanted it removed from the penal code,[12] by the fifth edition he argues that born criminals 'are impervious to every social cure and must be eliminated for our own defence, sometimes by the death penalty' (*ibid*, p. 354). His words confirm the Darwinian basis to his theory: the death penalty is not about deterrence or retribution, as in pre-classicist thought, but functions to facilitate the process of natural selection. This argument clearly paves the way for the implementation of eugenicist policies, which held that the only way of eliminating 'inferior' races or individuals was to exterminate them, either through execution or mass sterilisation. Such thinking led to the Holocaust in Germany in the 1930s and 1940s where millions of Jews, together with Roma, homosexuals, disabled people, Jehovah's Witnesses, communists and anarchists, were murdered by the Nazis. The use of biologically deterministic theories by the Nazis to justify the killing of so many people and the influence of Lombroso on German criminology in this period has, not surprisingly, been described by Nicole Rafter (2008) as 'criminology's darkest hour'. German theorists 'accepted Lombroso's idea of the born criminal, the biologically and mentally abnormal incorrigible who remains socially dangerous for life', and whilst he died in 1909, 'his social-defense philosophy and hereditarian views meshed smoothly with the eugenics ideas that became popular in Weimer Germany' (*ibid*, pp. 180, 181).

Early critiques of Lombroso and the ideas of individual positivism

Lombroso's theory attracted much controversy and was widely criticised by the leading social scientists of the day and not infrequently ridiculed in the press (see Box 3.3). Gabriel Tarde, Henri Joly, Georg von Mayr and W.A. Bonger in Europe and Frances Kellor and W.E.B. Du Bois in the United States were among those who were scathing of the methods and findings of biologically deterministic approaches to criminality.

Frances Kellor, an early contributor to the Chicago School of Sociology (see Chapter 4), who had conducted her own prison research, described Lombroso's findings as 'untrustworthy' (1900a,b, p. 530) and urged the American academy to pay more attention to French studies of criminality, which had 'less sympathy with the study of the body, physiognomy, speech, handwriting, sensibilities etc.' and believed 'that the great causes of crime are found not so much in an innate tendency to commit crime as in a lack of resistance to the pressure of social and physical life' (1970, p. 4). More sardonically, Herbert Bloch and Gilbert Geis were to comment that 'the best criticism of Lombroso remains that of the French anthropologist Paul Topinard (1830–1911) . . . who, when shown a collection of Lombroso's pictures of asymmetric and stigmatic criminals, remarked wryly that the pictures looked no different than those of his own friends' (1970, p. 89). Moritz Benedikt, the neurologist, previously a supporter of Lombroso, was also to mockingly suggest that 'an enlarged median occipital fossetta [first identified in Villella's skull] might just as well be used to hypothesize a predisposition to haemorrhoids instead of criminality' (cited

> **Box 3.3 Extract from *The New York Times*, 4 Aug. 1907**
>
> ## LOMBROSO TRICKED AGAIN?
>
> Photo of "Soleilland's Hand" May Be That of Somebody's Else
>
> Special Cablegram
>
> Paris. Aug. 3 – Prof Cesare Lombroso, the well-known Italian criminologist, has written to Le Temps on behalf of Soleilland, the man sentenced for assaulting and murdering a little girl, the daughter of a couple with whom he was on friendly terms.
>
> Lombroso calls attention to the peculiar shape of Soleilland's right hand, the outer edges of which instead of being slightly convex, is quite straight and forms a continuation of the line of the forearm. There is a wide gap between the third and fourth fingers, and the second and third are the same length. Instead of two oblique lines on the palm, there is only one straight line. All these signs are peculiar to what is called in neuropathy the monkey hand, as usually found in the lower apes, epileptics, idiots and born criminals.
>
> Lombroso thinks these indications, taken in conjunction with the peculiar shape of the iris of Soleilland's eye, prove that the prisoner is a degenerate and only slightly responsible for the crime.
>
> Unfortunately the weak point in Prof. Lombroso's argument is that Bertillion, the head of the Police Anthropometrical Department, says he has never photographed Soleilland's hands, and it is extremely probable that the distinguished Italian is the victim of a practical joker.
>
> Meanwhile Soleilland's spirits are reviving and he is telling his warders that when his sentence is commuted and he is sent out to New Caledonia or Guiana he hopes to settle down, lead a new life, and own a donkey cart.

in Rafter and Gibson, 2004, p. 6). After Lombroso's death *The Times* reported that 'the abnormal novelties and phantasms' of his 'early writings, the almost grotesque exaggerations in which he indulged, the fanaticism with which he dogmatized, gained quickly for his theories a reputation which has steadily waned in the light of scientific research' (28 June 1911).

In 1913 Lombroso's standing as a major theoretician of criminality took a further blow with the publication of the research of Charles Goring, the deputy medical officer of H.M. Prison Parkhurst, which achieved widespread newspaper coverage in Europe and the United States. Goring's book, *The English Convict*, was based on ten years of study, with the utilisation of statistics compiled from 3,000 convicts. His conclusion was that 'there is no such thing as a "criminal type"' (*The New York Times*, 2 Nov 1913, p. 13). Further, Dutch criminologist Willem Bonger pointed out in 1939 that 'no one comes into the world with "criminality" in the way in which one is born with a certain colour of eyes, and so forth. *Crime is something completely different*' (1943 ed, p. 27; author emphasis).

However, despite such disparaging comments, Lombroso's 'criminal man' found his way into popular culture. Rose et al cite this example from one of Agatha Christie's books which illustrates the concept of 'othering' in the sense of physically caricaturing those who are representative of 'dangerous' views, in this case communism:

> In an early book (*The Secret Adversary*, 1922) we find her clean-cut young upper-class English hero secretly observing the arrival of a Communist trade unionist at a rendezvous: 'The man who came up the staircase with a soft-footed tread was quite unknown to Tommy. He was obviously of the very dregs of society. The low beetling brows, and the criminal jaw, the bestiality of the whole countenance were new to the young man, though he was a type that Scotland Yard would have recognised at a glance.' Lombroso would have recognised him too
>
> (1990, p. 54)

Box 3.4 An extraordinary meeting: Lombroso and Leo Tolstoy

In August 1897 Lombroso travelled to Moscow to attend the Twelfth International Medical Congress. This was a huge event attracting in excess of 7,000 delegates from countries that included France, Germany, Austria, England, Italy and America. Lombroso, according to a correspondent reporting for the *Journal of the American Medical Association*, was 'one of ten great names' addressing the Congress, and his session elicited some of 'the greatest amount of enthusiasm', to the extent that when he got up to speak 'such were the demonstration of applause that it was some minutes before [he] could be heard' (Caldwell, 1897, p. 655). He presented his thesis on the link between madness and genius, drawing on examples of 'great men', such as Dante

(Siegel, 2013). For Lombroso, genius, like criminality, was a sign of degeneracy. In his 1891 book, *Man of Genius*, he described genius as 'a true degenerative psychosis belonging to the group of moral insanity' and that it, too, was marked by 'physical signs of degeneracy' such as shortness of stature; thus he noted, Montaigne and Beccaria were short, as were Mozart, Beethoven, Balzac and Blake, and 'Albert Magnus was of such small size that the Pope, having allowed him to kiss his foot, commanded him to stand up, under the impression that he was still kneeling' (pp. 6–7).

In Moscow, Lombroso sought to confirm his ideas on madness, degeneracy and genius by visiting the great Russian novelist Leo Tolstoy at his home at Yasnaya Polyana. Lombroso had referred to Tolstoy in *Man of Genius*: writing that Tolstoy had confessed 'that philosophic skepticism had led him into a condition approximating to madness' (1891, p. 50). He also remarked that he had found 'in Tolstoy's writings so many points relevant to my theory [for instance, inherited disease, caprices and eccentricities in youth, epileptic fits with hallucinations, mental irritation], that I could hope to find evidence of it in the famous artist's life' (cited in Sirotkina, 2003, p. 78). Lombroso's visit was first opposed by the Moscow authorities, who saw Tolstoy as a potentially dangerous opponent of the tsarist regime. However, as Irina Sirotkina writes, when Lombroso went to argue his case, the general in charge of granting permits to travel 'made one last attempt' to dissuade him by 'asking "Don't you know that Tolstoy's head is not all right?",' to which Lombroso replied, '"that is why I want to see him: I am a psychiatrist"', to the general's apparent delight (*ibid*, p. 76; see also Tolstoy, 1953). Thus, once again, we have an example of how the label 'mad', like 'criminal', is utilised to silence and condemn those who dare to question the workings of the state. As the Ober-Procurator of the Holy Synod wrote in a letter to the tsar, in relation to Tolstoy's vision of a peasant utopia in which private property was abolished, 'Tolstoy is a fanatic with his own mad views, and, unfortunately, he seduces and leads into madness thousands of naïve people. . . . Mad people who believe in Tolstoy are obsessed, just like himself, by the spirit of untamed propaganda, and they want to transform his teaching into action and inspire the peasants' (cited in Sirotkina, 2003, p. 76).

On arrival at Yasnaya Polyana, Lombroso found himself faced with a man who bore little similarity to the 'cretinous and degenerate looking' (Mazzarello, 2001, p. 983; Mazzarello, 2011) man of genius. Tolstoy was clearly in full possession of his faculties. His attitude to Lombroso was, as Paolo Mazzarello notes, 'calm, correct and friendly' (2001, p. 983), yet the meeting seems to have gone awry from the start. Tolstoy invited Lombroso to swim with him and was surprised when his visitor was unable to keep up. Describing Lombroso as an 'old man', although he was some years younger than himself, Tolstoy recalled turning around to see 'my old man was floundering about in the water, but somehow making no progress' and was forced to drag him from the water (*ibid*, p. 983). Swimming aside, the two writers went on to argue over Lombroso's theories on the origins of criminality: Tolstoy condemned his ideas as 'nonsense' and was to record in his diary, 'Lombroso came. He is an ingenuous and limited old man', adding later 'all this is an absolute misery of thought, of concept and of sensibility' (Mazzarello, 2001, p. 983). Lombroso's account of the dispute was to make reference to 'the angry and evil look in Tolstoy's eyes throughout our argument' (1984 ed, pp. 185–189). According to the diaries of Sophia, Tolstoy's wife, the visit ended with Lombroso being taken back to the station by a family friend, Vasilij Alekseevich Maklakov, which led to an 'unpleasant incident' and 'ugly conversation' when Lombroso accused Maklakov of theft after giving him his wallet to buy a ticket (2010 ed, p. 918).

After his meeting with Lombroso, Tolstoy rewrote his last novel, *Resurrection*, which was previously in draft form. Published in 1899, it seems highly probable, given the book's content and didactic tone, that his argument with Lombroso on the causes of crime had a profound impact on him. Indeed, the novel can be interpreted as Tolstoy's attempt to put forward an alternative narrative with regards to criminality and criminal justice. For Tolstoy 'criminals' are largely products of social circumstance and the hypocritical and oppressive way that they – typically the poor and powerless – are labelled and condemned by the state. *Resurrection* is relentless and unsparing in its portrayal of the inhumanity and brutality inherent in the system. Unlike Lombroso's depiction of the prostitute woman as a 'born criminal' and of criminal women as 'ferocious', cruel, and with 'muscular strength', one of the central characters in *Resurrection*, Katúsha Maslova, is a prostitute as a result of circumstance. She was born illegitimate, into poverty, orphaned in childhood and becomes a servant. She is 'taken advantage of' at the age of 16 by her employers' nephew, a young nobleman, Prince Dmítri Ivánovitch Nekhlúdoff, which leads to a pregnancy and her removal from the household. Maslova places her child in an orphanage. Maslova's choice is a bleak one – and not uncommon for women in her situation – it is that of prostitution or starvation. Prostitution is not about 'a lack of modesty and moral insanity' (Lombroso and Ferrero, 1895 ed, p. 216), but arises from impoverishment and 'ends for nine out of ten women in painful disease, premature decrepitude, and death' (Tolstoy, 1899, 2014 ed, p. 10). Maslova is accused of theft from a drunken man in a brothel, who dies. Although innocent as a result of a judicial error, Maslova receives a sentence of hard labour in Siberia. Not only is she not a 'criminal woman' in the Lomborosian sense but the system of justice that confronts her is not one of fairness and rationality in the classicist sense. The prosecutor is ill prepared, having spent the night at the brothel where Maslova worked playing cards with a friend; he is a 'fearful blockhead' who presents a Lombrosian assessment of Maslova as having within her 'the germs of criminality' (Tolstoy, 1899, 2014 ed, p. 84). The judge is determined to get the trial over as quickly as possible so he can meet his mistress before 6 p.m. Neither prosecutor nor judge are particularly interested in whether justice is served or not.

By coincidence, Nekhlúdoff, the cause of Maslova's downfall, is on the jury at her trial. He is riddled with guilt over the role that he has played in her plight and aims to right his wrongs. He follows her to Siberia, and the book is largely about his journey – both spiritual and literal – as he witnesses the horrors of prison life: rats, solitary confinement, floggings, disease and deaths from ill treatment. Nekhlúdoff reflects on the science of criminality and concludes that what he sees amongst the prisoners – drunkenness, cruelty and other vices – are not due to 'degeneration or to the existence of monstrosities of the criminal type', but were the result of circumstance (those who criminology classifies as 'criminal type' are those 'who society has sinned' (1899, 2014 ed, p. 384)). He reads the works of Lombroso, Garofalo, Ferri, Maudsley and others and finds no answer to his, and Tolstoy's, central question, 'why, and with what right, do some people lock up, torment, exile, flog and kill others, while they are themselves just like those whom they torment, flog and kill?' (*ibid*, p. 384). It is not about whether they have 'free will or not' or that 'signs of criminality could be detected by measuring skulls or not' (*ibid*, p. 384). The system is unjust and serves itself ('what revolted him were the men in courts etc. who got large salaries') and the upper classes. We see the behaviours of the upper classes not as crimes: hence, 'the rich boast of their wealth i.e. robbery; the commanders in the army pride themselves on victories i.e. murder; and those in high places vaunt their power, i.e. violence' (*ibid*, p. 179).

Tolstoy's advocacy for social justice in *Resurrection*, his critique of positivist criminology, his focus on the situation of the poor and the need to abolish private property, together with his virulent opposition to punishment, make him not only an 'unorthodox criminologist', as

> John R Fuller (2009) describes him, but one whose ideas are in line with those that come under the umbrella of critical criminology.
>
> **Further Reading:**
>
> Fuller, J. R. (2009) 'Leo Tolstoy and social justice', *Contemporary Justice Review*, pp. 321–330

Creating the 'other': the presentation of the Irish

Dominant cultural identities are bolstered through the stigmatising process of 'othering' groups or individuals perceived as different. This is clearly dangerous in terms of creating stereotypes about specific racial and ethnic groups. As it has been shown throughout this chapter, Lombroso and his colleagues, in attempting to link the 'criminal man' to the alleged physical features of Black and Indigenous populations, equating them to a primitive and more savage past, are practitioners of the concept of 'othering'. Racial inequality becomes enshrined through the depiction of the inferior 'other': by presenting the 'other' as 'primitive, lawless and uncivilized', colonialism is thus considered justified.

The identification of a 'criminal type' through a focus on facial features, which was first popularised by the physiognomists (see Box 3.1) and then developed in the work of Lombroso, was also used – as was illustrated by the response to peasant brigandage in Southern Italy – against groups perceived as threats to the dominant social order. 'Othering' works to repress and control subversive and potentially threatening factions from within and outside of a state. Thus, as Lewis Curtis shows in *Apes and Angels: The Irishman in Victorian Caricature* (1971), we find the Irish in English cartoons portrayed initially as harmless drunks. But as the campaign for Irish independence grows, they are caricatured as ape-like or monsters. As Curtis argues,

> [T]his Victorian image of the Irish was . . . only one product of a polygonal prism of images which refracted much the same light in as many different directions as there were outgroups for Europeans and Englishmen to worry about. No matter if the people or races being measured or physiognomized lived in Europe, Africa or Asia, or America, the refracted image worked in the same way to enhance the self-esteem of the beholder at the expense of those being stereotyped.
>
> (1971, p. 14)

Hence, in this cartoon from *The Tomahawk* (18 December 1869), which is entitled 'The Irish Frankenstein', the ape-like monster has 'Fenianism' written across his chest.

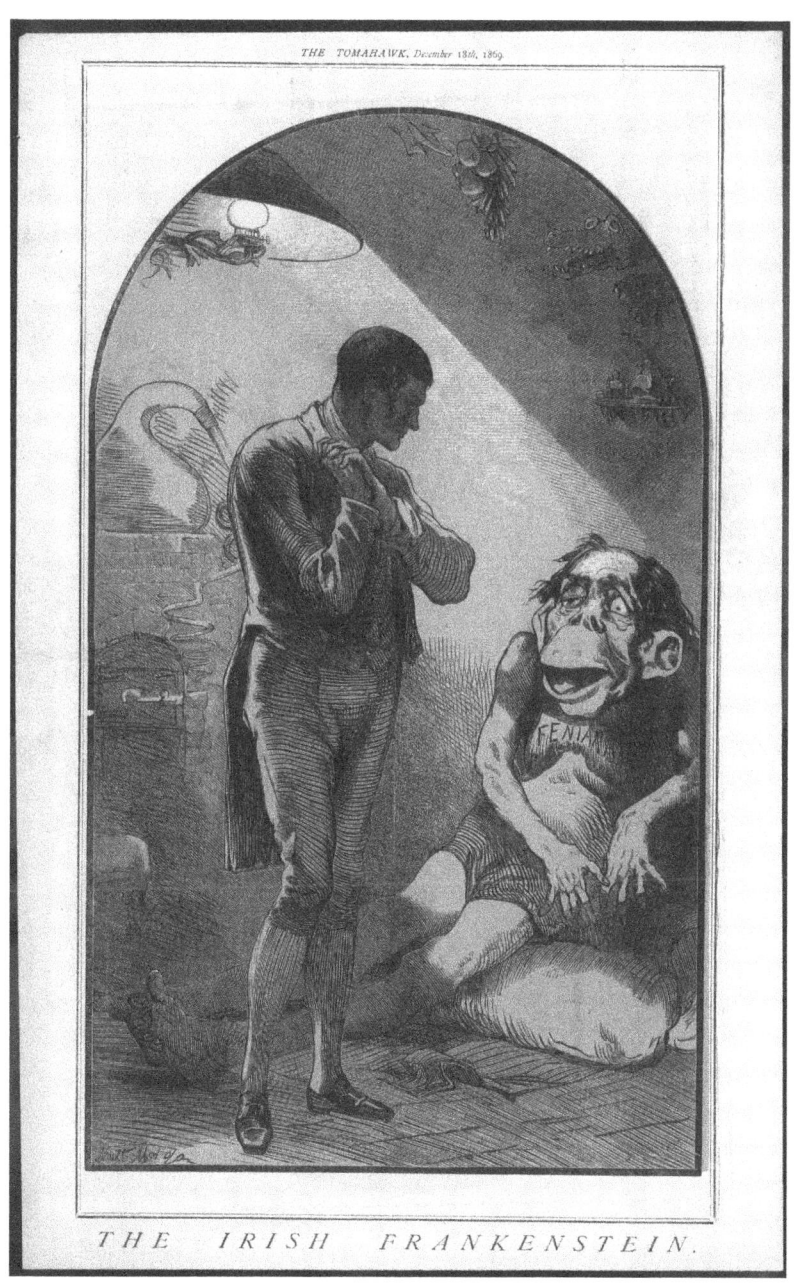

Figure 3.3 'The Irish Frankenstein', from *The Tomahawk*, 18 December 1869.

Figure 3.4 'The Irish Frankenstein' from Punch magazine, 20 May 1882.

Next is another 'Irish Frankenstein', published in *Punch* magazine (20 May 1882) after the Phoenix Park murders in 1882 of Thomas Henry Burke and Lord Frederick Cavendish, senior government officials, by 'The Invisibles', a splinter group of the Irish Republican Brotherhood.

Caricatures of the Irish 'as a cross between a garrotter and a gorilla' (Spielmann, 1895, pp. 105–106) worked to support the notion that the Irish were 'uncivilized' and therefore incapable of self-rule.

'The persistence of the positivist paradigm': the twentieth century and beyond

In more contemporary times, Lombroso's theories of the criminal man are frequently dismissed as 'bizarre' (Jupp, 1989, p. 2), 'fanciful' (Heidensohn, 1985, p. 114), 'simple and naive' (Lilly et al, 1989 ed, p. 29) and 'an amusing and slightly unfortunate episode in the development of criminology' (Smart, 1976, p. 32), yet a biological positivist stance has remained. As Frances Heidensohn notes, 'the persistence of the positivist paradigm is one of the most marked features of twentieth century social science' and, of course, this is true into the twenty-first (see Young, 2011). Indeed, Jock Young suggests that of all the branches of sociology and psychology, criminology appears to be the discipline in which 'the problem of unchecked positivism is greatest' (2004, p. 20).

The majority of studies in the first half of the twentieth century located the determining factors within the individual offender identifying the causes of crime to be biological and/or psychological. The idea of a connection between biology and criminality was seen, for example, in the work of Earnest Hooton (1939), William Sheldon (1949) and Sheldon Glueck and Eleanor Glueck (1930, 1934, 1950). Hooton found, amongst other physical factors, that criminals were smaller than non-criminals (1939, Vol. 1, p. 329). Race for him was likewise a determining factor:

> it is possible that Negroes and Negroids racially are more susceptible to criminalistic infection, so that antisocial behaviour is likely to manifest itself more commonly than in whites in individuals who are not obviously stunted, undernourished, and of a generally inferior constitutional and biological endowment.
>
> *(ibid*, p. 369)

This assertion met with strong criticism from Robert Merton and M.F. Ashley-Montague, who pointed to the selective use of data in Hooton's work: for the various factors are 'introduced or neglected in accord with the disposition of the investigator' (1940, p. 406). Sheldon, studying delinquent male youths, distinguished three main types of human physique: muscular active types (mesomorphs), thin physiques (ectomorphs) and fleshier, fat builds (endomorphs). Mesomorphs, he proposed, were more likely to be delinquent. The work of Sheldon and Eleanor Glueck supported this: they found as a result of a comparative study of delinquents and non-delinquents that delinquents had narrower faces, wider chests, larger and broader waists, bigger forearms and upper arms than non-delinquents. Their approach, however, was broadly multi-factorial – thus, not only was bodily structure important but so was personality development, the school, the family and so forth.

Edwin Sutherland entered into a heated debate with the Gluecks to the extent that Laub and Sampson described the exchange as the equivalent of an 'intellectual shoot-out' (1991, p. 1404). In Sutherland's review of the Gluecks's *Later Criminal Careers* (1937) for the *Harvard Law Review* – a book that was an extension of their research on male prisoners at the Massachusetts Reformatory – he particularly took issue with the Gluecks's emphasis on 'mental condition' as an explanatory factor. Sutherland observed that the first diagnosis was conducted by a psychiatrist at the institution who 'had a heavy case load and little time for careful examinations, and also had a general bias toward interpretation of delinquency as due to mental pathology'; the second diagnosis given five years after the ending of parole could only have been 'secured by reading the reports of the field investigators' (1937, pp. 184–186). Not only is this shoddy research but the classification of abnormality, as Sutherland shows, is highly questionable: 'for instance, 55 of the 235 mentally abnormal cases are alcoholics; why should the authors assume that an alcoholic is mentally abnormal? Alcoholism may be due to mental abnormality, but it may, also, be due to other conditions and processes' (*ibid*).

A few years earlier in 1934 the Gluecks published *Five Hundred Delinquent Women*, a study of women detained at the Massachusetts Reformatory for Women. This, as Nicole Rafter and Mary Gibson reflect, 'returned to Lombroso's practice of judging female deviance more stringently than male deviance and according to primarily sexual criteria', concluding that extramarital sexuality is indicative of 'biological inferiority and heredity' (2004, p. 25). For 'defective delinquents' their solution was to impose life sentences, to 'prevent biologically inferior women from reproducing their bad heredity' (*ibid*, p. 25). Rafter and Gibson conclude that the Gluecks 'reiterate nearly all of [Lombroso's] major ideas and carry his hereditarian implications to an eugenical conclusion' (*ibid*).

Other perspectives in this period were more centred on the psychology of the individual. Many of these were particularly influenced by Freudian psychoanalysis and thus attributed criminal behaviour to defects in the ego or superego (see Alexander and Healy (1935)). Despite critiques – such as that of Sutherland's – of methodology, dubious classification and spurious assumptions, psychological theories were to remain in fashion, probably due to the expansion of the medical field and the availability of patients to study. A host of studies followed which attempted to identify certain psychological or personality traits as predictors of criminality, such as emotional instability, aggressiveness, immaturity, excitability, mechanical aptitude, etc., and criminals were accordingly categorised as 'psychopaths', 'sociopaths' and 'anti-social' personalities (Mooney, 2000). However, after World War II research committed to uncovering the biological basis of human behaviour started to receive less attention. This may well have been due to its association with eugenics and to criminology's 'darkest hour' – although Lilly et al (2011 ed) comment that it may also have been because the biological sciences were eclipsed by advances in the natural sciences, especially physics (space travelling being of much more interest than the behaviour of individuals) and the growth of social sciences.

By the 1960s and 1970s the situation changed again. In the 1960s Hans Eysenck, who is without doubt the leading psychological positivist of the twentieth century, put forward arguments that combined psychology with biological determinism. In *Crime and Personality* (1964), he proposed that there were two basic personality types – extraverts and introverts – which are genetically based. Extraversion, he argued, was linked to anti-social behaviour and criminality. The sociable, outgoing, sensation-seeking, lively extravert is considered to respond to conditioning situations, such as punishment by parents, teachers and peers, less readily than introverts. The introvert tends to be more reflective and self-examining and is therefore more susceptible to conditioning which results in conformity. Eysenck suggested that there was a relationship between psychoticism and criminal behaviour: 'the general personality traits subsumed under psychoticism appear clearly related to anti-social and non-conformist conduct' (1987, p. 31; Eysenck and Gudjonsson, 1989).

With respect to women, Eysenck chose to test his extraversion-introversion hypothesis on groups of married and unmarried mothers. Being an unmarried mother was indicative of promiscuity and, therefore, deviance. From a study conducted by Sybil B. G. Eysenck, he found,

> The unmarried mothers were. . . [discovered to be] both more extraverted and also to have much higher degrees of emotionality than did the married mothers. When compared with the general population norms too, it was found again that the unmarried mothers tended to fall into the psychopathic quadrant, i.e., were high on neuroticism and high on extraversion.
>
> (1964, p. 132)

Thus, we find in Eysenck's work an attitude towards women that yet again bears a similarity to that of Lombroso and Ferrero's.

The mid-1970s saw the publication of E.O. Wilson's hugely successful book *Sociobiology*. This outlined the new discipline of sociobiology: it was to be 'the systematic study of the biological basis of all forms of social behavior, including sexual and parental behavior, in all kinds of organisms including humans' (1975, p. 1). It was to extend neo-Darwinism into the study of human behaviour and animal societies (*ibid*). This coincided with a renewed enthusiasm for the field of genetics. Richard Dawkins's *The Selfish Gene*, with the message – as the title implies – that genes are selfish, came out a year later. *The Selfish Gene*'s success is such that in 2017 the Royal Society declared it one of the most inspiring science books of all time. *The Selfish Gene*, as Lilly et al comment,

> opened up the path to a return to varieties of Darwinism, proposing that virtually all of human behavior could be understood as biologically determined activities of individuals directed toward reproduction so that their 'selfish' genes would be passed on to future generations.
>
> (2011 ed, p. 352)

The buzz that was generated over developments in sociobiology provided the impetus for the use of evolutionary theory to study crime, especially violence (see Daly and Wilson, 1988; Burgess and Draper, 1989; Daly and Wilson, 1994; Wilson and Daly, 1992; Dutton, 1995; Wilson and Daly, 1998). At one point evolutionary theorists had such a grip on the field of family violence that the only theoretical contribution to Lloyd Ohlin and Michael Tonry's edited collection, *Family Violence* (1989), was Burgess and Draper's 'The Explanation of Family Violence: The Role of Biological, Behavioral and Cultural Selection'. Evolutionary theory suggests that human behaviour, like the rest of the animal kingdom, is a product of natural selection. If violence was merely a pathology, it would have been selected out. Accordingly it must bestow a Darwinian advantage. This, as Margo Wilson and Martin Daly suggest, is evident in cases of domestic violence. Marriage is presented as being primarily a reproductive alliance and, as such, 'parental investment' helps us understand how this form of violence can occur. For a major threat to a man's evolutionary 'fitness' is the possibility that his 'mate' will become pregnant with another man's child, an event that will prove costly in terms of parental investment should he fail to detect what has happened and accept the child as his own, for this will prevent the passing on of his genes. Males in species such as our own, where parental investment is high, have been selected to be intolerant of cuckoldry. Men are therefore likely to direct threats or actual physical violence at their rivals, their wives or both. For Daly and Wilson, 'the use of a credible threat of violence . . . can . . . deter a wife from pursuing courses of action that are not in the man's interest (1994, p. 269). Hence, domestic violence is related to male sexual proprietariness and has clearly been successful in terms of monopolising female reproductive capacity and increasing the possibility of confidently identifying offspring, or else it would have been selected out. In other words, what is bad for the wife might be good for the species. The flaws in this line of reasoning have been widely discussed (Sayers, 1982; Rose et al, 1990; Mooney, 2000). On a most obvious level it does not explain why one of the most typical scenarios where domestic violence is enacted is when the woman is pregnant (see Bewley and Gibbs, 1997; Mooney, 2000). How evolutionary theory could explain how violence occurs in situations which would surely damage a man's genetic stock is a mystery. As a theoretical explanation of domestic violence, it is a short step from 'blaming the victim', for if women had not been unfaithful and cuckolded their husbands in past generations, violence would not have evolved as an adaptive function. Moreover, as Steven Rose and colleagues point out, it presents a very depressing picture of human nature:

> By arguing that each aspect of human behavioural repertoire is specifically adaptive, or at least was so in the past, sociobiology sets the stage for the legitimation of things as they are. We are the products of eons of natural selection. Dare we, in our hubris, try to go against the social arrangements of nature in its wisdom has built into us? There is a reason why we are entrepreneurial, xenophobic, territorial.
>
> (1990, p. 264)

In terms of domestic violence, by seeing this form of behaviour as an inevitable part of human existence, as an 'evolved adaptation', there is little that can be done about it. The assumption is that men cannot help their violence! However, as Janet Sayers (1982) and others argue, people are constantly changing and constructing their own identities: we and the societies that we live in are in a constant state of flux.

In the mid-1980s the idea that the criminal is somehow wicked by nature was to resurface in James Q. Wilson and Richard Herrnstein's *Crime and Human Nature* (1985). In *Crime and Human Nature*, Wilson and Herrnstein state 'our intention is to offer as comprehensive an explanation as we can manage of why some individuals are more likely than others to commit crime' (1985, p. 20). Wilson was an advisor to the Reagan and George H.W. Bush administrations and as such was a particularly influential figure at the time. Although their approach is multi-causal, involving, for example, family rearing and cultural factors, they lay great stress on what they term 'constitutional factors' which they maintain predispose individuals to become criminals. The biological positivist stance of Wilson and Herrnstein is illustrated by the following statement:

> The existence of biological predispositions means that circumstances that activate behaviour in one person will not do so in another, that social forces cannot deter criminal behaviour in 100 percent of the population, and that the distribution of crime within and across societies may, to some extent, reflect underlying distribution of constitutional factors.

> Crime cannot be understood without taking into account predispositions and their biological roots.
>
> (*ibid*, p. 103)

It is not surprising that their work has been described as 'the new scientific revolution of the "born again" Lombrosians' (Young, 1994, p. 70), with Lilly et al commenting that 'Wilson and Herrnstein's perspective harkens back to the theories of Lombroso, Hooton, Sheldon and the Gluecks' (1989 ed, p. 196). Indeed, in *Crime and Human Nature* Wilson and Herrnstein lend support to the notion that criminals can be differentiated from non-criminals by body type:

> Wherever it has been examined, criminals on average differ in physique from the population at large. They tend to be more mesomorphic (muscular) and less ectomorphic (linear), with the third component (endomorphy) not clearly deviating from normal. Where it has been assessed, the 'masculine' configuration called andromorphy also characterizes the average criminal.
>
> (1985, p. 89)

They reproduce William Sheldon's 1949 photographs of body types, together with evidence from twin and adoptive studies, to bolster their claim that crime has a genetic basis – 'the criminality of the biological parents is . . . more important than that of the adoptive parents, suggesting a genetic transmission of some factor or factors associated with crime' (*ibid*, p. 96). With regard to how constitutional factors affect criminality, Wilson and Herrnstein claim they affect the ability to consider future and immediate rewards and punishment. Thus, young men who are aggressive, impulsive and of low intelligence are more at risk than those who have developed 'conscience'; by this they mean an 'internalized constraint against certain actions, the violation of which causes feelings of anxiety' (*ibid*, p. 217). Conscience is taken as indicating a higher level of cognitive and intellectual development. The family is seen as able to 'moderate and magnify any natural predispositions' (*ibid*, p. 217) through early conditioning; we, therefore, also have in tandem the 'bad families produce bad children' argument.

For Lilly et al the work of Wilson and Herrnstein was representative of a 'growing trend' in the United States to 'root crime in human nature' (1989, p. 199). They interpreted this trend as indicative of the ethos of individualism and the corresponding opposition to social welfare policies that were increasingly prevalent in American society:

> 'Failure' – whether by being poor, or perhaps by being criminal – is seen either as a matter of choosing a profligate lifestyle or as a product of defects in the individual's character or endowment. The danger of such

thinking is not only that it erroneously overlooks the social sources of human behaviour but also that it eases social conscience: Because individuals are to blame for their actions, no need exists to question the justice of the prevailing social arrangements or to support policies that call on citizens to share their advantages with the less fortunate.

(*ibid*, pp. 194–195)

In the 1990s overtly racist views of criminality – a 'scientific racism' – were to re-emerge with Herrnstein's collaboration with Charles Murray, which resulted in their jointly authored *The Bell Curve: Intelligence and Class Structure in American Life* (1994), and in Philippe Rushton's book *Race, Evolution and Behavior* (1995). Herrnstein and Murray sanctimoniously write that *The Bell Curve* deals with subjects that are 'among the more sensitive in contemporary America – so sensitive that hardly anyone writes or talks about them in public' (p. xxi). This is, of course – though it may have been unwittingly intended – somewhat of a truism: racist attitudes attract strong sentiments, and it is arguably a mark of progress that they are not a feature of public debate and are not given a platform within the academy. *The Bell Curve* revived the old controversy on intelligence and social pathology, a relationship that had also been dismissed by Edwin Sutherland (1931, 1947) and others in the first half of the twentieth century. Low IQ, Herrnstein and Murray allege, contributes to a host of problems, including crime, poverty, welfare dependency, unemployment, illegitimacy and broken homes, and that racial and ethnic differences in IQ scores had a large genetic component. Ignoring the controversies over the value of IQ tests, the questions used and the way that they are calculated, it was, they said, scientifically proven that 'criminal offenders had average IQs of about 92, eight points below the mean' and 'more serious offenders generally have lower scores than more casual offenders' (p. 235). Their meaning was transparent. As the political commentator Francis Wheen, in article for *The Guardian* newspaper on Murray's 'scientific racism', put it,

> *The Bell Curve* runs to more than 800 pages but can be summarized in a few sentences. Black people are more stupid than white people: always have been, always will be. This is why they have less economic and social success. Since the fault lies in their genes, they are doomed to be at the bottom of the heap now and forever.
>
> [Murray's] insidious achievement has been to make racism respectable by dressing it up in the alluring garb of science and dispassionate scholarship.
>
> (2000, 10 May)

This is, of course, something that we have seen throughout the history of individual positivism. For Murray, the existing social structure becomes about differences in intelligence between races and classes, rather than about social inequity: there is nothing that can or should be done to counter racial and class-based disparities. Indeed, Wheen (2000) observes that, in a previously published manifesto *What It Means to Be a Libertarian*, Murray proposed the abolition of all social security and welfare and the repeal of all legislation protecting civil rights or outlawing racial discrimination.

Philippe Rushton's *Race, Evolution and Behavior* was warmly endorsed by the doyen of behaviourist psychology, the late Hans Eysenck. Shaun Gabbidon, in his insightful, *Criminological Perspectives on Race and Crime* (2010), illustrates the level that Rushton's ideas, which use E.O. Wilson's (MacArthur and Wilson, 1967) r/K selection theory, suggest that the differences between races, including propensity to criminality, is linked to migrations out of Africa and that 'aggression, impulsive behaviour, low self-control, low intelligence, and lack of following rules are all associated with criminals and, according to Rushton, those who fall under the r-strategy: black people' (2010, p. 42). Gabbidon, likewise, points out that the claims made by Rushton cannot help but 'return us to the days of Lombrosoism and the eugenics movement' (*ibid*, p. 44).

As time marches on, we are increasingly living, as Nikolas Rose remarks, 'inescapably in a biologized culture' (2000, p. 6). This relates not just to 'the sicknesses of human beings, but also their personalities, capacities, passions and the forces that mobilize them – their "identities" themselves – appear at least potentially to be explicable in biological terms, and increasingly in terms of their genetic make-up' (*ibid*). The marketplace has witnessed a boom in biotechnology stocks as corporations seek ways to make profits from the proliferation of new work in genetic engineering (Lilly et al, 2011 ed,). Since the beginning of the twenty-first century there has been a flurry of studies based on the biological basis of human behaviour within criminology; this is variously labelled 'biocriminology', 'biosocial criminology' and, more recently given advances in neuroscience, 'neurocriminology'. In 2012 John Paul Wright and Francis Cullen wrote an article on the future of biosocial criminology for the *Journal of Contemporary Criminal Justice* on how biologically informed studies of crime were gaining momentum, with more articles being published in traditional criminology journals, more books on the subject, more students trained in the area and more conference panels at leading criminology conferences. There is no question that biosocial research is on the rise: simultaneously celebrated and condemned.

Proponents of this work have tried to separate themselves from what Wright and Cullen describe as 'the script', which they suggest has previously 'tainted' any developments in this area. The 'script' goes something like this, 'biological theorizing is a "dangerous" idea because it created Nazism, was used to justify racism and sexism, and led to the dangerous eugenics movement in the United States' (2012, p. 237), which is admittedly in line with much of my narrative in this chapter. For Wright and Cullen, the advantages of biosocial criminology are that it is 'rooted' in 'science and empirical observation', which has less to do with 'ideology' (*ibid*), unlike other subsections of the discipline. Political ideology, or what are termed 'sacred values', is seen as having played too great a role within the discipline and, indeed, has generally permeated the academy. Wright and Cullen grumble that 'virtually every study ever completed on the political orientation of university faculty has found that liberal ideology is the dominant ideology on college campuses across the United States; in fact in many academic fields, it is virtually the only ideology' (*ibid*, p. 240). The impact of this, they claim, is that biological theorists, 'honest scholars[,] have been publicly sanctioned, their lives threatened, or their careers terminated for violating sacred values' (*ibid*, p. 242). Their list of 'honest scholars' includes 'Larry Summers, at the time president of Harvard University [who] created a firestorm when he suggested the possibility that women are underrepresented in the top science programs because they are dissimilar to men in certain mental abilities' and 'more pertinent to criminology, James Q. Wilson (1975) [who] was lambasted for his book *Thinking About Crime*' and 'Richard Herrnstein and Charles Murray (1994) [whose] *The Bell Curve* . . . generated accusations of racism' (*ibid*, p. 243). Whether Murray did badly out of the controversy or not is perhaps a moot point: *The Bell Curve* was a best-seller, Murray is regularly interviewed; has a niche on the public speaking circuit, having fed into popular prejudice; and currently holds the F.A. Hayek Emeritus Chair at the American Enterprise Institute, a conservative think tank. Wright and Cullen, in their championing of biological theorists, are seemingly oblivious to the harm the work of their 'honest scholars' has caused or could potentially cause.

Much of the research in this area today does not focus on crime per se but on violent, aggressive and anti-social behaviour. It attempts to identify the biological processes, genetic markers and other factors that put individuals at risk for such behaviour (Mason and Frick, 1994; Beaver et al, 2009; Owen, 2012). Anti-social behaviour, it is argued, is consistently shown to be modestly to highly heritable (Mason and Frick, 1994; Wright and Cullen, 2012). The research includes adoption studies, hormonal research, neurophysiology, neuropsychology, attention deficit disorder, brain dysfunction and life-course studies (see Rose and Abi-Rached, 2013).

Adrian Raine, a leader in 'neurocriminology', conducts brain imaging studies of violent criminals. He suggests brain imaging allows the assessment of brain functioning in violent individuals, and from this it appears that the frontal brain regions are involved as well as the temporal cortex (Raine et al, 1997). Interviewed in 2014 for Terry Gross's *Fresh Air* show on National Public Radio (NPR) in the United States, Raine said, 'just as there's a biological basis for schizophrenia and anxiety disorders and depression, I'm saying here there's a biological basis also to recidivist violent offending'. This has certainly caught the public's imagination: Roberta Williams, widow of one of 'Australia's most notorious gangsters', Carl Williams, allowed experts to examine the brain of her husband: she said, 'I believe it's to help with research

... and might explain why guys like Carl do the violent things they do' (*Sky News*, 26 April 2010, cited in Rose and Abi-Rached, 2013, p. 165). While it has long been accepted by biological researchers that there is 'overwhelming evidence for genetic influences on criminal and other anti-social behaviours' (Barker et al, 2010, p. 30), the search for the specific genotype is gaining momentum. In 2014 researchers in Finland published an article in *Molecular Psychiatry* claiming to have found two genes associated with criminality. The two genes were the MAOA gene – that previous work has called the 'warrior gene' because of its supposed link to aggressive offending – and a variant of cadherin 13 (CDH13) (Hogenboom, 2014, see also Barker et al, 2010). Critics of this work point out that up to half of the population could have one of the genes involved: Jan Schnupp of the University of Oxford said that to call these alleles 'genes for violence' is a massive exaggeration (BBC News, 24 October 2014). Yet biological theorists suggest that by establishing links between biological abnormalities and propensity for violence, this will facilitate the identification of those at risk, resulting in preventive intervention and effective treatment proposals.

For Nikolas Rose these new biological conceptions of pathological conduct are bound up with a new 'public health' conception of crime control: this is not a 'new eugenics but a control strategy that aims to identify, treat and control individuals predisposed to impulsive or aggressive conduct' (2000, p. 5). This 'new biology of control' results in 'socio-political interventions [that] are legitimated not in the language of law and rights, but in terms of the priority of protecting "normal people" against risks that threaten their security and containment'(Rose, 2007, p. 249). The implications of the 'overstated rhetoric' of molecular biology and neurogenetics are disturbing, for these invite the opening up of 'new control possibilities' involving the introduction of risk predictor techniques:

> While full-scale screening of the inhabitants in the inner cities might be too controversial to contemplate in most jurisdictions, the example of Attention Deficit Hyperactivity Disorder, at least in the US, suggests the likelihood of proposals for genetic screening of disruptive schoolchildren, with pre-emptive treatment a condition of continuing schooling. Or one might imagine post-conviction screening of petty criminals, with genetic testing and compliance with treatment made a condition of probation or parole. Or one can envisage scenarios in which genetic screening is a condition for employment or insurance, or genetic therapy is offered to disruptive or delinquent employees as an alternative to termination.
>
> (Rose, 2007, p. 250)

There is little, if any, recognition by biological theorists that 'violence', 'anti-social behaviour' and 'aggression' are subjective concepts – their meanings change over time, from culture to culture, and what is 'violence' or 'anti-social behaviour' or 'aggression' to one person will not be to another. Even definitions of 'schizophrenia', 'anxiety disorder', 'depression' and attention deficit hyperactivity disorder (ADHD) – which are frequently discussed in terms of their 'biological roots' – are highly contested. To suggest that human behaviour is primarily determined by our biology undermines what it means to be a human being: we have creativity, the ability to choose to respond and act differently in the same circumstances. We are not predicable – often we are unpredictable. People turn 'factors' into narratives – they are even capable of turning such factors on their heads (Young, 2011; Duster, 2005). As David Matza argued, the individual is

> capable of creating and assigning meaning, able to contemplate his surroundings, and even his own condition, given to anticipation, planning and projecting man – the subject -stands in a different and more complex relationship to circumstance . . . his distinctive capacity is to reshape, strive toward creating, and actually transcend circumstance.
> (Matza, 1969, pp. 92–93)

Complex human behaviour cannot be simply reduced to internal individual factors. In moving away from a positivist model, it might be better to substitute 'behaviour' for 'action': behaviour is always caused by something, in the sense that eating is caused by hunger, but 'action' always involves 'interaction' – it conveys the complexities of the 'heated moment of experience' (Goffman, 1967, p. 261, see Kontos, 2020).

This is not, of course, to suggest that individual/biological/psychological factors have no relevance. Important arguments have been made, for example, with regard to the impact of environmental toxins on the brain – as in lead exposure – leading to behavioural consequences (see Atkin, 2018 on the Flint, Michigan, water crisis) and the effects of repeated head trauma on National Football League (NFL) athletes (Taibbi, 2012).[13] As Robert Merton acknowledged, 'biological and personality differences . . . may be significantly involved in the incidence of deviate conduct' (1938, p. 672). The point is that we must look to the bigger picture, 'the social and cultural matrix', and hence it is important to 'abstract from other factors', to consider what James S. Plant spoke of as 'the "normal reaction of normal people to abnormal conditions"'(Merton, 1938, p. 672). Biological positivism, 'whatever its other deficiencies, clearly begs one question. It provides no basis for determining the non-biological conditions which induce deviations from prescribed patterns of conduct' (*ibid*). Further, probably the most persuasive argument against biological perspectives is, as Elliott Currie points out, the tremendous variation of crime across different societies: no one, he writes, 'has ever credibly shown that such a biological characteristic (or set of characteristics) exist . . . that would explain why so many people are murdered in, say Russia or El Salvador than in Finland or Chile' (2016, p. 34).

Finally, it is essential that we recognise – despite the objections of 'biocriminologists' or 'biosocial criminologists' or 'neurocriminologists' – that biological theories of criminality can lead us into dangerous territory. Wright and Cullen might protest that 'most of the outrageous acts' of 'criminology's darkest hour' occurred fifty to one hundred years ago and 'would not seem possible in 21st-century America (e.g. a call for eugenics would not find a receptive audience, including among biosocial criminologists)' (2012, p. 241): but as this section on contemporary developments highlights, this work is not so distant from the ideas of early biological positivism, and the criticism of it being Lombrosian or neo-Lombrosian is found warranted. It might not be eugenics, but it is easy to see how it fits with a desire to control 'undesirable' populations.

In the United States and much of the Global North we have witnessed a rise in the far-right and the mainstreaming of racist discourse. There are many people who are only too happy to read the 'scientific racism' of Murray, Rushton and others of their ilk: 'delighted to find their prejudices confirmed by apparently irrefutable statistical research' (Wheen, 2000, p. 1). It would be, as Lilly et al argue, 'the height of arrogance for the rising biosocial criminology to insist that it is free from all value judgements' (2011 ed, p. 353) – its values are obvious when we consider the type of crime it regards as important and its positivistic definition of what constitutes 'scientific' research. Certainly, as they note, it is those ideology-based theories – Marxist, critical, anarchist, feminist, left realist – that have

> alerted us to the role of social power in determining which criminological theories thrive, and they have made it clear the appeal of biosocial theory to the powerful, who are much more willing to support and reward criminologists who support what used to be called the 'Establishment'.
>
> (*ibid*)

Troy Duster, in his 2005 American Sociological Association presidential address, observed that governmental support for social science was declining, whilst that for biological research on violence was increasing. This may be, as Lilly et al further suggest, 'because biology promises "harder" findings but it also may involve the fact that social science research is more critical of existing power structures and sources of inequality' (2011 ed, p. 382). For Duster, 'sociologists can stand on the sidelines, watch the parade of reductionist science as it goes by and point out that it is all "socially constructed" but 'that will not be good enough to rain on this parade, because of the imprimatur of legitimation increasingly afforded to the study of so-called basic processes within the body' (2006, p. 10).

What we must not do is forget history and the devastating impact that policies that focus on the individual have had under the guise of controlling or eliminating undesirable individuals from the population. With this in mind,

I am concluding this chapter with a quotation on the *Buck v. Bell* ruling from the epilogue to Stephen Jay Gould's book *The Mismeasure of Man* (1981):

On the Buck v. Bell *ruling*

In 1927 Oliver Wendell Holmes, Jr., delivered the Supreme Court's decision upholding the Virginia sterilization law in *Buck v. Bell*. Carrie Buck, a young mother with a child of allegedly feeble mind, had scored a mental age of 9 on the Stanford-Binet. Carrie Buck's mother, then 52, had tested at mental age 7. Holmes wrote, in one of the most famous and chilling statements of our century:

> We have seen more than once that the public welfare may call upon the best citizens for their lives. It would be strange if it could not call upon those who already sap the strength of the state for these lesser sacrifices. . . . Three generations of imbeciles are enough.

Buck v. Bell is a signpost of history, an event linked with the distant past in my [Gould's] mind . . . I was therefore shocked by an item in the *Washington Post* on 23 February 1980 – for few things can be more disconcerting than a juxtaposition of neatly ordered and separated temporal events. 'Over 7,500 sterilized in Virginia' the headline read. The law that Holmes upheld had been implemented for forty-eight years, from 1924 to 1972. The operations had been performed in mental health facilities, primarily upon white men and women considered feeble-minded and antisocial – including 'unwed mothers, prostitutes, petty criminals and children with disciplinary problems'.

Carrie Buck, now 72, lives near Charlottesville. Neither she nor her sister Doris would be considered mentally deficient by today's standards. Doris Buck was sterilized under the same law in 1928. She later married Matthew Figgins, a plumber. But Doris Buck was never informed. 'They told me,' she recalled, 'that the operation was for an appendix and rupture.' So she and Matthew Figgins tried to conceive a child. They consulted physicians at three hospitals throughout her child-bearing years; no one recognized that her Fallopian tubes had been severed. Last year, Doris Buck Figgins finally discovered the cause of her lifelong sadness.

One might invoke an unfeeling calculus and say that Doris Buck's disappointment ranks as nothing compared with millions of dead in wars to support the designs of madmen or the conceits of rulers. But can one measure the pain of a single dream unfulfilled, the hope of a defenceless woman snatched by public power in the name of an ideology advanced to purify a race. May Doris Buck's simple and eloquent testimony stand for millions of deaths and disappointments and help us to remember that the Sabbath was made for man, not man for the Sabbath: 'I broke down and cried. My husband and me wanted children desperately. We were crazy about them. I never knew what they'd done to me'.

(1981, pp. 335–336)

The theoretical approaches that have been considered thus far, with the exception of the work of Guerry and Quetelet, have largely centred on the individual. To again quote from Robert Merton's seminal paper, 'Social Structure and Anomie', 'nonconformity is assumed to be rooted in original nature' with 'conformity by implication the result of a utilitarian calculus or unreasoned conditioning' (1938, p. 672). In the following chapters I start to move away from such discussions to those that concentrate on the social structure, with the aim of providing an understanding of how crime is socio-culturally induced. For these approaches, the micro-situation of the individual is contextualised within the macro-context of the wider social structure.

Notes

1 This is not to suggest that Comte's work should be equated with 'raw empiricism' (Thomson, 2010), especially given the critiques of criminological positivism outlined in this chapter. For as Turner (2006) points out, Comte recognised that 'if it is true that every theory must be based upon observed facts, it is equally true that facts cannot be observed without the guidance of some theory'(Comte, 1854, p. 4).
2 It should be noted, however, that although working independently of Quetelet, Guerry made similar inferences from the data. See A.-M. Guerry (1882, 2002 ed) *Essay on the Moral Statistics of France*, New York: Edwin Mellen (edited by H.P.Witt and V.W. Reinking). The introduction to this edition includes an essay 'Inventing Sociology: A-M Guerry and the *Essai sur la statistique morale de la France*' by H.P. Witt, which discusses the contribution of Guerry's work, his relationship with Quetelet and his influence on Durkheim.
3 For a more complete discussion of Quetelet see Piers Beirne's article 'Adolphe Quetelet and the Origins of Positivist Criminology' *American Journal of Sociology*, (1987), Vol. 92, No 5, pp. 1140–1169.
4 See also the translation by Nicole Hahn Rafter and Gibson (2004) of Lombroso's other main publication on crime, *Criminal Woman, the Prostitute and the Normal Woman*, written with his son-in-law (Gina's husband), Guglielmo Ferrero, in 1895.
5 According to Wolfgang (1960), whilst Auguste Comte's concern was with social organisation, and for him, 'the age of sociology had arrived' (see Turner, 2009), there is a biological basis to some of Comte's ideas, and he was known for his support of the work of Franz Joseph Gall.
6 Lombroso does acknowledge this in some of his writings: in his essay on homicide he describes brigandage 'as a sort of wild justice, substituting its own savage methods for the civil justice that is lacking' (1898, p. 1).
7 Surprisingly it was not until the 2006 version by Mary Gibson and Nicole Hahn Rafter that a comprehensive English translation of *Criminal Man* became available for the first time, despite having gone through five editions. This certainly contrasts with the multiple, although often problematic, translations of Beccaria's seminal work. The volume mentioned in the text by Lombroso's daughter, Gina Lombroso-Ferrero, provides only a summary of *Criminal Man*, and this is regarded as being a rather simplistic account of his

theories. *Crime, Its Causes and Remedies* published in 1911 is also an incomplete version, translating only one volume of the fifth edition of *Criminal Man*. However, this did not stop Lombroso's ideas from being popularised in Britain and North America, as is evident from numerous articles published in leading newspapers and journals. In 1889 *The Times Newspaper* carried an article on the 'positive school of criminology' and the 'leader of the movement', Professor Lombroso (11 Sept. ed, p. 10). This was followed both by wide debate and contributions by Lombroso himself, for example, to *The New York Times*, *Chicago Daily Tribune*, *Pall Mall Magazine* and *Popular Science Monthly*. He also gained fame through the English edition of *The Man of Genius* in 1891, in which he argued that genius was an inherited form of insanity or mental aberration.

8 As an aside, it should be noted that Lombroso was aware of the work of Gall and that of Guerry and Quetelet – all, for example, are referred to in *Criminal Man* (1876 and subsequent editions).

9 Regicides or attempted regicides have historically been symbolic of the 'ordinary' person's desire for social change (Mooney, 2014).

10 Bailkin's 'Making Faces: Tattooed Women and Colonial Regimes' (2005) explores the complex relationship between tattooing and colonialism.

11 Brockway did acknowledge the influence of Lombroso on his ideas; in his autobiography he commented that 'world-wide inquiry into the causes of crime arising from defectiveness of the criminals, particularly the investigations of Lombroso quickened my own inquiring attitude and stimulated rationality of the reformative procedure' (1969 ed, p. 215). However, as the reformatory opened in 1876, the same year that *Criminal Man* was first published, it seems likely that Brockway was inspired by the general movement away from the classicist focus on the criminal act that was occurring in the United States at this time, particularly in relation to the treatment of juveniles who were regarded as in need of more specialised treatment. For example, the Michigan Law of 1861 argued for discrimination in prison treatment between those aged sixteen to twenty-one years and older criminals; this was put into practice at the Detroit House of Corrections, where Brockway was the superintendent between 1861 and 1872.

12 It is noteworthy that Francis Cullen is a contributor to Robert Lilly et al's text *Criminological Theory: Context and Consequences*

13 See also Nikolas Rose's 2014 interview on the Human Brain Project at: https://blogs.lse.ac.uk/usappblog/2014/01/31/nikolas-rose-human-brain-project/e

Chapter 4

Chicago School of Sociology
An explosion of ideas

> *In 1840, Chicago was little more than a mud village on a swamp – there were only four and a half thousand people living there, and it was to be swept away both by floods and fire. The Great Fire of 1871 is generally considered a landmark event: a large section of the city was destroyed and a major new city emerged from the ruins. Yet by the late nineteenth century, the city had grown to over one and half million and had become the second largest city in the USA. With migration from all over the country and all over the world, it became the classic melting pot: Poles, Germans, Jews, Italians, Czechs, Lithuanians, Irish, Scandinavians accounting for half of its population. And by 1930, it had grown to well over three million.*
>
> (Plummer, 1997, p. 3)

Chicago was seen by the end of the 1900s as the archetypical 'modern' city. Its hosting of the 1893 World's Columbian Exposition, to mark the 400th anniversary of Christopher Columbus's arrival in North America, served to cement the city's reputation as a growing economic and cultural force. It was to rival that of the 1889 Paris World's Fair in its extravagance and sheer number of exhibits. Sometimes called the 'Chicago World's Fair' or the 'Fair that Changed America', it is estimated that one in four Americans visited its nearly 700-acre site to marvel at the wonders of the Ferris Wheel, electricity, neon lights, the first voice recorders and other extraordinary inventions on display (Novak, 2013; Neal, 2017).[1] Yet it was also a city of the most unimaginable poverty and destitution. Jane Addams and Julia Lathrop wrote of the desperation of the 'winter of panic' of 1893 to 1894 as the financial depression that affected the country was compounded by the numbers left unemployed and stranded – 'the inevitable human *débris*' (Lathrop, 1895, 2007 ed, p. 48) – at the close of the fair. They witnessed the 'working people who suddenly found themselves without work and their savings exhausted' and 'the poor, always on the edge of pauperism, who at last found themselves pushed into the black abyss' (Addams, 2004 ed, p. 48). This was, Addams recalled, the winter that W.H. Stead, a frequent visitor to the Hull House settlement, penned his 'indictment' of Chicago, *If Christ Came to Chicago*, exposing its harshness, misery and 'crooks' (1894, 1910 ed, p. 106). It was this juxtaposition of the excitement of the dawning of a new age, with all of its materialist trappings, alongside the situation of many of the city's residents, their 'weariness, their chill and hunger' (Lathrop, 1895, 2007 ed, p. 128), that was to form the backcloth to Chicago sociology.

Sociology, to put it simply, is the systematic study of human social life. It is concerned with how society hangs together: how society is ordered. And this has meant that, from its origins, it has had a parallel concern with social disorder, which is evident in much of the early work of what became known as the Chicago School of Sociology. This chapter's main focus is on the beginnings of the Chicago School to the 1930s. The core ideas that emerged in this period have remained important to much sociological criminology in the contemporary period: continuing to inform the ways in which criminality and deviance are both researched and understood within an urban context.

Chicago School of Sociology

The Chicago School of Sociology was instrumental in establishing sociology in the United States and for providing an analysis of criminality and other social problems. Indeed, it is suggested that in the early part of the twentieth century American sociology was Chicago sociology (Coser, 1978; Smith, 1988). The output of work was quite extraordinary, and the importance of the city of Chicago to the production of sociological ideas cannot be overstated. As Ken Plummer (1997) has pointed out no city before or since the mid-1930s has been so thoroughly subjected to social investigation. The city of Chicago was to be observed, experienced, mapped, measured and analysed (Smith, 1988) and solutions to its social problems proposed. There are two strands to the Chicago School of Sociology: that of the University of Chicago's Sociology Department and work that came out of the Hull House settlement, founded by Jane Addams and Ellen Gates Starr in 1889. Hull House is described as being for 'women sociologists what the University of Chicago was for men sociologists: the institutional center for research and social thought' (Deegan, 1988, 2005 ed, p. 33), although from its earliest days women also played a role within the university. Yet until the 1980s the work of the women of Hull House and their influence on Chicago sociology was largely underestimated, dismissed as social work or ignored. This is despite the fact that *Hull House Maps and Papers* (1895), which mapped and documented the nationalities, wages and social conditions of a Chicago neighbourhood, was to have a major influence on the university sociologists.

Whilst the Chicago School of Sociology has often been solely equated with the work of the university sociologists, and especially that of the male academics, with Hull House presented as a separate enterprise, these were not intellectually separate spaces. There was a continuous exchange of ideas between the university sociologists and Hull House. Jane Addams taught at the university, and Katharine Bement Davis, as a university doctoral student, taught classes at the settlement. Charles Zeublin, first appointed to the Sociology Department in 1892, lived at the settlement and was a contributor to *Hull House Maps and Papers* (1895). John Dewey, George Herbert Mead, W.I. Thomas, Albion Small, Charles Henderson, Thorstein Veblen, Edward Bemis – university men – were all frequent visitors to Hull House. Ernest Burgess, the 'father' of the concentric zone model of the city, was a one-time Hull House resident. Edwin Sutherland was an officer of the Juvenile Protection Association of Chicago for about six months in 1906, which was then based at Hull House (Deegan, 2003). The settlement was a lively meeting place for scholars, practitioners and activists. Although we can never fully know what was discussed in these meetings or over fireside chats, there is little doubt that the intellectual climate provided by Hull House played a significant role in the development of sociological thought at this time. Visitors included W.E.B. Du Bois, Ida B. Wells, Marianne and Max Weber, Beatrice and Sidney Webb, Ramsay MacDonald, Samuel Barnett, Eugene Debs, Emma Goldman, Peter Kropotkin and Charlotte Perkins Gilman.[2]

Is the Chicago School of Sociology actually a 'school'? This question has incited a significant amount of debate. The term 'school' is a retrospectively applied label. Everett Hughes, a graduate student in the 1920s and later faculty member at the university, recalled, 'I don't remember where or when I first heard of the Chicago School. The phrase was invented by others, not the Chicago people' (Cavan, 1983, p. 407). Ruth Shonle Cavan (1983), another Chicago graduate, notes that it was first employed in 1930, but it was not until the 1950s that 'Chicago School' entered into general usage (Harvey, 1986; Plummer, 1997). Howard S. Becker, another Chicago graduate, argues that a 'school' implies consistency and coherence, with 'theory inform[ing] the research done in its name' and that those who follow on 'embellish the theory and its associated body of thought' (1999, p. 4). Hence, 'when sociologists speak of a Durkhemian school, they mean to indicate with good reason, that everything connected with that school of thought was of a piece' (*ibid*, p. 4). This is not true of Chicago – the body of work is much too varied and disparate. There is debate, as has been implied, 'over who was and was not a member, whose work was influential and whose was marginal' and, additionally, 'how far qualitative and quantitative methods were central' (Delamont, 1992, p. 40). Becker's preferred term for the work of Chicago's Sociology Department is 'school of activity'. Further, until 1929 sociology and anthropology were a joint department (Cavan, 1983), and students were often taught and mentored by faculty from other departments. Thorstein Veblen – who guided the work of a number of sociology doctoral students – was recruited to teach political economy. However, the central motif around which most ideas were generated was the city and the impact of the urban environment. Although wide-ranging in focus and interpretation – as this chapter will illustrate – this does to some extent give a degree of coherence to the work generated in the formative years of Chicago sociology.

The University of Chicago

The University of Chicago was established in 1890. It was just a short walk from the university to the World's Fair. The university was well funded from the start, with endowments from the American Baptist Education Society and John D. Rockefeller Sr., a devout Baptist, who some have suggested is the wealthiest man in American history. Rockefeller's first contribution totalled $1,000,000, with $800,000 designated for non-professional graduate instruction and fellowships (Letter from John D. Rockefeller, 16 Sept. 1890) This 'magnificent gift' was 'hailed with a profound rejoicing by the Board of Trustees' (*The President's Report*, 1892–1902, p. 508). On 8 Nov. 1892, the university as 'a slight recognition of the indebtedness to Mr. Rockefeller', decided that the words 'Founded by John D. Rockefeller' be used in connection with the name of the university in all official reports, publications and correspondence (*ibid*, p. 536).[3]

The first president of the university was William Rainey Harper, a theology scholar and member of the Baptist clergy. Rockefeller, having first met Harper in 1886, was impressed with his 'energy and ideas' (University of Chicago, 1992). Mary Jo Deegan has described Harper as 'an aggressive upstart who used persuasion, money and promises of institutional power to lure prominent often young, scholars to the "wild" West' (2005, p. 1). It certainly was not long before it had acquired an impressive faculty and Harper had silenced those critics who suggested that to put a top university in Chicago 'would be only the next thing to putting it in the Fiji Islands' (cited in Fitzpatrick, 1990, p. 33).

Although Chicago was to have an undergraduate degree programme, it was, following the lead of Clark University in Massachusetts, to prioritise research and graduate study, aiming to advance a national and international reputation. Its Sociology Department was founded in 1892 and placed under the directorship of Albion Small, who – in keeping with the university's Baptist origins – had at one time considered ordination into the Baptist ministry. Small's department was to represent the consolidation of sociology as an area of academic study in the United States. Prior to this, sociology had existed as 'an amorphous area of study', comprising 'a little bit of history, a dash of political economy, and a pinch of social amelioration' (Deegan, 2005, p. 1).

Very much aware of his position at the helm of a fledgling discipline, Albion Small established the *American Journal of Sociology* in 1895, with a welcome in the first edition to 'the era of sociology' (Small, 1895, p. 1). He was also a founder of the American Sociology Society (ASS) (now known as the American Sociological Association [ASA]), serving as its president in 1912 and 1913.[4] It is of note that this development within U.S. academia occurred at roughly the same time that Durkheim was establishing sociology as a discipline in France. The first edition of *L' Aneé sociologique* came out just three years after the *American Journal of Sociology*. In a sense this period represents a 'bittersweet moment' in the history of sociology, for the academicisation of the subject resulted in a tension between the studying of social life purely as a knowledge-gathering exercise – to be read about in journals and books – and the promotion of social inquiry as a tool to aid the understanding and amelioration of the social problems of the day. Chicago's emphasis on doctoral training for the 'would be academic scholar' was to contribute to the professionalism of social science (Bulmer, 1984, p. 7) and to the input of academics into the developing criminal justice and social welfare professions.

Women of the university

Significantly, the university founders stated that their intention was to provide 'equal privileges to both sexes', and women were to constitute nearly a quarter of its first cohort of students (*The President's Report*, 1901).[5] Whilst the men associated with the Sociology Department are well known – Small, Dewey, Thomas, W.F. Ogburn, Robert Park, Ernest Burgess, Clifford Shaw, Henry McKay, Frederic Thrasher, Walter Reckless, Edwin Sutherland and Herbert Bulmer – to name some of the key figures – in recent years there has been more recognition of the contributions of the women who studied and taught at the university in its early days. As Grant et al have commented, 'an important component of contemporary feminist scholarship is the rediscovery of the lost contributions of women. . . . [This] new scholarship has documented both the influence of women on the formation of the discipline of sociology and the distinctive orientation of their research and writing' (2002, p. 69). For Mary Jo Deegan this period in Chicago's history represents a 'golden era for women in sociology', which in turn resulted in a 'golden era for women in criminology' (2003, p. 18).

Marion Talbot championed women's education with the slogan that it should be 'no more, no less' than a man's (cited in Helvie-Mason, 2010). She was co-founder of the American Association of University Women and appointed Assistant Professor and Assistant Dean of Women at Chicago in 1892, becoming Dean of Women in 1893. Even though women continued to enter the university in ever-increasing numbers and were highly successful, it was by no means without difficulty. In 1902 Harper proposed a plan for gender segregation: his commitment to the inclusion of women students within the university had not extended to an acceptance of men and women being taught together. The university's religious foundations and the faith of many of its top administrators, as well as concerns that women students might outpace the men academically, were largely responsible for this development.[6] 'Another factor' for Harper was that 'the association of a large number of young men and women' may prove a 'distraction and a disadvantage' (*The President's Report*, 1902, p. cix). Young men were disadvantaged, he argued, because girls mature early and 'are apt to be patronizing toward the boys, and the latter are self-conscious and embarrassed in the company of girls' (*ibid*, p.

xx). Marion Talbot was one of the most vocal and active campaigners against Harper's proposal. She headed a committee of inquiry and, together with fifty-seven other instructors, urged for the matter to be reconsidered, for it represented 'the first step in the over-throw of co-education' (The University of Chicago Library, 2009). The policy of gender segregation was implemented but abandoned a few years later, having been judged as 'unworkable' (*ibid*).

At Chicago, Talbot created a culture of support for women students and instructors and was tireless in her fight to attain equality in terms of funding, appointments and fellowships throughout her career. She was key to securing social policy positions for many of the university's graduates. An associate editor of the *American Journal of Sociology* from its establishment until her retirement in 1925, Talbot's academic interests lay in the 'overlap between urban studies, town planning and home economics' (Delamont, 1992, p. 43).

Annie Marion MacLean: the 'mother of contemporary ethnography'

One of Talbot's mentees was Annie Marion MacLean.[7] She was awarded an MA in 1897 and in 1900 became the second woman to receive a PhD from the University of Chicago. From 1903 MacLean taught as part of the university's extension faculty. Despite Talbot's efforts, few women were granted full-time faculty appointments at the university. MacLean's research and publications record were impressive. Her specialist interests largely centred on women's working lives and women's relationship to the state. Her biographer, Mary Jo Deegan, describes her alliance with W.E.B. Du Bois and the National Association for the Advancement of Colored People (NAACP), observing that she was responsible for one of the first community-based studies of a Black town, presenting the findings at the 1903 Atlanta Conference organized by Du Bois, who praised the 'value' of her work. Although a pioneer of mixed methods – the use of qualitative, experimental and quantitative methods – within social research, her early ethnographic work is quite exceptional and pre-dates that which is usually associated with the Chicago School. Certainly, Hallett and Jeffers (2008) point out that given that much of her work was completed between 1897 and 1910, she really was ahead of her time: Thomas and Znaniecki's *The Polish Peasant in Europe and America*, often cited as the university's first empirical sociological study, was not published until 1918. MacLean's research was decades before the ethnographies produced during the Park and Burgess years. Hallett and Jeffers refer to MacLean as the 'neglected mother of contemporary ethnography' (*ibid*, p. 3).

In the late 1800s and early 1900s MacLean published two studies in the *American Journal of Sociology* based on participant observation. The first, entitled 'Two Weeks in Department Stores' (1899), had involved working 'undercover' as a shop worker to provide a 'true picture' of those who work in department stores, for, as she put it, 'it is common for those who purchase to think nothing at all about the clerk in attendance, or the conditions under which the goods were produced' (p. 721). Powerfully documenting the harsh and exploitative environment and the weariness of the workers, some of whom were children, she ends with the plea, 'we should not rest until the bad stores improve or go out of business' (p. 741). In this paper MacLean documents the constraints placed on the lives of women workers. By using the actual words uttered by the department store clerks, she pulls the reader into their world and in so doing we gain an understanding of the terrible dilemmas women faced as they tried to cope with poverty wages and the ever-present temptation of prostitution:

> It was common to hear such expressions as this uttered in agonized seriousness: 'If I don't get more wages I'll have to go bad. But I'd hate to disgrace my family'. Lecherous men were always around ready to offer aid. They came, professedly to buy, but it was not the wares of the store they wanted. The young and pretty girls yielded most easily. They would weep, sometimes, and say: 'Good people look down on us. But they don't know – they don't know. We have to earn our living'.
> (MacLean, 1899, p. 736)

The second study was 'The Sweat-Shop in Summer' (1903): for this MacLean took on the role of a 'toiler' in a series of sweatshops. In this section, she elaborates on her methodological approach. For it is only by 'participating' in the world of the 'toiler' that 'meaning' can be given to their experiences:

> I had visited over a hundred of these places, and I already knew the aspects they present to the observer, but a few minutes visit can never teach on the hardships of the workers.
>
> We may gasp when we are told of women who toil twelve or fourteen hours for a mere pittance, but, after all, it is without meaning until one has experienced the weary eyes and dizzy head and aching back. This caused by a long day's sewing in badly ventilated and poorly lighted room. My poor cramped shoulders made me understand the women who sang 'Song of the Shirt', and only too many of our present-day toilers know what it means to 'stitch, stitch, stitch, in poverty, hunger and dirt'. And, who makes them do it? We do. Our mad craze for cheapness has cheapened life.
> (1903, pp. 304–305)

She believed producing an 'honest portrayal of the conditions under which the people work' would prove to 'be of inestimable value to all' (*ibid*, p. 289). Such research had the potential to provide 'a rational ground for constructive action' and for the 'toiler himself it may mean hope in the future' (*ibid*, p. 290). 'The Sweat-Shop in Summer' included photographs of the workers, making Annie Marion MacLean one of the first sociologists to incorporate

Figure 4.1 'A Young Toiler' from 'A Sweat-Shop in Summer', *American Journal of Sociology*, 1903, p. 304.

visual imagery into her ethnography. She was also very much aware of her privileged position as a researcher: in a later study of a factory she wrote, 'it was, not after all, my life. As one of the forewomen said, "You do not have to stay here; you can do what gives you joy"' (1923, p. 444).

'Two Weeks in Department Stores' and 'The Sweat-Shop in Summer' are forceful critiques of the workers' conditions and of 'modern' society. What 'I saw', MacLean wrote, was a 'group of human beings working under conditions not fit for human beings' (1903, p. 298). 'A Sweat-Shop in Summer' is a damning indictment of the level of structural violence endured by the poor and powerless. Although not citing Marx and Engels directly, MacLean's exposés of the hardships faced by the workers bear a similarity to Engels's account of working-class life in *The Condition of the Working Class in England in 1844* (1845) and reflects to an extent Marx's theories of alienation and the impact of industrialisation on the worker (see Hallett and Jeffers, 2008). It is of significance that MacLean was a close friend of Florence Kelley,[8] a Hull House resident and lifelong socialist, who translated *The Condition of the Working Class in England in 1844* from its original German and contributed a chapter on 'the sweating-system' for *Hull House Maps and Papers* (1895). In 'Four Months in a Model Factory' MacLean concluded,

> Freedom is a large question, and I suppose few of us are really free: but that man is least free, it seems to me, who earns his bread as a cog in a machine over which he as a man has not the slightest controlling voice; where he can be dropped without notice at some one's whim or because orders are short; and where he can have, consequently, no sense of security. I do not believe the world was made to be dominated by machines. It was made for human beings, and if the method of making machines takes one cubit from the spiritual stature of a man, then, I say, scrap the machines and save the man.
>
> (1923, p. 444)

Not only is MacLean important in terms of her own research but she had a direct influence on Edwin Sutherland as his teacher on an introduction to sociology correspondence course, taught as part of the university's extension programme. As Sutherland wrote, 'I had no courses in sociology in college and no other courses in sociology elsewhere except this correspondence course' (cited in Deegan, 2014, p. 40).[9] As Deegan suggests, given Sutherland's later role as a leader in criminology, and his presidency of the ASA, MacLean's teaching should be interpreted as having had a 'deep impact' on the development of the discipline (*ibid*, p. 41).

University women, criminology and criminal justice policy: a mixed legacy

MacLean's classmates, Frances Kellor and Katharine Bement Davis, were to write more specifically on crime and crime policy. Unlike many of her fellow graduate students, Kellor, raised by a single mother in poverty, was familiar with hardship. She began her studies at Chicago in 1898 under the mentorship of Charles Henderson. Henderson was the author of *An Introduction to the Study of the Dependent, Defective and Delinquent Classes* (1893), a book that although sceptical of Lombroso, did support determinist arguments, albeit with more emphasis placed on psychological, social and environmental factors in the development of criminality. It is probably true to say that, like many of those starting to write on crime and delinquency in this period, Henderson was trying to arrive at some kind of mid-way position that took both individual and social explanations seriously. Kellor was to thank him for inspiring and guiding her work (1901a, p. viii).[10]

Kellor was a highly motivated student. Within her first year at Chicago she published two papers in the *American Journal of Sociology*. As a junior scholar she aimed firstly to improve sociology's reputation as a respectable 'science'. For, as she put it, 'one of the charges most frequently brought against sociology is that it consists only of theories, and these often of doubtful practicability' (1900a, p. 527). Second, she intended to show that criminology was much more than the 'popularly believed' phase of 'anthropometric' study (1900a, p. 301) as represented by Lombroso and his colleagues. The problem, she argued, was that few had extended the subject to include the social and economic environment (*ibid*). Although Kellor adopted Lombroso's methods in her research, she did so in order to scientifically test and then refute his belief in the hereditary basis of criminality, with confidence. Comparing the characteristics of women inmates at five institutions across the United States (the reform school at Geneva, the penitentiary at Joliet, the workhouse at Cincinnati, Ohio State Penitentiary at Columbus and the workhouse and penitentiary at Blackwell's Island, New York City) with those of women students – making this one of the first serious studies of women offenders – she concluded that anthropomorphic measurements revealed there was no 'criminal type' and the psychological tests, 'touching on the vital functioning of the individual, do not reveal defects and variations which discourage educational and reformatory measures' (1900b, p. 58). This was important, given the number of those working in crime policy who were to regard some 'criminals' as beyond help and, consequently, were supportive of eugenicist principles. Kellor therefore was to provide an important counterargument to biological determinism and emerges as an early contributor to the development of sociological criminology in the United States. It was her contention that the ideas of Lombroso and Ferri and the other European 'investigators' were influential in the States because the discipline of criminology was still in its infancy (1900b). It is noteworthy that despite criticisms by Chicago's male sociologists of Lombroso and hereditary explanations, and the emphasis that was to be placed on the 'science' of sociology, little, if any, reference is made to Kellor's research or writing. There are no citations for her in Park and Burgess's *Introduction to the Science of Sociology* (1921) or in Burgess's 'The Study of the Delinquent as a Person' (1923) despite his lengthy discussion of Lombroso, Ferri and Tarde.

In line with feminist criminology in the contemporary period, Kellor observed that women criminals were treated more harshly than men because of their sex:

> It is a prevailing opinion that when women are criminal they are more degraded and more abandoned than men. . . . [T]his seems due rather to the difference in the standards which we set for the two sexes. We say woman is worse, but we judge her so by comparison with the ideal of woman, not with a common ideal. For instance, I have included swearing and use of tobacco as bad habits among women; among men we should not consider them in the same light.
>
> (1900b, p. 679)

Further, in a series of articles for *The Arena* (1901b) magazine and in her book *Experimental Sociology. Descriptive and Analytical: Delinquents* (1901a) Kellor was to enter into the debate on the so-called rise in criminality amongst African Americans. Influenced by W.E.B. Du Bois, she warned of the dangers of taking statistics at their face value and drew attention to disparities in the administration of justice between the North and South and in the treatment of African Americans in comparison to whites. In the South the legacy of slavery and a racist criminal justice system had to be considered. Penalties in the South 'are extreme and negroes are serving life sentences for crimes which receive penalties from between one to five years in the North'. In the South 'a negro may be serving a three year sentence for stealing half a dozen ears of corn to feed his mule' (1901b, p. 154). She referred to a 'Southern Officer' whose words were illustrative of the extent of racial prejudice in the Southern states:

> 'If two white men quarrel and one murders the other, we imprison the culprit and then pardon him; if a white man murders a negro, we let him off; if a negro murders a white man, we lynch him; if a negro murders a negro, we hang or imprison him.' The penal system is so lucrative to the states that the tendency is to imprison rather than hang, unless public sentiment demands it. When white men are arrested for gambling they are usually released or lightly fined; but if found gambling with negroes they get the full penalty of the law, 'just for the indignity of the thing.' This prejudice creeps in almost unconsciously.
>
> (*ibid*)

Kellor was additionally concerned with exposing the terrible conditions in prisons in the South, with women inmates being beaten and given amphetamines to keep them working. Her solution was a 'practical philanthropy' (her description). For the privileged classes had a duty to ensure that African Americans had access to education and employment opportunities and that social work and crime prevention initiatives were expanded into poor communities. In 1906 Kellor founded, with S.W. Layten, the National League for the Protection of Colored Women, which aimed to help African American women in urban areas, especially those who had migrated to the cities of the North and were at risk of exploitation. She went on to become secretary of the New York State Immigration Commission, and then in 1910 was put in charge of the Bureau of Industries and Immigration.

Yet whilst Kellor's study of the African American experience was seen as 'at the leading edge of a new direction in the national black crime discourse' (Muhammad, 2010, p. 88), there was, as with so many of her generation, a disturbing side to her commentaries. Although she directly blames the legacy of slavery, Kellor argues that the 'the negro's criminality is that of an underdeveloped race', with 'that of whites . . . characterized by a capacity born of development' (1901b, p. 31). As Khalil Gibran Muhammad points out in his highly informative book, *The Condemnation of Blackness*, at the same time that Kellor 'discounted race traits and made significant strides toward an environmental or sociological perspective on black criminality, part of her analysis reified the inferiority of blacks even as criminals' (2010, p. 100). Hence, 'negroes are notorious thieves, but they remain months and years in stockades that would not hold ordinary northern safe blowers twenty-four hours' (1901b, p. 31; cited in Muhammad, 2010, p. 100). With respect to women, Kellor is extremely critical of women who have abortions, for this 'lowers the moral standard of the women of a nation' and, in a statement that bears the hallmarks of a Lombrosian sexism, suggests that for married women, abortion 'shows a decrease in the maternal sentiment which has preserved women from much crime and degradation' (1898, p. 80).

Katharine Bement Davis was born into a family of social reformers. Her grandmother, Rhoda Denison Bement, managed an underground station for slaves fleeing from the South before the Civil War and, as an associate of Elizabeth Cady Stanton, had attended the historic Seneca Falls Women's Rights Convention in 1848. Both Davis's grandmother and mother were staunch advocates for women's suffrage. As Davis once said, 'I never knew what it was to be anything but a suffragist' (*The New York Times*, 6 January 1914, p. 12). Her first introduction to Chicago was the World's Columbian Exposition. She had gone there to develop and run the New York State Workingman's Model Home exhibit. This was a life-sized house in which real people – a man, a woman and two children – were placed as representative of a 'typical' working family. The exhibit, in which the costs of the house, furniture, food (including lists of what the family should be eating) and clothing were all itemised, was extremely popular with visitors (Barnes, 1981).

Following her success in Chicago, Davis was recruited to head up the St. Mary's Street College Settlement in Philadelphia which was modelled on the Hull House settlement. The settlement was located in the Seventh Ward of Philadelphia, in which a quarter of the city's African American population resided. Davis was to develop a reputation as an energetic activist on behalf of the poor and an advocate for better housing conditions.[11] This section of the city was to form part of the research basis for W.E.B. Du Bois's *The Philadelphia Negro* (1899), and Du Bois was to live at the settlement while Davis was there[12]. Settlement records reveal Davis actively supported Du Bois's research, and they were to remain fond acquaintances.[13]

Davis was to return to Chicago in 1895 to undertake graduate studies in political economy and sociology, mentored by Thorstein Veblen. She felt particularly drawn to Veblen, who she said was 'sympathetic and made one think' (cited in Fitzpatrick, 1990, p. 53). Interestingly, given attempts to 'silence' radical thought within the academy (see Box 4.1), Davis noted that 'it was said in the Department that he was the only man in the world that the

---

Box 4.1 Silencing the academy: the case of Edward Bemis

Edward Bemis was a tenured professor in the university's extension programme, teaching courses in sociology and political economy. His appointment was officially terminated at the end of 1894. The 1890s were politically turbulent years for the city of Chicago: the financial depression was taking its toll. In May 1894 workers at the Pullman Car Works factory walked off the job in protest at their poor wages and restrictive living conditions. They were joined in their action by the Railway Operatives Union, led by the socialist leader Eugene V. Debs. As one of the workers said to Debs's men: 'we struck because we were without hope' (cited in Grossman, 2011). They felt they were 'owned' by George Pullman, the factory owner who had set up housing for his workers. 'We were born in a Pullman house . . . and when we die we shall be buried in the Pullman cemetery and go to a Pullman hell' (*ibid*). Bemis was somewhat on the fence when the unrest started, but once the railway operatives decided to strike, he spoke out in opposition to the railway corporations: 'if the railroads would expect their men to be law-abiding, they must set the example. Let their open violation of the interstate commerce law and their relations to corrupt legislatures and assessors testify to their part in this regard' (cited in Schwendinger and Schwendinger (1974, p. 492). This attracted the attention of President William Rainey Harper, who wrote an angry letter to him indicating that his relations with local businesses and supporters of the university were being affected: your words, he said, have 'caused me a great deal of annoyance. It is hardly safe for me to venture into any of the Chicago clubs. I am pounced upon from all sides' (*ibid*).

Bemis was in favour of the state ownership of utilities and openly criticised the monopoly of the Rockefeller-controlled Standard Oil Company. The university denied Rockefeller's involvement in Bemis's firing – suggesting he was simply an incompetent instructor – but it does seem likely that he was removed in anticipation of Rockefeller's displeasure. The financial hold that Rockefeller had on the university was such that it was referred to in some quarters as the 'Standard Oil Institution'. Certainly, it was a bit of a coincidence that at the time of Bemis's firing, Harper was trying to secure further funding from Rockefeller. Indeed, a notable amount of social research was funded by the Rockefeller family, including, for example, the work of Katharine Bement Davis in New York City and the Bureau of Social Hygiene.

Bemis, himself, had no doubts that his situation was because of concerns over wealthy donors and potential donors to the university: he claimed that Harper had said, 'it is all very well to sympathize with the workingmen, but we get our money from those on the other side, and we cannot afford to offend them' (*The New York Times*, 25 October, 1894, p. 16). Albion Small supported Harper's position, revealing, as Mary Jo Deegan suggests, the level that he was co-opted 'by his conservative allegiance to the administration and his search for "academic" legitimacy' (1988, p. 173).

Eugene Debs was quite clear that the Bemis affair had exposed the failings of the university:

> If the American university has failed in doing its share in solving the 'great labor problem' no laborious research is required to find a plausible reason for its shortcomings, and recent humiliating incidents transpiring in the operation of the Chicago University, became sufficiently explanatory to satisfy the most exacting. The dismissal of Prof. Bemis proclaims the fact that the American University is not equipped to solve labor problems, but is arrogantly hostile to labor.
> (Debs, 1970, p. 56; cited in Schwendinger and Schwendinger, 1974, p. 494)

This was not the last instance of an attempt at 'silencing' by Chicago. In 1908 Charles Zeublin was also forced to resign from his position at the university. He had publicly advocated for more control for the workers. In a letter from the new president of the university, Harry Pratt Judson, Zeublin was reprimanded for his embarrassing speeches and told 'it is impossible to differentiate the lecturer on the public platform who bears the name of the University from the University itself'

(Judson to Zeublin, 7 March 1908, cited in Deegan, 1988, p. 178). Although it is difficult to fully assess the impact of this 'silencing' on the development of the discipline, as well as the series of Red Scares which affected both the university and Hull House, it is likely that the result was a more cautious approach to theory and policy. When Henry Carter Adams was dismissed from Cornell University for supporting labour following the city of Chicago's Haymarket Massacre, he suggested that 'fellow social scientists . . . avoid controversial topics and become technical experts for legislators or regulatory commissions' (Lengermann and Niebrugge-Brantley, 1998, p. 16). And according to Robert Westbrook, John Dewey advised colleagues after the Bemis affair 'that the injection of moralism and an inflammatory tone into criticism of the established order would get them into hot water' (cited in Schultz, 2007, p. 16). For Schwendinger and Schwendinger the Chicago sociologists were working at the behest of capital and the 'political repression of radical scholarship within the academy has been one of the most important factors determining the nature of American sociology throughout its entire history' (Schwendinger and Schwendinger, 1974, p. 490).

Further Reading:

Schwendinger, H. and Schwendinger, J. (1974) *The Sociologists of the Chair: A Radical Analysis of the Formative Years of North American Sociology*, New York City: Basic Books

trustees and the faculty would dare permit to lecture on socialism, because no one knew when he got through which side he was on, and you couldn't possibly get it out of him by questioning!' (*ibid*). Her dissertation, which drew on the work of Veblen and that of the other male Chicago sociologists, was on farm labour in Bohemia. To complement her studies, Davis spent a year at the University of Berlin and in Vienna – many of the Chicago PhD students were to study in Berlin, and Chicago sociology was heavily influenced by German scholarship. In her research, Davis discussed the 'greed' of the estate owners and the terrible conditions that the workers laboured under, together with the exploitation of child labourers (Fitzpatrick, 1990, p. 55). On her return to Chicago, Davis collected statistical data on the housing conditions of the city's Bohemian immigrants for a committee headed by Jane Addams (Deegan, 2003).

In 1900 Josephine Shaw Lowell, a noted philanthropist and penal reformer from Boston, contacted Marion Talbot to see if she knew someone trained in sociology under Veblen, Small, Henderson, Vincent and Charles Zueblin[14] (Deegan, 2003) to take on the position of the first superintendent of the recently built New York State Reformatory for Women at Bedford Hills. Lowell had adopted Elizabeth Fry's mission to push for women inmates to be housed separately from men and under the care of female custodians. Indeed, Lowell drew directly from Fry's book, *Observations on the Visiting, Superintendence and Government of Female Prisoners* (1827), in her 1880 paper, 'Reformatories for Women'. Talbot was to suggest Katharine Bement Davis for the position. However, if Lowell can be seen as following in the footsteps of Fry, this is not the case for Davis or the other Chicagoean women who were to become involved in criminal justice reform. For them, policy was to be informed by scientific research. The philanthropic penal reformer in this period was becoming a thing of the past (Freedman, 1984; Mooney and Shanahan, 2020). As Fitzpatrick (1990) notes, the nature of Lowell's approach to Talbot underscored this change in strategy. Sociological inquiry was 'increasingly perceived as relevant to social welfare', with activists such as Lowell now placing 'a high value on those who could bring their university training to bear on social problems' (*ibid*, p. 77).

At Bedford Hills, Davis was to introduce a number of progressive reforms. She emphasised that women presented much less of a problem than men when it came to criminality. Women formed 12 per cent of the prison population and were mostly incarcerated for disorderly conduct and prostitution (Davis, 1913a, 1913b). Ellen Fitzpatrick writes that in a 1905 address to the National Prison Association, Davis argued that women law breakers were 'the victims of destructive social and economic forces' and 'rehabilitation depended on recognition of this social fact' and once 'the problems in American cities were resolved . . . there would be "little need" for professional meetings devoted to methods of dealing with criminal behavior' (1990, p. 97). For Davis it was important to provide economic and educational opportunities for inmates as part of their rehabilitation; she herself taught classes on the democratic process to the women at Bedford Hills. She stressed the need for comfortable prison housing with access to natural light and little in the way of restraint. Davis also got rid of what she described as the unjust, immoral and indefensible policy of racial segregation in the face of considerable opposition from New York City officials (*The New York Times*, 18 December 1914, p. 10; McCarthy, 1997). At this time, most prisons with a notable number of African American inmates enforced a strict policy of segregation.

With the financial support of John D. Rockefeller Jr., in 1911 Davis founded the Laboratory of Social Hygiene at Bedford Hills in order to advance the scientific study of prostitution and criminality amongst women. She recruited fellow University of Chicago graduates, Jessie Taft and Virginia Robinson, to work there. Their brief was to investigate those factors that lead women into criminality and offences associated with prostitution in order to proscribe an appropriate rehabilitative and therapeutic regime. As *The New York Times* put it, their intention was to discover why the woman had gone wrong: 'Was she the victim of inescapable poverty? Was she reared in wretched surroundings? Was she forced into evil ways by others? Has she some physical deficiency? Ought she be imprisoned at all? Is she mentally clouded?' (23 January 1912, p. 7). The 'laboratory' method was typical of the university sociologists and used to research education, children, psychology and physiology (Deegan, 2003). Kellor (1901a) had stressed the importance of the 'laboratory method' in conducting her study on women offenders, which was in keeping with her emphasis on the need to be 'scientific' – to collect data that are testable – when conducting social research.

Davis's 'success'[15] at Bedford Hills and growing reputation in the field of prison reform led to her appointment as New York City's commissioner of corrections in 1914. She was the first woman in the United States to hold a senior office in corrections, six years before women got the right to vote. In an interview for *The New York Times*, Davis described her new position as commissioner as presenting 'a vast opportunity for progressive work' for 'everybody knows New York's prison institutions to be little better than medieval' and, as such, 'I hope to bring them up to something nearer to the highest modern standard' (Marshall, 1914, pp. 6–7).[16] Although Davis was considered a progressive advocate for penal reform,[17] a significant component of her research and crime policy exemplifies the extent that a positivist ideology had taken root in the nascent field of criminology in the United States and is indicative of a move away from structural considerations. At the Laboratory of Social Hygiene many of the women following the administration of IQ tests were found to be psychologically unstable or 'mentally defective', as well as simply incorrigible. At intake women were to be diagnosed and classified by 'experts' with the results used to inform 'treatment' and sentencing. It was essential, Davis argued, for an individualised approach to sentencing: treatment needed 'to fit the criminal rather than make punishment fit the crime' (1913a, p. 403). She was, following the lead of Zebulon Brockway, the founder of the New York State–based Elmira reformatory, to become a major proponent of indeterminate sentencing. She believed that it was important for the inmate to be held until she demonstrated reform, for 'the prisoner should recognize that her only hope of freedom is in preparing herself to lead an industrious, self-supporting life. The hope of this should be kept ever before her' (*ibid*, p. 407). This, she believed, would help

> rid the streets of New York and our large cities of soliciting, loitering, and public vice than anything that could be devised. For there is nothing the common prostitute fears so greatly as to know that if she offends and is caught, she will be subject to the possibility of prolonged confinement.
> (*ibid*, p. 408)

More ominously, Davis noted that the Bedford Hills research, and other studies, show a high proportion of 'mental defectives' amongst the inmates:

> This means women who are not superficially different from other women but who have the minds of children and who bring into the world illegitimate children who, if the laws of heredity mean anything, are liable in their turn to become a burden upon the community.
>
> (ibid, p. 404)

By enforcing an individualized approach, this group – the 'social menace' – were to be removed from the general population of prisoners and confined to separate institutions, preferably for the duration of their lives, as this 'would relieve the state from the ever increasing burden of the support of their illegitimate children' (*ibid*, p. 408). Her comments on the 'social menace' within the inmate population resulted in the endorsing of an impossiblist positivist ideology – when nothing could be done the only option was confinement and the prevention of reproduction. With assumptions being made over the 'desirable' versus the 'undesirable' elements within society, we glimpse at that strand of penal reform that was concerned with 'nation-building' (see Bosworth, 2010). Not surprisingly, Davis was to become aligned with the eugenics movement. Those with the potential of becoming worthy citizens were to be given indeterminate sentences with the aim of working towards successful rehabilitation; those with 'irredeemable' traits were to be removed. Katharine Bement Davis's mentor, Josephine Shaw Lowell, was likewise an advocate of eugenics: 'what right', she asked, 'have we to-day to allow men and women who are diseased and vicious to reproduce their own crime' (cited in Rafter, 2009, p. 245).[18] The number of 'progressives' in this period who were to seriously entertain eugenicist principles is quite remarkable.

Men of the university

Albion Small was to publish in 1894, with George Vincent, a PhD student, what is considered to be the first American sociology textbook, *Introduction to the Study of Society*. Described as a 'laboratory guide' (1894, p. 15), it was largely to aid the teaching of the subject, with the inclusion of lists of 'subjects for investigation' by the student at the end of each section. This is one of the first uses of the word 'laboratory' by the university sociologists to describe their approach to sociological inquiry, and it was to remain a constant theme. The *Annual Register* of the University of Chicago for 1904 described the city of Chicago as 'one of the most complete social laboratories in the world' for 'no city in the world presents a wider variety of social problems' (p. 287). The concept of 'laboratory' became more central through the work of Robert Park, who taught at the university from 1914 until 1932. 'Laboratory' is still used today to describe the university's research centres (see https://urbanlabs.uchicago.edu).

Small and Vincent's *Introduction to the Study of Society* was to 'present the inchoate science' of sociology, 'as thus far an interrogation of social reality' (1894, p. 31). 'Sociology' emerged with the 'so-called industrial revolution', for as Small and Vincent contend, it was in this period that inequality became more 'obtrusive' (*ibid*, p. 34). Factories resulted in the concentration 'of great numbers of a single class of workmen in the same location' and, as such, 'the social and industrial contrasts between employer and employed become wider and more distinct' (*ibid*). The subsequent 'poor man's protest' in his own poverty results in 'a demand for sociology' (*ibid*). This 'demand' therefore stems from the experience of social inequality. Hence, most sociologists believe in the importance of constructing a general science of society to contribute to the solving of social problems (Small, 1912).

While Small was undoubtedly sympathetic to Marx ('one of the few really great thinkers in the history of social science' [1912, p. 17]) and Small and Vincent express support for 'socialists who attribute all poverty, vice and crime to our present economic arrangements' (1894, p. 271), they depict crime in *Introduction to the Study of Society* as against the social contract and, typically, the result of a failure of responsibility on behalf of the offender towards society. Some crime, however, is characterised as pathological. To an extent, all crime for Small and Vincent is pathological because it represents a pathological stain on a social system that by and large is seen as working. Small and Vincent argue that to attribute crime to 'economic arrangements' ignores both individual responsibility and other determining factors. For example, a 'heavy burden of responsibility for vice, crime and pauperism rests upon the family for its failure through many generations to furnish normal individuals to society' (1894, p. 278). Thus, we see a combination of classicist and positivist discourses in their presentation of crime and criminality. The solution for 'unsocial individuals, thieves, burglars, brawlers, murderers, and others who refuse to be governed by the regulations which must be observed if society is to exist and make progress' are for them to 'be arrested, tried, and withdrawn from society in jails and prisons' (1894, p. 164), although they admit such measures – i.e. a 'period of isolation' – often fail to 'induce better conduct' (*ibid*).

The Park and Burgess years

Some twenty years after Small and Vincent's textbook, Robert Park and Ernest Burgess penned what students came to call the 'green bible', or as Alan Sica called it, 'the totem for the Chicago tribe': *Introduction to the Science of Sociology* (1921). This huge book – 1,040 pages and weighing several pounds – was to sell over 30,000 copies by 1943, an extraordinary feat, equivalent to the selling of 332,000 copies or more today, given the relative change in enrolment in sociology courses (Sica, 2012). Despite the well-documented neglect of both women members of the university and those associated with Hull House (Deegan, 1988) it continues to be usual for criminology textbooks to start with the work of Robert Park when discussing the Chicago School. He certainly proved an inspiration for generations of scholars. Humorously, Howard S. Becker liked to tell people that when he arrived at Chicago for graduate school, 'I went out on the University of Chicago Midway and fasted for seven days, at which time the spirit of Robert E. Park appeared and revealed to me the kind of sociologist I was to become' (1970, p. v).

By all accounts, Park, an ex-newspaper reporter, had the air of 'a casually dressed absent-minded professor, but as soon as he opened his mouth he captured his students' attention' (Bovenkerk, 2010, p. 49). He insisted that they go out into the city ('Why go to the North Pole or climb Everest for adventure when we have Chicago?' [Park, cited in Lindner, 1996, p. 3]) to observe the social world in all of its glory. One of his graduate students was to attribute this quotation to him, which has become one of the most repeated quotations in the history of social research:

> Go and sit in the lounges of the luxury hotels and on the doorsteps of the flophouses; sit on the Gold Coast settees and on the slum shakedowns; sit in the Orchestra Hall and in the Star and Garter Burlesque. In short, gentlemen, *go get the seat of your pants dirty in real research.*
> (Lee, 2017, p. 51; author emphasis)[19]

And, like Annie Marion MacLean, who had got 'the seat of' her 'pants dirty in real research' years earlier, out into the city Chicago's students went, which resulted in some of the most enthusiastically received ethnographic studies within the disciplines of sociology and criminology. Nels Anderson's *The Hobo* (1923), Frederic Thrasher's *The Gang* (1927), Louis Wirth's *The Ghetto*, Clifford Shaw's *The Jack Roller* (1930) and Paul Cressey's *The Taxi Dance Hall* (1932) were all produced in the university's Park and Burgess period, and one or the other was responsible for writing the book's preface or introduction (Deegan, 2007). It was not necessary, however, for this research to encourage social change. For Park and Burgess, the city as 'social laboratory' was to mean scientific detachment, with the city and its inhabitants treated merely as objects for study. As Ernest Burgess wrote in his comparison of natural to social sciences:

> In chemistry, physics, and even biology the subjects of study can be brought into the laboratory and studied under controlled conditions. . . . The objects of social science research, as persons, groups, and institutions, must be studied under controlled conditions. . . . The objects of social science research, as persons, groups, and institutions, must be studied if at all in the laboratory of community life.
> (1925, p. 47)

For Louis Wirth, 'the ghetto' was a 'laboratory specimen' (1928, p. 287; see Gieryn, 2006). A position that was underscored by Chicago professor William F. Ogburn in his American Sociological Society presidential address of 1929:

> Sociology as a science is not interested in making the world a better place in which to live, in encouraging beliefs, in spreading information, in dispensing news, in setting forth impressions of life, in leading the multitudes, or in guiding the ship of state. Science is interested directly in one thing only, to wit, discovering new knowledge.

This contrasts with that of the early university sociologists and of Jane Addams and her colleagues at Hull House.

HUMAN ECOLOGY

Robert Park's 'tramping about in cities' was to make him think of 'the city, the community and the region, not as a geographical phenomenon merely but as a kind of social organism' (1952 ed, p. 1). The study of this was termed 'human ecology': an 'attempt to apply to the interrelations of human beings a type of analysis previously applied to the interrelations of plants and animals' (Park, 1936, p. 1).[20] For it is 'not man, but the community; not man's relation to the earth which he inhabits, but his relations to other men, that concerns us most' (Park, 1952 ed, p. 165). The city is characterised by symbiotic relationships of mutual interdependence and an inter-relationship that is complex: 'every community has something of the character of an organic unit. It has a more or less definite structure and it has a life history in which juvenile, adult and senile phases can be observed', it is a 'superorganism' (Park, 1936, p. 4). This 'superorganism' was 'an amalgamation of a series of subpopulations differentiated either by race, ethnicity, income group or spatial factors' (Hayward, 2001, p. 31). The balance of communities could change for, like plant and animal communities, they were affected by 'processes of competition, invasion, succession and segregation' (Park et al, 1925, p. 145), and it is in studying these 'processes' that we begin to understand their impact on human behaviours, including criminality. If we think back to the start of this chapter and the discussion of the development of the 'modern' city, the comment of Vold et al on how this process can be related to colonised countries has an obvious resonance: for 'the history of America is a process of invasion, dominance, and succession by Europeans into the territory of Native Americans' (2001, p. 119).

THE CONCENTRIC ZONES MAP OF THE CITY

Following on from Park's analysis, his colleague Ernest Burgess was to explore how cities come to be spatially organised. Burgess was responsible for what Mike Davis described as 'the most famous diagram in social science' (1998,

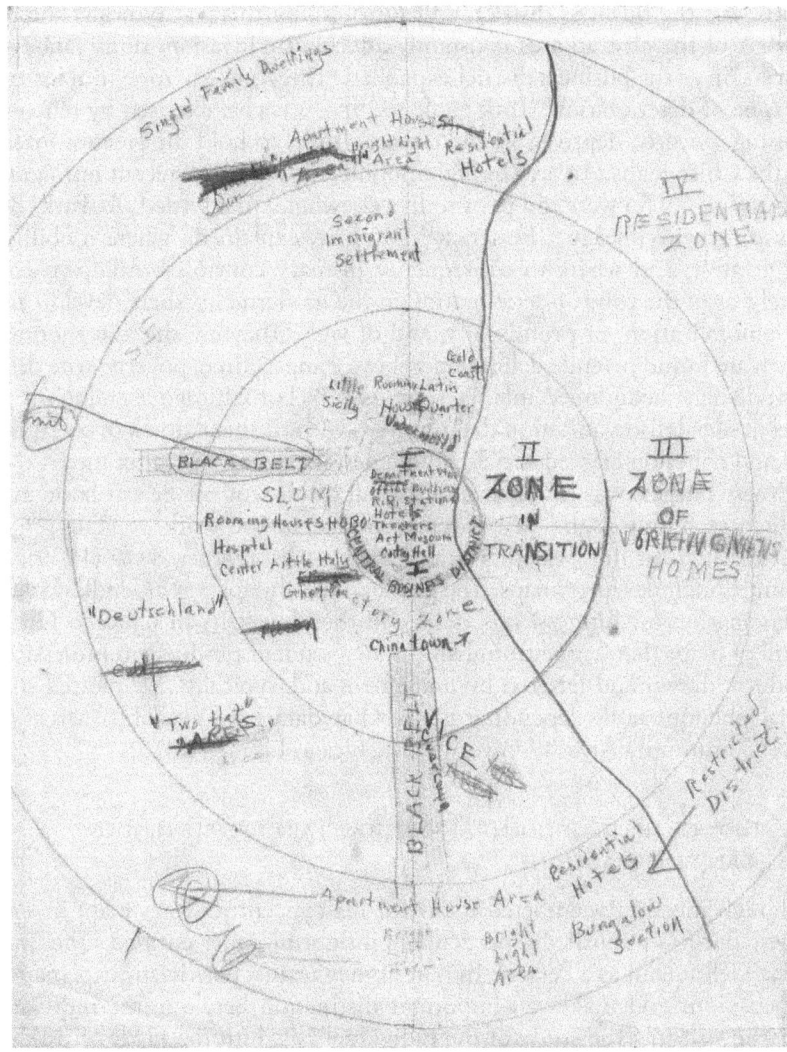

Figure 4.2 Map of the radial expansion and the five urban zones, this hand-drawn map is believed to be the earliest illustration of the concentric zones model developed by Ernest Burgess. Ernest Watson Burgess Papers, University of Chicago.

p. 364): the concentric zones map of the city. First published in the *Proceedings of the American Sociological Society* in 1923, Burgess suggested the city did not just grow at its edges but rather tended to expand from its centre in a series of concentric patterns, or 'zones', that resemble a bull's eye. The city's expansion was the result of the invasion of each zone by the next one. At the centre was the business district, and surrounding this was typically the oldest part of the city, an area constantly affected by invasion, dominance and succession as the business district expanded. This zone – a 'zone in transition' or 'zone of deterioration' (Park et al, 1925) – was characterised by tenement housing, poverty, deprivation and disease. It was to hold the greatest interest for the Chicagoans. An area of high mobility, it was where recent immigrants into the city, who were too poor to live elsewhere, first settled. As Park, Burgess and their colleague, Roderick McKenzie, explained, 'where mobility is the greatest, and where in consequence primary controls breakdown completely, as in the zone of deterioration in the modern city, there develop areas of demoralization, of promiscuity, and of vice'. They are the 'the regions in which are found juvenile delinquency, boys' gangs, crime, poverty, wife desertion, divorce, abandoned infants' (*ibid*, p. 59). For Chicago sociologists, the level of social disorganisation that occurred with the breakdown of social control and cohesion created social pathologies, including that of crime.

Ernest Burgess was to make sure that all of his students learnt basic mapmaking techniques, and maps were included in the work of many of the Chicago men in this period. Clifford Shaw's *Delinquency Areas* (1929), for example, includes forty maps. The production of maps was an endless source of fascination for Burgess. His archive in the University of Chicago Library is full of maps that 'range from hand-drawn student products to professional products drawn and lettered by draftsmen' and 'typically . . . plotted some social phenomenon, depending upon what data were available, across the city's Community Areas' (University of Chicago Library, 2015).

THE STUDY OF THE DELINQUENT AS A PERSON: 'I AIN'T FEEBLE-MINDED; I JUST CAN'T DO FRACTIONS'

Although mostly remembered today for his concentric zones map, in 1923 Ernest Burgess published a particularly insightful paper entitled 'The Study of the Delinquent as a Person'. In it he argues against positivistic explanations of behaviour and makes an important distinction between 'the individual' and 'the person'. The study of the individual falls into the fields of psychology and psychiatry and is 'of the reaction of the organism to its environment' (p. 662) and focuses on 'certain traits' (p. 665). The person is the 'product of social interaction with his fellows' (*ibid*), and this is the concern of sociology. He uses the case of a boy called George to elaborate on this distinction. George is struggling with mathematics, 'an individual handicap', and this 'gets its meaning in its effect upon the status of the boy in his social group' (p. 663). Burgess includes a lovely quotation from George in which he objects to being labelled 'feeble-minded': ' "They put me in the feeble-minded room", he said, "and I ain't feeble-minded; I just can't do fractions" ' (*ibid*). Burgess writes movingly of the impact of 'loss of status' on a person – 'the collapse of one's social world', which is 'perhaps the greatest catastrophe in the life of the person' (p. 677). Burgess concludes, 'the criminal . . . is first of all a person, and second a criminal' (p. 680). Considering the influence that physiological approaches had on criminology, the labelling of those who were poor or criminal as 'mentally defective' or 'incorrigible' or both – and the implications of this in terms of 'othering' and 'dehumanisation' – and the slippery slope to eugenicist arguments, Burgess's 'study of the delinquent as a person' is extraordinary for this time.

SOCIAL DISORGANISATION

Clifford Shaw and Henry McKay, students of Park and Burgess in the 1920s, were to work extensively on juvenile delinquency. They sought to test Burgess's theory that crime was greater in areas of disorganisation by mapping juvenile delinquency court data onto the concentric zone model. They found that delinquency rates were, indeed, greatest in the zone of transition and declined with increasing distance from the city centre as neighbourhoods became more affluent. Socially disorganised neighbourhoods, they found, tended to create and support delinquent behaviour, contrasting with more stable, socially cohesive neighbourhoods, i.e. those characterised by lower levels of mobility. Shaw and McKay further argued that socially disorganised neighbourhoods led to situations which encouraged the cultural transmission of 'criminal values' (Lilly et al, 2007, p. 39). Delinquent values, they argued, are 'transmitted down through successive generations of boys, in much the same way that language and other social forms are transmitted' (Shaw and McKay, 1942, p. 166).

Clifford Shaw, also author of *The Jack Roller* (1930), a life history of a 'delinquent Chicago boy', was well known for the sensitivity of his research and for 'the kindness and generosity' with which he treated his subjects (Snodgrass, 1976, p. 8), putting him at odds with those who encouraged detachment and scientific objectivity. Some of the 'delinquents' became close friends of his: one remembered, 'we were such good friends, I'm sure if hell is a bad place, Shaw will send me a message' (cited in Snodgrass, 1976, p. 8).

DIFFERENTIAL ASSOCIATION

Edwin Sutherland, first taught by Annie Marion McLean and then Charles Henderson, was to develop the idea of social disorganisation and tie it to Shaw and McKay's perspective on the intergenerational transmission of delinquent values. Noting that social disorganisation was 'one of the best of explanations of [high] crime rates', he suggested that the term 'differential social organization' was more apt, for

> A group may be organized for criminal behavior or organized against criminal behavior. Most communities are organized for both criminal

and anti-criminal behavior, and in that sense the crime rate is an expression of the differential group organization.

(Sutherland and Cressey, 1966, p. 77)

Following on from this, Sutherland coined the term 'differential association' to explain how crime is learned through social interaction: 'differential group organization as an explanation of variations in crime rates is consistent with the differential association theory of the processes by which persons become criminals' (*ibid*, p. 77). As Lilly et al (2007) explain, inner-city areas experience 'culture conflict', with two different cultures, the criminal and the conventional, competing for the support of those who live there. A person therefore 'becomes delinquent because of an excess of definitions favorable to violation of the law over definitions unfavorable to the violation of the law', and 'this is the principle of differential association' (Sutherland and Cressey, 1966, p. 75). Sutherland was responsible for one of the first textbooks in criminology, *Principles of Criminology*.[21] Originally published in 1924, this went to several editions and was extensively revised as the discipline developed. Although a prolific scholar, Sutherland's most critically acclaimed publications are *The Professional Thief* (1937), written while at Chicago, and *White Collar Crime* (1949). As Ken Plummer shows in his critical assessment of the Chicago School, the work of the Park and Burgess years helped to inform the next generation of sociological and criminological thought (see, 1997, p. 18).

CRITIQUING THE PARK AND BURGESS YEARS

The writing of the men of the Chicago School of Sociology has over the years been extensively debated and critiqued.

GENDER, CLASS AND POWER

Whereas men in the early Chicago years studied women, albeit often from a biologically deterministic perspective or without recognition of women's socio-economic situation, Robert Park did not study women and was known for his sexist treatment of women academics (Deegan, 1988). His students were, likewise, neglectful when it came to researching women (*ibid*). Their concern was largely with the male delinquent.

Moreover, as Lilly et al point out, there is 'a tendency for this strand of Chicago sociology to present 'the spatial distribution of groups in the city as a "natural" social process' (2007, p. 44), when exploring the downside to urban growth, e.g. criminality. In so doing, and through affording scant attention to how criminal culture originated in the first place, they serve to divert attention from the role that class domination and power 'can play in creating and perpetuating slums and the enormous economic inequality that pervades urban areas' (*ibid*).

Critics of Shaw and McKay have noted that they took 'social disorganization' for granted and were overly concerned with the internal conditions of disorganised areas (Snodgrass, 1976). Hence, when they did venture into policy with the Chicago Area Project (CAP), their focus was on the inner workings of the communities and the development of short-term intervention, typically centring on how to improve behaviour in 'problem' areas. Their emphasis, as John Snodgrass illustrates, was on 'self-help from within' (*ibid*, p. 15) and thus 'was not addressed to broader types of social action and in particular did not seek to deal directly with the forces destroying and disorganizing the community' (*ibid*). Snodgrass contends that

> some of the procedures of the CAP are uncomfortably reminiscent of the coercive techniques commonly associated with authoritarian political regimes; for instance taking down the names and addresses of all the boys in an area and organizing block councils in order 'to have little groups of neighbours living in the same block who can meet with us when a boy gets into difficulty and thus bring to bear upon that case some public disapproval of his act'.
>
> (*ibid*, p. 17)

The aim of CAP was not to change the political and economic conditions of those living in 'slums' but to 'force individuals to adapt to American society' (*ibid*).

Further, Thomas Gieryn (2006) contrasts the urban sociology of Park and Burgess et al to that of the more recent L.A. School, as represented by the work of Mike Davis, Michael J. Dear, Allen J. Scott and Edward Soja. For them, the city is a contested space: it is not just somewhere to observe but is 'a place for everybody . . . to struggle over . . . a contested terrain, where groups with competing interests and varying amounts of terrain fight to win control over defining the place' (*ibid*, p. 27). Theirs is not a 'pre-political neutrality', as typified by Chicago's laboratory model, for 'blame is squarely placed on powerful evil-doers who somehow manage to benefit from the chaos' of the city (*ibid*). Hence, Mike Davis (2002) 'describes developers as "criminal", banks plot to "rob the world", the energy sector lusts after "superprofits" and even worries about the natural environment becom(ing) a "hypocritical attempt by the rich to use ecology to detour Vietnam-era growth in their luxury enclaves"' (Gieryn, 2006, p. 27). The L.A. school, Gieryn argues, is about 'immediate activism and mobilized resistance', being on the side of the 'have-nots': Davis 'courts the have-nots (and those more advantaged audiences who sympathize with their plight)' (*ibid*, p. 27). The message conveyed is that 'we are on your side, comrades in arms' (*ibid*, p. 27).

The Hull House settlement

The Hull House settlement was located at the corner of Polk and Halsted streets, an impoverished neighbourhood of Chicago. Populated by many recent immigrants to the United States: Irish, Germans, Bohemians, Italians, Greeks, Poles, Russian Jews and Mexicans, it must have seemed a world apart from the university. Lloyd Lewis recalls that 'aristocratic friends, members of the old Yankee ruling class of the city, had advised Jane Addams not to make this plunge into the slums. They said it would make her unacceptable in the homes of the "best people"' (1940, p. 110). If anything, such advice – with its transparent class prejudice – would make Addams and Starr more determined to make a success of the settlement.

Addams and Starr modelled Hull House on the famous Toynbee Hall settlement in the East End of London, which Addams visited while on a trip to Europe with Starr. Toynbee Hall was the idea of Samuel Barnett, a Church of England vicar, and his wife, Henrietta, who had come to the realisation that long-term social change could not be achieved by the individualised, frequently haphazard philanthropy that was in place (Toynbee Hall, 2018). Their aim was to bring privileged, educated, young people to 'reside in the poorer quarter of London for the sake of influencing the people there toward better local government and a wider social and intellectual life' (Addams, 1895, p. 9). The Barnetts believed that if the 'haves' lived in close proximity to the 'have-nots' in settlements that this would serve as a bridge between the classes, encouraging understanding and, given fears over the potential for class conflict, would promote a more harmonious society. 'Distance', Samuel Barnett said, 'made friendship between the classes impossible' (Barnett, 1919, p. 307). Associates of Toynbee Hall included Beatrice Webb, Charles Booth and Clement Attlee, who was to go on to become prime minster in 1945. Significantly, Charles Booth and the residents of Toynbee Hall, including Beatrice Webb (then Potter), who was his cousin, resolved not only to help the impoverished classes (poverty for him was 'the problem of all problems')[22] but also to survey London's poverty and map its extent. For Booth – as was to be the case for Jane Addams and her colleagues – the acquiring of social information was the first stage towards its resolution (Bales, 1999). The first survey was completed in 1886. Its findings and maps of London's poverty were published in *Life and Labour of the People in London*, which eventually went into seventeen volumes. As it has been pointed out, the mapping of the social environment became increasingly popular in the nineteenth century, with the first crime maps attributed to A-M Guerry and Adriano Balbi in 1829, followed by Adolphe Quetelet in 1832 and Henry Mayhew's of London in the 1860s (see Bales, 1999; Friendly, 2007). Booth's work was to exert the most influence on the residents of Hull House.

To a large extent Jane Addams reflected the views of the Progressive era in which she lived: a period in U.S. history which dated from the late 1800s to the 1920s. As Lilly et al note, Progressives 'were critical of the human costs wrought by America's unbridled industrial growth' and were troubled by the situation of the urban poor' (2008, p. 41). It was blatantly obvious that not all segments of society were benefitting from the 'new' America. Many families were suffering from the harsh realities of poverty, starvation, 'slum' accommodation, child labour, exploitation in the sweatshops, corruption in government and business and racial prejudice. As was previously indicated by Katharine Bement Davis's address to the National Prison Association in 1905 and the perspective of Frances Kellor, Progressives believed that 'the poor were pushed by their environment – not born – into lives of crime' (*ibid*, p. 35). The fault was largely placed on the prevailing economic conditions that created gross disparities in wealth: the Rockefellers, Carnegies and the Vanderbilts had amassed huge fortunes on the backs of the labouring poor. The present situation, as Jane Addams said, amounted to a 'social crime' (1895, p. 139).

Addams, however, was no revolutionary. Progressives were reformists, wanting to affect change but within the existing social order. For Addams, the settlement was an effort 'to add the social function to democracy' (1892, p. 1). It prevented the labour movement from degenerating into class war. As she argued, 'a class working for a class, and against another class, implies that within itself there should be trades working for trades, individuals working for individuals', and once this happens 'the universal character of the movement is gone from the start' (1895, p. 148). However, while not quite a 'comrade in arms' to Chicago's have-nots, she certainly was on their side. Politically her views were akin to those of Samuel Barnett and the Fabian socialism of Beatrice and Sidney Webb. Yet probably as a result of the leftish intellectual climate provided by Hull House and some of its visitors, together with the level of activism that was engaged in on behalf of the poor,

> [T]here was always to be heard a protest – sometimes a blast, sometimes a growl – about their perilous fostering of radicalism. That certain reactionaries always wanted 'to run Jane Addams out of town' was true from 1889 till her death in 1935.
>
> (Lewis, 1940, p. 13)

Addams's support of Abraham Isaak, the editor of an anarchist newspaper, and other anarchists rounded up following the 1901 assassination of President William McKinley in all likelihood fuelled this perception. Hull House was denounced as a 'hot-bed' of anarchism, stones were thrown at its windows and she received hundreds of abusive letters, which, she said, 'made my mail a horror every morning' (cited in Knight, 2010, p. 120).

Theory and practice

In *Sociology and Pragmatism*, C. Wright Mills writes on John Dewey's perspective that ' "Social theory" must not be "an idle luxury" but a "guiding method of inquiry and planning" ' (1964, p. 432). Mills's statement could easily be applied to Jane Addams, who was close to Dewey, himself one of the trustees of Hull House. Dewey's daughter Jane, named after Addams, said his 'faith in democracy as a guiding force in education took on shape and a deeper meaning because of Hull House and Jane Addams' (cited in Mills, 1964, p. 307). In her article 'A Function of the Social Settlement', Jane Addams quotes Dewey at length in support of her belief on the importance of using sociological knowledge for social action: 'knowledge is no longer its own justification, the interest in it has at last transferred itself from accumulation and verification to its application to life' (1899, p. 324).

Mary Jo Deegan has shown how Addams and her settlement colleagues, together with women such as Annie Marion MacLean, built on the work of John Dewey and the other Chicago pragmatists, most notably G.H. Mead, who dominated the early years of Chicago sociology, to create a feminist pragmatism. Deegan defines feminist pragmatism as 'an American theory uniting liberal values and a belief in a rational public with a cooperative, nurturing, and liberating model of the self, the other, and the community', with education and democracy emphasised 'as significant, nonviolent mechanisms to organize and improve society' (2014, p. 59). For Addams, people sharing the same neighbourhood develop a shared experience. The self emerges from communication with others (*ibid*). For Addams 'life can be learned only through experience and social life, only though interactive participation in society' (Lengermann and Niebrugge-Brantley, 1998, p. 75). The 'modern' city, however, presented an alien environment for many of its inhabitants: its transient nature; the lack of familial, social and community ties; and the level that work and hardship made it difficult to make and maintain friendships and support networks, resulted in anonymity, loneliness and depression. Not surprisingly, for Addams, boys found solace in the companionship of gangs, while others ended up defeated or slid into lives of criminality, prostitution or alcoholism, as 'no one can safely live without companionship and affection' (1911, p. 34).

The current era, Addams argued, necessitated a 'social ethic': that people 'must learn to identify their interests with the common good, and the common good must be defined so as to recognize an injury to one is an injury to all' (Lengermann and Niebrugge-Brantley, 1998, p. 74). Feminist pragmatism provided the foundation for the development of the 'social justice maternalism' from which the notion of the modern welfare state developed (Deegan, 2014; Oakley, 2017). Further, at the centre of Addams's concept of the 'self' is the notion of human agency. As Lengermann and Niebrugge-Brantley state, she 'understands the individual social being as an embodied, agentic subjectivity motivated by interests and ethics' (1998, p. 78) and is dismissive of the idea of the individual as socially determined. The individual is 'willful, desirous, irrepressible', and 'the capacity of the individual to hold to her or his purposes even in the most repressive or degrading circumstances is an object of wonder to her' (*ibid*, p. 85, 78).

Addams and her settlement colleagues were to reject the University's conception of the 'laboratory', although those at the university sometimes described the settlement as a 'social laboratory' – partly as a result of its location. She was fearful of the University swallowing the settlement and turning 'it into one more laboratory: another place in which to analyze and depict, to observe and record' (1899, p. 47).[23] For Addams and her associates at Hull House, research was not to be carried out for its own sake. Research was for the betterment of society. As Agnes Sinclair Holbrook wrote,

> insistent probing into the lives of the poor . . . and the personal impertinence of many of the questions asked, would be unendurable and unpardonable were it not for the conviction that the public conscience when roused must demand better surroundings for the most . . . long-suffering citizens of the commonwealth.
>
> (1895, pp. 13–14)

People and their neighbourhoods should not be treated merely as research objects, with little concern for their well-being. As Michael Hill notes, Addams considered Hull House's visitors neighbours, never to be seen as 'guinea pigs, lab rats or impersonal others' (2005, p. 93). Research was to arise out of the experience of being immersed in neighbourhoods. The importance of doing this was underscored by one settlement worker, who wrote, 'from the settlement I have gained that subtle, interpretative method of dealing with facts which I believe can only come by steeping one's self in the standards, manners, and customs of races, and by entering into the community life of a neighborhood' (Richmond, 1917, p. 300).

A women-centred approach

Moreover, Addams's sociological thought was women-centred. It reflects a concern with the lives of women – as domestics, factory workers, sweatshop workers, charity workers, housewives, mothers (Lengermann and Niebrugge-Brantley, 1998). This leads her to write forcefully of the difficulties facing women, especially when torn between the need to earn a wage and the responsibilities of being a mother.

> I cannot recall without indignation a recent experience. I was detained late one evening in an office building by a prolonged committee meeting

of the Board of Education. As I came out at eleven o'clock, I met in the corridor of the fourteenth floor a woman whom I knew, on her knees scrubbing the marble tiling. As she straightened up to greet me, she seemed so wet from her feet up to her chin, that I hastily inquired the cause. Her reply was that she left home at five o'clock every night and had no opportunity for six hours to nurse her baby. Her mother's milk mingled with the very water with which she scrubbed the floors until she should return at midnight, heated and exhausted, to feed her screaming child with what remained within her breasts.

(1910a, p. 345)

In 'If Men Were Seeking the Franchise' (1913) Addams notes how women, particularly poor women, are both devalued and powerless in 'every man-ruled city'. Presenting arguments similar to those of Josephine Butler (1896) in England, she points out how easy it is for a 'homeless young girl looking for lodging to be arrested for soliciting the streets', subject to 'harassing questions' and medical examinations. That women who are seeking their living as prostitutes find themselves 'set aside as outcasts', whereas their male clients are never arrested, nor indeed are they even considered lawbreakers (1913, 2002, p. 233).[24]

For Addams, the level of devaluation experienced by women in a male-dominated world renders them vulnerable to economic exploitation and abuse. If change is to occur, values associated with 'femininity' – nurturing, homemaking, peace making, communication and cooperation – needed to be elevated. 'Masculinity' – associated with militarism, war, violence and domination – threatened to damage the fabric of society. 'Justice', Addams argues, 'between men or between nations can be achieved only through understanding and fellowship, and that a finely tempered sense of justice, which alone is of any service in modern civilization, cannot possibly be secured in the storm and stress of war' (1922, p. 4). Hence, she was to declare herself a pacifist and opposed U.S. entry into World War I, resulting in her being included in Archibald Stevenson's 'traitors list' of individuals holding 'dangerous, destructive, and anarchistic sentiments'. Addams's meetings with soldiers showed there was nothing essentialist in the act of violence. Indeed, she controversially declared that the only way young men in war were able to overcome their revulsion about what they were doing was because they were 'given stimulants' (1915, 2002 ed, p. 339). It was, Addams felt, women who could change things and 'defend those at the bottom of society who, irrespective of the victory or defeat of any army, are ever oppressed and overburdened' (*ibid*, p. 351).

Hull House Maps and Papers by the Residents of Hull House

Hull House Maps and Papers: A Presentation of Nationalities and Wages in a Congested District of Chicago Together with Comments and Essays on the Problems Growing Out of the Social Conditions, to give the project its full title, was published in 1895. Deegan suggests it is *Hull House Maps and Papers* (*HHMP*) that 'established the Chicago tradition of studying the city and its inhabitants' (1988 ed, p. 55). It is 'one of the classics of social science' (Fink, 1997, p. 18). Largely directed by Florence Kelley, it adapted Charles Booth's methods to map the wages and nationalities of the area around Hull House: it was therefore the Hull House residents who pioneered the mapping techniques usually associated with Park, Burgess and their students (see Bursik, 2009).

The essays included in *HHMP* are on, for example, 'The Sweating System', 'Wage Earning Children', 'The Bohemian People in Chicago', 'Art and Labour' and Jane Addams's 'The Settlement as a Factor in the Labor Movement'. Kelley's on 'The Sweating System' and 'Wage Earning Children' (with Alzina Stevens) provide a blunt indictment of the impact of industrial capitalism. It is of interest that Kelley communicated with Friedrich Engels throughout the *HHMP* project. 'Wage Earning Children' documents the abuse of children in the factories or when working as newsboys and bootblacks and the case of the young girl who worked until midnight for one of 'the best known candy stores', forced to walk home 'across the worst district of Chicago' to her 'terrified mother at one o'clock on Christmas morning' (1895, p. 77). The lack of recognition given to *HHMP*, and the subsequent research and mapping by Hull House, by Park and Burgess and the men of the Chicago School has been described by Deegan as amounting to 'academic dishonesty' (1988 ed, p.46).

Improving social conditions

The aim of Hull House, as stated in its incorporation papers, was 'to provide a center for a higher social life: to institute and maintain educational and philanthropic enterprises, and to investigate and improve the conditions in the industrial districts of Chicago' (Lewis, 1940, p. 110). The residents ran children's clubs, free kindergartens, a penny savings bank, a lodging house and an employment bureau, as well as teaching courses in literature, music and painting. They were responsive to the needs of the local community: as Addams wrote in *Twenty Years at Hull House*,

> We early found ourselves spending many hours in efforts to secure support for deserted women, insurance for bewildered widows, damages for injured operators, furniture from the clutches of the installment store. The settlement is valuable as an information and interpretation bureau. It constantly acts between the various institutions of the city and the people for whose benefit these situations were erected. . . . From the first it seemed understood that we were asked to perform the humblest neighborhood services. We were asked to wash new-born babies, to prepare the dead for burial, to nurse the sick, and to 'mind the children'.
> (1911, p. 167, 109)

Certainly, they were not afraid to get the 'seat of their pants dirty' in direct action: Ellen Gates Starr found herself 'locked up' for 'disorderly conduct' whilst supporting, 'arm-in-arm', striking women garment workers (*The New York Times*, 3 March 1914).

On a wider level, those associated with Hull House amount to 'a veritable Who's Who of American reform' (Elshtain, 2002, p. xxvi). Florence Kelley, who had gone to Hull House to escape an unhappy marriage, became the chief factory inspector of Illinois and then went on to become the secretary of the National Consumers League.[25] Alice Hamilton presided over medical matters and became a pioneer in investigating health and safety in the workplace and industrial diseases. Grace Abbott was the first head of the Immigrants Protection League. Julia Lathrop was the major lobbyist behind the establishing of the first juvenile court, Cook County Juvenile Court. She went on to become chief of the U.S. Children's Bureau, appointed by President Taft. Sophonisba Breckinridge, born into a family of social reformers, took on a number of roles: for example, city health inspector and probation officer for the juvenile court. She also helped to found the Chicago School of Civics and Philanthropy for the education of social workers (Lengermann and Niebrugge-Brantley, 1998). Jean Bethke Elshtain comments that Jane Addams and Hull House's significance were such that 'nearly every piece of major reform in the years 1895–1930 comes with Jane Addams's name attached in one way or another' (2002, p. xxv).

Crime policy

Both Lathrop and Addams were motivated by their horror of children and teenagers ending up in prison; some they found were as young as 9 years old (Lathrop, 1912). They argued for a separate system, to have a 'kindly concern for the young' and for them not to be labelled as 'criminals'. Hence, one of the first judges at Cook County Juvenile Court, Richard Tuthill, stated, 'kindness and love for the children must be used in this work' (Grossman, 2014). The idea, as Ron Grossman wrote, 'that a juvenile court could be more like a parent than a prosecutor was revolutionary' (*ibid*) and should make us reflect on the current U.S. penal system that still tries children as adults. In 1909 Addams was appointed the first woman president of the National Conference of Charities and Corrections. On many occasions she expressed her displeasure at the savagery of punishment and revenge that characterised the criminal justice system. She pointed out that the United States spends more dollars 'on its policemen, courts and prisons than upon all its works of religion, charity and education' and if some of this money was re-directed to help those in need when they are young, it 'might save the State thousands of dollars and the man untold horrors' (1913, 2002 ed, p. 232). This is similar to arguments that are heard today over the excessive cost of the prison system and the level to which it destroys lives, especially young people's lives.

Painting a rosy picture?

However, again, we must be cautious of presenting too rosy a picture. It is questionable how far these mostly privileged women managed to bridge the gap between themselves and their neighbours. Treviño and McCormack (2016) document that the doors of Hull House were initially closed for the summer so that Starr and Addams could leave the heat of Chicago and visit friends and family. Of course, no such respite was available for their neighbours. On meeting her hero Tolstoy in Russia in 1896, Jane Addams was forced to confront the ambiguous relationship between her socio-economic position and her work in Chicago. She relates that Tolstoy asked of her,

> [W]ho 'fed' me, and how did I obtain 'shelter'? Upon my reply that a farm a hundred miles from Chicago supplied me with the necessities of life, I fairly anticipated the next scathing question (from Tolstoy): 'So you are an absentee landlord? Do you think you will help the people more by adding yourself to the crowded city than you would by tilling your own soil?'
>
> (1911, p. 268)

There was no getting away from the fact that the women of Hull House were largely women of privilege and it was this that allowed them to *choose* a life of living amongst the poor. Tony Platt (1969) has been particularly disparaging of their legacy, especially the founding of the juvenile court system. Describing them as 'child savers', he wrote that their work resulted in measures to control the urban poor: they 'helped to create special judicial and correctional institutions for the labeling, processing, and management of "troublesome" youth' and, 'in doing so, (they) invented . . . new categories of youthful misbehaviour' (*ibid*, pp. 3–4).

Never far from controversy, in 1901 Jane Addams was to attract the criticism of Ida B. Wells. Addams had published an anti-lynching piece in the *New York Independent*, writing forcefully against the brutality and cruelty of the lynching of African Americans and, in keeping with her general line on the impact of bodily punishment on the populace, how severe punishment leads to further violence. Despite acknowledging Addams's 'good intentions', Wells (1901) exposed her 'unfortunate presumption' that lynching had occurred in response to 'criminal acts'. Wells, by reprinting public records from the *Chicago Daily Tribune* on the allegations that prompted lynching, illustrated that the majority of these so-called criminal acts were completely fabricated. Addams was thus guilty of the 'perpetuation of a racist myth' (Hamington, 2005, p. 168). The realisation of this must have caused both disquiet and disappointment – given that by most accounts Wells and Addams appear to have been close, working on a number of projects together.[26]

Hull House, as previously implied, opened its doors to a wide range of leftists, but their intention was not to 'rock the boat' in terms of overthrowing the prevailing class arrangements, but to achieve more parity within the existing social order. This may be the reason why, as Schultz notes, 'there are . . . none of the voices of the protesting socialists, anarchists and trade unionists who were already rising in anger against their conditions' (2007, p. 32) in *HHMP*. It is also possible that to be seen as too 'revolutionary' may have resulted in a backlash against the work that they were trying to do in the Polk and Halsted neighbourhood.

Contributing to an intellectual climate

The level that Hull House was dismissed at the time (and is often not given full credit for its work and insights today) is in keeping with the level of sexism within the academy and the wider political culture.[27] Burgess described their research as 'little more than the discovery and reporting to the public that the feelings and sentiments of those living in the slums were, in reality, quite different to those imputed to them by the public' (1964, p. 5).[28] Park suggested it was 'practical rather than theoretic' and that they simply 'created a new and romantic interest in the slum' (1974, cited in Deegan, 1988, p. 65).[29] Perhaps even worse, President Theodore Roosevelt referred to Addams as 'poor bleeding Jane' and 'a progressive mouse' (cited by Curti, 1961, p. 240). Such characterisations are clearly unjust and incorrect. As this chapter has shown, the work of Jane Addams and Hull House contributed to the 'explosion of ideas' that are representative of the Chicago School of Sociology. Addams was a member of the ASS from its start in 1895, contributing numerous articles to the *American Journal of Sociology* (including in its first volume a piece entitled 'A Belated Industry' (1896), which dealt with domestic labour). She was the author of nine books concerned with sociological theory and analysis (Lengermann and Niebrugge-Brantley, 1998). And although no women held the highest offices of the ASS/ASA from 1906 to 1931, 'eight women did hold elected positions on the executive committee, and they all engaged in work influenced by Jane Addams' (Deegan, 1981, p. 18). In contrasting the intellectual concerns of Hull House to those of the Park and Burgess years, it is possible to identify what have become some of the core components of a feminist research methodology and that of the approach of critical criminology. The need to treat the 'researched' as human beings and for research to be linked to social action has, for example, been shown to be of utmost importance. The start of a split between mainstream sociology and that which is more focused on advancing social change also becomes evident in this period. Further, scholarship has demonstrated the relevance of Addams's emphasis on justice, participation, community, cooperation, respect and trust to the more recent development of peace-making criminology (Frey, 2007).

Achieving a better tomorrow?

Finally, the work of Hull House makes us think about how we can achieve a better world and the role of intellectuals and the academy in trying to make this happen. For Jane Addams it is essential to keep moving forward:

> It is as though we thirsted to drink at the great wells of human experience, because we knew that a daintier or less potent draught would not carry us to the end of the journey, going forward as we must in the heat and jostle of the crowd.
>
> (Addams, 1902, 2002, p. 9)

Yet at the same time it underscores the limitations of a reformist approach to social problems. For many of the issues that Jane Addams and her colleagues were concerned with remain with us today. Henry Steele Commager, in his forward to the 1961 edition of *Twenty Years at Hull House*, compared Jane Addams to Alice with the Red Queen in Lewis Carroll's *Through the Looking Glass*:

> More and more [Addams] came to feel like Alice with the Red Queen: no matter how fast she ran, she was still in the same place; the poverty, the slums, the crime and vice, the misgovernment, the illiteracy, the exploitation, the inhumanity of man to man – all these were still there.
>
> (p. xvi, cited in Schneiderhan, 2011)

Commager's observation remains relevant today. We must continue to pose the question: how far have we come? As Nancy Fraser pointed out in *Justice Interruptus* (1997), reform that focuses on the surface transfer of resources in a 'Band-Aid' fashion will only result in superficial changes. For example, the transfer of resources from the employed to the unemployed by housing subsidies or welfare payments, without changing the relationship of class, does not lead to long-term change and, in fact, simply reaffirms the division between the classes. The realisation that social problems are embedded within the social fabric and relate to structures of power is central to much of radical politics. However, the question of what fundamental changes are needed to ultimately transform the situation of injustice that confronts us is both complex and contested. The next chapter further explores the development of sociological criminology through the work of Durkheim, Du Bois, Merton and Tannenbaum – these theorists, though in differing ways, were concerned with the manifestation and impact of power within the existing social order and how social inequality is experienced, and helped advance the conversation on how social justice could be achieved. And, as we will see in the final chapters, strands of radical feminism and critical criminology – the latter having largely emerged from early sociological theories – were to focus on the pursuit of transformative remedies in order to affect change at the level of the social structure.

Notes

1 The 1893 World's Columbian Exposition is a site of controversy for its emphasis on the achievements of the Industrial Revolution, Western 'civilisation', endorsement of consumption and its displays of the natives of other lands as curiosities and primitive (Rothstein, 2013). Its celebration of America excluded African Americans, which led Ida B. Wells, Frederick Douglas, Ferdinand Lee Barnett and Robert W. Rydell to write the protest pamphlet, *The Reason Why the Colored American is not in the World's Columbian Exhibition*. In the preface Wells wrote:

> The exhibit of the progress made by a race in 25 years of freedom as against 250 years of slavery, would have been the greatest tribute to the greatness and progressiveness of American institutions which could have been shown the world. The colored people of this great Republic number eight million – more than one-tenth the whole population of the United States. They were among the earliest settlers of this continent, landing at Jamestown, Virginia in 1619 in a slave ship, before the Puritans, who landed at Plymouth in 1620. They have contributed a large share to American prosperity and civilization. The labor of one-half of this country has always been, and is still being done by them. The first credit this country had in its commerce with foreign nations was created by productions resulting from their labor. The wealth created by their industry has afforded to the white people of this country the leisure essential to their great progress in education, art, science, industry and invention.

> Those visitors to the World's Columbian Exposition who know these facts, especially foreigners will naturally ask: Why are not the colored people, who constitute so large an element of the American population, and who have contributed so large a share to American greatness, more visibly present and better represented in this World's Exposition? Why are they not taking part in this glorious celebration of the four-hundredth anniversary of the discovery of their country?(1893, p. 1)

In response fair officials agreed to a special day for African Americans, which for Wells and others, was little more than a token gesture – too late and not enough.

Moreover, the glossiness of the exhibition contrasted with the desperate poverty of many of Chicago's residents. The fair's president, Harlow Higinbotham, refused to give the poor waifs of the city a day's free admission, believing they would scare visitors away (Kasson, 2015, p. 102) and serving to underscore its elitism.

2 Charlotte Perkins Gilman arrived at Hull House as a guest of Jane Addams and they were to remain lifelong friends. She was in many ways a woman ahead of her time (see Lemert, 2000; Deegan and Podeschi, 2001). Whilst I am unable in this book to give consideration to her work, it should be noted that she pioneered ideas that we today associate with 'ecofeminism' and, as such, her insights are of relevance to current developments in green criminology.

3 Rockefeller's patronage continued: in December 1900, *The New York Times* reported on his generous 'Christmas gift' to the university of $1,500,000 to be made 'available immediately' (23 Dec. 1900, p. 13). According to C. Wright Mills, by 1919 Rockefeller had given over thirty four and half million dollars to the university (1964, p. 59). Rockefeller was to describe the university as 'the best investment I ever made' (Beam, 2008, p. 38).

4 Indeed, as Martin Bulmer notes, 'of the 40 presidents of the ASS, no less than 19 were either former graduate students or current or former staff of the University of Chicago, and in some cases two of these' (1984, p. 43).

5 This covers the first ten years of the University of Chicago.

6 By 1902 women were the majority of students elected to the Phi Beta Kappa honour society (The University of Chicago Library, ND).
7 Annie Marion MacLean was born on Prince Edward Island in 1869, moving to Nova Scotia as a child. She was the first Canadian to receive a PhD in sociology (Deegan, 2014).
8 See Deegan 2014.
9 The extension programme, involving correspondence courses, was devised by Harper to teach non-traditional students who would otherwise be prevented from advanced education (Fitzpatrick, 1990).
10 However, again, Henderson, like so many others, remains a problematic figure. Shaun Gabbidon, in his book *WEB Du Bois on Crime and Justice*, draws attention to Henderson's 1904 statement in which he argues,

> There could be no doubt that one of the most serious factors in crime statistics is found in the condition of the freedmen of African descent, both North and South. The causes are complex. The primary factor is racial inheritance, physical, mental inferiority, barbarism and slave ancestry and culture.
>
> (2017, p. 7)

11 While at the settlement in Philadelphia, Davis smashed all the windows of a condemned building in protest at the city's lack of action in remedying the housing situation.
12 Du Bois did not particularly take to settlement life: it involved, he said, living 'in the midst of poverty, and crime. Murder sat on our doorsteps, police were our government and philanthropy dropped in with periodic advice' (Du Bois, 1968, p. 195).
13 Letter from Katharine Bement Davis to W.E.B. Du Bois, 14 April 1924 at: http://credo.library.umass.edu/view/full/mums312-b024-i351.
14 According to Mary Jo Deegan (2003), Davis did not, in fact, study with Zueblin.
15 Although Katharine Bement Davis's work at Bedford Hills was generally praised, concerns were raised about the punishments inflicted on the women. Davis admitted to the use of solitary confinement: under her administration a disciplinary building was constructed with soundproof cells ('ice-box' doors), where women would sometimes be 'handcuffed to their cots' (*The New York Times*, 21 December 1919, p. 14). She also said that 'on one or two occasions I have personally superintended the washing out of a girl's mouth when she had persisted in using indecent language' and believed that '"dipping girls'" heads in water . . . was a proper form of punishment in certain cases' (*ibid*).
16 Whilst overseeing corrections for New York City, Davis was to come into contact with Frank Tannenbaum, who was incarcerated in Blackwell's Island penitentiary (see Chapter 6).
17 In 1915 Davis was named one of three most-noted women of America by the Panama-Pacific Exposition, the other two being Jane Addams and Zekia Nuttall, for her work on penal reform.
18 As Morris (2015) points out, Albion Small was to expose sociologists to the ideas of the leading eugenicist, Francis Galton, by publishing his paper, 'Eugenics, Its Scope and Aims', in the 1904 *American Journal of Sociology*. Galton's ideas were to reach an even wider sociological audience through the publication of his paper, 'Eugenics as a Science of Progress', in Park and Burgess's textbook, *Introduction to the Science of Sociology*, with sections of the book given over to the discussion of this 'new science' (1921, p. 144; Morris, 2015). Schwendinger and Schwendinger also refer to Small's commitment 'to a program of physical and moral "engineering" or "eugenics"' (1974, p. 234).
19 In Lee (2017) the controversy surrounding the source for this quotation is outlined. It is usually attributed to Howard Becker, a graduate student of Park's, not to be confused with Howard S. Becker, who was a Chicago graduate student in the late 1940s/1950s.
20 'Human ecology' was not a new concept. It appears in Small and Vincent (1894).
21 Later taken over by Donald Cressey but remained 'a direct extension of the work done by Professor Sutherland' (1966, p. v).

22 Although often attributed to Charles Booth, it is believed that his wife, Mary, came up with the phrase (Gay, 1994). Another example, of the failure to recognise the contribution of a woman.

23 In the 1970s/1980s 'laboratory' came to be associated with the controversial multi-factorial positivist research on family violence carried out at the University of New Hampshire under the directorship of Murray Straus. Their research unit was named the 'Family Research Laboratory', thus underscoring their belief in 'scientific objectivity' in the study of social problems – a notion that has been heavily critiqued by feminists, critical criminologists and left realists (see Mooney, 2000).

24 Jane Addams writes this in the third person – as the views of 'conscientious women responsible for the State in which life was considered of more value than wealth' (1913, p. 232).

25 See K. Kish Sklar (1995) *Florence Kelley and the Nation's Work*, New Haven and London: Yale University Press.

26 Recently, scholars have rightly pointed out that the racist phrases and attitudes that 'slipped' into Addams's writing should not be gently dismissed as a 'product of the time' (Barnett, 2018), especially given her alliance with the eugenicist movement.

27 Keith Hayward suggests that the reason for the neglect of Jane Addams and Hull House within the criminological canon – despite the spatial dimension of the work and use of mapping techniques – is the result of 'criminology's fascination with technology, in this case the scientism associated with the statistical methods of demography and human ecology as applied to the "city as social laboratory"' (2012, p. 444)

28 Given Burgess's later antipathy to Hull House, it is noteworthy that he wrote a poem, a eulogy, for Jane Addams after her death – reprinted in full in Deegan (2005 ed, p. 150) – in which he acknowledges Addams's influence and the intellectual climate provided by Hull House, writing,

> On one not-to-be-forgotten afternoon
>
> I heard you tell of Tolstoi and world peace
> Years after your dinner guest at Hull House. I.
> Tongue-tied and inarticulate, could not speak
> Of my love and reverence. We talked of many things.
> Great topics, but small to me in your presence.
> Lady of Hull House, hostess to the stranger.
> ...
> The world was drawn there, to see and talk with you.
> Peter Kropotkin. Altgeld. John Burns, Breshkovska.
> The high and low knocked and your door and entered.

It is interesting that three of the figures Burgess chose to cite were very much part of radical revolutionary politics of the later nineteenth century: Peter Kropotkin, Mme. Breshkovsky (one of the leaders of the Russian Revolution who Emma Goldman called 'Babushka' [Grandmother]) and John Burns, an English trade unionist who encouraged direct action against unemployment and was one of the leaders of the London Dock Strike. John Peter Altgeld was the first Democrat elected to the state of Illinois and was responsible for the appointment of Florence Kelley as chief factory inspector in Illinois to regulate the sweatshops in acknowledgement of the importance of Hull House's activist work (https://hullhouse.uic.edu/hull/urbanexp/).

29 Furthermore, in his 2008 American Society of Criminology address Robert Bursik points out how extraordinary it is that not a single reference is made to Jane Addams's 'highly relevant intergenerational research' in any of Clifford Shaw's life histories, which focused on the children of immigrants (2009, p. 12). Bursik proposes that, 'given the major influence his work had during the first half of the twentieth century', it is likely that Shaw's 'opinion

of Addams . . . may be at least partially responsible for her currently marginal status as a criminologist' (*ibid*). He observes that it is of interest that 'Shaw's office at the Institute for Juvenile Research was at worse only a 15-minute walk from Hull House' (*ibid*). Bursik also draws attention to the neglect of Ruth Shonle Cavan, a student of Ernest Burgess, receiving her PhD from Chicago in 1926. He writes that 'despite her extensive publications record and existence of [the ASC's] prestigious award named in her honor, I suspect that only a handful of ASC members, including some of the award winners themselves, can describe any of her major contributions' (*ibid*, p. 8).

Chapter 5

Developing a sociological criminology
Durkheim, Du Bois, Merton and Tannenbaum

Frank Tannenbaum begins *Crime and the Community*, which was published in 1938, with 'criminology has been the happy hunting ground for all kinds of theories' (p. 3). He makes the point that much criminological discourse has been fixated on there being 'a qualitative difference between the nature of the criminal and the non-criminal' (*ibid*). The category of 'criminal' is contrasted to the designation of 'good citizen', that is the person who is sanctioned as 'acceptable' to society or the nation-state. In the work of Durkheim, Du Bois, Merton and Tannenbaum we find this contrast problematised. They advance a sociological criminology that is concerned with meaning and power, that provides a conception of humanity within situations and an understanding that human beings respond to life problems which arise from social structures that are not always of their making. Crime for these theorists is not a 'given': crime and the criminal are social constructs. Indeed, their position can be seen as embracing what Peter Berger described as 'the first wisdom of sociology', that 'things are not what they seem' (1963, pp. 23–24) – the idea that social reality 'has many layers of meaning and the discovery of each new layer changes the perception of the whole' (*ibid*). The sociological and criminological imagination of Durkheim, Du Bois, Merton and Tannenbaum was a reaction to the times in which they lived and an attempt to make sense of the individual and social crises with which they were confronted. Yet their insights remain of importance as we try to make sense of the complexities of today's society and the challenges that face us.

Émile Durkheim

> M. Durkheim, tall, thin and fair, is already bald. His voice at the start was feeble and subdued, but gradually, under the pressure of the ideas he was expressing, it rose grew animated and warm, until it seemed capable of filling a vast vessel.
> (M. Perreur, 11 March 1893)

> He was questioned first about his Latin thesis on Montesquieu, the examiners paying tribute to its 'probing study of the texts, the excellence of its method and the clarity of

its exposition' but questioning his own 'personal, ingenious and bold[...] didate defended himself with much vigour and the jury was unan[...] the precision of his ideas, the sureness of his speech, and the sincerit[...] ardour which he manifested throughout. We were agreed in consid[...] one of the best successful doctoral candidates we have announced fo[...] less to add, we were unanimous.

(Doyen's Report, 8 March 1893, in Lukes, 1973, pp. 297–299)

In Europe André-Michel Guerry and Adolphe Quetelet were among the first to emphasize the importance of researching society as a whole in order to understand human behaviour. Auguste Comte had given sociology its name, but it is Émile Durkheim who is credited for advancing the subject of 'sociology' as an academic discipline in its own right. He was to do for France what Albion Small had done for Chicago. It was Durkheim who was responsible for introducing the first course on sociology in France at the University of Bordeaux, where he was appointed in 1887 to teach social sciences and education, and who went on to found, edit and contribute to France's first journal of sociology, *l'Aneé sociologique* (1898). As Durkheim was to write, *l'Aneé*, by embracing the 'entire field', was able 'to establish a standard which sociology must, and will, achieve' (1895, 1938 ed, p. xiii). The quotations at the start of this chapter refer to Durkheim's doctoral defence at the Sorbonne in Paris. This consisted of a short Latin dissertation on Montesquieu and a longer thesis on the division of labour in society, which was to become his first major publication. The questioning of his work was by all accounts extremely rigorous, but as we can see the defence, especially that of the division of labour in society, was a great success. *La Petite Gironde* in Bordeaux reported that 'we are happy to state that, thanks to M. Durkheim, sociology has finally won the right to be mentioned at the Sorbonne' (Lukes, 1973, 1985ed, p. 299).

Durkheim's contribution to sociology is immense. It is his ideas, together with those of Max Weber and Karl Marx, that are often presented in sociology textbooks as providing the theoretical framework for modern sociology (Morrison, 2006; Eller, 2016). Indeed, as Eller wryly comments, 'the triumvirate of Marx, Durkheim and Weber . . . continue to stalk the discipline [of sociology], as every introductory textbook recounts their contributions and, often enough, refracts each sociological topic through their three lenses' (2016, p. 168).

Durkheim was concerned with questions relating to social development, methodology, the sociology of economics and law, education, suicide, 'primitive' and 'civilised' mentalities, ethics, the role of the intellectual, the social characteristics of knowledge, social psychology, democracy and the role of the state. As Beirne and Messerschmidt point out, the titles of his major works – the aforementioned *The Division of Labour in Society* (1893), *The Rules of Sociological Method* (1894), *Suicide* (1897), *Professional Ethics and*

Civil Morals (1900) and *The Elementary Forms of Religious Life* (1912) – reveal 'the breath of Durkheim's interests' (1995, p. 371). Moreover, his insights and analyses on crime and punishment have had an immense impact on criminology. Durkheim, together with the contributions of the early Chicago School of Sociology, provided the foundations for the development of much sociological criminology in the present period.

Émile Durkheim was born on 15 April 1858 in the town of Épinal, along the banks of the Moselle River, into an Orthodox Jewish family. His father, Moïse Durkheim, was chief rabbi of the Vosges and Haute-Marne, his grandfather had been a rabbi, as had his great grandfather, and at first it seemed that Durkheim would follow a religious path. For a while during his boyhood he studied at a rabbinical school. However, he had stopped practicing Judaism by the time he came to leave secondary education and was to marry his wife, Louise, in a civil ceremony – although religion and questions of morality remained central to his sociological thought.

Durkheim lived during a period of extraordinary political, economic and social upheaval. By the time he was in his early teens he had witnessed the defeat of France in the Franco-Prussian War (referred to in France as the War of 1870), the resulting overthrow of Louis-Napoléon and the collapse of the Second French Empire. The war, one of the most disastrous in the history of France, threw the country into utter turmoil. Épinal, being a border town, was briefly occupied by German troops and was subsequently the focus of a huge wave of immigration following the surrender of Alsace-Lorraine to Germany. Racial and class conflicts surfaced with a vengeance. The situation in Alsace-Lorraine led to virulent anti-Semitism as the Jews were blamed for the defeats, something that Durkheim described as having observed 'at close hand' being 'myself of Jewish origin' (1899, p. 60). In Paris, the Siege, which took place towards the end of the war, had brought famine (Otto von Bismarck having been fully prepared to see hundreds of thousands die of starvation), disease and numerous other privations to the city. This, alongside widespread unemployment, distrust of the authorities and the reactionary direction of the National Assembly and an increasingly restless working class that was beginning to question its situation, resulted in rebellion and the establishment by the people of the Paris Commune on 18 March 1871.

The communards, joined by mutinous National Guardsmen and disenchanted members of the petty bourgeoisie, set about creating a more equitable system of government that reflected the interests of the workers. Workers' councils were established, workplaces turned into cooperatives, night work limited, guaranteed support provided for the poor and sick, education was to be accessible to all without interference from the church or state, bureaucracy abolished and the salaries of all administrative and government officials were to be kept at the level of the wages of a worker, amounting to no more than 6,000 francs a year. For Karl Marx, the Paris Commune 'was essentially a working-class government, the product of the struggle of the producing against the appropriating class, the political form at last discovered under which to work out the economical emancipation of labor' (2005 ed, p. 171). Less than three months after the commune was established, Paris was attacked by government troops. Over 30,000 men, women and children were murdered, shot in the street, with thousands more arrested and either executed or forced into exile. It is estimated that Paris lost 100,000 of its workers, one-seventh of its adult male working population (Wilson, 2007). The brutal repression of the commune showed, as Engels wrote, 'the savagery of which the ruling class is capable as soon as the working class dares to come out for its rights' (1891, introduction). The response to the Commune sent shockwaves throughout France and led to a further deterioration in the relationship between the classes. Durkheim, whose maternal grandfather survived the Siege of Paris and was a member of the commune, never wrote specifically on the commune but was a known supporter of Gambetta, who advocated an amnesty for all communards in prison or in exile (Stedman Jones, 2006). As Steve Fenton reflects, the War of 1870 and the commune had a tremendous impact on Durkheim's generation, 'the first being a severe blow to national pride and self-confidence, the second dramatizing the potential for violent class conflict' (1984, p. 8). The fear of violent class action spread to England and the United States. It was presented as one of the arguments for the establishment of the settlement movement: Samuel Barnett of Toynbee Hall hoped that the settlement would provide a progressive alternative to 'revolutionary schemes' which 'turn the world upside down' (Abel, 1979).

It was hoped that the Third Republic, which came into being after the fall of Louis-Napoléon, would bring stability after the events of 1870–1871. It was the eighth regime since 1789. In the years following the French Revolution there had been three monarchies, two empires and two republics (Bellah, 1973). However, the political climate was to remain highly charged. As Anthony Thomson documents, 'Monarchists and Bonapartists attacked the government from the right; on the left, socialists sought political legitimacy and a revolutionary movement known as "syndicalism" kept alive the image of the Commune and the aspirations of the working class' (2010, p. 207). The economy was also changing rapidly. France went through a rapid period of industrialisation which affected the cities and rural areas. People migrated from the countryside in the hope of new opportunities.

Yet by the 1870s the key stages of industrialisation were virtually over, and by 1882 the country had plummeted into a depression, one of the worst in the history of France and from which it was not to recover until 1890. France's economic fortunes had been seriously damaged by the loss of the mines and industries of the Alsace-Lorraine region and the need to pay a war indemnity of five billion francs to the Germans. The stock market crashed, and France was forced to borrow from the Bank of England. Diseases in the wine and silk crops seriously harmed the rural economy.

In spite of this, the late 1800s in France were also a period in which people's aspirations rose. Education reform was made a priority for the new republic. Control was removed from the Catholic Church, and the emphasis was placed on creating a free, mandatory and secular system of education. The aim was to raise standards for *all* of France's citizens, and special attention was given to those in small towns and rural areas where the delivery of education was poor or non-existent. As Thomson notes, this was 'an important step towards opening all fields, particularly intellectual ones, to persons of talent regardless of class' (2010, p. 208). On the surface, it is also easy to see France at this time as being on an economic upturn. Roads were improved and the railways expanded, increasing communication between the provinces and cities. The country became a major colonial power, achieving control over parts of Indo-China and North and West Africa. Technological prowess was celebrated at the World Exhibition held in Paris in 1889, which commemorated the one hundredth anniversary of the French Revolution. The exhibition was marked by the unveiling of the Eiffel Tower, 'that great symbol of modern industrial enterprise and engineering power' (Sumner, 1994, p. 8). This is, of course, similar to that which was to occur in Chicago with the 1893 opening of the World's Columbian Exposition.

In Paris it was the era of the *belle époque* which was associated with decadence and amusement, fashion, theatre, film and art. Artists, writers and would-be artists and writers flocked to the city. The Moulin Rouge, home of the can-can, was established in 1889. But the 'golden age' was largely for those with money and sat uneasily alongside the predicament of those low down in the class structure. Baudelaire's idle 'dandy' whose only concern is to 'chase along the highway of happiness' shared the city with those who were most affected by the Depression: the poor who lived in 'slum' accommodations, were poorly paid, endured atrocious working conditions and poor health and, unlike previous generations, were less accepting of their lot. It was a society of contradictions and conflicts, of uncertainty, as the old ways of life gave way to the new. It was, as Durkheim was to write, 'one of those critical phases' in history, a time of 'crisis' (1961 ed, p. 101).

Émile Durkheim's work is largely centred on making sense of and documenting the impact of this crisis, understanding its historical basis and, above all, the need for social reconstruction. He believed the War of 1870 produced a 'shock' that 'reanimated men's minds' towards this latter goal (1972 ed, p. 12). In his article on the 'Sociology in France in the Nineteenth Century', Durkheim wrote 'of all the countries of Europe, [France] is the one where social organization has been most completely uprooted; we have made of it a tabula rasa, and on the field thus laid bare we must raise an entirely new edifice' (1900, p. 22).

Politically Durkheim was a democratic reformist. Although there are aspects of his thought that are not dissimilar to that of Karl Marx, Durkheim – given France's history and the fairly recent events of the Paris Commune which had brought the country to the brink of civil war – was also fearful of the chaos that violent class conflict could result in. His preference was for 'orderly, continuous social change in the direction of greater social justice' (Bellah, 1973, p. xvi)[1] and as such was a lifelong supporter of the Third Republic. The Third Republic has been erroneously presented as leaning towards conservatism; however,

> to be a conservative in the 1880s meant specifically *not* to be committed to the Third Republic. . . [it] stood for an appropriation of the ideals of the French Revolution and their stable institutionalism in a social order, to be in favor of the Third Republic meant that one was necessarily a democrat, a political liberal, and if not a socialist at least concerned with major reforms of social and economic order, all of which Durkheim was.
> (*ibid*, p. xvi)

Box 5.1 A note on Durkheim and the Chicago School of Sociology: the establishment of a discipline

Émile Durkheim was writing at roughly the same time as those of the early Chicago sociologists, a period in which both France and the United States can be characterised as still finding their feet in terms of the establishment of liberal democratic society. The cities of Paris and Chicago were experiencing the excitement of the dawning of the 'modern' age, while being confronted by the abject poverty of many of their inhabitants and a growing sense of the potential for violent class revolt, fuelled by the events of the Paris Commune. This provides the context to the intellectual endeavours of these early sociologists and the 'dawning' of the 'era' of sociology – the desire to study and make sense of the societal changes that were occurring and to be part of their respective countries' 'reconstruction' after the ravages of war. As George Davy wrote, Durkheim felt 'he must teach a doctrine, have disciples and not just students, play a role in the social reconstruction of France' (1820, p. 183). Durkheim's political position is thus akin to much of the social democratic reformism that characterised the early years of Chicago sociology. Moreover, with sociology as a discipline in its infancy, both Chicago's Albion Small and Durkheim were intent on consolidating it as a recognised and respectable area of academic study. Indeed, Durkheim was an advisory editor of the *American Journal of Sociology* from its earliest days until the First World War (Lukes, 1973). His ideas were also to receive considerable attention at the third meeting of the newly inaugurated British Sociological Society in 1904 (*ibid*). One of Durkheim's major texts, *The Rules of Sociological Method* (1895), was, as Kai Erikson noted, 'intended as a working manual for persons interested in the systematic study of society' (1966, p. 3). Stressing the importance of 'sociological training', it was not to be 'an auxiliary of any other science; it is itself a distinct and autonomous science' (Durkheim, 1895, 1938 ed, p. 45). The responsibility was immense, for as Durkheim wrote in 1900, *'[T]he word ["sociology"] is on everyone's lips . . . the thing has become popular. People's eyes are fixed on the new science and they expect much from it'* (cited in Lukes, 1973, p. 396, author emphasis).

Further Reading:

Durkheim, E. (1895, 1938 ed) *The Rules of Sociological Method*, New York: The Free Press, conclusion.

Small, A. (1895) 'The era of sociology', *American Journal of Sociology*, Vol. 1, No. 1, pp. 1–15.

Society, social facts and social integration

For Durkheim to move along the path towards social reorganisation and France's reconstruction, we must first recognise the importance of society. However, what he meant by 'society' is not straightforward. Although sometimes Durkheim utilises the word to refer to a specific social group, he emphasised that society is not just 'the group of individuals that compose it and their dwelling place'; it is, 'above all a composition of ideas, beliefs and sentiments of all sorts which realize themselves through individuals' (Bellah, 1973, p. ix). Society, while realising itself through individuals, exists over and above individuals; it was there before we were born and will outlast us (*ibid*). It is not, Durkheim said in 1885, 'a substance more or less transcendent' but 'a whole composed of parts' and 'the first problem for the sociologist is to decompose this whole, to enumerate its parts, to describe and class them, to seek how they are grouped and divided' (p. 632). The basis of the sociological method is therefore the study of social phenomena or 'social facts'. Social facts are 'general throughout a given society'; they are 'common ways of acting, thinking, and feeling' that exist independently of the individual. Their origin is society as a whole; they are not rooted in biology or individual consciousness. For example, 'the church member finds the beliefs and practices of his religious life ready-made at birth; their existence prior to his own implies their existence outside of himself'. A 'social fact' is also 'every way of acting, fixed or not, capable of exercising on the individual an external constraint'.

Indeed, it is 'recognised by the coercive power which it exercises or is capable of exercising over individuals' (Durkheim, 1938 ed, pp. 1–13).

In emphasising the 'bigger picture', that is the importance of studying the social structure and social phenomena, Durkheim's work breaks with individualism both as a mode of analysing society and as a basis for political order. He was critical of the 'analytical individualism' of those approaches discussed in the earlier sections of this book which attempt to either explain social action as the result of biological or psychological forces, as in individual positivism, or support the notion of a social contract freely entered into by atomised individuals who were weighing up the costs and benefits of their behaviour, as in neo-classicist or utilitarian perspectives. Indeed, Taylor, Walton and Young argued that 'Durkheim's central achievement was to spell out the elements of social explanation at a time when political and ethical philosophy, the "science" of political economy, and the positive schools were united under the banners of individualism' (1973, p. 67).

Hence in *The Rules of Sociological Method* (1895), through the elaboration of the concept of 'social fact', Durkheim emphasises that the world is not simply the result of individual action, 'if we consider social facts as things, we consider them social things. . . . We have . . . refused to identify the immateriality which characterizes [social facts] with the complex immateriality of psychological phenomena; we have, furthermore, refused to absorb it, with the Italian school, into the general properties of matter' (p. 162). For Durkheim utilitarian theories failed to grasp the realities of an industrial age. He was, as Taylor, Walton and Young note, well aware that 'a society divided into different interest groups, on an inequitable basis, was not a society in which "just contracts" between individuals and society could be struck' (1973, p. 67). Contractarian approaches assume there is an orderly basis to society; this, according to Durkheim was idealistic, bearing 'no relation to the facts', for 'the observer does not meet it along his road, so to speak. Not only are there no societies which have such an origin, but there are none whose structure presents the least trace of a contractual organization' (1895, 1964 ed, p. 202).

Utilitarian theory, reflected Anthony Giddens writing on Durkheim, 'gives prominence to the emergence of individualism, but mistakenly attempts to formulate an abstract social theory on this basis: in fact a society composed of egoistic or self-seeking, individuals would be no society at all' (1972, p. 2). In more contemporary times this vision of a 'society' composed of atomised individuals was evident in the political philosophy of Margaret Thatcher: as she saw it, 'there is no such thing as society. There are individual men and women and there are families' (*Women's Own*, 1987, cited in *The Guardian*, 8 April 2013). For Durkheim, 'one has an easy time in denouncing as an ideal without grandeur this shabby commercialism which reduces society to the status of a vast apparatus of production and exchange' (1898, p. 7).[2]

In *The Division of Labour in Society* – which Robert Merton described as 'one of the peak contributions of modern sociology' (1934, p. 328) – Durkheim outlines the evolution of society from *mechanical* to *organic* solidarity. Pre-industrial society was characterised by mechanical solidarity. Representative of an old way of life in which traditions, customs and kinship ties bonded people together, labour in such a society was relatively undifferentiated, with solidarity strengthened through similarity. Over time, industrialisation results in an increasingly varied and complex society. Labour becomes more highly differentiated until its structure is that of an 'advanced organism' (Giddens, 1972, p. 8). As the traditional bonds that hold society together are eroded, mechanical solidarity gives way to organic solidarity, a process that leads to increased individuation. The characteristics of mechanical solidarity were not completely erased, however, for these are ideal types. Nor was society rendered obsolete; far from it. In modern society solidarity becomes structured around difference: integration is achieved through the functional interdependence of its people for their 'specialized pursuits make them rely on one another' (Macionis and Plummer, 2008, p. 110).

Society and punishment

Under mechanical solidarity the law is repressive. Criminal behaviour is that which deviates from 'collective sentiments', norms and rules. What is, or is not, sanctionable is morally agreed upon. Violation of consensual norms and rules is met with harsh punishment; 'the intensity of punishment is greater to the degree that a society belongs to a less developed type' (Durkheim, 1972 ed, p. 129), which was, as we have seen, the case for pre-revolutionary France. As David Garland notes, 'the existence of strong bonds of moral solidarity are the conditions which cause punishments to come about, and, in turn punishment results in the reaffirmation and strengthening of these same bonds' (1990, p. 28). Punishment for Durkheim is an 'emotional reaction' (1893, 1972 ed, p. 124). A society based on mechanical solidarity punishes to 'avenge itself' (*ibid*). Hence, he asks, '[I]s not the very common punishment of *lex talionis* a mode of satisfying the passion for vengeance?' (*ibid*). In contrast, a society based on organic solidarity, being more highly differentiated, lacks consensual norms and rules. Here the law is required to arbitrate among people with divergent opinions and beliefs. As such, law becomes more restitutive and less repressive. For, as Newburn points out, 'under conditions of organic solidarity, where restitutive law is the norm, crime and deviance disturb social order rather than moral sentiments and rehabilitative, restorative action by officials is necessary in order to restore the status quo' (2017, p. 582). The development of restitutive law is 'testimony . . . to the growth of individuality of interest, function and identity' (Taylor et al, 1973, p. 77), which occurs in more advanced societies. Society no longer uses punishment to avenge itself, but to defend itself:

> [T]he suffering which it inflicts is in its hands no longer anything but a methodical means of protection. It punishes, not because chastisement

offers it any intrinsic satisfaction, but so that the fear of punishment may paralyze those who contemplate evil. It is no longer anger, but a well thought-out precaution which determines repression.

(Durkheim, 1893, 1972, p. 124)

The person who violates or disregards the law is not made to suffer in relation to his wrong doing; he is simply sentenced to comply.

(*ibid*, p. 135)

For Durkheim, the prison – which is rarely featured in more primitive, traditional societies – becomes central to dealing with offending behaviour, replacing the death penalty and torture. Whereas crime in primitive society is a community responsibility, in more advanced societies, 'responsibility becomes an individual matter' and 'from then on, measures are necessary to make sure that the individual concerned does not flee to escape sanction; and as at the same time they are less shocking to public morality, prisons appear' (Durkheim, 1972 ed, p. 131). The emergence of the prison as a feature of liberal democratic society and the replacement of harsh punishment – the 'cruel and unusual' – by institutional confinement has been noted by numerous commentators from the penal reformers of the eighteenth century onwards (Eddy, 1801). The originality of Durkheim's thought lies in the way he sees punishment as having a moral, emotional and expressive dimension outside of merely being an instrument of crime control (see Garland, 1990; Valier, 2002; Newburn, 2017). As David Garland points out, Durkheim argues, 'that despite the appearance of modern punishment, and whatever the contrary intentions of its administrators, the elementary characteristics he identified in primitive societies still underpin our practice and give it its true meaning' (1990, p. 28). While penal reformers were concerned with removing moral censure from the administration of penal law, Durkheim attempts to show that social morality – albeit 'unspoken, latent, taken for granted' (*ibid*, p. 28) – is a feature of modern society and thus 'to bring into view these submerged moralities . . . helping to elucidate punishment's moral significance and moralizing social functions' (*ibid*, pp. 28–29).[3] Moreover, Newburn (2017) comments that Durkheim helps to draw attention to the political role of punishment by observing its use in the shoring up of particular forms of authority.

The perils of modern society

The move from mechanical to organic solidarity has several undesirable consequences. One is increased individuation, in which the individual throws 'aside the tyranny of the group' and descends into 'a rampant individualism – a cult of the individual – where there is no agreed moral order with agreement as to just rewards and where individuals compete unfairly in an unequal society' (Young, 2013, pp. 4–5; Giddens, 1972). In modern society there is 'a lack of regulation and norms themselves which exhort individuation at the expense of the collective good' (Young, 2013, pp. 4–5). It is from this situation that anomie emerges.

Anomie has been described as one of the most influential theories in explaining the causes of crime and deviant behaviour: for it is anomie that 'attempts to pinpoint the genesis of crime and deviance in the dominant ethos of society and in the fundamental contradictions which exist within the social order' (Young, 2013, p. 2).[4] Although in his early works Durkheim seems to equate anomie with a state of normlessness,[5] anomie is, as Young has shown, more complex than this. The organic needs of individuals are, by their 'very nature, satiable and limited'; it is 'socially induced aspirations' that are potentially insatiable (*ibid*). There are two main forms of anomie: the *anomie of injustice* and the *anomie of the advantaged*.[6] The anomie of injustice relates to the disjunction that occurs between aptitude and merit and the distribution of rewards in society. As Frank Pearce clarifies in *The Radical Durkheim*, it is the institutions of inherited wealth that 'create a gap between the needs of the social order, its legitimations and the actual experience of its subjects, subverting the possibility that they could make a rational commitment to the social order' (2001, p. 78). This underscores the necessity of understanding the contradiction between available opportunities and individual merit in a society marked by the existence of inherited wealth and the impact of this on individuals faced with inequitable opportunities. The anomie of the advantaged, on the other hand, critiques 'the utilitarian perspective that endorses unrestrained self-seeking and which has no meaningful endpoint nor any substantial or tangible object' (Mooney and Young, unpublished). As Durkheim put it in this evocative section,

> From top to bottom of the ladder, greed is aroused without knowing where to find ultimate foothold. Nothing can calm it, since its goal is far beyond all it can attain. Reality seems valueless by comparison with the dreams of feverished imaginations; reality is therefore abandoned, but so too is possibility when it in turn becomes reality. A thirst arises for novelties, unfamiliar pleasures, nameless sensations, all of which lose their savor once known.
>
> (Durkheim, 1952 ed, p. 256)

Such a condition results from the rapid expansion of markets, industry and technological development. As Durkheim explained, whereas in the past, 'the producer could gain his profits only in his immediate neighborhood', and this 'restricted amount of possible gain could not much overexcite ambition', today, 'he may assume to have almost the entire world as his customer', and thus, 'how could passions accept their former confinement in the face of such limitless prospects?' (*ibid*). The resulting 'state of crisis and anomy'[7] (original spelling) becomes 'constant and, so to speak, normal' (*ibid*). Anomie is most pronounced when there is an increase in prosperity and in times of economic crisis. The levels of crime, suicide, rebellion, deviance and so on become indicative of the strength or weakness of moral regulation and social integration. For Durkheim in order to achieve integration, inheritance should be abolished and the division of labour itself be developed, together with the establishment of new social practices. Inherited wealth results in 'unjust contracts' between 'men', 'being based on power and wealth rather than natural aptitude and abilities' (Taylor et al, 1973, p. 88). There cannot, Durkheim argued, 'be rich and poor at birth without there being unjust contracts' (1964 ed, p. 384). The achievement of a 'moral individualism', as Wilkinson states, is imperative if the health of society is to be improved, 'the possibility for our moral unity lies in nurturing of a broader sympathy for all human sufferings' (2010, p. 44). This formed the backcloth to Durkheim's take on the case of Alfred Dreyfus, which rocked France at the end of nineteenth century.

The 'normal' and the 'pathological'

In his classic text, *Wayward Puritans*, Kai Erikson emphasises the importance of Durkheim's commentary on the 'normal' and 'pathological' elements in 'the life of society' and how this relates to our definitions of deviance or crime (1966, p. 3). There is nothing intrinsic to 'crime'. Behaviour, Durkheim pointed out, that looks abnormal to the psychiatrist or the judge

> does not always look abnormal when viewed through the special lens of the sociologist; and thus students of the new science [sociology] should be careful to understand that even the most aberrant forms of individual behavior may still be considered normal from this broader point of view.
>
> (*ibid*)

At any point in time 'the "worst" people in the community are considered its criminals, the "sickest" its patients, no matter how serious these conditions may appear according to some universal standard' and, as such, 'deviance can be defined as behavior which falls on the outer edge of the group's experience, whether the range of that experience is wide or narrow' (1966, p. 26). As such, in *The Rules of Sociological Method* Durkheim asks the reader to

> Imagine a society of saints, a perfect cloister of exemplary individuals. Crimes, properly so called, will there be unknown; but faults which appear venial to the layman will create there the same scandal that the ordinary offense does in ordinary consciousness. If, then, this society has the power to judge and punish, it will define these acts as criminal and will treat them as such.
>
> (1964 ed, pp. 68–69)

Crime,[8] therefore, is 'normal' to society because it is simply that which offends 'collective sentiments' (*ibid*, p. 67). As Erikson argues, even 'if a community were able to simply to lop off its most marginal people – banishing them to another part of the world, for instance, or executing them by the carload – it is unlikely that the volume of deviation in the community would really be reduced' (1966, pp. 26–27). For

> either new ranks of offenders would move into the vacuum in place of departed fellows (as England discovered when it tried a policy of wholesale transportation to the colonies) or the agencies of control would focus on a new target area and develop an interest in the behavior taking place there.
>
> (*ibid*)

Moreover, Durkheim suggested that crime and acts of deviance serve to bond people together through common indignation:

> Crime brings together upright consciences and concentrates them. We have only to notice what happens, particularly in a small town, when some moral scandal has been committed. They stop each other in the street, they visit each other, they seek to come together to talk of the event and to wax indignant in common. From all the similar impressions which are exchanged, for all the temper that gets itself expressed, there emerges a unique temper . . . which is everybody's without being anybody's in particular. This is the public temper.
>
> (1933 ed, p. 102)

Finally, 'crime' can help play a role in the progressive development of society, for those who rebel against established norms – and are labelled 'criminal' or 'deviant' – can help pave the way for social change as the 'functional rebel'. Socrates was condemned a criminal by Athenian law; 'however', as Durkheim writes, 'his crime, namely the independence of his thought, rendered a service not only to humanity but to his country' (1895, 1938 ed, p. 71), for 'it served to prepare a new morality and faith which the Athenians needed, since the traditions by which they had lived then were no longer in harmony with the current conditions of life' (*ibid*). Nor was Socrates unique. Recalling the time of the *ancien régime* and the transformation to a more 'enlightened' society, Durkheim argues,

> It would not have been possible to establish the freedom of thought we now enjoy if the regulations prohibiting it had not been violated before being solemnly abrogated. At that time, however, the violation was a crime, since it was an offense against sentiments still very keen in the average conscience. And yet this crime was useful as a prelude to reforms

which daily became more necessary. Liberal philosophy had as its precursors the heretics of all kinds who were justly punished by secular authorities during the entire course of the Middle Ages and until the eve of modern times.

(*ibid*, pp. 71–72)

L'affaire Dreyfus

The clash between the 'old' France, as represented by right-wing traditionalists, and the 'new', that is, those intent on upholding the values of the French Revolution and the Republic, was to come to a head with *l'affaire Dreyfus*. As with *l'affaire Damiens*, high-profile events that attract intense public and media interest can tell us much about underlying tensions within society, especially those arising from race, class and gender.[9] *L'affaire Dreyfus* was to become the subject of international attention, and Durkheim, on the side of Dreyfus, was to become heavily involved with it. The public nature of Durkheim's activism and his writings in relation to the case serve to refute those critics who have charged him with conservatism, which, as Steven Lukes (1973) and others argue, is a misrepresentation, the result of a selective reading of his work (see also Young, 2013).

Alfred Dreyfus was a French army captain who was the victim of a terrible miscarriage of justice. He was convicted by a secret military court in 1894 of high treason for selling secrets on military strategy and technology to Germany. Dreyfus was condemned to imprisonment on Devil's Island, off the coast of South America. Before his deportation he was publicly humiliated: in front of troops at the École militaire he was ceremoniously stripped of his rank, the braids and buttons struck from his uniform and his sword broken. On Devil's Island Dreyfus was kept in solitary confinement. The guards were not allowed to talk to him and, as a result, he lost the ability to speak. He was shackled to his bed at night. His diet was so atrocious that his teeth fell out. The Devil's Island penal colony was to become known as the 'Dry Guillotine' (Adams, 2016). Its very existence and Dreyfus's treatment there are indicative of the fact that – despite the ideals of Beccaria and Voltaire a century or more before – brutal punishment did not end with the *ancien régime*.

The evidence against Dreyfus, an Alsatian Jew, was flimsy from the start – based on a letter found in a wastepaper basket by a cleaner in the German embassy in Paris. Yet even after a more obvious culprit was identified Dreyfus's conviction was upheld, the army chiefs 'being more interested in preserving the image of the army than in rectifying their error' (Vallier, 2002, p. 33). Later, the Germans confirmed 'that no relations or connections of any kind ever existed' between Dreyfus and any German agent (*The New York Times*, 9 Sept. 1899, p. 1). The case symbolised the problems facing France: the right wing was gaining ascendancy – Dreyfus's 'alleged espionage was cited as evidence of the failings of the republic' (Vallier, 2002, p. 32) – alongside a resurgence in anti-Semitism. It was no coincidence that Dreyfus was the first Jew to rise to the General Staff of France's army (Fields, 2002) and had a German accent. French nationalism, fuelled by the Church, was pitted against the Jews. Jews were 'othered', seen as not properly French, even anti-French. Newspapers published racist caricatures: the Jew was 'hunchbacked, hook-nosed, bug-eyed, his face diabolical' (Wiesel, 1987, p. 4). Dreyfus's crime was portrayed 'as evidence of Jewish treachery' (Vallier, 2002, p. 32). There were attacks on synagogues and Jewish-owned businesses. The 'public temper' that Durkheim referred to reached frenzied proportions. People demonstrated in the streets against the Jews, and Dreyfus's defence lawyer was shot in the back on his way to court (Vallier, 2002). Even after Dreyfus was exonerated, he was shot by a right-wing journalist while attending a memorial ceremony for Émile Zola – fortunately he was not seriously wounded (*The New York Times*, 5 June 1908, p. 1). Durkheim, himself an Alsatian Jew, saw the Jew as a convenient scapegoat for the series of social and economic crises that had beset France: anti-Semitism, he wrote, was 'the consequence and the superficial symptom of a state of social malaise' for 'when society undergoes suffering, it feels the need to find someone whom it can hold responsible for its sickness, on whom it can avenge its misfortunes: and those against whom public opinion already discriminates are naturally designated for this role' (1899, p. 60). This is how 'othering' functions. As Durkheim noted, when Dreyfus's was found guilty,

> There was a surge of joy on the boulevards. People celebrated as a triumph what should have been a cause for public mourning. At last they knew whom to blame for the economic troubles and moral distress in which they lived. The trouble came from the Jews.
> (*ibid*, p. 61; cited in Lukes, 1973, p. 345)

After Dreyfus's conviction was upheld, incensed by the terrible situation, Émile Zola published an open letter to Félix Faure, the President of France, with the headline 'J'accuse' in the newspaper *L'Aurore*. In it he describes the case as a 'stain' on the 'cheek' of France, contrasting the events with the president's 'triumph of our World Fair which will crown our great century of work, truth and freedom' (13 Jan. 1898). He provides a point-by-point outline of the level of injustice that has occurred, accusing the military of a cover-up and warns of the dangers of anti-Semitism:

> It is a crime to poison the minds of the humble, ordinary people, to whip reactionary and intolerant passions into a frenzy while sheltering behind the odious bastion of anti-Semitism. France, the great and liberal cradle of the rights of man, will die of anti-Semitism if it is not cured of it. It is a crime to play on patriotism to further the aims of hatred. And it is a

crime to worship the sabre as a modern god when all of human science is laboring to hasten the triumph of truth and justice.

(*ibid*)

As with the difficulties that faced Voltaire and other committed artists, Zola was condemned for his stand against injustice. Convicted of libel, he fled to England before his sentencing. The day after Zola's letter, *L'Aurore* carried the 'Manifesto of the Intellectuals', signed by prominent artists, writers, scientists, lawyers and professors, which protested the 'violation of judicial procedure' (14 Jan. 1898).

Although not a signatory to the 'Manifesto', Durkheim the sociologist, as Karen Fields observed, 'became Durkheim the activist' (2002, p. 439). He was an early member of the Ligue pour la Défense des Droits de l'Homme and founded the Bordeaux branch of the Ligue. The Ligue was described as 'the most effective and durable creation of all this Dreyfusiste agitation' (Miquel, 1964, p. 51), and members were of the view that Dreyfus's conviction and Zola's persecution 'were all a travesty of republican justice and a victory for the forces of reaction' (Lukes, 1973, p. 347). Durkheim was known for his fiery speeches: they became 'rallying points for the student supporters of Dreyfus' (Bellah, 1973, p. xxxvi). It is also suggested that he used his friendship with Jean Jaurès, the prominent socialist leader, to elicit the support of Jaurès and the socialists for the cause.

In 1898 the noted historian Ferdinand Brunetière published 'Après le Procès', in which he defended the military, described the social order as under threat from 'individualism' and 'anarchy' and scoffed at the intellectuals (Dreyfusards) who doubted the justice of the Dreyfus trial and conviction (Lukes, 1969). He argued the army 'was vital for French security, prosperity and democracy' (*ibid*, p. 17) and 'the army of France, today as of old, is France herself . . . our armies have made us what we are . . . it is in their blood . . . that national unity has been formed, cemented and consolidated' (1898, cited in Lukes, 1969, p. 17). Further, Brunetière contended that 'prejudice against Freemasons, Protestants and Jews was a natural and legitimate reaction to their "domination" in the spheres of politics, law, education and administration, and that the Jews themselves were partly responsible for anti-Semitism' (Lukes, 1969, p. 17). The Dreyfusard intellectuals were also attacked by Catholic agitators, who critiqued the 'ignoble race of these academics . . . who spend their lives teaching error and in corrupting souls, and, in due course society as a whole' (cited in Lukes, 1969, p. 16). Maurice Barrès suggested, '[T]he great culprits who should be punished, are the "intellectuals", the "anarchists of the lecture platform", the "metaphysicians of sociology". A band of arrogant madmen' (*ibid*).

In response to Brunetière and others, Durkheim penned 'Individualism and the Intellectuals' (1898). Described by Lukes as 'a Dreyfusiste manifesto and an eloquent defence of liberalism' (1973, p. 339), this insightful article does not directly address the Dreyfus case. He begins with 'let us . . . leave on one side the minutely detailed arguments which have been exchanged from side to side; let us forget the Affair itself and the melancholy scenes we have witnessed' (1898, 1969 ed, p. 20). It is the wider symbolism of the case that concerns Durkheim: 'the problem confronting us goes infinitely beyond the current events' (*ibid*). In 'Individualism and the Intellectuals' he explains what is meant by a 'sociology of individualism', which he sees 'as going beyond the philosophical ethics of the past, by treating moral beliefs and practices as social facts' (Lukes, 1973, p. 339). Individualism was 'itself a social product, like all moralities and all religions' (*ibid*). The individual is 'a product of society, rather than its causes' (Durkheim, 1898, 1969 ed). The 'individualist, who defends the rights of the individual, defends at the same time the vital interests of society; for he is preventing the criminal impoverishment of that final reserve of collective ideas and sentiments that constitutes the very soul of the nation' (*ibid*, p. 27). Thus the 'Rights of Man' need to be upheld. For the ideals on which the Republic was founded cannot be renounced 'without renouncing ourselves, without diminishing ourselves in the eyes of the world, without committing real moral suicide' (*ibid*, p. 28). Above all, as 'a consequence of a more advanced division of labour', what we have in common with each other is our *humanity*. In a strident passage Durkheim argues,

> [T]he idea of the human person, given different emphases in accordance with the diversity of national temperaments, is therefore the sole idea that survives, immutable and impersonal, above the changing tides of particular opinions; and the sentiments which it awakens are the only ones to be found in almost all hearts . . . there remains nothing that men may love and honour in common, apart from man himself.
>
> (*ibid*, p. 26)

'Individualism and the Intellectuals' ends with a plea for action: 'may the common danger we confront at least help us by shaking us out of our torpor and giving us again the taste for action' (*ibid*, p. 30) and yet 'already . . . one sees initiatives awakening within the country, men of good will seeking one another out' (*ibid*). Let us hope, he says, that France learns from current events and avoids falling 'into that sterile inaction for which we are now paying' (*ibid*). This was not to be the case. The tide of anti-Semitism did not recede. Five years after Dreyfus's death in 1935 anti-Semitism was to become the official policy of France's collaborationist Vichy government, which assisted in the deportation of 76,000 Jews, including Alfred Dreyfus's granddaughter, to the death camps of Nazi Germany (Riding, 2006).

Figure 5.1 Alfred Dreyfus (Hulton Archive/Stringer/Getty).

Durkheim's legacy

Durkheim's insights into the problems of the modern age resonate today, faced as we are with the crises created by mass consumerism and greed, the development of the market and increased competition on a global scale and an ever-increasing gap between those with wealth and those who struggle at the edges of society, together with an upsurge in racism and the 'othering' of marginalised groups. He provides us with an understanding of how crime and deviance are socially constructed and the social significance of this in terms of collective indignation, exclusion and the potential role of the 'rebel'. The literature on anomie is vast, and the concept was to significantly influence the work of Robert Merton. Sadly, despite his many achievements, Durkheim was to die at the relatively young age of 59, seemingly of a broken heart.

Less than a month after the start of the First World War, on 13 August 1914, Germany invaded Belgium and Northern France. Durkheim was again to become actively partisan. This time, he strongly supported the French army and the cause of national defence, immersing himself in writing pamphlets, and organising committees for the publication of documents on the war 'to neutral countries and [to] neutralize, as far as possible, Germany's bold and lying propaganda' (*Letter* 30 Oct. 1914, cited in Lukes, 1973, p. 549). He was, however, the subject of 'at least two scurrilous attacks' as a native of Alsace-Lorraine and for being a Jew with a German name (*ibid*, p. 177). According to Lukes, the first was a piece in *Libre Parole* (19 Jan. 1916) in which he was described as 'a *Boche* with a false nose, representing the *Kriegsministerium* whose agents are swarming throughout France' (*Letter* 26 Jan. 1916, cited in Lukes, 1973, p. 157). But the real blow came with the death of his adored son, André. André was a brilliant young man, a talented linguist: Durkheim had revelled in their 'intellectual intimacy'. André had been serving in the army on the Bulgarian front when he went missing. Durkheim's anguish is revealed in a number of letters to friends: in one he writes that he was fixated by 'the image of this exhausted child, alone at the side of a road in the midst of night and fog . . . that seizes me by the throat' (*Letter* to Georges Davy, cited in Lukes, 1973, p. 555). André was declared dead in April 1916. Durkheim never recovered. As Steven Lukes writes, 'he died on the 13 November [1916] . . . his work unfinished, having lost in the course of the war, many of his closest collaborators and finest students' (1973, p. 559) and his son.

Across the Atlantic

W.E.B. Du Bois

W.E.B. Du Bois was born in 1868, ten years after Durkheim, in the state of Massachusetts and died in 1963 in Ghana. Du Bois was the first African American to be awarded a PhD from Harvard in 1895: his thesis was on the African slave trade to the United States and the enforcement of slave trade laws. During his studies at Harvard he spent two years in Germany, studying with Max Weber. He was in Europe at the height of the Dreyfus trial, and having followed the case carefully, said it 'led me on to conceive of the plight of other minority groups' (1968, p. 30). It was 'part of the disturbed world in which I lived' (*ibid*, p. 48). Whilst there is no evidence that Durkheim and

Du Bois ever met, Karen Fields, in imagining a conversation between these two men, points to a number of similarities, chiefly that 'both men thought, taught, and wrote with passion about what democracy required amid the social and above all economic turbulence of the late-nineteenth century world' (2002, p. 441). Both believed 'that upholding the value of humanity as such is the central problem of their time' (*ibid*, p. 437), and 'each lived on a racially defined edge of his society (*ibid*, p. 441).

Du Bois was among a number of early African American scholars who wrote on crime. Other notable figures include Monroe Work, Kelly Miller, E. Franklin Frazier and Ida B. Wells (see McMurry, 1980; Greene and Gabbidon, 2000). However, as Shaun Gabbidon, Helen Taylor Greene and Vernetta D. Young point out, 'the perspectives of African Americans' were and 'remain on the periphery of their discipline' (2002, p. xi).[10] Certainly, until the fairly recent work by Gabbidon (1996, 2007) and Laura Hanson (2010) there was scant recognition of Du Bois as a criminologist. Indeed, Hanson suggests that Chicago's Robert Park, who shared Booker T. Washington's 'accommodationist' perspective on race, was in all likelihood 'disinclined to champion the more radical views espoused by Du Bois' (2010, p. 57), contributing to his exclusion from the criminological canon. The reality is that Du Bois's work should be seen, as Biko Agozino writes, as a 'rallying cry that we need to pay attention to minority perspectives not just for what [they] may contribute to the ending of oppression but also for what the experience of the struggles against oppression may contribute to our discipline' (2017, p. x).

Many early African American sociologists, like their white counterparts, were influenced by Durkheim and Chicago sociology, with social disorganisation, anomie and social ecology featuring in their analyses (Gabbidon et al, 2002; Carrabine et al, 2014). Mary Jo Deegan (1988) has outlined the impact that the women of Hull House, where Du Bois was a frequent visitor, and the pragmatism of Jane Addams, G.H. Mead, W.I. Thomas and especially William James had on Du Bois's intellectual development. It was James who Du Bois credited with guiding 'me out of the sterilities of scholastic philosophy to realist pragmatism' (1968, p. 133). Du Bois was also to affect the work of the Chicago School. Aldon Morris and others have shown that Park's 'Marginal Man' (1928) was directly influenced by Du Bois's concept of 'double consciousness' (Morris, 2015). As Julian Go notes, 'Park just did not bother to cite it' (Go, 2016, p. 4). Du Bois's discussion in *The Philadelphia Negro* (1899) of the migration of African Americans from the Southern to Northern states and the impact that this had also bears a similarity to the later sociological analyses of the Park and Burgess years of Chicago sociology.

Du Bois came from a middle-class family and lived in what has been described as a 'friendly town' with comparatively few signs of overt racism (Hanson, 2010), but it was in 'the early days of rollicking boyhood' that his consciousness of what it meant to be Black emerged. In this impassioned passage from the 'Strivings of the Negro People' (1897), in which he describes the feelings of being excluded from the 'dazzling opportunities' of his white contemporaries, it is easy to identify the motivation for his later thought and activism on behalf of African Americans:

> I remember well when the shadow swept across me. I was a little thing, away up in the hills of New England, where the dark Housatonic winds between Hoosac and Taghkanic to the sea. In a wee wooden schoolhouse, something put it into the boys' and girls' heads to buy gorgeous visiting-cards – ten cents a package – and exchange. The exchange was merry, till one girl, a tall newcomer, refused my card, – refused it peremptorily, with a glance. Then it dawned upon me with a certain suddenness that I was different from the others; or like, mayhap, in heart and life and longing, but shut out from their world by a vast veil. I had thereafter no desire to tear down that veil, to creep through; I held all beyond it in common contempt, and lived above it in a region of blue sky and great wandering shadows. That sky was bluest when I could beat my mates at examination-time, or beat them at a foot-race, or even beat their stringy heads. Alas, with the years all this fine contempt began to fade; for the world I longed for, and all its dazzling opportunities, were theirs, not mine. But they should not keep these prizes, I said; some, all, I would wrest from them. Just how I would do it I could never decide: by reading law, by healing the sick, by telling the wonderful tales that swam in my head, – some way.

Du Bois saw his future to be somewhat rosier than that of the other Black boys:

> With other black boys the strife was not so fiercely sunny: their youth shrunk into tasteless sycophancy, or into silent hatred of the pale world about them and mocking distrust of everything white; or wasted itself in a bitter cry, Why did God make me an outcast and a stranger in mine own house? The 'shades of the prison-house' closed round about us all: walls strait and stubborn to the whitest, but relentlessly narrow, tall, and unscalable to sons of night who must plod darkly against the stone, or steadily, half hopelessly watch the streak of blue above.
> (From *The Atlantic*, August, 1897)

Du Bois's experiences of exclusion as a child and an adult[11] led him to stress the need for a separate Black social development, 'a form of biculturalism within "one Nation"' (1897; Thomson, 2010, p. 283).

In 1903, in his seminal essay *The Souls of Black Folk*, Du Bois famously wrote that 'the problem of the twentieth century is the problem of the color line' (1965 ed, p. 221). Yet the 'problem of the color line' for Du Bois was not just confined to 'nine millions [sic] Americans and settled when their rights and opportunities are assured', for 'a glance over the world at the dawn of the new century will convince us that this is but the beginning of the problem – that the color-line belts the world and the social problem of the twentieth century is to be the relation of the civilized world to the dark races of mankind' (2014 ed, pp. 111–112). While each racial group's experience will have historically specific characteristics, Du Bois pointed out that the 'color-line' manifested itself in numerous ways across the world, whether between 'the brown Turanians of India' and their 'yellow conquerors' (*ibid*, p. 113) or the 'most curious and complicated race conflict between Germans, Hungarians, Czechs, Jews, and Poles' (Du Bois *ibid*, p. 119). Thus, the 'problem of the color line' can also be seen as relating to the situation of the Southern Italians (as discussed in Chapter 3), the anti-Semitism of Durkheim's France and the subsequent rise of Nazi Germany.[12] The implications of the 'color line' were clearly articulated throughout Du Bois's many writings. In terms of the contemporary relevance of the 'color-line' in the United States, Vann R. Newkirk II noted in the new introduction to the 2017 edition of *The Souls of Black Folk* that 'from Barack Obama's presidency to the rise of Black Lives Matter to Donald Trump's election amid a furor over voting rights, white nationalism, and racism, the color line is still the country's core subject'.

Slavery and the convict lease system

Du Bois's PhD thesis was published in 1896 as *The Suppression of the African Slave Trade to the United States of America, 1638–1870* in Harvard's Historical Studies series.[13] This book, which he modestly described as a 'small contribution to the scientific study of slavery and the American Negro' (1896, p. 1), is a thorough consideration of the history of the slave trade, the introduction of laws to suppress it and the 'moral apathy . . . an indisposition to attack the evil' (*ibid*, p. 195) that affected the enforcement of legislation. Evident at the national and international level, this apathy amounted to 'criminal negligence' and resulted in few incidents of severe punishment. In the south of the country there was direct sabotage, for as was 'boldly' declared by those opposing antislavery legislation, 'a large majority of people in the Southern States do not consider slavery as even an evil' (*ibid*, p. 96). 'Northern greed', Du Bois was to argue, together with 'Southern credulity', created a situation that would 'circumvent any law, human or divine' (1891, 1982 ed, p. 27).

Throughout *The Suppression* Du Bois emphasises the necessity for moral courage. As he later wrote, he saw life at this time as 'a series of conscious moral judgements' (1954, 'Apologia'): 'I wanted the young nation to call "the whole moral energy of the people into action" instead of accepting a "bargain" on "one of the most threatening of the social and political ills" which faced the nation' (*ibid*). Yet as George Lavan notes, the struggle that he presents is ultimately 'more materialist than idealist' (1955, p. 105). Hence, 'the history of slavery and the slave-trade after 1820' must, Du Bois argued, 'be read in the light of the industrial revolution' (1896, p. 150) and especially in terms of enormous advances in cotton manufacture. This turned Southern slavery 'from a family institution to an industrial system' (*ibid*, p. 152). And here lies the problem, for in 'compromising with slavery in the beginning, and of the policy of laissez-faire pursued thereafter . . . healthy, normal, economic development' did not occur 'along proper industrial lines'. Slavery became intertwined with 'the economic forces of an industrial age' (*ibid*). The 'rise of the African slave-trade to America' allowed the colonists to 'rapidly' and 'ruthlessly' exploit the country's resources (*ibid*, p. 194).

Later, in 1954, when *The Suppression* was republished, Du Bois included an 'Apologia' for failing to realise the significance of Freud and Marx. This he put down to poor teaching: at Harvard, Marx was mentioned 'in passing' and 'in Germany I heard more of Marxism but in rebuttal of his theories rather than in explanation' (1954, 'Apologia'). 'Consequently', he did not fully understand, 'the psychological reasons behind the trends of human action which the African slave trade involved', which would, he suggested, have strengthened his arguments on the exercising of moral judgement and the importance of 'that classic word of Marx on the colonies as the source of primary capitalistic accumulation' (*ibid*). The ideas articulated in *The Suppression* can be seen as providing the impetus for Du Bois's analysis of the convict lease system, which he described as 'the spawn of slavery' (1901, 2017 ed, p. 117).

The convict lease system was established in the Southern states allowing prisons and reformatories to lease convicts to private individuals and companies. Given that the Thirteenth Amendment of the United States Constitution forbade slavery and involuntary servitude, 'except as a punishment for crime where of the party shall have been duly convicted', Du Bois's observation seems entirely justified. He pointed out that the convict lease system – the 'chain gang' – allowed white people to continue to profit from the labour of African Americans. A discriminatory and harsh criminal justice system ensured a ready supply of convict labourers. Seventy per cent of all prisoners in the South were Black – which can partly be explained 'by the fact that accused Negroes are . . . easily convicted and get long sentences, while whites . . . continue to escape the penalty of many crimes even among themselves' (1901, 2017, p. 120). Du Bois documented the conditions of the prisoners, who 'often had scarcely any clothing, they were fed on a scanty diet of corn bread and fat meat and worked twelve or more hours a day'. He described the case of a young girl who was repeatedly assaulted by several of her guards, eventually dying in childbirth while in camp' (*ibid*, p. 119). The convict lease system was simply 'slavery by another name' (Blackmon, 2008). And since Du Bois many scholars have focused on the links between slavery, prison labour and mass incarceration. It is, as Angela Davis has written, 'through the prison system the vestiges of slavery have persisted' (1996, p. 26; see also, 1999).

Certainly contemporary scenes of Black prisoners working in the fields at prisons such as Angola make it hard to avoid 'the stench of slavery and racial oppression' (Benns, 2015, p. 1).

The Philadelphia Negro

In 1896 Du Bois accepted the position of assistant in sociology at the University of Pennsylvania to conduct a study of Philadelphia's African American population. Katharine Bement Davis, who headed the Philadelphia College Settlement at the time of the research and was subsequently part of the Chicago School, published the first serious review of Du Bois's study and that of his colleague, Isabel Eaton, for the *Journal of Political Economy*. The project, as she explained in her review, was a collaboration between the University of Philadelphia and the College Settlement and had arisen out of the concerns of a 'number of men and women of Philadelphia interested in social reform, for a foundation of definite knowledge on which to base their efforts' (Davis, 1900, p. 248). The intention behind it was to do for the African American in Philadelphia what Charles Booth had done for London's poor in *Life and Labour of the People in London* (1902) and the *Hull House Maps and Papers* (1895) for Chicago. Eaton, who had worked closely with Jane Addams at Hull House, focused largely on the '[N]egro[14] in domestic service' given the high numbers working in this capacity (Davis, 1900, p. 248).[15] In her review, Davis praises Du Bois for producing 'probably one of the most important contributions, we have yet had toward the study of the [N]egro problem in the US': it demonstrates his abilities as a social scientist 'to reach the facts of the case, to see them in their true proportions, to separate cause from effect, to trace out the action of special environments, and beyond this, to set forth the results of his study in a clear, concise, and scientific manner' (*ibid*). She drew attention to his exploration of poverty and low wages, 'the causes of poverty are largely historical in character. Low wages are explained when we consider the few occupations to which [N]egroes are limited and the great competition that ensues' (*ibid*, p. 251). The level of prejudice that African Americans experienced from whites is particularly highlighted, with the trade unions having prevented them from membership, and the difficulties in becoming more socially mobile, it being almost impossible for an African American family 'to rent a house on a good residence street, in a respectable neighborhood occupied chiefly by whites' (*ibid*, p. 253).

Du Bois's research displayed a methodological sophistication, which was particularly advanced for the time: making use of a number of methods – house-to-house surveys, mapping, historical and media data, officially collected data (e.g., arrest and prison statistics), general observation and participation observation. In the first chapter he admits to the difficulties of conducting social research. Surveys are subject to 'many sources of error: misapprehension, vagueness and forgetfulness, and deliberate deception on the part of the person questioned' (1899, p. 3). The researcher is never completely objective and must remain aware of this throughout the process: 'he must ever tremble lest some personal bias, some moral conviction or some unconscious trend of thought due to previous training' affect the researcher's interpretation (*ibid*, p. 3). The degree of reflection shown by Du Bois on the problems of research is remarkable and in line with contemporary debates over the problems of objectivity, the hidden figure in survey research and the importance of methodological triangulation, that is, the use of multiple methods to 'correct to some extent the errors of each' (1899, p. 3; Mooney, 2000).

In the chapter on 'The Negro Criminal' Du Bois advances a number of explanations to explain the Black crime rate, both historically and in the present period. He opens the chapter with,

> Crime is a phenomenon of organized social life, and is the open rebellion of an individual against his social environment. Naturally then, if men are suddenly transported from one environment to another, the result is lack of harmony with the new conditions; lack of harmony with the new physical surroundings leading to disease and death or modification of physique; lack of harmony with social surroundings leading to crime.
>
> (p. 166)

Crime is socially situated: it arises from the social environment of the individual and is also a form of resistance to that environment. In a subsequent work Du Bois wrote more strongly that what 'we call crime' is 'social protest and revolt' (1901, 1982 ed., p. 116), thus anticipating the explanations for crime given by those holding a Marxist, anarchist or conflict criminological perspective. In *The Philadelphia Negro*, drawing from old colonial records, Du Bois documented historical incidents of insubordination (City Ordinance 1732, cited by Du Bois, 1899, p. 236) and outright rebellion from slaves. Outbreaks of disorder and rioting were frequently met with harsh punishment: 'whipping of Negroes at the public whipping post was frequent, and so severe was the punishment that in 1743 a slave brought up to be whipped committed suicide' (*ibid*, p. 237).

In discussing the more recent situation, crime, Du Bois stresses, 'is a phenomenon that stands not alone, but rather as a symptom of countless wrong social conditions' (*ibid*, p. 242). Similar to the later Chicago School, Du Bois refers to crime as emanating from the social disorganisation – 'a lack of harmony with the new conditions' – that results from migration into the cities and the rapid expansion of the urban environment. Increases in crime have generally been found to correlate to the 'increased complexity of life, in industrial competition, and the rush of great numbers to large cities' (*ibid*, p. 240). However, his is a more pointed political analysis: the role played by the legacy of slavery, poverty and racial prejudice in both criminality and the social construction of crime have to be fully taken on board in analysing the African American experience, for 'in the case of the Negro there were special causes for the prevalence of crime: he had lately been freed from serfdom, he was the object of stinging oppression and ridicule, and paths of advancement open to many were closed to him', and as a consequence, 'the class of the shiftless, aimless, idle, discouraged and disappointed was proportionately larger' (*ibid*, p. 241). The effect of emancipation 'was that of any social revolution: a strain upon the strength and resources of the Negro, moral, economic and physical, which drove many to the wall' (*ibid*, p. 283). It is not, therefore, a straightforward cause-and-effect relationship: it is about understanding how the individual responds to their social circumstances – the level of social disorder and 'strain' that occurs – which is the starting point for much sociological criminology in the contemporary period.

Both racial prejudice and public opinion are seen by Du Bois to play a role in the social construction of crime. He points out that African Americans are more likely to be treated harshly than whites and that white-collar crime is rarely prosecuted:

> In convictions by human courts the rich always are favored somewhat at the expense of the poor, the upper classes at the expense of the unfortunate classes, and whites at the expense of Negroes. We know for instance that certain crimes are not punished in Philadelphia because the public opinion is lenient, as for instance embezzlement, forgery, and certain sorts of stealing; on the other hand a commercial community is apt to punish with severity petty thieving, breaches of the peace, and personal assault or burglary.
>
> (*ibid*, p. 249)

Moreover, the popularly held assumption that being Black equates to criminality results in wrongful arrest, miscarriages of justice and the likelihood of a brutal response by the police. As Du Bois notes, 'whoever snatches a pocketbook on a dark night is supposed to be black' (*ibid*, p. 263) and includes this 'typical' case:

> W. M. Boley, colored, thirty years old, who said he resided in Mayesville, South Carolina, was a defendant before Magistrate Jermon, at the City Hall, yesterday, on the charge of assault with intent to steal. Detective Gallagher and Special Policeman Thomas testified that their attention was attracted to the prisoner by his actions in a crowd at the New York train gate at Broad street station on Saturday. He had with him several parcels which he laid on the floor near the gate, and they said they saw him make several attempts to pick women's pockets, and arrested him. The man however proved by documentary evidence that he was

a clergyman, a graduate of Howard University, and financial agent of a Southern school. He was released.

(*ibid*, p. 268)

And that of William Drumgoole, who allegedly stole a pair of shoes from a store. Drumgoole, 'colored, aged thirty-one years, of Lawrenceville, Va., was shot in the back and probably fatally wounded late yesterday afternoon by William H. McCalley, a detective, employed in the store of John Wanamaker, Thirteenth and Chestnut streets' (*ibid*, p. 259). Laura Hanson comments on the importance of Du Bois's 'sociological observations' in *The Philadelphia Negro* 'about the gaping disparity between white and Black groups in American society' in the creation of 'a platform for future discussions surrounding equality and social inclusion for the Black community (2010, p. 55). The incidents that Du Bois draws on for *The Philadelphia Negro* from over one hundred years ago bear a depressing similarity to the struggles faced by African Americans today.

Post-Philadelphia: the Atlanta School

Although Du Bois had not yet published *The Philadelphia Negro*, he was appointed to a faculty position at Atlanta University. His brief was to establish a sociology programme and to participate in the development of the university's curriculum. He was also offered the opportunity to institute a series of conferences focusing on the African American experience, known as the Atlanta conferences. Alongside these activities Du Bois embarked on an ambitious research programme for the study of the African American, which included the replication of studies of different facets of the African American experience every ten years – involving his students in the fieldwork (Gabbidon, 1996, 2007). Early research carried out by the Atlanta School included that on mortality in cities, the social and physical conditions of life in the city, 'efforts of Negroes for social betterment', 'the Negro in business', 'the Negro church' and 'the Negro common school' (1903b; 1980 ed p. 125). There was a strong community feel to the work: for not only was Du Bois committed to the education of a new generation of Black sociologists, who were in fact only one generation removed from slavery, but was also – in Hull House style – concerned with benefiting the local community. As he noted with pleasure, 'as time passed, it happens that many uplift efforts were ... based on our studies: the kindergarten system of the city of Atlanta, the Negro business league and various projects to better health and combat crime' (Du Bois, 1968, p. 26).

Like the early Chicagoans, he described this centre of 'activity'[16] as a 'laboratory', believing Atlanta University to be ideally located, given that it was 'situated within a few miles of the geographical centre of the Negro population of the nation, and, is, therefore, near the centre of the congeries of human problems which cluster around the black American' (1903b, 1980 ed, p. 125). The training for students was rigorous, equipping them with the skills necessary to 'study systematically conditions of living right around the university' (1903b, 1980, pp. 158–159). Hence, undergraduates spent two years 'with a course in economics . . . Here the methods of study are largely inductive, going from fieldwork and personal knowledge to the establishment of the main principles' (*ibid*). Whilst there is discussion over whether Atlanta is a 'School' or not, this is somewhat unwarranted: for Du Bois's vision for a teaching strategy and a research agenda and the influence that Atlanta sociology was to have on Black scholars surely makes it as much of school as the 'Chicago School' (Gabbidon, 1996, 2007; Wright II, 2017). Atlanta produced a recognisable body of work that was committed to increasing the visibility of the African American experience. For Du Bois, as Gabbidon writes, had

> [Both] a vision and a missionary drive. In his intellectual vision, his social scientific research would serve as a precursor to social policy. His missionary drive was his belief that, in affecting social policy through his research, he would be contributing to uplifting his people . . . Du Bois was convinced that, when the facts (his findings) were presented to policy makers, the plight of many African Americans could no longer be ignored.
> (2007, p. 29)

Du Bois inspired a generation of Black sociologists, who had come to embrace sociology as 'an intellectual discipline as a weapon of liberation' (Morris, 2015, p. 59). As Aldon Morris cites, a talented Black student, Jessie Fauset, was to write to Du Bois after the publication of *The Souls of Black Folk* (1903a): 'We have needed someone to voice the intricacies of the blind maze of thought and action along which the modern educated colored man or woman struggle' (*ibid*, p. 60). However, the research of the Atlanta School was for many years not given the recognition it was due:[17] the 'color-line' meant 'we rated', as Du Bois said in 1968, 'as Negroes studying Negroes, and after all what had Negroes to do with America or science' (*ibid*, p. 228)?

Box 5.2 The necessity of activism, the transformation of society and the 'Red Scare'

For Du Bois, academia could never be enough. When a impoverished Black man named Sam Hose was lynched in 1899 after being accused of killing his landlord's wife, Du Bois went to the *Atlanta Constitution* to put in a statement about the lynching. While on the way he heard that Hose's knuckles were being exhibited in a local grocery store further down the road. He turned around, realising 'one could not be a calm, cool and detached scientist while Negroes were lynched, murdered, and starved' (1968, p. 222). In 1905 Du Bois co-founded the Niagara Movement to campaign for social and political change. Its 'Declaration of Principles', largely written by Du Bois, included,

> PROTEST: We refuse to allow the impression to remain that the Negro-American assents to inferiority, is submissive under oppression and apologetic before insults. Through helplessness we may submit, but the voice of protest of ten million Americans must never cease to assail the ears of their fellows, so long as America is unjust.
> COLOR-LINE: Any discrimination based simply on race or color is barbarous, we care not how hallowed it be by custom, expediency or prejudice. Differences made on account of ignorance, immorality, or disease are legitimate methods of fighting evil, and against them we have no word of protest; but discriminations based simply and solely on physical peculiarities, place of birth, color of skin, are relics of that unreasoning human savagery of which the world is and ought to be thoroughly ashamed.
> 'JIM CROW' CARS: We protest against the 'Jim Crow' car, since its effect is and must be to make us pay first-class fare for third-class accommodations, render us open to insults and discomfort and to crucify wantonly our manhood, womanhood and self-respect. (Niagara Movement, 1905).

The Niagara Movement was to provide the foundation for the National Association for the Advancement of Colored People (NAACP) of which Du Bois, Jane Addams, Ida B. Wells, John Dewey, Florence Kelley, W.I. Thomas and Charles Zeublin were among the co-founders. Du Bois became director of publications for the NAACP in 1909. As editor of the organization's magazine, *The Crisis*, he published stories of lynching[18] and other brutalities and injustices committed against African Americans that were often ignored by the mainstream press.

Du Bois's career was long and varied,[19] and over its course – although he had always been sympathetic to socialism – he became more closely aligned with Marxism. He asked in a 1933 piece for *The Crisis*, 'what shall we say of the Marxian philosophy and of its relation to the American Negro'? answering,

> The Marxian philosophy is a true diagnosis of the situation in Europe in the middle of the 19th Century despite some of its logical difficulties. But it must be modified in the United States of America and

especially so far as the Negro is concerned. The Negro is exploited to a degree that means poverty, crime, delinquency and indigence. And that exploitation comes not from a black capitalist class but from the white capitalists and equally from the white proletariat.

(Du Bois, 1933, 1996, p. 151)

After World War II, the United States was gripped by another Red Scare as hysteria was whipped up over a perceived threat from communists, who were seen as threatening capitalism and American 'values'. Du Bois, who had visited a number of communist countries, including the Soviet Union, was placed under Federal Bureau of Investigation (FBI) surveillance. In 1951 his Peace Information Center, which was established to 'tell the people of the United States what other nations were doing and thinking about war' (Du Bois, 1968, p. 357), was condemned as a front for communist activities. Du Bois and his fellow members were indicted for failing to register the Peace Information Center under the 1938 Foreign Registrations Act. As the poet Langston Hughes was to write, 'Somebody in Washington wants to put Dr. Du Bois in jail. Somebody in France wanted to put Voltaire in jail. Somebody in Franco's Spain sent Lorca, their greatest poet, to death before a firing squad' (1951, cited in Gabbidon, 2017, p. 55).

Du Bois did in fact join the Communist Party of the USA but not until he was 93 years old, writing in his application letter to Gus Hall,

I have been long and slow in coming to this conclusion, but at last my mind is settled.

Capitalism cannot reform itself; it is doomed to self-destruction. No universal selfishness can bring social good to all

Communism – the effort to give all men what they need and to ask of each the best they can contribute – this is the only way of human life.

And responds to the impact of the 'Red Scare' with, the 'aims' of the Communist Party of the USA are 'not crimes. . . . No nation can call itself free which does not allow its citizens to work for these ends' (Letter, 1 Oct. 1961).

Du Bois was not alone in being placed under surveillance. C. Wright Mills, Franklin Frazier, Talcott Parsons and Robert Merton, to name a few, were all being watched by the FBI for their supposed communist leanings. Jock Young, who retrieved Merton's FBI file, was struck by both the detail and length of time that he was under surveillance. He describes the FBI investigation as having a 'Monty Pythonesque quality about it and centred on the full-scale investigation between 1952 and 1954 of Talcott Parsons as the suspected leader of a communist cell at Harvard. Seemingly, Merton was supposed to have been placed at Columbia University by members of the Harvard cell' (2010, p. 96). Monty Python aside, as with the earlier 'Red Scares', the effect was, as Young suggested, 'chilling' for 'it involved academic highflyers and the foot soldiers, it affected the content of lectures and of books, it urged a movement towards "hard" data and natural scientific method . . . its long term effects have been like a trauma which have distorted and differentiated American sociology' (2013b unpublished). Indeed, with respect to Merton's 'Social Structure and Anomie', Young[20] suggests it is telling that Marx is not mentioned: 'it was Marxism without Marx'. It has all the 'Marxist elements: contradiction, ideology, incessant ends, the fetishism for money, institutionalism yet amoral individualism' (*ibid*). As Laurie Taylor pointed out, 'it accurately described the machine but didn't explain what it was doing there in the first place and who took the profit' (1971, p. 148; cited in Young, 2013b, unpublished).

Further Reading:

'Application for membership in the communist party by WEB Du Bois', at: www.cpusa.org/party_info/application-to-join-the-cpusa-by-w-e-b-du-bois-1961/

Keen, M. (1999) *Stalking Sociologists*, Westport: Greenwood Press.

'The Niagara movement: Declaration of principles', at: http://scua.library.umass.edu/collections/etext/dubois/niagara.pdf

Recently, within criminology there are calls to build on Du Bois's work on the impact of racial oppression – the 'color line' – and to use his legacy as the foundation for the development of a Black criminology. James Unnever, Shaun Gabbidon, Katheryn Russell-Brown and Akwasi Owusu-Bempah outlined the basic tenets of a Black criminology in an article for *The Criminologist*, the American Society of Criminology's newsletter: the 'basic function' of a Black criminology, they wrote, 'is to enable criminologists to tackle the difficult and controversial questions of how the "color line" affects African American offending and the United States' justice system' (2019, p. 3). Theoretically, a Black criminology should adopt a broad theoretical framework, 'similar to a feminist criminology that embraces multiple methodologies and theoretical orientations'; it should lead scholars 'to revisit whether they have sufficiently incorporated race and racism into their analyses of crime' and be integrated into the curriculum of graduate programmes (*ibid*, pp. 1–6). It is envisaged that the institutionalization of a Black criminology will enable the discipline to move beyond its white essentialist orientation.

A snapshot of 1930s America

The 1930s began with the Great Depression and ended with World War II. At the height of the Depression, triggered by the Wall Street Crash of 1929, fifteen million people were unemployed in the United States. Bread lines and soup kitchens became familiar sites. The Dust Bowl, the drought and dust that hit the Midwest, destroying agricultural production, exacerbated the situation. Thousands were left homeless. In the South lynching continued.

In 1932 Franklin D. Roosevelt was elected president of the United States. Roosevelt's values were very much in line with the Progressive era. Intent on advancing a reformist agenda, he put forward the 'New Deal' to improve the lives of the working people and stabilise the economy. The 1930s were also to witness advances in communication: the radio became a feature of many American homes. News came across the airwaves rather than through print media. People were exposed to stories of celebrities and of a 'better' world, filled with the consumer goods of the day. The development of mass communication helped to feed aspirational desires. Poverty and hardship went hand in hand with a 'new' consumerism. The term 'American Dream' was coined in 1931 by author James Truslow Adams, who saw it idealistically as 'that dream of a land in which life should be better and richer and fuller for everyone with opportunity for each according to ability or achievement' (cited in Clark, 2007). It came to be associated with having 'two children, a marriage, and a three-bedroom house with the infamous white picket fence.'[21]

With war around the corner, the decade was politically tumultuous. The rise of the Nazis in Germany emboldened their supporters in the United States, who held rallies in which they proclaimed their American patriotism and pro-Nazi views. Rife with anti-Semitism, they blamed the country's economic problems on the Jews. Roosevelt was denounced, and the New Deal was named the 'Jew Deal'. Violent opposition to these rallies was organised by socialists and communists (who also sometimes fought each other), and there was fear amongst the establishment that such 'Red' elements were a threat to the existing social order. The largest rally occurred in 1939 when some 20,000 pro-Nazi supporters held a 'Pro-America Rally' in Madison Square Gardens, New York City, which was met with protests from thousands of demonstrators.

Figure 5.2 The 'American Dream' (H. Armstrong Roberts/Getty).

In 1938 Robert Merton published 'Social Structure and Anomie' in the *American Sociological Review*, which is probably the most cited sociological article of all time and was to have a profound impact on criminological thought. Also in 1938 Frank Tannenbaum published *Crime and the Community*. Tannenbaum's analysis of the 'the dramatization of evil' would provide the foundations for labelling theory.

Robert Merton and the American Dream

Robert Merton was born Meyer Schkolnick in a 'depressed area' of South Philadelphia that he described as a 'benign slum' (Cullen and Messner, 2007, p. 15). Merton's parents were Jewish immigrants and owned a small grocery store. Merton's name change came about as a result of his early side-line as a magician at children's parties when he adopted the name 'Robert K. Merlin', which led to 'Robert Merton'. Merton was very aware of the impact of anti-Semitism, and the name change might well have been, as David Greenberg, has suggested, a 'strategy for upward mobility' (Young, 2010, p. 89). Likewise, it is possible, as Cullen and Messner suggest, to have related to his own experiences with differential opportunity: 'Merton might have seen his own local environment as benign but also may have been aware that ascending in the cosmopolitan world beyond his neighborhood would require the more "innovative adaptation" of hiding his Jewish heritage' (2007, p. 33). Studying first at Temple College[22] (now Temple University), which was established for 'the poor boys and girls of Philadelphia', and then Harvard, sociology appealed to him. Like so many of the early sociologists, it allowed him to contextualise 'the crisis of the world around him: the Great Depression on the one hand and the social organization of anti-Semitism on the other' (Young, 2010, p. 90). Yet his early living conditions led Merton to see 'slum life' as organised rather than disorganised: it was a world that functioned despite poverty and deprivation.

At Harvard, Merton was Pitirim Sorokin's teaching assistant. Sorokin, who was due to present a paper on French sociology, asked Merton to review Durkheim's work. This, explained Merton, made him into 'a transatlantic Durkheim' and 'laid the groundwork for what would become [his] own mode of structural and functional analysis' (cited in Young, 2010, p. 91). As he was to state, his goal in trying 'to follow in [Durkheim's] large footsteps and consequently wobble a bit in these excessively spacious areas' was to develop Durkheim's theory of anomie, for he did not 'afford explicit and methodical guidance to the various signs of anomie' (1957, p. 164). 'Social Structure and Anomie' (1938) was written when Merton was 27 years old and at Harvard. He introduced its themes to his class, which included Albert Cohen[23] and Richard Cloward. Merton was to conceive anomie 'as a breakdown in the cultural structure, occurring particularly when there is an acute disjunction between the cultural norms and goals and the socially structured capacities of members of the group to act in accord with them' (Merton, 1957, p. 162). For Merton, crime, therefore, 'is a meaningful, creative response to a situation, it is a product not of lack of socialization [as in a social positivistic framework] but a socialization into a culture which involves the pursuit of incessant goals and constant frustration' (Young, 2010, p. 93). It is not poverty that leads directly to crime for – as Quetelet showed – many poor communities have less crime than more affluent ones, and the economic upturn in the second part of the nineteenth century did not lead to less crime. The problem lies with the 'American Dream', the assumption that anyone can succeed if they work hard, despite their background: it is about the gap between the widespread cultural belief in a meritocracy and the actual, grossly unequal class system. The acceptance of the American Dream results in

> [F]irst the deflection of criticism of the social structure onto one's self among those so situated in the society that they do not have full and equal access to opportunity; second, the preservation of a structure of social power by having individuals in the lower social strata identify themselves not with their compeers, but with those at the top and third, providing pressure for conformity with the cultural dictates of unslacked ambition by the threat of less than full membership in the society for those who fail to conform.
>
> (1957, p. 139)

Moreover, in line with Durkheim's 'insatiable aspirations', there is with the American Dream 'no final stopping point', for 'the measure of "monetary success" is conveniently indefinite and relative' (*ibid*, p. 136). He describes individuals living in this context as responding or adapting in a variety of ways: *conformity* (pursuing culturally ascribed goals by approved means, e.g. hard work and talent), *innovation* (the attempt to achieve wealth and power by unconventional means, e.g. through drug dealing or corrupt practices as with the 'Robber Barons'), *ritualism* (the lowering of one's horizons, involving the 'abandoning or scaling down of the lofty cultural goals of great pecuniary success and rapid social mobility' and, thus, allaying the status anxiety that results from 'ceaseless competitive struggle' (*ibid*, p. 149), *retreatism* ('the rejection of cultural goals and institutional means', in this category, Merton includes 'pariahs, outcasts, vagabonds, tramps, chronic drunkards and drug addicts' (*ibid*, p. 153)) and finally *rebellion* (this leads individuals 'outside the environing social structure to envisage and seek to bring into being a new, that is to say, a greatly modified social structure'; it implies 'alienation from reigning goals and standards' (*ibid*, p. 155). Rebellion can occur on a small scale and also be more endemic within society; thus:

> When rebellion is confined to relatively small and relatively powerless elements in a community, it provides a potential for the formation of subgroups, alienated from the rest of the community but unified within themselves. The pattern is exemplified by alienated adolescents teaming up in gangs or becoming part of a youth movement with a distinctive subculture of its own.
>
> (*ibid*, p. 191)

And,

> When rebellion becomes endemic in a substantial part of the society it provides a potential for revolution, which reshapes both the normative and the social structure.
>
> (*ibid*, p. 191)

> In our society, organized movements for rebellion apparently aim to introduce a social structure in which the cultural standards of success would be sharply modified and provision would be made for a closer correspondence between merit, effort and reward.
>
> (*ibid*, p. 155)

Merton has come to be criticised for putting too much emphasis on background structural factors. Jack Katz, for example, argued in *Seductions of Crime* that this led to the experience of the 'act' itself (the 'foreground') being ignored, 'the positive, often wonderful attractions within the lived experience of criminality' (1988, p. 3). Crime is complex and, as such, Katz wrote, 'neither academic methods or academic theories seem to be able to grasp why . . . killers may have been courteous to their victims just moments before the killing . . . or how it makes sense to kill when only petty cash is at stake' (*ibid*). Crime, for many, is exciting; it is thrilling; it is seductive (*ibid*). For cultural criminologists this was to become a core component of their analysis of crime and deviance.

However, there is no doubt that Merton left an extraordinary mark on criminology, especially with respect to the development of subcultural theory. For example, Albert Cohen (who was also taught by Edwin Sutherland) builds on Merton's structurally situated actors and their 'goals and aspirations' by introducing humiliation, frustration, energy, transgression and rage to explain the behaviour of 'delinquent boys'. In *Delinquent Boys: The Culture of the Gang* (1955) the school is identified as a prime source of meritocratic disappointment, with working-class boys being judged by a 'middle class measuring rod'. As such, 'certain children are denied status in respectable society because they cannot meet the criteria of the respectable status system' (1955, p. 121). The response is the creation of 'a delinquent subculture [that] takes its norms from the larger culture but turns them upside down' (*ibid*, p. 28). Hence,

> Those values which are at the core of 'the American way of life', which help to motivate behaviour which we most esteem as 'typically American', are among the major determinants of that which we stigmatize as 'pathological'. More specifically, it holds that the problems of adjustment to which the delinquent subculture is a response are determined, in part, by

those very values which respectable society holds most sacred. The same value system, impinging upon children differently equipped to meet it, is instrumental in generating both delinquency and respectability.

(*ibid*, p. 137)

The response of the 'delinquent boy' is to become part of a delinquent subculture: to join with others who are similarly affected. He is able to achieve a 'kind of sectarian solidarity' though his participation in the subculture of the delinquent gang. The delinquent subculture provides a 'criteria of status which these children *can* meet' (*ibid*, p. 121; original emphasis). Although Cohen sometimes refers in more general terms to 'children' or 'the delinquent', the 'delinquent is typically a rogue male' and 'his conduct may be viewed not only negatively, as a device for attacking and derogating the respectable culture; positively it may be viewed as the exploitation of modes of behavior which are traditionally symbolic of untrammeled masculinity' (*ibid*, p. 140).[24] Cohen's exploration of masculinity and femininity in *Delinquent Boys* and, indeed, in his call for future research on masculinity and the 'problems of achieving masculinity' (*ibid*, p. 169), makes his work a precursor to studies of masculinity and crime that emerged in the 1990s (Messerschmidt, 1993; Kimmel, 1993).

Richard Cloward in the late 1950s and in *Delinquency and Opportunity* (1960, with Lloyd Ohlin) developed Merton's idea of differential opportunity structures, showing that just as young people have differential access to legitimate opportunities, this is also true of illegitimate opportunities. Cloward, in fact, suggested to Merton that he had been 'half right', that 'while he had correctly explained the pressures on lower-class youth to commit delinquency, he had not accounted for the range of subcultures available to such youth or the rationale for choosing one over the other' (Brotherton, 2010, p. 148). Moreover, Young notes that Cloward and Ohlin turned the Mertonian theory of anomie into social policy through Mobilization for Youth, 'a multimillion dollar funded project [which] was launched in the Lower East Side of Manhattan in the early 1960s, that aimed to directly reduce delinquency by expanding job opportunities' (2010, p. 97). This project was denounced in 1964 by the *New York Daily News* as a 'commie' front, with its offices raided and staff interrogated. Interestingly, Stephen Pfohl was to point out, 'What could be more American than trying to incorporate people into the opportunity structure as a whole?', with Young retorting, 'what could be more American than government intervention against any project which suggests transformative change' (2011, p. 215)?

The spirit of anomie, as Young comments, is also to be found at the 'heart' of Phillipe Bourgois's *In Search of Respect* (1995), Steven Messner and Richard Rosenfeld's *Crime and the American Dream* (2001), and in his own work, *The Exclusive Society* (1999) and *The Vertigo of Late Modernity* (2007). Left realist criminology was also strongly influenced by Merton in its exploration of the experience of relative deprivation, especially within the inner city.

Frank Tannenbaum and 'the dramatization of evil'

Frank Tannenbaum, like so many others in the history of criminology, is often excluded from contemporary overviews of criminological theory.[25] However, his exploration of 'The Dramatization of Evil' in *Crime and Community* (1938) provides the basis for labelling theory. Matthew Yeager (2016) points to how Merton took up Tannenbaum's ideas in his 'self-fulfilling prophecy' (1948), as did Edwin Lemert in the 1950s.

> **Box 5.3 Frank Tannenbaum: convict criminologist**
>
> As Matthew Yeager's fascinating biography (2016) of Frank Tannenbaum documents, he is thought of as the 'first convict criminologist'. In Chapter 4 the work of Katharine Bement Davis was discussed – the Chicago School graduate who became the first female commissioner of corrections for New York City. Bement Davis came into contact with Tannenbaum after he was incarcerated in Blackwell's Island penitentiary in 1914. Tannenbaum was then a young Industrial Workers of the World (IWW) member and an associate of Emma Goldman and Alexander Berkman. Tannenbaum was serving a year's sentence on Blackwell's Island, having been arrested for 'unlawful assembly and disturbing the peace' for invading a church with his 'army of unemployed workers' (see Mooney and Shanahan, 2020). He wrote about his experiences at Blackwell's for the journal *The Masses*, describing how he had become 'the most broken spirited person imaginable' (1915, p. 8) in the prison. He was behind at least two prisoner uprisings while he was there in protest over the dreadful conditions and bullying by the guards. Davis placed Tannenbaum and the other instigators in 'the cooler' (solitary confinement) to starve them into submission, contrasting with her earlier commitment to humanitarian values, evidenced through her settlement work and associations with W.E.B. Du Bois, Jane Addams and other progressives of the time. 'The cooler', Tannenbaum wrote, drove inmates crazy, 'when I got out of the cooler after seven days I was so weak I couldn't stand' (1915, p. 8). 'Miss Davis', he said with sarcasm, had 'humanized the cooler' by dividing the one piece of bread you were allowed a day, into two so you could be fed twice!
>
> On his release, Tannenbaum was to become an active critic of the prison system and befriended Thomas Mott Osborne, the penal reformer, who supported his application to Columbia University. In 1924 he published *Darker Phases of the South*, in which he exposed the brutality of Southern prisons – the chain gangs, the convict lease system

and the prison farms. *Darker Phases* shows the influence of W.E.B Du Bois, with whom he was friends – the connections between Bement Davis, Du Bois, Tannenbaum and other progressive intellectuals of the day, as was apparent from the Hull House meetings, is intriguing in considering how ideas develop.

Du Bois actively supported Tannenbaum's research in the South, introducing him to Florence Kelley and others who might be of help (Letter W.E.B. Du Bois to Florence Kelley, 22 May 1923). In *Darker Phases* Tannenbaum describes the problem of the 'color line' as seen through the Southern prison system – with the 'colored population . . . predominant. The management is white' (1924, p. 83) and also the situation of poor whites. He suggests that the prejudice and violence directed towards the Black population had arisen in part from the resentment that poor whites felt about their own situation – the level of deprivation and lack of control over their lives – and was fuelled by an 'underlying apprehension that the South will be outstripped in the population by the colored as against the white. It is fear of losing grip upon the world, of losing caste, of losing control' (1924, p.162; see Earle's excellent book *Convict Criminology*, 2016 – chapter 2). This has a particular resonance in terms of contemporary politics, as seen in Trump's United States and the resentment expressed towards immigrants throughout the Global North. The fear, especially amongst working-class whites, of losing control, of losing status is widely discussed in the sociological literature (Young, 1999; Ware and Black, 2002; Earle, 2016). Further, anticipating some of the ideas of Jack Katz (1988) and cultural criminologists, Tannenbaum suggests – while condemnatory of their actions – that poor whites find excitement in the spectacle of violence: 'they are starved emotionally. They desperately crave some excitement, some interest, some passionate outburst' (1924, p. 25) to escape their situation. And part of the awfulness and 'the danger of the Ku Klux Klan is that it dramatizes and perpetuates this state of excitement' (*ibid*, p. 26).

At Columbia, Tannenbaum completed a doctorate in 1928 and became a professor. However, his move into the academy did not go unchallenged by comrades. Elizabeth Gurley Flynn, the labour radical, suggested, Tannenbaum's 'labor career' ended once his fine was paid for disturbing the peace: up he went to Columbia; 'the poor and lowly', she suggested, 'remained with us' (cited in Yeager, 2016, p. 100). His subsequent toning down and move away from radical activism may well have been the result of Red Scares: Columbia at this time was under pressure to remove 'Red' faculty, and Tannenbaum would have been on the list of IWW supporters. It is highly possible that he thought it was all too risky. Yet he was to continue to provide commentary on the South, on slavery and race relations, and, as Yeager points out, Tannenbaum's position on the prison remained consistent: 'he was opposed to the architecture of the American penitentiary and thought that most offenders ought not to be incarcerated', and he was a member of the American League to Abolish Capital Punishment and an advocate of re-entry policies (2016, p. 103).

Convict criminology in the academy

'You don't know anything about it, do you? It's all a game to you . . . Prison. You think because you've spoken to a few cons you understand it all. Well, you don't, you just don't' ('Jeff Bridges' to the criminology lecturer in Stan Cohen's *Against Criminology*, 1988, p. 299).

Along with Tannenbaum, there are many ex-prisoners who have entered the academy, with Angela Davis and John Irwin being perhaps the best known (see the entry on Irwin in *Fifty Key Thinkers in Criminology* [2010]). There are also, of course, many who have written about their prison experiences and used them to encourage debate on the function of imprisonment for academic, activist and lay audiences. In the early 1900s Tannenbaum's anarchist comrade, Emma Goldman, likewise spent time in Blackwell's penitentiary and was also part of Jane Addams's Hull House intellectual scene in Chicago. Her article, 'Prisons: A Social Crime and Failure' (1917), engages with criminological literature and presents a powerful argument for the abolition of prisons. Peter Kropotkin's anarchist criminology was also informed by his prison experiences and provide the backcloth to his *Are Prisons Necessary?* (1887) Kropotkin had been sentenced for alleged anti-tsarist activities to the notorious Peter and Paul Fortress in St Petersburg.

As a subdiscipline of criminology, convict criminology (CC) was founded in 1997 in the United States (Ross and Richards, 2003), with a British Convict Criminology group established in 2011/2012 by Rod Earle, Sacha Darke and Andy Aresti. While agreeing that Tannenbaum can be referred to as the first convict criminologist, CC notes 'the convict criminologist label is achieved through a process of self-identification, not by third party ascription' (2016, p. 492). Appropriating the moniker 'new' from Taylor, Walton and Young's *New Criminology* (1973), in recognition of the necessity of radical and provocative discourse within criminology, convict criminologists in the United States have described 'CC' as a 'new criminology' led by former prisoners who are now academic faculty, engaged 'in research that illustrates the experiences of prisoners and ex-cons, attempts to combat the misrepresentations of scholars, the media and government, and to propose new and less costly strategies that are more humane and effective' (Richards and Ross, 2003; convictcriminology.org, 2016). It consists of those 'who believe that convict voices have been ignored, minimized, or misinterpreted in scholarly research on jails, prisons, convicts, correctional officers, and associated policies and practices that affect these individuals' (*ibid*, p. 491). Within criminology there are those who think 'because you've spoken to a few cons you understand it all'. Of key importance to CC is the stigma attached to being previously incarcerated: 'felons and ex-convicts are "invisible minorities," as the stigma, disadvantage, and prejudice suffered are not readily apparent until discovered or "outed"' and 'though other stigmatized groups have gained some protections in the US, this is not true for felons' (*ibid*, p. 492; Ross et al, 2011; Richards, 2018). Other areas of concern are with

> how the problem of crime is defined; solutions proposed; the devastating impacts of those decisions on the men and women "labeled" criminals who are locked in correctional facilities, separated from loved ones, and prevented from fully reintegrating into the community; record high rates of incarceration; overcrowding of penal institutions; a lack of meaningful programming inside and outside of prison; and the structural impediments to successful re-entry that results in a revolving door criminal justice system.
> (convictcriminology.org, 2016)

Frank Tannenbaum, when asked in 1950 about his thoughts on progress in penology, said,

> You'd have to ask if the aims of society are better accomplished now by prisons or in the 18th century. I think there's been no progress or little.
> (cited, Yeager, 2016, p. 103)

Further Reading:

Earle, R. (2016) *Convict Criminology*, Bristol: Policy Press.
Yeager, M. (2016) *Frank Tannenbaum: The Making of a Convict Criminologist*, Oxon: Routledge.

Tannenbaum was always, as Erich Goode observes, 'on the side of the little guy, the underdog, and against the massive institutions that were crushing human freedoms and liberties' (1994, p. 95). In referring to society and criminology's 'search for the scapegoat', he notes how we distinguish between the 'normal' and 'abnormal' to shore up our own values and how those who are 'different' are considered a threat to the orderly workings of society:

> The projection of the idea of normal or good is merely the passing of moral judgement upon our own habits and way of life. The deviate who is a communist, a pacifist, a crank, a criminal, challenges our scheme of habits, institutions, and values. And unless we exclude him and set him apart from the group, the whole structure of our orderly life goes to pieces. It is not that we do not wish to be identified with him: we cannot be identified with him and keep our own world from being shattered about us.

Thus, again, we are presented with an understanding of how criminology has 'othered' those who are seen as different and/or a threat:

> [The] theories of the criminologists are understandable. They have imputed an evil nature to the evil doer, whatever the terms upon which that nature was postulated – possession by the devil, deliberate evil doing, physical stigmata, intellectual inferiority, emotional instability, poor inheritance, glandular unbalance. In each case we had a good explanation for the 'unsocial' behavior of the individual, and it left unchallenged our institutional set-up, both theoretic and practical.
>
> (1938, pp. 7–8)

In lower-class neighbourhoods, Tannenbaum argued, most boys become involved in a variety of mischievous activities: 'breaking windows, annoying people, running around porches, climbing over roofs, stealing from pushcarts, playing truant – all are items of play, adventure, excitement (*ibid*, p. 17). However, even though this behaviour is normal to the boys, to the community it 'take[s] on the form of a nuisance, evil, delinquency' resulting in 'the demand for control, admonition, chastisement, punishment, police, court, truant school' (*ibid*). The community's attitude hardens and demands suppression. A shift occurs from

> seeing the definition of the specific acts as evil to a definition of the individual as evil, so that all of his acts come to be looked on with suspicion . . . from the community's point of view, the individual who used to do bad and mischievous things now has become a bad and unredeemable human being.
>
> (*ibid*)

The boy, in response, feels a 'sense of grievance and injustice' for being misunderstood, mistreated and punished, but he also comes to a recognition that he is subject to a different definition as a human being than other boys in the neighbourhood. It results in a process of self-identification. The 'delinquent becomes bad because he is defined as bad and because he is not believed if he is good' (*ibid*, pp. 17–18). The boy who has been 'tagged' in this way responds with antagonism and rebellion, and he 'becomes the thing he is described as being' by escalating the severity of the acts he is involved in. It does not matter whether the valuation of him is made by those 'who would punish or those who would reform' (*ibid*, p. 20). And 'the harder they work to reform the evil, the greater the evil grows under their hands' (*ibid*). The child's subsequent isolation leads him to find companionship with similarly defined boys, 'and the gang becomes his means of escape' (*ibid*). It is the process of social control that creates this situation; it results in an amplification of the original act, 'making it the source of a new series of experiences that lead directly to a criminal career' (*ibid*). Thus, Tannenbaum shows how 'primary deviance' results in 'secondary deviance'. The best approach is to avoid 'the dramatization of evil' for, as Erich Goode writes, 'they will grow up to be just fine' (1994, p. 95).

The idea that labelling produces deviance was to be further developed in the 1950s and 1960s, especially through the work of Edwin Lemert (1951, 1967), Howard S. Becker (1963) and John Kitsuse (1971). The emphasis was to be placed more fully on the social reaction to crime (Tannenbaum included a discussion of structural factors in terms of crime causation). Social reaction could involve public opinion, families, mass media and those of official agencies, e.g. police, courts, prisons and social workers. This work also helped to form the basis for the emergence of moral panic theory (Young, 1968; Cohen, 1972). It showed that the process of labelling is a political act, as Becker noted, 'the questions of what rules are to be enforced, what behavior regarded as deviant, and which people labelled as outsiders must . . . be regarded as political' (1963, p. 7). However, by focusing on the social reaction to crime, labelling was seen as neglecting what led up to the act in the first place (Carrabine et al, 2014). Early work was also mostly concerned with the young male delinquent.

Further, it should be acknowledged, especially when evaluating the legacy of Durkheim, Merton and Tannenbaum, that theories that have focused on the social and cultural context to the criminal act and those concerned with the social construction and reaction to the act have come under criticism for being inattentive to the victim. As feminists and left realists have pointed out, crime has a very real impact on victims' lives. Erich Goode reflects on this reality in detailing the near- fatal mugging of Frank Tannenbaum at the age of 75: an incident which horribly marred the last years of his life. Goode asks,

> Was Tannenbaum's attacker aware of his theory of crime? Had he been a victim of 'round up the usual suspects'? Was he a misunderstood underdog? Was he, perhaps, a mischievous adolescent, engaged in exuberant high jinks? Or did he, perhaps, start out as a mischievous youngster, only

to be unjustly and capriciously labeled? As a result, was he forced to see himself as a true criminal? Is this why he mugged and nearly killed a 75 year old man . . . Irony can be cruel, and it was especially cruel with the work and death of Frank Tannenbaum.

(1994, pp. 95–96)

Nonetheless, it is largely due to the work of Durkheim, Du Bois, Merton and Tannenbaum that sociological criminology was to advance theoretically as a discipline. Many of their insights were to form the backcloth for the development of deviancy theory in the 1950s and 1960s in the United States, which in turn provided the impetus for the 'new' critical criminology which was to take off in the 1970s in the UK. Albert Cohen's *Delinquent Boys* (1955) highlighted, to some extent, the significance of masculinity and femininity in understanding delinquent behaviour, which was to become of importance to feminist criminologists. In the previous chapter, when discussing the women of the Chicago School, feminist values and some of the core principles that have come to be identified with feminist theorising and, especially, the development of a distinct feminist research methodology were evident. In the following chapter I offer a more comprehensive overview of feminism and how feminists have attempted to redress the gender imbalance in the study of crime.

Notes

1 Lukes suggests that politically Durkheim's views reveal a sympathy to the reformism of Jean Jaurès, the French socialist leader (1969, p. 18).
2 Durkheim particularly takes issue with the 'narrow utilitarianism' of Herbert Spencer (1898, p. 20).
3 Durkheim's essay on *Two Laws of Penal Evolution* (1900) provides further insights into his perspective on the evolution of punishment (see Wilkinson, 2010).
4 See Young (2013) 'The Durkheimian Legacy' for the way in which the concept of 'anomie' has often been 'narrowed' or misinterpreted in contemporary scholarship at: www.malcolmread.com/JockYoung/durkheims_legacy.pdf.
5 As Mathieu Deflem points out, 'etymologically, the concept is derived from the Greek "anomia", which, containing the root term "nomos", literally means a lack of law or, more broadly, deregulation and/or normlessness' (2015, p. 718)
6 Before Jock Young's death in 2013, we were working on a paper, 'Realism with Energy, Culture with Realism', which centred on the development of the ideas of Durkheim, Merton and Mills and their relevance to left realism and cultural criminology.
7 'Anomy' – spelling as in the original
8 Durkheim was to be subjected to a number of attacks by Gabriel Tarde. This is discussed by Lukes (1973) and Beirne (1993). Durkheim believed Tarde had misconstrued his views on the nature of crime, especially the contention that crime was normal. In his rebuttal in 'Crime and Social Health', he clarified that crime was normal because it was 'linked to the fundamental conditions of all social life' (cited in Lukes, 1973, p. 309). Lukes suggests the roots of this debate were personal, possibly arising from academic jealousy.
9 See Lynn Chancer's *High-Profile Crimes* (2006) in relation to more contemporary cases, for example, those of O.J. Simpson and the Central Park Five.

10 When Gabbidon and Greene (2001) conducted a citation analysis to uncover the extent of references to early African American scholarship in American criminology texts published between 1918 and 1960, they showed that African American graduates from the University of Chicago's 'Chicago School', including Charles Johnson, E. Franklin Frazier, Monroe Work and Earl R. Moses, were cited the most often. African American scholars were also typically cited in discussions of either race or culture, with 'work on the effects of social, economic, and political conditions such as slavery, segregation, racism and oppression on crime and criminality, especially among African Americans' being generally not cited. As they suggest, 'while claims that African American scholarship cannot be found in mainstream publications might be somewhat overstated as they relate to early American criminology texts, *the most important themes found in the writings of African Americans were excluded*' (p. 301; author emphasis).

Two of the most extensively referred to early African American sociologists are Charles Johnson, author of the now 'classic' study of the Chicago Race Riots of 1919 (*The Negro in Chicago*, 1922), and E. Franklin Frazier (*The Negro Family*, 1932), both worked closely with Robert Park. Frazier served as president of the American Sociological Society in 1948.

11 Du Bois attended Fisk University as an undergraduate, having been denied entry to Harvard 'where less-talented whites easily secured a place' (Thomson, 2010, p. 283). Later at Harvard for his doctoral studies, he was prevented from joining the Glee Club because of his race (*ibid*). Further, on completion of his PhD, 'like most African American scholars, he was unable to locate a permanent position at any white school' (Gabbidon, 2017, p. 4).

12 In 'The Crisis of May, 1933', Du Bois wrote of Germany,

> It seems impossible that in the middle of the 20th Century a country like Germany could turn to race hate as a political expedient. Surely, the experience of America is enough to warn the world . . . One has only to think of a hundred names like Mendelssohn, Heine, and Einstein to remember but partially what the Jew has done for German civilization. It all reminds the American Negro that after all race prejudice has nothing to do with accomplishment or desert, with genius or ability. It is an ugly, dirty thing. It feeds on envy and hate.
>
> (p. 117)

And in the *Pittsburgh Courier*,

> There is a campaign of race prejudice carried on, openly, continuously and determinedly against all non-Nordic races, but specifically against the Jews, which surpasses in vindictive cruelty and public insult anything I have ever seen; and I have seen much . . . There has been no tragedy in modern times equal in its awful effects to the fight on the Jew in Germany. It is an attack on civilization, comparable only to such horrors as the Spanish Inquisition and the African slave trade.
>
> (19 December 1936)

13 *The Suppression of the African Slave Trade to the United States of America, 1638–1870* was the first volume in Harvard's Historical Studies series.

14 The 'N' in Negro is not capitalised in Davis's article. This is likely to have caused Du Bois some irritation: in *The Philadelphia Negro* he writes, 'I believe eight million Americans are entitled to a capital letter' (1899, p. 1).

In the mid-1920s Du Bois undertook a letter writing campaign insisting that newspaper, magazine and book editors capitalize the 'N' (Tharps, 2014).

15 Mary Jo Deegan (2001) comments that Isabel Eaton's contributions have largely been overlooked. She, in fact, wrote the final eighty-two pages of *The Philadelphia Negro*. Katharine Bement Davis's (1900) review represents one of the few serious acknowledgements of Eaton's work. Deegan points out that Du Bois did not share the biases of the largely male scholars who reviewed *The Philadelphia Negro* and thought highly of her (Du Bois, 1899, p. iv; Deegan, 2001).

16 To use Howard S. Becker's (1970) word for the body of research associated with the Chicagoans.
17 The works of Gabbidon (1996, 2007) especially and those of Wright II (2002; 2017), Hanson (2010) and Morris (2015) make for essential reading, highlighting not only Du Bois's exclusion, and that of the Atlanta School, from the history of the discipline but also the importance of Du Bois's ideas in terms of contemporary criminological discourse.
18 It is incredible given the horror of lynching, the legacy of racism, the structural violence, actual violence and discrimination faced by African Americans in the United States, and the obvious need for reparations, that despite nearly 200 anti-lynching bills being introduced in Congress from 1882 to 1986, none were approved. In June 2018, the Senate's three African American members – Cory Booker, Kamala Harris and Tim Scott – introduced a "'The Justice for Victims of Lynching Act of 2018' to make that willful, collective act of murder punishable as a federal crime, resulting in harsher sentencing under existing hate crime statutes'" (Dingle, 2018). As they put it: Sen. Harris, 'Lynching is a dark, despicable part of our history, and we must acknowledge that, lest we repeat'; Sen. Booker, 'It's a travesty that despite repeated attempts to do so, Congress still hasn't put anti-lynching legislation on the books. This bill will right historical wrongs by acknowledging our country's stained past and codifying into law our commitment to abolishing this shameful practice' and Sen. Scott, 'This measure is certainly well past due and I am glad to be able to join in efforts that will underscore the severity of this crime. This piece of legislation sends a message that together, as a nation, we condemn the actions of those that try to divide us with violence and hate' (Dingle, 2018; *The New York Times*, 2018, 28 June). The work of Ida B. Wells and Monroe Work highlighted the extent of lynching at the time. Frank Tannenbaum also wrote of lynching in the *Darker Phases of the South* (1924). Monroe Work, of the Tuskegee Institute, documented every known lynching between 1900 and 1931 – see www.monroeworktoday.org.
19 In 1934 Du Bois resigned from the NAACP after a falling out with its leadership. Becoming more radical, he believed the NAACP was failing to address the needs of the masses. Arguing against the NAACP's commitment to integration he wrote in *The Crisis* in favour of voluntary segregated communities. In 1944 Du Bois returned to the NAACP as director of special research, to be dismissed four years later, probably due to his increased support for leftist organisations. Thomas Holt (1999) suggests Du Bois's advocacy of the 'leftish Southern Negro Congress (at a time of rising hysteria about Communism and the onset of the Cold War)' was a major factor.
20 Young makes the point that:

> Great thinkers are inevitably the subject of textbooks and revision. The patina of time leads to an accumulation of representations, some pursued with such energy as to have a life of their own. So has it been with Merton, so that anomie has become 'strain' theory, parts of 'SSA' ('Social Structure and Anomie') have become bowdlerized to represent the whole and writers of both the left and right have spun the work out of recognition. Thus Merton has been characterized unjustly as a conservative, as making a fundamental break with Durkheim, as a leading sociological positivist – all of which are wildly off the mark at least as far as his early writings are concerned.
>
> (2010, p. 89)

21 Cited at: https://transformationoftheamericandream.weebly.com/1930s.html
22 Merton wrote that 'like many other Temple College students during the Great Depression, I was a dedicated socialist' (1997, p. 286). Young described Merton's socialism as 'grounded in Marxism learnt, first of all, from the "shoemaker intellectual" at the street corner where he grew up' and refers to his extremely 'battered copy of *Das Kapital, Volume 1* with a private index of 100 pages' (2010, p. 91). Merton was a lifelong friend of Alvin Gouldner, the Marxist sociologist, who was to write *The Coming Crisis of Western Sociology* (1970) and the introduction to Taylor, Walton and Young's *The New Criminology* (1973).

23 There is a fascinating interview with Robert Merton by Albert Cohen, conducted at John Jay College of Criminal Justice in 1997, available at: www.youtube.com/watch?v=Wdgfg485ekU
24 In discussing male and female sex roles in *Delinquent Boys*, Albert Cohen builds on the earlier discussion of Talcott Parsons (1947), who stressed the assertion of masculinity or 'masculine protest' in the creating of anti-social behaviour (see A. Cohen on Parsons, 1955, pp. 162–169).
25 Tannenbaum, for example, despite his significance in terms of both CC and labelling theory, does not have an entry in K. Hayward, S. Maruna and J. Mooney (2010) *Fifty Key Thinkers in Criminology*, Oxon: Routledge.

Chapter 6

Feminism
Redressing the gender imbalance

French women revile Lombroso

> *This afternoon the ladies composing the group of champions of woman's rights called 'La Solidarite des Femmes' met in conclave in the Town Hall of the Saint Sulpice District for the purpose of protesting against some of the ideas put forth by Dr Cesare Lombroso in his last book 'La Donna Delinquente'. The learned Italian has already written on 'L'Uomo Delinquente' and his deductions were generally received with favour in this country. Now, however, that he has entered upon the study and classification of the other sex, Mme. Potonie Pierre and her friends are up in arms. They are particularly annoyed at the doctor's statement to the effect that women being organised for special functions, it is safe to conclude that they ought to be kept out of the political sphere of action. Prof. Lombroso also made the sweeping assertion that women were not gifted with the synthetical as opposed to the analytical faculty . . . A letter of protestation is to be sent to Dr Lombroso and in this epistle he will be roundly told what an influential section of the women of France think about him and his theories.*
>
> New York Times, 14 Jan. 1894, p. 9

Eugenie Potonie Pierre, who led the demonstration against Lombroso's ideas in France, was one of the most prominent women's rights activists of the 1890s. As is evident from the newspaper report above, Potonie Pierre and *La Solidarite des Femmes* were concerned not just with how women were represented in *La Donna Delinquente*, but how Lombroso's ideas regarding women's 'nature' implied they were unsuitable for full participation in the public sphere. This presentation of women was common to both Enlightenment and much individual positivist thought, from Lombroso to the work of Hans Eysenck. Even though women associated with the early Chicago School of Sociology did participate in public life, their path was not an easy one. Although many of the women were to take on prominent roles in organisations concerned with social welfare and public policy, they were often denied full-time faculty appointments. Social welfare and policy-related occupations were typically seen as more 'fitting' for women's nature – i.e. woman as the 'nurturer', the 'carer', concerned with upholding and improving the 'domestic' life of the nation. The noted Chicagoen W.I. Thomas was fearful of women's increased participation in public life and 'emancipation', believing it to result in a rise of 'immorality' in young women and men (1923, 1961 ed, pp. 84–85). Robert Park and Ernest Burgess scathingly referred to the work of the women of Hull House as 'social work', which served to detract from its intellectual content, and the influence that it had on their work and that of other Chicagoens (Deegan, 1988). As a result, it is only in the last thirty years that we have seen a gradual acknowledgement of the role played by the women of the Chicago School of Sociology in the development of both sociology and criminology.

The activism and writings of early feminists and those involved in the campaign for women's suffrage consistently challenged misconceptions regarding women's nature and fitness for public life. It is notable that the majority of the Chicagoen women were highly active in the women's suffrage movement: Jane Addams, for example, was well known for her involvement with International Suffrage Alliance and became the first vice president of the National American Women Suffrage Association in 1911. Katharine Bement Davis came from a family that had long supported the cause for women's suffrage, and her appointment as New York City's Commissioner of Corrections in 1914 was hailed as a tremendous step forward for women's rights.

This chapter focuses on the contributions of nineteenth-century feminists to our understanding of the position of women in social life and their more specific experiences of crime and the criminal justice system (whether as offenders or victims) and the legacy of this work in terms of key feminist dates in the 'modern' period. In order to contextualise these contributions, it is necessary to first consider the meaning of the words 'feminist' and 'feminism'.

'Feminist' and 'feminism'

Eugenie Potonie Pierre was responsible for organising two congresses (in 1892 and 1896) to discuss women's role in society; these congresses were particularly significant in that they were widely described as 'feminist'. For although the first self-described 'feministe' was the suffrage campaigner, Hubertine Auclert, who employed the term from 1882 in her monthly journal *La Citoyenne*, this appears to be the first time 'feminist' entered into popular discourse (Offen, 2000). Newspapers from this period show that prior to this time 'feminist' discussions were referred to as 'women's rights' or the 'women's movement', whereas from the mid-1890s 'feminist' began to be more commonly used.[1]

Since this time, there has been much debate over the meanings of 'feminist' and 'feminism'. Finn Mackay acknowledges that 'the term [feminist] means different things to different people, it also freights meaning and is charged with symbolism, not all of it positive' (2015, p. 3). Nevertheless, for the majority of feminists, at the heart of feminism has to be a commitment to making the world a better place for women. For whilst care must be taken not to negate differences of privilege between women, it is tricky not to think of feminism without this overarching goal. As Michèle Barrett wrote in 1980, 'feminism is very hard to conceive of without the experiential dimensions of women's sense of oppression and without a vision of change' (p. v). This is central to feminism's 'political project'.

As we have seen in the chapter on classicist theories, in reference to the writings of Mary Astell and the activism of Olympe de Gouges, examples can be found throughout history of those who have supported feminist principles in the sense of arguing against discrimination on the basis of sex and for women to be granted equality with men. However, as a social movement feminism has typically – and controversially – been split into three waves: the first wave was in the nineteenth and early twentieth century, the second from the 1960s into the 1980s and a third from the late 1980s/early 1990s to the present. 'First wave' feminism was largely concerned with the campaign for the vote, rights to education and property and more participation for women in public life. 'Second wave' feminism largely served to challenge post–Second World War expectations about women's role as homemakers and mothers and their financial dependence on men. It emphasised the necessity for women to have contraceptive choice and access to abortion, highlighted the inequalities that continued to persist between women and men in the public and private spheres and the impact of men's violence against women. Many of those involved in the first and second waves were concerned with issues related to crime and criminal justice and in the second wave were instrumental in developing a feminist approach to criminology. What the third wave represents is somewhat contested: for some the problem is chronological in the sense that it can be difficult to know when the second wave ended and the third began and whether it should simply be seen as 'a natural progression of feminist thought' following the critiques of postcolonial and Black feminists in the 1980s (Burgess-Proctor, 2006, p. 37), who exposed the ethnocentricity of the first and second waves, and the subsequent incorporation of multicultural, multiracial and intersectionality approaches (see, for example, Crenshaw, 1989; Ruiz and Dubois, 2000; Thomson, 2010). For others it also involves women's, particularly young women's, right to assert themselves sexually in whatever way they choose and reclaims derogatory words such as 'slut' and 'bitch' (The Righteous Babes 1998), an emphasis on transgendered politics, a rejection of the gender binary and an acknowledgment of the 'multiple and complex experiences that could be represented through the terms "gender" and "woman"' (Ellison, 2016, p. 337).

It is more commonplace today to speak of 'feminisms'. This, together with increased emphasis on fluid and multiple identities, has been taken to signify a clear move away from the politics of the second wave and the assumption of a collective identity involving collective action, which are the defining features of a social movement. This can be seen as potentially risking the fragmentation and disintegration of the feminist movement as a whole.

Even though in this chapter I make use of the timeframes that the 'waves' fall into, it is important to acknowledge that the wave narrative is extensively critiqued. It is considered to obscure those individual examples of feminist resistance to male oppression that have occurred throughout history and cultures to present, for the most part, a history of the activities of white women in the 'West' at the expense of other movements that have occurred outside of the 'waves' and mainstream politics, especially those of Black, minority and working-class women, as well as feminist movements in other countries that have taken place at different times (Ruiz and Dubois, 2000).

As with the other historical periods covered in this book, it is necessary to be mindful of the degree to which the discipline of criminology and, indeed, academia in general has been exclusionary. Where, for example, are the contributions of Ida B. Wells to discussions on violence? Born into slavery in 1862 Mississippi, Wells became an anti-lynching campaigner, touring the United Kingdom to raise awareness and establishing the British Anti-Lynching Committee. She was, as we saw in the last chapter, an associate of Jane Addams, and was also active in the campaign for women's suffrage in the United States, founding the Alpha Suffrage Club of Chicago. She confronted the racism of the suffrage movement by refusing to march at the back with other Black delegates during a demonstration organised by the National American Women Suffrage Association in 1913 (National Women's History Museum, 2017). Or those of Harriet Tubman? Tubman was responsible for leading hundreds of slaves to freedom as a 'conductor' on the Underground Railroad in the 1850s, a 'mode of action . . . in opposition to the violent world and racist discourses that elite plantation owners had created to rationalize the institution of slavery' (Taylor, 2010, p. 63). Her activism is described by Ula Y. Taylor as adding 'a thread of militancy to the future tapestry of revolutionary black feminisms' (*ibid*). She, too, was involved in women's organisations and in the campaign for suffrage and as an 'advocate of increased attention to the needs of the poor and aged persons . . . was also in the vanguard of the human rights struggle' (*ibid*, pp. 63–64). Given that human rights has been a key area of concern for criminology since its earliest days, the lack of attention afforded to this work is both extraordinary and short-sighted. The exploration of structural violence and social resistance is necessary if we are to fully understand the multi-faceted nature of crime and deviance. Grant et al (2002) have pointed out that even though Black women like Wells worked with academics and wrote sociologically important texts, their exclusion from the academy has meant the sociological and criminological relevance of their contributions have gone unacknowledged.

The nineteenth century

One of the main concerns of feminism in the nineteenth century was the granting of equal rights to women. With this it represented a direct challenge to the application of the principle of formal equality on which modern liberal democracy is founded. The American Declaration of Independence states, 'all men are created equal, that they are endowed by their Creator with certain unalienable Rights, that among these are Life, Liberty and the pursuit of Happiness'. However, 'man' meant a property-owning male, and it was he who had 'rights' and was considered 'equal' to other bourgeois men. In fact, there was agreement amongst the principal Enlightenment thinkers that women's biological make-up meant that they could not be considered rational individuals (Bryson, 1992). An early example of protest against the gender-biased implementation of the notion of formal equality occurred in 1848 at the first convention on women's rights at Seneca Falls in the United States, organised by Elizabeth Cady Stanton and Lucretia Mott. At the Seneca Falls convention sixty-eight women and thirty-two men signed the Declaration of Sentiments, drawn up by Stanton and based on the American Declaration of Independence. The document called for women to be given the same rights as men in relation to education, employment and the vote (see Box 6.1). This, of course, bears a similarity to Olympe de Gouge's 1791 Declaration of the Rights of Woman and the French Citizen, which adapted the words of the Declaration of the Rights of Man in order to draw attention to the lack of equality afforded to women in the 'new' France.

Box 6.1   Excerpt from the 'Declaration of Sentiments'

We hold these truths to be self-evident: that all men and women are created equal; that they are endowed by their Creator with certain inalienable rights; that among these are life, liberty, and the pursuit of happiness; that to secure these rights governments are instituted, deriving their just powers from the consent of the governed. Whenever any form of government becomes destructive of these ends, it is the right of those who suffer from it to refuse allegiance to it, and to insist upon the institution of a new government, laying its foundation on such principles, and organizing its powers in such form, as to them shall seem most likely to effect their safety and happiness.

The history of mankind is a history of repeated injuries and usurpations on the part of man toward woman, having in direct object the establishment of an absolute tyranny over her. To prove this, let facts be submitted to a candid world.

He has never permitted her to exercise her inalienable right to the elective franchise.

He has compelled her to submit to laws, in the formation of which she had no voice.

He has withheld from her rights which are given to the most ignorant and degraded men – both natives and foreigners.

Having deprived her of this first right of a citizen, the elective franchise, thereby leaving her without representation in the halls of legislation, he has oppressed her on all sides.

He has made her, if married, in the eye of the law, civilly dead.

He has taken from her all right in property, even to the wages she earns.

He has so framed the laws of divorce, as to what shall be the proper causes, and in case of separation, to whom the guardianship of the children shall be given, as to be wholly regardless of the happiness of women – the law, in all cases, going upon a false supposition of the supremacy of man, and giving all power into his hands.

After depriving her of all rights as a married woman, if single, and the owner of property, he has taxed her to support a government which recognizes her only when her property can be made profitable to it.

He has monopolized nearly all the profitable employments, and from those she is permitted to follow, she receives but a scanty remuneration. He closes against her all the avenues to wealth and distinction which he considers most honorable to himself. As a teacher of theology, medicine, or law, she is not known.

He has denied her the facilities for obtaining a thorough education, all colleges being closed against her.

Further Reading:

'Declaration of sentiments and resolutions woman's rights convention, held at Seneca Falls, 19–20 July 1848', The Elizabeth Cady Stanton and Susan B. Anthony Papers Project, at: http://ecssba.rutgers.edu/docs/seneca.html

The suffragette movement

In the United Kingdom early feminist activism has largely come to be associated with the activism of the suffragette movement over women's right to the vote. Members of the Women's Social and Political Union (WSPU), founded by Emmeline Pankhurst in 1903, chained themselves to railings, set fire to post boxes, broke windows, heckled government ministers, disrupted Parliament and marched for their cause. Many of the suffragettes were imprisoned and while there continued their protest by going on hunger strike. However, the suffragettes and their supporters were involved in much more than this: their experiences in prison and with the police led them to be critical of the treatment of women offenders by the criminal justice system and to argue for women police officers and the reform of the prison system. They also campaigned on issues related to violence against women and prostitution. Like other groups who have questioned or were seen as a threat to the maintenance of the established social order (i.e. that represented by white male privilege),

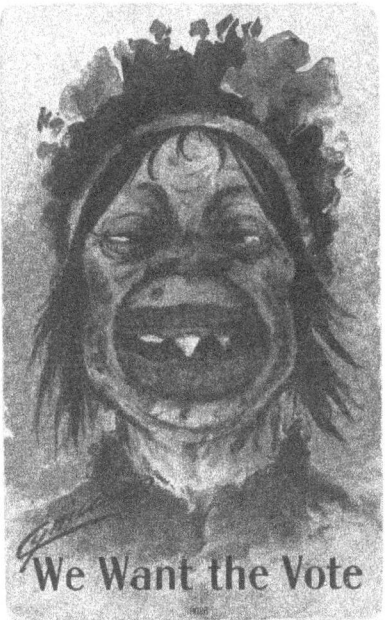

Figure 6.1 A postcard sent to Christabel Pankhurst with the message 'Don't you think that you had better sew a button on my shirt', 1909, Museum of London. The picture, in a similar way to the cartoons of the Irish, is illustrative of the Lombrosian demonisation and 'othering' of those who dare to resist the prevailing social order.

the suffragettes were to find themselves 'othered': they were routinely depicted in the press and on picture postcards as sterile 'old maids' or even monsters in an attempt to suppress and detract from their cause.

The use of surveillance tactics against the suffragettes

Surveillance techniques are today commonly associated with neo-classicist approaches to criminality and utilised in the so-called 'fight against crime'.

Figure 6.2 A secretly taken photograph of suffragettes Evelyn Manesta and Lillian Forrester, Manchester Prison, 1913. As Casciani (2003) notes, 'the photographer was hiding in a van as the women took exercise in the yard'. The National Archives, UK.

Figure 6.3 ID sheets that were used to help police officers identify suffragettes. The National Archives, UK.

In 2003 an exhibition of material from the National Archives in the United Kingdom[2] commemorating the votes for women movement showed that the suffragettes were one of the earliest groups to be subjected to covert photography as a means of monitoring their activities. Dominic Casciani suggests that the suffragette movement was, in all likelihood, the first 'terrorist' organisation to be subjected to secret surveillance photography in the UK, and perhaps even the world (2003). In 1912 photographs were taken of suffragettes using a long-lens camera both inside and outside of prison, enabling the pictorial compilation of lists of key suspects; the militancy of their action being seen as a direct attack on the foundations of the British Empire. The meetings held by suffragettes were also infiltrated by police spies, and Carole Tulloch, the exhibition's curator, amusingly records that Scotland Yard eventually assigned a plainclothes officer on a motorbike to follow the suffragettes: 'He was able to make some notes but failed to keep up with the suffragettes because he had not been given a bike with an automatic starter motor'!

Feminist activism in Europe

Similar campaigns and discussions over the position of women occurred elsewhere in Europe. In France, Hubertine Auclert argued for political rights and also denounced the subordination of women in marriage. Article 213 of the French Civil Code read that the 'the wife must obey the husband'. In Germany Anita Augspurg and Minna Cauer, two of the country's most prominent activists, likewise declared their opposition to marriage, arguing that it degraded and 'enslaved' women. Again in opposition to positivist conceptions of women's nature, Madeleine Pelletier, a French physician and leading feminist activist, advanced social constructionist arguments with respect to how we acquire gender identity: the emphasis being that we are *made*, not born. As Claudine Mitchell notes in her article 'Madeleine Pelletier: The Politics of Sexual Oppression' (1989), Pelletier believed gender identity was acquired by a complex process of social conditioning and that if femininity and masculinity are socially and culturally produced, then feminism could make significant gains in the critiquing of such processes. Pelletier published 'The Sociological Factors of Feminine Psychology' in 1908 in which she described the unequal way in which girls and boys are brought up by their parents, as well as the lack of appreciation of mothering and differences in the education, both intellectual and sexual, of young men and women. Pelletier was also concerned with class-based differences and used 'the example of working class girls being made to serve their brothers to demonstrate the inculcation of female subordination in working class families (whereas) middle class girls were encouraged to focus on the presentation of self – on dress, cleanliness, demeanour, manners' (Mitchell, 1989, p. 77). She saw the emphasis on personal appearance as leading to another form of oppression: the evaluation of the female body through the male gaze. Pelletier, as did many European feminists, experimented with more masculine forms of dress in order to distance herself from traditional concepts of femininity.

Early feminism, crime and criminal justice

As noted earlier, much early feminist action was concerned with issues related to crime and criminal justice. Although the suffragette movement is often seen as representing the start of 'first wave' feminism and was at its peak in the late 1800s/early 1900s, it is argued that the birth of a recognisable women's movement in the UK occurred somewhat earlier with the campaign against the Contagious Diseases Acts (Kossew Pichanick, 1977; Bindel, 2006).

The Contagious Diseases Acts and the work of Josephine Butler

> *'Whatever people may say of me, the main object of my life has been the fight against injustice.'*
>
> Josephine Butler[3]

The Contagious Diseases Acts of 1864, 1866 and 1869 were passed with the intention of preventing venereal diseases in the armed forces. The Vagrancy Act of 1824 had introduced the term 'common prostitute' for women sex workers,[4] a derogatory and stigmatising label that continued to be used in the UK until 2007 (Kevan, 2007). The first Contagious Diseases Act stated that any woman suspected of being a 'common prostitute' within a specified radius of selected garrison towns and naval ports could be approached by a police officer, expected to consent to an internal examination for venereal disease or be brought in front of magistrates. The definition of 'common prostitute' was unclear and, as such, the police had wide discretionary powers (Walkowitz and Walkowitz, 1973). Moreover, as Walkowitz and Walkowitz note, 'at trial, the burden was on the woman to prove she was virtuous – that she did not go with men, whether for money or not' (1973, p. 74). If the woman was found to be suffering from a disease, she was ordered to be confined to a certified 'lock' hospital, which had specialist wards, for a period of three months. If she objected to any stage of the process, she risked imprisonment.

The first Act attracted little in the way of public attention. According to Helena Wojtczak (2009), newspapers simply reported that 'The Contagious Bill passed its reading' and 'by an extraordinary "coincidence", a Bill for the prevention of contagious diseases in cattle was also being debated around that time, and under precisely the same name . . . and so of course people assumed that any mention of those words in the newspapers referred to the diseases of cows' (*ibid*, p. 6). The subsequent Acts extended the legislation to cover more garrison towns and naval ports, widened the radius around the designated areas where women could be apprehended and allowed for longer detention in a 'lock' hospital. Given that only women could be labelled 'common prostitutes' and the Acts specifically addressed the conduct of women, the sexual double standard was blatant. Harriet Martineau, the early sociologist[5] and women's rights advocate, was to write a series of letters for the progressive newspaper, *Daily News*, in which she stated the assumption behind the Acts was the belief that men were 'pre-destined fornicators' with uncontrollable sexual urges that needed to be provided for, like their 'need of food and clothing', and accordingly warranted protection from the consequences of their lust (cited in Butler, 1896, pp. 9–10). As Walkowitz and Walkowitz have argued, the Acts reflected the 'desire of military authorities to safeguard a "healthy imperial race"' and also the turning inwards of 'imperialist compulsions toward the domestic colonization of the poor' and that 'it is within the general atmosphere of social intolerance and institutionalized violence that the treatment of the lower-class prostitute becomes comprehensible' for the 'prostitute's legal status bore the taint of the outcast stripped of civil personality and constitutional rights' (1973, p. 75). The Act did not, of course, just protect soldiers and sailors but all male clients of prostitutes, who were seen as a threat to the 'health' of society. By the late 1860s disquiet with the Acts was growing rapidly. Jacob Bright, the Liberal minister of Parliament (MP), was reported as having 'bitterly complained' of the manner in which the Acts were introduced: 'they have been brought forward either late at night or late in the Session, and every effort has been made to stifle discussion' (Parl. Deb. vol. 203, 20 July 1870; cited in Hamilton, 1978, p. 19) and that women were 'induced by fraud and cajolery to sign a voluntary submission (to an internal examination)' (cited in Wojtczak, 2009). Josephine Butler was to become a leading figure in the movement against the Contagious Diseases Acts and the state legislation of prostitution.

Josephine Butler was born in 1828 into a wealthy yet progressive family that had been active in the abolitionist campaign against slavery. As was the case with many Victorian feminists, she was to draw parallels between slavery and the situation of white women forced into prostitution.[6] Moving to Liverpool with her husband in 1866, she had witnessed how poor women often had little choice but to turn to prostitution in order to support their children, and she was shocked by the treatment they received. As Julie Bindel pointed out, she was deeply disturbed at 'the way servant girls were often sexually assaulted by the men they worked for, and then left destitute when they got pregnant' (2006, p. 34).[7] She helped prostitutes on the streets and in workhouses, often opening her home to them as a place of refuge. Butler was unhappy with the methods of religious charities, who would often preach to 'fallen women' that they should repent or risk eternal damnation, saying, 'rather I would begin by making them women first; by restoring their womanhood . . . it is we, not they, who ought to cover our faces and blush as they pass us by; for the sin of society is ours' (1874, p. 61, cited in Jordan and Sharp, 2003, p. 5). Eventually Butler was to establish her own House of Rest for those who were sick and dying and an Industrial Home where 'women could earn a small income and receive training for "honest occupations"' (Jordan and Sharp, 2003, p. 2).

Butler became secretary of the Ladies National Association for the Repeal of the Acts and embarked on an impressive campaign of letter writing, public speaking and the lobbying of Parliament. The high-profile nature of her work led her to become, as Julie Bindel wrote, 'the first publicly recognized feminist activist in Britain' (2006). Moreover, although she was concerned to equate women's social position and poverty with prostitution, she emphasised that its cause lay with men. At the start of her campaign, when she was asked by a man, 'Can you ever reclaim prostitutes?' she is said to have retorted 'that prostitutes often came to her and asked if men could ever be reclaimed' (*ibid*). Not surprisingly Sheila Jeffreys, who is active in current feminist campaigns against the international sex industry, described her to Bindel as a pioneer, for 'even today, few dare to mention that prostitution is caused by and protected for the sake of men, not women' (*ibid*). Butler was the driving force behind the famous 'Ladies' Protest' against the Acts, which was supported by over 2,000 women, including such notable figures as Harriet Martineau, Florence

Nightingale and the penal reformer Mary Carpenter. The protest pointed out that the Acts violated women's constitutional rights, for they amounted to a 'momentous change in the legal standards hitherto enjoyed by women in common with men' and, in relation to the vagueness of the definition of 'common prostitute', that the 'law is bound in any country professing to give civil liberty to its subjects, to define clearly an offense which it punishes' (Butler, 1896, p. 18). Further they argued that it was 'unjust to punish the sex who are the victims of a vice and leave unpunished the sex who are the main cause, both of vice and its dreaded consequences' and that the 'measures' employed were simply 'cruel' (*ibid*, p. 19). Following the protest, an MP told Butler,

> Your manifesto has shaken us very badly in the Houses of Commons. . . . We know how to manage any other opposition in the House or in the country, but this is very awkward for us – the revolt of the women. It is quite a new thing, what are we to do with such an opposition as this.
> (*ibid*, p. 19)

Many thought it unbecoming that women should be talking of sexual matters and that 'the revolt of women' was a troubling sign of the times, which it undoubtedly was given the activism of the women's suffragette movement that was to come. Butler – as is the fate of many who choose to oppose the establishment and to shake up the status quo – often found herself subjected to vitriolic abuse. One journalist called her 'indecent', a 'shrieking sister, frenzied, unsexed and utterly without shame' (cited in Yeandle et al, 2016, p. 113). Nevertheless, she remained undaunted and received international support from a number of prominent figures, including Victor Hugo, who wrote from Paris, 'I am with you, madam and ladies. . . . Protest! Resist! Show your indignation' (Butler, 1896, p. 25). Finally, in 1886 the Acts were repealed.

Following the success of the campaign against the Contagious Diseases Acts, Butler and her associates continued to fight on behalf of prostitutes. She argued for the age of consent to be raised from 13 to 16 years of age to protect young girls from sexual exploitation and against the sexual trafficking of women to the continent. Butler is in many ways the 'mother' of 'second wave' and recent radical feminist campaigns against the sexual exploitation of women through prostitution, which present prostitution as abuse and as damaging to *all* women (see for example, Barry, 1995; Bindel, 2006, 2017; Jeffreys, 2009). As Butler put it, 'the degradation of these poor unhappy women is not degradation for them alone; it is a blow to the dignity of every virtuous woman too, it is a dishonor done to me, it is the shaming of every woman in every country of the world' (1896, p. 137). Women's involvement in sex work is, however, a contentious area for contemporary feminism. Some feminists, mostly socialist, liberal and sex-positivist feminists, and prostitutes' rights organisations believe that it should be seen as a legitimate occupation that women – as rational agents – can freely choose in a bid to uphold the rights of women to do what they please with their bodies, to normalise the practice and consequently remove the stigma associated with prostitution. It is considered a valid job that is certainly not worse and may make better economic sense for women than working for barely subsistence level pay in other occupations (COYOTE, 2004). Sex-positive feminists who are sometimes associated with 'third wave' feminism have argued that sex workers should be seen as subverters, rather than victims, of the patriarchal social order (see Bazelon, 2016).

Violence against women

In the United Kingdom, the suffragettes, partly through the very public nature of their activism, often found themselves subjected to male violence. As Barbara Caine documents, women suffragettes 'had their breasts crushed and squeezed, and there were reported cases of rape' (2001, p. 776). On 18 November 1910, a day that became known as 'Black Friday', many suffragettes were physically and sexually assaulted by both the police and members of the public as they tried to march on Parliament. Such personal experiences led to a much greater understanding amongst women involved in the movement of the level of violence perpetrated by men against women. One suffragette, Nina Boyle, was particularly vocal on the subject. She concluded, after analysing reported cases of violence, that no crime received such a low level of punishment as that of violence against women. Boyle led the campaign for women police officers, which she hoped would result in a more serious attitude towards violence against women and a greater level of fairness in the treatment of women both as victims and offenders.

Feminists, however, did not just focus on violence in public space. For many, the issue of 'wife beating' was of great concern. Frances Power Cobbe, Matilda Blake and Mabel Sharman Crawford were core members of the campaign against wife beating, contributing articles and lobbying Parliament in an effort to raise public and governmental awareness (Doggett, 1992; Mooney, 2000). Indeed, for these 'first wave' feminists, wife beating was to become a central issue and key to understanding the oppression of women in late Victorian society.

In the United States many 'first wave' feminists campaigned against wife beating as part of the general demands of the temperance movement (see Gordon, 1988; Pleck, 1983). As Elizabeth Pleck notes, their aim was to increase protection for women and to ensure male offenders received harsher punishments while seeing the roots of the problem as residing in the structure of the family, male sexuality and drunkenness; they argued that the wives of drunks, who were often physically abused, 'had the right to divorce their husbands on the grounds of cruelty or *habitual drunkeness*' (1983, p. 453, author emphasis). The linking of wife beating to individual factors such as drunkenness can, however, be seen as serving to divert attention from wider structural causes, weakening the recognition of wife beating as a major social problem requiring intervention in its own right.

Frances Power Cobbe's work did much to highlight the extent and severity of the violence inflicted on many wives in England. Significantly, Cobbe was one of the first to understand the importance of 'naming' and defining women's experiences of violence in order to effectively convey the nature and the impact of the problem. In her influential article, 'Wife-Torture in England' (1878), Cobbe uses the phrase 'wife torture' to

> impress my readers with the fact that the familiar term 'wife-beating' conveys about as remote a notion of the extremity of the cruelty indicated as when candid and ingenuous vivisectors talk of 'scratching a newt's tail' when they refer to burning alive, or dissecting out the nerves of living dogs or torturing ninety cats in one series of experiments.
>
> (p. 72)[8]

She also stated that without intervention, 'Wife-*beating* is the mere preliminary canter before the race . . . Wife-*beating* in process of time, and in numberless cases, advances to Wife-*torture*, and the Wife-torture usually ends in Wife-maiming, Wife-blinding, or Wife-murder' (*ibid*, original emphasis). In this article Cobbe cites numerous reports of particularly horrific cases; for example:

> James Mills cut his wife's throat as she lay in bed. He was quite sober at the time. On a previous occasion he had nearly torn away her left breast.
>
> James Lawrence, who had been frequently bound over to keep the peace and who had been supported by his wife's industry for years, struck her on the face with a poker, leaving traces of the most dreadful kind when she appeared in court.
>
> Fredrick Knight jumped on the face of his wife (who had only been confined a month) with a pair of boots studded with hobnails.
>
> (*ibid*, p. 74)

Nineteenth-century feminists also questioned the image of the battered woman as 'nagging' and 'provocative', which was frequently put forward to the courts:

> I have no doubt that every husband who comes home with empty pockets and from whom his wife needs to beg repeatedly for money to feed herself and her children, considers that she 'nags' him. I have no doubt that when a wife reproaches such a husband with squandering his wages in the public-house, or on some wretched rival, while she and her children are starving, he accuses her to all his friends of intolerable 'nagging,' and

that, not seldom having acquired from him the reputation of this kind of thing, the verdict of 'Serve her Right' is generally passed upon her by public opinion when her 'nagging' is capitally punished by a broken head.
(Cobbe, 1878, p. 68)

The unjust, and often sexist, manner in which women are presented and then blamed for their victimisation continues to be an area of concern for feminists.

These early activists, in emphasising the inadequacy of the law in terms of its response to cases of wife beating, advocated the need for women to be granted an exit from their violent marriages. Thus, Cobbe subsequently fronted a campaign for the introduction of separation orders. With the assistance of Alfred Hill, a Birmingham magistrate and the son of an old friend, she drafted a bill 'for the Protection of Wives whose Husbands have been convicted of assaults upon them'. Her proposals became part of the Matrimonial Causes Act, which was passed in 1878. However, Cobbe did not believe that the achievement of this act would resolve the problem of wife beating, although it would engender 'some alleviation of their wretched condition' (1878, p. 82). In her autobiography, she stated, 'I hope that at least a hundred poor souls each year thus obtain release from their tormentors' (1904, p. 598). In fact, Cobbe and her colleagues were wary of criminal sanctions imposed on men, for these had the potential to make the offender's wife and children suffer due to the level of women's economic dependence on men and could also leave them at risk of reprisals. Hence, as Mabel Sharman Crawford argued in 1893, 'the fine imposed taxed the means required for the support for the offender's family' and 'the sentence of imprisonment entailed on her the penalty of hard labour to keep herself and her children from starvation' (pp. 292–299). 'Let us be aware', she noted, of how a woman 'may well shrink with dread from the thought of being subjected in a few months time to the vengeful fury of the punished tyrant on his release from prison' (p. 293). To underscore the dangerousness of the situation, Crawford detailed the number of cases of husbands who had killed their wives after serving prison sentences for assaulting them. If real change was to occur, this had to be at the level of the social structure. For although Cobbe often cited the orthodox explanations for wife beating put forward at the time – alcohol, prostitution, overcrowding and the degradation of working-class life – she believed the major cause resided in the unequal status of women, in particular, that of wives. Thus, 'the notion that a man's wife is his PROPERTY, in the sense in which a horse is his property, is the fatal root of incalculable evil and misery' (1878, p. 62; original emphasis). And, like many other nineteenth-century feminists, she insisted that change would not occur as long as

> the position of a woman before the law as wife, mother and citizen, remains so much below that of a man as husband, father and citizen,

that it is a matter of course that she must be regarded by him as inferior and fail to obtain from him such a modicum of respect as her mental and moral qualities might win did he see her placed by the State on an equal footing.

(ibid, p. 61)

Being interwoven with the demands of the women's suffrage movement, there was a strong belief in the educational value of being granted formal equality with men. It was hoped that if husbands saw their wives being granted equality by the state, they would be less inclined to regard them as *their* property, and this would reduce women's susceptibility to abuse and encourage women's resistance.

Thus, 'first wave' feminists in the UK, through the dedicated nature of their activism, made wife beating into a matter of societal concern. By providing an understanding of the seriousness of the problem and its impact on the lives of women, they challenged popular misconceptions and affected legislative change, but did not lose sight of the wider structural conditions that underpinned male violence towards women in the home, which had to be tackled if the problem was to be resolved.

A critique of the treatment of women in prison

There is a long history of women prison reformers. Elizabeth Fry is probably one of the best known of the early reformers. A Quaker – as were many of the early prison reformers – from a wealthy family, she worked tirelessly to improve the situation of incarcerated women. Visiting the women in London's Newgate Prison in 1813, she was horrified by the 'filth' of their conditions and pledged to do everything that she could to help. She brought the prisoners bedding and clothing and in 1817 established the Association for the Improvement of Female Prisoners in Newgate, which led to the founding of a school and the employment of women in sewing, spinning and knitting, with any profits from these activities being returned to them (Cooper, 1981). Fry argued for women prisoners to be separated from male prisoners and guards, with a female matron put in charge, aided by the assistance of women visitors. Largely motivated by Christian charity, she believed in the salvation of the prisoner and encouraged other women to likewise become involved, for under their 'fostering care' many a prisoner 'has become completely changed, rescued from a condition of depravity and wretchedness, and restored to happiness as a useful and respectable member of the community' (1827, p. 4). Her book *Observations on the Visiting, Superintendence and Government of Female Prisoners* (1827) became a guide for many middle- and upper-class women who were to form their own reformist organisations (Bosworth, 2004). Fry further encouraged women to become involved in the visiting of other institutions such as hospitals, workhouses and asylums, for this might serve as 'an important check on a variety of abuses which are far too apt to creep into the management of these establishments' (Fry, 1827, p. 4).

Fry, having witnessed the plight of women prisoners being forced aboard boats to be shipped to New South Wales, became part of the movement to abolish the transportation of prisoners. This barbaric practice, which saw 25,000 women sent to Australia between 1787 and 1852, led to the separation of families, with no children over the age of 7 being allowed to accompany their mothers, and although the shackling of women prisoners was prohibited, women found themselves placed in irons for the duration of the journey (Fry, 1827). However, whilst Fry is often regarded as an example of an early feminist campaigner for her efforts on behalf of women prisoners and the public nature of her work, her focus was on improving the day-to-day conditions that women encountered rather than engaging with their experiences of structural oppression. Her emphasis was largely on the need for women prisoners to be compliant, to conform to society's expectations; hence she stated that the object of the Association for the Improvement of Female Prisoners in Newgate was 'to form in them, as much as possible, those habits of sobriety, order, and industry, which may render them docile and peaceable while in prison, and respectable when they leave it' (1847, p. 262). The intention of early prison reformers was for the prison to rehabilitate the 'criminal' or 'fallen' woman to a more socially acceptable vision of femininity and womanhood, constructed around modesty, submissiveness and being a 'good wife and mother'.

A few decades later, hundreds of suffragettes were to be imprisoned as a result of the militancy of their actions. Despite the attempts of reformists such as Fry, the prison life they encountered was extremely harsh, and they were exposed to the level of ill treatment that women inmates were subjected to on a daily basis. As is true today, many of the prisoners they encountered had been convicted of non-violent petty crimes, were poor and had suffered sexual and physical abuse.

The well-known suffragette Lady Constance Lytton wrote in her autobiography *Prisons and Prisoners: Some Personal Experiences:*

> Who were the women who, day by day, trod the very stones on which my feet now stood.... How and why had they broken the law, in what ways were they enemies of Society? Child-burdened women who were left without money, without the means or opportunity or physical power to earn it, who had stolen in order to save their lives and that of their children, – thieves! Women who from childhood had been trained to physical shame, women who at their first adolescence had born children by their own fathers.... Women who had been seduced by their employers. Women deceived and deserted by their friends. Women employed by their own parents for wage earning prostitution.
>
> (1914, pp. 62–63)

As with violence against women, these social injustices were seen by Lytton and other feminists in this period to have arisen directly from the unequal status of women in society: a symbolic manifestation of the suffragettes' cause.

> Before they took to these muddy lanes have they not been driven out from their fair road? What was their training, what their choice from the start? Are not the doors of the professions and many trades still barred to them? Their right to work, a fair value for their work, is it not denied to them? When they undertake the burdensome but joyous labour of maternity, is there any security to them of physical respect and choice, of economic security, of rewardful honour and social influence? Where is the recognition of the woman's great service, how is she helped to render it suitably and efficiently; does the State, the race, the family, the individual, see to it that she has her reward.
>
> (*ibid*, p. 63)

Lytton was to stress the importance of acknowledging the implications of class prejudices and barriers, arguing that these were deeply injurious to both individuals and society as a whole and that, when imprisoned, women of her social standing received much better treatment than working-class women. To demonstrate this, she travelled to Liverpool and Manchester, her 'first experience of meetings in a really poverty stricken district' (1914, p. 235) and adopted the persona of Jane Warton, a working-class seamstress. As Jane Warton she was arrested for suffragette activities, sentenced to hard labour and, on going on hunger strike, subjected to force feeding without any medical examination. This contrasted to Lady Lytton's earlier experiences, for when imprisoned under her real name, she was well treated and underwent numerous medical checks due to her weak heart.

On a practical level, many of the suffragettes used what voice they had to argue against unnecessary and degrading prison procedures, such as the level of searching, restrictions on sanitary provisions and the cutting of women's hair. They also protested their own treatment; having been labelled 'insane' by the authorities, they fought for the right to be considered political prisoners. Further, as noted earlier, many of the suffragettes continued their campaign of civil disobedience by going on hunger strike, which resulted in forcible feeding. This was, as the feminist historian June Purvis documents, a brutal process:

> The hunger striker was held down on a bed by wardresses or tied to a chair which they tipped back. Then a rubber tube was either forced up the nose or down the throat and into the stomach. The latter method was particularly painful because a steel gap was pushed into the mouth and screwed open, as wide as possible. Tissue in the nose and throat was nearly always

Figure 6.4 'The Modern Inquisition —Treatment of Political Prisoners Under a Liberal Government'. Protest poster against the treatment of women suffragettes, published by The Women's Social and Political Union, 1910, Museum of London.

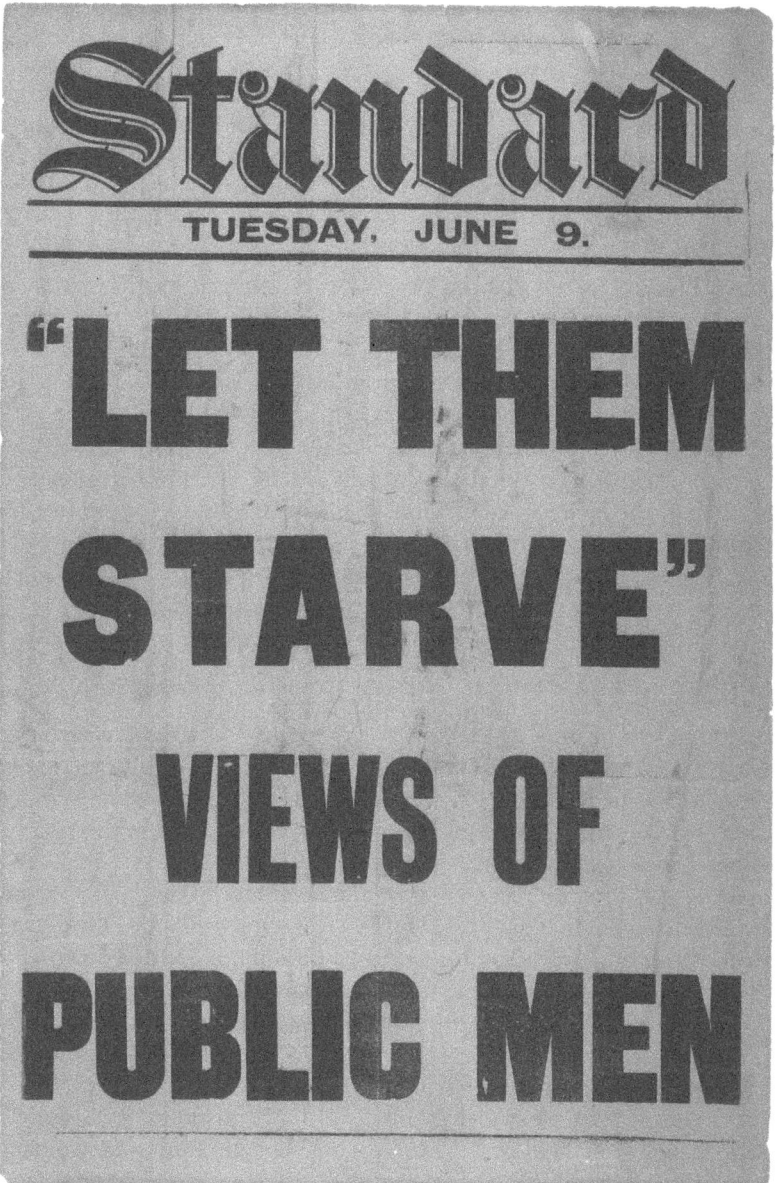

Figure 6.5 Newspaper billboard from the *Evening Standard*, 1914. This refers to the response of the authorities – the 'public men' – to the hunger-striking suffragettes, Museum of London.

damaged, while sometimes the tube was accidentally inserted into the windpipe, causing food to enter the lungs and endangering life.

(*The Guardian*, 6 July 2009)

Letters from suffragettes reveal the nasal tube was often dirty: Dorothy Pethick recalled that it was not sanitised between feedings, with the tube and the jug which contained the liquid left near a window on an open tray. The treatment, she said, was 'agonising', 'callous', 'careless' and 'violent' (*Letter*, 1 November, 1909).[9] Some women, such as Grace Roe and Kitty Marion, were to endure the procedure over 200 times (Purvis, 2009).

Alyson Brown has pointed out that for the suffragettes, such experiences provided further examples of male injustice and were part of the political situation that had brought them into prison in the first place. Taken to its extreme, forcible feeding could be seen as an 'invasion of a female body by the oppressive hands of the state and even a form of violation or rape' (2002, p. 627). The poster pictured here depicts the practice as 'torture', the late nineteenth- and early twentieth-century equivalent of the water torture used at the time of the Spanish Inquisition. It is similar to some of the treatment that Jean Calas was subjected to in the eighteenth century and has again been used against political prisoners in U.S. detention centres, such as Guantanamo Bay.

Feminism in the contemporary period

Even though feminism as a social movement might not have been as recognisable in the years following the high-profile campaigns of the suffragettes, feminist ideals remained. Ann Logan's *Feminism and Criminal Justice: A Historical Perspective* documents how a number of leading suffragettes in the UK, some of whom had 'experienced first-hand the criminal justice system in courts and prisons during their struggle for women's votes' (2006a, p. 1), went on to become magistrates, which she regards 'as a logical outcome of the struggle for women's suffrage and citizenship rights' (2006b, p. 834). Women understood their role as being an 'important indicator of their status as citizens' (2006a, p. 1), but also that there was much more to the job than was generally assumed. They were, therefore, instrumental in professionalising the role of the lay magistracy and became involved in wider reform measures. Margery Fry, for example, was a founder member of the Magistrates' Association, an education advisor at Holloway Prison for women in London, a campaigner against the death penalty and pioneered the idea of compensation for victims of crime. Logan further shows how women penal reformers in the UK, like many of the early Chicago women sociologists, were at the forefront of the need to commission 'scientific' studies and university-based research to follow up ex-offenders and to assess the rates of recidivism. Logan's analysis of the level that women were involved in the judicial system, either as magistrates or in other roles; their concerns over the treatment of women and children within the system; and the emphasis placed on social welfare lends support to her argument that the concept of 'penal-welfarism' within criminology (Garland, 1985; Bailey, 1987) and the relationship between penal policy and the welfare state should be re-evaluated to take account of feminist contributions. For even though the time between 1945 and 1959 is often seen as 'the nadir of feminism' as a movement, feminist ideals were 'alive and well', although admittedly women had to adapt to the 'cautious, conservative and constitutional values of the time as well as to cope with the passing of the suffrage generation' (Logan, 2006a, p. 4).

In the United States, feminist ideals in the pre–World War II period were strongly evident in the work of women associated with Jane Addams and the Hull House settlement, and after the war through the activities of women such as Anna Kross. Kross had been active in the women's suffrage movement in New York City. A social reformer and advocate for family courts and rehabilitation measures, she became Commissioner of Corrections for the city in 1954 (McCarthy, 1997). As a young lawyer, Kross had volunteered assistance to women brought into the women's night court and later as commissioner stated publicly that prostitution was a social issue and should not be dealt with by the criminal justice system and, controversially for the time, that 90 per cent of those held at the Women's House of Detention in New York City should never have been arrested. The feminism that Logan describes, and that is evident in Kross's activities, is that of a liberal feminism concerned with equal rights before the law and 'a "welfare" feminism that was concerned with women within the existing system' (Jackson, 2011, p. 155).

The late 1960s onwards

The late 1960s is recognised as an important time within feminist history. It is seen as marking the start of a tremendous growth in feminist ideas and the development of feminism as a distinct social theory. Stevie Jackson has described feminist social theory as that which 'addresses the broad question of how and why women come to be subordinated, and offers analyses of the social and cultural processes through which that subordination is perpetuated' (1993, p. 3). For many 'second wave' feminists, a key concept for exploring the principles and structures which underpin women's subordination was that of patriarchy. Originally used in its literal sense to mean 'rule by fathers' to justify the absolute authority of monarchs in the time of the *ancien régime*, in 'second wave' feminism, the concept of 'patriarchy' was 're-discovered. . . . as a "struggle concept", because the movement needed a term by which the totality of oppressive and exploitative relations which affect women could be expressed, as well as their systematic character' (Mies, 1986, p. 37). As such, patriarchy is usually taken to refer to the way in which male supremacy and the subordination of women are organised within society. In criminology

Frances Heidensohn (1985) notes that patriarchy can be used in two ways: to explain women's experiences in the criminal justice system and the gendered nature of a large amount of criminal victimisation.

Within contemporary feminism a range of perspectives and theoretical positions can be identified, and care must be taken not to see feminism as a unified body of thought. However, in this section, it is necessary to briefly touch on some core theoretical strands in order to explore how feminism has sought to redress the gender balance within criminology. Many of the issues that concerned nineteenth-century feminists, especially those relating to violence and the treatment of women by the criminal justice system, continued to be the focus of feminist campaigns in the 'second wave' and into the present period.

Liberal feminism

Liberal feminism, as illustrated by Logan (2006a) in her discussion of women penal reformers, is an extension of the liberal project of the Enlightenment to include women. It was argued from the beginnings of feminist thought that as women are rational beings like men, they should have the same legal and political rights. A consideration of the Seneca Falls Declaration of Sentiments shows how easy it is to fit the arguments of some of those involved in the 'first wave' into the equal rights agenda of liberal feminism. In the 1970s the campaign in the United States for the Equal Rights Amendment, which proposed that equal rights under the law shall not be denied by any state on account of sex, is seen as an obvious example of liberal feminist ideals in action in this period (see Gregory, 1986).[10] Liberal feminism has continued to argue for equality in employment and for maternity leave, child care and pension rights. In the United Kingdom the Fawcett Society, which promotes 'women's equality and rights at home, at work and in public life', has shown, for example, how women remain under-represented in terms of the higher professions of the criminal justice system. The study *Sex and Power 2013: Who Runs Britain* found that only 15.6 per cent of high court judges were women and there was only one woman Supreme Court Justice.

One of the problems inherent in liberal feminism, as with the liberal or classicist position in criminological discourse, is that of the 'classicist contradiction': that is the contradiction between formal and substantive equality. Liberal feminists have been accused of 'reflecting only the concerns of middle-class white women who are privileged in every way other than their sex, and of ignoring the inequalities amongst men and the realities of class and race oppression' (Bryson, 1992, p. 168). Liberal feminism, unlike other 'feminisms', for example, socialist, radical, Black and postcolonial, does not sufficiently critique the existing social structure; it aims to reform rather than to overthrow. Indeed, as a result of this, it is often referred to as 'bourgeois feminism' for 'its goal is to obtain sexual equality within the economic and political framework of capitalism' (Gregory, 1986, p. 65).

Socialist feminism

Some of the impetus for the development of a socialist feminism arose from a disillusionment with liberal politics and the promotion of an equal rights agenda without questioning existing social arrangements. Jeanne Gregory, for example, has forcefully highlighted the dangers of arguing for equal rights in a capitalist society:

> Gains secured under the equal rights banner are inherently fragile as individuals or groups with competing rights claim equal legitimacy. A woman's right to choose an abortion is challenged in terms of the rights of the unborn fetus. Fathers compete with mothers for an extension of rights in relation to their children. Such divisions cannot be resolved within the framework of competitive individualism that capitalism breeds.
> (1986, p. 65)

Socialist feminism, which comprises a number of Marxist and non-Marxist socialist positions, came to prominence in the 1970s. In this period, as Lynne Segal points out, 'radical socialist politics of some sort were integral to a feminist outlook in Britain' (1987, p. 44). What unites the various socialist 'feminisms' is the belief that women's situation is influenced by its socio-economic context and that this context needs to be changed if we are to see an improvement in women's lives and social positions. A socialist feminism is evident in the work of many of those involved with the Hull House settlement: theirs was a shared belief in the necessity of economic and social improvement and political action. Moreover, Hull House, described as a 'commune of women', represented for some of the women who lived there a means by which they could be freed from financial dependence on men.

In the 1970s socialist feminist debates centred on the application of Marxist theory to feminism. Marxism examines society in terms of the material conditions of production; that is, the circumstances under which labour is organised and goods are produced. In capitalist society, the fundamental social divide is that of class, analysed in terms of the exploitation of working-class (proletarian) labour by the bourgeoisie (those who own the means of production). Class struggle is presented as the principal force driving history and is seen as eventually resulting in an egalitarian (socialist) society in which oppression is eradicated. Marxist feminists have attempted either to assimilate feminism into a Marxist critique of capitalism or to develop Marxist theory to encompass the politics of the women's liberation movement (see Jackson, 1993). The latter group have been described by some commentators as Marxist feminists (Maynard, 1989).

Thus, many Marxist feminists have focused their attention on the position of women in the labour market. It has been argued that women are concentrated in badly paid, low-status, part-time positions often because they are regarded as financially dependent on husbands, even though this may not reflect the reality of their situation (see Maynard, 1989; Donovan, 1997). The Marxist concept of a reserve army of labour has been applied to women, locating the specificity of women's paid labour within the general Marxist model of capital accumulation (Beechey, 1977; Bruegal, 1979). Women are seen as being brought into and out of paid work as the interests of capital dictates (that is, in terms of economic expansion and recession). As Anne Phillips and Barbara Taylor comment, women are presented as the 'super-exploitables' (1980, p. 80) in capitalist society. The societal perception of men as the major 'breadwinners' and women as primarily housewives who may be working for a little extra 'pin-money' to supplement their housekeeping can be seen as reinforcing women's economic dependency on men and necessitating the finding of a husband. Charnie Guettel, a Canadian Marxist feminist, has highlighted the wider implications of this:

> [S]ince she lacks access to subsistence jobs for herself . . . she must defer to her mate and males in general . . . where [women] must live, with whom, and by means of what, these are determined by economic factors, and they in turn determine the parameters of male-female relationships.
> (1974, pp. 49–50)

This analysis can be utilised to explain women's economic dependence on men and highlights how difficult it is for a woman to leave an abusive relationship and provide for herself and her children financially (see Mooney, 2000).

In criminology, class-based studies have additionally proven useful in understanding aspects of women's criminality. Historically women have been found to commit mostly non-violent property offences or those connected with prostitution; both are seen as resulting from the poverty created by their disadvantaged economic situation (Carlen, 1988; Cook, 1987). Susan Edwards's 1987 research, for example, showed an increase in the level of offences related to prostitution during the period of Margaret Thatcher's Conservative government in Britain; this had to be seen as primarily caused by the deterioration of women's economic position. The government, which aimed to advance market society, had reduced the 'safety net' of the welfare state at a time of rising levels of unemployment and economic recession.

Social class position has likewise been used to explain the violence of men. Elizabeth Wilson (1983) and Lynne Segal (1989, 1990) present violence as a result of the frustrations generated by class inequality. Wilson comments, 'the working class youth's aggression – "bovver" – becomes a front to conceal his inner desperation and to protect him from a hostile world that condemns him, essentially to failure' (1983, p. 231). Julia Schwendinger in *Rape and Inequality* (1983) (with Herman Schwendinger) adopted a Marxist feminist approach to show 'that the incidence of violence against women compounds with the degree of sexual inequality in a given context', with the blame for inequality placed on the devastating hold that corporate capitalism has on the United States (cited in Barak and Pagni, 2010, p. 163). Further, Lynne Segal argued with reference to domestic violence that 'what we are confronting here is the barbarism of private life reflecting back to the increased barbarism of public life as contemporary capitalism continues to chisel out its hierarchies along the familiar groves of class, race and gender' (1990, p. 271). For socialist feminists,

> It is social cooperation, not excessive individualism, that would form a better basis for social life and for relations between the sexes, and would best meet the needs of most of us, women and men together.
>
> None of this will happen so long as our society is run on the profit motive, which is the elevation of greed as the basic social principle.
>
> (Wilson, 1983, p. 242)

Radical feminism

Radical feminism developed towards the end of the 1960s and, as Andrea Jaggar (1983) notes, contrasted to liberal and traditional Marxist conceptions of feminism, which were based in philosophical traditions that are over three hundred and one hundred years old, respectively. The theoretical impetus for radical feminism came, in part, from women's experiences of sexual domination in the New Left organisations which had sprung up during this decade. Jeanne Gregory comments that the neglect of women's issues by the male Left in the United States directly led to a 'mushrooming' of feminist organisations; thus,

> The Chicago group was . . . conceived in anger, following a political convention at which a women's resolution was considered too insignificant to merit discussion. The chairman patted one of the women on the head and told her: 'Cool down little girl. We have more important things to talk about than women's problems'. The 'little girl' did not cool down. Instead, she [Shulamith Firestone] became a radical feminist and wrote *The Dialectic of Sex*. You could not ask for a more vivid demonstration of the inter-relationship between the political and the theoretical than this!
>
> (1986, p. 64)

Radical feminism is rooted in the experiences of women and, as such, is considered to be a theory that is *of* and *for* women (Bryson, 1992). Indeed, Catharine MacKinnon argues that it is the only true feminist theory:

> Feminism has been widely thought to contain tendencies of liberal feminism, radical feminism, and socialist feminism. But just as socialist feminism has often amounted to traditional Marxism . . . applied to women – liberal feminism has been liberalism applied to women. Radical Feminism is feminism.
>
> (1989, p. 117)

For radical feminists, it is the male oppression of women that is the most fundamental form of domination. Patriarchy is therefore central to their analysis of women's position in society. It is patriarchy, not capitalism, that is held responsible for women's oppression, and patriarchy pre-dates capitalism. Men as a group are seen to dominate women as a group and are the beneficiaries of women's continued subjugation. As Kate Millett comments in *Sexual Politics*,[11] 'sex is a status category with political implications' (1977, p. 24). Men are presented as oppressing women in all areas of life; important to this is the idea that 'the personal is political', which serves to highlight women's oppression in their private lives and personal relationships. 'The personal is political' clearly presents a challenge to conventional political theory, including liberal and traditional forms of Marxist feminism, which consider political power to be connected with the state or paid employment – in other words, the public sphere. For radical feminists, women are dominated not only in the public sphere but also in their private lives; furthermore, such domination is intimate and bodily. For the majority of radical feminists, patriarchal domination is considered to involve the male appropriation of women's sexuality and bodies, as well as acts of violence. In criminology, radical feminist ideas have particularly affected discussions on violence against women.

One of the main criticisms of radical feminism is that of essentialism, particularly with respect to conceptions of masculinity. In much of the early writing there is the assumption that men are all the same. Susan Brownmiller's arguments, for example, in *Against Our Will: Men, Women and Rape* (1975), whilst having considerable influence, have been attacked for biological essentialism. She suggests that men rape because they have the biological capacity to do so, which is an individual positivist position. Hence, 'men's structural capacity to rape and women's corresponding structural vulnerability are as basic to the physiology of both sexes as the primal act of sex itself . . . when men discovered they could rape, they proceeded to do it' (*ibid*, pp. 13–14). Since this time, radical feminists, especially in Britain, have been concerned to stress that the criticism of biological essentialism is a misrepresentation of radical feminist analyses: violence, as Jalna Hanmer, Jill Radford and Betsy

Stanko (1989) point out, is a product of the social construction of masculinity (see also Walby, 1990; Jordan, 2010 on Brownmiller).

Radical feminism and violence against women

Like nineteenth-century feminists, radical feminism in the 'second wave' did much to highlight the extent and impact of violence against women. Male violence is seen as the basis of men's control over women. Early analyses, particularly those of U.S. radical feminists, tended to focus on the subject of rape (Griffin, 1971; Medea and Thompson, 1974; Reynolds, 1974). They argued against the positivistic theories of rape, which suggest that rape is an exceptional occurrence carried out by a few abnormal men (that is, by those with an inadequate or asocial personality). Thus, Andrea Medea and Kathleen Thompson stress the widespread nature of rape and maintain,

> It is time, then, for women to stop thinking of rapists as sick or crazy men. You might very easily have dated [one] or your daughter might or your elder sister. [He] might have been the man you married or [the men] egging him on might have been friends of yours. The rapist is the man next door.
>
> (1974, p. 36)

Violence against women is seen as keeping all women in a state of fear because it is impossible for a woman to tell which men are safe and which are rapists or batterers. As Susan Griffin argues, 'rape is a kind of terrorism which severely limits the freedom of women and makes women dependent on men' (1971, p. 7). It leads women to seek the protection of one man against all others. Jan Reynolds further develops the social control thesis by suggesting that societal distinctions over what is seen as 'appropriate' and 'inappropriate' female behaviour mean that women who violate the traditional female role expectations are targeted: 'rape is a punitive action directed toward females who usurp or appear to usurp the culturally defined prerogatives of the dominant male role' (1974, p. 66). Women who fail to conform, for example, by being sexually promiscuous or assertive, are more at risk. Male violence denies women their freedom and autonomy, an argument elaborated by Betsy Stanko, who demonstrates how women's lives are structured around concerns for personal safety,

> Wherever women are, their peripheral vision monitors the landscape and those around them for potential danger. On the street, we listen for footsteps approaching and avoid looking men in the eyes. At home, women are more likely than men to ask callers to identify themselves before opening the front door and to search for ways to minimize conflict with potentially violent partners. . . . Women's lives rest upon a continuum of

unsafety. . . . For the most part, women find they must constantly negotiate their safety with men – those with whom they live, work or socialise, as well as those they have never met.

(1990, p. 85)

For Frances Power Cobbe in the nineteenth century, choice of language in the naming and defining of wife beating was key to the way in which the problem was to be conceptualised and socially understood.

'Second wave' radical feminist work was likewise to challenge conventional definitions of violence and legal categories. Liz Kelly's *Surviving Sexual Violence* (1988) is today a classic within feminist literature for its detailed critique and exploration of definitions of male violence. Stressing the importance of using women's voices ('if we are to reflect in our definition the range and complexity of what women experience as abusive we must listen to what they are saying' [1988, p. 71]), she noted that conventional definitions of violence and legal categories 'reflect men's ideas and limit the range of male behaviour' seen as unacceptable 'to the most extreme, gross and public forms' (*ibid*, p. 138). As such, women find themselves caught between their own experiences, which they regard as abusive, and the dominant male discourse that defines such behaviour as normal or expected. Kelly, who refers to a 'continuum of sexual violence' in order to link the various forms of male violence together, described sexual violence as any behaviour 'experienced by the woman or girl, at the time or later, as a threat, invasion or assault, that has the effect of hurting her or degrading her and/or takes away her ability to control intimate contact' (*ibid*, p. 41). What is central to radical feminist discourses on violence against women is how *women* themselves define their experiences.

The level that the problem of male violence was underestimated was of great concern to radical feminists, for it had the potential to undermine the construction of male violence against women as a major social problem, which had implications for the amount of resources deemed necessary to tackle it. In the 'first wave', feminists had called attention to the 'hidden figure' that exists with respect to such violence: as Cobbe wrote, 'there are, for every one of these *published* horrors, at least three or four which *never are reported at all*, and where the poor victim dies quietly of her injuries like a wounded animal, without seeking the mockery of redress offered her by the law' (1878, pp. 73–74, emphasis in original). The problem of the hidden figure was repeatedly restated in the 'second wave', with feminists pointing out that women do not report for a wide variety of reasons, for example, because of fear of reprisals from the man, or his friends and family, the loss of family support, concerns over official intervention, distrust of the police or that the police will consider their case too trivial, the belief that what they have been subjected to does not match the official definition of 'domestic violence', that it will add to the trauma of the original assault and so on (Mooney, 2000). The research of Diana Russell (1982) in the United States on rape in marriage carried out towards the end of the 1970s and Jalna Hanmer and Sheila Saunders's survey of violence against women in a neighbourhood of Leeds in the UK, which was published as *Well Founded Fear* in 1984 were therefore ground-breaking in terms of uncovering the extent of male violence against women, exposing the level of the hidden figure and also in their advocating of the need for a sensitive, women-centred research methodology.

With respect to rape and arguments for improvements in the criminal justice system, Sue Lees's work on rape trials in the UK is particularly important. Through research conducted at the Old Bailey Criminal Court in London, she showed the frequency with which the victim's sexual history was introduced in an attempt to discredit her evidence (the 'inappropriate' behaviour argument). Much of the cross-examination of the woman was degrading and, as Lees observed, the implications of some of the questions are subtle, as is apparent in this example where the complainant was asked about her red shoes,

> The defence asked: 'You would admit these shoes are not leather. They are at the cheaper end of the market'. If her shoes were cheap, the implication was that she must be cheap too.
> (Lees, in *The Guardian*, 16 Feb. 1999)

Lees fought for the government to restrict evidence concerning a woman's sexual history and for better training for judges and barristers. She believed that, given the sensitive nature of such cases, there should be special prosecutors for rape trials

However, involvement with criminal justice reforms is a contentious area for radical feminists. Some radical feminists

> have argued that the state and the law, the legal mechanism and the police are part of a patriarchal structure, under which attempts at legal reform are only tinkerings within the overall system of control and regulation – so legal change serves only to perpetuate the basic conditions of patriarchy.
> (Edwards, 1989, p. 15)

Related to this, there is concern, especially in the United States, over 'carceral feminism':[12] a feminism aligned with a 'law and order' agenda, with a focus on policing, prosecution and imprisonment as a way of dealing with crimes against women. For as is well documented, the police are often the instigators of violence, and prisons and jails are violent institutions, and as Alex Press points out, given the current situation in which 'the United States incarcerates people – especially black and brown people – at *unparalleled rates*, and our president [Trump] *embraces and publicizes* racist explanations for social problems' (original emphasis), this will simply lead to the 'locking up of more poor and working-class people' (1 Feb. 2018) leaving those in power relatively unscathed, and engaging with the criminal justice system has the potential to make things worse, not better, for women. The necessity of problematising the role of the state and recognising it as an agent of social control, and the level that it affects Black and minority women, is key to much feminism in the contemporary period.

What is consistent within the radical feminist literature from the late 1960s into the 1980s is the need for women-centred services, such as Women's Aid and Rape Crisis in the UK, and for women's collective support and action and for long-term structural change at the level of the patriarchal social order. Hence, 'our strength must be in our women's groups and organisations. We have to organise to protect ourselves and our children from all forms of male violence and control (Hanmer and Saunders, 1984, p. 112). And Liz Kelly contends,

> It was never the intention of those of us who chose to work in this area in the 1970s that our work became limited to 'band aid' solutions: as Maria Zavala puts it, 'a MASH unit, patching up the wounded and sending them back to the front line' . . . No matter how effective our services and support networks, no matter how much change in policy and practice is achieved, without a mass movement of women committed to resisting sexual violence in all its forms there will continue to be casualties in the 'shadow war' and women's and girl's lives will continue to be circumscribed by the reality of sexual violence.
>
> (1988, p. 238)

Feminism and criminology

The development of contemporary theory in criminology in the 1970s was marked in the UK by the publication of Ian Taylor, Paul Walton and Jock Young's *The New Criminology* (1973), and in terms of feminist theorising, Carol Smart's *Women, Crime and Criminology: A Feminist Critique* (1976) was, as Sandra Walklate has put it, 'a critical *tour de force*' (2010, p. 279). There were, of course, feminist studies on specific areas of crime before this date, as is evident from the discussion of the contributions of nineteenth-century feminists and the work of women associated with the Chicago School of Sociology. In the 'second wave' period, commentaries on sexual violence by Griffin (1971), Medea and Thompson (1974), Reynolds (1974) and Brownmiller (1975) in the United States were influential. The work of Frances Heidensohn on women and crime in the late 1960s in Britain must also be acknowledged. In 1968 she published her first paper, 'The Deviance of Women: A Critique and an Enquiry' in the *British Journal of Sociology*. Even though Heidensohn described 'The Deviance of Women' in an interview that

I conducted with her for *Fifty Key Thinkers in Criminology* (2010) as prefeminist in its approach, in the sense of lacking the vocabulary and conceptual analysis provided by feminism of the 1970s, it is a remarkable paper, in that it addresses the major themes for the study of women and crime and deviance. It critiques both the neglect and sexist treatment of women in historical and contemporary theoretical debates on criminality. Whilst women and crime featured in the research of those associated with the early days of the Chicago School of Sociology, and there were the wonderful ethnographies, for example, by Annie Marion MacLean, this work was affected by the male dominance of the academy and, as such, never reached the prominence of, say, Clifford Shaw's *The Jack Roller* (1930) or Edwin Sutherland's *The Professional Thief* (1937). In 'The Deviance of Women', Heidensohn suggested that what was now needed was 'a crash programme in research which telescopes decades of comparable studies of males' (1968, p. 171) that would serve to 'broaden our view of deviance in general' (*ibid*).

It was Carol Smart's book that was to be the first to systematically theorise on issues relating to women, crime and criminal justice *within* the academic discipline of criminology. Smart studied sociology at Portsmouth Polytechnic in, as Sandra Walklate notes, the 'turbulent 1970s – just as 'second wave' feminism was taking hold on academics and activists alike' (2010, p. 278) before going on to study for her Master's and PhD at the University of Sheffield, where one of her lecturers was Ian Taylor. She wrote *Women, Crime and Criminology* as a Master's student (*ibid*). Let us consider the key arguments she presented.

Smart's central thesis was that, in comparison to the amount of work on male criminality, women and crime was a neglected area. It was neglected due to the relatively low numbers of women who commit crime and the mainly trivial nature of their offences. Female criminality was not a threat to the social order and therefore was not considered a social problem in the same way as male criminality. As Smart comments, women and girl offenders 'present less of an irritation to the police, the courts and the penal system and consequently there has been little official requirement or support for studies of female criminality' (*ibid*, p. 3). The male orientation of criminology was, of course, by no means unique in the social sciences. However, Smart argued, as criminology is a policy-driven discipline, this had particularly serious implications for women, 'which extend beyond the narrow confines of academia to the actual treatment of women in the courts and penal institutions' (*ibid*, p. 1). She took particular issue with the way in which women offenders are frequently presented as mentally ill and how mental illness is seen as a type of deviant behaviour appropriate to women to the extent that it is seen as 'an equivalent or alternative form of behaviour to criminality' (*ibid*, 146). Pathologising female criminality served to focus the problem of crime on the individual rather than society. For example, when Holloway Prison in London was redeveloped in the 1970s, it reflected 'views about women offenders being physically or mentally sick, or both' (Heidensohn and Silvestri, 2012, p. 353) and thus requiring, in line with positivist conceptions, a therapeutic regime. Additionally, there were, and still are, only a small number of women's prisons, meaning women were likely to be placed many miles from their homes, making it difficult to maintain the family and friendship links considered essential to successful rehabilitation. The pathological presentation of female criminality was to lend itself to an emphasis on treatment, and often this also meant being re-socialised into a stereotypical feminine role.

As with the neglect of women offenders, Smart drew attention to the way in which rape had been ignored in the criminological literature: 'there are relatively few studies within the traditional body of criminological literature concerned with examining the reasons why men commit rape, under what circumstances rape occurs and what the effects on the victim may be' (*ibid*, p. 78). Again, Smart showed how positivistic accounts tended to dominate, with 'the stereotypical rapist . . . thought to be a sexual psychopath, having little in common with other men' (*ibid*, p. 94). And the woman, especially if the offender was a known man, more often than not found herself blamed for the attack:

> his victim is often thought to have little in common with ordinary women, it being assumed that only a foolish or reckless woman would be found in circumstances where a rape may take place or that only a sexually promiscuous woman would dress or act in a manner likely to arouse uncontrollable sexual desire.
>
> (*ibid*, p. 94)

Such presentations of both the offender and victim affected the attitudes of the police and courts. Smart concluded *Women, Crime and Criminology* by discussing the possibility of formulating a 'feminist criminology,'[13] noting how the new, critical, radical and working-class criminologies that were emerging at this time still failed to include a feminist perspective or seriously consider women. Like Heidensohn, she called for more research in the area of women and crime, which she stressed must be 'situated in the wider moral, political, economic and sexual spheres which influence women's status and position in society' (*ibid*, 185).

Since the 1970s the situation has changed considerably. Courses on 'Women and Crime' or 'Gender and Crime' are taught in criminology and criminal justice departments in universities around the world. There is a tremendous amount of feminist writing, research and policy within the discipline,[14] some of which I have touched upon. Frances Heidensohn and Marisa Silvestri have described feminists as contributing some of the 'strongest' and 'most lively and important' (2012, p. 361, p. 263) work to criminology. Feminists have provided a focus on the offending behaviour of women and girls and explanations for their low criminality in comparison to men (see, for example, Carlen, 1985, 1988, 1990, 2002). They have shown – as did nineteenth-century feminists – that women enter prison having already been exposed to some of the more brutalising aspects of human experience (Walklate, 2004) and demonstrated the level that women resist structures of control imposed on them (Bosworth, 1999). Feminists have consistently exposed the sexist way in which women are treated by the criminal justice system, whether as victims or as offenders, and that, even in more contemporary times, being seen as conforming to the stereotypes of the 'respectable woman' or the 'good wife or mother' affects decision-making in the courts (Carlen, 1994; Walklate, 1995; Lees, 1996). Studies of women working within the criminal justice system have highlighted occupational challenges and the sexism that women can be subjected to (Brown and Heidensohn, 2000; Westmarland, 2001). Further, historical analyses such as that by Mary Bosworth of *Hôpital de la Salpêtrière* in Paris from 1684 to 1916 have called attention to the importance of recording women's experiences to provide a fuller understanding of the 'development and legitimacy of imprisonment today and in the past' (2001, p. 265). Feminists have also provided a focus on the myriad but inter-related forms of violence experienced by women from men and within a male-dominated social order, with work in the contemporary period highlighting, to refer to a few of the areas covered, that of femicide (Radford and Russell, 1992), honour-based violence (Gill et al, 2014; Siddiqui, 2016), rape as a 'weapon of war' (Lees, 1996) and sex trafficking (Kelly and Regan, 2000). Throughout this impressive body of work is an emphasis on the placing of the voices and experiences of women at the centre, whether in terms of the actual process of doing the research (Kelly, 1988; Mooney, 2000; Ortiz-Rodriguez, 2016) or ensuring a 'woman-wise' approach to penal policy (Carlen, 1994).

Moreover, in the previous chapter, in contrasting the research of Chicago's Hull House to those of the Park and Burgess years, some of the core components of a feminist research methodology were identified, namely the need to treat the 'researched' as human beings rather than 'lab rats'. In more contemporary feminism many valuable criticisms have been made by feminists of the research methods used in mainstream social science (see Mooney, 2000). As Stanley and Wise have argued, the conventional relationship in which personal involvement is minimised and objectivity is emphasised 'is obscene because it treats people as mere objects, there for the researcher to do research "on". Treating people as objects – sex objects or research objects – is morally unjustifiable' (1983, p. 168). It is said of conventional positivistic research that 'it appears to some critics that social scientists are suffering from "physics envy", and therefore try to be as methodologically hard as their brothers in the natural sciences in an attempt to prove that they too, are objective scientists' (Yllo, 1988, p. 34). To reiterate, the concern of feminist social scientists – whether they take a qualitative, quantitative or mixed-methods approach – is with women's experiences and the validating of those experiences. Instead of objectivity or 'value-free' research, radical feminists have especially argued for 'conscious partiality': it is made explicit that their values guide their work, and the political commitment to the ending of the oppression of women is made explicit (Mooney, 2000).

Feminism is additionally credited with influencing much contemporary criminological theory, most notably that of left realism and work on masculinities. Feminist research is acknowledged to have shaped left realism's perspective on the victim of crime. Roger Matthews and Jock Young have said how feminist studies on rape, domestic violence and sexual harassment brought home to them 'the limits of the romantic conception of crime and the criminal', as conveyed by some strands of critical criminology in the 1970s and 1980s by showing the impact that men's violence has on women (1986, p. 2). Moreover, in terms of research methodology, the feminist emphasis on the need for sensitive methods, especially the necessity of using committed, considerate interviewers to gain more reliable results, shaped the design of local victimisation surveys pioneered by left realists (Mooney, 2000).

Following feminist theorising on the causes of crime and the involvement of men in campaigns against men's violence, the 1990s witnessed a growth in the study of the social construction of masculinity or, as is preferred, masculinities, for there are many ways in which masculinity can be constructed (see, for example, Hearn and Morgan, 1990; Newburn and Stanko, 1994; Messerschmidt, 1993, 1997; Jefferson, 1997; Collier, 1998 and work by socialist feminists such as Lynn Segal, 1990, and Bea Campbell, 1993). Criminology has long been criticised by feminists for being overwhelmingly concerned with the male offender, but men have rarely been scrutinised as gendered subjects, that is in terms of their masculinity – in other words, what it means on an individual and societal level to be a man and how this relates to crime and criminality. Jalna Hanmer, Jill Radford and Betsy Stanko, feminists who have written extensively on men's violence, argued, as we have seen, in their defence of radical feminism against the claim of biological essentialism, that violence is part of how men choose to construct their masculine identity, and called for men 'to examine and reject their misogynistic construction of masculinity' (1989, p. 4). As Sandra Walklate observes, a focus on how masculinity is constructed 'foregrounds' men as the problem, thus forcing the question:

> What is about men, not as working class, not as migrant, not as underprivilege individual, but as men that induces them to commit crime? Here it is no longer women who are judged by the norms of masculinity and found to be 'the problem'. Now it is men and not humanity who are openly acknowledged as the objects and subjects of investigation.
> (Grosz, 1987, p. 5, cited in Walklate, 1995, p. 160)

Admittedly there were precursors to this 'new' approach. Madeleine Pelletier in the 'first wave' feminist period, discussed social constructionist arguments with respect to how we acquire gender identity. Talcott Parsons (1947), Edwin Sutherland (1947) and, as we saw in the last chapter, Albert Cohen (1955) referred to differences in male and female roles and how this affected involvement in delinquency and crime. However, Parsons, Sutherland and Cohen lack a notion of power as being structured along gendered lines.

The Australian sociologist Raewyn Connell's work (1987, 1995) is considered to have 'kick-started' much of the debate in this area (Collier, 2004). Connell focuses on the core themes of patriarchy, oppression, domination and exploitation in which men are regarded as being the superior and women the inferior in society. As Loraine Gelsthorpe and Frances Heidensohn observe, 'this at once draws together feminist perspectives on the social construction of gender and puts the contestation of power at the centre of an analysis of masculinities' (2007, p. 388). Connell argues that masculinity is organised and practised in a variety of ways depending on the particular context (for example, within the workplace, school or family). In *Gender and Power* (1987) she develops the concept of 'hegemonic masculinity' which is exemplified by the characteristics of heterosexuality, physical prowess, authority, toughness, competition and success through work and relationships. Hegemonic masculinity represents the culturally idealised form of masculinity within society and is 'understood as the pattern of practices (i.e. things done, not just a set of role expectations or an identity)' (Connell and Messerschmidt, 2005, p. 832). This allows men to continue to subordinate women. It embodies 'the currently most honoured way of being a man' and requires 'all other men to position themselves in relation to it' (*ibid*). As Richard Collier comments, the utilisation of this concept makes it possible to address the diversity of men's lives, 'whilst at the same time recognising the existence of a culturally exalted form of (heterosexual) masculinity' (2004, p. 290).

Hegemonic masculinity explains how certain groups of men are able to occupy positions of power and how these are then legitimised and replicated both socially and culturally. As one of the most influential feminist thinkers, Simone de Beauvoir famously argued in *The Second Sex* (1949), this culturally idealised form of masculinity is always constructed in relation to women, and also, for Connell, 'subordinated masculinities'. These subordinated masculinities need not be clearly identified; 'indeed, achieving hegemony may consist precisely in preventing alternatives gaining cultural definition and recognition as alternatives, confining them to ghettos, to privacy, to unconsciousness' (1987, p. 186). However, a prime example of subordinated masculinity is that of the gay man, a subordination that 'involves both direct interaction and a kind of ideological warfare' (*ibid*). Illustrations of some of the interactions include police harassment, street violence and economic discrimination, which are 'tied together by the contempt for homosexuality and homosexual men that is part of the ideological package of hegemonic masculinity' (*ibid*). Hegemonic masculinity defines relationships between men and men and women and, though not achieved 'at the point of a gun' (*ibid*), hegemonic masculinity may be maintained through the threat of force and use of force, for example, in the form of violence against women and against gay men.

James Messerschmidt built on many of Connell's ideas to apply them more systematically to criminality, and the two have since collaborated to develop many of the earlier concepts. Like Carol Smart, Frances Heidensohn and other feminists working within the discipline, Messerschmidt, in his now-classic 1993 book *Masculinities and Crime*, is critical of the gender-blind nature of much conventional criminology, whether it be the historical work of Lombroso or the later perspectives of Robert Merton, Travis Hirschi or Edwin Schur. He puts forward the idea of gender as 'situational accomplishment' ('masculinity is accomplished, it is not something done to men or something settled beforehand' [*ibid*, p. 80]) and presents crime as a means, for some men, of 'doing gender'. Messerschmidt argues that men's resources for accomplishing masculinity vary depending on how they are positioned in society and, as such, 'a sociology of masculinity must acknowledge that socially organized power relations between men are historically constructed on the basis of class, race and sexual orientation' (*ibid*, p. 83). As men situationally accomplish masculinity in response to their social structural position, various forms of crime can be seen as providing a resource within the context of the street, workplace and the family for 'doing masculinity'. Messerschmidt ends *Masculinities and Crime* by recommending social change at both the institutional and interactional levels in order to reduce gender, as well as class and racial inequalities. He quotes the proposals first put forward by Connell for a 'practical politics of gender for heterosexual men'; these are clearly in line with many of the feminist arguments discussed in this chapter and serve to take up the challenge posed by Hanmer et al for men to question and 'reject their misogynistic construction of masculinity' (1989, p. 4). These include sharing child care; working for equal pay; challenging misogyny and homophobia and sexual harassment in the workspace; supporting the redistribution of wealth; creating a culture that is safe for women, gays and lesbians; supporting battered women's shelters and rape crisis intervention centres; and so on (Messerschmidt, 1993, p. 186). The need to lay out such strategy vividly shows that there is still much to be done in terms of achieving an equitable society.

In the more contemporary period there has been an emphasis on the need to include – or indeed have as a starting point – a broader understanding of the multiplicity of oppressions that are experienced by *all* women (and men), especially those from Black or minority backgrounds (Sokoloff and Dupont, 2005; Burgess-Proctor, 2006; Parmar, 2016). Indeed, Heidensohn and Silvestri point out that 'the proper treatment of race, gender and punishment' is crucial for the development of feminist theorising within criminology (2012,

p. 361), and an intersectional, multicultural or multiracial lens has been adopted by many feminists (see Bosworth, 2007; Henne and Troshynski, 2013; Rehman et al, 2016). It is also recognised that the 'feminist political project' has yet to be realised and there is a continuing need to keep up the pressure on the political establishment to ensure that women's experiences of crime and criminal justice are not 'forgotten or marginalised' (Heidensohn and Silvestri, 2012, p. 361). Although this moves me away from a focus on the historical context of criminological thought, it is necessary – especially given the exclusionary nature of much criminology – to address these wider concerns. For it is imperative as we move forward that both feminism and criminology take on board the significance of 'difference' and the importance of political action.

Rethinking 'feminism'

The 1980s and early 1990s represent a period of intense reflection and debate for many feminists and activists on the feminist movement as a whole and how it conceptualised women's experiences. For some this was seen as paving the way for a 'third wave' of feminism. The emphasis placed by the feminist movement on the importance of collective action and the resulting need to mobilise 'all women' in the fight against male oppression was seen as glossing over, to put it mildly, the significance of other forms of oppression, especially those arising from race, ethnicity, immigration status and class. Many of the criticisms came from Black and postcolonial feminists. Both the 'first' and 'second waves' of feminism were characterised as being too ethnocentric, as being preoccupied with the concerns of white, middle-class, educated, 'First World' women and as having essentialised women. As Sokoloff et al (2004) note, 'essentialism occurs when a voice – typically a white, heterosexual and socioeconomically privileged voice – claims to speak for everyone' (p. 12).

In her 1981 book, *Women, Race and Class*, Angela Davis powerfully illustrated how feminists prominent in the 'first wave' in the United States remained defenceless, 'even after years of involvement in progressive causes – to the pernicious ideological influence of racism', with, for example, Elizabeth Cady Stanton and Susan B. Anthony assuming that 'the abolition of the slave system elevated Black people to a position in U.S. society that was comparable in almost every respect to that of middle-class white women' (p. 76). Feminists in the 'second wave' were criticised for resurrecting the dangerous myth of the Black rapist: as was evidenced in the advice Diana Russell gave to white women in *The Politics of Rape* (1975): '[I]f some black men see rape of white women as an act of revenge or as a justifiable expression of hostility toward whites. I think it equally realistic for white women to be less trusting of black men than many of them are' (*ibid*, p. 179). Furthermore, bell hooks argued that feminist theory had emerged 'from privileged women who live at the center, whose perspectives on reality rarely include knowledge and awareness of the lives of women and men who live at the margins' (1984, p. xvii); it was middle-class white women who were able to 'employ a rhetoric of commonality that made their condition synonymous with "oppression"' (*ibid*, p. 5). The feminist emphasis on a commonality to women's experiences was undoubtedly effective in, for example, changing the perception of male violence as an individual pathology to that of a structurally embedded social problem and the creating of community-provided support and solidarity for many women, but it also resulted in 'exclusion, prejudices and prohibitions' (Hewitt, 2000, p. 4).

In the UK, Valerie Amos and Pratibha Parmar, in a 1984 paper that is now recognised as a 'turning point' (Howe, 2008), challenged feminism in the UK to reflect on its roots in imperialism, the level that 'gains made by white women have been and still are at the expense of Black women', that large numbers of Black women who had been excluded from participating from the movement in a meaningful way, that Black women's experiences had not been sufficiently accounted for and that there was a failure 'to adequately deal with the contradictions inherent in gender and class relations within the context of racist society' (Amos and Parmar, 1984, pp. 3–19, 3–5). Postcolonial feminist Chandra Talpade Mohanty (1991) also pointed to the way in which the feminist movement had neglected racism and imperialism and the specificity of historical context and its resulting impact: 'black, white and other third world women have very different histories with respect to the particular inheritance of post-fifteenth-century Euro-American hegemony: the influence of slavery, enforced migration, plantation and indentured labor, colonialism, imperial conquest and genocide' (p. 10). And continuing with the critique of assumptions of commonality, as Howe (2008) notes, 'homogenising the class, race, religion and material practice of women in the Third World' (p. 46), for Mohanty and others, created 'a false sense of the commonality of oppressions, interests and struggles between and among women globally' (Mohanty, 1988, pp. 77–78).

A brief caveat should at this point be introduced, for the understandable tendency to reflect on and re-characterise the feminist movement as a wholly white, middle-class movement also runs the risk of rendering invisible the contributions that women who were not from such privileged backgrounds have made to the feminist movement (Ruiz and Dubois, 2000; Hewitt 200) and to feminist activism against male violence in particular (Osmundson, 2016) in both the 'first' and 'second waves'. Certainly, many of those whose work I have drawn from in documenting the history of radical and socialist feminism in the UK were mindful of the compounding impact of other forms of oppression and argued for a more inclusive approach (Mackay, 2015). Nevertheless, this was a pivotal moment in the history of feminism leading to a greater and more complex comprehension of the various manifestations of structural oppression and inequality, how they intersect and differentially affect the lives of women. As Adrian Howe put it, 'the time had come to move away from celebrating universality in order to work through the implications of differences among women's experiences' (2008, p. 45).

In both the 'first' and 'second waves' of feminism, the family was identified as the principal site of women's oppression. This is perhaps not surprising given the emphasis placed on the need to raise awareness of men's violence against women in the home and its implications, for this form of violence is almost, by definition, going to be situated within the family, and women's economic dependence on men is consistently found to compound the problems women face in such situations (Mooney, 2000). However, the insistence by some feminists, most notably Michèle Barrett in *Women's Oppression Today* (1980), on its centrality as a site of oppression was considered to be an over-generalisation and lacking in relevance to the lives of Black women. For Black feminists, whilst the family is undoubtedly a site of male violence (Mama, 2000), it is also a place of refuge and resistance to racism, and it is the violence and coercion of a racist state in terms of immigration laws and police practices that are particularly oppressive to Black and minority women, rather than the family per se (Carby, 1982; Bhavani and Coulson, 1986). As Howe (2008) pointed out, it was wrong to present the family as the *main* source of oppression for *all* women, for as Amos and Parmar (1984) and others had shown for Asian women, 'the British state through its immigration legislation had destroyed Asian families, separating husbands from wives, parents from children, and demanding proof that arranged marriages were genuine' (p. 45). However, the impact of the family and the cultural expectations placed on women remain a terrain that can be difficult to navigate due to negative stereotypes about women and men from different backgrounds (Ortiz Rodriguez, 2016).

In the United States, the necessity of recognising the oppressive nature of the state in the lives of women of color was to be particularly stressed. For as Natalie Sokoloff and Ida Dupont write in terms of domestic violence, 'as a member of a devalued racial identity, some women of color, particularly African American women, may fear that calling the police will subject their partners to racist treatment by the criminal justice system as well as confirm racist stereotypes of Blacks as violent' (2005, p. 43). A push for increased criminalisation under the guise of 'taking domestic violence seriously' as a social problem risked arrest of victims and more aggressive policing, resulting in the 'use of force, mass incarceration, and brutality' in communities of color (Ritchie, 2000, p. 135; Coker, 2001). Black women, it was argued, suffer patriarchal and sexual oppression from Black men but are also fighting alongside them against racial oppression and it was imperative for feminism to take account of this (Rice, 1990). Further, Yolanda Ortiz-Rodriguez's research on battered Latina women in New York City reveals how current institutional procedures and immigration policies pose a real threat to undocumented Latinas: threats that range from 'structural barriers such as lack of language proficiency to institutional racism based on anti-immigrant sentiments to having their families torn apart through deportation' (2016, p. 23).

In the late 1980s Kimberlé Crenshaw in the United States coined the term 'intersectionality' to clarify how the lives of women of color are affected by multiple systems of oppression, especially those based on gender, race, class, age, sexual orientation and religion. Like many feminists working in the area of crime, the impetus for Crenshaw's analysis arose from personal experiences. As a young student involved in Black radical politics, she was on the receiving end of violence from a boyfriend ('after a messy break-up, in my 10th floor dorm room with the plate glass window. I landed just a foot short of it, the first of many near misses that could have changed my life forever' (2005, p. 312). For Crenshaw the politics of gender and race both compounded and confused the experience. In one of her first uses of 'intersectionality' Crenshaw employed the following analogy to explain its significance: 'discrimination like traffic though an intersection may flow in one direction, and it may flow in another' and 'if an accident happens in an intersection, it can be caused by cars traveling from any number of directions and sometimes from all of them' (1989, p. 149). Crenshaw (1991, 1997) outlined three aspects of intersectionality to demonstrate how the lives of battered women of color are situated between the categories of race and gender: (i) structural intersectionality, which describes the structural impact of domination; (ii) political intersectionality, the politics brought about by a specific system of domination; and (iii) representational intersectionality, the way in which those who are dominated are represented. To explore this further, structural intersectionality can be seen 'in the way in which the burdens of illiteracy, responsibility for child care, poverty, lack of job skills, and pervasive discrimination weigh down many battered women of color who are trying to escape the cycle of abuse' (1991, p. 115). Political intersectionality can be recognised by the suppressing of information about domestic violence in the communities of women of color 'in the name of anti-racism' which 'leaves unrevealed, and thus unaddressed in public discourse within our communities, the real terror in which many women of color live' (*ibid*, p. 116). Finally, representational intersectionality is revealed in the stereotypical images of women of color in popular culture. An example of this is *Tales from the Darkside: The Movie* where the 'Black woman . . . is an animal, or worse yet, a monster. The Asian-American woman is passive' (*ibid*); this leads to the 'othering' of women of color and provides a further illustration of how power is exercised over them, thus serving once again to underscore the importance of 'othering' in criminological discourse. As Crenshaw argues, such images 'function to create counter narratives to the experiences of women of color that discredit our claims and render the violence that we experience unimportant' (*ibid*, p. 253). They not only serve to devalue the experiences of women of color but also 'reproduce it by providing viewers with both conscious and unconscious cues for interpreting the experiences of "others"' (*ibid*).[15] Whilst intersectionality is today widely debated and applied (Walby et al, 2012), it has become one of the most recognised conceptual paradigms associated with contemporary feminism (Fernandes, 2010).

The importance of recognising a 'multiplicity of oppressions' is extended to include the situation and experiences of trans people. Trans, as the scholar activist Emi Koyama writes, is 'used as an inclusive term encompassing a wide range of gender norm violations that involve some discontinuity between one's sex assigned at birth to her or his gender identity and expression' (2001, p. 1). Koyama has argued for a transfeminism, which is defined as 'a movement by and for trans women who view their liberation to be intrinsically linked to the liberation of all women and beyond' and calls for trans women 'to openly take part in the feminist revolution'. Leon Laidlaw (2016) observes the 'cisnormative assumption [that] reinforces rigid cultural norms associated with men and women' have rendered trans people invisible. Given the need for inclusivity within criminological discourse, it is important that this invisibility is confronted. For Black trans people, this invisibility is even more pronounced (Ellison, 2016). Trans people have high rates of violence and harassment against them and are at increased risk of coming in contact with the criminal justice system through, for example, increased surveillance by law enforcement. This increases their likelihood of coming under the orbit of state control by being targeted for petty offences, such as public disorder or loitering; through participation in criminalised industries, such as sex work; and the tendency for the police to stereotype and profile trans gender people as criminals (Miles-Johnson, 2015; Laidlaw, 2016). However, there is disagreement amongst feminists over trans inclusion: some feminists are critical of the trans movement and have resisted the inclusion of trans women in feminist or women-only spaces (Jeffreys, 2012), while others, for example, Judith Butler (2014) and Sally Hines (2017) point out that trans people challenge repressive gender norms and are fully aligned with feminist principles. Indeed, Butler has spoken of the dangers of 'feminist policing of trans lives and trans choices' (Williams, 2015) for this is clearly in contravention of the feminist commitment to the advancing of social justice (Radcliffe Richards, 1982). For Koyama (2001), the involvement of trans women will ultimately expand the scope of the feminist movement.

Achieving the feminist 'political project'

It is true to say that many of the goals of feminism remain unmet. The Women's Liberation Conference that took place in the UK in 1978 drew up a list of demands that included 'freedom for all women from intimidation by the threat or use of male violence; an end to all the laws, assumptions and institutions which perpetuate male dominance and men's aggression towards women' (Walby, 2011, p. 28). Yet male violence against women persists. We are confronted with the knowledge that one in three women will encounter male violence in the home at some point in their lives, one in ten in the course of a year (Mooney, 2000), and that it causes the deaths of two women a week in the UK, three women a day in the United States (Vagianos, 2015; Sisters Uncut, 2016). In *International Feminist Perspectives in Criminology*, Frances Heidensohn and Nicole Rafter note that the feminist project in criminology is ultimately one of 'self-obsolescence' for if the discipline was fully 'engendered and crime control policy transformed as feminists recommend, they could retire from the field' (1995, p. 14), yet they stress the immensity of the task involved. Moreover, when Heidensohn was asked if she thought the feminist enterprise had been successful, she shook her head and asked how could it be when we have so many women in prison (Mooney, 2000).

Yet although there is more to be done, feminism has not failed. From the 'first' to 'second wave' and into the present phase, feminists have been behind support services and policies that have helped countless women. The significance placed on difference and the emergence of multiracial, multicultural and intersectional perspectives within feminism (and the critiques of the past) have by and large created new energy, resulting in key theoretical and policy developments. If we take the area of violence, whereas feminists from the nineteenth century onwards consistently advocated for short-term initiatives (e.g. refuges and shelters) and for long-term structural change to achieve the eradication of male violence, it is the current phase, with its emphasis on structural oppression and inequality (as manifested along the lines of gender, race, ethnicity and class) that has moved the latter to 'the front and center of their efforts' (2013, p. 572). As Gretchen Arnold and Jami Ake, in their perceptive article on the battered women's movement in the United States, suggest, the approaches characteristic of this period consistently advocate for 'changing the cultural and structural underpinnings of violence in order to get it to end once and for all, rather than intervening after it has taken place' (*ibid*). Furthermore, the recent resurgence of radical feminist activism in the UK, led by a new generation of feminists, has kept the focus on men and the need to examine how masculinity(ies) is constructed within the existing social order, and that efforts must be directed at confronting the behaviour and attitudes of men and at changing gender relations in order to affect social change (Mackay, 2015).

The new radical feminist politics: 'The suffragettes wouldn't stand for this'

The new radical feminist politics that have emerged in recent years are committed to an intersectional feminism, which recognises 'the complexity of identity' and the creating of solidarity amongst women through political protest (Mackay, 2015, p. 108). In 2004 Finn Mackay founded the London Feminist Network, a feminist networking and campaigning organisation that was behind the revival of the Reclaim the Night marches, a feature of 1970s campaigning against rape and male sexual violence. The Reclaim the Night marches – which attracted more marchers than in their heyday in the 1970s and 1980s – called attention to the fact that there has been little change in the levels of male violence against women and that women are still all too often blamed for their victimisation.[16]

The continued growth of feminist activism is also evident through the activities of the organization Sisters Uncut, which was established in 2014 to protest, in the short term, the austerity measures introduced by the UK government that resulted in spending cuts to domestic violence services and, in the long term, to 'fight male oppression and violence'. Sisters Uncut's *Feministo* again emphasises the importance of both difference and solidarity:

> Every woman's experience is specific to her; as intersectional feminists we understand that a woman's individual experience of violence is affected by race, class, disability, sexuality and immigration status. . . . We stand united with all self-defining women who live under the threat of domestic violence, and those who experience violence in their daily lives . . . we are women, we will not be silenced. We stand united and fight together, and together we will win.[17]

Sisters Uncut have pointed out that two in three women in the UK are being turned away from refuges and that thirty-four refuges have closed under the Conservative government. The cuts to public spending have made

> it harder for women to leave dangerous relationships and live safely. Safety is not a privilege. Access to justice cannot become a luxury. Austerity cuts are ideological but cuts to domestic violence services are fatal. Doors are being slammed on women fleeing violence. Refuges are being shut down, legal aid has been cut, social housing is scarce and private rents are extortionate.[18]

Sisters Uncut have organised demonstrations in response to the cuts, for example, occupying empty council flats, most recently in Hackney, North London, to highlight the accommodation difficulties facing battered women. Inspired by the direct action of the suffragettes, a recent demonstration saw 'Sisters' wearing the traditional suffragette colours of purple and green, symbolically chaining themselves to the gates of Parliament and holding up placards showing domestic violence statistics, with one reading 'The Suffragettes Wouldn't Stand for This' and letting off purple and green smoke bombs (Sisters Uncut, 2016) (see Figure 6.6). As one Sisters Uncut activist, Emma Smith, said, 'The suffragettes took direct action because they couldn't wait any longer for the right to vote. We are taking direct action because we can't wait any longer for women's safety: our sisters are dying' (*ibid*).[19] They were joined at the demonstration by Helen Pankhurst, the great-granddaughter of

Figure 6.6 Reclaiming the direct action campaigns of the suffragettes.[20]

Figure 6.7 Sisters Uncut's die-in on the red carpet of *Suffragette*, October 2015, Getty Images.

Emmeline Pankhurst. At the 2015 premiere of the movie *Suffragette*, which was about women's suffrage in the UK, Sisters stormed the red carpet. By staging a 'die-in', their intention was to 'use the publicity of the night to remind the world that the fight is far from over' (Kwei, *The Independent*, 8 October 2015) (see Figure 6.7). Although they were not protesting the movie itself – it is told from the perspective of a white working-class woman – they also wanted to draw attention to the fact that 'the all-white cast erases the contribution and achievements of women of colour in the movement' (*ibid*). Sarah Kwei, a Sister, asks, 'where was Sophie Duleep Singh and her Indian sisters, who led the Black Friday deputation to the Houses of Parliament in 1910' (*ibid*)? Further, *Suffragette*'s promotional film shoot included the slogan 'I'd rather be a rebel than a slave', as if 'being a slave is some sort of lifestyle choice' (*ibid*). Sisters Uncut organises, as Kwei says,

> in the spirit of the Suffragettes themselves and feel certain that had they been alive today, they would have been down there with us. These were their tactics, and we feel proud and humble to be carrying the flame in the continued fight for liberation.
>
> (*ibid*)

Notes

1 For example, in *The New York Times* the word 'feminist' was first used in 1897 in a review of Paul Hervieu's play *The Law of Man* (1897, p. 17).
2 The National Archives are in Kew, Surrey. They are the official archives of the UK government.
3 Josephine Butler to her son, George. Cited in J. Jordan and I. Sharp, eds., 2003, *Josephine Butler and the Prostitution Campaigns: The Ladies' Appeal and Protest*, p. 2.
4 'Sex worker' is the preferred term for many feminists and activists given the negative connotations associated with the word 'prostitute'. However, as I am largely dealing with historical material, I have chosen to keep with the language that was used at the time.
5 Harriet Martineau argued for the right of a woman to 'claim her privileges as an intellectual being'; although Martineau is often typically remembered as the translator of Comte's work into English, she wrote a number of influential papers and books, including her 'most sociological book', *Society in America* (1837), which was based on two years of travel in the United States (Thomson, 2010, pp. 124, 125).
6 Such a comparison is clearly problematic, given the history of slavery and its legacy, especially for African Americans in the United States, and is inattentive to the level of sexual violence experienced by enslaved women. In Victor Hugo's letter to Josephine Butler on prostitution, he writes, 'the slavery of black women is abolished in America but the slavery of white women continues in Europe' (Butler, 1896, p. 25).
7 This was, as we saw in the discussion of Leo Tolstoy, the fate that was to befall the female protagonist of his novel *Resurrection*, written in all likelihood to provide a counter-narrative to Lombroso's theories of criminality.
8 Cobbe, towards the end of her life, became prominent in the anti-vivisection movement, creating The British Union for the Abolition of Vivisection Society in 1898.
9 In J. Marlow (Ed) (2015) *Suffragettes: The Fight for Votes for Women*, London: Virago

10 Moreover, in the 1960s, the writings of Betty Freidan critiqued the role of women in American society by drawing attention to the dissatisfaction felt by suburban housewives whose lives, despite gains in education and contraception, were still defined by housekeeping and child rearing, making them financially dependent on their husbands and thus unequal to men and unable to fully participate in the public sphere.
11 First published in 1969, *Sexual Politics* and Firestone's *The Dialectics of Sex* (1970) made major contributions to the development of radical feminist theory.
12 The term 'carceral feminism' was coined by Elizabeth Bernstein (2007). It is particularly used against those advocating for the criminalisation of sex work.
13 A feminist criminology?

The debate over whether there should be a sub-discipline known as 'feminist criminology' was extensively discussed (see Heidensohn, 1994) in the 1980s and early 1990s in the UK. Allison Morris and Loraine Gelsthorpe repeatedly put forward the view (see Morris, 1987; Gelsthorpe and Morris, 1988; Gelsthorpe and Morris, 1990) that a 'feminist criminology' cannot exist because neither criminology nor feminism presents a unified set of principles and practices:

> Criminology, like feminism, encompasses disparate and sometimes conflicting perspectives. The history of criminology well reflects these. In contrast, the tensions and conflicts within feminism are seen as indicative of an inchoate, unrigorous and 'indisciplined' discipline. There is no one specific feminism just as there is no one specific criminology.
>
> (*ibid*, p. 2)

Thus, Gelsthorpe and Morris believe the phrase 'feminist perspectives in criminology' more accurately describes the body of feminist work that has contributed to the subject. However, in recent years it has again become common to refer to feminist work in criminology as 'feminist criminology', hence the journal title for the American Society of Criminology's Women and Crime Division is *Feminist Criminology*.

14 For a more complete summary of feminist work in criminology in the UK see L. Burman and L. Gelsthorpe (2017) 'Feminist criminology: Inequalities, powerlessness and justice' in A. Liebling, S.Maruna and L. McAra (Eds.) *The Oxford Handbook of Criminology*, Oxford: Oxford University Press and for a global perspective, R. Barberet *Women, Crime and Criminal Justice: A Global Enquiry*, 2014, Oxon: Routledge.
15 The idea of intersectionality should also be utilised to reflect on our own identities. As Finn Mackay writes, being conscious of our own identities and where we are situated in relation to the 'fractures' of race, class, sexuality and so forth and how these bring us 'varying levels of privilege compared to others is an important political reflection' for feminists and the feminist movement as a whole. For 'when we consider ways that certain elements of our identity have brought us access, or resulted in us being excluded, we can extend this awareness to analyse whether and in what ways we may be part of excluding others' (2015, pp. 17–18).
16 See 'Why Reclaim the Night' at www.reclaimthenight.co.uk/why.html
17 Sisters Uncut, *Feministo*, (2016) http:www.sistersuncut.org/feministo
18 Sisters Uncut, *Feministo*,
19 Sisters Uncut www.sistersuncut.org/2016/06/08/we-are-the-suffragettes-sisters-uncut-chain-themselves-to-parliament-at-government-art-launch/ (accessed 17 July 2017)
20 Sisters Uncut (@sistersuncut-Instagram), http://scontent.cdninstagram.com/

Chapter 7

Confronting the establishment
The emergence of critical criminology

Critical criminology developed at a significant point in time: the late 1960s and 1970s. This was a period of political and social upheaval in which young people in particular developed an increased awareness of the oppressive power of the state and the levels of discrimination experienced by those from Black, minority or impoverished backgrounds who often found themselves held responsible for the 'ills' of society. The rapid expansion of higher education in the UK meant that those from working-class origins were entering the academy in much greater numbers than ever before: politicised by the events of the time, they wanted their voices heard. Many of those who were to become involved in the UK's National Deviancy Conferences (NDC), which took place between 1968 and 1973, came from the working class and were the first members of their families to go into higher education.[1]

The prominence of the civil rights movement in the United States and the launch of campaigns against the Vietnam and Cambodian wars and Ian Smith's racist government in Rhodesia had a profound impact. The London School of Economics (LSE), the focus of much student radicalism,[2] was closed down for a time in 1967 following a student sit-in over the disciplinary measures taken against two student union officials involved in earlier protests against the new director of the university, Walter Adams, a known associate of Ian Smith's regime. The student union officials: David Adelstein, a third-year student from Manchester reading economics, and Marshall Bloom, an American civil rights activist who was studying for a Master's in sociology, had been suspended. Hundreds of students took part in the demonstrations, with some going on hunger strike.[3,4] In 1970 at Kent State University in the United States four students were killed and nine others wounded by the Ohio National Guard following protests against the American invasion of Cambodia, an atrocity that reverberated across the world and caused considerable outrage amongst the younger members of the British academy.

The massive political unrest that occurred in Paris in 1968 especially caught the imagination of the NDC founders and was the focus of much discussion at the inaugural conference held later that year. The Paris events began as an occupation at the University of Paris at Nanterre, where students and activists were protesting a number of issues, including overcrowding at the university and the arrest of six members of the National Vietnam Committee. Their action spread to other universities and lycées, and the leaders called for solidarity with the working classes, who continued to suffer from appallingly low pay and poor conditions despite the post–Second World War economic boom. The protests spilled on to the streets, leading to violent confrontations with the police. Strikes broke out throughout the country, effectively closing down Paris and Lyon (Sreenan, 1993). The government of President Charles de Gaulle was brought to near collapse; North Atlantic Treaty Organization (NATO) troops were mobilised on the French border.

In this moment, obvious social injustices were no longer to be ignored. The era was marked by widespread questioning of 'establishment' views and lack of conformity to accepted opinions and values. This provided the impetus for critical criminology and the need for a radical – and indeed a potentially revolutionary – political framework. For some, this was to mean the restructuring of society along socialist lines and the need for active resistance against the state. The roots of critical criminology are varied, but largely originate from Marxist or neo-Marxist theories.

The historical context: poverty, resistance and the transformation of society

Karl Marx and Friedrich Engels

> *Marx is the towering figure of modern social theory. It is no exaggeration to claim that all subsequent theory is a debate with his legacy.*
>
> (Lea, 2010, p. 18)

Karl Heinrich Marx was born in Trier, Germany, on 5 May 1818 into a middle-class family. He first studied jurisprudence at the University of Bonn before going on to attend the University of Berlin, where he became interested in philosophy and influenced by the ideas of G.W.F. Hegel. He spent his early working years as a radical journalist, editing the Cologne-based *Rheinische Zeitung*, where the political content of his articles eventually led to the journal's closure. In October 1843 Marx left for Paris, where he embarked on his lifelong collaborative relationship with Friedrich Engels.

Persecuted by the police and censors for their involvement in the communist movement and the oppositional nature of their writings, Marx and Engels moved from one European capital to another before establishing themselves in England. Engels, who was from Barmen, in the Rhine Province, had previously lived in Manchester, where he had been sent by his father to manage his cotton mill.[5] This experience exposed him to the acute levels of poverty in which the British working class lived and formed the basis for his seminal work, *The Condition of the Working Class in England in 1844* (1845). Originally intended for a German audience, it was translated into English in 1885 by the American social activist Florence Kelley. As discussed in Chapter 4, Kelley was later to reside at Hull House and was the director of the *Hull House Maps and Papers* (1895) project. She remained close to Engels, as is evident from their lengthy correspondence that lasted until just before his death in 1895. It was in England that Marx wrote his greatest work, *Capital: A Critique of Political Economy* (1867).

Marx and Engels on crime

Marx and Engels's primary concern was with political economy and how capital and labour related to each other within the context of capitalism; as John Lea puts it, 'they were revolutionaries concerned to analyse the dynamics of nineteenth century capitalism for the purpose of understanding how it was to be superseded by a communist society' (2010, p. 19). As such, it is perhaps not surprising to find little systematic discussion of crime in their writings – there were much bigger things with which to be concerned with! Nevertheless, this is not to say that Marx was uninterested in the subject and unaware of current debates. Quetelet's work, which, as we saw in Chapter 3 provided an analysis of crime statistics and raised important points with regard to the experience of deprivation, certainly seems to have influenced Marx's thinking. In the *New York Daily Tribune* Marx uses Quetelet's work to support the contention that the causes of crime are to be found in the current structure of society:

> Mr Quetelet in a calculation of the probabilities of crime published in 1829, actually predicted with astonishing certainty, not only the amount but all the different kinds of crime committed in France in 1830. That it is not so much the particular political institutions of a country as the fundamental conditions of the modern *bourgeois* society in general, which produce an average amount of crime in a given national fraction of society. . . . Now, if crimes observed on a great scale thus show, in their amount and their classification, the regularity of physical phenomena – if as Mr Quetelet remarks, 'it would be difficult to decide in respect to which of the two' the physical world and the social system 'the acting causes produce their effect with the utmost regularity' – is there not a necessity for deeply reflecting upon an alteration of the system that breeds these crimes.
>
> (17–18 February 1853)

Moreover, Engels explores the problem of crime amongst the poor in some depth in *The Condition of the Working Class in England in 1844* (1845). Many of the later points raised by Marx (1867) and by Marx and Engels (1848, 1998 ed) on crime appear to derive from this text.

As is indicated in the passage from the *New York Daily Tribune*, crime results from the conditions created by modern bourgeois society. Whilst 'socialist' themes are to be found in the work of key Enlightenment figures – who also experienced persecution and censorship by the authorities – and Beccaria was certainly aware of class-based inequality and the problem of private property, the establishment of liberal democracy failed to deal with the gap between formal equality and the substantive inequalities as experienced by many people (the 'classicist contradiction'). The enormous changes that resulted in the overthrow of the *ancien régime* and feudal society transformed the material forces of production, leading to increased industrialisation, but they did not alter social relations. Prevailing inequalities in the distribution of wealth result in an imbalance of power within society and the continuing exploitation of those with fewer economic resources. In the *Manifesto of the Communist Party*, Marx and Engels write, 'the modern bourgeois society that has sprouted from the ruins of feudal society has not done away with class antagonisms' (1848, 1998 ed, p. 35). Indeed,

> the bourgeoisie . . . has put an end to all feudal, patriarchal, idyllic relations. It has pitilessly torn asunder the motley feudal ties that bound man to his 'natural superiors', and has left remaining no other nexus between man and man than naked self-interest, than callous 'cash payment' . . . . It has resolved personal worth into exchange value and, in place of the numberless indefeasible chartered freedoms, has set up that single, unconscionable freedom – free trade. In one word, for exploitation, veiled by religious and political illusions, it has substituted naked, shameless, direct, brutal exploitation.
>
> (*ibid*, pp. 37–38)

As Engels was to argue in *The Condition of the Working Class in England in 1844*, the classicist principles of free choice and participation in the social contract is, for the proletariat, a myth,

> The bourgeoisie has gained a monopoly of all means of existence in the broadest sense of the word. What the proletarian needs, he can obtain only from the bourgeoisie, which is protected in its monopoly by the power of the state. The proletariat is, therefore, in law and in fact, the slave of the bourgeoisie, which can decree his life or death. It offers him the means of living, but only for an 'equivalent', for his work. It even lets him have the appearance of acting from a free choice, of making a contract with free, unconstrained consent, as a responsible agent who has attained his majority.
>
> (1845, p. 51)

For Marx and Engels, we have to understand this social context in order to make sense of crime. The advance of capitalism resulted in human misery – the awfulness of lives lived in poverty. Crime is not willed in voluntaristic fashion, as the classicist would maintain; it is not the 'result of pure arbitrariness' but is 'the struggle of the isolated individual against the prevailing social conditions' (Marx and Engels, 1845, p. 367). Moreover, '[i]t depends on the same conditions that rule. The same visionaries who see in right and the law the domination of some independently existing, general will can see in crime the mere violation of right and law' (*ibid*). Some commentators have described this as Marx's 'primitive rebellion thesis', implying 'that crime is a primitive form of rebellion against the dominant social order; one that may eventually develop into conscious revolutionary activity' (Vold et al, 2001 p. 252). Marx, however, does not explicitly state this and was somewhat of a moralist when it came to criminality: both Marx and Engels preferred to see crime as a manifestation of contempt for the inequalities created by bourgeois society. Thus, as Engels wrote, 'the contempt for the existing social order is most conspicuous in its extreme form – that of offences against the law' (1845, p. 81): 'the working-man lived in poverty and want, and saw that others were better off than he . . . Want conquered his inherited respect for the sacredness of property and he stole' (*ibid*, pp. 502–503). The idea of crime as overt rebellion or a form of resistance emerged in the work of later critical commentators. For example, for Du Bois, what 'we call crime is social protest and revolt' [1901, 1982 ed, p. 116]), a notion that was further developed in the 1970s by British Marxist historians, especially by Edward Thompson and his colleagues.

However, the impact of capitalism is not straightforward. For while it is the bourgeoisie who are to gain from the transformation of society to a capitalist mode of production, as capitalism advances the number of capitalist magnates diminish – i.e. power and wealth become concentrated amongst the few – and, as Marx wrote in *Capital*, it is this diminishing 'number of magnates of capital, who usurp and monopolise all advantages of this process of transformation'. With this 'grows the mass of misery, oppression, slavery, degradation, exploitation' but alongside this also 'grows the revolt of the working class, a class always increasing in numbers, and disciplined, united, organised by the very mechanism of the process of capitalist production itself'. Increased centralisation of the means of production and the development of labour 'reach a point where they become incompatible with their capitalist integument': 'this integument is burst asunder' and the 'knell of capitalist private property sounds' (1867, 1921 ed, p. 788, 789).

For Marx and Engels the 'criminal man' is 'both determined and determining' (Taylor et al, 1973, p. 213), at once determined by the material conditions and self-determining in his resistance and response to those conditions. This duality separates their analysis from both the voluntaristic approaches of classicist criminology and the crude economic determinism of social positivism. For Marx, 'men make their own history, but they do not make it just as they please; they do not make it under circumstances chosen by themselves, but under circumstances directly encountered, given and transmitted from the past' (1852, p. 15).

Hence, in *Capital*, we find Marx lamenting the fate of the child print workers who, having been used simply as commodities as the dictates of capitalism demand, are expelled from the industry once their usefulness is over and end up with few options but to go into a life of crime:

> [Their] sole business is either to spread the sheets of paper under the machine, or to take from it the printed sheets. They perform this weary task, in London especially, for 14, 15 and 16 hours at a stretch, during several days in the week and frequently for 36 hours, with only two hours rest for meals and sleep! . . . As soon as they get too old for such child's work, that is about 17 at the latest, they are discharged from the printing establishments.
>
> (1867, p. 531)

Despite their attempts to gain employment, having no other skills and through 'their ignorance and brutality, and by their mental and bodily degradation' caused by working in the print from such a young age, they, unsurprisingly, become 'recruits of crime' (*ibid*).

Engels, likewise, in *The Condition of the Working Class in England in 1844* presented crime as arising out of the brutalising circumstances of poverty:

> when the poverty of the proletarian is intensified to the point of actual lack of the barest necessaries of life, to want and hunger, the temptation to disregard all social order does but gain power . . . Want leaves the working-man the choice between starving slowly, killing himself speedily, or taking what he needs where he finds it – in plain English, stealing.
>
> (1845, p. 74)

He portrays the grimness of life in the boarding houses and slums of the major British cities in graphic detail and presents crime – theft, domestic and sexual violence – and vice, in the form of prostitution and drunkenness, and child neglect as resulting from the moral degeneration of working-class life in capitalist societies. In the boarding houses,

> Into every bed four, five, or six human beings are piled, as many as can be packed in, sick and well, young and old, drunk and sober, men and women, just as they come, indiscriminately. Then come strife, blows, wounds, or, if these bedfellows agree, so much the worse; thefts are

arranged and things done which our language, grown more humane than our deeds, refuses to accord.

(1845, p. 192)

And 'the social order makes family life impossible for the worker', for

> In a comfortless, filthy house, hardly good enough for mere nightly shelter, ill-furnished, often neither rain tight nor warm, a foul atmosphere filling rooms overcrowded with human beings, no domestic comfort is possible. The husband works the whole day through, perhaps the wife also and the elder children, all in different places; they meet night and morning, all under perpetual temptation to drink; what family life is possible under such conditions? Yet the working-man cannot escape from the family, must live in the family, and the consequence is a perpetual succession of family troubles, domestic quarrels, most demoralizing for parents and children alike. Neglect of all domestic duties, neglect of the children, especially.... And the children growing up in this savage way, amidst these demoralizing influences, are expected to turn out goody-goody and moral in the end.

(*ibid*, p. 81)[6]

Some of the examples included by Engels highlight the acute desperation of the poor:

> On Monday, Jan. 15th, 1844, two boys were brought before the police magistrate, being in a starving condition, they had stolen and immediately devoured a half-cooked calf's foot from a shop. The magistrate felt called upon to investigate the case further, and received the following details from the policeman: The mother of the two boys was the widow of an ex-soldier, afterwards policeman, and had had a very hard time since the death of her husband, to provide for her nine children. She lived at No. 2 Pool's Place, Quaker Court, Spitalfields, in the utmost poverty. When the policeman came to her, he found her with six of her children literally huddled together in a little back room, with no furniture but two old rush-bottomed chairs with the seats gone, a small table with two legs broken, a broken cup, and a small dish. On the hearth was scarcely a spark of fire, and in one corner lay as many old rags as would fill a woman's apron, which served the whole family as a bed. For bed clothing they had only their scanty day clothing. The poor woman told him that she had been forced to sell her bedstead the year before to buy food. Her bedding she had pawned with the victualler for food. In short, everything had gone for food.

(*ibid*, p. 26)

Friedrich Engels took his analysis of crime further in terms of extending what is meant by crime, arguing that crime is not simply that which is perpetuated by individuals. For the current social arrangements which exist at the behest of bourgeois society are inherently criminal. Engels used the utterly chilling phrase 'social murder' to describe the many deaths that occur each year that result from the dreadful living and working conditions that so many are forced to endure. Society 'has placed the workers under conditions in which they can neither retain health nor live long; that it undermines the vital force of these workers gradually, little by little, and so hurries them to the grave before their time' (*ibid*, p. 63).

Moreover, while still emphasising that crime is largely concentrated amongst the proletariat, Engels considered the impact of white-collar crimes, such as food and tobacco adulteration, fraud, unsafe factory conditions and the rape of women employees. These all disproportionately affect the working classes. With respect to food adulteration, for example,

> the rich are less deceived because they can pay the high prices of the large shops which have a reputation to lose and would injure themselves more than their customers if they kept poor or adulterated wares; the rich are spoiled, too, by habitual good eating, and detect adulteration more easily with their sensitive palates.
>
> (*ibid*, p. 47)

The rich and the poor are also dealt with differently by the law:

> If a rich man is brought up, or rather summoned, to appear before the court, the judge regrets that he is obliged to impose so much trouble, treats the matter as favourably as possible, and, [if] he is forced to condemn the accused, does so with extreme regret etc. etc. and at the end of it all is a miserable fine, which the bourgeois throws upon the table with contempt and then departs. But if the poor devil gets into such a position as involves appearing before the Justice of the Peace – he has almost always spent the night in the station-house with a crowd of his peers – he is regarded from the beginning as guilty; his defence is set aside with a contemptuous 'Oh! we know the excuse', and a fine imposed which he cannot pay and must work out with several months on the treadmill. And if nothing can be proved against him, he is sent to the treadmill, none the less 'as a rogue and a vagabond'.
>
> (*ibid*, p. 169)

The institution of the law is presented throughout both Marx and Engels's writings as generally supporting bourgeois interests, both ideologically and practically. In a series of early articles for the journal *Rheinische Zeitung*, Marx discusses the law that was introduced on the theft of wood by the

Rhineland parliament in 1842. The demand for wood had increased with industrialisation, and this new law turned what had once been a 'customary right' of forest dwellers to collect fallen wood from the forest floor into a criminal offence. This led to the criminalisation of the poor, the innocent. Marx argues, 'if the law applies the term theft to an action that is scarcely even a violation of forest regulations' then 'the poor are sacrificed to a legal lie'. The customary right of gathering wood was effectively being privatised by the bourgeoisie for their own ends; the provincial assembly, instead of taking into consideration the rights of all citizens, was 'representing a definite particular interest',[7] that of the forest owner. In the preface to *A Contribution to the Critique of Political Economy* (1859), Marx said the theft of wood was one of the issues that inspired him to 'turn his attention to economic questions'.

Thus, although Marx and Engels never fully elaborated their ideas on crime[8], there is clearly much to be gleaned from their writings. In the early 1900s it fell to the Dutchman Willem Adriaan Bonger to further explore the legitimacy of Marxism as the theoretical basis for an understanding of crime and criminality.[9]

W.A. Bonger

Willem Adriaan Bonger was born in Amsterdam in 1876. As Patrick Hebberecht (2010) notes, it was as a law student at the University of Amsterdam that he developed an interest in social justice and became a socialist and a member of the Sociaal-Democratische Arbeiderspartij (the Social Democratic Workers Party). Throughout his life Bonger was to remain passionately committed to political and social activism (*ibid*). His doctoral thesis, which he defended in 1905, was on criminality and economic conditions. This was published in English, in the United States, as *Criminality and Economic Conditions* in 1916. Bonger's other key texts include *An Introduction to Criminology* (1935) and *Race and Crime* (1942). John Wigmore commented in the introduction to *Race and Crime* that Bonger stood out amongst his generation 'as a preeminent specialist in the sound analysis of statistics, and the leading exponent of the philosophy of crime as a social and not a biological phenomenon' (1942, p. vi).

In *Criminality and Economic Conditions* Bonger critiques Lombroso and the Italian School at length for focusing on individual biological and physiological factors and for largely overlooking the wider economic system and its influence on 'social organisation' (his term) and criminality (Hebberecht, 2010). There is, Bonger argued, 'no stigmata belonging to criminals only, nor is there any criminal type; the atavistic hypothesis is one of the profoundest errors' (1916, p. 122). For 'primitive peoples are neither thieves nor murderers and our ancestors, consequently, may be regarded as cleared of the same charge' (*ibid*, p. 657). He writes forcefully against heredity arguments and their eugenicist implications, which were gaining support, especially in the United States:

> That heredity plays a great part on the scene of criminality has never been proved. Have the advocates of 'sterilization', one should be inclined to ask, never heard of Australia, where a considerable number of inhabitants are descended from the worst of criminals, and where yet the rate of criminality is low?
>
> (*ibid*, p. xxvii)

Although many of those transported were not 'the worst of criminals', this does not detract from Bonger's argument. His contempt for such theories is palpably clear throughout his work: 'the effect of "sterilization" seems to be as useful as the efforts to stop with a bottle a brook in its course', for the 'roots' of crime 'are found outside man, in society' (1916, p. xxvii).

To clarify how the capitalist system of production affects society and criminality, Bonger, like Engels, stressed the 'brutalizing treatment' of the 'working man' by the bourgeoisie, the levels of abject poverty and 'filthy' living conditions (1916, p. 26), and he also made use of the concepts of 'altruism' and 'egoism'. With respect to the latter, Bonger was influenced by Karl Kautsky, who put forward the idea 'that levels of altruism in society are determined by strong social instincts and sentiments' (Hebberecht, 2010, p. 60). 'Altruism' was evident in traditional pre-capitalist societies that emphasised shared conditions, a 'uniformity of interest' and a feeling of community (1916, p. 397). Capitalist societies, on the other hand, are 'based upon exchange' and 'such a mode of production cannot fail to have an egoistic character', for

> A society based on exchange isolates the individuals by weakening the bond that unites them. When it is a question of exchange the two parties interested think only of their own advantage even to the detriment of the other party.
>
> (*ibid*, p. 418)

Capitalism is responsible for the creation of 'egoism', and crime 'is an egoistic act, that is to say an act which injures the interests of others' (*ibid*, p. 646); it places self-interest above the interests of others. It is this competitive system that is responsible for damaging 'altruism' and 'undermines the moral strength of the people' (Hebberecht, 2010, p. 61).[10] Bonger was, however, at pains to stress that 'the egotistic tendency does not *by itself* make a man a criminal . . . it is possible for the environment to create a great egoist, but this does not imply that the egoist will necessarily become criminal' (1916, p. 418; author emphasis). Capitalism results in 'man' becoming 'very egoistic and hence more *capable of crime*, than if the environment had developed the germs of altruism' (*ibid*; original emphasis): what it does, therefore, is set the stage for a 'criminal thought' to be converted into an act of criminality.

Bonger sees crime as more prevalent amongst the proletariat, for the more a social class is subject to discriminatory economic and social conditions, the more likely 'egoism' will lead to a 'criminal thought' and subsequently a criminal act. Yet the bourgeoisie are not exempt: 'egoism' affects all social classes, and economic, sexual, political and pathological crimes are committed by both the powerless and the powerful. The present economic situation 'has unshackled egoism . . . it reaps what is sows' (*ibid*, p. 189). Indeed, Bonger was one of the first European criminologists to consider the crimes of the bourgeoisie, especially those of fraud and fraudulent bankruptcy (Taylor et al, 1973; Hebberecht, 2010). In such cases, 'what [white-collar criminals] get by honest business is not enough for them, they wish to become richer' (1916, p. 138).

Further, it is difficult to determine what 'crime' is and what its overall impact is, for in a capitalist society crime does not necessarily refer to acts that are 'immoral' or 'anti-social': definitions of 'crime' reflect the interests of the bourgeoisie. The crimes of the bourgeoisie are legitimised, whereas those of the proletariat criminalised. As Bonger wrote,

> In every society which is divided into a ruling class and a class ruled, penal law has been principally constituted according to the will of the former. . . . In the existing penal code, hardly an act is punished if it does not injure the interests of the dominant classes.
>
> (1916, pp. 379–380)

As Hebberecht observes, this was 'an extremely innovative sociological concept of crime' (2010, p. 59) and anticipates the title of Jeffrey Reiman's 1979 *The Rich Get Richer and the Poor Get Prison* (Lanier and Henry, 1998).

On women, whilst Bonger adopts many of the attitudes towards women that were typical of his time, seeing women as more 'passive' than men and responsible for the home and child care,[11] he does acknowledge the level that women are oppressed within capitalist society by men, their economic situation and the legal system:

> The great power of a man over his wife, as a consequence of his economic preponderance, may equally be a demoralizing cause. It is certain that there will always be abuse of power on the part of a number of those whose social circumstances have clothed with a certain authority. How many women there are now who have had to endure the coarseness and

bad treatment of their husbands, but would not hesitate to leave them if their economic dependence and the law did not prevent.

(1916, pp. 462–463)

Stan Cohen asked where Willem Bonger would have stood in terms of more contemporary radical criminological discourse. The answer, Cohen felt, lay in the left realist programme 'because this is a criminology reconstituted for a leftist social democracy' (1998, p. 125). There are, he points out, in *Introduction to Criminology* many references to 'the damaging and demoralizing effects of crime, and its cost to the body politic, the suffering caused to victims and offenders alike' (*ibid*, p. 126), which fits a left realist agenda. 'Certainly', Bonger 'had little time for the notion of the criminal as a social rebel' (*ibid*).

For Bonger, 'crime is the consequence of economic and social conditions' and the way to combat it is 'by changing these conditions' (*ibid*, p. 669). He ends *Criminality and Economic Conditions* by quoting Quetelet and expressing optimism for the future:

'It is society that prepares the crime', says the true adage of Quetelet. For all those who have reached this conclusion, and are not insensible to the sufferings of humanity, this statement is sad, but contains a ground of hope. It is sad because society punishes severely those who commit the crime which she has herself prepared. It contains a ground of hope, since it promises to humanity the possibility of someday delivering itself from one of its most terrible scourges.

(*ibid*, p. 672)

Box 7.1   Death of a criminologist: W.A. Bonger

Bonger's last book, *Race and Crime*, was published three years after his death in 1943. In it he laments the ascendency of criminological anthropological thought under the Nazi regime. The book attempts to provide a counter-narrative to the increasing popularity of theories linking crime and race in criminological discourse. Bonger questions accepted notions of what race is, the subjectivity of the label of crime and, as in his earlier work, the role of powerful groups – represented by the state – in designating certain behaviours as 'crimes' and applying punishment. Without understanding this, he argues, it is impossible to enter into a meaningful discussion. Bonger dismisses both physical and psychological differences between races and draws attention to the 'blunders' of Lombroso and more contemporary theorists. He argues it is a 'great nonsense to speak of criminal and non-criminal races' (1943,

p. 28). Admittedly, there are flaws in his analysis (see Hawkins, 1995), but it is impossible not to see the political intentions behind this slim text. In the introduction Bonger expresses desperation over the current situation:

> Pettiness and lunacy dominate the whole subject [of race and crime]. No trace of science remains. Bestial passions and baseless prejudices have led to situations which but a short time ago would have been considered totally impossible. In certain countries the Jews are robbed and mistreated in hundreds of thousands. They are killed or driven out for no other reason that that they differ anthropologically from the rest of the population. A part of mankind has fallen back to the Middle Ages when just such a primitive irrationality was uppermost in men's minds. But this is much more dangerous now that it formerly was, for now men have the means of modern technique and publicity at their disposal.
>
> (1943, p. ix)

A member of Comité van Waakzaamheid, a 'political movement of vigilance against the emerging Nazism', Bonger was well aware that he was on the list of people who would be arrested by the Nazis (van Swaaningen, 1995, p. 74). Indeed, according to J.M. Van Bremmelen (1955), after September 1939 Bonger's name was mentioned on a number of occasions by the Bremer radio as an arch-enemy of Nazi Germany. Yet he refused to leave the Netherlands, and five days after the Nazis invaded, on 15 May 1940, he committed suicide with his wife. In a note that he left to his son he wrote, 'I don't see any future for myself and I cannot bow to this scum which will now overmaster us' (*ibid*, p. 302).

Georg Rusche and Otto Kirchheimer

Georg Rusche and Otto Kirchheimer's *Punishment and Social Structure* (1939) was mainly based on the ideas of Rusche, which were first outlined in Rusche's 'Arbeitsmarkt and Strafvollzug' (1933), a proposal to the Frankfurt Institute of Social Research. *Punishment and Social Structure* was, as Dario Melossi has put it, 'to become – to friend and foe – the certified *bona fide* Marxist view on punishment' (2009, p. xxi). Rusche (born in Hanover in 1900) and Kirchheimer (born in Heilbronn, Germany in 1905), and the Frankfurt Institute, were to be displaced following Hitler's rise to power. Kirchheimer, as did many of the Frankfurt Institute's members, ended up in New York. Rusche went first to Paris, then to London and Palestine, before back to London (Melossi, 2003).[12] In 'Arbeitsmarkt and Strafvollzug', Rusche argued that the problem with criminologists – despite producing 'valuable insights about the individual and social causes of crime and the sociopsychological functions of punishments' – is that they have not 'connected to economic theory, nor are they historically orientated . . . they unconsciously characterize the social system as eternal and unchanging rather than a historical process' (1980 ed, p. 11). The 'economic theory of punishment' that Rusche puts forward suggests that those in power utilise penal strategies that relate to their political-economic systems, especially in terms of how labour markets are organised and the economic and social situation of the proletariat, and deploy 'state strategies for facilitating social control, as these develop within specific modes of production' (Michalowski and Carlson, 1999, p. 218; Rusche, 1933). These ideas were developed further in *Punishment and Social Structure*. In the introductory section to this text Rusche and Kirchheimer stress the need to first break the 'bond' between crime and punishment:

> Punishment is neither a simple consequence of crime, nor the reverse side of crime, nor a means which is determined by the end to be achieved. Punishment should be understood as a social phenomenon freed from both its juristic concept and its social ends. We do not deny that punishment has specific ends, but we do deny that it can be understood from its ends alone . . . Punishment does not exist; only concrete systems of punishment and specific practices exist.
> (2009 ed, p. 5)

They go on to outline what became known as the 'Rusche-Kirchheimer hypothesis' (Michalowski and Carlson, 1999), which maintains that

> every system of production tends to discover punishments which correspond to its productive relationships. It is thus necessary to investigate the origin and fate of penal systems, the use or avoidance of specific punishments, and the intensity of penal practices as they are determined by social forces, above all by economic and then fiscal forces.
> (Rusche and Kirchheimer, 2009 ed, p. 5)

In identifying three core historical eras – the early Middle Ages, in which fines and penance typified systems of punishment; the later Middle Ages, where corporal punishment and the death penalty become more common; and the Age of the Enlightenment that saw the birth of the penitentiary – Rusche and Kirchheimer illustrate how changes in the dominant mode of production result in changes in the dominant mode of punishment. At the start of this book I focused on the brutality of punishment in the pre-Enlightenment era: Rusche and Kirchheimer held that in the later Middle Ages there was no shortage of labour and 'as the price paid for labour decreased, the value on human life became smaller and smaller (2009 ed, p. 20) and punishment became 'the most cruel form of suppression' (*ibid*, p. 23), as is evidenced by the use of torture and the death penalty. Indeed, 'the hard struggle for existence molded the penal system in such a way as to make it one of the means of preventing too great an increase of population' (*ibid*, p. 20). Citing Von Hentig, they suggest the system 'acted as a kind of artificial earthquake or famine in destroying those whom the upper classes considered unfit for society' (*ibid*). Punishment thus functions as part of a complex system of social control: 'the penal system of any given society is not an isolated phenomenon subject only to its own special laws' (*ibid*, p. 207). It forms 'an integral part of the whole social system, and shares its aspirations and its defects' (*ibid*). The power of the ruling class is henceforth reinforced through systems of punishment. As Rusche put it in his 1933 piece, 'criminality certainly occurs throughout all social classes' but it is 'clear that the criminal law and the daily work of the criminal courts are directly almost exclusively against those people whose class background, poverty, neglected education, or demoralization drove them to crime' (1980 ed, p. 11). 'The history of the penal system', he writes, 'is more than a history of the alleged independent development of legal "institutions". It is the history of the relations of the "two nations" as Disraeli called them, that constitute a people – the rich and the poor' (*ibid*, p. 13). Depressingly, *Punishment and Social Structure* concludes with 'the futility of severe punishment and cruel treatment may be proven a thousand times, but *so long as society is unable to solve its social problems, repression, the easy way out, will always be accepted*' (2003 ed, p. 207, author emphasis).

Punishment and Social Structure has been criticised for being too economically deterministic. David Garland, for example, pointed out that there is 'contemporary evidence which shows a wide variation in penal practice between societies which share similar economic conditions' (1990, p. 107).[13] Nevertheless, it was described by Foucault in *Discipline and Punishment* as a 'great work', and he credits it with providing 'a number of essential reference points': such as 'we must first of all rid ourselves of the illusion that penality is above all (if not exclusively) a means of reducing crime' and

> we must analyse rather the 'concrete systems of punishment', study them as social phenomena that cannot be accounted for by the juridical structure of society alone, nor by its fundamental ethical choices; we must situate them in their field of operation, in which the punishment of crime is not the sole element.
>
> (1975, p. 24)

We need to study punishment in terms of how it has been practised historically. Dario Melossi also observes that it is significant that after Foucault pays homage to *Punishment and Social Structure* he proceeds to outline some of his most important concepts, namely the 'political economy of the body' and of the 'microphysics of power' (2003, p. xxvii). In the United States the book had a particular influence on the work of Thorsten Sellin,[14] especially *Slavery and the Penal System* (1976), and radical criminologists associated with the Berkeley School of Criminology in the late 1960s/1970s. Indeed, Melossi notes that it was mainly in the United States that *Punishment and Social Structure* garnered attention[15] – his own writing on Rusche and Kirchheimer being published in the 'critical criminology' journal *Crime and Social Justice* in the 1970s. In Tony Platt and Paul Takagi's anthology of papers *Punishment and Penal Discipline: Essays on the Prison and the Prisoners' Movement* (1980), Melossi's paper on 'Punishment and Social Structure' was included alongside a translation of Rusche's 'Arbeitsmarkt and Strafvollzug' an introductory discussion of Rusche and Kirchheimer and some of the 'best work' from *Crime and Social Justice*. The editors described the purpose of this volume was to reflect on 'our progress and problems' in the 'construction of a Marxist analysis of punishment' (1980, p. vii),[16] which the editors saw as being in a fledgling stage of development.[17] In the early 1980s Randall Shelden drew on both Du Bois and Rusche and Kirchheimer in his analysis of penal changes in Tennessee, 1830–1915. Shelden (1981) argued that when the United States changed from a slave economy to a capitalist economy after the Civil War, imprisonment became the dominant system of punishment. As occurs with societies in the first stages of capitalist development, in the South there was a need for 'an abundant and steady source of *cheap* and *forced* labor' (1981, p. 613, author emphasis). One source of this labour were those confined in Southern prisons 'and utilized by a unique form of forced labor, the convict lease system' (*ibid*).

It was not until the late 1960s and early 1970s, with the consolidation of a 'critical criminology' that the value of Marxist ideas to the study of crime, deviance and punishment were to be more fully realised within the discipline of criminology.

The rise of critical criminology

For Marxists, as we have seen, the focus is on the economy and the capitalist structure of society. As Rick Matthews succinctly comments, from a Marxist perspective 'crime can only be understood as occurring within a specific set of social and economic conditions' and, as such, 'the nature, form and extent of crime is dependent on the way in which society organizes itself' (2003, p. 3). The majority of critical criminologists likewise support the conception of crime as having a materialist basis.

Alongside Marxist ideas, critical criminologists were strongly influenced by the new American deviancy theory of the especially creative period of 1955 to 1965 (see Ferrell et al, 2008). This had two strands: subcultural theory, particularly the writings of Albert Cohen and Richard Cloward and the early work of Robert Merton, and the labelling theorists, for example, Howard S. Becker, John Kitsuse and Edwin Lemert, who built on the ideas of Frank

Tannenbaum. The former focused on the deviant act, the latter on reactions to the act. The innovation of critical criminologists was to put both strands together and to place this within a Marxist inspired macro-context which examined the dynamics of society as a whole. This was the function of *The New Criminology*: its aim was to create 'a fully social theory' of crime and deviance. The impact of American deviancy theory is highlighted by Stan Cohen in his description next of how the National Deviancy Conferences (NDC) came about.

The National Deviancy Conferences

> In the middle of the 1960s, there were a number of young sociologists in Britain attracted to the then wholly American field in the sociology of deviance. The ideas in such works as Becker's *Outsiders* and Matza's *Delinquency and Drift*[18] seemed to make sense across a whole range of teaching and research interests, particularly in 'marginal' areas such as drugs, sexual deviance, youth culture and mental illness. Official criminology was regarded with attitudes ranging from ideological condemnation to a certain measure of boredom. But being a sociologist – often isolated in a small department – was not enough to get away from criminology: some sort of separate subculture had to be carved out within the sociological world. So, ostensibly for these reasons (although this account sounds suspiciously like colour-supplement history), seven of us met in July 1968, fittingly enough in Cambridge in the middle of the Third National Conference of Teaching and Research, organised by the Institute (of Criminology) and opened by the Home Secretary. We decided to form a group to provide some sort of intellectual support for each other to cope with collective problems of identity.
>
> (S. Cohen, 1981, p. 194)

This 'intellectual support' was consolidated around the NDC.[19] As Cohen recalls, the conferences were brought into being by a group of young academics who were both excited by the developments in North American radical sociology and disillusioned with establishment criminology as represented by the Institute of Criminology at Cambridge University under the directorship of Leon Radzinowicz. The Third National Conference of Teaching and Research on Criminology had been dominated by the largely positivist views of the establishment, concerned with the pathology of the offender. The seven founding individuals, who met as part of that breakaway faction at the conference, were Stan Cohen, Kit Carson, Mary McIntosh, David Downes, Jock Young, Paul Rock and Ian Taylor, all of whom became well known in the fields of criminology and the sociology of deviance. Leon Radzinowicz said of the NDC that 'at the time, it reminded me a little of naughty schoolboys, playing a nasty game on their stern headmaster' (1999, p. 229). He unsurprisingly was not invited to participate. Young has described the NDC as 'anarchistic and antinomian, set deep in the counter culture of the time' and also 'hectic, irreverent, transgressive and, above all, fun' (2002, p. 252). Between 1968 and 1973 there were fourteen conferences producing an extraordinary outpouring of innovative work that would ultimately transform the discipline of criminology in Britain. It attacked positivist and classicist discourses and was concerned with how the criminal justice system was selective and fundamentally flawed, particularly with respect to its focus on the crimes of the working class while ignoring those of the more powerful groups in society. In terms of explorations in the sociology of deviance, there was an emphasis on youth and class that generated papers, for example, on football hooliganism and working-class youth (Taylor, 1968), drug use (Young, 1968), hippies (Hall, 1970) and motorbike subculture (Willis, 1972). However, there were no restrictions in terms of discipline and, as such, there were important contributions to cultural studies, anti-psychiatry and the sociology of sexualities.

The NDC played a vital role in terms of the development of critical criminology in Britain, leading to two important theoretical strands: the 'new' criminology of Taylor, Young, Paul Walton and others, and the work of the University of Birmingham's Centre for Contemporary Cultural Studies, under the directorship of Stuart Hall, on the theorisation of youth subcultures, resistance and moral panics. Taylor, Walton and Young's *The New Criminology* (1973) has been described as the 'major manifesto of NDC Marxism' (Payne et al, 1981, p. 105); in its introduction the authors directly acknowledge that it is a 'product of discussions and developments in and around the National Deviancy Conference' (1973, p. xv). Similarly, Steve Redhead (1995) has described the ventures into youth culture and subcultures by the Centre for Contemporary Cultural Studies (CCCS) as having originated from the research into politics and deviance that was carried out by the NDC. Many of those associated with the CCCS were active participants in the NDC. Stuart Hall gave papers at the NDC's fifth symposium in April 1970 and at the twelfth symposium in January 1973. Phil Cohen, 'the other most influential and seminal theorist in this period of CCCS work' (Redhead, 1995, p. 33), presented his path-breaking study of working-class youth culture in October 1970. Paul Willis, who went on to write the now-classic ethnography of working class 'lads', *Learning to Labour* (1977), gave his paper on 'A Motor Bike Subculture' at the ninth symposium in January 1972. The 'new' criminology and the work of the Birmingham Centre for Contemporary Cultural Studies has had a lasting impact on debates on criminology, deviance and narratives of social control, both nationally and internationally.

The New Criminology

The ideas of Marx and Engels are evident throughout *The New Criminology*.[20] In over thirty years this key text in the history of critical criminology in Britain has not been out of print. It was followed by *Critical Criminology* in 1975, a series of essays edited also by Taylor, Walton and Young and featuring contributions by commentators such as Herman and Julia Schwendinger, William Chambliss and Tony Platt, who were known for their leftist views on crime and social control in the United States. This text was designed to explore and debate the ideas presented in *The New Criminology*.

A major influence was the work of Alvin Gouldner, especially 'The Sociologist as Partisan' (1968) and *The Coming Crisis of Western Sociology* (1970). In 'The Sociologist as Partisan' Gouldner had criticised Howard S. Becker's Presidential Address to the Society for the Study of Social Problems, 'Whose Side Are We On?', for his 'identification with the underdog' which is, he wrote, equivalent to that of 'the Great White Hunter who has barely risked the perils of the urban jungle to bring back an exotic specimen' (1968, p. 106). He is like a 'zookeeper' who 'displays his rare specimens'. And 'like the zookeeper, he wishes to protect his collection, he does not want spectators to throw rocks at the animals behind the bars. But neither is he eager to *tear down the bars* and *let the animals go*' (*ibid*; author emphasis). This is the problem of career liberals within the academy. Sociologists such as Becker represent, as Jock Young put it, 'the zoo-keepers of deviance' (1969). For Gouldner 'radical sociologists' are those who want to study the 'overdog', the 'leader', the 'power elites', the 'masters of men'; 'radical sociologists differ from liberals in that, while they take the standpoint of the underdog, they apply it to the study of overdogs' (1968, p. 111). In *The Coming Crisis of Western Sociology* Gouldner called for a reflexive sociology: 'an historically sensitive sociology' in which the sociologist is 'aware of their historically evolving character, and of their place in a historically evolving society' (1970, p. 507). Its 'historical mission' is that of helping individuals 'in their struggle to take possession of what is theirs – society and culture – and of aiding them to know who they are and what they may want' (*ibid*, p. 509).

As an aside, although the 'zookeeper' critique is undoubtedly a valid one, it perhaps should not obscure Becker's contribution to 'making sociology relevant to society'. Becker (2003) observed that the problem is that people typically want 'a *panacea*, which (to give a technical definition) is something that gets rid of what you don't like without upsetting all the other arrangements that are satisfactory to you, in short, without costing anything' (p. 5, original emphasis), and thus when the chairperson of a Canadian Royal Commission on the illicit use of recreational drugs told him he wanted to get 'rid of such use and that he did not want to be told to legalize it (which all his previous consultants had told him was the simple way to solve that problem)', Becker was to tell him,

> He could do it by suspending civil liberties, searching people randomly on the street and making random searches of houses, and then shooting on the spot any people found to be in possession of drugs. He said, 'Are you telling me that anything less than that won't work?' I said, 'Yes, and you're not willing to live with the consequences of such a decision,

supposing you could get it approved, so why don't you start talking seriously and stop posturing?'

(ibid)

The New Criminology was to set the stage for a fully social theory of crime and deviance. Alvin Gouldner wrote the forward. In *The New Criminology*, Gouldner said, it is 'made thoroughly clear' that the study of criminology should involve 'the *critical understanding* of both the larger and of the broadest social theory; it is not the study of some marginal exotic or esoteric group, be they criminals or criminologists' (Taylor et al, 1973, p. x; original emphasis). Gouldner's 'exotic' or 'esoteric' was a reference to his critique of Becker.

The New Criminology argued for theory to be placed in its wider social and historical context: we need to fully comprehend the nature of crime and the reaction to it. *The New Criminology* critiques the major criminological theories – classicism and positivism – and some of the more recent approaches of the time, for example, labelling theory and the 'new' conflict theories. It takes issue with those that set the individual apart from society and fail to provide a sense of history; indeed, the social and historical actor is seen as 'almost totally absent in existing criminological theory' (*ibid*, p. 269). The major 'enemy' is establishment criminology which endorses a positivistic explanation for crime, presenting it as largely the result of social or personal pathology and advocating correctionalism (that which involves correcting the behaviour of the individual through criminal sanctions or rehabilitation) as a means of dealing with it. As Taylor et al were to elaborate in *Critical Criminology*, correctionalism 'is irretrievably bound up with the identification of deviance with pathology, or that, where it is not, it collapses into a mindless relativism' (Taylor et al, 1975, p. 44). For the new criminologists the causes of crime are to be found outside of the individual, in the social structure, that is, in the 'inequalities of wealth and power, and in particular of inequalities in property and life-chances' (Taylor et al, 1973, p. 281) created by contemporary capitalist society and, as such, the solution must involve the restructuring of society.

Hence Taylor, Walton and Young write 'with Marx, we have been concerned with the social arrangements that have obstructed, and the social contradictions that enhance, man's chances of achieving full sociality' (*ibid*, p. 270). And in *Critical Criminology* they acknowledge more fully the importance of utilising Marxism to create a social theory of crime:

> The superiority of Marx's work lies not in his individual genius but rather in his *method*.[21] In part, this method rests on a refusal to separate out thought from society. Thus, for Marx, theoretical reflection is either obfuscation or an exercise in practical reasoning. Marx insists upon two features of any properly social analysis. Firstly, he says that, 'to be radical is grasp things at the root. For man the root is Man himself'. Second, he

observes that man is inseparable from society. It follows that to analyse crime, for example, requires we examine man's position in *society*.
(Taylor et al, 1975, p. 45)

The goal should therefore be to create a socialist society in which material differences are removed and equality is emphasised. As the causes of crime are located in the conditions created by capitalism, the only way that crime could possibly be abolished is by abolishing capitalism. Moreover, a socialist society should be one that embraces and does not criminalise human diversity. For

> it *is* possible to envisage societies free of any material necessity to criminalize deviance . . . there are forms of human diversity which, under capitalism, are labelled and processed as criminal but which should not be subject to control in societies that proclaimed themselves to be socialist.
> (*ibid*, p. 20; emphasis in original)

Examples of diversity would include homosexuality, drug use, gambling and other forms of hedonistic or oppositional behaviour. This would clearly necessitate a reduction in the level of state control: an important theme in contemporary critical criminology.

Box 7.2 *The New Criminology*: A new approach to theory

The formal and substantive requirements of theory

After examining and exposing the flaws in the major criminological theories Taylor, Walton and Young's final chapter of *The New Criminology* outlined the formal requirements of a fully social theory of crime and deviance. Additionally, it indicated some of the substantive requirements of the theory; this would be further clarified by Young in *The New Criminology Revisited* (1998). The emphasis is on the structural origins of the act and of the reaction to the act.

The formal requirements of theory

The formal requirements of theory should be able to point to and account for the connections between:

1   The wider origins of the deviant act, 'in other words, to place the act in terms of its wider structural origins'.

2   Immediate origins of the deviant act, to 'be able to explain the different events, experiences or structural developments that precipitate the deviant act'.
3   The actual act, to explain the relationship between the behaviour and the causes, 'a working class adolescent, for example, confronted with blockage of opportunity, with problems of status frustration, alienated from the kind of existence offered out to him in contemporary society, may want to engage in hedonistic activities or he may choose to kick back at a rejecting society (e.g. through acts of vandalism)'.
4   Immediate origins of social reaction, i.e. how the act is responded to.
5   The wider origins of deviant reaction, i.e. 'the position and attributes of those who instigate the reaction against the deviant'.
6   The outcome of the social reaction on the deviant's further action.
7   The nature of the deviant process as a whole, how 1–6 connect together.

(Taylor et al, 1973, pp. 270–278)

The substantive requirements of theory

Theory should acknowledge the following:

1   Human beings are both determined and determining.
2   A pluralistic diverse society.
3   A class society based on inequalities of wealth and power.
4   A sequential, processual model that is historical and open-ended.
5   A dialectic between structure and consciousness, that is, it would relate typical sets of motives (consciousness and ideologies) to situated actions (given historical contexts).
6   Holistic view of society and of the individual: the fully social conception of human action.
7   Theory must be isomorphic (that is, symmetrical) – given same explanation of social reaction and action for the theorist and the object of study.
8   Empirical base: must both utilise and endeavour to explain all types of deviancy.
9   It must involve a criminology that is aware of history and the sociohistorical position of the theorists: which will treat crime not as a technicality or a surface problem needing correction, but deal with society as a totality.

(Young, 1998, p. 24)

The Centre for Contemporary Cultural Studies

Birmingham University's CCCS was, like the 'new' theorists, Marxist leaning; the writings of Antonio Gramsci played a particularly important role in the development of the theoretical background to its work. Indeed, Stuart Hall has described the CCCS as a 'Gramscian project' (1990, p. 17). The Gramscian concept of hegemony was seen as fundamental in terms of understanding how power is constructed in society. Hegemony refers to the way in which power is achieved and legitimated through consent as opposed to coercion. This relates not only to the acquiring of control at the level of the economy, 'the decisive nucleus of the economic activity', but how those who hold the power are able to impose their values – their interpretation of the world – such that these are accepted by subordinated groups. The role of ideas is key to achieving power by consent. As Hall wrote in 1987, '[t]he nature of power in the modern world is that it is *also* constructed in relation to political, moral, intellectual, cultural, ideological, sexual questions'; thus, 'the question of hegemony is always the question of a new cultural order' (pp. 20–21, original emphasis).

The CCCS aspired to be in line with Gramsci's concept of the 'organic intellectual'. The 'organic intellectual' contrasted to the traditional intellectual who was elitist and distant from the masses: traditional intellectuals wrote 'without feeling the elementary passions of the people, understanding them and therefore explaining and justifying them in the particular historical situation' (Gramsci, 1971 ed, p. 418), Organic intellectuals arose 'organically' from their class grouping and gave a voice to the interests, culture, values and concerns of the people. They were, as Colin Webster commented, 'much closer to the everyday, to "common sense" knowledge and popular culture than their traditional counterparts' (2010, p. 199). Many of those involved in the CCCS, as with the NDC, originally came from the less privileged sections of society; their backgrounds were largely working class, and most were graduate students rather than full-time faculty. They were more in touch with the 'dirty outside world', and their aim, as Hall reflected, was to 'use the enormous advantage given to a tiny handful of us in the British educational system who had the opportunity to go into universities and reflect on [real] problems, to spend that time usefully to try to understand how the world worked' (1990, p. 17). Moreover,

> [They] took to heart the Gramscian injunction that the practice of an organic intellectual would have to be to engage with the philosophical end of the enterprise, with knowledge at its most testing. Because it mattered, we had to know more than they knew about our subject at the same time as we took responsibility for translating that knowledge back into practice.... Neither the one nor the other alone would do. And that

is because we tried, in our extremely marginal way up there on the eighth floor in the Arts Faculty Building, to think of ourselves as a tiny piece of a hegemonic struggle. Just one tiny bit of it. We didn't have the illusion we were where the game really was. But we knew that the questions we were asking were of central relevance to the questions through which hegemony is either established or contested.

(*ibid*, p. 18)

The CCCS, under Hall's leadership, has been described as a 'powerhouse in contemporary sociology' and as 'interdisciplinary *par excellence*, iconoclastic, and immensely innovative' (Ferrell et al, 2008, p. 46). In addition to those names already mentioned, others associated with the CCCS included Angela McRobbie who (with Jenny Garber) produced ground-breaking work on girls and subcultures, Dick Hebdige, Tony Jefferson, John Clarke, Paul Gilroy, Chas Critcher, Paul Corrigan and Dave Morley. Constantly moving between the disciplines of sociology, criminology, literary studies and social history, they made use of Marxist literature in order to provide a fuller understanding of the role that ideology played in the construction of the hegemonic process: Richard Hoggart on how to 'read' working-class culture; Raymond Williams and the importance of expressing the creativity inherent in popular culture and how this relates to people's identities; the work of Claude Levi Strauss and Roland Barthes and the concept of 'bricolage'; and from English social historians such as Edward Thompson came the idea of 'writing history from below'. The exploration and incorporation of critical ideas from a range of sources being necessary to flesh out aspects of contemporary human experience.

Edward Thompson's 'writing from below' was very much in line with the role of the 'organic intellectual': it is of history written from 'the material experience of the common people, rather than "from above" in the committee chambers of high office' (Pearson, 1978, p. 119). As Barry Godfrey has stated, the Marxist-oriented 'history from below' movement 'sought to rescue the voices of the poor' (2011, p. 209) from what Thompson described in *The Making of the English Working Class* as the 'enormous condescension of posterity' (1972, p. 12).[22] The 'gaze' of the CCCS was thus 'wide in focus; it disdained the narrow optic of orthodox criminology' (Ferrell et al, 2008, p. 46). Yet despite such a cross-disciplinary approach and multiplicity of research interests – Teddy boys, mods and rockers, drugs, mugging and so on – the theme that united those associated with the CCCS was how order was reproduced in capitalist Britain in the post-war period (Downes and Rock, 2007).

From a critical criminology perspective, the two main texts are the collaboratively written *Resistance Through Rituals* (1975) and *Policing the Crisis* (1978). Both attempt to provide a social theory in the sense of focusing on the structural origins and context of the act of deviance or crime and the reaction to it. *Policing the Crisis* is more developed in its approach and addresses to a large degree the formal requirements of theory as outlined in *The New*

Criminology to the extent that it allows the reader to 'assess the claim that critical criminology is superior to alternative approaches' (Downes and Rock, 2007, p. 235).

The focus in *Resistance Through Rituals*, edited by Hall and Jefferson, is on the style-centred youth cultures that emerged after the Second World War. The importance of understanding culture in its historical context is highlighted in the first chapter of the book. Drawing on Thompson (1960) and Marx's *The German Ideology*, John Clarke et al write

> Culture is the way, the forms, in which groups 'handle' the raw material of their social and material existence. . . . 'Culture' is the practice which realizes or *objectivates* group-life in meaningful shape and form. . . . The 'culture' of a group or class is the peculiar and distinctive 'way of life' of the group or class, the meanings, values and ideas embodied in institutions, in social relations, in systems of beliefs, in mores and customs, in the uses of objects and material life. . . . A culture includes 'maps of meaning' which make things intelligible to its members. These 'maps of meaning' are not simply carried around in the head: they are objectivated in the patterns of social organisation and relationship through which the individual becomes a 'social individual'. Culture is the way the social relations of a group are structured and shaped: but it is also the way those shapes are experienced, understood and interpreted.
>
> (1975, p. 10–11; original emphasis)

The number and variety of youth cultures, or subcultures, were seen as collective responses to the material conditions in which youth, especially those from the working class, encountered in British society. For as Colin Webster points out, the 'changes in popular culture and the emergence of a new consumer culture' that occurred in this period 'gave the appearance of freedom of choice and "classlessness"', but simply disguised the 'real relations of class and power' that still existed (2010, p. 200). The reality for many working-class young people was educational disadvantage, 'compulsory miseducation', unemployment, jobs with no prospects, the increasing routinisation and specialisation of labour, low levels of pay and the loss of skills valued in previous generations. However, unlike the American subcultural theorists, the authors of *Resistance Through Rituals* did not see the subculture as a 'solution' to these problems: 'sub-cultural strategies cannot match, meet or answer the structuring dimensions emerging in this period as a whole' (Clarke et al, 1975, p. 47). For Clarke et al, when post-war subcultures confront the structural problems inherent in their class position, 'they often do so in ways which reproduce the gaps and discrepancies between real negotiations and symbolically displaced "resolutions". They "solve", but in an imaginary way, problems which at the concrete material level remain unresolved' (*ibid*, pp. 47–48).

Thus, Jefferson's ethnography of the Teddy boy provides a rather sad portrayal of the Teddy boys response to their 'social plight'. The adoption of a rather upper-class style of dress – a variation on the Saville Row Edwardian suit – serves to 'cover' the 'gap between largely manual, unskilled, near-lumpen real careers and life-chances, and the "all-dressed-up- and-nowhere-to-go" experience of Saturday evening' (1975, p. 48). When fights erupted, Jefferson found them as having largely arisen from perceived or actual insults to the Teddy boys appearance and style of dress. These incidents become understandable once we take on board the Teddy boys' 'plight' and the symbolic importance attached to their clothes. As Jefferson writes,

> My contention is that to lads traditionally lacking in status and *being further deprived of what little they possessed* there remained only the self, the cultural extension of the self (dress, personal appearance) and the social extension of the self (the group). Once threats were perceived in these areas, the only 'reality' or 'space' on which they had any hold, then the fights, *in defence of this space* become explicable and *meaningful* phenomena.
>
> (*ibid*, p. 82; emphasis in original)

The social reaction to youth culture was as much of a preoccupation for the CCCS as the documentation of its origins and manifestation. As they observed, mainstream or 'dominant' society did not 'calmly sit on the sidelines throughout the period and watch the subcultures at play' (*ibid*, p. 71). Youth came to symbolise social change. Whilst social change in post-war Britain was seen as largely positive – for example, increased affluence and choice – it also threatened the traditional ordering of society leading to social anxiety. The result of this was the creation of moral panics – 'a spiral in which the social groups who perceive their world and position as threatened, identify a "responsible enemy", and emerge as the vociferous guardians of traditional values' (*ibid*, p. 72) – around the new and highly visible youth subcultures. As Clarke et al argued, events associated in particular with the rise of Teddy boys and mods were 'classic moral panics', and each 'was seen as signifying, in microcosm, a wider and deeper social problem – the problem of youth as a whole' (*ibid*). Moral panics, likewise, occurred around the 'rebellious' behaviour of middle-class youth leading to heightened concerns over permissiveness, drugs, sexuality and pornography. Whereas working-class youth groups were thought symptomatic of the depth of civil unrest, middle-class groups 'with their public disaffiliation, their ideological attack on "straight society", their relentless search for pleasure and gratification . . . were interpreted as action, more consciously and deliberately, to undermine social and moral stability' (*ibid*). They damaged the very fabric of society. The result of such moral panics was the beginnings of a more punitive law-and-order society in which young people were often the target of increasing levels of social control. This theme was to be developed further in *Policing the Crisis*.

Policing the Crisis: Mugging, the State and Law and Order, to give the book its full title, was published as part of the Critical Social Studies series edited by Walton and Young and is regarded by many as the seminal text of the CCCS. Whereas *Resistance Through Rituals* is remarkable for its youthful (no pun intended) enthusiasm for its subject matter, *Policing the Crisis* is a much more scholarly enterprise. The aim of the book was to examine the social phenomenon of 'mugging' – to understand its social context and meaning and especially why at the particular historical moment of the early 1970s British society was reacting to it in such an extreme way. It illustrates how the themes of race, class and youth were all 'condensed into the image of "mugging"' (Hall et al, 1978, p. viii), what this symbolised and its resulting impact on the development of a law-and-order society. Its impetus was the severe sentencing handed down to three young men of mixed ethnicity, Paul Storey, James Duignan and Mustafa Fuat, who had 'mugged' a man on his way home from a pub in Handsworth, Birmingham, leaving him robbed and seriously injured. It was a very brutal attack. Storey, judged to be the 'ring-leader', who was 16 years old, received a sentence of twenty years, the other two those of ten years. The case received a tremendous amount of news coverage:

PRIMARY NEWS

JAILED FOR 20 YEARS – SHOCK SENTENCE ON A MUGGER AGED 16 *(Daily Mirror*, 20 March 1973)

20 YEARS FOR MUGGERS – Boy 16 weeps after sentence *(Daily Express*, 20 March 1973)

20 YEARS FOR THE MUGGERS AGED 16 *(Sun*, 20 March 1973)

20 YEARS FOR BOY, 16, WHO WENT MUGGING FOR FUN *(Daily Mail*, 20 March 1973)

16 YEAR OLD BOY GETS 20 YEARS FOR MUGGING (*Guardian*, 20 March 1973)

20 YEARS FOR 16 YEAR OLD MUGGER – five cigarettes and 30p from victim *(Daily Telegraph*, 20 March 1973)

Figure 7.1 News coverage of the Handsworth 'mugging' from S. Hall et al, 1978, p. 83

From this incident, the authors examine the use of the word 'mugging', a label appropriated from the United States although originating in Victorian England, and not, of course, a recognised criminal offence (Mooney, 1992). The label, with its imported American connotations relating to 'the race conflict; the urban crisis; rising crime, the breakdown of "law and order"; the liberal conspiracy; the white backlash' (Hall et al, 1978, p. 27) was used to suggest rising levels of street crime and as indicative of a society that was rapidly racing out of control. As the *Birmingham Evening Mail* reported on 20 March 1973, 'Britain seems to be edging too close for comfort to the American pattern of urban violence' (*ibid*, p. 26).

Hall and his colleagues sought to examine the statistical basis for the 'mugging' panic. They showed the offence closest to the label 'mugging', that of 'robbery or assault with intent to rob', did not rise as dramatically as was reported. In actuality, the increase that occurred was largely caused by the conflating of non-violent offences, such as 'snatches' and pick-pocketing, with those of 'robbery or assault with intent to rob'. This was also to occur in Brixton, London, in the 1980s. Here again the figures were conflated, resulting in a seemingly steep rise in violent street offences. The heavy-handed police tactics employed in a bid to combat the 'rise' – including increased use of racially targeted stops and searches – were a major factor behind the subsequent Brixton riots (Mooney, 1992). For the authors of *Policing the Crisis*, if the so-called 'rising tide of mugging' (Hall et al, 1978, p. 26) of the early 1970s was without foundation, what on earth was going on? The answer to this was a 'moral panic' over mugging and the supposed criminality of Black youth.

As in *Resistance Through Rituals*, the 1970s are presented as a time of heightened social anxiety in which the traditional way of life was under threat. Older people felt acutely the loss of close family ties, respect, discipline, a sense of community and 'Englishness'. And whilst this was perceived as a period of increased affluence in which 'poverty as a way of life was widely said and thought to be disappearing', it 'refused to disappear; indeed, not long after it was, magically, rediscovered' (*ibid*, p. 158). As a result, 'mugging' came to represent a society that had 'slipped "out of control"' (Clarke, 2008, p. 311), and the 'Black mugger' became the convenient 'folk devil', the scapegoat, on which social anxieties could be projected. It is therefore not surprising that the state, confronted by a 'crisis in hegemony', becomes more punitive, launching into a 'war on crime' in order to re-establish its legitimacy and authority.

The result of the 'crisis' is therefore a drift towards 'law and order society' and the rise of the 'exceptional' state in which

> the state has won the right, and indeed inherited the duty, to move swiftly, to stamp fast and hard, to listen in, discreetly survey, saturate and swamp,

charge or hold without charge, act on suspicion, hustle and shoulder, to keep society on the straight and narrow.

(Hall et al, 1978, p. 323)

This is, the authors conclude, 'the social, the ideological content of social reaction in the 1970s. It is also the *moment of mugging*' (*ibid*; original emphasis).

Finally, even though Hall and his co-workers stress that *Policing the Crisis* 'is *not* a book about why or how muggers, as individuals, mug' (*ibid*, p. 27), the end does deal with the causes of crime which are emphatically presented as arising from inequalities within the social structure. The Black labour force are the 'super-exploitables' of the present economic situation. For young Black men, the realities of their situation are all too apparent; having gone through the British education system, they are better equipped than their parents' generation 'to take their place beside the white peers of their own class in the ranks of skilled and semi-skilled labour', yet 'they feel the closure of the occupational and opportunity structure to them – on grounds not of competence but of race. . . . In their experience English society is "racist" – it works *through race*' (*ibid*, p. 354; original emphasis).

They end up doing 'shit work', and as the economic crisis deepens, their destiny is to 'become the unemployed reserve army of their class' (*ibid*, p. 356). Crime is the 'perfectly predictable and quite comprehensible consequence of this process' (*ibid*, p. 390). For many young Black men 'hustling' and petty crime come to represent both a survival strategy and a form of resistance to the mainstream culture. In its analysis of both the causes of crime and the social reaction to crime in a particular historical period, *Policing the Crisis* comes closer to providing a 'fully social theory of crime' than had hitherto occurred.

Anarchism and criminology

> *Anarchism: The philosophy of a new social order based on liberty unrestricted by man-made law; the theory that all forms of government rest on violence, and are therefore wrong and harmful, as well as unnecessary.*
>
> Emma Goldman, 1911, p. 3)

Whilst I have largely focused on traditional Marxism or neo-Marxism, the need to deconstruct and understand the role of the state meant that anarchist ideas were likewise influential in the development of critical criminology. Stan Cohen, Jock Young, David Downes and Ian Taylor were all to write for the paper, *Anarchy*, with Jock Young's 'The Zookeepers of Deviancy' being first published in the April 1969 edition.

Early anarchists, such as William Godwin, Mikhail Bakunin and Peter Kropotkin attacked the authority of the state and legal control. Peter Kropotkin described William Godwin as 'the first to formulate the political and economical conceptions of anarchism, even though he did not give that name to his ideas' (1905, p. 289). For Godwin, Kropotkin wrote, 'laws are not a product of the wisdom of our ancestors; they are the product of their passions, their timidity, their jealousies and their ambition', and 'the remedy they offer is worse than the evils they pretend to cure . . . as to the State, Godwin frankly claimed its abolition' (*ibid*, p. 289). Godwin commended the action of Robert-François Damiens and those of other attempted regicides – or 'political assassins' as he preferred to call them – as selfless acts of courage and expressed his utter disgust at those who were 'summoned to deliberate how a human being might be destroyed with the longest protracted and most . . . agony' (1798, p. 13). It is, however, the writings of Kropotkin and Emma Goldman that are more directly relevant to criminological discourse and especially to critical criminology.

Peter Kropotkin, as Jeff Ferrell, points out, was a 'gentle soul and ardent revolutionary, esteemed scientist and imprisoned activist', all of which influenced his criminology (2010, p. 32). Lombroso (1897) saw Kropotkin as an exception to his general rule on the nature of anarchists: 'it is easy to understand that the anarchist movement is composed for the most part (except for a very few exceptions, like Reclus and Kropotkin) of criminals and madmen, and sometimes of both together'. Kropotkin (1887). meanwhile, had made it very clear what he thought of Lombroso's ideas: 'we cannot', he wrote, 'consider society as entitled to exterminate all people having defective structure of brain and still less to imprison those who have long arms'. 'Criminal insanity', Kropotkin pointed out, occurs throughout society, in 'respectable homes, and palaces' as well as insane asylums (*ibid*). The only difference is 'the circumstances under which they were born and have grown up'. Crime is not a pathology or inherited 'like a certain bump of criminality' (*ibid*). And as should be reflected upon when considering biological explanations,

> These affections of the mind, the cerebrospinal system, etc., might be found in their incipience among us all. The great majority of us have some one of these maladies. But they do not lead a person to commit an anti-social act unless external circumstances give them a morbid turn.
>
> (1887)

It is 'society' that

> Is responsible as a whole for any anti-social act committed by any of its members. We have our part in the glory of our heroes and geniuses; we also share in the acts of our assassins. It is we who have made them what they are, – the one as well as the other.
>
> (*ibid*)

Jeff Ferrell (2010) observes that Kropotkin's writing on crime anticipates both differential association and labelling theory, which were to appear a century later.

At the heart of Kropotkin's vision was that human beings and their evolution as social beings were largely defined by 'mutual aid'. He argued 'that mutual cooperation has remained the social dynamic essential for survival and progress' and 'if oppressive social institutions could be changed, then, this human tendency could once again flourish – and the prevalence of criminality could be greatly diminished' (Ferrell, 2010, p. 34). In *Mutual Aid: A Factor of Evolution* Kropotkin, wrote that 'man' is

> guided in his acts, not merely by love, which is always personal, or at the best tribal, but by the perception of his oneness with each human being. In the practice of mutual aid, which we can retrace to the earliest beginnings of evolution, we thus find the positive and undoubted origin of our ethical conceptions; and we can affirm that in the ethical progress of man, mutual support not mutual struggle – has had the leading part. In its wide extension, even at the present time, we also see the best guarantee of a still loftier evolution of our race.
>
> (1902, Chapter 9)

In this Kropotkin positions himself against the Darwinist 'survival of the fittest' models of evolution. Indeed, he suggests that Darwin's vision might be more about the competitiveness of his own British society than the realities of the natural world (Ferrell, 2010).

It is notable that the intellectual circle around Jane Addams and Hull House debated anarchist ideas and warmly welcomed Peter Kropotkin on his visit to Chicago. Jane Addams described Kropotkin as the most 'distinguished' of the 'wonderful procession of revolutionists' who visited Hull House, 'who have impressed me, as no one else has ever done' for their courage to pour 'forth blood that human progress might be advanced' (1961 ed, pp. 261, 262). Emma Goldman was also acquainted with Jane Addams and wrote to her of 'our dear great comrade' on Kropotkin's stay at Hull House (7 April 1901).

Emma Goldman, in 'Anarchism: What It Really Stands For', wrote that 'crime is naught but misdirected energy', and as long 'as every institution of today, economic, political, social, and moral, conspires to misdirect human energy into wrong channels; so long as most people are out of place doing the things they hate to do, living a life they loathe to live, crime will be inevitable', and 'all the laws on the statutes can only increase, but never do away with crime' (1911, p. 7). To understand crime, we need to 'know of the process of despair, the poverty, the horrors, the fearful struggle [of] the human soul' (*ibid*). Goldman, who was imprisoned several times for political activism, vociferously denounced the prison. Prison, she questioned, as 'a social protection? What a monstrous mind ever conceived such an idea?' (1917, p. 3).

She pointed out, as many critics of the prison have throughout the twentieth and twenty-first centuries, the ridiculous cost of such institutions and that it clearly was not working given the high rates of recidivism and persistence of crime. It is, Goldman wrote, 'an excessive national expense' and 'a complete social failure' (*ibid*). Acknowledging that the basis of punishment and the justification of imprisonment rests 'on the notion of free will, the idea that man is at all times a free agent for good or evil; if he chooses the latter he must be made to pay the price': a philosophy, she contends, that has resulted in 'the most cruel and brutal tormentor of human life' (*ibid*, p. 9). The impact of imprisonment is that 'year after year the gates of prison hells return to the world an emaciated, deformed, will-less ship-wrecked crew of humanity, with the Cain mark on their foreheads, their hopes crushed, all their natural inclinations thwarted' (*ibid*, p. 10)

Despite the obvious relevance of the arguments of Kropotkin and Goldman, the relationship between anarchism and criminology is relatively unexplored within criminology, rarely appearing in criminology textbooks. In the late 1970s Hal Pepinsky suggested a 'communist anarchism as an alternative to the rule of law', and Larry Tifft put forward an anarchist sociology differing from 'Marxist sociologies whose advocates dwell on separation and struggle but also assume unity and recommitment to structure after the struggle ends'; an anarchist sociology contends that we perpetuate humankind's present injuries, harms and pain, precisely to the extent that we commit ourselves to structure and appropriation, rather than to revolution as a continuous process – one emphasizing both the sovereignty of each and the unity of all – to a never-ending struggle with life's inevitable dualities' (1979, p. 393) and suggested state justice be replaced by a more fluid arrangement stemming from human needs, leading to 'a continuous process of anarchy and justice' (*ibid*, p. 400; see also Tifft and Sullivan, 1980).[23] Jeff Ferrell in the 1990s built on the work of the Paul Feyerabend (1975), the anarchist science philosopher, to develop 'an anarchist criminology aimed especially at examining the interplay between state/legal authority, day-to-day resistance to it, and the practice of criminality'.[24] And there is a direct lineage to be traced from the anarchism of Peter Kropotkin, Emma Goldman, Feyerabend and others, together with those of *The New Criminology* and the Birmingham School, to the cultural criminology of Jeff Ferrell, Keith Hayward and Jock Young (2010). The influence of anarchism is also seen in the work of contemporary prison abolitionists and critics of state harm (e.g. Sim, 2009; criticalresistance.org, 2019).

In 1969 Paul Goodman wrote in *Anarchy*,

> So Bakunin, Kropotin, and the other anarchists were right after all: the real enemies have proved to be the State (whose health is war). Overcentralised organisation, the authoritarian personality of the people. The call is for grass-roots social structures, spontaneity and mutual aid, direct

action and doing it for yourself, education for self reliance, and agitation for freedom. Marxists now talk a good deal about alienation and liberals have picked it up, especially 'youth alienation', but this is what the anarchists were always talking about. They knew it by human feeling and common observation.

(p. 124)

Problematising critical criminology

From the outset commentators – some of whom were on the same side politically – suggested there were a number of problems with critical criminology. Paul Hirst took issue with the Marxist roots of much critical criminology, arguing that 'there is no "Marxist theory of deviance", either in existence, or which can be developed within orthodox Marxism' (1975, p. 204), a claim that was strongly rebutted by Taylor et al (1975) and others keen to apply Marxist ideas to crime and deviance. Although Taylor et al acknowledged 'that a return to Marx in criminology must inevitably raise the thorny issue of how one engages in the "reading" of Marx' – Hirst offered a 'narrow' analysis, when what is important is the 'nature of liberation as a whole' (1975, p. 234). What critical theorists attempt to do

> is to move criminology away from a focus on the 'criminality' of the poor, the pathologizing of 'deviant' behaviour into categories derived from biology, psychology or positivistic sociology, and to abolish the distinction between the study of human deviation and the study of the functioning of states, and ruling-class ideologies as a whole.
>
> (*ibid*)

Probably more damaging, however, is the neglect of women, which must lead to a questioning of the level that critical criminology can be thought of as a 'fully social theory of crime'. With the exception of McRobbie and Garber's chapter on girls and subculture, *Resistance Through Rituals* reflects a fixation with the young male deviant. McRobbie and Garber discovered that for girls, culture is constructed around the home, the bedroom is the teenage girl's 'hang out'. However, for the young male researchers of the time, this rendered them less exciting than the lads on the streets. As McRobbie later commented, there was little interest in the sociology of the family or what went on in the domestic sphere, 'only what happened out there on the streets mattered' (1980, p. 39).

As I noted previously, Carol Smart in *Women, Crime and Criminology: A Feminist Critique* (1976) berated the failure of the 'new, critical, radical and working class criminologies' to seriously consider women and feminist theory. The emphasis on male deviance meant that although the oppressive violence of authority was a constant theme for Taylor, Walton and

Young and those associated with the CCCS, the victimisation of women by men was afforded scant attention (Mooney, 2000). In many ways this neglect of women was typical of its time. As Frances Heidensohn discovered in the late 1960s when starting to research women and crime, her choice of topic was often greeted with puzzlement and incomprehension or, at best, 'polite disinterest' (Mooney, 2010, p. 257), although one would have hoped, given the commitment of critical criminology to radical politics and social justice, that this would not have been the case here. For as Jeanne Gregory pointed out, 'a criminology rooted in Marxism is equipped with a sophisticated set of conceptual tools for analysing oppression and would . . . seem ideally suited to understanding the oppression of women' (1986, p. 62). Unfortunately, the male-centredness of the academy meant for the most part that critical criminology and feminist theory in Britain developed separately.

Critical criminology: developments in Europe and the United States

The importance of *The New Criminology* and the CCCS in the development of critical criminology cannot be overstated; however, critical thinking in relation to crime and deviance was not just a British phenomenon. Similar approaches developed at roughly the same time in Europe and across the Atlantic. With respect to continental Europe, critical criminology began to emerge in some countries by the end of the 1960s. However, as René van Swaaningen argues in the informative *Critical Criminology: Visions from Europe*, it has a somewhat uneven history, for 'the extent to which social critique in academia emerges has to do with the level of welfare and actual political constellation in a particular country' (1997, p. 74). Thus, the dictatorships of Salazar and Caetano in Portugal or of the Greek colonels 'did not offer much common ground' and, as such, 'the phase of a "euphoric left" did not affect these countries' (*ibid*, p. 74). From the late 1960s until 1980, the development of a critical criminology was more evident in Germany, Italy, the Netherlands and Scandinavia. For example, in Germany Fritz Sack (1972) provided a critique of labelling theory and suggested it needed to be contextualised in relation to Marxist theory in order to properly understand how crime is defined. In Italy, the home, as we have seen, of much early theorising on crime, the work of Massimo Pavarini, Dario Melossi and Alessandro Baratta was particularly influential in its exploration of the relationship between Marxist theory and criminology.

In Scandinavia and the Netherlands critical criminology developed around the prison abolitionist movement, pioneered by Nils Christie and Thomas Mathieson from Norway and Herman Bianchi and Louk Hulsman from the Netherlands, which critiqued legal definitions of crime and argued against punitive responses to what are seen as criminalised social problems. From an abolitionist's perspective, punishment is not justified as a form of social control because it is founded on the flawed assumption that crime will be prevented by inflicting pain. Moreover, for abolitionists, the prison, which is central to our current system of punishment, should be abolished and replaced by more democratic and community-based forms of intervention, such as victim–offender mediation schemes (Hulsman, 1995, personal communication).

Across the Atlantic, critical criminology surfaced in the work of Julia and Herman Schwendinger (1974, 1977), Tony Platt (1974), William Chambliss (1975), Richard Quinney (1973) and David Greenberg (1976, 1981). The Berkeley School of Criminology at the University of California (the Schwendingers, Platt, Paul Takagi, Barry Krisberg, Elliot Currie and Gregg Barak, to name a few of those associated with the school) became well known for its radical orientation. As well as Marxists, the Berkeley School included Maoists, left liberals, moderate liberals, social democrats and anarchists (Schwendinger et al, 2002, p. 42). As Julia and Herman Schwendinger recall, this group

> generated a vibrant intellectual climate. Fundamental political and economic questions were raised about America's class, gender and racial inequality. And interaction between radical students and staff brought about the critical mass that produced an Enlightenment- like explosion of rich theoretical ideas about the nature of crime and criminal justice.
>
> (*ibid*, p. 43)

Their radicalism, however, was met with opposition from conservative forces both within and outside of the university, committed to a 'friendly fascism' that had been 'bred by decades of McCarthyism and the Cold War' (Schwendinger et al, 2002, p. 48). Herman Schwendinger and others were denied tenure as a direct result of their political views (Schwendinger's having been expressed in *Sociologists of the Chair: A Radical Analysis of the Formative Years of North American Sociology* [1974, with Julia Schwendinger]), the budget was cut and the school eventually disbanded. Interestingly, Stan Cohen, Mario Simondi from Italy and Karl Schumann from Germany, all well known for their contributions to critical criminology, were visiting scholars at the Berkeley School in 1970 sharing an office. Thus, at Berkeley we have a coming together of key people involved in the emergence of North American and European critical criminology and, as van Swaaningen notes, even though they did not know each other previously, they shared 'a dissatisfaction with the dominant law-and-order interests' which determined the criminological agenda and 'a positive commitment to social justice' (*ibid*, p. 82).[25] Such a commitment to social justice remains central to critical criminology.

Box 7.3 The Berkeley School: a critical teaching agenda 1972–1973

In the fall–winter quarters of 1972–1973, Tony Platt, Barry Krisberg and Paul Takagi revamped Berkeley's Introduction to Criminology course. The syllabus was published in the *Newsletter of the Union of Radical Criminologists* under the heading 'The New Criminology: A Course Outline'. It had previously been taught as a public relations course for non-majors, featuring a conventional survey of the field (Platt et al, 1973). As the authors of the course wrote, it covered the following in the first quarter:

> The Definition of Crime (Who Are the Real Criminals?); Ideology and Scholarship; Theory and Practice; The Crimes of Imperialism; The Crimes of Capitalism; The Crimes of Racism; The Crimes of Sexism; and Crimes by the State ... we argued that the traditional (legal) definition of crime and criminology was grounded in liberal conceptions of society, served to legitimize inequality and exploitation, and restricted the field of criminology to narrow and technocratic social engineering. We argued instead for a human rights definition of crime which expanded the legal definition to include system crimes (the political economy) and state crimes. We proposed that legally defined 'criminals' were the victims of larger crimes such as imperialism and racism which denied whole classes of people (even countries) their full human potentiality and right to survival, self-determination and dignity.
>
> *(ibid, p. 11)*

In the second quarter they 'examined social control and the criminal justice system, emphasizing a class analysis, historical perspective and political economic framework' and included topics such as 'Marxist Perspectives on Social Control', 'The Political Economy and the Rise of Modern Social Control Agencies' and 'The Rise of the Modern Criminal Justice System'. As Platt et al note, 'liberal theories of control were presented and critically rejected' (*ibid*, pp. 11–12). They assembled their own reader, which included a core of radical texts, for example, George Jackson *Soledad Brother*; Mao Tse-Tung, *On Practice*; Frantz Fanon, *The Wretched of the Earth*, 'Colonial Wars and Mental Disorders'; Harry Magdoff, 'Imperialism: A Historical Survey'; Ralph Miliband, *The State in Capitalist Society*; and Juliet Mitchell, 'Women: The Longest Revolution' and showed movies such as the *Battle of Algiers* and *The Murder of Fred Hampton*. Nearly 600 students took the first part of the course, over 300 the second, making it 'the largest number ever to take a criminology course at Berkeley' (*ibid*, p. 11).

Addressing the politics of the time: critical criminology: from the 1980s to the early 2000s

There is no doubt that critical criminology has had, and continues to have, a considerable impact on the study of crime and deviance and the reaction to these phenomena both nationally and internationally. From the early 1980s critical criminology provided the background for a number of important developments in theory. In the UK these actively challenged the law-and-order policies of the Thatcher and New Labour governments.

Left realism

In 1979 Margaret Thatcher became prime minister of Britain with an administration of the radical right, close in politics to Ronald Reagan but perhaps more sharply defined and acerbic. This was a Conservative government intent on advancing market society and cutting back on the welfare state. A largely law-and-order platform had secured Thatcher's election, yet throughout the next ten years there was a continuously rising crime rate. Between 1980 and 1985, for instance, there was a 35 per cent increase in crimes known to the police, and there was widespread public concern about crime and disorder. Riots, largely resulting from racial tensions and bad relations with the police against a background of high unemployment and deprivation, had affected many major British cities. As well as Brixton, in 1981 there were large-scale riots in the St Paul's district of Bristol, Moss Side in Manchester and the Toxteth area of Liverpool. While central government was Conservative, many of the metropolitan councils were Labour controlled and radicalised by the high unemployment rates generated by the government's monetarist policies. Not only poverty but crime and disorder characterised the conditions of people living in inner-city areas of England and Wales. It was therefore of great concern to these Labour councils to tackle the problem of crime whilst curbing the excessive use of police powers, which they viewed as the major cause of the riots, as well as allowing a plethora of police malpractices. It was out of this context that left realism emerged, intent on identifying problems of crime and policing in urban areas, committed to putting law-and-order issues high on the Labour agenda but seeking crime control policies which were progressive and non-authoritarian.

The founding text of left realism is *What Is to Be Done About Law and Order?* (Lea and Young, 1984) which was directly influenced by Ian Taylor's *Law and Order: Arguments for Socialism* (1982). Much of the work came out of the Centre for Criminology at Middlesex Polytechnic and the criminologists who worked there, including Jock Young, John Lea, Roger Matthews and Kate Painter, together with Brian MacLean, a visiting Canadian professor, and Richard Kinsey from the University of Edinburgh. Parallel work was evident in North America, particularly that of Elliott Currie, and Walter

DeKeseredy, Marty Schwartz and Shahid Alvi, and in Australia in the research and writing of Dave Brown, Kerry Carrington and Russell Hogg.

Elliott Currie's *Confronting Crime*, published in 1985, was particularly important to the development of left realism. In *Confronting Crime* Currie provided a counter-argument to conservative approaches to crime and disorder and the liberal/classicist belief that crime is not a problem. *Confronting Crime* pointed out the inadequacies of right-wing perspectives in the United States that at best degenerated into a wistful nostalgia for the past 'or, worse, into self-righteous, punitive brutality that finds expression in the resurgent demands for more corporal punishment, harsher discipline in the family and the schools, and the indiscriminate use of prisons as the holding pens for an urban underclass we have decided "to give up on"' (cited in Brown, 1985). In exploring the complex relationship between crime and inequalities and the need to confront structural problems, *Confronting Crime* was to provide, as Gregg Barak (1986) put it, a text that the American left could use to 'rebuff' those on the right.

At the core of left realism was the acknowledgement of the need to take crime seriously with respect to its impact on communities and particularly on women. It embraced the need for an activist – not revolutionary – approach with the advocating of short-term interventions, as well as long-term structural change, aimed at improving the quality of life of those in inner-city areas. Left realism aimed to listen to the concerns of ordinary people and to reclaim the politics of crime and disorder from the Right. It set itself against the new administrative criminology, pioneered by Home Office criminologists, which was doubtful about the validity of the causes of crime and tended to downplay the problem, seeing fear of crime as more of a problem than crime itself (Young, 1992); that of 'right realists', such as James Q. Wilson, who had put forward a multitude of causes but with an emphasis on individual factors, so that the focus was placed on the individual rather than the social structure, which meant that there was no need to make 'social changes which would be politically unacceptable' (Young, 1992, pp. 30–31); and the control theory of Travis Hirshi, who abandoned causation 'to the extent that it is identified with motivation', with cause metamorphosing from 'active desire into absence of restraint' (*ibid*). For James Q. Wilson, intervention was to occur where there is a possibility of a gain without radically disturbing the social order, and with this in mind he suggested, with George Kelling (Wilson and Kelling, 1982), zero tolerance against disorderly behaviour, the incapacitation of repeat offenders in prison and strong action against first-time drug users rather than the addicts themselves who he portrayed as past saving (Wilson and Herrnstein, 1985). He argued for order to take priority over justice, whereas left realism was to argue that only a just society could in the long run tackle the crime problem and this necessitated substantial structural change and, in the short term, police interventions are only effective within the rule of law where policing is seen as just and democratic.

Left realism starts with the problems as people experience them: it therefore treats 'seriously the complaints of women with regards the dangers of being in public places at night, it takes note of the fears of the elderly with regard burglary, it acknowledges the widespread occurrence of domestic violence and racist attacks' (Young, 1986, p. 24). Furthermore, realists argue that we must take 'seriously' a whole range of crime from street crime to suite crime, from crimes of the poor to those of the state and of corporations. Incivilities and harassment are also of great significance: indeed, it is noted that incessant acts of what are sometimes considered 'lesser' crimes can be more harmful than the single burglary or act of violence.

Crime is seen as having a substantial impact: fear of being victimised shapes people's lives, for example, people avoid going out after dark and feel unsafe in their own homes. These fears are presented by left realists as rational: those who fear crime greatest tend to suffer most from crime. In doing this, they distinguish between risk rates and impact rates and in terms of the latter, those who are most likely to experience crime – women, minority communities and the working class – suffer a greater degree of impact because of their relatively vulnerable position in the social structure. They tend to have less access to money and resources and suffer from other social problems. As such, it is pointed out that,

> If we were to draw a map of the city outlining areas of high infant mortality, bad housing, unemployment, poor nutrition, etc, we would find that all these maps would coincide and that further, the outline traced would correspond to those areas of high criminal victimisation.
>
> (Young, 1992, p. 52)

The well-known problem of the hidden figure of crime unknown to the police led realists to suggest that 'to base criminological theory, or social policy for that matter, on the majority of official figures is an exercise in "guesstimates" and tealeaf gazing' (Young, 1988, p. 164). Pioneering the local crime survey, for left realists this approach had the potential to present us with a much clearer picture of the extent of crime than that available from official statistics. Crime, it was observed, is focused both geographically in certain areas, particularly that of the inner city, and socially in certain groups. Statistics which conflate low and high crime areas tend to obscure the fashion in which crime is pinpointed within the population. The best-known examples of left realist crime surveys are the Merseyside Crime Survey (Kinsey, 1985), Islington Crime Survey (Jones et al, 1986) and Broadwater Farm Survey (Lea et al, 1988). Many of these surveys were commissioned and funded by left-wing local authorities such as Islington Council and Haringey Council in London. The Broadwater Farm survey was commissioned by Haringey Council after the Broadwater Farm Estate riot in 1985.

Left realists contend that criminology must embrace the totality of the criminal process if it is to reflect the reality of crime. For realists, criminology must consider the fact that crime must involve formal and informal control systems (the reaction to crime), as well as offenders and victims (the criminal action). This is called the four points of 'the square of crime'. Other criminological theories, largely those dubbed 'establishment criminology', are described as suffering from the problem of 'partiality' in that they focus on just one part of the square: formal control (as in classicism), informal social control (as in new administrative criminology/rational choice/control theory), the offender (as in positivism) and the victim (as in routine activities theory). Realism is concerned with stressing the social causes of crime. A significant influence on the theory was the work of Merton (1938) and Cloward and Ohlin (1960) on anomie and relative deprivation (see Lea, 1992). Although left realists do not advocate monocausality, relative deprivation is presented as a major cause of crime. As Jock Young comments, it occurs, 'when people experience a level of unfairness in their allocation of resources and utilize individualistic means to attempt to right this condition. It is a reaction to the experience of injustice' (1997, p. 488).

Crime can therefore occur anywhere within the social structure – it is not the monopoly of the poor; for relative deprivation is experienced throughout the classes. John Lea (1992) related the concept of relative deprivation to white-collar and corporate crime. It is not dependent on absolute levels of deprivation: indeed, realists stress that the crime rate was low in the 1930s despite extreme levels of poverty. On the whole, however, left realists emphasise the importance of working-class crime and, thus, it is pointed out that 'it is among the poor, particularly the lower working class and certain ethnic minorities who are marginalised from the "glittering prizes" of the wider society, that the push towards crime is greater than elsewhere in the social structure' (*ibid*, pp. 487–488). Establishment criminology, it is noted – in its many varieties from positivism to new administrative criminology and control theory – ignores the causes of crime in the wider structure of society, choosing to locate it in the microstructure of society (the family, the school) or in the individual's biological or psychological predisposition. The delinquency of young people, for example, is blamed by establishment criminology on the maladministration of the control of the young (whether in schools or the family) and in the inherent nature of individuals. This takes attention from the criticism of the wider society while reversing the direction of causality: it is not a problematic society which causes delinquency, but delinquents who cause problems for society. For left realists, crime is located in the nature of market capitalism – in its unequal class structure and in the rampant individualism that the market engenders, which results in a class structure that systematically frustrates the meritrocratic ideals which serve to legitimate the system and within the core values of a competitive individualism, which shape and guide people's anger and frustrations (Mooney, 2000).

And in a patriarchal system where the hegemony of dominance of men over women when threatened results in violence and aggression towards women.

Following on from this left realism influenced the development of a feminist realism – which combined concepts derived from radical feminism and left realism (see Mooney, 2000; Walklate, 1992; Ahluwalia, 1992). In *Gender, Violence and the Social Order* (2000) I used a feminist realist framework to help explain the prevalence and impact of men's violence against women in domestic relationships: for radical feminism points to the causes of domestic violence, whilst realism helps to explain the factors that prevent women from leaving violent men and why men are able to get away with such violence. Violence is central to the maintaining of patriarchal order. It is a powerful means of subordinating women and serves as key mechanism of social control. The left realist stress on structural inequalities helps to explain why women have less access to money and resources and are frequently economically dependent on men and/or the state. A feminist realist position argues for both short-term interventions – which can include alternative accommodation, a more sensitive criminal justice response and so on – and long-term structural change. A feminist realist perspective is also seen in the work of North American left realists, for example, that of Walter DeKeseredy and Marty Schwartz.

Throughout the Conservative administrations of Margaret Thatcher and John Major left realists kept up their attack on the government. The crime rate continued to rise upwards: by 1991 the number of crimes known to the police passed the five million mark. It did not take much mental agility to correlate such a qualitative leap with the recession and a government intent on creating a market society (Mooney, 1997). But – in alliance with establishment criminology – government ministers suggested the causes lay elsewhere. John Major stated it was futile to seek the causes of crime in the wider society – instead, he said we should look at the problems in the family and rather surprisingly blamed socialism – by this he meant the welfare state. The neo-liberal explanation was that the welfare state had created a dependency culture of single mothers and feckless fathers, which in turn had created a maladjusted population. The accent was on blame and exclusion, not on absorbing the 'underclass' into society, and the crime prevention measures suggested by new administrative criminologists – which put the onus on the individual in the war against crime – were endorsed.

In this period left realists critiqued what they felt was the tendency of some critical criminologists – who left realists termed 'left idealists' – to minimise the importance of working-class crime by one-sidedly emphasising the crimes of the powerful, such as those of the ruling class, the police, corporations and state agencies. Left realists applied the label 'left idealism' to this strand of critical thinking not as a comment on its perceived utopianism, but philosophically because of a stress on ideas rather than material reality (Young, 1986). Left realists basically charged left idealists with ignoring the everyday struggles of working people while waiting for the revolution. This particular criticism disappointingly led to a rather acrimonious period of debate between criminologists on the left: splits between those who are ostensibly on the same side are not helpful when trying to affect political change.

What drove prominent left realists, such as Jock Young, to move away from engagement with Labour Party politics, local government policy and eventually a realist agenda was the election of Tony Blair and the New Labour government in 1997. Tony Blair is famous for his couplet 'tough on crime, tough on the causes of crime', which is essentially a left realist statement. Blair first used the couplet in a 1993 article in *The New Statesman*, 'Why Crime Is a Socialist Issue'. The last line it was hoped would mean that the causes of crime would be located in the deep structure of society. But this was not so: 'socialism' soon went from Blair's vocabulary, and the first line of the couplet meant punishment and the maintenance of a large-scale prison system; the second located the causes of crime within the family and poor parenting. J.Q. Wilson, with his zero-tolerance policing strategies, influenced central government policy, together with John Dilulio (1995), the right-wing advocate of the American Prison experiment, and Charles Murray.[26] Taking on board much of the Conservative rhetoric about the underclass and fecklessness, New Labour found Murray's idea of 'underclass' attractive, i.e. those who were 'unwilling to work rather than as, in the social democratic version of William Julius Wilson, those cut off from work' (Matthews and Young, 2003, p. 39). As left realists argued genuine social inclusion was not to be confused with New Labour's policies of coercive inclusion in the labour market at poverty wages or forcefully created families backed by the threat of hostel accommodations for single mothers. New Labour's flirtation with Murray, in particular, whose 1994 book *The Bell Curve* caused outrage with his claim that Black Americans had lower IQs than white and advocation for the abolition of welfare payments to single mothers, was profoundly disturbing. Home Secretary Jack Straw, despite protests, agreed to share a speaking platform with Murray while he was on visit to the UK at the invitation of *The Sunday Times* (Burrell, 2000; Wheen, 2000). Jock Young (2000) questioned at the time of Murray's visit why 'alarm bells' were not going off, given the extraordinary racial focus of the United States' 'carceral experiment'. The figures of one in three African Americans in prison, on probation or parole, he said, were 'staggering' – and if you included 'have ever' figures and focused on poor Blacks, there must be 'sizeable slices' of the United States where to be 'untouched by the law' would be 'regarded as strange'. It is ridiculous, he said:

> To attempt to learn crime control from the United States is rather like travelling to Saudi Arabia to learn about women's rights. The one lesson to be learnt is not to travel down this path of punishment, to realise that if it takes a gulag to maintain a winner-takes- all society, then it is society that must be changed rather than the prison expanded.[27,28]

The 'exceptional' state

Policing the Crisis and later work produced by the CCCS (for example, *The Empire Strikes Back* (1982)) gave rise to further analysis of the complexities of the role of and use (or misuse) of power by the state. In Phil Scraton's edited volume *Law, Order and the Authoritarian State* (1987) the coercive power of the British state under Margaret Thatcher's Conservative government is explored through its introduction of a range of repressive criminal justice policies and practices that impacted along the axes of class, race and gender. In *The Coercive State: The Decline of Democracy in Britain* (1988) Paddy Hillyard and Janie Percy-Smith focused more widely on legislative changes within and beyond the framework of the welfare state and the criminal justice system.

There was, as David Whyte (2010) demonstrates, a precursor to this line of thinking to be found in the work of Louis Proal's *Political Crime*, published in 1898. In this book Proal highlights how the law was used as an instrument of colonial power by the British. His words – which, as Whyte observes, make one think of Bertolt Brecht or Woodie Guthrie – are strident in their denunciation of the use of the law by the state:

> Barbarous peoples make use of arms to kill and rob; people who think themselves civilised make use of laws. The law is an murderous as firearms, as potent an instrument of destruction as the axe, and depredations go under cover of it as highway robbery under cover of a forest. Murder and robbery have been made part of the law; proscription and spoliation have been given legal shape.
> (Proal, cited in Whyte, 2010, p. 4)

Proal shows how 'the "monstrous" suppression of the Irish people was given ... a legal shape' (cited in Whyte, 2010, p. 4)

In the early 1990s it was in Paddy Hillyard's work on the Northern Ireland situation that we were to see the main ideas of *Policing the Crisis* brought up to date, with the development of the 'exceptional' state. As Stuart Hall commented, Hillyard's contemporary exploration of the 'exceptional state' 'picks up on an uncertainty in *Policing* about committing itself as to when precisely the "drift" towards a law and order society became an "exceptional state" and whether the latter has arrived and is now the "normal" state of affairs' (2009, p. xvi). Hillyard (1993, 2009) uses the same schema as *Policing the Crisis* for identifying the elements by which an 'exceptional state' can be identified. The essential elements of an exceptional state are seen in

> the continuing resort to law, the increasing use of a wide range of personnel in the exercise of informal control, intensified surveillance of the population and the widespread shift away from the ordinary criminal law

to the use of "counter-terror" law are all essential elements of an exceptional state.

(p. 142)

Further, as time has gone on, with the rise of a 'surveillance society', we now have a situation in which 'real-time surveillance of large sections of the population is now possible, further enhancing the disciplinary, authoritarian society described in *Policing the Crisis*' (*ibid*, p. 130). Hillyard's conclusion is that whilst surveillance is a 'key element' by which an 'exceptional state' can now be recognised, together with an expansion of informal social control and the move from the use of the criminal law to the counter-terrorism law' the actual *defining point* of an *exceptional state* in the British context was 'the capacity to sanction and then condone the widespread killings of its own citizens in an attempt to control Irish political violence' (*ibid*, p. 142).

The 'exceptional' state and its impact on citizens lead to a renewed focus on state crime or state violence, where the state is treated as a 'criminal actor' in its own right (Hallsworth and Lea, 2012, p. 189). As Penny Green and Tony Ward point out, 'not only do modern states claim a monopoly of violence . . . they also perpetuate or instigate most of the world's serious violent crime: the infliction of pain, injury or death in contravention of legal or moral norms' (2009, p. 96). For such a monopoly to occur, it is necessary that the agencies that perpetuate it have 'their coercive power authorized by the state' (*ibid*, p. 97; see also Ryan and Ward, 1989). Whilst 'in much of the world public compliance is secured through consensual forms of governance', coercive government is 'rarely far from the surface', and they make use of Robert Cover's (1986) example. Cover describes how most convicted defendants walk to the cells, 'without significant disturbance to the civil appearance of the event' yet it is 'grotesque to assume that the civil façade is "voluntary" . . . most prisoners walk into prison because they know they would be dragged or beaten if they do not walk' (p. 1601).

There has in recent years been a growth of critical scholarship on the multifaced nature of state crime, including war crimes (as in Ruth Jamieson's ground-breaking work on the criminology of war, 1998, 1999), genocide,[29] human rights abuses, environmental abuse and that associated with colonialism and its aftermath. The previous lack of attention by criminology to what Wayne Morrison describes as 'great crimes', such as those of war and genocide, lends support, on the one hand, to the discipline being a 'mere servant of state power' (2004, p. 74) or, on the other, that when confronted by the horror of 'great crime', for example, that of the Holocaust or Rwandan genocide, it is found to be simply too 'unsettling' and, therefore, 'silence' may be 'understandable since language appears unable to do "justice" to the horror and terror of it' (*ibid*, p. 77).

In Jamieson and McEvoy's (2005) work they show how modern state crime, like the modern state, is a 'slippery concept', that it is not the monolithic entity it is often perceived to be. As such, 'a criminology of "state crime" requires a subtle and pluralistic notion of the state intersecting with other sectors in both the commission of and response to deviant actions' (*ibid*, p. 504). The complexities of state crime are illustrated, for example, by the situation in Northern Ireland in which many high-profile killings attributed to Loyalist paramilitaries were found to be carried out by members of the locally recruited regiment of the British Army (the Ulster Defence Regiment) and, in some cases, the Royal Ulster Constabulary, and in the former Yugoslavia atrocities committed during the war which were thought to be the acts of paramilitaries were, in fact, 'carried out by 'crack [Serbian] professional soldiers masquerading as local volunteers' (Sherwell, 1992)' (*ibid*, p. 506). Such groups, they point out, 'do not supinely follow state directives on each and every killing'; indeed, 'they often have a dynamic of their own in their targeting and operational strategies' (*ibid*, p. 512). In such instances, the 'creation' of 'space for innovative sadism' that ensues as in Loyalist "romper rooms"',[30] 'which were drinking clubs where Catholic civilians were kidnapped, tortured and mutilated (sometimes while the drinkers watched) and their bodies later dumped' (*ibid*), or the depraved acts of sexual violence by Bosnian-Serb paramilitaries becomes 'useful in both distancing the state from its proxy actors (what self-respecting state would condone such actions?) as well terrorizing the host community from which the insurgent groups derive'(*ibid*). Hence, 'the image of ill-disciplined, out-of-control, sectarian paramilitaries, irregulars or death squads who are 'beyond the reach' of the state' becomes 'materially and symbolically convenient in the denial of state crime' (*ibid*).

Criminology, as Green and Ward reflect, has a 'woefully myopic understanding of violence'. Violence 'needs to be understood in relation to long-term historical changes, global configurations of culture and state formation, and its global and local economic context' (*ibid*, p. 104). Significantly, they point out, that with good reason critical criminology – as I have documented – has shied away from studying individual motivation; however, in an effort to understand the structural nature of crime and criminal justice practice, critical criminology has tended to throw the baby out of the bathwater by largely ignoring war crimes, genocide and torture, which demand a detailed examination of individual motivation and action (*ibid*).

For example, we need to give attention to how the process of dehumanisation and 'othering' facilitate such acts of violence (Green and Ward, 2005, 2009; see also Mooney and Young, 2005, on war and terrorism) and, along this line, how states employ a range of methods to obfuscate their responsibility in the commission of state crime through the 'othering' of both perpetrators and victims (Jamieson and McEvoy, 2005). In order to counter state violence, Green and Ward suggest, we look to civil society: 'in addition to trade unions, political movements and human rights based NGOs, we must also include those elements of civil society committed to challenging political and social processes in which minorities and their cultures are systematically devalued' (2009, p. 104).

In much of the theoretical work on the state within a 'peacetime' context, the criminal justice system is identified as the major apparatus of state control. In Joe Sim's *Punishment and Prisons: Power and the Carceral State* (2009), the brutality of the prison is emphasised; the prison remains 'a place where the old, punitive mentalities, and the often unaccountable infliction of physical and psychological pain' have stayed 'central to the institution's organization and the everyday interactions that many staff (have) with the confined' (p. 107). Those who are incarcerated are predominantly 'the unemployed, the homeless, the mentally disturbed, the institutionally brutalised, the sexually traumatised and the substance dependent' (*ibid*, p. 118). They are the people who have already had their fair share of disadvantage; the prison is about the 'penal management of poverty and inequality' (*ibid*). This, together with the often-heard argument that prison does not work in terms of reducing the crime rate or recidivism, led Sim and others (see Ryan and Ward, 2015) to propose an abolitionist stance towards the prison system along the lines of that pioneered by the organization Radical Alternatives to Prison (RAP), which was founded 'on the strong breeze of the counterculture' in the UK in 1970 (Ryan and Ward, 2015, p. 108), and that of critical criminologists in continental Europe, as in the writings of Nils Christie and Thomas Mathieson from Norway and Herman Bianchi and Louk Hulsman from the Netherlands.

Moreover, many British critical criminologists, as did those associated with the abolitionist movement in continental Europe and feminist scholars, critiqued what we mean by 'crime' and the extent of which our definitions are still determined by the legal system. Hillyard, Pantazis, Tombs and Gordon proposed that we should move 'beyond criminology' and a consideration of 'crime' per se to the study of social harm; that is to 'focus on all the different types of harm people experience from the cradle to the grave' (2004, p. 1). This includes harm associated with the state and with corporations, those that occur in the workplace, those that arise from poverty and so on. They suggest it is nonsensical to separate out those harms that meet the definition of criminal from all other harms: all harm should be considered together; otherwise, 'a very distorted view of the world will be produced' (*ibid*, p. 2). For instance, it makes no difference whether a person dies from an act that is deliberately intended or is accidental or through indifference, 'they are still dead with all the social and economic consequences for their family and friends' (*ibid*, p. 1). A notion of social harm helps us to move away from an individualised conception of crime and justice focused on discrete events in specific locales to an understanding of the global implications of structural iniquity. For example, as Sandra Walklate (2016) observes, 'harm from terrorist attacks is firmly put in perspective when set against the harm caused by malnutrition and starvation' (p. 54). The 'brute fact' that more people die every day from the effects of diarrhoea than were killed in 9/11 serves as 'a graphic and worthwhile reminder that the scale of discussions about many Western "catastrophes" still pale in comparison with the daily conditions in less economically developed parts of the world' (Wilkinson, 2009, p. 96). This underscores how 'boundaries of concern tend to be set with the plight of advanced nations in mind' (*ibid*) and how the experiences of those in the Global South are rendered less visible, and certainly are not seen as 'criminal events'. Trying to correct this imbalance within criminological discourse emerges as an important theme for southern criminology, which is discussed in the next chapter. Finally, at the core of critical criminology is a commitment to instigating structural change. Largely for those critical criminologists discussed in this chapter there is the belief that when we are dealing with issues of crime and justice that affect so many lives, we cannot sit on the sidelines.

Notes

1 Jock Young, for example, was from a Scottish mining family.
2 On 11 February 1965 Malcolm X gave a lecture at the LSE, which 'became more profound when eleven days later, he was assassinated in New York' (see: www.alumni.lse.ac.uk/s/1623/interior-hybrid.aspx?sid=1623&gid=1&pgid=1008).
3 See: http://news.bbc.co.uk/onthisday/hi/dates/stories/march/13/newsid_2542000/2542639.stm
4 In 1969, having returned to the United States, Marshall Bloom committed suicide after receiving his call-up papers for military service in Vietnam.
5 The English cotton industry was largely supplied by slave labour from the Southern states of America. Marx was to write in the *New York Daily Tribune*, 'as long as the English cotton manufactures depended on slave-grown cotton, it could be truthfully asserted that they rested on a twofold slavery, the indirect slavery of the white man in England and the direct slavery of the black men on the other side of the Atlantic' (14 Oct. 1861). It also relied on child labour. It is somewhat ironic that Marx and Engels were to derive part of their livelihood from the income generated from Engels Sr's cotton mills.
6 If we refer back to Chapter 3 and Enrico Ferri's discussion of poverty and its impact on family life in Italy, we will see this bears a striking similarity to Engels's account of the English working class, which is, of course, not surprising given Ferri's early socialist position.
7 Articles from Rheinische Zeitung (1842), Proceedings of the Sixth Rhine Province Assembly.
8 The lack of a more systematic approach to crime in the work of Marx and Engels resulted in debate over whether crime and deviance are in fact justifiable concerns for Marxist theorists. This is particularly illustrated by Paul Hirst's critique of *The New Criminology*.

> There is no 'Marxist theory of deviance', either in existence, or which can be developed within orthodox Marxism. Crime and deviance vanish into general theoretical concerns and the specific scientific object of Marxism. Crime and deviance are no more a scientific field for Marxism than education, the family or sport. The objects of Marxist theory are specified by its own concepts: the mode of production, the class struggle, the state, ideology etc.
>
> (1975, p. 204)

However, given the development of Marxist ideas in the work of Bonger in the early 1900s, Rusche and Kirchheimer in the 1930s, and the large body of Marxist-orientated critical criminology that emerged from the late 1960s onwards such an argument seemingly has little validity.

9 Paul Stretesky in *Radical and Marxist Theories of Crime*, further points to the early writings of M.A. Reisner, who 'argues that the Russian proletariat could derive a revolutionary form of law from an understanding of its class position' and P.I. Stuchka, who held 'that law was a reflection of social interests and more specifically the interests of the dominant class' in the early 1900s (2017, Introduction).
10 This bears a certain similarity to Durkheim's anomie theory (Lanier and Henry, 1998).
11 In fact the working-class woman's absence from the home in order to take on paid labour as a result of the demands of capitalism is seen by Bonger as having led to the demoralisation of the children of the working class: 'when there is no one to watch a child, when he is left to himself, he becomes demoralized' (1916, p. 318). The implication is that a woman's place is in the home. See Messerschmidt's (1988) critique on socialist writings on women, gender and crime.
12 Dario Melossi has written extensively on Georg Rusche and the importance of his analysis in constructing a Marxist theory of punishment. Melossi additionally has contributed a wealth of biographical information on Rusche and, indeed, notes that he was a somewhat 'shady' character, who, after the war, taught in schools for refugee children or in 'special' schools, frequently moving on after being suspected 'for his relationships with the children' (2009, p. xv).
13 A useful discussion and defence of Rusche and Kirchheimer against the charge of 'materialist reduction' (see also Garland, 1990) is that by Roger Matthews in *Doing Time: An Introduction to the Sociology of Imprisonment* (1999).
14 Thorsten Sellin wrote the introduction to the 1939 U.S. edition of *Punishment and Social Structure*.
15 Rusche and Kirchheimer are not mentioned in *The New Criminology* (1973) – the chapter on Marxism focuses on Marx and Engels and Bonger. Rusche and Kirchheimer's 'economic theory of punishment' was, however, to influence criminologists in the UK in the 1980s – see for example S. Box and C. Hale 'Economic Crises and the Rising Prison Population in England and Wales, *Crime and Social Justice*, 1982,17, pp. 20–35, and C. Hale 'Economy, Punishment and Imprisonment', *Contemporary Crises*, 13, pp. 327–350.
16 *Punishment and Penal Discipline* (1980) includes contributions by Dario Melossi, Russell Hogg, Ivan Jankovic and Herman and Julia Schwendinger and Gregory Shank who discussed Thorsten Sellin's penology.
17 David Greenberg's edited collection *Crime and Capitalism: Readings in Marxist Criminology*, published in 1981, was also a highly significant work, serving to initiate further debate in the United States on what was to constitute a Marxist criminology.
18 David Matza's *Delinquency and Drift* was published in 1964. He was hired by the University of California, Berkeley in 1962. In 1967 Matza took a sabbatical at the LSE to write *Becoming Deviant*. Stan Cohen, Jock Young, Frances Heidensohn and Mike Brake were all graduate students at the LSE (see Mooncy, 2010). Matza's writing with Gresham Sykes (1957, 1961) produced the key sociological concepts of 'techniques of neutralization' and 'subterranean values', which I utilised in terms of making sense of domestic violence (2007) and were employed by Stan Cohen in *States of Denial* (2002) to explain how 'normal' Germans could bring themselves to be involved in the mass slaughter of the Jews, and by Jock Young (2004) to explain terrorism.
19 First called the National Deviancy Symposium.
20 In *The New Criminology* Taylor, Walton and Young engage with Bonger but largely see him as too positivistic and economically deterministic, which seems a rather simplistic dismissal of what is a wide body of work and glosses over his analysis of the subjectivity of the concept of 'crime' and the importance of both culture and time in terms of understanding this (see van Swaaningen, 1995). Van Swaaningen (1995) suggests that the criticisms raised in *The New Criminology* may be because the authors did not have access to the full range of Bonger's writing.

21 Unless indicated otherwise, emphasis is as in the original text.
22 As Barry Godfrey points out in 'Critical historical perspectives on crime' the publication of *Albion's Fatal Tree* by Hay, Linebaugh, Rule, Thompson and Winslow in 1975, and the start of 'the history from below' movement, represented the beginning 'of a huge growth in the number of historians exploring the impact of legal changes on the lives of the working classes' (2011, p. 209). For these largely Marxist scholars, the law and its administration were about the maintenance of an unequal class system. Hence, 'this school of history saw the law as being the tool whereby countryside agricultural labourers and then, later factory workers were forced into new work disciplines and wage slavery' (*ibid*).
23 Hal Pepinsky later adapted his ideas into peace-making criminology, which he presents as 'the opposite of the prevailing "war-making" paradigm in criminology, which is the science and art of identifying, isolating and subduing offenders or would-be offenders' (2013, p. 307; see also J. Ferrell's (1998) overview). Larry Tifft and Dennis Sullivan (1998) also endorse peace-making criminology and the model of restorative justice as an alternative to state-controlled punishment.
24 See Jeff Ferrell (1998) 'Against the Law: Anarchist Criminology' accessed at: https://theanarchistlibrary.org/library/jeff-ferrell-against-the-law-anarchist-criminology
25 Mario Simondi, Stan Cohen and Karl Schumann, with Ian Taylor, were instrumental in creating a European version of the NDC – the European Group for the Study of Deviance and Social Control. Described by Stan Cohen as 'an instrumental force in bringing together like minded scholars', the European Group held its first meeting in Florence in 1972 and still holds annual conferences today (see europeangroup.org).
26 A key research influence on the Labour Party was the work of David Farrington, who in an article with Michael Tonry (Farrington and Tonry, 1995) prioritises above all 'development prevention' as the major strategy to combat crime: that is intervention in the family and the school to ensure the development of the child occurs in a way which is 'normal' and, *ipso facto*, non-delinquent. Thus, Jack Straw, the Home Secretary, at a Nexus Conference on the Third Way held in London, talked of how good schools occur in poor areas because of good head teachers and that poverty does not link with crime because many impoverished families have good parenting skills. Time and time again under New Labour the rising statistics of one-parent families, teenage pregnancies and divorces were placed against the rise in crime and the 'obvious conclusions' drawn (Mooney, 2003, p. 107).
27 Jock Young ended his association with the Labour Party by cutting up his membership card and throwing it out of the window of his Hackney home, only for some hopeful soul to tape it back together and post it through his letter box.
28 Towards the end of his life Young was returning to more of a left realism position – he was concerned about how little contemporary criminology, even that which is ostensibly leftist and progressive – evidenced commitment to a notion of praxis and the concerns of ordinary working people.
29 See Morrison (2004), Esparza (2018).
30 Labelled 'romper rooms' after a popular children's television programme (see Bruce, 1992; Jamieson and McEvoy, 2005, p. 512).

Chapter 8

From theoretical innovations to political engagement

In 2011 critical criminology was described by Jock Young in *The Criminological Imagination* as 'flourishing', with the most insightful textbooks having been written from a critical criminology perspective, for example, Mark Lanier and Stuart Henry's *Essential Criminology* (2004, Ian Taylor's *Crime and Context* (1999), René van Swaaningen's *Critical Criminology: Visions from Europe* (1997), Wayne Morrison's *Theoretical Criminology: From Modernity to Post-Modernism* (1999), John Lea's *Crime and Modernity* (2002) and Rob White and Fiona Haines's *Crime and Criminology* (2008), to name a few. These books have hopefully helped to inspire a progressive teaching agenda within the academy. Certainly, they were representative of 'massively needed' work, for 'in the age of the Gulag and punitive turn' it is critical criminology that can provide the 'counter-voice' (Young, 2011, p. 217) to neo-liberalism and conservativism and the persistence of the positivist paradigm.

As a discipline, criminology is tainted by the 'bogus of positivism' and 'the nomothetic impulse' which being at the heart of positivism has resulted in a quest for generalisability, independent of and indifferent to nation or locality (Mooney, 2014; Walklate, 2016). And whilst critical criminology may be 'flourishing', we are, at the same time, in the midst of a biosocial revolution in criminology: 'never before in the history of criminology has as much research been published by a group of scholars working from a singular perspective in such a short period of time as has been by biosocial criminologists' (Beaver et al, 2015, p. 6). This is particularly worrisome given the current president of the United States, Donald Trump, believes in the 'racehorse theory of human development', that 'if you put together the genes of a superior woman and a superior man, you get superior offspring' (Fang and Rieger, 2016) and puts his success down to being of good genetic stock. In a series of video clips posted by the *Huffington Post* he says, 'You know, I'm proud to have that German blood', 'Great stuff'. To a room full of British business leaders Trump remarked on how they had 'all got such good bloodlines' and must have 'amazing DNA'. A leaked conversation revealed him to describe those from Haiti and some African nations as being from 'shithole countries'. Why, he demanded to know, should they be allowed into the United States rather than people from Norway, who would be a better fit (Hirschfeld Davis et al, 2018).

Moreover, as Sandra Walklate points out, the projection of American (liberal) values, particularly concerning individualism, affects criminological pursuits everywhere: this 'not only denies culture, it also facilitates the comfortable and comforting liberal analyses of othering and/or dehumanization found within criminology' and is particularly pertinent to thinking about violence, 'a thinking that generates presences and absences of violence' in its various forms (2016, p. 57). This has to be a concern in this political moment when there is a widespread resurgence of far-right sentiment together with the continued reinforcement of the superiority of Global Northern countries. Let us not forget that criminology is, for the most part, a policy-oriented discipline – one that is concerned with 'crime', what it means and what to do about it – that is rooted in a difficult history. Without trying to sound too dramatic, we ignore the political implications of criminology – both bad and good – at our peril.

The history of criminology is a story of exclusion, misery, despair and silence, but it is also one that has featured resistance and oppositional scholarship. And it was with the latter in mind that I chose in the last two chapters to provide a focus on feminist activism and a largely Marxist- or neo-Marxist-oriented critical criminology. In the spirit of advancing the discussion of the 'criminological imagination' I shall now turn to explore some recent approaches that fall under the 'umbrella' of critical criminology and are indicative of the continued need for theoretical innovation within the discipline – not only to advance debate but also to help frame a counter-narrative to the more unsettling politics of our time. My story of the foundations of criminological thought will then conclude by turning to some of the challenges that confront criminologists as we move through the twenty-first century.

Never boring: cultural criminology

> *The study of crime has been preoccupied with a search for background forces, usually defects in the offenders' psychological backgrounds or social environments, to the neglect of the positive, often wonderful attractions within the lived experiences of criminality . . . The social science literature contains only scattered evidence of what it means, feels, sounds, tastes or looks like to commit a particular crime. Readers of research on homicide and assault do not hear the slaps and curses, see the pushes and shoves, or feel the humiliation and rage that may build toward the attack, sometimes persisting after the victim's death.*
>
> (Jack Katz, *Seductions of Crime: Moral and Sensual Attractions of Doing Evil*, 1988, p. 3)

Katz's provocative words were meant as a challenge to macro-criminological theories. We must not be preoccupied with background causes but the foreground, what is happening in the moment – 'the lived experiences of criminality'. Criminology has tended to overlook the interpersonal drama of the criminal event. Positivism ignores its complexities: why, Katz, asks, 'are people who were not determined to commit a crime one moment determined to do so the next' (pp. 3–4). And then there are those such as Howard S. Becker who have 'turned crime into an abstraction and then study the abstraction' (Ferrell et al, 2008, p. 18). We must remind ourselves 'of crime's *fearsome foreground*' (*ibid*; author emphasis). Katz's *Seductions of Crime* was to influence the phenomenological focus of cultural criminology, and his later *How Emotions Work* (1999) helped to remind criminologists of the importance of taking on board the 'emotional meanings of everyday life' (see Ferrell et al, 2008).

For emotions do not, as Katz writes, 'derive from personality traits' but 'flow most directly from an initially sensual being in a social world' (1999, p. 44). Through 'emotions a person both attends to the immediate situation and orients to transcendent dimensions of the moment's experience' (*ibid*, p. 34). Using the example of becoming 'pissed off' when driving, an 'inescapable fact of life' in traffic-congested Los Angeles, Katz describes the emotional dynamics that define the experience of anger. 'Flipping someone off' or 'giving the finger', for example, is made sense of by individuals through a narrative of 'righteous indignation', 'prejudicial stereotypes' and the 'socio-emotional logic of revenge scenarios' (*ibid*, p. 46). Using 'the right metaphor' functions 'as a bridge that allows anger to pass naturally from one driver to another'; thus, to 'simply say that the victim's anger is "displaced" is to leave confused the temporal and causal ordering of emotional change' and 'obscures the practical story-creating work' through which the encounter is understood (*ibid*, p. 69).

Cultural criminology is perhaps the most-cited development in critical criminology in the contemporary period, which, although pioneered in the United States, emerged as a joint enterprise between British and North American criminologists (Ferrell and Sanders, 1995; Presdee, 2000; Ferrell et al, 2004; Ferrell, 2005; Ferrell et al, 2008). It builds on the 'new criminology', the work of the Birmingham School (CCCS) and draws from sociological criminology, interactionist sociology, cultural studies, postmodernism, critical theory, ethnographic work and media/textual analysis (see Ferrell, 1999). As the name 'cultural criminology' implies, crime and deviance and the reaction to them are viewed as 'cultural projects'. Whereas conventional criminology takes culture away from crime and deviance, cultural criminology puts it back in – culture being seen as 'the stuff of collective meaning and identity' (Ferrell et al, 2008, p. 2). Taking a Katzian perspective, human agency and creativity are foregrounded. With its focus on culture and crime and deviance, or to put it another way, 'on meaning and transgression', cultural criminology provides an important perspective into the nature of social life and interaction. It is positioned precisely at 'those points where norms are imposed and threatened, laws enacted and broken, rules negotiated and renegotiated', and this

> inevitably exposes the on-going tension between cultural maintenance, cultural disorder, and cultural regeneration – and so, from the view of

> cultural criminology the everyday actions of criminals, police officers and judges offer not just insights into criminal justice but important glimpses into the very process by which social life is constructed and reconstructed . . . this subject matter in turn reveals the complex, contested dynamic between cultures of control (control agencies' downward symbolic constructions) and cultures of deviance (rule breakers' upwards counter-constructions).
>
> (*ibid*, pp. 4–5)

Cultural criminology sets itself against the criminological binary of the 'rational calculator' and the 'mechanist actor' counter-posing 'a naturalness'. As Young comments, 'the actual experience of committing crime, the actual outcome of the criminal act bears little relationship to these narrow essentialisms' (2011, p. 105). Such conceptions of criminality fail to capture the feelings of, say, anger, humiliation, excitement, fear and the rush of adrenalin. Cultural criminology presents itself as embracing a naturalistic and existentialist position that contrasts to that of conventional criminology. It is illustrated, therefore, in the 'struggle between the forces of rationalization and that of existential possibility and lived lives' (Hayward and Young, 2004, p. 266).

It is a criminology for the twenty-first century, a period that is characterised by 'the rise of a more individualistic, expressive society, where vocabularies of motives, identities and human action begin to lose their rigid moorings in social structure', which is occurring at the same time that 'the subject begins to be dominated by precisely its opposite, a positivistic fundamentalism bent on rendering human action into the predictable, the quantifiable, the mundane' (Hayward and Young, 2004, p. 263). The boring. Cultural criminology in this context becomes all the more apposite, for its concern is with the creativity that typifies the *now*, together with the extraordinary proliferation of the mass media and its transformative impact on human subjectivity. Indeed, in late modernity the virtual community exists alongside and is as real as the traditional concept of community – friends and neighbours – and, accordingly, vocabularies of motive, points of reference and identities become globalised (Ferrell et al, 2008). Yet this does not mean cultural criminology lacks structure – quite the contrary. Cultural criminologists build on C. Wright Mills's emphasis on the necessity of putting human beings in their historical and structural settings by providing an understanding of the context of crime and deviance in the contemporary period.

What is required is 'Merton with Energy, Katz with Structure' (Young, 2003): that is, an analysis of the structures and sentiments that lead to vindictiveness and transgression. The 'job' of cultural criminologists 'is to emphasize both structure and agency and trace how each constitutes the other' (*ibid*, p. 408). Hence, the need to critique 'the insipid rationalistic nature of current neo-liberal discourses' and provide a reformulation of 'Mertonian notions of anomie in terms of energy, resentment and tension' (*ibid*, p. 389).

The transgressive is thus placed within a structural context. In today's world, economic and cultural globalisation result in material inequalities and ontological resentment which heightens both relative deprivation and crises of identity, which creates feelings of unfairness and humiliation that are perceived as threatening. This results in behaviour that is transgressive rather than instrumental. With respect to the 'better off': because 'of insecurities of identity, position and the level of sacrifices demanded in their daily life', tension is experienced and, as such, the politics of exclusion become more vicious and 'punishment becomes vindictive rather than instrumental and rational' (*ibid*).

Despite concerns that cultural criminology has leant more towards exploring subcultural nuances at the expense of political engagement, structural change and the incorporation of praxis, for Ferrell, Hayward and Young, political engagement is paramount. There is 'no neat choice between political involvement and criminological analysis' (*ibid*, p. 13). Individual and collective resistance to the mechanisms of social control are highlighted and explored throughout cultural criminology.[1] It is a resistance that takes various forms. Early on in the development of cultural criminology Jeff Ferrell (1995) showed how those involved in the production of urban graffiti are engaged in a process of resistance to the increasing segregation and control of urban environments and work to subvert legal and political attempts to control them. The collective production of graffiti is both an act of confrontation and resistance to existing arrangements and serves to construct an alternative to the prevailing social, cultural and economic order. Further, cultural criminology itself signifies a form of 'intellectual resistance' providing 'a diverse counter-reading and counter-discourse' (Ferrell, 1999, p. 396) on the conventional, and often reactionary, constructions of crime and criminality. It is pitched against the forces of 'professionalization', the bureaucratisation of research through the 'iron-cage' of institutional review boards, 'the structuring of funding, the santization of quantitative methods, which seek to distance the criminologist from his or her object of study' (Hayward and Young, 2004, p. 266) – all of which create a stranglehold on creative and progressive research within the discipline. Although cultural criminologists do not contend that capitalism structures all social life (attention must likewise be given to patriarchy and racism in order to provide an understanding of crime and inequality), it is 'the currently ascendant form of economic exploitation' (*ibid*, p. 14) and must therefore be confronted as such. In *Cultural Criminology: An Invitation* Ferrell, Hayward and Young set out their position thus:

> If ever we could afford the fiction of 'objective' criminology – a criminology devoid of moral passion and political meaning – we certainly cannot now, not when every bloody knuckle leaves marks of mediated meaning and political consequence. The day-to-day inequalities of criminal justice, the sour drift towards institutionalized meanness and legal retribution,

the on-going abrogation of human rights in the name of 'counter-terrorism' and 'free trade' – all carry criminology with them, willingly or not. Building upon existing inequalities of ethnicity, gender, age, and social class, such injustices reinforce these inequalities and harden the hopelessness they produce. Increasingly crafted as media spectacles, consistently marked as information or entertainment, the inequitable dynamics of law and social control remain essential to the maintenance of political power, and so operate to prop up the system that produces them.

(2008, p. 13)

'Beyond the horizon, across the divide': Southern criminology and green criminology

Southern criminology

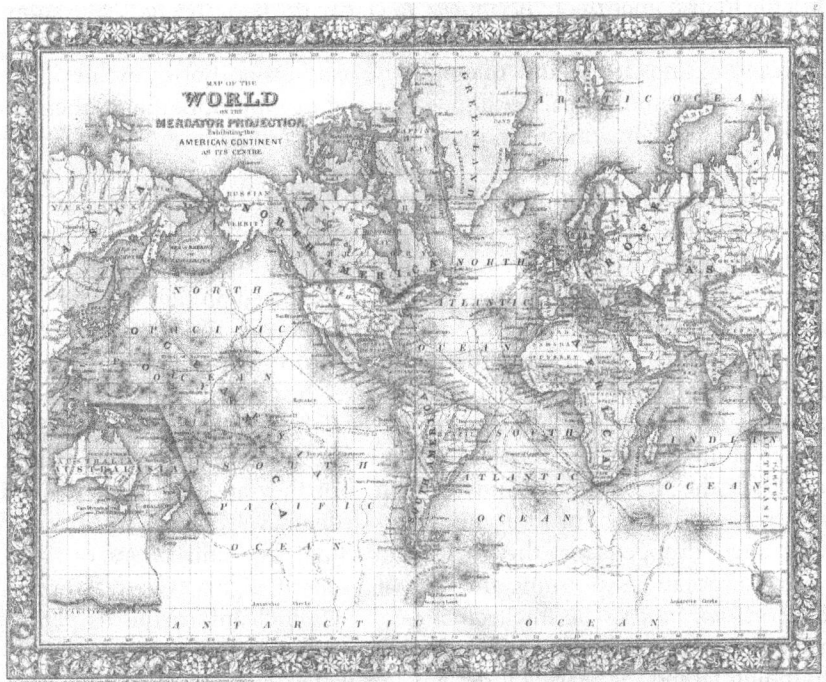

Figure 8.1 Samuel Augustus Mitchell map of the world on the Mercator projection, circa 1866. *When the updated version was replaced with the Peters projection map, 'the students view of the world suddenly changed, the USA was small. Europe too had suddenly shrunk. Africa and South America appeared narrower but also much larger than usual' (The Guardian, 23 March 2017).*

The foundations of what we have come to know as sociological, and therefore, criminological theory originated in the Global North. Historically this presented itself as 'universal knowledge' and, accordingly, the actual experience of colonisation is compounded by a colonisation of ideas. In the chapter on positivism it was noted how the nineteenth century was the 'golden age' of cartography in the Global North: the privileging of the Global North over the Global South was pictorially reinforced by the once commonly used Mercator projection map, which represented Europe and North America as much larger than they actually are – indeed it was only in 2017 that Boston schools in the United States replaced it with the more accurate Peters projection map (Walters, 2017).

In *Southern Theory* Raewyn Connell rejects the language of 'North/South', 'East/West' as ambiguous terminology which fails to disguise the realities of global division: for they are expressions that 'refer to the long-lasting pattern of inequality in power, wealth and cultural influence that grew historically out of European and North American imperialism' (2007a, p. 212). Connell uses the hybrid 'metropole/periphery' to clarify the pattern (*ibid*). She adopts the term 'southern theory' to 'call attention to periphery-centre relations in the realm of knowledge' and 'to emphasise relations-authority, exclusion and inclusion, hegemony, partnership, sponsorship, appropriation – between intellectuals and institutions in the metropole and those in the world periphery' (*ibid*, pp. viii–ix).

Sociological knowledge in the Global North, Connell argues, 'formed itself on ethnocentric assumptions that amounted to a gigantic lie – that modernity created itself within the North Atlantic world, independent of the rest of humanity', with the result that, 'models constructed on the basis of the lie, such as functionalist sociology, modernisation theory and neoclassical economics, were then exported to the rest of the world with all the authority of the most advanced knowledge and all the weight of First World wealth and power (2007a, pp. vii–ix). She acknowledges that the hegemony of metropolitan thinking does not eradicate all others, for alternative ways of thinking about the world are certainly evident. But they are easily marginalised, 'as African discussions of indigenous knowledge have shown – intellectually discredited, dropped from the curricula of schools and universities, or ripped off by corporations pursuing intellectual property rights (Odora-Hoppers, 2002)' (*ibid*, p. xi). The intellectual canon, Connell informs us, is perhaps not quite what we have been taught in our schools and universities – the 'founding fathers' of Marx, Durkheim and Weber, along with Comte, Spencer, Tönnies and Simmel, do not provide the full picture of sociology's 'origin' story. Many of the classic texts did not present the 'founding fathers' in this way. The 'Green Bible' of the Chicago School (Park and Burgess, 1924) listed works that were representative of the developing discipline of sociology with Simmel and Durkheim included but not Marx, Weber or Pareto. Indeed, she points out 'only one work by Weber was mentioned in this thousand-page volume, and then only in the notes' (*ibid*, p. 5). Interestingly in Durkheim's *L'année sociologique* between 1898 and 1913 only a fraction of the content was on recent or contemporary societies of Europe and North America,

> Twice as many of the reviews concerned ancient and medieval societies, colonial or remote societies, or global surveys of human history. Studies of holy war in ancient Israel, Malay magic, Buddhist India, technical points of Roman law, medieval vengeance, Aboriginal kinship in central Australia and the legal systems of primitive societies were more characteristic of sociology as seen in *L'année sociologique* than studies of new technology or bureaucracy.
>
> (*ibid*, p. 7)

What you start looking back and returning to primary texts, things are never quite the same as you have been led to believe. For Connell, sociology 'reflected in the most direct way, the social relations of imperialism': this does not, of course, mean 'that all sociologists were outright racists, though certainly some were [as were some criminologists, as we have seen]. Others, Du Bois and Durkheim among them, suffered the effects of racism'. The point is 'rather that racial hierarchy on a world scale was a perception built into the concept of "progress" and was a central part of what sociology was thought to be about' (2007a, p. 11).

Analysing recent contributions to theoretical work on globalisation, Connell exposes the Westo-centric bias of Northern theorising: the processes of globalisation are often seen as affecting *all of us* with the result that the systematic violence of the metropole is overlooked and its effect on those on the periphery, the non-metropolitan experience, is erased. She provides the example of Ulrick Beck's *What Is Globalization?*, which ends with a short essay on 'The Brazilianization of Europe' (2000, pp. 161–163).[2] As Connell points out,

> This does not discuss Brazil at all, but uses the name to evoke a horrific scene of social fragmentation, violence, and selfishness, which the European readers, surely, do not want. The remarkable social and educational reconstruction efforts undertaken *by the Brazilians*, in the aftermath of a violent military dictatorship and in the teeth of corporate power, does not enter Beck's argument.
>
> (2007b, p. 380; original emphasis)

In Michael Hardt and Antonio Negri's *Empire* Lukács, Benjamin, Adorno, Wittgenstein, Foucault and Deleuze are considered 'helpful for thinking about the transition from the possible to the real', but not 'Gandhi, not

Fanon, in fact no one with a black face, no women, and no one from outside Europe' (*ibid*, p. 379).

The study of crime in the Global South has received scant attention by the Global North (Schulte-Bockholt, 2011). As Stan Cohen wrote in 1988, 'criminologists have either ignored the Third World completely or treated it in a more theoretically primitive fashion' (p. 172). The importance of Indigenous theories of crime in the advancement of criminological theory in the contemporary period is well documented (see Willis et al, 1999); however, the level that this work is recognised by scholars in the Global North is questionable. Hence, while Raewyn Connell's concern was with sociology, Kerry Carrington, Russell Hogg and Maximo Sozzo (2016) illustrate how her argument applies equally to criminology.

Criminology, like sociology, they point out, has produced 'readings from the centre' which make universal claims yet 'fails to reflect their geo-political specificity' (Connell, 2007a, p. 44; Carrington et al, 2016, p. 2). The aim of a 'southern criminology' is thus to remedy these absences by advancing original and more diverse thinking to research agendas in criminology, producing a more inclusive approach. This is not done uncritically. For Carrington and colleagues are aware of the risk of creating an essentialist and reductionist approach to the Global North while having a romantic take on the Global South (See McLennan's critique, 2013, 2018). Southern criminology is intended to be used in a reflexive way to illuminate the power relations that are entrenched in the hierarchical production of criminological knowledge that privileges that from the Global North. The intention is not to dismiss the conceptual and empirical foundations of criminology but to de-colonise 'the toolbox of available concepts, theories and methods' (Carrington et al, 2016, p. 3).

In the Global South criminology has been unduly influenced by that from the Global North, which not only has limited the development of criminology but has resulted in the neglect of key criminological issues that affect both the North and South. The classicist foundations of criminology were based on the notion of a stable nation-state where free and equal individuals had contracted together to create a state that would protect their interests and create a harmonious society. Violence from outside was largely ignored or not seen as 'violence' and discussions of 'justice' confined to domestic or national contexts. As Carrington et al, write,

> Taking a high level of internal peace for granted, as the very condition of its existence, criminology rarely inquired into how those conditions were brought about (or not) in different historical or geo-political settings. How states were made, how their rule (through justice institutions and otherwise) was exerted and how the reach of their power was extended into new worlds were left unexamined. Rather, criminology largely confined its attention to the relatively minor delinquencies that troubled the

internal peace of stable liberal states (mostly without seriously threatening them) to the more efficient measurement of these problems (crime statistics, surveys and the like) and to refining the instruments for policing, controlling, punishment and treating those (mostly poor, young and marginal) individuals and groups who transgressed (Garland, 2001).

(2016, p. 8)

The result, as Southern criminologists point out, is a scarcity of scholarship on colonial penal practices; penal transportation, the genocide of Indigenous people and how these relate to imperialism and nation building; internal wars, the splintering of communities and displacement of people, the high numbers of Indigenous people who are either incarcerated or subject to other forms of criminal justice sanction; and the Islamisation of criminal justice that is taking place in the world (see, for example, Morrison, 2004; Mir-Hosseini, 2011; Jamieson, 2014; Cunneen, 2015 Carrington et al, 2018). The complex legacy of colonialism and de-colonialisation has to move to the centre of the criminological stage. Indeed, as Carrington et al (2017) so rightly note, Global North countries like the United States and Canada share the same features of racial segregation and exclusion as colonial settler societies. Moreover, the derision that those from the Global South are still subjected to underscores the importance of southern criminology.

Southern criminology is a comparatively new approach for criminology, but its aim is not to simply add one more 'criminology' to an already overburdened list, which could potentially lead to a fragmentation of the critical criminology agenda, but to create a political project, as well as theoretical and empirical work that aims to 'bridge global divides' and bring 'democratizing epistemology by levelling the power imbalances that privilege knowledges produced in the metropolitan centres of the Global North, particularly those located in the Anglo world' (Carrington et al, 2017, p. 15). Already innovative approaches to policy have been highlighted in the Global South, as is evidenced by Kerry Carrington's (2019) research study on women's police stations in Argentina. Women's police stations are illustrative of a feminist justice project (which allies with many of the core principles of feminist realism) that are run mostly by women police officers: the voices of the women they serve are central to the whole process, and the criminal justice system is presented as only one of a range of possibilities for women in terms of making decisions about what is best for themselves and their children in situations of domestic violence.

Likewise, in Ecuador there are potential lessons to be learnt from their the response of Rafael Correa's government to gangs: Ecuador's policy on gangs was one of inclusion rather than exclusion and is correlated with some startling results in the reduction of the homicide rate. Whereas in the United States gang members are criminalised and gangs pathologised, Ecuador legalised gangs, allowing 'the gangs to remake themselves as cultural associations that could register with the government, which in turn allowed them to qualify for grants and benefit from social programming, just like everybody else' (Samuel, 2019). David Brotherton has been following the Ecuadorean situation since the election of Rafael Correa in 2007. Correa won the presidency on the platform of the Citizens' Revolution and had announced that 'instead of just focusing on law and order, security will be based on social security' (Brotherton, interview with Sigal Samuel, 2019). Brotherton said that in Ecuador there was 'this fascinating phenomenon going on of peaceful coexistence': there were

> a number of the senior guys [from gangs] who were working with the government or in the police force. Some were doing crime analysis. Some were in college studying constitutional law and social work. Some were getting into entrepreneurship, becoming caterers or graphic designers.
> (Samuel, 2019)

Brotherton elaborates,

> It's all about a progressive, rational policy for social control. There's this idea known as 'deviance amplification' – basically, when you want to stop a behavior, the worst thing you can do is prohibit it. Social inclusion is the most productive means of social control. You have to have a system where most of people's engagement with the authorities is as positive as possible.
> (*ibid*)

We need, as Brotherton and Gude point out, to 'take seriously the hopes and agency of youth who, as Robert Merton (1938) long ago warned, will build innovative subcultures if their dreams are denied or deferred' (2018, p. 20). This work provides another perspective on the state, for in this context we move from the vision of an authoritarian, or an 'exceptional' state, to a situation in which

> The state can't just say, 'This is the American dream, you can do it, so do it.' The state has to say, 'I want you, and I'm going to help you in these concrete ways, and I'm going to win your trust'.
> (Brotherton Interview, Samuel, 2019)

The possibilities of southern criminology are exciting to critical criminologists. The examples of the impact of feminism and women's voices on policy in Argentina and the inclusionary politics of Ecuador are indicative of the possibility of achieving positive change: that the use of the 'criminological imagination' can 'make a difference' to people's lives. Further, as Sandra Walklate, citing Katja Aaas, argues, once the 'theoretical blinkers' are lifted,

> The global does not therefore present itself as a smooth, unified surface, a plane of immanence accessible through a zoom function, but rather as a dynamic multiplicity of surfaces and tectonic boundaries. It is in

these meeting points and frictions between the global north and south, between licit and illicit words, that criminology has an opportunity to gain (and provide other social sciences with) invaluable insight into the nature of the contemporary world order.

(Aaas, 2012, p. 14, in Walklate, 2016)

Thinking about the planet: 'greening' criminology

> In January 2019 at Davos the World Economic Forum [its mission is to improve 'the state of the world'] David Attenborough issued the warning that humankind has the power to exterminate whole ecosystems 'without even noticing', and implored world leaders to treat the natural world with respect. He outlined how the connection between the natural world and urban societies had been 'remote and widening' since the industrial revolution, in that humans do not realise the effect of their actions on the global ecosystem. It was he said 'difficult to overstate' the urgency of the environmental crisis. 'The Garden of Eden in no more'.
>
> At the same forum Dutch historian, Rutger Bregman pointed out that 1,500 people had travelled by private jet to the Davos World Economic Forum to hear David Attenborough talk about climate change. Why, he questioned, was no one talking about raising taxes on the rich? 'It feels like', he said that, 'I am at a fire fighters conference and no one's allowed to speak about water'. 'Most wealth is not created at the top, but merely devoured there'.
>
> What Bregman said, put simply, was the Davos emperors have no clothes. They talk a lot about how something must be done about inequality [and environment problems] and the need to address social unrest, but cavil at the idea they might be a big part of the problem.
>
> *The Guardian, Jan. 2019*[3]

The question of how to save the planet, when faced with the increasingly obvious effects of global warming, loss of biodiversity, pollution, deforestation and soil degradation, is arguably the most pressing one of our time. As Nigel South put it, 'the most serious crime that humanity is currently committing is against itself and its future generations' (1998, p. 213). Green criminology is that which is 'concerned with crimes and harms affecting the environment, the planet and the associated impacts on human and non-human life' (Carrabine et al, 2014, p. 389). Global in focus and attentive to the relevance and impact of social inequity – both current and historical – it overlaps with many of the concerns of southern criminology. The quotations provided earlier are useful in helping us understand the need for a critical green criminology – they underscore the necessity of seeing the 'bigger picture'. Bregman's comments illustrate the importance of 'studying up' (Connell, 2007a), of critiquing elites, the wealthy, of corporations. Bregman was, in fact, driven to publicly express his opinions after giving a private dinner talk at the forum and seeing the incredulity and scorn on the faces of technology chief executives when he mentioned taxes: 'one American looked at me as if I was from another planet,' he said.

The term 'green criminology' was first introduced by Michael Lynch in a 1990 article for the *Critical Criminologist* – he described 'green criminology' as reflecting 'existing traditions' within criminology while 'fostering emergent directions' (Brisman and South, 2014, p. 3). Lynch's intention was to expose and confront a 'variety of class related injustices that maintain an inequitable distribution of power while destroying human life, generating hunger, uprooting and poisoning the environment of all classes, peoples and animals' (1990, p. 3). Some years later Nigel South talked of a 'green vision' for criminology to be placed 'alongside other recent sources of change and critique in the field (e.g. feminism, minority representation, postmodernism, advocacy of human rights)' (1998, p. 212). For the situation is that

> The earth and its resources are being wasted and over-exploited by processes in which human beings are commodities in chains of production and distribution, and profit is put before sense or sensibility. In these processes, multiple and numerous crimes, violations, deviations and irregularities are perpetrated against the environment, yet go largely unchecked.
> (*ibid*, pp. 213–214)

Criminology therefore has to acknowledge 'the finite nature of the earth's resources and how this fits with global and socio-economic trends which have profound implications for the social sciences' (*ibid*, p. 225). This demands, as South put it, 'a new academic way of looking at the world but also a new global politics' (2010, p. 242).[4]

However, both Lynch and South recognised that a green criminology was not a new strand of criminological thinking as such: there are a number of criminologists who have previously studied environmental crimes, and research on corporate crime has provided important insights (Ruggiero, 1996; South and Beirne, 2006). In the early 1970s Robert Iseman wrote about the difficulties of getting environmental pollution seen as a 'crime' in the United States and making corporations responsible. Environmental pollution, he pointed out, is not necessarily visible: the damage that is done 'cannot easily be identified by the public' (1972, p. 65). Thus, much of society 'still considers environmental offenses to be "morally neutral if not blameless"' (*ibid*), and while

> Ten years ago, when the dire implications of pollution were not as apparent, environmental offenses could be accurately placed in the same *malum prohibitum* category as antitrust and housing code violations. But today pollution can almost be classified as *malum in se*, something wrong in and of itself like robbery, assault or murder. On at least three occasions

polluted air has caused mass death as a result of temperature inversions. In addition, pollution has been linked to emphysema, bronchitis and asthma, cyanosis, hepatitis, encephalitis, heart disease, polio, pneumonia and the common cold, cancer, increased deaths, and is believed to seriously aggravate many previously acquired afflictions.

(*ibid*, p. 67)

Corporate executives, he observed, 'speak out against violence in the streets and are not brought to account for their responsibility in producing a scale of violence [environmental pollution] that utterly dwarfs street crime' (*ibid*, p. 94). The ineffectiveness of legislation is underscored by the report that one company deliberately cut back their furnaces when they received notice of a forthcoming air pollution inspection' but 'as soon as the monitoring was completed there was business and pollution as usual' (*ibid*, p. 68) Today, while the problems of corporate and state accountability remain, the public, at least, is becoming more aware of the impact of environmental crime, even though frustrated and unsure about what to do about it. The latter is exacerbated by the indifference – and indeed opposition to green initiatives – of the governments of Donald Trump and Jair Bolsonaro in Brazil.

Significantly, for the development of a critical green criminology, we find in the writings of Karl Marx that the exploitation of the workers is analysed alongside that of nature (see Foster, 1999; 2000; 2015; Saito, 2017). In *Capital*, Marx wrote

> Capital cares nothing for the length of life of labour-power. All that concerns it is simply and solely the maximum of labour-power, that can be rendered fluent in a working day. It attains this end by shortening the extent of the labourer's life, as a greedy farmer snatches increased produce from the soil by robbing it of its fertility.
>
> (Vol. 1, 1867, 2018 ed, p. 179)

As such,

> All progress in capitalistic agriculture is a progress in the art, not only of robbing the labourer, but of robbing the soil; all progress in increasing the fertility of the soil for a given time, is a progress towards ruining the lasting sources of that fertility. The more a country starts its development on the foundation of modern industry, like the United States, for example, the more rapid is this process of destruction. Capitalist production, therefore, develops technology, and the combining together of various processes into a social whole, only by sapping the original sources of all wealth-the soil and the labourer.
>
> (*ibid*, p. 328)

For John Bellamy Foster, the 'green Karl Marx' is largely seen in Marx's concept of metabolic rift, which he developed from the writings of Justus Von Liebig, the German agricultural chemist (Slater and McDonough, 2008). A metabolic rift is the 'irreparable rift in the interdependent process of soil metabolism, a metabolism proscribed by the natural laws of life itself' (*Capital*, Vol. 3, 1977 ed, p. 949). It ensues when

> nutrients from the soil are naturally transferred to agricultural products in the process of growth and, as nutrients embodied in the commodity form, are then transported from their local ecosystems through trade to urban centres of consumption . . . if they are not replaced there will be (gradual) deterioration of the soil.
> (Slater and McDonough, 2008, p. 169)

This, Marx argued, was the situation in Ireland. Colonialism, therefore, has an ecological dimension: the soil of Ireland was effectively being colonised. The 'clearing of the estate of Ireland', the expulsion of the Irish peasantry from the land and the establishment of capitalist farms, are for the 'one purpose of English rule in Ireland' (Marx to Engels, 1867). 'Since the exodus' Marx wrote, 'the land has been underfed and overworked . . . So result . . . gradual deterioration and exhaustion of the source of national life, the soil' ('Notes for an undelivered speech on Ireland' in Slater and McDonough, 2008, p. 169). Further, in *Capital* he pointed out

> It must not be forgotten that for a century and a half, England has indirectly exported the soil of Ireland, without even allowing its cultivators the means of replacing the constituents of the exhausted soil.
> (Marx, 2018 ed, Vol. 1, p. 860)

Moreover, the colonisation of the soil has affected the health of Ireland's people:

> With the exhaustion of the soil, the population has deteriorated physically. There has been an absolute increase in the number of lame, blind, deaf and dumb, and insane in the decreasing population.
> (Marx, 1971 ed)

As Slater and McDonough note, in linking environmental deterioration to health problems, Marx appears 'not only as a historical analyst of colonialism but, also, perhaps, as a theorist of environmental modernity' (2008, p. 170). The same problem of soil degradation has persisted – a recent UN report suggested that if current rates of degradation continue, all of the world's topsoil could be gone within sixty years (Arsenault, 2017, see Crook et al, 2018).

Karl Marx also attended some of the lectures on solar energy by John Tyndall, who is today referred to as a founding figure of climate science. According to John Bellamy Foster's informative 'Marxism and Ecology: Common Fonts of a Great Transition', in these lectures, 'Tyndall reported on his experiments demonstrating for the first time that carbon dioxide emissions contributed to the greenhouse effect' (2015, p. 6). Marx 'took detailed notes on how the shifting isotherms on the earth's surface due to climate change led to species extinction over the course of earth history' and 'how anthropogenic regional climate change in the form of desertification contributed to the fall of ancient civilizations, and considered the way this would likely play out within capitalism' (*ibid*). Marx asserted that classical liberal political economy 'treated the natural conditions of production (raw materials, energy, the fertility of the soil, etc.) as "free gifts of nature" to capital' and based his 'critique on an open-system thermodynamics, in which production is constrained by a solar budget and by limited supplies of fossil fuels – referred to by Engels as "past solar heat" – that was being systematically "squandered"' (*ibid*). In *Capital*, Marx argued, we are 'not the owners of the earth' and 'have to bequeath it in an improved state to succeeding generations as *boni patres familias*' (Vol. 3, 1977 ed, p. 911).

In terms of subject matter, today green criminology embraces a broad range of research areas, including animal abuse, loss of biodiversity, pollution, deforestation, the extraction and exploitation of natural resources, state-corporate collusion, global warming and climate change, resistance to environmental harm and the criminalisation of protest (South and Brisman, 2013; Brisman and South, 2014; Beirne et al, 2018). Like strands of contemporary critical criminology, green criminologists have widened the conventional focus of criminology from interpersonal and street crimes to those of the state, as well as how human activities affect local and global ecosystems (South and Beirne, 1998). Indeed, for Nigel South, criminology should also 'be taking seriously old crimes and new violations', for example, dog fights, badger baiting and other ' "animal spectacles" for entertainment', as well as those that have arisen from late modernity's consumption society – the ' "throwaway", "discard and dispose" society' which has translated into 'the highly profitable area of illegal waste transfer and disposal' (1998, p. 226).

Similar to the conception of social harm associated with the work of critical scholars such as Paddy Hillyard and Steve Tombs (a 'focus on the different types of harm which people experience from cradle to the grave' (Hillyard et al, 2004, p. 1), 'harm' for many green criminologists is seen as a more useful category than that of 'crime'. What is meant by 'crime' is too narrow and fails to capture the myriad and multi-faceted nature of that which causes 'harm'. As Carrabine et al clarify, 'a green criminology counts among its avenues of investigation the "why, how and when" of the generation and control of such harms and related exploitation, abuse, loss and suffering' and incorporates an intersectional approach encompassing gender inequalities, racism, speciesm and classism (2014, p. 396). It emphasises the widespread harm, for example, of air pollution exposure which affects far more people than that conventionally defined as crime, e.g. homicide. Green criminology's focus therefore is not just on questions of legally defined crime but also on 'questions concerning rights, justice, morals, victimization, criminality, and the use of administrative, civil and regulatory justice systems' (Nurse, 2015, introduction).

The connection of genocide to ecocide is explored in the writing of a number of green criminologists, serving to emphasise the enormous damage that is being inflicted on the planet (see White and Heckenberg, 2014; Brisman and South, 2014; Crook et al, 2018). As South comments, 'ecocide' was not an unknown concept to environmental debate and is a '"word of warning" and signal of late modern awareness of the ecocidal tendencies of advanced (and now many developing) nations' (2009, p. 14; Crook et al, 2018). The Eradicating Ecocide campaign has highlighted numerous examples of ecocide and the impact that it has had worldwide. The campaign defines ecocide as the 'loss or damage to, or destruction of ecosystem(s) of a given territory(ies), such that peaceful enjoyment by the inhabitants has been or will be severely diminished'. Ecocide is:

> [A] crime against the living natural world – ecosystem loss, damage or destruction is occurring every day; for instance, the Athabasca Tar Sands. Ecocide is a crime against the Earth, not just humans. Further, ecocide can also be climate crime: dangerous industrial activity causes climate ecocide. . . . Unlike crimes against humanity, ecocide has severe impact on inhabitants, not just humans.
> (eradicatingecocide.com, 2010–2018)

The campaign calls for 'ecocide' to be accepted as a crime within international law. Ecocide particularly affects Indigenous people who, as Crook et al write, 'depend on the health of their local environment not only for their own physical well-being but also for their spiritual and cultural vitality' (2018, p. 303). Ecocide as a method of genocide 'attempts to undermine the life, existence and resistance of Indigenous populations – where killing the buffalo, fish and other means of subsistence are textbook counterinsurgency "starvation" tactics as part of a larger extermination strategy' (Dunlap, 2018, p. 557). Modern-day examples of Marx's 'metabolic rift' affecting Indigenous people are found in 'the process of "extreme energy", whereby energy extraction methods grow more intense, unconventional and riskier over time as the easier-to-extract conventional sources are depleted – all of which are associated with the insatiable demand for fossil fuels on the global markets rooted in a system of "fossil capitalism"' (Crook et al, 2018, p. 308). This is evident in the oil-extraction projects carried out at Standing Rock in North Dakota,

United States, and Athabasca Tar Sands in Northern Alberta, Canada. At Standing Rock sacred land of the Sioux tribe was bulldozed. The Athabasca Tar Sands project affected the Mikisew Cree First Nation, Athabasca Chipewyan First Nation, Fort McMurray First Nation, Fort McKay Cree Nation, Beaver Lake Cree First Nation, Chipewyan Prairie First Nation and the Metis (Indigenous Environmental Network, 2019). It has resulted in

> [A]n artificial division and fragmentation of the local ecosystem in order to extract oil, regardless of the anti-ecological effects that the resultant unnatural throughput and transfer of energy and materials has on the local environment and, critically, on the local indigenous population. The environmental externalities, for instance, in the local waterways, have had a crippling impact on both the physical and cultural well-being of the local indigenous population and have been associated with significant levels of colon cancer, leukaemia and lymphoma.
>
> (Crook et al, 2018, p. 308)

With Indigenous people being sacrificed for oil money, this amounts to a 'slow industrial genocide' (Indigenous Environmental Network, 2019). As a Mikisew Crew First Nation member in Canada, George Poitras, said,

> If we don't have land and we don't have anywhere to carry out our traditional lifestyle, we lose who we are as a people. So *if there's no land*, then it's the equivalent in our estimation to *genocide of a people*.
>
> (Cited in Crook et al, 2018, p. 308; original emphasis)

The connections between green criminology and southern criminology are underscored by the devastation caused by Cyclone Idai in March, 2019. Described as the worst weather disaster in the history of the Southern Hemisphere, it caused extensive flooding, wiping out the city of Beira in Mozambique, leaving 1.7 million or more affected, hundreds of thousands displaced and at least 1,000 killed in Mozambique, Zimbabwe and Malawi. Nearly a year's worth of rain came down in just a few days, 'an extreme weather event that climate scientists say is consistent with models of climate change' (*Democracy Now!*, 22 March 2019). As Dipti Bhatnagar, from Friends of the Earth International, said in an interview with Amy Goodman from *Democracy Now!*,

> In Mozambique, we've always known we are going to be really impacted by climate change. We are a downstream country. We are a very, very flat country. And we have faced floods before. And we knew that this is going to be our fate, that as our oceans warm and as the atmosphere warms, this is going to have direct impacts on our people.

Our people have contributed almost nothing to the climate crisis. But this is the irony of the climate crisis, that it affects those who did not do anything to create it, and it affects those the most. So the poorest and most vulnerable people on the planet are going to be affected the most.

We're pushing for repayment of the climate debt, which means we didn't create the crisis, so those who did give us the finance to be able to actually deal with this on the ground. And you know we want to fight for people centered renewable energy for our people.

And we really want to call out those who are responsible. So this is about the rich countries. Amy, where you are sitting at the moment, the United States. This is about Europe and Australia and Japan. And for years your societies have built up your societies using the fossil fuels, and now we know this is what it's caused in the atmosphere. So we call out the rich countries. . . *this is about historical responsibility*.

(author emphasis)

Concluding thoughts

In exploring the historical foundations of criminological theory, I have attempted to show how crime, the nature of 'justice' and what Stephen Pfohl (1985) described as 'recipes for appropriate action' are subjects of perennial interest and debate. That theory does not emerge spontaneously but in relation to distinct social, political, economic and cultural situations. I have illustrated the limits and dangers of criminological approaches that search for the solutions to crime within the individual and that 'reform' – although often initiated by 'good' people – is often little more than a 'Band-Aid' making some difference to the lives of a few (and not necessarily positive) but ultimately fails to achieve the long-term structural change that is necessary if we really are to work towards 'a better tomorrow'. There have been tremendous theoretical innovations in the field of criminology in the recent period, especially within critical criminology, that challenge some of the premises on which the discipline is founded, but we still need to ask if enough has been achieved.

In 1961 Henry Steele Commager remarked in his commentary on Jane Addams that there was still poverty, the 'slums', crime, misgovernment, exploitation, 'the inhumanity of man to man'. In the chapter on feminism, I noted how the feminist political project remained far removed from its goals all the time women continued to die as a result of male violence or misogynistic practices. A recent report revealed the number of women being killed by their male partners in the United States was rising, with 1,527 killed in 2017 (Holson, 2019). The legacy of the violence of colonialism remains evidenced, in part, by the high rates of incarceration of Indigenous, Black and minority people; oppressive state practices; and the continuing appropriation of

Indigenous lands. Political engagement, or lack of engagement, has been the subject of much discussion in recent years – with critical criminology being especially called to task. The latter is not surprising. For, as has been apparent throughout the discussion of critical criminology, it consistently emphasises the importance of political engagement and its activist credentials.

Critical criminology – in all of its various manifestations – is founded on the belief that unless structural change occurs and we move towards a more equitable society, there will be 'nothing new under the sun': those at the bottom will stay at the bottom and the criminal justice system will remain disproportionately focused on them, while those at the top will continue to get away with creating political, economic, social and environmental havoc.

Political engagement

Joanne Belknap argued in her American Society of Criminology (ASC) Presidential Address of 2014 that what had to happen was a more 'activist criminology' to engage 'in social and/or legal justice at individual, organizational, and/or policy levels, which goes beyond typical research, teaching, and service' (2014, p. 5). She pointed out that as a discipline 'there is a growing diversity among criminologists and this has had a powerful impact on expanding the scope and depth of the field', citing key work such as that of Greene and Gabbidon's *African American Criminological Thought* (2000), which identifies African American pioneers such as Ida B. Wells, W.E.B. Du Bois, Monroe Work, William Julius Wilson, Darnell Hawkins and others who are noted for their dedication to the achievement of justice. This is in line with an activist critical criminology – which should seek both to educate and work for change. However, Belknap observed that this is occurring at the same time that academic and university climates are working against 'our commitment to advancing social and legal justice' (2014, p. 1). As John Laub said in his Presidential Address to the ASC in 2003, the discipline of criminology is now one in 'which "career concerns" are center stage in the field – for example, publication counts, the amount of external funding generated, departmental rankings and so forth' (2004, p. 3). Reflecting on the British situation, convict criminologist Rod Earle despairingly remarked that 'criminology departments now resemble corporate fitness gyms where academics pump intellectual iron ahead of advertising campaigns inflating the employability of their products' (2016, p. 1501). In such a climate it would seem that there is little space for activism.

A couple of years after Belknap's address, Darnell Hawkins, in a provocative piece for the ASC's magazine *The Criminologist*, drew attention to the 'disciplinary cautiousness' (2016, pp. 3–4) that he believes now characterises criminology. Looking back, he noted that four decades ago when he began his career, 'one of the things that impressed me most was the presence and high visibility of those conflict theorists, critical criminologists, and Marxian (now a bad word) scholars who were a vital part of the discipline' (*ibid*). Critical criminology 'arose in response to the civil rights movement and anti-Vietnam War initiatives of the 1960s' and before that many of the 'insights of pioneering American [and European] criminologists arose in response to similar early 20th century discourse regarding racial and ethnic inequalities, crime, and immigration' (*ibid*). Certainly, the National Deviancy Conferences (NDC), as Joe Sim notes, sought to advance 'a forum for a more critically engaged, politically interventionist criminology' (2009, p. xxi). Today's 'disciplinary silence', Hawkins argues, is apparent from its minimal involvement in the policing crisis, which has seen 'a seemingly endless body count of largely adolescent and young adult African American males who have died at the hands of American law enforcement' (*ibid*) – Philando Castile, Freddie Gray, Tamir Rice (who was only 12 years old), Michael Brown and Eric Garner, to cite some of the high-profile cases of the last few years. 'Oh, newly minted critical criminological brothers and sisters, where are you?' wrote Hawkins, 'you have work to do' (*ibid*).

To some extent Hawkins's comments might seem an unfair characterisation, as there are certainly many examples of critical criminologists and feminists engaging in some of the most pressing issues of the day. We should, for example, consider the powerful research and campaigning of Phil Scraton on behalf of the families of the 1989 Hillsborough tragedy; Kim Cook's advocacy on behalf of those exonerated from death row in the United States; Brotherton's critique of the United States' deportation regime; Marcia Esparza's Historical Memory Project, which preserves the collective memory of war, genocide and state violence in Latin America; and the commitment of the late Sue Lees to highlighting the treatment of rape victims in court. Lees confronted politicians and judges and publicised the issue in newspapers and through television documentaries: she never wavered in her campaigns, even when her public exposure of serial rapists led to hate mail and threats on her life. And, there is the recent work of those involved in Black revolutionary criminology, prison abolitionist debates and convict criminology, especially British convict criminology, which has forged strong links with voluntary organisations, NGOs (non-governmental organisations) and campaign groups that work on behalf of ex-cons (Aresti and Darke, 2016). Responding to Belknap, Matthew Ball (2016) references the intrinsically activist research of queer criminologists that addresses the level of injustice experienced by queer communities. While David Rodríguez Goyes (2016) has outlined a 'green activist criminology' based on epistemologies of the Global South, calling for criminologists to confront the difficulties of being an activist criminologist within the academy, which has not only historically attempted to silence radical thought but reflects a traditional concept of what constitutes 'acceptable knowledge'.

Nevertheless, Hawkins's point is an important one that all criminologists should reflect on. I started this book with 'justice' in the time of the *ancien régime* and how the treatment of women as witches and use of torture served to remind us of the cruelty that people can inflict on one another. The level of inhumanity expressed in the case of Robert-François Damiens who attempted to stab the king of France in 1757 was beyond awful. The Enlightenment promised to rid society of such barbarity. People were to be treated with 'compassion and humanity'. As a manifesto, Beccaria's *On Crimes and Punishments* is commendable for its opposition to the frequently cruel and arbitrary way in which 'justice' was administered. Yet today in Donald Trump's United States the policies of his presidency have caused, amongst other atrocities, intolerable suffering to asylum seekers and undocumented immigrants in the name of 'law and order' and 'national security'. Thousands of children have been forcibly separated from their parents or guardians at the border between the United States and Mexico. Witnesses have described scenes of children surrounded by metal fences, with foil sheets instead of blankets. A toddler lying alone on the ground in a detention centre screaming for her mother with a guard standing over her, obeying orders delivered from up high to not comfort the children. And while in the custody of U.S. Border Patrol a little girl, Jakelin Caal Maquin, aged seven from Guatemala, died from dehydration and shock.

Martin Garbus, a lawyer providing legal help at the Dilley, Texas, Immigration Center wrote in an article for *The Nation* in March 2019 of how the women he saw from the northern triangle of Central America – Honduras, Guatemala and El Salvador – had come not to save themselves from poverty and violence but their children from sexual abuse, rape, violence and possibly murder in their home countries. They thought they would be safer in the United States, after all the words on the Statue of Liberty – given by the people of France in honour of the shared history of the two countries – state 'Give me your tired, your poor. Your huddled masses yearning to breathe free'. Nearly everyone Garbus saw, some 500, was sick. They had crossed the Rio Grande, and on arrival agents had taken them in their sodden clothes to what is called the '*hielera*' or 'icebox', a 'refrigerated building, a large processing center, where they had to sleep on the concrete floor or sit on concrete benches . . . prodded by agents all night and day, deliberately kept awake', forbidden to go to the bathroom, often soiling themselves. After that they went to the '*perrera*' or 'doghouse' where they were put in cages 'as though they were animals'. What the women and children were experiencing, Garber said, 'evoked the careful, calculated and precise torture' of Franz Kafka's *In the Penal Colony*, where

> Kafka describes the efficiency and errors of the executioner's machine of torture as the needles cut deeply into his victim's body. Here at the detention center we don't hear the screams or see the blood spurting out of the deep traumas being inflicted on their already traumatized bodies. I saw the silent screams in their eyes.

When we are confronted with a world that seems, as Joe Sim put it, 'devoid of the human and the humane', it has to be the responsibility of those on the left to try to do something about it. It thus seems appropriate to end this survey of criminological thought with the oft-quoted words of Karl Marx from *Theses on Feuerbach* (1845):

> *'The philosophers have only interpreted the world, in various ways; the point is to change it.'*

Notes

1 There is some debate over what 'resistance' means in cultural criminology – see Hayward and Schuilenburg, 2014.
2 Although this perhaps takes on a different connotation, given the recent election of the extreme right-winger Jair Bolsonaro to the presidency of Brazil, who is making allies with Trump and the right in the United States and in Europe.
3 Compiled from reports in *The Guardian* newspaper by Martin Farrer, Larry Elliott, Graeme Wearden, Kalyeena Makortoff.
4 See also https://greencriminology.org/950-2/

References

abbé Barruel (1799) *Memoirs Illustrating the History of Jacobinism*, New York: Hudson and Goodwin
Abel, E. (1979) 'Toynbee Hall, 1884–1914', *Social Service Review*, Vol. 53, No. 4, pp. 606–632
Adams, J. (1786) *Diary of John Adams*, Jul. 20
Adams, L. (2016) 'Return to Devil's Island: The toughest penal colony of all time', *Sabotage Times*, Jul. 26
Addams, J. (1892) 'The subjective value of a social settlement', *The Forum*
Addams, J. (1895) 'Prefatory note', in Residents of Hull House (Ed), *Hull House Maps and Papers*, New York: Thomas Y. Crowell Co.
Addams, J. (1899) 'A function of the social settlement', *The Annals of the American Academy of Political and Social Science*, Vol. 13, pp. 33–55
Addams, J. (1901) 'Respect for law', *New York Independent*, Jan. 3
Addams, J. (1902) *Democracy and Social Ethics*, New York: Palgrave Macmillan
Addams, J. (1910a) 'Immigrants and their children', in *Twenty Years at Hull House*, New York: Palgrave Macmillan
Addams, J. (1910b, 1961 ed) *Twenty Years at Hull House*, New York: Palgrave Macmillan
Addams, J. (1911) 'The social situation', *Religious Education*, pp. 145–152
Addams, J. (1913, 2002 ed) 'If men were seeking the franchise', in J. B. Elshtain (Ed), *The Jane Addams Reader*, New York: Basic Books
Addams, J. (1915, 2002 ed) 'Address of miss Addams at Carnegie Hall', in J. B. Elshtain (Ed), *The Jane Addams Reader*, New York: Basic Books
Addams, J. (1922) *Peace and Bread in Time of War*, New York: Palgrave Macmillan
Addams, J. (1935, 2004 ed) *My Friend, Julia Lathrop*, Urbana and Chicago: University of Illinois Press
Agozino, B. (2003) *Counter-Colonial Criminology: A Critique of Imperialist Reason*, London: Pluto Press
Agozino, B. (2014) 'Indigenous European justice and other Indigenous justices' (Special Issue on 'Indigenous Perspectives and Counter-Colonial Criminology'), *African Journal of Criminology and Justice Studies*, Vol. 8, No. 1, pp. 1–19
Agozino, B. (2017) 'Editor's preface', in S. Gabbidon (Ed), *WEB Du Bois on Crime and Justice*, Oxon: Routledge
Ahearne, M. (1994) *Beccaria*, Occasional Paper, Centre for Criminology: Middlesex University
Ahluwalia, S. (1992) 'Counting what counts', in J. Lowman and B. MacLean (Eds), *Realist Criminology*, Toronto: University of Toronto Press

Ainsworth, W. H. (1844) *Ainsworth's Magazine*, Vol. 5–6
Alexander, F. and Healy, W. (1935) *Roots of Crime*, New York: Alfred A. Knopf
Alvi, S. (2000) *Youth and the Canadian Criminal Justice System*, Toronto: Anderson Publishing
American Civil Liberties Union (2019) *The Convention Against Torture*, accessed at: https://www.aclu.org/other/commentary-convention-against-torture-report
Amnesty International (2015) *American Torture Story*, accessed at: www.amnestyusa.org/pdfs/AmericanTortureStoryToolkitFall2015.pdf
Amos, V. and Parmar, P. (1984) 'Challenging imperial feminism', *Feminist Review*, Vol. 17, pp. 3–19
Anderson, N. (1923) *The Hobo*, Chicago: University of Chicago Press
Anon., (1757) *Pièces originales et procédures du procès, fait à Robert-François Damiens*, Paris: Pierre Guillaume Simon, at: http://chnm.gmu.edu/revolution
Aresti, A. and Darke, S. (2016) 'Practicing convict criminology: Lessons learned from British academic activism, *Critical Criminology*, Vol. 24, No. 4, pp. 533–547
Arnold, G. and Ake, J. (2013) 'Reframing the narrative of the battered women's movement', *Violence Against Women*, Vol. 19, No. 5, pp. 557–578
Arsenault, C. (2017) 'Only 60 years of farming left if soil degradation continues', accessed at: www.scientificamerican.com/article/only-60-years-of-farming-left-if-soil- degradation-continues/
Ashcroft, B., Griffiths, G. and Tiffin, H. (2003) *Post-colonial Studies: The Key Concepts*, Oxon: Routledge
Astell, M. (1986 ed) 'Reflection on Marriage and Other Writings', in B. Hill (Ed), *The First English Feminist*, Aldershot: Gower
Atkin, E. (2018) 'Did flint's water crisis damage kids' brains?', *The New Republic*, Feb. 14, accessed at: https://newrepublic.com/article/147066/flints-water-crisis-damage-kids-brains
Bahr, E. (1988) 'In defense of enlightenment: Foucault and Habermas', *German Studies Review*, Vol. 11, No. 1, pp. 97–109
Bailey, V. (1987) *Delinquency and Citizenship: Reclaiming the Young Offender, 1914–1948*, Oxford: Clarendon Press
Bailkin, J. (2005) 'Making faces: Tattooed women and colonial regimes', *History Workshop Journal*, No. 59, Spring, pp. 33–56
Balbi, A. and Guerry, A-M. (1829 ed) *Statistique comparée de l'état de l'instruction et du nombre des crimes dans les divers arrondissements des académies et des cours royales de France*, Paris: Jules Renouard
Baldoli, C. (2009) *A History of Italy*, London: Macmillan
Bales, K. (1999) 'Popular reactions to sociological research: The case of Charles Booth', *Sociology*, Vol. 33, No. 1, pp. 153–168
Ball, M. (2016) 'Queer criminology as activism', *Critical Criminology*, No. 24, p. 473
Barak, G. (1986) 'Is America ready of the Currie challenge', *Crime and Social Justice*, No. 25, pp 200–204
Barak, G. and Pagni, C. (2010) 'Julia Schwendinger and Herman Schwendinger', in K. Hayward, S. Maruna and J. Mooney (Eds), *Fifty Key Thinkers in Criminology*, Oxon: Routledge
Barber, W. H. (1993) 'Voltaire: Art, thought, and action', *Modern Language Review*, Vol. 88, No. 4, pp. xxv–xxxvi
Barberet, R. (2014) *Women, Crime and Criminal Justice: A Global Enquiry*, Oxon: Routledge
Barbier, E. J. F. (1847–56), *Journal historique et anecdotique du règne de Louis XV*, Paris: J Renouard et cie.
Barker, C. and Jane, E. (2016) *Cultural Studies: Theory and Practice*, London: Sage

Barker, L., Tuvblad, C. and Raine, A. (2010) 'Genetics and crime', in E. McLaughlin and T. Newburn (Eds), *The Sage Handbook of Criminological Theory*, London: Sage

Barnes, J. (1981) *Katharine B. Davis and the Working Man's Model Home of 1893*, Rochester: Rochester History

Barnett, H. (1919) *Canon Barnett*, Boston and New York: Houghton Mifflin Co.

Barnett, J. (2018) *Gender and Crime Presentation*, New York: CUNY Graduate Center

Barrett, M. (1980) *Women's Oppression Today*, London: Verso

Barry, K. (1995) *The Prostitution of Sexuality*, New York: New York University Press

Bazelon, E. (2016) 'Should prostitution be a crime?', *New York Times*, May 5

Beam, A. (2008) *A Great Idea at the Time*, New York: Public Affairs

Beaver, K., DeLisi, M., Wright, J. P. and Vaughn, M. (2009) 'Gene-environment interplay and delinquent involvement', *Journal of Adolescent Research*, Vol. 24, No. 2, pp. 147–168

Beaver, K., Nedelec, J., da Silva Costa, C. and Vidal, M. M. (2015) 'The future of biosocial criminology', *Criminal Justice Studies*, Vol. 28, No.1, pp. 6–17.

Beccaria, C. (1801 ed) *An Essay on Crimes and Punishments*, London: E. Hodson

Beccaria, C. (1880 ed) *An Essay on Crimes and Punishments*, A New Translation by James Farrer, London: Chatto & Windus

Beccaria, C. (1995 ed) *On Crimes and Punishments and Other Writings*, Cambridge: Cambridge University Press

Becker, H. S. (1963) *Outsiders*, New York: The Free Press

Becker, H. S. (1970) *Sociological Work: Method and Substance, Essays by Howard S. Becker*, New York: Transaction Pub.

Becker, H. S. (1999) 'The Chicago school, so-called', *Qualitative Sociology*, Vol. 22, No. I, pp. 3–12

Becker, H. S. (2003. 2016 ed) 'Making sociology relevant to society', Paper to the 2003 meeting of the European Sociological Association, *Journal of Criminal Justice and Popular Culture*, Vol. 18, No. 1, pp 1–8

Bedau, H. (2004) 'Bentham's theory of punishment', *Journal of Bentham Studies*, Vol. 7, pp. 1–17

Beechey, V. (1997) 'Some notes on the female wage labourer in capitalist production', *Capital and Class*, Vol. 3, pp. 45–66

Behar, R. (1987) 'Sex and sin, witchcraft and the devil in late-colonial Mexico', *American Ethnologist*, Vol. 4, No. 1, pp. 34–54

Beirne, P. (1987) 'Adolphe Quetelet and the Origins of Positivist Criminology', *American Journal of Sociology*, Vol. 92, No. 5, pp. 1140–1169.

Beirne, P. (1993) *Inventing Criminology*, New York: SUNY Press

Beirne, P. and Messerschimdt, J. (1995, 2014 ed) *Criminology: A Sociological Approach*, Oxford: Oxford University Press

Beirne, P., Brisman, A., Sollund, R. and South, N. (2018) 'Editors' introduction: "For a green criminology" – 20 years and onwards', *Theoretical Criminology*, Vol. 22, No. 3, pp. 295–297

Belknap, J. (2014) 'American Society of Criminology, Presidential Address', *Criminology*, 2015, Vol. 53, No. 1, pp. 1–22

Bellah, R. (1973 ed) *Emile Durkheim on Morality and Society*, Chicago: University of Chicago Press

Bellamy, R. (1995) *Introduction to on Crimes and Punishments and Other Writings*, Cambridge: Cambridge University Press

Benns, W. (2015) 'American slavery, reinvented', *The Atlantic*, Sept. 21, accessed at: https://www.theatlantic.com/business/archive/2015/09/prison-labor-in-america/406177/
Bentham, J. (1791, 2008 ed) *Panopticon, or the Inspection House*, London: Dodo Press
Bentham, J. (1823, 1879 ed) *Introduction to the Principles of Morals and Legislation*, London: W. Pickering
Bentham, J. (1843) *The Works of Jeremy Bentham*, Edinburgh: William Tait
Bentham, J. (1864 ed) *Theory of Legislation*, London: Trubner & Co.
Bentham Project, (2010) accessed at: www.ucl.ac.uk/bentham-project/
Ben-Yehuda, N. (1980) 'The European witch craze of the 14th to 17th centuries: A sociologist's perspective', *American Journal of Sociology*, Vol. 86, No. 1, pp. 1–31
Berger, D. and Losier, T. (2018) *Rethinking the American Prison Movement*, London: Routledge
Berger, P. (1963) *Invitation to Sociology*, New York: Doubleday
Bernstein, E. (2007) The sexual politics of the 'New Abolitionism', *Differences*, Vol. 18, No. 3, pp. 128–151
Bewley, C. and Gibbs, A. (1997) 'The role of the midwife', in S. Bewley, J. Friend and G. Mezey (Eds), *Violence Against Women*, London: Royal College of Midwives
Bhavani, K-K. and Coulson, M. (1986) 'Transforming socialist feminism: The challenge of racism', *Feminist Review*, Vol. 20, pp. 81–92
Bindel, J. (2006) 'A heroine for our age', *The Guardian*, Sept. 21, art 1
Bindel, J. (2017) *The Pimping of Prostitution*, London: Palgrave Macmillan
Blackmon, D. (2008) *Slavery by Another Name: The Re-Enslavement of Black Americans From the Civil War to World War II*, New York: Doubleday
Blackstone, W. (1769, 1860 ed) *Commentaries on the Laws of England*, Oxford: Clarendon Press
Bloch, H. and Geis, G. (1970) *Man, Crime and Society*, New York: Random House
Blumbers, D. (1964) ' "Dear Mr. Engels" unpublished letters, 1884–1894 of Florence Kelley (- Wischnewetzky) to Friedrich Engels', *Journal of Labor History*, Vol. 5, No. 2, pp. 103–133
Bonger, W. (1916) *Criminality and Economic Conditions*, Boston, MA: Little, Brown and Co.
Bonger, W. (1936) *An Introduction to Criminology*, London: Methuen
Bonger, W. (1943) *Race and Crime*, Newark, NJ: Patterson Smith
Booth, C. (1902 ed) *Life and Labour of the People in London*, London: Palgrave Macmillan
Bosworth, M. (1999) 'Agency and choice in women's prisons', in S. Henry and D. Milovanovic (Eds), *Constitutive Criminology at Work: Applications to Crime and Justice*, New York: SUNY Press
Bosworth, M. (2001) 'The past as a foreign country? Some methodological implications of doing historical criminology', *British Journal of Criminology*, Vol. 41, No. 3, pp. 431–442
Bosworth, M. (2004) *Encyclopedia of Prisons and Correctional Facilities*, London: Sage
Bosworth, M. (2007) *Race, Gender and Punishment*, Brunswick, NJ: Rutgers University Press
Bosworth, M. (2010) *Explaining U.S. Imprisonment*, London: Sage
Bovenkerk, F. (2010) 'Robert park', in K. Hayward, S. Maruna and J. Mooney (Eds), *Fifty Key Thinkers in Criminology*, London: Routledge
Brace, C. L. (1874) *Dangerous Classes of New York*, New York: Wynkoop & Hallenbeck Publisher
Breck Perkins, J. (1897) *France under Louis XV*, Cambridge: Cambridge Scholars Pub.
Brisman, A. and South, N. (2014) *Green Cultural Criminology*, Oxon: Routledge
Brockway, Z. (1870) 'The ideal of a true prison system for a State', a Paper read before the *National Congress on Penitentiary and Reformatory Discipline* at Cincinnati, Oct. 12
Brockway, Z. (1917, 1969 ed) *Fifty Years of Prison Service; An Autobiography*, New York: Charities Publications

Brotherton, D. (2010) 'Richard Cloward', in K. Hayward, S. Maruna and J. Mooney (Eds), *Fifty Key Thinkers in Criminology*, London: Routledge

Brotherton, D. and Gude, R.,(2018) 'Social Inclusion from Below: The Perspectives of Street Gangs and their Possible Effects on Declining Homicide Rates in Ecuador' *CUNY Academic Works*

Brown, A. (2002) 'Conflicting objectives: Suffragette prisoners and female prison staff in Edwardian England', *Women's Studies*, Vol. 31, No. 5, pp. 627–644

Brown, L. (1985) 'Confronting crime: An American challenge', *LA Times*, accessed at: https://www.latimes.com/archives/la-xpm-1985-12-15-bk-689-story.html

Brown, J. and Heidensohn, F. (2000) *Gender and Policing: Comparative Perspectives*, London: Palgrave Macmillan

Brownmiller, S. (1975) *Against Our Will: Men, Women and Rape*, New York: Simon & Schuster

Bruce, S. (1992) *The Red Hand: Protestant Paramilitaries in Northern Ireland*, Oxford: Oxford University Press

Bruegal, I. (1979) 'Women as a reserve army of labour', *Feminist Review*, Vol. 3, pp. 12–23

Bryson, V. (1992) *Feminist Political Theory*, London: Palgrave Macmillan

Bufacchi, V. and Arrigo, J. (2006) 'Torture, terrorism and the state: A refutation of the ticking bomb argument', *Journal of Applied Philosophy*, Vol. 23, No. 3, pp. 1–19

Bulmer, M. (1984) *The Chicago School of Sociology*, Chicago: University of Chicago Press

Burgess, E. W. (1923) 'The study of the delinquent as a person', *American Journal of Sociology*, Vol. 28, No. 6, pp. 657–680

Burgess, E. W. (1925) 'The growth of the city: An introduction to a research project', in R. Park and E. W. Burgess (Eds), *The City*, Chicago: University of Chicago Press

Burgess, E. W. (1964) 'Research in urban society: A long view', in E. W. Burgess and D. J. Bogue (Eds), *Contributions to Urban Sociology*, Chicago: University of Chicago

Burgess, R. and Draper, P. (1989) 'The explanation of family violence: The role of biological, behavioural and cultural selection', in L. Ohlin and M. Tonry (Eds), *Family Violence*, Chicago: University of Chicago Press

Burgess-Proctor, A. (2006) 'Intersections of race, class, gender and crime: Future directions for feminist criminology', *Feminist Criminology*, pp. 27–47

Burrell, I. (2000) 'Anti-racists urge Straw to pull out of debate with 'deplorable' scholar', *The Independent*, May 5

Bursik, R. J. (2009) 'The Dead Sea scrolls and criminological knowledge: 2008 Presidential address to the American Society of Criminology', *Criminology*, Vol. 47, pp. 5–16

Butler, J. (1896) *Personal Reminiscences of a Great Crusade*, London: H. Marshall

Butler, J. (2014) 'Interview with Judith Butler on gender identity', *The Transadvocate*

Caine, B. (2001) Feminism in London, circa 1850–1914, *Journal of Urban History*, Vol. 27, No. 6, pp. 765–778

Caldwell, W. S. (1897) 'Letter from Moscow: The Twelfth International Medical Congress, *Journal of the American Medical Association*, Sept. 25

Campbell, B. (1993) *Goliath*, London: Methuen

Campbell, B., McKeown, L. and O'Hagan, F. (1994) *Nor Meekly Serve My Time: The HBlock Struggle, 1976–1981*, Belfast: Beyond the Pale

Campbell, P. R. (1996) *Power and Politics in Old Regime France, 1720–1745*, London: Routledge

Carby, H. (1982) 'White women listen! Black feminism and the boundaries of sisterhood' in Centre for Contemporary Cultural Studies (Eds), *The Empire Strikes Back*, London: Hutchinson

Card, C. (2008) 'Ticking bombs and Interrogations', *Criminal Law and Philosophy*, Vol. 2, No. 1, pp. 1–15

Carey, D. and Festa, L. (Eds) (2009) *The Postcolonial Enlightenment*, Oxford: Oxford University Press

Carlen, P. (1985) *Criminal Women*, Cambridge: Polity Press

Carlen, P. (1988) *Women, Crime and Poverty*, Milton Keynes: Open University Press

Carlen, P. (1990) *Alternatives to Women's Imprisonment*, Milton Keynes: Open University Press

Carlen, P. (1994) 'Why study women's imprisonment? Or anyone else's', *British Journal of Criminology*, Vol. 34 (Special Issue), pp. 131–140

Carlen, P. (2002 ed) *Women and Punishment*, Cullompton, Devon: Willan

Carr, E. H. (1961) *What Is History?* New York: Vintage Press

Carrabine, E., Cox, P., Fussey, P., Hobbs, D., South, N., Thiel, D. and Turton, J. (2014) *Criminology: A Sociological Introduction*, Oxon: Routledge (3rd Edition)

Carrington, K., Hogg, R. and Sozzo, M. (2016) 'Southern criminology', *British Journal of Criminology*, Vol. 56, No. 1, pp. 1–20

Carrington, K. and Hogg, R. (2017) 'Deconstructing criminology's origin stories', *Asian Journal of Criminology*, Vol. 12, No. 3, pp. 181–197

Carrington, K., Hogg, R. and Sozzo, M. (2018 ed) 'Southern criminology', in W. DeKeseredy and M. Dragiewicz (Eds), *Routledge Handbook of Critical Criminology*, Oxon: Routledge

Carrington, K., Hogg, R., Scott, J. and Sozzo, M., (Eds) (2018) *The Palgrave Handbook of Criminology and the Global South*, London: Palgrave

Carrington, K. (2019) 'Women's police stations in Argentina', accessed at: https://research.qut.edu.au/pgv/

Carrithers, D. (2001) 'Montesquieu and the liberal philosophy of jurisprudence', in D. Carrithers, M. Mosher and P. Rahe (Eds), *Essays on The Spirit of Laws*, New York: Rowman & Littlefield

Carrithers, D., Mosher, M. and Rahe, P. (2001) *Essays on the Spirit of Laws*, New York: Rowman & Littlefield

Casanova, G. (1791, 1932 ed) *The Memoirs of Giacomo Casanova*, New York City: Garden City Publishing Co.

Casciani, D. (2003) 'The history of the suffragettes', *BBC*, at: http://news.bbc.co.uk/2/hi/uk/3153388.stm

Cavan, R. S. (1983) 'The Chicago school of sociology, 1918–1933', *Urban Life*, Vol. 11, No. 4, p. 407

Centre for Contemporary Cultural Studies (1982) *The Empire Strikes Back*, London: Routledge

Chambliss, W. (1975) 'Toward a political economy of crime', *Theory and Society*, Vol. 2, No.1, pp. 149–170

Chancer, L. (2006) *High Profile Crimes*, Chicago: University of Chicago Press

Chauhan, R. S. (2005) *". . . And he Shall Rule Over Thee" The Malleus Maleficurum and the Politics of Misogyny, Medicine and Midwifery (1484 to Present)*, Simon Fraser University

Cimino, G. and Foschi, R. (2014) 'Northerners versus Southerners: Italian anthropology and psychology faced with the "Southern Question"', *History of Psychology*, Vol. 17, No. 4, pp. 282–293

Cizova, T. (1962) 'Beccaria in Russia', *Slavonic and East European Review*, p. 40

Clark, J. (2007) 'In search of the American dream: Articles by Eleanor Roosevelt and others take up the question of what constitutes the American ideal', *The Atlantic*, Jun.

Clarke, J. (2008) 'What's the problem? Precarious youth: Marginalisation, criminalisation and racialisation', *Social Work and Society*, Vol. 6, No. 2, pp. 306–314

Clarke, J., Hall, S., Jefferson, T. and Roberts, B. (1975) 'Subcultures, cultures and class: A theoretical overview', in S. Hall and T. Jefferson (Eds), *Resistance Through Rituals*, London: Hutchinson

Clarke, R. (1980) 'Situational crime prevention: Theory and practice', *British Journal of Criminology*, Vol. 20, No. 2, pp. 136–147

Clarke, R. (2010) 'Crime science', in E. McLaughlin and T. Newburn (Eds), *The Sage Handbook of Criminological Theory*, London: Sage

Clarke, R. and Cornish, D. (2001 ed) 'Rational choice', in R. Paternoster and R. Bachman (Eds), *Explaining Criminals and Crime*, Los Angeles: Roxbury

Clemens, J. (2017) 'Bentham, torture, modernity', *Cogent Arts & Humanities*, No. 4

Cloward, R. and Ohlin, L. (1960) *Delinquency and Opportunity*, New York: Free Press

Cobbe, F. P. (1878) 'Wife torture in England', *Contemporary Review*, pp. 55–87

Cobbe, F. P. (1904) *Life of Frances Power Cobbe, as Told by Herself*, London: Swan Sonnenschein & Co.

Cohen, A. (1955) *Delinquent Boys: The Culture of the Gang*, Glencoe, IL: Free Press

Cohen, S. (1972) *Folk Devils and Moral Panics*, London: Martin Robertson

Cohen, S. (1981) 'Footprints on the sand: A further report on criminology and the sociology of deviance in Britain', in M. Fitzgerald, G. McLennan and J. Pawson (Eds), *Crime and Society: Readings in History and Theory*, London: Routledge and Kegan Paul

Cohen, S. (1988) *Against Criminology*, New Brunswick, NJ: Transaction Publishers

Cohen, S. (1998) 'Intellectual scepticism and political commitment: The case of radical criminology' in P. Walton and J. Young (Eds), *The New Criminology Revisted*, London: Macmillan

Coker, D. (2001) 'Crime control and feminist law reform in domestic violence law: A critical review', *Buffalo Criminal Law Review*, Vol. 4, No. 2, pp. 801–860

Collier, R. (1998) *Masculinity, Crime and Criminology*, London: Sage

Collier, R. (2004) 'Masculinities and crime: Rethinking the 'man' question', in C. Sumner (Ed), *The Blackwell Companion to Criminology*, Cambridge: Blackwell Publishing

Compton, L. (1978) 'Offences against oneself', *The Journal of Homosexuality*, Vol. 3, No. 4, pp. 389–406

Comte, A. (1822, 2017 ed) 'Plan of the scientific operations necessary for the reorganizing of society', in G. Bishchof (Ed), *Auguste Comte and Positivism: The Essential Writings*, London: Routledge

Connell, R. (1987) *Gender and Power*, Stanford, CA: Stanford University Press

Connell, R. (1995) *Masculinities*, Los Angeles, CA: University of California Press

Connell, R. (2007a) *Southern Theory*, Cambridge: Polity Press

Connell, R. (2007b) 'The Northern theory of globalization', *Sociological Theory*, pp. 368–385

Connell, R. (2014) 'Using southern theory: Decolonizing social thought in theory, research and application', *Planning Theory*, Vol. 13, No. 2, pp. 210–223

Connell, R. and Messerschmidt, J. (2005) 'Hegemonic masculinity: Rethinking the concept', *Gender and Society*, Vol. 19, No. 6, pp. 829–859

Cook, D. (1987) 'Women on welfare: In crime or injustice', in P. Carlen and A. Worral (Eds), *Gender, Crime and Justice*, Milton Keynes: Open University Press

Cooper, R. A. (1981) 'Jeremy Bentham, Elizabeth Fry and English prison reform', *Journal of the History of Ideas*, Vol. 42, No. 4, pp. 675–690

Cornish, D. and Clarke, R. (1986) *The Reasoning Criminal: Rational Choice Perspectives on Offending*, New York: Springer

Coser, L. A. (1978) 'American trends', in T. Bottomore and R. Nisbet (Eds), *A History of Sociological Analysis*, New York: Basic Books

Cover, R. (1986) 'Violence and the word', *Yale Law Journal*, Vol. 95, p. 1601

COYOTE (2004) 'Testimony on prostitution', at: www.coyotela.org/what_is.html

Crawford, M. S. (1893) 'Maltreatment of wives', *Westminister Review*

Crenshaw, K. (1989) 'Demarginalizing the intersection of race and sex: A Black feminist critique of antidiscrimination doctrine, feminist theory and antiracist politics', *University of Chicago Legal Forum*, p. 139

Crenshaw, K. (1991) 'Mapping the margins: Intersectionality, identity politics, and violence against women of color', *Stanford Law Review*, pp. 1241–1299

Crenshaw, K. (1997) 'Beyond racism and misogyny: Black feminism and 2 Live Crew', in D. Tietjens Meyers (Ed), *Feminist Thought: A Reader*, London: Routledge

Crenshaw, K. (2005) 'Reflection', in R. Kennedy, J. Edleson and C. Renzetti (Eds), *Violence Against Women: Classic Papers*, Boston, MA: Allyn & Bacon

Cressey, P. G. (1932) *The Taxi-Dance Hall*, Chicago: University of Chicago

Crimmins, J. (1990) *Secular Utilitarianism: Social Science and the Critique of Religion in the Thought of Jeremy Bentham*, Oxford: Clarendon

Crimmins, J. (2013) 'Jeremy Bentham', in G. Claeys (Ed), *Encyclopedia of Modern Political Thought*, Thousand Oaks: Sage

Crimmins, J. (2015) 'Jeremy Bentham', *Stanford Encyclopedia of Philosophy*, accessed at: https://plato.stanford.edu

Crook, M., Short, D. and South, N. (2018) 'Ecocide, genocide, capitalism and colonialism: Consequences for indigenous peoples and global ecosystems environments', *Theoretical Criminology*, Vol. 22, No. 3, pp. 298–317

Cullen, F. T. and Messner, S. F. (2007) 'The making of criminology: An oral history of Merton's anomie paradigm', *Theoretical Criminology*, Vol. 11, pp. 5–37

Cunneen, C. (2015) 'The place of Indigenous people: Locating crime and criminal justice in a colonizing world', in D. Baker, A. Harkness and B. Harris (Eds) *Locating Crime in Context and Place: Rural and Regional Perspectives* Leichardt: Federation Press

Currie, E. (1985) *Confronting Crime*, New York City: Pantheon

Curti, M. (1961) 'Jane Addams on human nature', *Journal of the History of Ideas*, Vol. 22, No. 2, pp. 240–253

Curtis, L. (1971) *Apes and Angels: The Irishman in Victorian Caricature*, Exeter: David Charles Pub.

D'Agostino, P. (2002) 'Craniums, criminals, and the "cursed race": Italian anthropology in American racial thought 1861–1924', *Comparative Studies in Society and History*, Vol. 44, No. 2, pp. 319–343

d'Argenson, (1857–1858) *Mémoires et journal inédit du Marquis d'Argenson*, 5 vols, Paris, (1859–1867), *Journal et mémoires du Marquis D'Argenson*, 9 vols, Paris

Daly, M. and Wilson, M. (1988) 'Evolutionary social psychology and family homicide', *Science*, Vol. 242, pp. 519–524

Daly, M. and Wilson, M. (1994) 'Evolutionary psychology of male violence', in J. Archer (Ed), *Male Violence*, Oxon: Routledge

Darnton, R. (2018) 'To deal with Trump, look to Voltaire', *New York Times*, Dec. 27, accessed at: https://www.nytimes.com/2018/12/27/opinion/trump-voltaire-enlightenment.html

Darwin, C. (1874) *Descent of Man*, London: John Murray

Davidson, I. (2004) *Voltaire in Exile*, New York: Grove Press

Davies, J. (2012) 'The fire-raisers: Bentham and torture', *Interdisciplinary Studies in the Long Nineteenth Century*, No. 15, pp. 1–25

Davis, A. (1981) *Women, Race and Class*, New York: Random House

Davis, A. (1996) 'Incarcerated women: Transformative strategies', *Black Renaissance /Renaissance Noir*, Vol. 1, p. 26

Davis, A. (1999) 'From the prison of slavery to the slavery of prison: Frederick Douglass and the convict lease system', in *Frederick Douglass: A Critical Reader*, Malden, MA: Blackwell Publishers

Davis, K. B. (1900) 'The condition of the Negro in Philadelphia', *Journal of Political Economy*, Vol. 8, No. 2, pp. 248–260

Davis, K. B. (1913a) 'A plan of rational treatment for women offenders', *Journal of the American Institute of Criminal Law and Criminology*, Vol. 4, pp. 402–408

Davis, K. B. (1913b) 'A study of prostitutes committed from New York City to the State Reformatory for Women at Bedford Hills', in G. Kneeland (Ed), *Commercialized Prostitution in New York City*, pp. 163–252. New York: Century

Davis, M. (1998) *Ecology of Fear: Los Angeles and the Imagination of Disaster*, New York: Random House

Davis, M. (2002) *Dead Cities*, New York: The New Press

Davy, G. (1920) 'Emile Durkheim: L'oeuvre', *Revue de metaphysique et de morale*, Vol. 27, pp. 71–112

Dawkins, R. (1976) *The Selfish Gene*, Oxford: Oxford University Press

Deegan, M. (1981) 'Early women sociologists and the American sociological society', *The American Sociologist*, Feb., pp. 14–24

Deegan, M. (1988) 'W.E.B. Du Bois and the women of Hull-House, 1895–1899', *The American Sociologist*, Vol. 19, No. 4, pp. 301–311

Deegan, M. (2001) 'The Chicago School of Ethnography', in P. Atkinson et al, *Handbook of Ethnography*, Thousand Oaks, CA: Sage

Deegan, M. (2003) 'Katharine Bement Davis (1860–1935)', *Women & Criminal Justice*, Vol. 14, No. 2–3, pp. 15–40

Deegan, M. (2005 ed) *Jane Addams and the Men of the Chicago School*, New Brunswick, NJ: Transaction

Deegan, M. (2007) 'The Chicago School of ethnography', in P. Atkinson, S. Delamont, A. Coffey, J. Lofland and L. Lofland (Eds), *Handbook of Ethnography*, London: Sage

Deegan, M. (2014) *Annie Marion MacLean and the Chicago Schools of Sociology, 1894–1934*, Oxon: Routledge

Deegan, M. and Podeschi, C. W. (2001) 'The ecofeminist pragmatism of Charlotte Perkins Gilman', *Environmental Ethics*, Vol. 23, No. 1, pp. 19–36

Deflem, M. (2015) 'Anomie', in *The Blackwells Encyclopedia of Sociology*, Cambridge: Blackwells

DeKeseredy, W. and Dragiewicz, M. (2011 eds) *Routledge Handbook of Critical Criminology*, Oxon: Routledge

Delamont, S. (1992) 'Old fogies and intellectual women: An episode in academic history', *Women's History Review*, Vol. 1, pp. 39–61

de Montaigne, M. (1580) 'Essay on cruelty', in M. Montaigne (Ed), (1910) *Essays of Montaigne*, New York: Edwin C. Hill

Dershowitz, A. (2001) 'Is there a torturous road to justice', *L.A. Times*, Nov. 8

Dershowitz, A. (2003) 'The torture warrant: A Response to Professor Strauss', *New York Law School Review*, Vol. 48, pp. 275–294

Dhawan, N. (2014) *Decolonizing Enlightenment: Transnational Justice, Human Rights and Democracy in a Postcolonial World*, Berlin: Barbara Budrich Publishers

Dickens, C. (1854) *Hard Times*, London: Chapman Hall

Dickens, C. (1859) *A Tale of Two Cities*, London: Chapman Hall

Dickie, J. (1992) 'A world at war: The Italian army and brigandage 1860–1870', *History Workshop Journal*, Vol. 33, No. 1, pp. 1–24

Dickie, J. (1999) *Darkest Italy: The Nation and Stereotypes of the Mezzogiorno, 1860–1900*, London: Palgrave Macmillan

Dingle, D. (2018) 'Kamala Harris, Cory Booker, Tim Scott introduce a bill that would make lynching a federal crime', accessed at https://www.blackenterprise.com/kamala-harris-cory-booker-lynching-federal-crime/

Doggett, M. (1992) *Marriage, Wife-Beating and the Law in Victorian England*, London: Weidenfeld and Nicolson

Donovan, J. (1997) *Feminist Theory*, New York: Continuum

Downes, D. and Rock, P. (1988 ed) *Understanding Deviance*, Oxford: Clarendon Press

Downes, D. and Rock, P. (2007 ed) *Understanding Deviance*, Oxford: Oxford University Press

Doyle, W. (1986) *The Ancien Regime*, London: Humanities Press

Draper, A. (2000) 'Cesare Beccaria's influence on English discussions of punishment, 1764-1789', *History of European Ideas*, Vol. 26, No. 3–4, pp. 177–199

Draper, A. (2002) 'An introduction to Jeremy Bentham', *Journal of Bentham Studies*, Vol. 5, No. 1, pp. 1–17

Draper, A. (2009) 'Punishment, proportionality, and the economic analysis of crime', *Journal of Bentham Studies*, Vol. 11, No. 1, pp. 1–32

Du Bois, W. E. B. (1891, 1982 ed) 'The enforcement of slave trade laws', *American Historical Association Annual Report*

Du Bois, W. E. B. (1896) *The Suppression of the African Slave Trade to the United States of America, 1638–1870*, Cambridge, MA: Harvard Historical Series

Du Bois, W. E. B. (1897) 'Strivings of the Negro people', *Atlantic*, Aug. accessed at: https://www.theatlantic.com/magazine/archive/1897/08/strivings-of-the-negro-people/305446/

Du Bois, W. E. B. (1899) *The Philadelphia Negro*, New York: Lippencott

Du Bois, W. E. B. (1901, 2017 ed) 'The spawn of slavery: The convict-lease system in the South', in S. Gabbidon (Ed), *WEB Du Bois on Crime and Justice*, Appendix 4, Oxon: Routledge

Du Bois, W. E. B. (1903a, 1965 ed), *The Souls of Black Folk*, Chicago: A.C McClurg & Co

Du Bois, W. E. B. (1903b, 1980 ed.) 'The laboratory in sociology at Atlanta University', *The Annals of the American Social Science*, Vol. 21, in W.E.B Du Bois (Ed), *Sociology and the Black Communnity*, Chicago: University of Chicago Press

Du Bois, W. E. B. (1933, 1996 ed) 'Marxism and the Negro problem', The Crisis, in C. D. Wintz (Ed), *African American Political Thought*, Armonk, NY: M.E. Sharpe

Du Bois, W. E. B. (1954 ed) 'Apologia', in *The Suppression of the African Slave Trade to the United States of America, 1638–1870*, New York: Social Science Press

Du Bois, W. E. B. (1968) *The Autobiography of W. E. B. DuBois: A Soliloquy on Viewing my Life from the Last Decade of its First Century*, New York, NY: International Publishers

Du Bois, W. E. B. (2014) *The Problem of the Color Line at the Turn of the Twentieth Century: The Early Essays*, New York: Fordham University Press

Dunlap, A. (2018) 'The "solution" is now the "problem": wind energy, colonisation and the "genocide-ecocide nexus" in the Isthmus of Tehuantepec, Oaxaca', *The International Journal of Human Rights*, Vol. 22, No. 4

Durkheim, E. (1893, 1933 ed) *The Division of Labor in Society*, New York: Palgrave Macmillan

Durkheim, E. (1895, 1938 ed, 1964 ed) *Rules of Sociological Method*, New York: The Free Press

Durkheim, E. (1897, 1952 ed) *Suicide*, London: Routledge, Kegan and Paul

Durkheim, E. (1898, 1969 ed) 'Individualism and the intellectuals', *Political Studies, Political Studies*, Vol. 17, No. 1, pp. 14–30

Durkheim, E. (1899) 'Anti-semistism and social crisis', *Sociological Theory*, Oct. 29, 2008

Durkheim, E. (1900) 'Sociology in France in the nineteenth century', Revue bleue, in R. Bellah (Ed), (1973) *Emile Durkheim on Morality and Society*, Chicago: University of Chicago Press

Durkheim, E. (1915 ed) *Elementary Forms of the Religious Life: A Study in Religious Sociology*, London: Allen and Unwin

Durkheim, E. (1961 ed) *Moral Education*, New York: The Free Press

Durkheim, E. (1972) *Emile Durkheim: Selected Writings* (Ed. A. Giddens), Cambridge: Cambridge University Press

Duster, T. (2005/6) 'Comparative perspectives and competing explanations: Taking on the newly configured reductionist challenge to sociology', *American Sociological Review*, Vol. 71, No. 1, pp. 1–15

Dutton, D. G. (1995) 'Intimate abusiveness', *Clinical Psychology: Science and Practice*, Vol. 2, pp. 207–224

Earle, R. (2016) *Convict Criminology*, Bristol: Policy Press

Eaton, I. (1899) 'Special report on Negro domestic service in the Seventh Ward, Philadelphia', in W. E. B. Du Bois (Ed), *The Philadelphia Negro*, New York: Lippencott

Eddy, T. (1801) *An Account of the State Prison or Penitentiary House, in the City of New-York*, New York: Isaac Collins and Son

Edwards, D. (1912) 'To make punishment fit the CRIMINAL, NOT THE CRIME; Miss Katherine B. Davis's experiments may bring about a clearing house for all offenders except murderers', *New York Times*, Sept. 1

Edwards, S. (1989) *Policing 'Domestic' Violence*, London: Sage

Eller, J. D. (2016) *Social Science and Historical Perspectives*, London: Taylor Francis

Ellison, T. (2016) 'The strangeness of progress and the uncertainty of blackness', in E. P. Johnson (Ed), *No Tea, No Shade*, Durham, NC: Duke University Press

Elshtain, J. B. (2002) *The Jane Addams Reader*, New York: Basic Books

Emsley, C. (2007) *Crime, Police and Penal Policy: European Experiences 1750–1940*, Oxford: Oxford University Press

Encylopedia of Diderot and d'Alembert, Collaborative Translation Project, Michigan Publishing, at: https://quod.lib.umich.edu/d/did/

Engels, F. (1845, 2009 ed) *The Condition of the Working Class in England, 1844*, Teddington: Echo

Engels, F. (1877) *Anti-Dühring*, New York, NY: International Publishers

Engels, F. (1891) 'Introduction', in K. Marx (Ed), *The Civil War in France*, Paris: International Library

Erickson, K. (1966) *Wayward Puritans*, London: John Wiley & Sons

Esparza, M. (2018) *Silenced Communities: Legacies of Militarization and Militarism in a Rural Guatemalan Town*, New York: Berghahn

Exum, M. L. (2002) 'The application and robustness of the rational choice perspective in the study of intoxicated and angry intentions to aggress', *Criminology*, Vol. 40, No. 4, pp. 933–966.

Eysenck, H. (1964) *Crime and Personality*, London: Paladin

Eysenck, H. (1987) 'The definition of personality disorders and the criteria appropriate for their description', *Journal of Personality Disorders*, Vol. 1131

Eysenck, H. and Gudjonsson, G. (1989) *The Causes and Cures of Criminality*, New York: Plenum Press

Fang, M. and Rieger, J. M. (2016) 'This may be the most horrible thing that Donald Trump believes', *The Huffington Post*, Sept. 28

Farge, A. (1994) *Subversive Words*, University Park, PA: Penn State Press

Farge, A. and Revel, J. (1991) *The Rules of Rebellion: Child Abductions in Paris in 1750*, Cambridge: Polity Press

Farrington, D. and Tonry, M. (1995) *Building a Safer Society: Strategic Approaches to Crime Prevention*, Chicago: University of Chicago Press

Fawcett Society (2013) *Sex and Power 2013: Who Runs Britain*, at: www.fawcettsociety.org.uk/sex-and-power-2013-who-runs-britain

Felson, M. (1998) *Crime and Everyday Life*, Newbury Park: Pine Forge Press

Felson, M. and Clarke, R. (1998) 'Opportunity makes the thief', *Police Research Series*, Vol. 98, Home Office

Fenton, S. (1984) *Durkheim and Modern Society*, Cambridge: Cambridge University Press

Ferguson, W. K. (1927) 'The place of Jansenism in French history', *The Journal of Religion*, Vol. 1, No. 7, Jan., p. 22

Fernandes, L. (2010) 'Unsettling "third wave" feminism: Feminist waves, intersectionality and identity politics in retrospect', in N. Hewitt (Ed), *No Permanent Waves: Recasting Histories of US Feminism*, Brunswick, NJ: Rutgers University Press

Ferrell, J. (1998) 'Against the law: Anarchist criminology', accessed at: https://theanarchistlibrary.org/library/jeff-ferrell-against-the-law-anarchist-criminology

Ferrell, J. (1999) 'Cultural Criminology', *Annual Review of Sociology*, Vo. 25, pp. 395–418

Ferrell, J. (2005) 'Cultural criminology', in *Blackwell Encyclopaedia of Sociology*, Oxford: Blackwell

Ferrell, J. (2010) 'Peter Kropotkin', in K. Hayward, S. Maruna and J. Mooney (Eds), *Fifty Key Thinkers in Criminology*, Oxon: Routledge

Ferrell, J., Hayward, K., Morrison, W. and Presdee, M. (2004 eds) *Cultural Criminology Unleashed*, London: Cavendish/Glasshouse

Ferrell, J., Hayward, K. and Young, J. (2008) *Cultural Criminology: An Invitation*, London: Sage

Ferrell, J. and Sanders, C. (1995) 'Culture, crime and criminology', in J. Ferrell and C. Sanders (Eds), *Cultural Criminology*, Boston: Northeastern University Press

Ferri, E. (1900 ed) *Socialism and Modern Science*, Chicago: C. H. Kerr & Co.

Ferri, E. (1905, 1917 ed) *Criminal Sociology*, Boston: Little, Brown, & Co.

Ferri, E. (1906 ed) *The Positive School of Criminology*, Chicago: C.H. Kerr & Co.

Feyerabend, P. (1975) *Against Method*, London: Verso

Fields, K. (2002) 'Individuality and the intellectuals: An imaginary conversation between W.E. B. Du Bois and Emile Durkheim', *Theory and Society*, Vol. 31, No. 4, pp. 435–462

Fink, L. (1997) *Progressive Intellectuals and the Dilemmas of Democratic Commitment*, Cambridge: Harvard University Press

Fisher, J. (2002) 'Tattooing the body, making culture', *Body and Society*, Vol. 8, No. 4, pp. 91–107

Fitzpatrick, E. (1990) *Endless Crusade: Women Social Scientists and Progressive Reform*, New York: Oxford University Press

Fogel, D. (1975) *We Are the Living Proof: The Justice Model for Corrections*, Cincinnati, OH: Anderson

Foster, J. B. (1999) 'Marx's theory of metabolic rift: Classical foundations for environmental sociology', *American Journal of Sociology*, Vol. 105, No. 2, pp. 366–405

Foster, J. B. (2000) *Marx's Ecology: Materialism and Nature*, New York: Monthly Review Press

Foster, J. B. (2015) 'Marxism and ecology: Common fonts of a great transition', *Monthly Review*, Vol. 67, No. 7

Foucault, M. (1975, 1977 ed) *Discipline and Punish: The Birth of the Prison*, London: Penguin
Fowler, J. (1896) *Life of Dr. Francois Joseph Gall*, London: LN Fowler & Co.
Fraistat, N. and Lanser, S. (2001) *Letters Written in France*, Peterborough: Broadview Press
Franklin, B. (1751) 'Felons and rattlesnakes', *The Pennsylvania Gazette*, May 9
Frazer, N. (1997) *Justice Interruptus*, London: Routledge
Frazier, E. F. (1939) *The Negro Family in the United States*, Chicago: University of Chicago
Freedman, E. B. (1984) *Their Sisters' Keepers*, Ann Arbor: University of Michigan Press
Frey, C. (2007) 'Jane Addams on peace, crime, and religion: The beginnings of a modern day peace making criminology', ETD Collection for the University of Nebraska
Friendly, M. (2007) 'A-M Guerry's moral statistics of France', *Statistical Science*, Vol. 22, No. 3, pp. 368–299
Fry, E. (1827) *Observations on the Visiting, Superintendence, and Government of Female Prisoners*, London: J & A Arch
Fry, E. (1847) *Memoir of the Life of Elizabeth Fry*, London: H. Longstreth
Fuller, J. R. (2009) 'Leo Tolstoy and social justice', *Contemporary Justice Review*, pp. 321–330
Gabbidon, S. (1996) *The Criminological Writings of W.E.B Du Bois: A Historical Analysis*, Ph.D. Dissertation, Indiana University of Pennsylvania
Gabbidon, S. (2007, 2017) *WEB Du Bois on Crime and Justice*, Oxon: Routledge
Gabbidon, S. (2010) *Race, Ethnicity, Crime and Justice*, Thousand Oaks: Sage
Gabbidon, S. and Greene, H. (2006) *Race and Crime*, London: Sage
Gabbidon, S. and Taylor, G. (2001) 'The presence of African American scholarship in early American criminology texts (1918–1960)', *Journal of Criminal Justice Education*, Vol. 12, No. 2, pp. 301–310
Gabbidon, S., Greene, H. and Young, V. (2002) *African American Classics in Criminology and Criminal Justice*, Thousand Oaks, CA: Sage
Gall, F. J. (1835 ed) *On the Function of the Brain and of Each of its Parts*, Boston: Marsh, Capon & Lyon
Garbus, M. (2019) 'What I saw at the Dilley, Texas, immigrant detention center', *The Nation*, Apr. 22
Garland, D. (1985) *Punishment and Welfare*, London: Gower
Garland, D. (1990) *Punishment and Modern Society*, Oxford: Clarendon
Garland, D. (1997) *The Culture of Control*, Chicago: Chicago University Press
Garland, D. (1999) 'The commonplace and the catastrophic: Interpretations of crime in late modernity', *Theoretical Criminology*, Vol. 30, No. 3, pp. 353–364
Garofalo, R. (1885, 1914 ed) *Criminology*, Boston: Little, Brown &Co.
Gatti, U. and Verde, A. (2012) 'Cesare Lombroso: Methodological ambiguities and brilliant intuitions', *International Journal of Law and Psychiatry*, Vol. 35, No. 1, pp. 19–26
Gay, P. (1994) *The Cultivation of Hatred*, London: W.W. Norton and Company
Geis, G. (1955) 'Pioneers in criminology VII – Jeremy Bentham (1748–1832)', *The Journal of Criminal Law, Criminology, and Police Science*, p. 159
Gelsthorpe, L. and Morris, A. (1988) 'Feminism and criminology in Britain', in P. Rock (Ed), *A History of British Criminology*, Oxford: Clarendon Press
Gelsthorpe, L. and Morris, A. (1990 eds) *Feminist Perspectives in Criminology*, Milton Keynes: Open University Press
Gibson, M. (2002) *Born to Crime: Cesare Lombroso and the Origins of Biological Criminology*, Westport: Praeger
Gibson, M. and Rafter, N. (2006) *Introduction to Lombroso's Criminal Man*, Durham, NC: Duke University Press

Giddens, A. (1972) 'Introduction', in *Emile Durkheim: Selected Writings*, Cambridge: Cambridge University Press

Gieryn, T. (2006) 'City as truth-spot: Laboratories and field-sites in urban studies', *Social Studies of Science*, Vol. 36, No. 1, pp. 5–38

Gill, A., Strange, C. and Roberts, K. (2014) *'Honour' Killing and Violence: Theory, Policy and Practice*, London: Springer

Glueck, S. and Glueck, E. (1930) *Five Hundred Criminal Careers*, Oxford: Knopf

Glueck, S. and Glueck, E. (1934) *Five Hundred Delinquent Women*, New York: Alfred A. Knopf

Glueck, S. and Glueck, E. (1950) *Unraveling Juvenile Delinquency*, New York: Commonwealth Fund

Go, J. (2016) 'The case for scholarly reparations', *Berkeley Journal of Sociology*, accessed at: http://berkeleyjournal.org/2016/01/the-case-for-scholarly-reparations/

Godfrey, B. (2011) 'Critical historical perspectives on crime', in W. DeKesereday and M. Dragiewicz (Eds), *Routledge Handbook of Critical Criminology*, Oxon: Routledge

Godwin, W. (1793, 1798 ed) *An Enquiry Concerning Political Justice and Its Influence on General Virtue and Happiness*, Vol. 1, London: J. and J. Robinson

Goldman, E. (1911) *Anarchism and Other Essays*, New York: Mother Earth Publishing

Goldman, E. (1917) *Prisons: A Social Crime and Failure*, New York: Mother Earth Publishing

Goffman, E. (1967, 2017 ed) *Interaction Ritual*, Oxon: Routledge

Golus, C. (2001) 'Rockefeller challenged others to give to University', *The University of Chicago Chronicle*, Oct. 18, accesssed at: http://chronicle.uchicago.edu/011018/donors.shtml

Gómez, A. (2014) 'José del Valle: A Benthamite in Central America', *Journal of Bentham Studies*, Vol. 16, No. 1, pp. 1–35

Goode, E. (1994) 'Round up the usual suspects: Crime, deviance, and the limits of constructionism', *The American Sociologist*, Vol. 25, No. 4, pp. 90–104

Goodman, A. (2019) 'Remember the South": Devastating Cyclone Idai. Another example of Global South paying for polluters', *Democracy Now!* Mar. 22

Gordon, L. (1988) *Heroes of Their Own Lives: The Politics and History of Family Violence* London: Virago

Goring, C. (1913) *The English Convict*, London: HMS

Gottfredson, M. and Hirschi, T. (1990) *A General Theory of Crime*, Stanford: Stanford University Press

Gould, S. J. (1981) *The Mismeasure of Man*, New York: W.W. Norton & Co.

Goyes, Rodríguez, D. (2016) 'Green activist criminology and the epistemologies of the South', *Critical Criminology*, Vol. 24, No. 4, pp. 503–518

Graham, L. J. (2000) *If the King Only Knew*, Charlottesville: University Press of Virginia

Gramsci, A. (1926, 2000 ed, 2005 ed) *The Southern Question*, New York: New York University Press

Gramsci, A. (1971 ed) *Selections from the Prison Notebooks*, New York: International Publishers

Grant, L., Stalp, M. and Ward, K. (2002) 'Women's sociological research and writing in the AJS in the pre-World War II era', *The American Sociologist*, Vol. 33, No. 3, pp. 69–91

Granucci, A. (1969) '"Nor cruel and unusual punishments inflicted" The original meaning', *California Law Review*, Vol. 57, No. 4, pp. 839–865

Green, P. and Ward, T. (2005 eds) *State Crime: Governments, Violence and Corruption*, London: Pluto Press

Green, P. and Ward, T. (2009) 'Violence and the state', in R. Coleman and D. Whyte (Eds) *State, Power and Crime*, London: Sage

Greenberg, D. (1976) 'One one-dimensional Marxist criminology', *Theory and Society*, Vol. 3, No. 4, pp. 611–621

Greenberg, D. (Ed) (1981 ed) *Crime and Capitalism: Readings in Marxist Criminology*, New York: Mayfield

Greene, T. H. and Gabbidon, S. (2000) *African American Criminological Thought*, Albany: SUNY Press

Gregory, J. (1986) 'Sex, class and crime: Towards a non-sexist criminology', in R. Matthews and J. Young (Eds), *Confronting Crime*, London: Sage

Griffin, S. (1971) 'Rape: The all-American crime', *Ramparts*

Grossman, R. (2011) 'The Pullman Strike', *Chicago Tribune*, accessed at: www.chicagotribune.com/news/nationworld/politics/chi-chicagodays- pullmanstrike-story-story.html

Grossman, R. (2014) 'Chicago ushers in new era in 1899 with nation's first juvenile court', *Chicago Tribune*, accessed at: http://articles.chicagotribune.com/2014-06-08/site/ct-juvenile-courts-flashback-0608-20140608_1_chicago-woman-young-offenders-new-era

Guerry, A-M. (1829 ed) *Statistique anti-vi de l'etat de l'instruction et du nombre des crimes*, Paris: Everat

Guerry A-M (1882, 2002 ed) *Essay on the Moral Statistics of France*, New York: Edwin Mellen

Guettel, C. (1974) *Marxism and Feminism*, Toronto: The Women's Press

Hall S. (1987) 'Gramsci and us', *Marxism Today*, Jun. 16–21

Hall, S. (1970) 'The Hippies: An American Moment', *NDC 5th Symposium*, Apr.

Hall, S. (1990) 'The emergence of cultural studies and the crisis of the humanities', *The Humanities as Social Technology*, Vol. 53, Oct., Summer, pp. 11–23

Hall, S. (2009) 'Preface', in R. Coleman, J. Sim, S. Tombs and D. Whyte (Eds), *State, Power, Crime*, London: Sage

Hall, S., Critcher, C., Jefferson, T., Clarke, J. and Roberts, B. (1978) *Policing the Crisis: Mugging, the State, and Law and Order*, London: Palgrave Macmillan

Hall, S. and Jefferson, T. (Eds) (1975) *Resistance Through Rituals*, London: Hutchinson

Hall, S. and Jefferson, T. (Eds) (2006 ed) *Resistance Through Rituals*, London: Routledge

Hallett, T. and Jeffers, G. (2008) 'A long neglected mother of contemporary ethnography: Annie Marion MacLean and the memory of method', *Journal of Contemporary Ethnography*, Vol. 37, No. 1, pp. 3–37

Hallsworth, S. and Lea, J. (2012) 'Reconnecting the king with his head', *Crime, Media, Culture*, Jul. 25, Vol. 8, No. 1, pp. 185–195

Hamilton, M. (1978) 'Opposition to the Contagious Diseases Acts, 1864–1886', *Albion*, pp. 14–27

Hamington, M. (2005) 'Public pragmatism: Jane Addams and Ida B. Wells on lynching', *The Journal of Speculative Philosophy*, Vol. 19, No. 2, pp 167–174

Hanmer, J., Radford, J. and Stanko, E. (1989) *Women, Policing, and Male Violence: International Perspectives*, London: Routledge

Hanmer, J. and Saunders, S. (1984) *Well-Founded Fear*, London: Hutchinson

Hanson, L. (2010) 'W.E.B. Du Bois', in K. Hayward, S. Maruna and J. Mooney (Eds), *Fifty Key Thinkers in Criminology*, London: Routledge

Harris Poll (2012) 'Poll on tattooing', at: https://theharrispoll.com/new-york

Harvey, L. (1986) 'The myths of the Chicago School', *Quantity and Quality*, Vol. 20, pp. 191–217

Hawkins, D. (1995) *Ethnicity, Race and Crime: Perspectives Across Time and Place*, New York: SUNY Press

Hawkins, D. (2016) 'Oh brother, where art though? Critical criminology, the policing crisis and the quiet after the storm', *The Criminologist*, Jan.–Feb, pp. 2–3

Hayward, K. (2001) 'The Chicago School', in E. McLaughlin and J. Muncie.(Eds), *Sage Dictionary of Criminology*, London: Sage

Hayward, K. (2007) 'Situational crime prevention and its discontents', *Social Policy & Administration*, Vol. 4, No. 3, pp. 232–250

Hayward, K. (2012) 'Five spaces of cultural criminology', *British Journal of Criminology*, Vol. 52, pp. 441–462

Hayward, K., Maruna, S. and Mooney, J. (2010) *Fifty Key Thinkers in Criminology*, Oxon: Routledge

Hayward, K., and Schuilenburg, M. B. (2014). To Resist = to Create? Some Thoughts on the Concept of Resistance in Cultural Criminology, *Tijdschrift over cultuur & criminaliteit*, Vol. 4, No. 1, pp. 22–36

Hayward, K. and Young, J. (2004) 'Cultural criminology: Some notes on the script', *Theoretical Criminology*, Vol. 8, No. 3, pp. 259–273

Hazlitt, W. (1825) *The Spirit of the Age*, London: Henry Colburn

Hearn, J. and Morgan, D. (1990) *Men, Masculinities and Social Theory*, London: Unwin Hyman

Hebberecht, P. (2010) 'Willem Bonger', in K. Hayward, S. Maruna and J. Mooney (Eds), *Fifty Key Thinkers in Criminology*, London: Routledge

Heidensohn, F. (1968) 'The deviance of women: A critique and an enquiry', *British Journal of Sociology*, Vol. XIX, No. 2, pp. 160–175

Heidensohn, F. (1985) *Women and Crime*, Basingstoke: Palgrave Macmillan

Heidensohn, F. (1994) 'Gender and crime', in M. Maguire, R. Morgan and R. Reiner (Eds), *The Oxford Handbook of Criminology*, Oxford: Clarendon Press

Heidensohn, F. and Rafter, N. (1995) *International Feminist Perspectives in Criminology*, Milton Keynes: Open University Press

Heidensohn, F. and Silvestri, M. (2012) 'Gender and crime', in R. Morgan, M. Maguire and R. Reiner (Eds), *The Oxford Handbook of Criminology*, Oxford: Clarendon Press (Fifth Edition)

Helvie-Mason, L. (2010) 'Pivotal communication: Marion Talbot's voice for educational equity', *Vitae Scholasticae*, Vol. 27, No. 2

Henderson, C. (1893, 1902 ed) *Introduction to the Study of the Dependent, Defective and Delinquent Classes*, London: D.C Heath

Henne, K. and Troshynski, E. (2013) 'Mapping the margins of intersectionality: Criminological possibilities in a transnational world', *Theoretical Criminology*, Vol. 17, No. 4, pp. 455–473

Herrick, J. (1985) *Against the Faith: Essays on Deists, Skeptics and Atheists*, London: Prometheus Books

Herrnstein, R. and Murray, C. (1994) *The Bell Curve*, New York: The Free Press

Hewitt, N. (2000) 'Beyond the search for sisterhood: American women's history in the 1990s', in V. Ruiz and E. C. DuBois (Eds), *Unequal Sisters: A Multicultural Reader in U.S. Women's History*, New York: Routledge

Hill, M. (2005) 'Harriet Martineau's Ambleside as a sociological laboratory', *Sociological Origins*, Spring, pp. 93–94

Hillyard, P. (2009) 'The "exceptional" state', in R. Coleman, J. Sim, S. Tombs and D. Whyte (Eds), *State, Power, Crime*, London: Sage

Hillyard, P. (1993) *Suspect Community*, London: Pluto Press

Hillyard, P., Pantazis, C., Tombs, S. and Gordon, D. (2004 eds) *Beyond Criminology: Taking Harm Seriously*, London: Pluto Press

Himmelfarb, G. (1968) 'The haunted house of Jeremy Bentham', in G. Himmelfarb (Ed), *Victorian Minds*, New York: Knopf

Hines, S. (2017) 'The feminist frontier: On trans and feminism', *Journal of Gender Studies*, Vol. 28, No. 2, pp. 145–157

Hirsch, A. (1991) *The Rise of the Penitentiary*, New Haven: Yale University Press

Hirschfeld Davis, J., Stolberg, S.G, and Kaplan, T. (2018) *Trump alarms lawmakers with disparaging words for Haiti and Africa*, New York Times, Jan. 11

Hirschi, T. (1969) *Causes of Delinquency*, New Brunswick, NJ; Transaction Publishers

Hirst, P. (1975) 'Marx and Engels on law, crime and morality', in I. Taylor, P. Walton and J. Young (Eds), *Critical Criminology*, London: Routledge & Kegan Paul

Hobsbawn, E. (1962) *The Age of Revolution, 1789–1848*, London: Weidenfeld & Nicolson

Hogenboom, M. (2014) 'Two genes linked with violent crime', *BBC*, Oct. 28

Holbrook, A. S. (1895, 2007 ed) 'Map notes and comments', in Hull House Residents (Ed), *Hull House Maps and Papers*, Urbana and Chicago: University of Illinois Press

Holmes, O. W (1900) *Montesquieu*, New York: D. Appleton and Company

Holson, L. (2019) 'Murders by intimate partners are on the rise, study finds', *New York Times*, Apr. 12

Holt, T. (1999) 'Du Bois, W.E.B', *American National Biography*

Hooton, E. (1939) *Crime and the Man*, Cambridge, MA: Harvard University Press

Howe, A. (2008) 'Violence against women: Rethinking the local-global nexus in feminist strategy', in M. Cain and A. Howe (Eds), *Women, Crime and Social Harm: Towards a Criminology for a Global Age*, Oxford: Hart

Hume, D. (1751) *An Enquiry Concerning the Principles of Morals*, London: A Millar

Iannantuoni, D. (2009) accessed at: www.nolombroso.org/

Indigenous Environmental Network (2019) accessed at: www.ienearth.org/

Iseman, R. (1972) 'The criminal responsibility of corporate officials for pollution of the environment', *Albany Law Review*, Vol. 37, No. 1, pp. 61–96

Jackson, L. (2011) 'Review of Logan's *Feminism and Criminal Justice: A Historical Perspective*', *Crime, History & Society*, Vol. 15, No. 1, pp. 155–158

Jackson, R. (1998) 'Jeremy Bentham and the New South Wales convicts', *International Journal of Social Economics*, Vol. 25, No. 2–4, pp. 370–379

Jackson, S. (1993) 'Feminist social theory', in S. Jackson (Ed), *Women Studies: A Reader*, London: Harvester Wheatsheaf

Jaggar, A. (1983) *Feminist Politics and Human Nature*, Brighton: Harvester Press

Jalata, A. (2013) 'The impacts of English colonial terrorism and genocide on Indigenous/ Black Australians', *Sage Open*, pp. 1–12

Jamieson, R. (1998) 'Towards a criminology of war in Europe', in V. Ruggiero, N. South and I. Taylor (Eds), *The New European Criminology*, London: Routledge

Jamieson, R. (1999) 'Genocide and the social production of immorality', *Theoretical Criminology*, Vol. 3, No. 2, pp. 131–146

Jamieson, R. (2014) *The Criminology of War*, Aldershot: Ashgate

Jamieson, R. (2015) 'Through the lens of war: Political imprisonment in Northern Ireland', in S. Walklate and R McGarry (Eds), *Criminology and War*, Oxon: Routledge

Jamieson, R. and McEvoy, K. (2005) 'State crime by proxy and juridical othering', *British Journal of Criminology*, Vol. 45, pp. 504–537

Jassie, K. (1996) *Popular Attitudes Toward Justice and Authority During the Old Regime and the French Revolution: Paris, 1720–1794*, PhD thesis, University of Wisconsin- Madison

Jefferson, T. (1975) 'Cultural responses of the Teds: The defence of space and status', in S. Hall and T. Jefferson (Eds), *Resistance Through Rituals*, London: Hutchinson

Jefferson, T. (1997) 'Masculinities and crime', in M. Maguire, R. Morgan and R.Reiner (Eds), *The Oxford Handbook of Criminology*, Oxford: Clarendon Press

Jeffreys, S. (2009) *The Industrial Vagina*, Oxon: Routledge

Jeffreys, S. (2012) 'Let us be free to debate trangenderism...', *The Guardian*, May 21, accessed at: https://www.theguardian.com/commentisfree/2012/may/29/transgenderism-hate-speech

Jenkins, P. (1984) 'Varieties of enlightenment criminology', *British Journal of Criminology*, Vol. 24, No. 2, pp. 120–130

John Howard Association (2019) 'Our history', accessed at: http/thejhc.org

Johnson, S. (2016) 'BRANDED: Trademark tattoos, slave owner brands, and the right to have "free skin"', (emphasis as in the original), *Michigan Telecommunications and Technology Law Review*, Vol. 22, No. 2

Jones, T., MacLean, B. and Young, J. (1986) *The First Islington Crime Survey*, Aldershot: Gower

Jones, A. (2006) *A Comprehensive Introduction to Genocide*, Oxon: Routledge

Jordan, J. (2010) 'Susan Brownmiller', in K. Hayward, S. Maruna and J. Mooney (Eds), *Fifty Key Thinkers in Criminology*, London: Routledge

Jordan, J. and Sharp, S. (2003 eds) *Josephine Butler and the Prostitution Campaigns: The Moral Reclaimability of Prostitutes*, London: Routledge

Joy, T. (2018) *The Problem with Privately Run Prisons*, Washington, DC: Justice Policy Institute

Jupp, V. (1989) *Methods of Criminological Research*, London: Unwin Hyman

Kaplan, S. (1982) 'The famine plot persuasion in eighteenth century France', *Transactions of the American Philosophical Society*. Vol. 72, No. 3, pp. 1–79

Kaplan, S. (1984) *Provisioning Paris*, Ithaca: Cornell University Press

Kasson, J. (2015) *Buffalo Bill's Wild West: Celebrity, Memory, and Popular History*, New York: Farrar, Straus and Giroux

Katz, J. (1988) *Seductions of Crime*, New York: Basic Books

Katz, J. (1999) *How Emotions Work*, Chicago: University of Chicago Press

Kelley, F. and Stevens, A. (1895, 2007 ed) 'Wage-earning children', in Residents of Hull House (Ed), *Hull House Maps and Papers*, New York: Thomas. Y Crowell Co

Kellor, F. (1898) 'Sex in crime', *International Journal of Ethics*, Vol. 9, No. 1, pp. 74–85

Kellor, F. (1900a) 'Psychological and environmental study of women criminals I', *American Journal of Sociology*, Vol. 5, No. 4

Kellor, F. (1900b) 'Psychological and environmental study of women criminals II', *American Journal of Sociology*, Vol. 5, No. 5

Kellor, F. (1901a) *Experimental Sociology, Descriptive and Analytical: Delinquents*, London: Macmillan and Co.

Kellor, F. (1901b) 'The criminal Negro', *The Arena*, Vol. 25

Kelly, L. (1988) *Surviving Sexual Violence*, Cambridge: Polity Press

Kelly, L. and Regan, L. (2000) *Stopping Traffic: Exploring the Extent of, and Responses to, Trafficking in Women for Sexual Exploitation in the UK*, London: Home Office

Kevan, P. (2007) '"Common Prostitute" erased from law', *Metro News*, 26 June

Kimmel, M. (1993) 'Invisible masculinity', *Society*, Vol. 30, No. 6, p. 28

Kinsey, R. (1985) *First Report of the Merseyside Crime Survey*, Liverpool: Merseyside County Council

Kish Sklar, K. (1995) *Florence Kelley & the Nation's Work*, New Haven and London: Yale University Press

Kitsuse, J. (1971) 'Deviance, deviant behaviour and deviants', in W. Filstead (Ed) *An Introduction to Deviance*, Chicago: Markham

Knepper, P. and Ystehede, P. (2013) *The Cesare Lombroso Handbook*, Oxon: Routledge

Knight, L. (2010) *Jane Addams: Spirit in Action*, New York: W.W. Norton & Co

Knowles, G. (2007) 'Friedrich von Spee', at: www.controverscial.com

Kontos, L. (2020) *New Deviancy Theory*, New York: Rowman & Littlefield

Kossew Pichanick, V. (1977) 'An abominable submission: Harriet Martineau's views on the role and place of woman', *Women's Studies: An Interdisciplinary Journal*, Vol. 5, No. 1, pp. 13–32

Koyamae, E. (2001) *The Transfeminist Manifesto*, accessed at: http://eminism.org/readings/pdf-rdg/tfmanifesto.pdf

Kropotkin, P. (1887) 'Are prisons necessary', accessed at: www.panarchy.org/kropotkin/prisons.html

Kropotkin, P. (1902) 'Mutual aid: A factor of evolution', accessed at: *The Anarchist Library*

Kropotkin, P. (1905) 'Anarchy', accessed at: www.panarchy.org/kropotkin/

Kwei, S. (2015) 'Why I protested with Sisters Uncut at the Suffragette premiere: We wanted to use the publicity of the night to remind the world that the fight is far from over', *The Independent*, Oct. 8, p. 22

Lacassagne, A. (1880) *Le tatouage: Etudes anthropologique et medico-legale*, Tattooing: Anthropologic and Forensic Studies. N.C. N.P.

Laidlaw, L. (2016) Trans representation and the criminological implications', Nov. 26, at: http//wwwrobson.crm.com

Lanier, M. and Henry, S. (1998, 2004 ed) *Essential Criminology*, Boulder, CO: Westview Press

Lathrop, J. (1895, 2007 ed) 'The cook county charities', in Residents of Hull House (Ed), *Hull House Maps and Papers*, Urbana and Chicago: University of Illinois Press

Lathrop, J. (1912) 'The Children's Bureau', *American Journal of Sociology*, Vol. 18, No. 3. Pp. 318–330

Laub, J. (2004) 'The life course of criminology in the United States: The American Society of Criminology 2003 Presidential Address', *Criminology*, Vol. 42, No. 1, pp. 1–26

Laub, J. and Sampson, R. (1991) 'The Sutherland-Glueck debate', *American Journal of Sociology*, Vol. 96, No. 6, pp. 1402–1440

Lavan, G., (1955) 'DuBois's early study of the slave trade', *Fourth International*, Vol. 16, No. 3, pp. 105–106.

Lavater, J. (1878 ed) *Essays on Physiognomy*, London: W. Tegg

Lawrence, P. (2012) 'History, criminology and the "use" of the past', *Theoretical Criminology*, Vol. 16, No. 3, pp. 313–328

Lea, H. (1901) *The History of the Inquisition of the Middle Ages*, 4 vols, New York: Franklin Square

Lea, J. (1992) 'The analysis of crime', in J. Young and R. Matthews (Eds), *Rethinking Criminology: The Realist Debate*, London: Sage

Lea, J. (2002) *Crime and Modernity*, London: Sage

Lea, J. (2010) 'Karl Marx and Frederick Engels', in K. Hayward, S. Maruna and J. Mooney (Eds), *Fifty Key Thinkers in Criminology*, London: Routledge

Lea, J., Jones, T. and Young, J. (1988) *Saving the Inner City: Broadwater Farm*, Middlesex Polytechic: Centre for Criminology

Lea, J. and Young, J. (1984) *What Is to Be Done About Law and Order?* Harmondsworth: Penguin

Lee, R. (2017) 'Beyond "get the seat of your pants dirty in real research": Park on methods', in P. Kivisto (Ed), *The Anthem Companion to Robert Park*, London: Anthem Press

Lees, S. (1996) *Carnal Knowledge: Rape on Trial*, London: Penguin

Lemert, C. (2000) 'Charlotte Perkins Gilman', in G. Ritzer (Ed), *The Blackwell Companion to Major Classical Social Theorists*, Oxford: Blackwells

Lemert, E. (1951) *Social Pathology: A Systematic Approach to the Theory of Sociopathic Behavior*, New York, NY: McGraw Hill

Lengermann, P. and Niebrugge-Brantley, J. (1998) *The Women Founders: Sociology and Social Theory, 1830–1930*, New York: McGraw-Hill

Lewis, L. (1940) 'The house that Jane Addams built', accessed at: www.swarthmore.edu/library/peace/DG001-025/DG001JAddams/series04.html

Lilly, J. R., Cullen, F. and Ball, R. (1989, 2007, 2011 eds) *Criminological Theory: Context and Consequences*, Thousand Oaks, CA: Sage

Limoli, D. A. (1958) 'Pietro Verri: A Lombard reformer under enlightened absolutism and the French Revolution', *Journal of Central European Affairs*, Vol. 18, pp. 254–280

Lindner, R. (1996) *The Reportage of Urban Culture: Robert Park and the Chicago School*, Cambridge: Cambridge University Press

Locke, J. (1690, 1924 ed) *Two Treatises of Government*, London: Dent

Logan, A. (2006a) *Feminism and Criminal Justice: A Historical Perspective*, London: Palgrave Macmillan

Logan, A. (2006b) 'Professionalism and the impact of England's first women justices, 1920–1950', *The Historical Journal*, Vol. 49, No. 3, pp. 833–850

Lombroso, C. (1871) *The White Man and the Man of Colour*, Sacchetto: Padua

Lombroso, C. (1876, 2006 ed) *Criminal Man*, Durham, NC: Duke University Press

Lombroso, C. (1891) *Man of Genius*, London: W. Scott

Lombroso, C. (1896) 'The savage origin of tattooing', *Popular Science Monthly*, Vol. 48, Apr.

Lombroso, C. (1897) 'Anarachy and its heroes', in A. Bérard, *Les mystiques de l'anarchie*, Lyon: A.-H. Storck

Lombroso, C. (1898) 'Why homicide has increased in the United States: Barbarism and Civilisation', *The North American Review*

Lombroso, C. (1902) 'The Last Brigand', in *Nuova Antologia*, 181, pp. 508–516

Lombroso, C. (1918 ed), *Crime, Its Causes and Remedies*, Boston: Little Brown

Lombroso, C. (1984 ed) in L. Opul'skaya (Ed), *Tolstoj nelle memorie dei contemporanei*, Moscow: Raduga

Lombroso, C. and Ferrero, G. (1876, 1911 ed) *Criminal Man*, London: GP Putnam's Sons

Lombroso, C. and Ferrero, G. (1893, 1895, 2004 ed) *Criminal Woman, the Prostitute and the Normal Woman*, Durham, NC: Duke University Press

Long, G. (1837 ed) *Penny Cyclopaedia*, Vol. 8, London: Charles Knight and Co.

Lukes, S. (1969) 'Durkheim's "Individualism and the Intellectuals"', *Political Studies*, Vol. 17, No. 1, pp. 14–30

Lukes, S. (1973, 1985 ed) *Emile Durkheim, His Life and Work*, London: Penguin

Lynch, M. (1990) 'The greening of criminology: A perspective on the 1990s', *Critical Criminologist*, Vol. 2, No. 3

Lyon, D. (2001) *Surveillance Society*, Buckingham: Open University Press

Lytton, C. (1914) *Prisons and Prisoners: Some Personal Experiences*, London: William Heinemann

MacArthur, R.H and Wilson, E.O. (1967) *The Theory of Island Biogeography*, Princeton, NJ: Princeton University Press
MacFarlane, C. (1844) *The French Revolution*, London: Charles, Knight and Company
Macionis, J. and Plummer, K. (2008) *Sociology*, London: Pearsons
Mackay, F. (2015) *Radical Feminism: Feminist Activism in Movement*, London: Palgrave Macmillan
MacKinnon, C. (1989) *Toward a Feminist Theory of the State*, Cambridge, MA: Harvard University Press
Mackinnon, J. (1902) *The Growth and Decline of the French Monarchy*, London: Longmans, Green and Co.
MacLean, A. M. (1899) 'Two weeks in department stores', *American Journal of Sociology*, Vol. 4, No. 6, pp. 721–741
MacLean, A. M. (1903) 'The sweat-shop in summer', *American Journal of Sociology*, Vol. 9, No. 3, pp. 289–309
MacLean, A. M. (1923) 'Four months in a model factory', *Century*, No. 106, pp. 436–444
Maestro, M. (1942) *Voltaire and Beccaria as Reformers of the Criminal Law*, New York: Columbia University Press
Maier-Katkin, D. (2003) 'On Sir Leon Radzinowicz reading Michel Foucault', *Punishment and Society*, Vol. 5, No. 2, pp. 155–177
Mama, A. (2000) 'Violence against Black women in the home', in J. Hanmer and C. Itzin (Eds), *Home Truths About Domestic Violence*, Oxon: Routledge
Mann, M. (2005) *The Darkside of Democracy*, Cambridge: Cambridge University Press
Manzoni, A. (1845) *The Column of Infamy*, London: Longman, Brown, Green and Longmans
Marshall, E. (1914) 'New York's first woman commissioner of correction', *New York Times*, Jan. 11, pp. 6–7
Marshall Project, (2015) at: www.themarshallproject.org/
Martin, J. J. (2014) 'Introduction: Manzoni and the making of Italy', in C. Povolo (Ed), *The Novelist and the Archivist*, London: Palgrave Macmillan
Martineau, H. (1837) *Society in America*, New York: Saunders and Otley
Marx, K. (1842, 1975 ed) 'Debates on the law of the theft of wood', in K. Marx and F. Engels, *Collected Works*, Vol. 1, London: Lawrence and Wishart
Marx, K. (1845, 1970 ed) *The German Ideology*, London: Lawrence and Wishart
Marx, K. (1852) *The Eighteenth Brumaire of Louis Bonaparte*, New York: International Publishers
Marx, K. (1867, 1921 ed, 1977 ed, 2018 ed) *Capital, a Critique of Political Economy*, Chicago: Charles H. Kerr & Co.
Marx, K. (1971 ed) 'Record of a speech on the Irish question delivered by Karl Marx to the German Workers' Educational Association in London on Dec. 16, 1867' in K. Marx (Ed), *Ireland and the Irish Question*, Moscow: Progress Publishers
Marx, K. (2005 ed) *The Paris Commune*, Socialist Labor Party of America, accessed at: www.slp.org/pdf/marx/paris_com.pdf
Marx, K. and Engels, F. (1975 ed) in S. W. Ryazanskaya (Ed), *Selected Correspondence*, Moscow: Progress
Marx, K. and Engels, F. (1848, 1998 ed.) *The Communist Manifesto*, London: The Communist League
Mason, D. and Frick, P. (1994) 'The heritability of anti-social anti-viol: A meta-analysis of twin and adoption studies', *Journal of Psychopathology and Behavioral Assessment*, Vol. 16, No. 4, pp. 301–323
Matthews, J. (2010) *Naples, Life, Death and Miracles*, at: www.naplesldm.com/bandits.php

Matthews, R. (1999) *Doing Time: An Introduction to the Sociology of Imprisonment*, London: Palgrave Macmillan

Matthews, R. (2003) 'Marxist criminology', in M. Schwartz and S. Hatty (Eds), *Controversies in Critical Criminology*, Cincinnati, OH: Anderson

Matthews, R. and Young, J. (1986 eds) *Confronting Crime*, London: Sage

Matthews, R. and Young, J. (Eds) (2003) *The New Politics of Crime and Punishment*, Cullompton: Willan

Matza, D. (1964) *Delinquency and Drift*, New York: Wiley

Matza, D. (1969) *Becoming Deviant*, Englewood Cliffs, NJ: Prentice Hall

Matza, D. and Sykes, G. (1961) 'Juvenile delinquency and subterranean values', *American Sociological Review*, Vol. 26, No. 5, pp. 712–719

Maxwell-Stewart, H. (2010) 'Convict transportation from Britain and Ireland 1625–1870', *History Compass*, Vol. 8, No. 11, pp. 1221–1242

Mayhew, H. (1861) *London Labour and the London Poor*, accessed at: www.bl.uk/collection-items/1861-edition-of-london-labour-and-the-london-poor-by-henry-mayhew

Maynard, M. (1989) *Sociological Theory*, London: Longman

Maynard, M. (1993) 'Violence towards women', in D. Richardson and V. Robinson (Eds), *Introducing Women's Studies*, Basingstoke: Palgrave Macmillan

Mazzarello. P. (2001) 'Lombroso and Tolstoy', *Nature*, Vol. 409, No. 6823, p. 983

Mazzarello, P. (2011) 'Cesare Lombroso: An anthropologist between evolution and degeneration', *A Functional Neurological*, Vol. 26, No. 2, pp. 97–101

McCarthy, T. (1997) *New York City's Suffragist Commissioner: Correction's Katharine Bement Davis*, accessed at: www.correctionhistory.org/html/chronicl/pdf/kbd01.pdf

McCarthy, T. (1997) New York Correction History Society, accessed at: www.correctionhistory.org

McLennan, G. (2013) 'Postcolonial critique: The necessity of sociology', *Political Power and Social Theory*, Vol. 24, pp. 119–144

McLennan, G. (2018) *Plenary at the New Zealand Sociology Conference*, Wellington, New Zealand

McLennan, R. (2008) *The Crisis of Imprisonment*, Cambridge: Cambridge University Press

McMullan, T. (2015) 'What does the panopticon mean in the age of digital surveillance?' *The Guardian*, Jul. 23

McMurry, L. (1980) 'A black intellectual in the New South: Monroe Nathan Work, 1866–1945', *Phylon*, Vol. 41, No. 4, pp. 333–344

McRobbie, A. (1980) 'Settling accounts with subcultures: A feminist critique', *Screen Education*, Vol. 34, pp. 37–49

McRobbie, A. and Garber, J. (1976) 'Girls and subcultures: An exploration', in S. Hall and T. Jefferson (Eds), *Resistance Through Rituals*, London: Hutchinson

McVicar, J. (1979) *McVicar by Himself*, London: Arrow

Medea, A. and Thompson, K. (1974) *Against Rape*, New York: Farrar, Straus & Giroux

Meier, R. and Geis, G. (1997) *Victimless Crimes? Prostitution, Drugs, Homosexuality, Abortion*, Los Angeles, CA: Roxbury Publishing Co.

Melossi, D. (2001) 'The global embeddedness of social control', *Theoretical Criminology*, Vol. 5, No. 4, pp. 403–424

Melossi, D. (2003) 'The simple "heuristic maxim" of an 'unusual human being', in G. Rusche and O. Kirchheimer (Eds), *Punishment and Social Structure*, New York: Columbia University Press

Melossi, D. (2008) *Controlling Crime, Controlling Society*, Cambridge: Polity

Melossi, D. (2009) in *Punishment and Social Structure*, New York: Columbia University Press
Merton, R. (1934) 'Durkheim's division of labor in society', *American Journal of Sociology*, Vol. 40, No. 3, pp. 319–328
Merton, R. (1938) 'Social structure and anomie', *American Sociological Review*, Vol. 3, pp. 672–682
Merton, R. (1957) 'Priorities in scientific discovery', *American Sociological Review*, Vol. 22, pp. 635–659
Merton, R. (1997) 'A life of learning', in K. Erikson (Ed) *Sociological Visions*, Lanham: Rowan & Littlefield
Merton, R. and Ashley-Montagne, M. F. (1940) 'Crime and the anthropologist', *American Anthropologist*, Vol. 42, No. 3, pp. 384–408
Messbarger, R. (1999) 'Reforming the female class: 'Il Caffe's "Defense of Women"', *Eighteenth-Century Studies*, Vol. 32, No. 3, pp. 355–369
Messerschmidt, J. (1988) 'From Marx to Bonger: Socialist writings on women, gender and crime', *Sociological Inquiry*, Vol. 58, No. 4, pp. 378–392
Messerschmidt, J. (1993) *Masculinities and Crime: Critique and Reconceptualization of Theory*, Langham, MD: Rowman & Littlefield
Messerschmidt, J. (1997) *Crime as Structured Action: Gender, Race, Class, and Crime in the Making*, London: Sage
Michalowski, R. J. and Carlson, S. M. (1999) Unemployment, imprisonment and social studies of accumulation: Historical contingency in the Rusche-Kirchheimer hypothesis', *Criminology*, Vol. 37, No. 2, pp. 217–250
Mies, M. (1986) *Patriarchy and Accumulation on a World Scale*, London: Zed Books
Miquel, P. (1964) *L'Affaire Dreyfus*, Paris: Presses Universitaires de France
Miles-Johnson, T. (2015) 'Policing transgender people', *Sage Open*, pp. 1–14
Millett, K. (1969, 1977 ed) *Sexual Politics*, London Virago
Mills, C. W. (1959) *The Sociological Imagination*, New York: Oxford University Press
Mills, C. W. (1964) *Sociology and Pragmatism*, New York: Paine-Whitman
Mir-Hosseini, Z. (2011) 'Criminalizing sexuality: Zina laws as violence against women in muslim contexts', *Sur International Journal on Human Rights*, Vol. 15, No. 1, pp. 7–34.
Mitchell, C. (1989) 'Madeleine Pelletier (1874–1939): The politics of sexual oppression', *Feminist Review*, No. 33, pp. 72–92
Mitchell Jr., S. A. (1866 circa) *Mitchell's New General Atlas, Containing Maps of the Various Countries of the World Plans of Cities, Etc. Embraced in Fifty-Five Quarto Maps. Forming a series of Eighty-Seven Maps and Plans. Together with Valuable Statistical Tables*, Philadelphia
Mohammad, K. G. (2010) *The Condemnation of Blackness*, Cambridge, MA: Harvard University Press
Mohanty, C. (1988) 'Under western eyes: feminist scholarship and colonial discourses', *Feminist Review*, Vol. 30, No. 1, pp. 61–88
Mohanty, C. (1991) 'Cartographies of struggle: Third World women and the politics of feminism', in C. Mohanty, A. Russo and L. Torres (Eds), *Third World Women and the Politics of Feminism*, Bloomington, IN: Indiana University Press
Monachesi, E. (1955) 'Cesare Beccaria', in H. Mannheim (Ed), *Pioneers in Criminology*, Newark: Patterson-Smith
Montaldo, S. (2013) 'The Lombroso Museum from its origins to the present day', in P. Knepper and P. Ystehede (Eds), *The Cesare Lombroso Handbook*, Oxon: Routledge
Montesquieu (1736–1743, 1977 ed) 'An essay on causes affecting minds and characters', in D. Carrithers (Ed), *The Spirit of Laws*, Berkeley: University of California Press

Montesquieu (1748, 1766 ed) *The Spirit of Laws*, London: J. Nourse and P. Vaillant
Mooney, J. (1992) *Street Robbery in Islington*, London: Middlesex Polytechnic
Mooney, J. (1997) 'Moral panics and the new right', in P. Walton and J. Young (Eds), *The New Criminology Revisited*, London: Macmillan
Mooney, J. (2000) *Gender, Violence and the Social Order*, London: Palgrave Macmillan
Mooney, J. (2003) 'It's the family stupid', in R. Matthews and J. Young (Eds), *The New Politics of Crime and Punishment*, Cullompton: Willan
Mooney, J. (2010) 'Frances Heidensohn', in K. Hayward, S. Maruna and J. Mooney (Eds), *Fifty Key Thinkers in Criminology*, London: Routledge
Mooney, J. (2014) 'A tale of two regicides', *European Journal of Criminology*, Vol. 11, No. 2, pp. 228–250
Mooney, J. and Shanahan, J. (2020) 'Rikers Island: The failure of a 'model' penitentiary', *Prison Journal*
Mooney, J. and Young, J. (2005) 'Imagining terrorism: Terrorism and anti-terrorism, two ways of doing evil', *Social Justice*, Vol. 32, No. 1, pp. 113–125
Mooney, J. and Young, J. (2013) 'Realism with energy, culture with realism', unpublished paper
Morgan, R. (2000) 'The utilitarian justification of torture', *Punishment and Society*, Vol. 2, No. 2, pp. 181–196
Morley, J. (1913) *Voltaire*, London: Macmillan and Company
Morris, A. (1987) *Women, Crime and Criminal Justice*, Oxford: Basil Blackwell
Morris, A. D. (2015) *The Scholar Denied: W. E. B. Du Bois and the Birth of Modern Sociology*, Oakland: University of California Press
Morrison, K. (2006) *Marx, Durkheim and Weber: Formations of Modern Social Thought*, London: Sage
Morrison, W. (1999) *Theoretical Criminology*, London: Cavendish
Morrison, W. (2004) 'Criminology, genocide and modernity', in C. Sumner (Ed), *The Blackwell Companion to Criminology*, Cambridge: Blackwell
Morrison, W. (2013) *Criminology, Civilisation and the New World Order*, Oxon: Routledge
Mudimbe, V. Y. (1988) *The Invention of Africa*, Bloomington, IN: Indiana University Press
Muhammad, K. G. (2010) *The Condemnation of Blackness*, Cambridge, MA: Harvard University Press
Murray, C. and Herrnstein, R. (1994) *The Bell Curve*, New York: Free Press
Naffine, N. (1990) *Law and the Sexes*, Sydney: Allen and Unwin
National Women's History Museum (2017) 'Ida B. Wells-Barnett', accessed at: www.womenshistory.org/education-resources/biographies/ida-b-wells-barnett
Neal, L. (2017) 'What remains of the 1893 Chicago world's fair today', at: http://allthatsinteresting.com/1893-chicago-worlds-fair
Newburn, T. (2017) *Criminology*, Oxon: Routledge
Newburn, T. and Stanko, B. (1994 eds) *Just Boys Doing Business? Men, Masculinities and Crime*, London: Routledge
Niagara Movement (1905) *Declaration of Principles*, at: https://glc.yale.edu/niagaras-declaration-principles
Norris, C. and Armstrong, G. (1999) *The Maximum Surveillance Society*, Oxford: Berg
Novak, M. (2013) 'Where the future comes from: A trip through the 1893 Chicago world's fair', at: https://paleofuture.gizmodo.com/where-the-future-came-from-a-trip-through-the-1893-chi-743942247

Nurse, A. (2015) *An Introduction to Green Criminology and Environmental Justice*, London: Sage

Oakley, A. (2017) 'The forgotten example of settlement sociology', *Research for All*, Vol. 1, No. 1, p. 20

Odora-Hoppers, C. (2002 ed), *Indigenous Knowledge and the Integration of Knowledge Systems: Towards a Philosophy of Articulation*, Claremont, South Africa: New Africa Book

Offen, K. (2000) *European Feminisms, 1700–1950: A Political History*, Stanford: Stanford University Press

Ogburn, W. F. (1929) 'American sociological society presidential address', at: www.asanet.org/sites/default/files/savvy/images/asa/docs/pdf/1929%20Presidential %20Address%20(William%20Ogburn).pdf

Ohlin, L. and Tonry, M. (1989 eds) *Family Violence*, Chicago: University of Chicago Press

Olshansky, B. (2002) *Secret Trials and Executions*, Canada: Center for Constitutional Rights

O'Malley, P. (2010) 'Jeremy Bentham', in K. Hayward, S. Maruna and J. Mooney (eds), *Fifty Key Thinkers in Criminology*, Oxon: Routledge

Okin, S. M. (1998) 'Gender, the public and private', in A. Phillips (Ed), *Feminism and Politics*, Oxford: Oxford University Press

Oriola, T. B. (2006) 'Biko Agozino and the rise of post-colonial criminology', *African Journal of Criminal and Justice Studies*, Vo. 2, No. 1

Ortiz Rodriguez, Y. (2016) *Help Seeking Latina Victims of Domestic Violence and the Programs That Serve Them in New York City*, PhD thesis, City University of New York

Ortiz Rodriguez, Y. and Mooney, J. (2018) 'Que diran? Making sense of the impact of Latinas' experiences of intimate partner violence in New York City', in K. Fitz-Gibbon, S. Walklate, J. McCulloch and J. Maher (Eds), *Intimate Partner Violence, Risk and Security*, Oxon: Routledge

Osmundson, L. (2016) 'Women of color: Leadership in the battered women's movement', *Community Action Stops Abuse*, at: http:/www.casa-stpete.org

Owen, T. (2012) 'The biological and the social in criminological theory', in S. Hall and S. Winlow (Eds), *New Directions in Criminological Theory*, Oxon: Routledge

Paine, T. (1791) *Rights of man*, New York: Eckler

Paolucci, H. (1963) *Introduction to On Crimes and Punishments*, London: Palgrave Macmillan

Park, R. E. (1928) 'Human migrationa and the marginal man', *American Journal of Sociology*, Vol. 33, No. 6, pp. 881–893

Park, R. E. (1936) 'Sucession, an ecological concept', *American Sociological Review*, Vol. 1, No. 2, pp. 171–179

Park, R. E. (1952) *Human Communities: The City and Human Ecology*, Glencoe, IL: Free Press

Park, R. E. (1974) 'The city as a social laboratory', in *Human Communities: The City and Human Ecology*, New York: Arno

Park, R. E. and Burgess, E. W. (1921, 1924 ed) *Introduction to the Science of Sociology*, Chicago: University of Chicago Press

Park, R. E., Burgess, E. W. and McKenzie, R. (1925) *The City*, Chicago: Chicago University Press

Parmar, A. (2016) 'Race, ethnicity and criminal justice: Refocusing the criminological gaze', in M. Bosworth, C. Hoyle and L. Zedner (Eds), *Changing Contours of Criminal Justice*, Oxford: Oxford University Press

Parsons, T. (1947) 'Certain primary sources and patterns of aggression in the social structure of the Western world', *Psychiatry*, X, May, pp. 167–181

Pateman, C. (1988) *The Sexual Contract*, Cambridge: Polity Press

Payne, G., Dingwall, R., Payne, J. and Carter, M. (1981) *Sociology and Social Research*, London: Routledge and Kegan Paul

Pearce, F. (2001) *The Radical Durkheim*, Toronto: The Canadian Scholars Press

Pearson, G. (1978) 'Goths and vandals – crime in history', *Contemporary Crises*, pp. 119–139

Pepinsky, H. (2013) 'Peacemaking criminology', *Critical Criminology*, Vol. 21, pp. 319–339

Pfohl, S. (1985) *Images of Deviance and Social Control: A Sociological History*, Englewood Cliffs, NJ: McGraw Hill

Pfohl, S. (1998) 'Deviance and social control course outline', at: https://www2.bc.edu/stephen-pfohl/deviance.html

Pfohl, S. (2003) 'Preface to B. Agozino', in *Counter-Colonial Criminology: A Critique of Imperialist Reason*, London: Pluto Press

Phelan, T. (1989) 'From the attic of the "American Journal of Sociology": Unusual contributions to American sociology, 1895–1935', *Sociological Forum*, Vol. 4, No. 1, pp. 71–86

Phillips, A. (1998) *Feminism and Politics*, Oxford: Basil Blackwell

Phillips, A. and Taylor, B. (1980) 'Sex and skill: Notes towards a feminist economics', *Feminist Review*, Vol. 6, pp. 79–8

Phillipson, C. (1923) Three Criminal Law Reformers: Beccaria, Bentham, Romilly, New York: J.M. Dent & Sons

Pick, D. (1986) 'The faces of anarchy: Lombroso and the politics of criminal science in post-unification Italy', *History Workshop Journal*, Vol. 21, No. 1, Mar., pp. 60–86

Pick, D. (1993) *Faces of Degeneration*, Cambridge: Cambridge University Press

Pick, D. (2004) 'Review of Mary Gibson's *Born to Crime*', *The American Historical Review*, Vol. 109, p. 641

Platt, A. (1969) *The Child Savers*, Chicago: University of Chicago Press

Platt, A. (1974) 'Prospects for a radical criminology in the United States', *Crime and Social Justice*, No. 1, pp. 2–10

Platt, A. and Takagi, P. (1980 eds) *Punishment and Penal Discipline: Essays on the Prison and the Prisoners Movement*, Berkeley, CA: Crime and Social Justice Associates

Platt, A. et al (1973) *Newsletter of the Union of Radical Criminologists*, Berkeley, CA

Pleck, E. (1983) 'Feminist responses to "crimes against women" 1868–1896', *Signs*, Vol. 8, No. 3, pp. 451–470

Plummer, K. (1997) *The Chicago School: Critical Assessments*, accessed at: https://kenplummer.com/publications/selected-writings-2/chicago-sociology/

Porta, P. and Scazzieri, R. (2002) 'Pietro Verri's political economy', *History of Political Economy*, Vol. 34, No. 1, pp. 83–110

Presdee, M. (2000) *Cultural Criminology and the Carnival of Crime*, London: Routledge

Purvis, J. (2009) 'Suffragette hunger strikes, 100 years on', *The Guardian*, accessed at: www.theguardian.com/commentisfree/libertycentral/2009/jul/06/suffragette- hunger-strike-protest

Quetelet, A. (1835, 1842 ed) *A Treatise on Man and the Development of His Faculties*, Paris: Bachelier

Quinney, R. (1973) 'Crime control in capitalist society', *Issues in Criminology*, Vol. 8, pp. 75–99

Quinney, R. and Wildeman, J. (1977) *The Problem of Crime*, New York: Harper & Row

Radcliffe Richards, J. (1982) *The Sceptical Feminist*, Harmondsworth: Penguin

Radford, J. and Russell, D. (1992 eds) *Femicide: The Politics of Woman Killing*, London and New York: Twayne

Radzinowicz, L. (1999) *Adventures in Criminology*, London: Routledge

Rafter, N. (2008) 'Criminology's darkest hour: Biocriminology in Nazi Germany', *Australian and New Zealand Journal of Criminology*, Vol. 41, No. 2, pp. 287–306

Rafter, N. (2009) *The Criminal Brain: Understanding Biological Theories of Crime*, New York: New York University Press

Rafter, N. and Gibson, M. (2004) *Introduction to Lombroso's Criminal Woman*, Durham, NC: Duke University Press

Raine, A. (2013) *The Anatomy of Violence: The Biological Roots of Crime*, New York: Knopf Doubleday

Raine, A., Bachsbaum, M. and Lacasse, L. (1997) 'Brain abnormalities in murderers indicated by positron emission tomography', *Biological Psychiatry*, Vol. 42, No. 6, pp. 495–508

Rancine, K. (2010) ' "This England and This Now": British Cultural and Intellectual Influence in the Spanish American Independence Era', *Hispanic American Historical Review*, Vol. 90, No. 3, pp. 423–454

Redhead, S. (1995) *Unpopular Cultures: The Birth of Law and Popular Culture*, Manchester: Manchester University Press

Rehman, Y., Kelly, L. and Siddiqui, H. (2016 eds) *Moving in the Shadows: Violence in the Lives of Minority Women and Children*, London: Routledge

Residents of Hull House (1895) *Hull House Maps and Papers*, New York: Thomas. Y Crowell Co.

Residents of Hull House (2007 ed) *Hull House Maps and Papers*, Urbana: University of Illinois Press: Urbana and Chicago

Reynolds, J. (1974) 'Rape as social control', *Catalyst*, Vol. 8, pp. 62–67

Rice, M. (1990) 'Challenging orthodoxies in feminist theory: A black feminist critique', in L. Gelsthorpe and A. Morris (Eds), *Feminist Perspectives in Criminology*, Milton Keynes: Oxford University Press

Richards, S. (2018) *Convict Criminology*, Oxford: Oxford Bibliographies

Richards, S. and Ross, J. (2003) *Convict Criminology*, Belmont, CA: Wadsworth

Richmond, M. (1917) *Social Diagnosis*, New York: Russell Sage

Riding, A. (2006) 'Dreyfus was vindicated, but what of the French?' *New York Times*, Jul. 7, p. A4

Ridley, G. (2002) 'Losing America and finding Australia', *Eighteen Century Life*, Vol. 26, No. 3, pp. 202–224

Ritchie, R. (2000) 'A Black feminist reflection on the anti-violence movement', *Signs*, Vol. 25, No. 4, pp. 1133–1137

Rock, P. (2005) 'Chronocentrism and British criminology', *British Journal of Sociology*, Vol. 56, No. 3, pp. 473–491

Rockefeller, J. D. (1890) *Letter in The Decennial Publications of the University of Chicago, Vol. 1* (1903), Chicago: University of Chicago Press

Rose, N. (2000) 'The biology of culpability: Pathological identity and crime control in a biological culture', *Theoretical Criminology*, Vol. 4, No. 1, pp. 5–32

Rose, N. (2007) 'Molecular biopolitics, somatic ethics and the spirit of biocapital', *Social Theory and Health*, Vol. 5, No. 1, pp. 3–29

Rose, N. and Abi-Rached, J. M. (2013) *Neuro: The New Brain Sciences and the Management of the Mind*, Princeton, NJ: Princeton University Press

Rose, S., Lewontin, R. C. and Kamin, L. (1990 ed) *Not in Our Genes: Biology, Ideology and Human Nature*, Harmondsworth: Penguin

Rosen, F. (1982) 'Jeremy Bentham: Recent interpretations', *Political Studies*, Vol. 30, No. 4, pp. 575–581

Rosenthal, G. (No Date), 'Auschwitz-Birkenau: The evolution of tattooing in the Auschwitz concentration camp', at: www.jewishvirtuallibrary.org/

Ross, J and Richards, S. (2003) *Convict Criminology*, Belmont, CA: Wadsworth

Ross, J., Richards, S., Newbold, G., Lenza, M. and Grigsby, R. (2011) 'Convict criminology', in W. DeKeseredy and M. Dragiewicz (Eds), *Routledge Handbook of Critical Criminology*, Oxon: Routledge

Rothman, D. (1980) *Conscience and Convenience: The Asylum and its Alternatives in Progressive America*, Boston: Little, Brown & Co.

Rothstein, E. (2013) 'Field museum looks back at Chicago's World Fair', *New York Times*, Nov. 1, Section C, p. 1

Rousseau, J-J. (1974 ed), *Emile*, London: Dent

Ruff, J. (2001) *Violence in Early Modern Europe 1500–1800*, Cambridge: Cambridge University Press

Ruggiero, V. (1996) *Organized and Corporate Crime in Europe: Offers That Can't Be Refused*, Aldershot: Dartmouth

Ruiz, V. and DuBois, E. C. (2000) *Unequal Sisters: A Multicultural Reader in US Women's History*, London: Routledge

Rusche, G. (1933, 1980 ed) 'Labor market and penal sanction: Thoughts on the sociology of criminal justice', in T. Platt and P. Takagi (Eds), *Punishment and Penal Discipline*, Berkeley, CA: Crime and Social Justice Associates

Rusche, G. and Kirchheimer, O. (1939, 2003 ed., 2009 ed). *Punishment and Social Structure*, New York: Columbia University Press

Rushton, P. (1995) *Race, Evolution and Behavior*, Brunswick, NJ: Transaction

Russell, D. (1975) *The Politics of Rape*, New York: Stein and Day

Russell, D. (1982) *Rape in Marriage*, New York: Palgrave Macmillan

Ryan, M. and Ward, T. (1989) *Privatisation and the Penal System: The American Experience and the Debate in Britain*, London: Macmillan

Ryan, M. and Ward, T. (2015) 'Prison abolitionism in the UK: They dare not speak its name', *Social Justice*, Vol. 41, No. 3, pp. 107–119

Sack, F. (1972) 'Definition von Kriminalität als politisches Handeln: Der labeling approach', *Kriminologisches Journal*, Jg. 4, pp. 3–31.

Saito, K. (2017) *Karl Marx's Ecosocialism*, New York: Monthly Review Press

Salvatore, R., Aguirre, C. and Joseph, G. (2001) *Crime and Punishment in Latin America*, Durham: Duke University Press

Samuel, S. (2019) 'Ecuador legalized gangs. Murder rates plummeted. A stunningly successful experiment has the potential to upend the mainstream US approach to deviance', Interview with D. Brotherton, VOX News

Sanderson, E. (1902) *Judicial Crimes*, London: Hutchinson & Co.

Savitz, L. and Johnston, N. (1982) *Contemporary Criminology*, New York: Wiley

Savitz, L., Turner, S. and Dickman, S. (1977) 'The origin of scientific criminology: Franz Joseph Gall as the first criminologist', in R. Meier (Ed), *Theory in Criminology*, London: Sage

Sayers, J. (1982) *Biological Politics*, London: Tavistock

Schulte-Bockholt, A. (2011) 'Latin American critical criminology', in W. Dekeseredy and M. Dragiewicz (Eds), *Routledge Handbook of Critical Criminology*, Oxon: Routledge

Schultz, R. (2007) 'Introduction', in *Hull House Maps and Papers*, Urbana and Chicago: University of Illinois Press

Schur, E. (1965) *Crimes Without Victims*, London: Prentice Hall

Schwendinger, H. and Schwendinger, J. (1974) *The Sociologists of the Chair*, New York: Basic Books

Schwendinger, J. and Schwendinger, J. (1983) *Rape and Inequality*, Beverley Hills, CA: Sage

Schwendinger, J., Schwendinger, H. and Lynch, M. J. (2002) 'Critical criminology in the United States: The Berkeley School and theoretical trajectories', in K. Carrington and R. Hogg (Eds), *Critical Criminology: Issues, Debates and Challenges*, Uffulme: Willan

Scraton, P. (1987) *Law, Order and the Authoritarian State*, Milton Keynes: Open University Press

Scraton, P. (2009) *Hillsborough: The Truth*, Edinburgh: Mainstream

Segal, L. (1987) *Is the Future Female?* London: Virago

Segal, L. (1989) 'The beast in man', *New Statesman and Society*, Sept. 8, pp. 21–23

Segal, L. (1990) *Slow Motion: Changing Masculinities, Changing Men*, London: Virago

Sellin, T. (1976) *Slavery and the Penal System*, New York: Elsevier

Shaw, C. (1929) *Delinquency Areas*, Chicago: University of Chicago Press

Shaw, C. (1930) *The Jack-Roller: A Delinquent Boy's Own Story*, Chicago: University of Chicago Press

Shaw, C. (1931) *The Natural History of a Delinquent Career*, Chicago: University of Chicago Press

Shaw, C. and McKay, H. (1942) *Juvenile Delinquency and Urban Areas*, Chicago: University of Chicago Press

Shelden, R. (1981) 'Convict leasing: An application of the Rusche-Kirchheimer thesis to penal changes in Tennessee, 1830–1915', in D. Greenberg (Ed), *Crime and Capitalism*, New York: Mayfield

Sheldon, W. (1949) *Varieties of Delinquent Youth*, New York: Harper & Brothers

Sherwell, P. (1992) 'Serbia's warlords walk tall in benighted Bosnia', *Sunday Telegraph*, Apr. 26

Sica, A. (2012) 'Book as totem: THE "Green Bible" one more time' (emphasis as in the original), *American Journal of Sociology*, Vol. 41, No. 5, pp. 557–560

Siddiqui, H. (2016) 'What will it take to end honour based violence in the UK', *Open Democracy*, Nov. 28

Siegel, D. (2013) 'The methods of Lombroso and cultural criminology', in P. Knepper and P. Ystehede (Eds), *The Cesare Lombroso Handbook*, Oxon: Routledge

Sim, J. (2009) *Punishment and Prisons: Power and the Carceral State*, London: Sage

Sirotkina, I. (2003) *Diagnosing Literary Genius*, Baltimore: JHU

Sisters Uncut, *Feministo*, (2016), accessed at: http:www.sistersuncut.org/feministo

Slater, E. and McDonough, T. (2008) 'Marx on nineteenth-century colonial Ireland: Analysing colonialism as a dynamic social process', *Irish Historical Studies*, No. 142, Nov. pp. 153–172

Small, A. (1895) 'The era of sociology', *American Journal of Sociology*, Vol. 1, No. 1

Small, A. (1912) 'Socialism in the light of social science', *American Journal of Sociology*, Vol. 17, No. 6, pp. 804–819

Small, A. and Vincent, G. (1894) *Introduction to the Study of Society*, New York: American Book Co.

Smart, C. (1976) *Women, Crime and Criminology*, London: Routledge, Kegan and Paul

Smith, D. (1988) *The Chicago School: A Liberal Critique of Capitalism*, London: Palgrave Macmillan

Smith, J. (2013) 'The enlightenment's "race" problem and ours', *New York Times*, Feb. 10, Blog

Snodgrass, J. (1976) 'Clifford R. Shaw and Henry D. McKay: Chicago criminologists', *British Journal of Criminology*, Vol. 16, No. 1, pp. 1–19

Sokoloff, N. and Dupont, I. (2005) 'Domestic violence at the intersections of race, class and gender', *Violence Against Women*, Vol. 11, No. 1, pp. 38–64

Sokoloff, N. Price, B. R. and Flavin, J. (2004) 'The criminal law and women', in B.R. Price and N. Sokoloff (Eds), *The Criminal Justice System and Women*, New York: McGraw Hill

South, N. (1998) 'A green field for criminology?' *Theoretical Criminology*, Vol. 2, No. 2, pp. 211–232

South, N. (2010) 'The ecocidal tendencies of late modernity', in R. Wright (Ed), *Global Environmental Harm: Criminological Perspectives*, Cullompton: Willan

South, N. and Beirne, P. (1998) 'Editors' introduction – green criminology', *Theoretical Criminology*, Vol. 2, No. 2, pp. 147–148

South, N. and Beirne, P. (2006 eds) *Green Criminology*, Hampshire: Ashgate

South, N. and Brisman, A. (2013 eds) *Routledge Handbook of Green Criminology*, Oxon: Routledge

Spielmann, M. (1895) *A History of Punch*, London: Cassell and Company

Sprenger, J. and Kramer, H. (1486, 1971) *Malleus Maleficarum*, New York: Dover

Spurr, D. (1993) *The Rhetoric of Empire*, Durham, NC: Duke University Press

Sreenan, D. (1993) 'France in 1968', *Workers Solidarity*, No. 39

Staff, J. D. (2007) 'Voltaire – Father of the innocence campaign', *Justice Denied*, No. 35, Winter, pp. 29–30

Stanko, E. (1990) *Everyday Violence*, London: Pandora

Stanley, L. and Wise, S. (1983) *Breaking Out: Feminist Consciousness and Feminist Research*, London: Routledge

Stead, W. H. (1894, 1910 ed) *If Christ Came to Chicago*, Chicago, Laird and Lee

Stedman Jones, S. (2006) 'Durkheim, the question of violence and the paris commune of 1871', *International Social Science Journal*, Wiley Online Library

Stretesky, P. (2017) *Radical and Marxist Theories of Crime*, Oxon: Routledge

Sumner, C. (1994) *The Sociology of Deviance: An Obituary*, Buckingham: Open University Press

Sutherland, E. (1931) 'Mental deficiency and crime', in K. Young (Ed), *Social Attitudes*, New York: Henry Holt

Sutherland, E. (1947) *Principles of Criminology*, Philadelphia: JB Lippincott

Sutherland, E. and Cressey, D. (1966, 1970 ed) *Principles of Criminology*, Philadelphia: Lippincott

Swiss, D. (2010) *The Tin Ticket*, New York: Penguin

Taibbi, M. (2012) 'NFL's fatal problem: It kills its workers', *RollingStone*, Sept. 3, accessed at: https://www.rollingstone.com/culture/culture-sports/nfls-fatal-problem-it-kills-its-workers-188967/

Tannenbaum, F. (1915) 'What I saw in prison', *The Masses*, pp. 8–9

Tannenbaum, F. (1924) *Darker Phases of the South*, New York, London: G.P. Putman's Sons

Tannenbaum, F. (1938) *Crime and Community*, New York: Columbia University Press

Tannenbaum, F. (1947) *Slave and Citizen*, Boston: Knopf Inc

Takaki, R. (1979) *Iron Cages*, New York, NY: Knopf

Taylor, I. (1968) 'Football mad: A speculative sociology of football hooliganism', *NDC 1st Symposium*, Nov.

Taylor, I. (1982) *Law and Order: Arguments for Socialism*, London: Palgrave Macmillan

Taylor, I. (1999) *Crime in Context*, Oxford: Polity Press

Taylor, I., Walton, P. and Young, J. (1973) *The New Criminology*, London: Routledge and Kegan Paul

Taylor, I., Walton, P. and Young, J. (Eds) (1975) *Critical Criminology*, London: Routledge & Kegan Paul

Taylor, U. (2010) 'Black feminisms and human agency', in N. Hewitt (Ed), *No Permanent Waves: Recasting Histories of U.S. Feminism*, Brunswick, NJ: Rutgers University Press

Treviño, A. J. and McCormack, K. (2016) *Service Sociology and Academic Engagement in Social Problems*, Oxon: Routledge

The Terrific Register (1825) *Dreadful Execution of Damiens*, Vol. 1, p. 1, London: Sherwood, Jones, and Co.

Thomas, W. I (1923, 1961 ed) *The Unadjusted Girl*, Boston, MA: Little, Brown and Company

Thompson, E. P. (1960) 'The long revolution', *New Left Review*, Vol. 9–10

Thomson, A. (2010) *The Making of Social Theory*, Oxford: Oxford University Press

Thrasher, F. M. (1927) *The Gang*, Chicago: University of Chicago Press

Tifft, L. (1979) 'The coming redefinitions of crime: An anarchist perspective', *Social Problems*, Vol. 26, No. 4, pp. 392–402

Tifft, L. and Sullivan, D. (1980) *The Struggle to be Human: Crime, Criminology and Anarchism*, MI: Cienfuegos Press

Tifft, L and Sullivan, D. (1998) 'Criminology as peacemaking: A peace-oriented perspective on crime, punishment and justice that takes into account the needs of all', *The Justice Professional*, Vol. 11, Nos. 1–2, pp. 4–34

Tocqueville, A. (1961 ed) *Democracy in America*, New York: Doubleday

Tolstoy, A. (1953) *Tolstoy: A Life of My Father*, accessed at: www.tolstoyfoundation.org/tolstoy_father.html

Tolstoy, L. (1899, 2014 ed) *Resurrection*, Ware: Wordsworth Editions

Tolstoy, S. (2010 ed) *The Diaries of Sophia Tolstoy*, New York: Harper Collins

Toynbee Hall (2018) 'Our history', accessed at: www.toynbeehall.org.uk/our-history

Turner, B. (2006) 'Classical sociology and cosmopolitanism', *British Journal of Sociology*, Vol. 57, No. 1, pp. 133–151

Twining, W. L. and Twining, P. E. (1973) 'Bentham on torture', *Northern Ireland Quarterly*, Vol. 24, pp. 305–356

United Nations (1948) *Universal Declaration of Human Rights*, accessed at: www.un.org/en/universal-declaration-human-rights/

University of Chicago (1892–1902) *The Presidents Report*, accessed at: www.lib.uchicago.edu/scrc/archives/publications/pubofficial/

University of Chicago (1992) 'William Rainey Harper (1865–1906)', in *The Presidents of the University of Chicago*, accessed at: www.lib.uchicago.edu/collex/exhibits/university-chicago-centennial-catalogues/presidents-university-chicago-centennial-view/william-rainey-harper-1856–1906/

University of Chicago (2009) 'Marion Talbot', accessed at: www.lib.uchicago.edu/collex/exhibits/exoet/marion-talbot/

University of Chicago Library (2015) 'Ernest Burgess archive', accessed at: http://news.lib.uchicago.edu/blog/2015/06/16/mapping-the-young-metropolis/2-burgess_portrait-sm/

Vagianos, A. (2015) '30 shocking domestic violence statistics that remind us it's an epidemic', *The Huffington Post*, Feb. 13, accessed at: http: www/huffingtonpost.com

Vallier, C. (2002) *Theories of Crime and Punishment*, London: Pearsons

Van Bremmelen, J. (1955) 'Pioneers in criminology: Willem Adriaan Bonger', *Journal of Criminal Law & Criminology*, Vol. 46, pp 243–302

Van Kley, D. (1984) *The Damiens Affair and the Unraveling of the Ancien Regime*, 1750–1770, Princeton, NJ: Princeton University Press

van Swaaningen, R. (1995, 1997) *Critical Criminology: Visions from Europe*, PhD thesis, London: Sage

Verri, P. (1804, 2014 ed), *Observations on Torture*, Paris: Viviane Hamy *Vitae Scholasticae*, Vol. 27, No. 2

Vitelli, R. (2009) 'Living in silence', in *Providentia*, Typepad. Inc

Vold, G. and Bernard, T. (1986 ed) *Theoretical Criminology*, Oxford: Oxford University Press

Vold, G., Bernard, T. and Snipes, J. (2001 ed) *Theoretical Criminology*, Oxford: Oxford University Press

Voltaire (1759) *Candide*, Paris

Voltaire (1763, 1994 ed) *A Treatise on Toleration*, New York: Prometheus Books

Voltaire (1764, 1901 ed) *A Philosophical Dictionary*, in J. Morley et al. (Eds), *The Works of Voltaire*, Vol. 8, London: E.R Du Mont

Voltaire (1801) 'The Commentary', in C. Beccaria, *An Essay on Crimes and Punishments*

Von Bar, C. L. (1916) *A History of Continental Criminal Law*, Boston, MA: Little, Brown & Co.

Von Hisrch, A. (1996) 'Giving criminals their just desserts', in J. Muncie, E. McLaughlin and M. Langan (Eds), *Criminological Perspectives: A Reader*, London: Sage

Von Spee, F. (1631, 2012) *Cautio Criminalis*, VA: University of Virginia Press

Walby, S. (1990) *Theorizing Patriarchy*, Oxford: Blackwell

Walby, S. (2011) *The Future of Feminism*, Cambridge: Polity

Walby, S., Armstrong, J. and Strid, S. (2012) 'Intersectionality: Multiple inequalities in social theory', *Sociology*, Vol. 46, No. 2, pp. 1–17

Walklate, S. (1989) *Victimology*, London: Unwin Hyman

Walklate, S. (1992) 'Appreciating the victim', in R. Matthews and J. Young (Eds), *Issues in Realist Criminology*, London: Sage

Walklate, S. (1995) *Gender and Crime*, Hemel Hempstead: Prentice Hall

Walklate, S. (2004) *Gender, Crime and Criminal Justice*, Cullompton, Devon: Willan (2nd Edition)

Walklate, S. (2010) 'Carol Smart', in K. Hayward, S. Maruna and J. Mooney (Eds), *Fifty Key Thinkers in Criminology*, London: Routledge

Walklate, S. (2016) 'Whither criminology: Its global futures?', *Asian Journal of Criminology*, Vol. 11, No. 1, pp. 47–59

Walkowitz, J. and Walkowitz, D. (1973) ' "We are not beasts of the field": Prostitution and the poor in Plymouth and Southampton under the Contagious Diseases Acts', *Feminist Studies, Women's History*, Vol. 1, No. 3–4, pp. 73–106

Walsh, A. (2003) 'The Holy Trinity and the legacy of the Italian school of criminal anthropology', *Human Nature Review*, Vol. 3, pp. 1–11

Walters, J. (2017) 'Boston public schools map switch aims to amend 500 years of distortion', *The Guardian*, Mar. 19

Walton, P. and Young, J. (1998) *The New Criminology Revisted*, London: Macmillan

Ward, T. and Green, P. (2016) 'Law, the state and the dialectics of state crime', *Critical Criminology*, Vol. 24, No. 2, pp. 217–230

Ware, V. and Black, L. (2002) *Out of Whiteness*, Chicago: University of Chicago Press

Waterson, D. (1994) 'The Tolpuddle Martyrs', *Australian Society for the Study of Labour History*, accessed at: https://www.labourhistory.org.au/hummer/no-5/tolpuddle-martyrs/

Webster, C. (2010) 'Stuart Hall', in K. Hayward, S. Maruna and J. Mooney (Eds), *Fifty Key Thinkers in Criminology*, London: Routledge

Welch, M. (2013) *Corrections: A Critical Approach*, Oxon: Routledge

Wells, I. B. (1893 ed), *The Reason Why the Colored American Is Not in the World's Columbian Exposition. The Afro-American's contribution to Columbian literature*, with contributions by F. Douglas, I. G. Penn and F. L. Barnett, at: http://digital.library.upenn.edu/women/wells/exposition/exposition.html
Wells, I. B. (1901) 'Lynching and the excuse for it', *New York Independent*, May 16
Westervelt, S. and Cook, K. (2012) *Life After Death Row*, Brunswick, NJ: Rutgers University Press
Westmarland, L. (2001) 'Blowing the whistle on police violence: Gender, ethnography and ethics', *The British Journal of Criminology*, Vol. 41, No. 3, pp. 523–535
Wetzell, R. F. (2000) *Inventing the Criminal: A History of German Criminology, 1880–1945*, Durham, NC: University of North Carolina Press
Wheen, F. (2000) 'The "science" behind racism', *The Guardian*, May 10
White, R. and Haines, F. (2008) *Crime and Criminology*, Oxford: Oxford University Press
White, R. and Heckenberg, D. (2014) *Green Criminology: An Introduction to the Study of Environmental Harm*, London: Routledge
Whyte, D. (2010) 'Dismantling the reasons of state', *Criminal Justice Matters*, Vol. 82, pp. 4–5
Wiencek, H. (2012) *Master of the Mountain: Thomas Jefferson and His Slaves*, New York: Farrar Straus Giroux
Wiesel, E. (1987) 'When hatred seized a nation', *New York Times*, Sept., Section 2, p. 1
Wilkinson, I. (2009) *Risk, Vulnerability and Everyday Life*, London: Routledge
Wilkinson, I. (2010) 'Emile Durkheim', in K. Hayward, S. Maruna and J. Mooney (Eds), *Fifty Key Thinkers in Criminology*, London: Routledge
Williams, C. (2015) 'Judith Butler on Gender and the Trans Experience', *Versobooks Blog*, 26 May
Williford, M. (1980) *Jeremy Bentham on Spanish America an Account of His Letters and Proposals to the New World*, Louisiana: Louisiana State University Press
Willis, C., Evans, T. and LaGrange, R. (1999) '"Down home" criminology: The place of indigenous theories of crime', *Journal of Criminal Justice*, Vol. 27, No. 3, pp. 227–238
Willis, P. (1972) 'A Motorbike Subculture', *NDC 8th Symposium*, Jan.
Willis, P. (1977) *Learning to Labour*, Aldershot: Gower
Wilson, C. (2007) *Paris and the Commune, 1871–78, The Politics of Forgetting*, London: Palgrave Macmillan
Wilson, E. O. (1983) *What Is to Be Done About Violence Against Women?* Harmondsworth: Penguin
Wilson, E. O. (1995) *Sociobiology*, Harvard: Harvard University Press
Wilson, J. Q. (1975) *Thinking About Crime*, New York, NY: Vintage Books
Wilson, J. Q. and Herrnstein, R. (1985) *Crime and Human Nature*, New York: Simon and Schuster
Wilson, J. Q. and Kelling G. (1982) 'Broken windows', *The Atlantic*, March, accessed at: https://www.theatlantic.com/magazine/archive/1982/03/broken-windows/304465/
Wilson, M. and Daly, M. (1992) 'The man who mistook his wife for a chattel', in J. H. Barkow, L. Cosmides and J. Tooby (Eds), *The Adapted Mind*, New York: Oxford University Press
Wilson, M. and Daly, M. (1998) 'Lethal and nonlethal violence against wives and the evolutionary psychology of male sexual proprietariness', in R. E Dobash and R. P. Dobash (Eds), *Rethinking Violence Against Women*, Thousand Oaks: Sage
Wirth, L. (1928) *The Ghetto*, Chicago: University of Chicago Press
Wojtczak, H. (2009) 'The contagious diseases act', accessed at: www.victorianweb.org/victorian/gender/contagious.html

Wolfgang, M. (1960) 'Cesare Lombroso', in H. Mannheim (Ed), *Pioneers in Criminology*, London: Stevens and Son Ltd.

Wright II, E. (2002) 'Why black people tend to shout! An earnest attempt to explain the sociological negation of the Atlanta Sociological Laboratory despite its possible unpleasantness', *Sociological Spectrum*, Vol. 22, No. 3, pp. 335–361

Wright II, E. (2017) *Du Bois and the Atlanta Sociological Laboratory*, Oxon: Routledge

Wright, J. P. and Cullen, F. (2012) 'The future of biosocial criminology: Beyond scholars' professional ideology', *Journal of Contemporary Criminal Justice*, Vol. 28, No. 3, pp. 237–253

Yeager, M. (2016) *Frank Tannenbaum: The Making of a Convict Criminologist*, New York: Routledge

Yeandle, P., Newey, K. and Richards, J. (2016) *Politics, Performance and Popular Culture: Theatre and Society in Nineteenth Century Britain*, Oxford: Oxford University Press

Yllo, K. (1988) 'Political and methodological debates in wife abuse research', in K. Yllo and M. Bograd (Eds), *Feminist Perspectives on Wife Abuse*, Newbury Park: Sage

Young, J. (1968) 'The role of the police as amplifiers of deviance, negotiators of reality and translators of phantasy', *NDC 1st Symposium*, Nov.

Young, J. (1969) 'The Zookeepers of Deviancy', *Anarchy*, April

Young, J. (1981) 'Thinking seriously about crime', in M. Fitzgerald, G. McLennan and J. Pawson (Eds), *Crime and Society*, London: Routledge

Young, J. (1986) 'The failure of criminology: The need for a radical realism', in R. Matthews and J. Young (Eds), *Confronting Crime*, London: Sage

Young, J. (1988) 'Risk of crime and fear of crime: A realist critique of survey-based assumption', in M. Maguire and J. Pointing (Eds), *Victims of Crime: A New Deal?*, Milton Keynes: Open University Press

Young, J. (1992) 'Ten points of realism', in J. Young and R. Matthews (Eds), *Rethinking Criminology: The Realist Debate*, London: Sage

Young, J. (1994) 'Incessant chatter: Recent paradigms in criminology', in M. Maguire, R. Morgan and R. Reiner (Eds), *The Oxford Handbook of Criminology*, Oxford: Clarendon Press

Young, J. (1997) 'Left Realist criminology: Radical in its analysis, realist in its polity', in M. Maguire, R.Morgan and R. Reiner (Eds), *The Oxford Handbook of Criminology*, Oxford: Clarendon Press (2nd ed)

Young, J. (1998) 'Breaking windows: Situating the new criminology', in P. Walton and J. Young (Eds), *The New Criminology Revisited*, London: Macmillan

Young, J. (1999) *The Exclusive Society*, London: Sage

Young, J. (2000) 'Charles Murray and the American prison experiment', at: www.malcolmread.com/JockYoung/

Young, J. (2002) 'Critical criminology in the twenty first century: Critique, irony and the always unfinished', in K. Carrington and R. Hogg (Eds), *Critical Criminology: Issues, Debates, Challenges*, Cullompton, Devon: Willan

Young, J. (2003) 'Merton with energy, Katz with structure', *Theoretical Criminology*, Vol. 7, No. 3, pp. 389–414

Young, J. (2004) 'Voodoo criminology and the numbers game', in J. Ferrell et al, (Eds), *Cultural Criminology Unleashed*, London: Glasshouse

Young, J. (2010) 'Robert Merton', in K. Hayward, S. Maruna and J.Mooney (Eds), *Fifty Key Thinkers in Criminology*, London: Routledge

Young, J. (2011) *The Criminological Imagination*, Cambridge: Polity Press

Young, J. (2013a) 'The durkheimian legacy', accessed at: www.malcolmread.com/JockYoung/
Young, J. (2013b) 'The big chill', unpublished paper
Zimring, F. and Hawkins, G. (1973) *Deterrence: The Legal Threat in Crime Control*, Chicago: University of Chicago Press
Zola, E. (1898) 'J'accuse', *L'Aurore*, Jan. 13

Newspapers and Periodicals

Chicago Daily Tribune
Daily News
The European Magazine and London Review
Extraordinary Gazette
Gazette d' Amsterdam
The Gazetteer and New Daily Advertiser
The Gentleman's Magazine and Historical Chronicle
The Guardian
Lloyd's Evening post and British Chronicle
London Chronicle
London Evening Post
London Gazette
The Masses
The Monthly Review
Morning Chronicle
Morning Post
Newcastle Weekly Courant
New York Daily Tribune
New York Independent
New York Times
Pall Mall Gazette
Pittsburgh Courier
Punch
The Times
The Tomahawk

Index

Note: Figures are indicated by page numbers in *italics*.

1984 (Orwell) 59
Abbott, Grace 164
Adams, John 46
Adams, Walter 267
Addams, Jane 133–134, 158–161, 164–167, 168n2, 170n24, 170n28–170n29, 191, 209, 211, 220, 222, 241, 297
Adelstein, David 267
Agozino, Biko 6, 34, 61, 85
Ahearne, Mike 72–73
Ake, Jami 262
American Dream 205–215
American Journal of Sociology 135
American Sociological Association (ASA) 135, 166
American War of Independence 29
Amos, Valerie 258
anarchism 295–299
ancien régime 5–21, *14*, 27n1, 29, 31, 63
Anderson, Nels 151
anomie 182–183, 204, 215n4–215n5
Anthony, Susan B. 257
anti-Semitism 174, 186–188, 193, 203, 205
Argentina 325
Aristotle 86
Arnold, Gretchen 262
Ashley-Montague, M.F. 117
Astell, Mary 63, 221
atavism 93–97, *95*
Athabasca Tar Sands 333
Atlanta School 198–203, 217n17
Attlee, Clement 158
Auclert, Hubertine 220, 227–228
Augspurg, Anita 228

Aussaresses, Paul 54–55
Australia 67–68

Bacon, Francis 45
Bakunin, Mikhail 296
Balbi, Adriano 87, 158
Ball, Matthew 336
banishment 66–68
Barak, Gregg 301, 304
Barnett, Ferdinand Lee 168n1
Barnett, Henrietta 158
Barnett, Samuel 158, 175
Barrès, Maurice 187
Barrett, Michèle 221, 259
Beccaria, Cesare 6–7, 35–47, *44*, 54, 60, 68, 71–75, 80n11, 337
Beck, Ulric 323
Becker, Howard 169n19
Becker, Howard S. 134, 169n19, 214, 282, 285–286, 318
Bedford Hills 147–149, 169n15
Bcirnc, Piers 86–88
Belknap, Joanne 335
Bellamy, Richard 50
Bell Curve, The (Herrnstein and Murray) 123, 308
Bemis, Edward 134, 144–146
Benedikt, Moritz 108
Bentham, Jeremy *44*, 47–59, 72, 81n12–81n13, 81n17–81n18, 84
Ben-Yehuda, Nachman 8
Berger, Peter 172
Berkeley School 302
Berkman, Alexander 209
Bernstein, Elizabeth 266n12
Bhatnagar, Dipti 333

Bianchi, Herman 300, 312
Bindel, Julie 230
biosocial criminology 124, 128
Blackstone, William 46–47
Blair, Tony 308
Blake, Matilda 232
Bloch, Herbert 108
Bloom, Marshall 267, 313n4
Boley, W. M. 197
Bolsonaro, Jair 329
Bonger, W.A. 110, 275–279, 313n8
Booker, Cory 217n18
Booth, Charles 158, 163, 170n22, 195
Borges, Dain 89
Bosworth, Mary 70, 253
Bourgois, Phillipe 208
Boyle, Nina 232
Brace, Charles Loring 103
Breckinridge, Sophonisba 164
Bregman, Rutger 327
brigandage 89–90
Bright, Jacob 230
Broadwater Farm Survey 305
Brockway, Zebulon Reed 106, 131n11, 148
Brotherton, David 326, 336
Brown, Alyson 240
Brown, Michael 336
Brownmiller, Susan 246
Brunetière, Ferdinand 187
Buck v. Bell 129–130
Bulmer, Martin 168n4
Burgess, Ernest 150–154, *153*, 154–155, 163, 166, 170n28, 220
Burke, Thomas Henry 117
Burns, John 170n28
Bursik, Robert 170n29
Bush, George W. 74
Butler, Josephine 162, 228–232

cadherin 13 126
Calas, Jean 32–34, 80n5, 240
Caldwell, Charles 92
Cambridge Analytica 59
CAP *see* Chicago Area Project (CAP)
Capital (Marx) 272
capitalism 271, 276–277
capital punishment 23, 30, 41–42, 47, 73–74, 107–108, 131n11, 240
carceral feminism 249–250, 266n12
Card, Claudia 55
Carlen, Pat 102
Carpenter, Mary 231

Carr, Edward 1
Carrington, Kerry 324–325
Carrithers, David W. 24
Casanova, Giacomo 12
Castile, Philando 336
Catherine the Great 45
Cauer, Minna 228
Cautio Criminalis 9–10
Cavan, Ruth Shonle 134, 171n29
Cavendish, Lord Frederick 117
CC *see* convict criminology (CC)
CCCS *see* Centre for Contemporary Cultural Studies (CCCS)
Centre for Contemporary Cultural Studies (CCCS) 284, 289–295
Chambliss, William 285, 301
Chancer, Lynn 215n9
Chauhan, Randeep Singh 10
Chicago, Illinois 132–133
Chicago Area Project (CAP) 157
Chicago School 108; African Americans and 216n10; class and 156–157; Durkheim and 177–178; feminism and 220; gender and 156–157; Hull House and 133–134, 158–166; human ecology and 152; men in 149–150; power and 156–157; as school 134; and University of Chicago 135–136; women in 136–149, *139*
Christie, Agatha 110
Christie, Nils 300, 312
city, concentric zones map of 152–154, *153*
Clarke, John 291
Clarke, Ron 76–78, 82n31
classicism: class bias in 62–64; criminal act in 66; gender bias in 62–64; influence of 34–35; modification of 70–71; positivism *vs.* 84
classicist contradiction 65–66
classicist criminology: contemporary application of 75–80; critique of 60–70; Enlightenment and origins of 29–59, *44*, *56*
Clemens, Justin 54
climate change 331, 333
Cloward, Richard 205, 208, 282
Cobbe, Frances Power 232–234, 248, 265n8
Cohen, Albert 79, 205, 207, 215, 217n24, 255, 282
Cohen, Stan 278, 283, 301, 315n25, 324
Collier, Richard 255
colonialism 27n7, 60–62, 330

colonial terrorism 82n21
Column of Infamy, The (Manzoni) 47, 52
Combe, George 92
Commager, Henry Steele 334
Commonplace Books (Jefferson) 46
Compton, Louis 51
Comte, Auguste 83–84, 89, 130n1, 130n5
concentric zones map 152–154, *153*
Condition of the Working-Class in England in 1844 (Engels) 270, 272
conformity 206
Connell, Raewyn 24, 255, 321, 323–324
Constitutio Criminalis Carolina 11, 27n9
Contagious Disease Acts 228–232
convict criminology (CC) 211–212
convict lease system 193–195
Cook, Kim 336
Cornish, Derek 76–77
Correa, Rafael 326
Crawford, Mabel Sharman 232
Crenshaw, Kimberlé 260
Cressey, Paul 151, 169n21
crime: in Beccaria 38–39
crime policy 164
crime prevention: in Beccaria 43
Criminal Man (Lombroso) 90–97, *95*
critical criminology: activism and 267; anarchism and 295–299; Berkeley School and 302; Bonger and 275–278; capitalism and 276–277; development of 267; developments in 300–302; Engels and 268–275; historical context of 268–282; Kirchheimer and 279–282; left realism and 303–308; Marx and 268–275; National Deviancy Conferences and 283–284; *New Criminology* and 283–287; politics and 303–313; prison and 312; problematisation of 299–300; rise of 282–299; Rusche and 279–282; violence and 310–311; women and 277–278, 299–300
Cullen, Francis 124–125
cultural criminology 317–321
Currie, Elliott 304
Curtis, Lewis 114
Cyclone Idai 333

Daly, Martin 120
Damiens, Robert-François 11–13, 16–21, 26–27, 29, 32, 34, 98, 296, 337
Darkside of Democracy, The (Mann) 61
Darwin, Charles 83, 89, 93, 105
Davies, Jeremy 54
Davis, Angela 195, 211, 220, 257
Davis, Katharine Bement 133–134, 140–141, 143–146, 149, 159, 169n11, 169n15–169n17, 195, 209, 216n15
Davis, Mike 152–153, 157
Davy, Georges 190
Dawkins, Richard 120
Dear, Michael J. 157
death penalty 23, 30, 41–42, 47, 73–74, 107–108, 131n11, 240
de Beauvoir, Simone 255
Declaration of Independence 29, 74, 223
Declaration of the Rights of Man and of the Citizen 29
Deegan, Mary Jo 135–136, 160, 191, 216n15
Deflem, Mathieu 215n5
de Gaulle, Charles 268
degeneracy 89
de Gouges, Olympe 64, 221, 223
DeKeseredy, Walter 307
delinquent: children as 207–208; as person 154–155
del Valle, José 81n12
Dershowitz, Alan 54
deterrence 22–23, 42, 52–53, 77, 108
Dewey, John 134, 160
Dhawan, Nikita 29
Dickens, Charles 13, 50
Diderot, Denis 24, 31, 62
differential association 155–156
Dilulio, John 308
Discipline and Punish: The Birth of the Prison (Foucault) 12, 14–15, 58
Dominican Order 8–9
Douglass, Frederick 168n1
Doyle, William 27n1
Draper, Tony 51
Dreyfus, Alfred *189*
Dreyfus Affair 185–188
Drumgoole, William 198
Du Bois, W.E.B. 137, 142, 144, 169n12, 190–203, 210, 216n11–216n12, 216n15, 217n17, 217n19
Dupin, Charles 87
Dupont, Ida 259
Durkheim, Émile 104, 135, 172–191, 206, 215n1–215n3, 215n8
Duster, Troy 128

Eaton, Isabel 195, 216n15
ecocide 332
ecology, human 152

Ecuador 325–326
Eddy, Thomas 68
egoism 276
Elmira reformatory 106–107, 148
Elshtain, Jean Bethke 164
Emile (Rousseau) 63
Emlyn, Sollum 52
Emsley, Clive 25
Encyclopédie 25–26, 35
Engels, Friedrich 25, 268–275
Enlightenment 5; critique of 60–70; as myth 30; and origins of classicist criminology 29–59, *44, 56*
Enquiry Concerning the Principles of Morals, An (Hume) 22
equality: formal *vs.* substantive 65–66
Erikson, Kai 178, 183–184
Essay on Causes Affecting Minds and Characters (Montesquieu) 23–24
Essay on Cruelty (Montaigne) 28n14
ethnography 137–140
evolution 83, 120
Eysenck, Hans 10, 119, 124, 219

Facchinei, Ferdinando 73
Farrington, David 315n26
Faure, Félix 186
Felson, Marcus 77
femininity 208
feminism: in 19th century 223; carceral 249–250, 266n12; in contemporary period 240–250; criminal justice and 228–240; criminology and 250–257, 266n13; in Europe 227–228; first wave 221, 232; left realism and 307; liberal 242–243; Lombroso and 219–223; race and 257–258; radical 245–250, 262–265, *264*; rethinking 257–261; second wave 221, 241; socialist 243–245; third wave 221; violence against women and 232–235; voting rights and 227–228, *225–227*; *see also* women
Fenton, Steve 175
Ferrell, Jeff 296–297, 315n24, 320–321
Ferrero, Gina Lombroso 93, 103
Ferrero, Guglielmo 88
Ferri, Enrico 88, 104–105, 313n6
Fields, Karen 186, 191
Fifty Key Thinkers in Criminology (Hayward, Maruna and Mooney) 3
Fitzpatrick, Ellen 147
Flynn, Elizabeth Gurley 210
Forrester, Lillian *226*

Foster, John Bellamy 330–331
Foucault, Michel 12, 14–15, 28n12, 58–59
France, Anatole 65
Franci, Carlo Sebastiano 63–64
Fraser, Nancy 167
Frazier, E. Franklin 191, 201, 216n10
free will 31, 62, 83–85, 89, 113, 198
French Revolution 29, 45–46
Freud, Sigmund 83, 118–119, 194
Friedan, Betty 266n10
Fry, Elizabeth 147, 235–236
Fuller, John R. 114

Gabbidon, Shaun 124, 169n10, 191, 199, 202, 216n10, 217n17
Gall, Franz Joseph 89, 91–92, 130n5
Galton, Francis 169n18
Garber, Jenny 290, 299
Garbus, Martin 337
Garland, David 28n12, 79, 180–181, 281
Garner, Eric 336
Garofalo, Raffaele 88, 104–105
Geis, Gilbert 108
Gelsthorpe, Loraine 255, 266n13
gender: Chicago School and 156–157; trans 261
gender bias 62–64
genius 111
genocide 332
George III of England 16
Gibson, Mary 96, 102, 118, 130n7
Giddens, Anthony 179
Gieryn, Thomas 157
Gilman, Charlotte Perkins 168n2
Glueck, Eleanor 118
Glueck, Sheldon 118
Go, Julian 191
Godfrey, Barry 290, 315n22
Godwin, William 296
Goldman, Emma 170n28, 295, 297–298
Gómez, Alejandro 81n12
Goode, Erich 212, 214–215
Goodman, Amy 333
Goodman, Paul 298–299
Goring, Charles 110
Gould, Stephen Jay 129–130
Gouldner, Alvin 217n22, 285–286
Goyes, David Rodríguez 336
Graham, Lisa Jane 21
Gramsci, Antonio 96, 105, 289
Gray, Freddie 336
Greenberg, David 205, 301
Green Bible 150, 322–323

green criminology 327–334
Greene, Helen Taylor 191, 216n10
Gregory, Jeanne 243, 245
Griffin, Susan 247
Grossman, Ron 164
Guerry, André-Michel 86–88, 130n2, 158, 173
Guettel, Charnie 244

Haeckel, Ernst 89
Hall, Gus 201
Hall, Stuart 284, 289, 294
Hanmer, Jalna 246–247, 249, 254
happiness principle 49–50
Hardt, Michael 323
Hard Times (Dickens) 50
Harper, William Rainey 135–136, 144
Harris, Kamala 217n18
Hawkins, Darnell 335–337
Hayward, Keith 79, 170n27, 320–321
Hazlitt, William 48–49
Hebberecht, Patrick 275, 277
Heidensohn, Frances 102, 117, 242, 250–252, 255–256, 262, 300
Henderson, Charles 134, 155
Herrnstein, Richard 121
Higinbotham, Harlow 168n1
Hill, Michael 161
Hillsborough tragedy 336
Hillyard, Paddy 309, 331
Hirschi, Travis 256
Hirst, Paul 299, 313n8
Hobbes, Thomas 45
Hobsbawn, Eric 80n1–80n2
Hoggart, Richard 290
hooks, bell 257
Hose, Sam 199–200
Howard, John 68
Howe, Adrian 258–259
Hughes, Everett 134
Hull House 133–134, 140, 158–167, 168n2, 170n28, 211, 220, 243, 253, 297
Hull House Maps and Papers 162–166
Hulsman, Louk 300, 312
human ecology 152
human nature 31, 36–37
human rights: Voltaire and 31–34
Hume, David 22, 61

Il Caffè (periodical) 36, 63
indignation 184
individualism 122–123, 187–188

innovation 206
intellectuals 21–27
IQ scores 123, 308
Ireland 330
Irish: othering of 114–117, *115–116*
Irwin, John 211
Iseman, Robert 328
Islington Crime Survey 305
Italian school 88–114, *91, 95*

Jackson, Stevie 241
Jaggar, Andrea 245
Jalata, Asafa 82n22
James, William 191
Jamieson, Ruth 310
Jansenists 18–19
Jaucourt, Louis Chevalier de 25–26, 54
Jaurès, Jean 215n1
Jefferson, Thomas 46
Jefferson, Tony 291–292
Jeffreys, Sheila 230
Jews 174, 186–188, 203, 216n12
Johnson, Charles 216n10
John XXII, Pope 8
Judson, Harry Pratt 145
"just desserts" 75–76

Kafka, Franz 337
Katz, Jack 79, 207, 210, 317–318
Kelley, Florence 140, 163–164, 170n28, 210
Kelling, George 304
Kellor, Frances 108–109, 140–143
Kent State massacre 267
Kirchheimer, Otto 279–282, 314n15
Kitsuse, John 214, 282
Koyama, Emi 261
Kramer, Heinrich 9
Krisberg, Barry 302
Kropotkin, Peter 170n28, 296–297
Kross, Anna 241
Kwei, Sarah 265

labelling 155, 213–214
Lacassagne, Alexander 99
l'affaire Dreyfus 185–188
Laidlaw, Leon 261
Lapi, Giovanni 44, *44*
L.A. School 157
Lathrop, Julia 164
Laub, John 335
Lavan, George 193
Lavater, Johann Caspar 85–86, 90

Layten, S.W. 143
left realism 303–308, 315n28
legal categorisation 65–66
Lemert, Edwin 214, 282
lettres de cachet 7
Lettres philosophiques (Voltaire) 33–34
liberal feminism 242–243
Ligue pour la Défense des Droits de l'Homme 187
Locke, John 31, 63
Logan, Ann 240
Lombroso, Cesare 10, 83, 88–114, *91*, *95*, 130n6, 131n11, 219–223
London School of Economics (LSE) 267
Louis XIV of France 6
Louis XVI of France 6
Louis XV of France 11, 19, 32
Lowell, Josephine Shaw 146–147
LSE *see* London School of Economics (LSE)
Lynch, Michael 328
lynching 217n18
Lytton, Constance 236–237

Mackay, Finn 221, 262, 266n15
MacKinnon, Catharine 246
MacLean, Annie Marion 137–140, 151, 155, 169n7, 251
Maier-Katkin, Daniel 15
Major, John 78, 307
Malcolm X 313n2
Malleus Maleficarum (The Witches' Hammer) (Kramer and Sprenger) 9, 27n7
Manesta, Evelyn *226*
Manifesto of the Communist Party (Marx and Engels) 270
Mann, Michael 46, 61
Manzoni, Alessandro 47–48, 52
MAOA gene 126
Marion, Kitty 240
marriage: rape in 248–249
Martineau, Harriet 62, 230, 265n5
Maruna, Shadd 3
Marx, Karl 72, 88, 150, 173–175, 194, 268–275, 329, 331
Marxism 243–244, 282, 313n8, 315n22
masculinity 208, 254–256
Mathieson, Thomas 300, 312
Matthews, Rick 282
Matthews, Roger 254
Matza, David 314n18
Maxwell-Stewart, Hamish 82n27–82n28
Mayhew, Henry 103, 158

McCalley, William H. 198
McKay, Henry 155, 157
McKenzie, Roderick 154
McKinley, William 159
McRobbie, Angela 290, 299
McVicar, John 79
Mead, George Herbert 134, 160, 191
Melossi, Dario 61, 69, 82n21, 281, 314n12
Merseyside Crime Survey 305
Merton, Robert 117, 127, 130, 179, 190, 201–202, 204–215, 217n22, 256, 282, 326
mesomorphs 118
Messbarger, Rebecca 63
Messerschmidt, James 256
Messner, Steven 208
Mexico 337
Middle Ages 280
Mill, James 49
Miller, Kelly 191
Millett, Kate 246
Mills, C. Wright 1, 160, 168n3, 201
Mitchell, Claudine 228
Mohanty, Chandra Talpade 258
Monachesi, Eli 45
Montaigne, Michel de 26, 28n14, 54
Montesquieu 22–24, 29, 45, 62, 173
moral statistics 86–88
Morel, Bénédict-August 89
Morellet, Andre 36, 71, 80n11
Morgan, Rod 52–53
Morris, Aldon 191, 199
Morris, Allison 266n13
Morrison, Wayne 310
Mosaic Law 8
Moses, Earl R. 216n10
Mott, Lucretia 223
Mozambique 333
Muhammad, Khalil Gibran 143
Murray, Charles 123–124, 308
Musolino, Giuseppe 90, 96
Mutual Aid: A Factor of Evolution (Kropotkin) 297

Nakaz (Catherine the Great) 45
National American Women Suffrage Association 220, 222
National Association for the Advancement of Colored People (NAACP) 200, 217n19
National Deviancy Conferences (NDC) 267, 283–284
Native Americans 61
natural selection 83

NDC *see* National Deviancy Conferences (NDC)
Negri, Antonio 323
neurocriminology 124, 128
New Criminology, The (Taylor, Walton and Young) 211, 250, 283–288, 314n15, 314n20
New Deal 203
Newkirk, Vann R., II 193
New South Wales 56–57, 67
Niagara Movement 200
Nicholson, Margaret 16
Nightingale, Florence 230–231
NoLombroso committee 98

Ogburn, William F. 152
Ohlin, Lloyd 120, 208
Olshansky, Barbara 74
O'Malley, Pat 50, 57
On Crimes and Punishments (Beccaria) 35–47, *44*, 60, 68, 72, 80n11
Ordinance of Villers-Cotterets 27n9
Oriola, Temitope Babatunde 62
Ortiz-Rodriguez, Yolanda 259–260
Orwell, George 59
Osborne, Thomas Mott 209
othering 59, 110, *225*; convict criminology and 213; of Irish 114–117, *115–116*
Owusu-Bempah, Akwasi 202

Paine, Thomas 13–14
Pankhurst, Christabel *225*
Pankhurst, Emmeline 265
Pankhurst, Helen 263
panopticon 55–59, *56*, 82n19
Paris Commune 174–177
Paris unrest (1968) 267–268
Park, Robert 149–154, 155, 163, 191, 220
Parmar, Pratibha 258
Parsons, Talcott 201, 217n24, 255
Passannante, Giovanni 97–98
Pateman, Carole 63
Peace Information Center 201
Pearce, Frank 182
Pelletier, Madeleine 228
penal code: in Beccaria 38
penitentiary 68–70
Pepinsky, Hal 298, 315n23
Percy-Smith, Janie 309
Pethick, Dorothy 240
Pfohl, Stephen 3, 62, 208, 334
Phillipson, Coleman 44

philosophes 24–27
Phoenix Park murders 117
phrenology 90–97, *91*, *95*
physiognomy 85–86
physique types 117–118
Piccato, Pablo 89
Pick, Daniel 89, 96–97
Platt, Tony 165, 282, 285, 301–302
Pleck, Elizabeth 232
Plummer, Ken 155
Poitras, George 333
political engagement 335–338
Pollak, Otto 10
Pope John XXII 8
positivism: classicism *vs.* 84–85; critiques of 108–110; cultural criminology and 317–318; development of 83; Ferri and 104–105; Garofalo and 104–105; individual 108–110; Lombroso and 88–114, *91*, *95*; persistence of 117–130
Potonie Pierre, Eugenie 219–220
poverty 78, 271–273, 306, 312
Presidio Modelo 58
Press, Alex 249
prison: critical criminology and 312; in Goldman 297–298; women in 235–240
private sphere: public *vs.* 64–65
Proal, Louis 309
Progressive era 159
prostitution 229, 265n4
psychoanalysis 118–119
public sphere: private *vs.* 64–65
punishment: in Beccaria 39–40; in Bentham 51; crime and 280; in Durkheim 180–181; mildness of 40
Purvis, June 237–240

Quetelet, Adolphe 86–88, 104, 158, 173, 205, 269
Quinney, Richard 301

race: biosocial criminology and 128; colonialism and 61; feminism and 257–258; state oppression and 259–260
Radford, Jill 254
radical feminism 245–250, 262–265, *264*
Radzinowicz, Leon 283
Rafter, Nicole 93, 102, 118, 130n7, 262
Raine, Adrian 125–126
Rancine, Karen 81n12
rape 246–249
rational-choice theory 76–80, 82n31

rebellion 206–207
Reclaim the Night 262–263
Redhead, Steve 284
Red Scare 199–202
regicide 11–16, *14*
Resurrection (Tolstoy) 112–114
retreatism 206
Ricardo, David 49
Rice, Tamir 336
Rights of Man (Paine) 13–14
ritualism 206
Robinson, Virginia 147
Rock, Paul 3
Rockefeller, John D. 135, 145, 147, 168n3
Roe, Grace 240
Rohan-Chabot, Chevalier de 7
Roosevelt, Franklin D. 203
Roosevelt, Theodore 61, 166
Rose, Nikolas 92, 126
Rosenfeld, Richard 208
Rousseau, Jean-Jacques 62–63
routine activities approach 77–78
Ruff, Julius 27n9
Rusche, Georg 279–282, 314n12, 314n15
Rush, Benjamin 85
Rushton, Philippe 123–124
Russell, Diana 248–249, 257
Russell-Brown, Katheryn 202
Rydell, Robert W. 168n1

Sack, Fritz 300
Saunders, Sheila 249
Sayers, Janet 121
Schkolnick, Meyer 205
Schnupp, Jan 126
Schofield, Philip 55
Schumann, Karl 301, 315n25
Schur, Edwin 256
Schwartz, Marty 307
Schwendinger, Herman 285, 301
Schwendinger, Julia 245, 285, 301
Scott, Allen J. 157
Scott, Tim 217n18
Scraton, Phil 309, 336
Segal, Lynne 243–245
Sellin, Thorsten 282, 314n14
Seneca Falls convention 223, 242
September 11 attacks 74
sex workers 229, 265n4
Shaw, Clifford 151, 154, 155, 157, 171n29, 251
Shelden, Randall 282

Sheldon, William 122
Silvestri, Marisa 252, 256
Sim, Joe 312, 336, 338
Simondi, Mario 301, 315n25
sin 7–8, 23
Sisters Uncut 263, *264*, 265
slavery 61–62, 193–195, 211
Small, Albion 134–135, 145, 149–150, 169n18, 177
Smart, Carol 102, 251–252, 256, 299
Smith, Emma 263
Snodgrass, John 157
Snowden, Edward 59
social class 71–75, 156–157, 244–245
social conditions 163–164
social contract 60, 66–70, 80n4
social disorganisation 155
social facts 178–180
social integration 178–180
socialist feminism 243–245
Society in America (Martineau) 62
sociobiology 119–120
Sociological Imagination, The (Mills) 1
Soja, Edward 157
Sokoloff, Natalie 259
Sorokin, Pitirim 205
soul 28n12
South, Nigel 327–328
Southern criminology 321–327
Spencer, Herbert 105, 215n2
Spirit of Laws, The (Montesquieu) 22–23
Sprenger, James 9
Spurzheim, Johann 92
Standing Rock protests 332–333
Stanko, Betsy 247, 254
Stanton, Elizabeth Cady 223, 257
Starr, Ellen Gates 133, 158, 164–165
statistics, moral 86–88
stigmata 100
Straus, Murray 170n23
Straw, Jack 315n26
Stretesky, Paul 314n9
suffragettes *see* voting rights
Sullivan, Dennis 315n23
surveillance 226–227, *226*, 310
Sutherland, Edwin 118, 134, 155–156, 251, 255
Swiss, Deborah 67
Sykes, Gresham 314n18

Taft, Jessie 147
Takagi, Paul 282, 302

Takaki, Ronald 82n21
Talbot, Marion 136–137, 146–147
Tale of Two Cities, A (Dickens) 13
Tannenbaum, Frank 169n16, 172, 204, 209–215, 217n18, 282–283
Tarde, Gabriel 215n8
tattooing 99–101
Taylor, Ian 250–251, 303, 315n25
Taylor, Laurie 202
Taylor, Ula Y. 222
Tedder, Ludlow 67
Thatcher, Margaret 78, 179, 303, 307, 309
Thirteenth Amendment 194
Thomas, W.I. 134, 191, 220
Thomasius, Christian 28n14
Thompson, Edward 290
Thomson, Anthony 175
Thrasher, Frederic 151
Tifft, Larry 315n23
Tolstoy, Leo 110–114, 165, 265n7
Tombs, Steve 331
Tonry, Michael 120
torture 11, 23, 27n9, 40–41, 74–75, 81n15, 81n18; in Bentham 52–55; in Manzoni 47–48
Toynbee Hall 158, 175
transgender 261
Treatise on Man and the Development of His Faculties, A (Quetelet) 87
trial: Beccaria on 42–43
Troubles, The 73–74
Trump, Donald 249, 316, 329, 337
Tubman, Harriet 222
Tuthill, Richard 164
Twining, P.E. 52
Twining, W.L. 52
Tyndall, John 331

Universal Declaration of Human Rights 73
University of Chicago 135–136
Unnever, James 202
utilitarianism 49, 52, 54, 57, 77, 81n12, 130, 179, 182

Vagrancy Act 229
Van Kley, Dale 11
Veblen, Thorstein 134, 144, 146
Verri, Pietro 36, 47, 80n5, 81n14
Villella, Giuseppe 93, 97
Vincent, George 149–150

violence: class inequality and 244–245; critical criminology and 310–311; against women 232–235, 247–250
Violence in Early Modern Europe 1500–1800 (Ruff) 27n9
Vives, Juan Luis 28n14
Voltaire 7, 10, 16, 29, 31–34, 43, 71, 74, 80n5, 187
von Bar, Carl Ludwig 7–8
Von Liebig, Justis 330
von Schönborn, Johann Philipp 10
von Spee, Friedrich 9–10, 28n14
voting rights 220, 222, 227–228, *225–227*, 240, *238–239*

Walklate, Sandra 250–251, 254, 312, 317, 326–327
Walsh, Anthony 84
Walton, Paul 250, 284
Washington, Booker T. 191
waterboarding 74–75
Webb, Beatrice 158–159
Webb, Sidney 159
Weber, Max 173, 190
Webster, Colin 289, 291
welfare model 76
Wells, Ida B. 165, 168n1, 191, 222
What Is History? (Carr) 1
White Man and the Man of Colour, The (Lombroso) 96
Whyte, David 309
will, free 31, 62, 83–85, 89, 113, 198
Williams, Carla 125–126
Williams, Helen Maria 82n26
Williams, Roberta 125–126
Willis, Paul 284
Wilson, Elizabeth 244–245
Wilson, E.O. 119–120, 124
Wilson, James Q. 121, 125, 304
Wilson, Margo 120
Wirth, Louis 151–152
witchcraft 8–11, 27n4–27n5, 27n7
Wojtczak, Helena 229
women: in Bonger 277–278; -centered approach 161–162; in Chicago School 136–149, *139*; in classicist thought 62–63; critical criminology and 277–278, 299–300; in Eysenck 119; in Lombroso 101–103; in prison 235–240; violence against 232–235, 247–250; voting rights of 220, 222, 227–228, *225–227*,

240, *238–239*; as witches 8–10; *see also* feminism
Women's Social and Political Union (WSPU) 225
Work, Monroe 191, 216n10
World's Columbian Exposition 132, 143, 168n1, 176
Wright, John Paul 124–125
WSPU *see* Women's Social and Political Union (WSPU)

Yeager, Matthew 209, 211
Young, Jock 2, 117, 202, 215n5, 217n20, 250, 254, 283–284, 295, 308, 313n1, 315n27–315n28, 316, 319–321
Young, Vernetta D. 191

Zeitung, Rheinische 313n7
Zeublin, Charles 134, 145
Zola, Émile 186